India's Economy

Raj Kapila (1932-2016)

India's Economy

Pre-liberalisation to GST

Essays in Honour of Raj Kapila

Editor

Uma Kapila

ACADEMIC FOUNDATION
NEW DELHI

www.academicfoundation.org

First published in 2017
by

ACADEMIC FOUNDATION
4772-73 / 23 Bharat Ram Road, (23 Ansari Road),
Darya Ganj, New Delhi - 110 002 (India).
Phones : 23245001 / 02 / 03 / 04.
Fax : +91-11-23245005.
E-mail : booksaf@gmail.com
www.academicfoundation.org

Disclaimer:
The opinions/views/findings expressed in this book are solely those of the authors and do not necessarily reflect the views of the publisher.

Cataloging in Publication Data--DK
Courtesy: D.K. Agencies (P) Ltd. <docinfo@dkagencies.com>

India's economy : pre-liberalisation to GST : essays in honour of Raj Kapila / editor, Uma Kapila.
pages cm
ISBN 9789332704312

1. India--Economic policy--1947- 2. Economic development--India. I. Kapila, Raj, honouree. II. Kapila, Uma, editor.

LCC HC435.2.I53 2017 | DDC 338.954 23

Typeset, printed and bound by The Book Mint, New Delhi.
www.thebookmint.in

Contents

III
Sectoral Issues

सत्यमेव जयते

Manmohan Singh
Member of Parliament
Rajya Sabha

FOREWORD

It gives me a great pleasure in writing the Foreword to the volume "India's Economy: Pre-liberalisation to GST—Essays in Honour of Raj Kapila".

Raj Kapila who had been a student of Delhi School of Economics (MA Programme, 1953-1955 batch) received excellent training under the guidance of some of India's leading economists. His passion for books—reading and writing—led him to set up the publishing house, Academic Foundation, in 1990 after his retirement.

I have seen Academic Foundation since its inception. The seed sown in 1990 has grown in to a beautiful tree which I am sure will continue to bear fruit for the academic community.

The festschrift edited by his lifelong partner Dr Uma Kapila is a fitting tribute to the memory of Raj Kapila. It is indeed heartening to see that the volume has contributions from a large number of our most distinguished and eminent economists. Each one of them has contributed immensely to the analysis of India's economic conditions and to policy formulation in their respective area of expertise.

The volume covers wide array of important issues, challenges and economic initiatives taken from time to time across various sectors of the Indian economy.

I congratulate the editor, Uma Kapila, and the Publishers Academic Foundation for bringing out this comprehensive volume spanning seven decades of India's economic development.

(Manmohan Singh)

New Delhi
25 August 2017

3, Motilal Nehru Place, New Delhi-110 011
Tel. : 2301-5470, 2301-8668 Fax : 2379-5152
E-mail : manmohan@gov.in

Raj Kapila (1932-2016)

Photo credit: Vinay Tandon

Raj Kapila: A Tribute

PULIN B. NAYAK

Raj Kapila, in whose memory this volume is being brought out, was born in 1932 in Ujhani, Badaun district, in Western Uttar Pradesh. He had his early school education in Lucknow and went on to graduate with Honours in Political Science from Government College, Simla. He then proceeded to do his Master's in Economics, being in the batch of 1953-1955, from the Delhi School of Economics (DSE). Those were the early days of the DSE and Raj was taught by a rich array of famous economists; V.K.R.V. Rao, P.N. Dhar, K.N. Raj and B.N. Ganguli, among many others. The youthful Raj Kapila was the Secretary of the 'Fraternity', a general body of students and teachers. It might be of some interest to know that as the President of the DSE Society, Prime Minister Jawaharlal Nehru was also the President of the 'Fraternity'.

Old timers of the DSE would fondly recall the Founder's Day, 14 November, on which, annually, the Prime Minister used to show up in the afternoon to have a tete-a-tete with the student body. There used to be no paraphernalia of any 'security', and Pandit Nehru used to be driven in his official Ambassador car without any accompanying motorcade. Describing the activities of one particular Founder's Day in the mid-1950s, Professor P.N. Dhar (1995: 19) writes: "One of the earliest and most memorable events of the Fraternity was a visit from Jawaharlal Nehru, who spent two informal hours with the members, discussing a variety of subjects, sitting on a writing table, his legs swinging free".

After completing his Master's, Raj joined the Planning Commission at the young age of 23 in 1955 and was straightaway made to work on the Second Five Year Plan and, in fact, to prepare a draft of Chapter 3 of the Plan. Those were the heady days of planning, and this is widely acknowledged to be the key and defining Plan with inputs from the celebrated physicist-statistician P.C. Mahalanobis. The Chairman was of course the Prime Minister himself and the Deputy Chairman was Shri Tarlok Singh. It should be mentioned that Pandit Nehru used to himself read through the drafts of the Plan documents quite carefully. Raj had also been tasked to prepare the additional taxation statements for the Ministry of Finance on behalf of the Planning Commission, which he did during his tenure there.

In this brief biographical sketch, it would not be possible to cover all details of Shri Raj Kapila's long walk through life, but it should be sufficient to say that Raj had a truly chequered career. From the Planning Commission, he moved on to the Ministry of Commerce and Industry and toured the country extensively to prepare industry outlook reports for various parts of the country. But Raj was deep down a restless soul and was not happy within the trappings of a government job. He was keen to quit this at the earliest opportunity and pursue an independent, constructive and meaningful vocation. He was frank enough to share this with the young lady who was to be his life partner, another alumnus of the DSE, who must have given her the intellectual as well as emotional support he was looking for. Raj's marriage took place in 1961, after which he resigned from his job and set up a publishing house to bring out a monthly journal on industry and trade. Dr Uma Kapila, a lifelong teacher of economics at the prestigious Miranda House of the Delhi University, was to be Raj's steady support and the constant factor all through his various business ventures and adventures and multiple jobs through his life.

In 1966, Raj Kapila authored an important book entitled: *The Time Demands: A Politico-Economic Analysis of*

Present-day India. It was based on first-hand information he had gathered by interviewing the key political personalities of the times, including the Prime Minister Smt Indira Gandhi, and most of her cabinet ministers, including Y.B. Chavan, Swaran Singh, C. Subramanian, M.C. Chagla, Humayun Kabir and Ashok Mehta, among others. A number of other leaders such as Morarji Desai, Ram Manohar Lohia, V.K. Krishna Menon, K. Kamaraj and M.R. Masani, were interviewed as well. In all, some 52 personages had been interviewed, and the book had been completed at breakneck speed with a great sense of urgency. It was released by Morarji Desai at Sapru House and had been well covered in the newspapers.

Raj had a long stint, from 1970 till 1982, as the Secretary of the Vanaspati Manufacturers Association of India. In this job, he had played an important role in convincing the government about decontrolling the vanaspati industry. In 1982, he joined as Advisor in the public sector Hindustan Vegetable Oil Corporation (HVOC) and took initiatives that led to the introduction of modern packaging in processed food and *vanaspati* industry.

But perhaps the greatest contribution of Raj Kapila was the setting up, in 1990, of the publishing company Academic Foundation, devoted to publishing quality books in economics and the social sciences generally; specially aimed at students, teachers and researchers, but also meant for the discerning citizens. Raj was always a voracious reader and a keen observer of the contemporary economic and political reality and it was his lifelong dream to set up a publishing house of substance. Academic Foundation has over the past 27 years grown from strength to strength and now has a major presence both nationally and internationally. Raj was helped in this major endeavour by his lifelong companion, Dr Uma ji, and their two very able and talented sons, Rituraj and Sanu.

Raj Kapila: A Tribute

ANAND PRAKASH

My association with Raj Kapila goes back to the time when I met him in the early 1980s as a fellow member of a Housing Society formed by a group of Delhi University teachers. He was active in its planning and management in capacity as spouse of a teacher, Dr Uma Kapila in Miranda House. Someone had put my name, too, in the governing body when annual elections took place in the society. As Raj Kapila and I formally met, we felt drawn towards each-other, he being a kind and well-meaning soul as well as accessible and cordial, and I quietly appreciative of his positive outlook on matters of collective interest. Soon, the two of us joined hands to oppose the lobby that appeared to us somewhat deficient in openness at the time. In his characteristic open style, Raj Kapila in the governing body meeting dwelt elaborately upon the course of action that would take the society to quick results. This garnered effective support in the governing body. To cut the long story short, the opposition lobby made it a fight to the finish, forgetting norms, and this we found rather distressing. As a result, we decided to make exit, agreed that such a 'fraternity' would not be worth being neighbours with! The decision cemented our friendship.

Soon, following this episode Raj Kapila (Kapila sahib to me) thought of launching a publication company that would eventually be known as Academic Foundation. In the pursuit, he showed mettle of a special kind. He thought big and was fond of taking up challenges. He also planned to the last detail, as if the venture had gone on in his mind, before he began executing it, as a well laid out dramatic sequence. At the time, I was the only one in his 'circle' who had links with literature. He suggested that I give him a couple of manuscripts for publication. One was indeed with me in the final form. It was my PhD thesis on literary theory, something new in those days of changed priorities, and the other would soon take shape since Sanu Kapila (Sanu to me), who attended my classes for DU's English Honours course, insisted I write my lectures on Emily Bronte's *Wuthering Heights* as chapters of the book of criticism they should publish. This was easy indeed and I agreed after initial hesitation. But I realised meanwhile that Sanu had discussed the issue threadbare with daddy Kapila sahib from the point of view of meeting the publication-deadline, and quietly the latter would drop a hint now and then that the manuscript be made ready early. This was usual with Raj Kapila; he would gently initiate the subject and leave it at that—much like the move of a management *guru* seeing that result should come sooner than anticipated!

Later, Academic Foundation went, understandably, in the direction of economics scholarship where its intellectual wealth grew at an enormous pace. In the journey to its successes, each an improvement on the previous one, Academic Foundation faced a number of obstacles though, most of them resource-related. However, Raj Kapila kept on taking risks, with unflinching support from Dr Uma Kapila, proving to him bedrock of inspiration and strength, and the duo saw to it that hurdles indeed produced trophies of achievement.

About the Editor/Contributors

Editor:

Uma Kapila has taught Indian Economy to undergraduate students for over forty-two years. She retired as Reader from the Department of Economics, Miranda House, University of Delhi. Presently, she is Editorial Director, Academic Foundation. An Honours Graduate from Miranda House, University of Delhi and MA and PhD from Delhi School of Economics (DSE), Dr Kapila has also served on the Planning Commission Study Group on "Agricultural Strategies in the Eastern Region of India for the Seventh Five Year Plan" (Perspective Planning Division). She is the author of the book *Oilseeds Economy of India* (1982) published by the Institute of Economic Growth (IEG), Delhi. A prolific writer, she has authored, and edited and co-edited with Raj Kapila, a number of books on India's economy, banking and finance. Edited by her and revised every year, the popular reference text, *Indian Economy Since Independence* is currently running into its 28th edition. She is editor of Academic Foundation's continuing series EDI (Economic Developments in India), a monthly update on Indian economy (230 volumes published till date).

Contributors:

Yoginder K. Alagh is Chancellor of the Central University of Gujarat, Professor Emeritus/Vice-chair, Sardar Patel Institute of Economic and Social Research, Ahmedabad and Chair Professor at Punjab University. From 1996 to 1998, he was the Minister of State (Independent Charge) for Planning and Programme Implementation, Science, Technology and Power, and until 2001, Member of the Rajya Sabha. He was Vice-Chancellor, Jawaharlal Nehru University, Member Planning Commission, Chairman BICP and Secretary to the Government and Chairman APC. Dr Alagh's professional experience is related to research, policymaking and administration of large research/policy formulation professional groups relating to macro policy and planning, industrial policies and reform, and agricultural planning and policy. He holds a doctorate in Economics from the University of Pennsylvania at Philadelphia. He has taught at that University, IIM Calcutta and at Swarthmore College. Extensively published in India and abroad, he writes a column for the Express Group and the Business Line.

Pulapare Balakrishnan, PhD from Cambridge University, is currently Professor of Economics at Ashoka University, Sonepat and Senior Fellow of Indian Institute of Management, Kozhikode. He works in the area of applied macroeconomics and his published work spans the inflationary process, the measurement of productivity growth, the transition to the market in post-communist Europe, agricultural involution in Kerala and economic growth in India. He has held appointments at Worcester College of Oxford University, the Indian Statistical Institute at Delhi and the Indian Institute of Management at Kozhikode. He has served as Country Economist for Ukraine at the World Bank and as a consultant to the ILO, RBI and UNDP. During 2010-2013, he was Director of the Centre for Development Studies, Thiruvananthapuram.

Sanjaya Baru one of India's most respected economic and political analysts, has been recently appointed secretary general of the Federation of Indian Chambers of Commerce and Industry (FICCI). He has been Chief Editor of major financial newspapers, a media advisor and spokesman of a Prime Minister of India; a professor at important universities and think tanks in New Delhi and Singapore, author of best-selling books, including *Strategic Consequences of India's Economic Performance* (Academic Foundation, 2006) and *The Accidental Prime Minister* (Penguin Viking, 2014). He was till recently Director for Geo-economics and Strategy, International Institute for Strategic Studies, London. He was a member of India's National Security Advisory Board.

Aditya Bhattacharjea is Professor and Head of the Department of Economics at the Delhi School of Economics, University of Delhi, where he teaches postgraduate courses in industrial organisation and Indian economic development. He earlier taught for many years at St Stephen's College, Delhi, and has been a visiting associate professor at Duke University, USA. His research interests include trade policy under imperfect competition, labour market regulation, and competition (antitrust) law and policy. His articles have appeared in leading law and economics journals. He was educated at St Stephen's College, University of Delhi, Jawaharlal Nehru University, the University of Cambridge, and Boston University, from where he obtained his PhD degree.

Rajesh Chadha is a Senior Fellow and Senior Research Counsellor at the National Council of Applied Economic Research (NCAER), New Delhi. Prior to joining NCAER in 2004, he was an Associate Professor of Economics at Hindu College, University of Delhi. His teaching and research career spans over 41 years. He has worked extensively on regional and multilateral international trade issues, foreign direct investment and agricultural markets. He is the Managing Editor of *MARGIN: The Journal of Applied Economic Research*, NCAER's international, peer-reviewed journal. He has been a Visiting Scholar at the Universities of Michigan, Melbourne, and Monash. He was nominated as GTAP Research Fellow (2004-2007) by the Global Trade Analysis Project, Purdue University, USA. He received his PhD from the Indian Institute of Technology, New Delhi.

Ramesh Chand is currently Member of NITI Aayog in the rank and status of Union Minister of State. He has a PhD in Agricultural Economics from Indian Agricultural Research Institute (IARI), New Delhi. He is Fellow, National Academy of Agricultural Sciences and Indian Society of Agricultural Economics. Prof Chand has 33 years of experience in research and teaching in the field of agricultural economics and policy. He has been involved in policy formulation for agriculture sector for the last 15 years. Prior to joining NITI Aayog, he was Director, National Institute of Agricultural Economics and Policy Research, New Delhi. He has authored 7 books and published more than 100 research papers in reputed national and international journals in the areas of: agriculture—production, growth, development and policy, and farmers issues, market and trade.

C.P. Chandrasekhar is a Professor of Economics at the Centre for Economic Studies and Planning, Jawaharlal Nehru University, New Delhi and Dean, School of Social Sciences, Jawaharlal Nehru University, New Delhi. His areas of interest include the role of finance and industry in development, and fiscal, financial and industrial policy reform in developing countries. He has published widely in academic journals and has co-authored several books. He is also a columnist for leading Indian magazines and newspapers.

Kanchan Chopra is former Director and Professor, Institute of Economic Growth, Delhi, where she was on the faculty for more than three decades. After receiving her PhD degree from the Delhi School of Economics, she specialised in the area of environment and development in which she has authored several books and research papers. She is Fellow of the Beijer Institute of Ecological Economics, Stockholm of the South Asian Network on Development and Environmental Economics and an elected Fellow of the Third World Academy of Sciences. Prof Chopra was Founder President of the Indian Society for Ecological Economics and in 2016 was the recipient of the Boulding Award of the International Society for Ecological Economics.

Bibek Debroy is an economist and was educated in Ramakrishna Mission School, Narendrapur; Presidency College, Kolkata; Delhi School of Economics and Trinity College, Cambridge. Presently he is Member, NITI Aayog, Government of India. He has worked in Presidency College, Kolkata (1979-1983), Gokhale Institute of Politics and Economics, Pune (1983-1987); Indian Institute of Foreign Trade, Delhi (1987-1993); as the Director of a Ministry of Finance/UNDP project on legal reforms (1993-1998); Department of Economic Affairs (1994-95); National Council of Applied Economic Research (1995-96); Rajiv Gandhi Institute for Contemporary Studies (1997-2005); PHD Chamber of Commerce and Industry (2005-06); and Centre for Policy Research (2007-2015). He has authored/edited several books, papers and popular articles and has also been a Consulting/Contributing Editor with several newspapers.

R.S. Deshpande is former Director of the Institute for Social and Economic Change (ISEC), Bangalore. He is currently Director of Centre of Development Studies at PES University, Bangalore. He holds a Bachelor of Science and Masters' Degree with a PhD in Economics. His specialisations include: agricultural development policy, agricultural price policy, WTO—agriculture & trade, rural policy and poverty, economics of drought-prone areas and rainfed regions, and economics of irrigation. Prof Deshpande is a recipient of PNASF Gold Medal for his contributions to Agricultural Policy and Sir M. Visvesvaraya Global Leadership Award in Karnataka for Excellence in Education. He was among the first two awardees as "Fellow of the Indian Society of Agricultural Economics". He was the President of the Platinum Jubilee Conference of the Indian Society of Agricultural Economics held at Ludhiana. He was the sole architect of Karnataka's Agricultural Policy 2006. He has authored/edited 17 books/monographs and more that 148 research papers published in national and international prestigious journals, 49 research studies and several participations in policy bodies at State and Country level in agricultural policymaking.

S. Mahendra Dev is Director and Vice Chancellor, Indira Gandhi Institute of Development Research, Mumbai. He is PhD in Economics from the Delhi School of Economics and did his post-doctoral research from Yale University. His research interests include: development economics, Indian economy, macro policies, inclusive growth, agricultural policies, poverty and inequality, rural development. Earlier he was Chairman of the Commission for Agricultural Costs and Prices, Government of India and Director, Centre for Economic and Social Studies, Hyderabad (1999-2008). He is member and Vice Chairman of Board of Trustees of International Food Policy Research Institute, Washington, D.C. He was Acting Chairman of the National Statistical Commission, Government of India. He has more than 100 research publications in national and international journals. He has been a member of several government committees in India, including the Prime Minister's Task Force on Employment and Committee on Financial Inclusion and member of Rangarajan Committee on Poverty.

Jayati Ghosh is professor of economics at the Centre for Economic Studies and Planning, School of Social Sciences, Jawaharlal Nehru University, New Delhi. She was educated at Delhi University, Jawaharlal Nehru University and the University of Cambridge, England where she obtained her PhD in 1983. Since 2002, she has been the Executive Secretary of International Development Economics Associates (IDEAS), an international network of heterodox development economists (*www.networkideas.org*). She is also involved in managing several public information websites including *www.macroscan.org*. Her current research interests include globalisation, international trade and finance, employment patterns in developing countries, macroeconomic policy, issues related to gender and development, and the implications of recent growth in China and India. She has authored several books and more than one hundred scholarly articles.

Bishwanath Goldar is Retired Professor of Economics of the Institute of Economic Growth, Delhi. He is the Chairman of the Standing Committee on Industrial Statistics set up by the Central Statistics Office, and is associated with several other official committees. He specialises in industrial economics and international trade. The bulk of his research has been on productivity, employment, wages and price-cost margin in Indian industries, energy efficiency in Indian industrial firms, impact of trade reforms on manufacturing, and foreign direct investment in India. Prof Goldar has an MA in Economics and PhD from Delhi School of Economics, University of Delhi.

Ashok Gulati is currently Infosys Chair Professor for Agriculture at Indian Council for Research on International Economic Relations (ICRIER). Formerly, he was Chairman of the Commission for Agricultural Costs and Prices (GoI). And for more than 10 years, he was Director at the International Food Policy Research Institute (IFPRI). He has been actively involved in policy analysis and advice, and was awarded 'Padma Shri'—a high civilian award, by the President of India for his services to the country.

Devendra B. Gupta is currently a Senior Consultant at National Council of Applied Economic Research (NCAER), New Delhi. He was associated with the Institute of Economic Growth (Professor of Economics and Director, Population Research Centre); Faculty of Management Studies, University of Delhi (S.P. Jain Chair), National Institute of Public Finance and Policy (HDFC Chair), Planning Commission (Advisor). He has been consultant with the World Bank, UNICEF, ESCAP, ILO-ARTEP, DFID, WHO. He has held visiting positions at Yale, Hull University (England), Hitotsubashi (Japan), Cambridge University. His primary areas of interest include: economic modelling, health and housing, water & sanitation, urban and land economics, small industry and developmental economics. He holds MA both in Economics and Economic Statistics from Delhi School of Economics and PhD from the University of Birmingham.

Vijay L. Kelkar currently serves as the Chairman, National Institute of Public Finance and Policy (NIPFP), New Delhi, Chairman, India Development Foundation, New Delhi, Vice President, Pune International Centre (PIC), Pune, Chairman, Janwani, Pune and the President, Indian Statistical Institute, Kolkata. He was appointed as Chairman of committee constituted on Revisiting & Revitalising the PPP Model of Infrastructure Development. Earlier, he was the Chairman, Forum of Federations, Ottawa (January 2010 to March 2013), Chairman of the Finance Commission in the rank of a Union Cabinet Minister (until January 2010), Executive Director for India, Sri Lanka, Bangladesh and Bhutan at the IMF (August 1999 to August 2002); Finance Secretary, GoI (1998-99); Chairman, Tariff Commission, GoI (1997-98): Secretary, Ministry of Petroleum & Natural Gas, GoI (1994-1997); Director & Coordinator, International Trade Division, UNCTAD, Geneva, Switzerland (1991-1994); Chairman, Bureau of Industrial Costs & Prices and Secretary to the GoI (1987-1991); Secretary, Economic Advisory Council to the Prime Minister, GoI (1985-1988). Dr Kelkar did his Bachelors of Engineering (BE) from the College of Engineering, Pune. He got his Masters degree from University of Minnesota and went on to do his PhD in economics from University of California, Berkeley. In January 2011, the President of India awarded him 'Padma Vibhushan', the second highest Civilian Award for distinguished and exceptional services to the Nation.

K.L. Krishna taught in Delhi School of Economics from 1958 to 2000 and had more than 50 PhD and MPhil students. He is PhD in Economics from University of Chichago (1963-1967). His fields of specialisation include: Econometrics (Methodology and Applications), Industrial Economics,

Economics of Productivity, Regional Inequality and Empirics of Trade. He was the Founder Member of the Centre for Development Economics (CDE), President of the Indian Econometric Society (1996-97) and Founder Managing Editor of the Journal of Quantitative Economics (1985-1995). He has authored more than 30 research papers on a variety of themes and edited many books. Currently, Prof Krishna is Chairman, Madras Institute of Development Studies, Chennai.

Nagesh Kumar is Director of Social Development Division, United Nations Economic and Social Commission for Asia and the Pacific (UNESCAP), Bangkok. He holds an additional charge as officer-in-charge of UNESCAP's South and South-West Asia (SSWA) Office, based in New Delhi. He earlier served as Chief Economist of UNESCAP and Director of Macroeconomic Policy and Development Division (MPDD) and Head of the SSWA Office. Before joining UNESCAP in 2009, Dr Kumar served as Director-General of Research and Information System for Developing Countries (RIS), a New Delhi-based policy think tank of the Government of India devoted to international economic and development issues for seven years. A PhD in Economics from the Delhi School of Economics, he is recipient of the Exim Bank of India's first International Trade Research Award in 1989 and a GDN Medal for best research awarded by the World Bank and the Japanese Government in 2000. He has written extensively on the development cooperation, developmental impact of FDI, industrial and technology development policies, the challenge of new technologies for development, on regional economic cooperation in Asia, and on WTO and development, among other themes.

Deepak Mohanty is an Executive Director in the Reserve Bank of India (RBI) currently overseeing areas of financial stability, risk management and enforcement. Earlier he oversaw monetary policy, economic research and statistics. He was Senior Adviser in the International Monetary Fund (IMF) and prior to that worked in various positions in economic research and was head of monetary policy department in the RBI. Dr Mohanty chaired several committees. He has a number of publications in professional journals and edited two books.

Pulin B. Nayak completed his Bachelor's and Master's in Economics from Delhi University and went to the University of Rochester, New York, in 1971 to pursue his doctorate. He completed his PhD in 1975 and had a brief tenure as Senior Economist at the National Institute of Public Finance and Policy (NIPFP), New Delhi. He then joined the faculty of the Delhi School of Economics (DSE) in 1978, and remained there till his retirement in 2015. During 1982-1984, he was the Agatha Harrison Fellow at St Antony's College, Oxford. He was Director of the DSE during 2005-2008. During 2013-14, he was a Member of the Prime Minister's Economic Advisory Council (PMEAC). His areas of interest have been public finance, microeconomic theory and economic development.

Anand Prakash, PhD, taught English Literature in Delhi University till retirement in 2007. He has written extensively on literary theory and cultural-aesthetic trends. His publications include: *Wuthering Heights: An Interpretation* (Academic Foundation 1993), *Marxist Literary Theory* (Academic Foundation 1994), *Approaches to Literary Theory: Marxism* (Worldview 2002), and *Muktibodh in Our Time* (Lokmitra 2012). Currently, he is editing *Journal of Literature Studies*. A poet and theatre person, he has scripted plays in English and Hindi; these have been staged at Shriram Centre, New Delhi, and also performed in Delhi slums.

Devender Pratap is an Associate Fellow at NCAER. His research interests include trade policy analysis/CGE modelling, GTAP Modelling/database, Social Accounting Matrix, Input Output Analysis, Construction of Benchmark Data-Sets for CGE Modelling, Macroeconometric Modelling and Agricultural. Livestock Economy. At NCAER, he has handled three major CGE models in a single and multi-country frameworks. He has been involved in the NCAER survey of Agricultural Markets in India.

Indira Rajaraman holds a PhD in Economics (January 1974) from Cornell University. She was Professor of Economics, IIM Bangalore (1976-1994), and RBI Chair Professor at the National Institute of Public Finance and Policy, Delhi (1994-2007), from where she retired at the age of 60. Subsequently, she was Member, 13th Finance Commission (2007-2009); and Member for a four-year term (2011-2015) of the Central Board of Directors and of the Technical Advisory Committee for Monetary Policy, Reserve Bank of India. Her research publications span development economics and macroeconomic—fiscal and financial sector—issues. Prof Rajaraman is currently an Independent Director on the Board of Tata Sikorsky Aerospace Limited, and a member of the India Advisory Board of the World Gold Council.

C. Rangarajan is a leading economist of India who has played a key role both as an academic and a policy maker. He has held several important positions which include Governor of Reserve Bank of India; Chairman, Economic Advisory Council to the Prime Minister; Governor of the state of Andhra Pradesh; and Chairman, 12th Finance Commission. Dr Rangarajan was Governor of the RBI during 1992-1997 when India embarked on wide-ranging economic reforms. He was President of the Indian Economic Association in 1988 and President of the Indian Econometric Society in 1994. He was awarded 'Padma Vibhusan' in 2002. He is currently Chairman, Madras School of Economics and Chancellor of the University of Hyderabad.

C.H. Hanumantha Rao holds a PhD from the Delhi School of Economics, University of Delhi (1962). He was Post-Doctoral Fellow, Department of Economics, University of Chicago (1966-67) and Fellow, Institute of Economic Growth, University of Delhi (1961-1992). He has been Hon. Professor, Centre for Economic and Social Studies, Hyderabad since 1992. His areas of interest are: Agricultural Economics, Development Planning and Policy. He has been a member of the Planning Commission, Finance Commission, on the Board of Directors of the RBI; Member, National Advisory Council; and Chancellor, University of Hyderabad. He was awarded 'Padma Bhushan' by the President of India in 2004 in the field of literature and education.

M. Govinda Rao, is currently, an Emeritus Professor, National Institute of Public Finance and Policy, New Delhi. He was a Member of the 14th Finance Commission, Government of India (2013-14) and a Member of Economic Advisory Council to the Prime Minister of India (2004-2012) and Director, National Institute of Public Finance and Policy (2003-2012). He is also an Adviser to the Centre for Public Policy, Indian Institute of Management and Counsellor, Takshashila Institution, Bangalore. Dr Rao is an expert in public finance and has written extensively on issues relating to fiscal policy, tax policy and reforms and fiscal decentralisation and federalism.

Surendra Laxminarayan Rao has degrees in Commerce (Bombay) and Economics (Delhi). A professional manager and applied economist, he is Distinguished Fellow Emeritus at The Energy Research Institute (TERI). He served at senior management levels in multinational companies for 28 years, has been a management consultant and teacher, designed and ran the National Management Programme, was Director-General of the National Council of Applied Economic Research, and the first Chairman of the Central Electricity Regulatory Commission. He has been on the boards of IIMB, IIML, IIIMK and other management education bodies; President of AIMA; on many corporate and other Boards, has written or edited 16 books and written many papers and articles.

Y.V. Reddy was Governor of the Reserve Bank of India from 2003-2008. He was Chairman of the 14th Finance Commission in 2013-14. Previously, he worked in the Government of India as Secretary in the Ministry of Finance, and in the Government of Andhra Pradesh as Principal Secretary. In 2010, he was awarded India's second highest civilian honour the 'Padma Vibushan'. Currently, he is Honorary Professor at the Centre for Economic and Social Studies, Hyderabad.

Khalil Musa Shaha holds a PhD in Economics, and is currently working as Data Bank Manager at Institute for Social and Economic Change, Bangalore. He has worked and published in the national and international journals and edited books on issues related to terms of trade, regional agricultural development, agricultural production and prices, market imperfections and farm sector distress, land, poverty, agricultural labour, common pool resources, and BRICS.

T.C.A. Srinivasa-Raghavan took his master's degree from the Delhi School of Economics in 1972. He worked as economics editor of Macmillan in the 1970s before turning to journalism in 1980 and has been the opinion page editor of several business papers since then. He is now retired from active journalism but continues to be a commentator on public affairs for the *Business Standard* and the Hindi portal of *Quint*. His history of monetary policy in India was published recently. In 2011, he wrote a book for the finance ministry on the Indian Economic Service and the history of economic policy in India. He has also written several research monographs and papers for think tanks.

M.S. Swaminathan is a plant geneticist by training. His contributions to agricultural renaissance in India have him being referred to as the leader of the green revolution movement and sustainable food security. He has served as Chairman of the UN Science Advisory Committee, as Independent Chairman of the FAO Council, and as President of the International Union for the Conservation of Nature and Natural Resources and of the Pugwash Conferences on Science and World Affairs. The International Association of Women and Development conferred on him the first international award for significant contributions to promoting knowledge, skill, and technological empowerment of women in agriculture and for mainstreaming gender considerations in agriculture and rural development. Prof Swaminathan was awarded the Ramon Magsaysay Award for Community Leadership in 1971, the Albert Einstein World Science Award in 1986, and the first World Food Prize in 1987. He is a Fellow of many of leading scientific academies of India and the world including the Royal Society of London, the US National Academy of Sciences and the Russian and Chinese Academy of Sciences.

Asuri Vasudevan was Special Adviser to the Governor, Central Bank of Nigeria, till end June 2012. Since then, he has been writing for financial dailies of India and Nigeria, and for Conferences. His major previously-held positions were: Executive Director, Reserve Bank of India (1996-2000) and Adviser to the Executive Director for India at the International Monetary Fund, Washington DC (1984-1989). He was member of India delegations to the IMF-WB meetings between 1984 and 1989 and 1993-2000 and member of the two Task Forces relating to International Standards and Codes of the erstwhile Financial Stability Forum at Bank for International Settlements (BIS), Basle. His book *Central Banking for Emerging Market Economies* (Academic Foundation 2003) has received acclaim as an important contribution to understanding of modern central banking. He has authored/edited books on deficit financing, strategy of development planning, external debt and money and banking, and has several articles on monetary and development policy issues.

Vijay Shankar Vyas is the Chairman of the Ajit Foundation, an institution working for last two decades for empowering youth. He has a PhD in economics and has taught at Bombay University, Sardar Patel University and Indian Institute of Management, Ahmedabad. He was awarded DLitt (*honoris causa*) by Maharana Pratap University of Agricultural Sciences, Udaipur. He was Director of Indian Institute of Management Ahmedabad and Chairman, Governing Board of the Institute of Development Studies, Jaipur. He has been Senior Adviser in the World Bank, Member of the Economic Advisory Council of the Prime Minister, Member of the Central Board of Reserve Bank of India and Deputy Chairman of the State Planning Board of Rajasthan. He was awarded 'Padma Bhushan' in 2006 by the President of India.

List of Tables and Figures

Tables

Figures

I
Prologue

1

Introduction

UMA KAPILA

I

Raj Kapila: A Life to Cherish

Raj Kapila (1932-2016) was a great visionary and a compassionate, loving and caring human being, who loved his family, friends and above all his country. He was a great planner, particularly with regard to his work, finances and time. Even if he had to suffer, he did not compromise. It was because of these rare qualities that he could calmly face and overcome adverse situations.

Raj and I had the good fortune of spending 55 years of our life together, sharing all the struggles and challenges with moments of joy along the way. It was because of his positive outlook that we could sail through even the hardest of times. Even when he was on wheelchair for nearly five years, during the last phase of his life, when enquired about his health, his prompt reply would always be "first class"!

Raj was always a keen observer of the contemporary economic and political reality. In his writings, discussions, right from college days, what was uppermost in his mind was India—Why we have not been able to solve our basic problems of poverty, unemployment, illiteracy? Where have we been lacking in policymaking or in implementation?

Raj's first book published in 1966 entitled: *The Time Demands: A Politico-Economic Analysis of Present-day India* was based on first hand information gathered by interviewing key political personalities of the time, academicians and senior bureaucrats. The author's preface in the book starts with the following opening verse of a poem:

God! Give us men, the time demands,
Strong minds, great hearts, true faith and willing hands;
Give us men, whom the lust for office does not kill,
Give us men, whom the spoils of office cannot buy,
Give us men who can have an opinion and a will.

— Josiah Gilbart Holland
(19th century American Poet & Novelist)

Six years later in 1972 Raj wrote another book: *India at Cross: After 25 Years of Independence* based on extensive interviews again with personalities from different fields. I am tempted to quote a paragraph from the introduction chapter entitled "Story of India since Independence":

> Intelligentsia is always the backbone of any society or country. But I am sorry to say that in our country the intelligentsia does not realize at all what is happening to the country and does not seem to be conscious of its moral duty to give a sort of leadership needed at the time. When the intelligentsia is indifferent to all that is happening today then I think there is no hope for the nation...

The point I wish to put across is that he, like every true nationalist, staunchly believed in keeping nation's interest first and foremost. In his thoughts and deeds, he was convinced that personal interest should never be at cost of millions who are ignored totally. He always stressed that no doubt we have come a long way, but we cannot lose sight of the persisting poverty, unemployment, inequality, illiteracy and poor health of our population along with other social problems perpetuating our society. He firmly believed that integrity, honesty and hard work should be the foundation stones of our society, politicians, and policy makers.

He lived his life like a brave soldier, and the end of his journey was as peaceful as anyone would wish it to be. Soon after he left, to fill up the vacuum, I rejoined our office. During one of our discussions, we decided to bring out a volume in his memory. I enthusiastically wrote to our economist friends, many of them Academic Foundation's authors, requesting them to contribute a paper in the area of their expertise, and the response was overwhelming. Academic Foundation owes a deep debt of gratitude to all the authors for their spontaneous response by sending in their contribution for this volume, and the final product in the form of the present volume is before all of you.

II

Roadmap to the Volume

The volume begins with a Foreword by Dr Manmohan Singh followed by tributes from Prof Pulin Nayak and Dr Anand Prakash, friends and academic peers of Raj Kapila.

The book with 31 chapters has three parts. Part I: Prologue in addition to the Introduction chapter carries the paper "The Saga of Delhi School of Economics (DSE)" by Prof K.L Krishna. As Raj Kapila belonged to DSE (1953-1955 batch of MA Students—and the School will be celebrating its 70 years), he chose to write about DSE for this memorial volume. This beautiful sketch of the School is indeed a treat for all the students and teachers of DSE.

The founding father of DSE, Prof V.K.R.V Rao, envisioned an institution of higher learning and research on socioeconomic issues on the lines of the London School of Economics. The seven decade story of the DSE with special focus on the recent quarter century when faculty research output on theoretical and applied issues have increased manifold would have made Prof Rao immensely proud and as editor of this volume, if I may add, would also have made Raj Kapila very happy.

Part II (chapter 3 to 21) of the volume devoted to the macro issues of India's economic development covers a wide array of issues. Starting with a crisp account of India's economic development (from the past into the present), the journey of India's economic reforms and how the 25 years of economic reforms have impacted poverty, inequality, growth and social opportunity, and regional inequality in development are discussed in detail. This is followed by a critique of opportunities and challenges arising from new measures such as digitisation, demonetisation, CCT (conditional cash transfer) and Goods and Services Tax (GST). The section also includes detailed discussion on monetary and fiscal policy, federalism, public debt, geo-economics of the trans-Atlantic financial crisis, policy regulations, demographic dividend, ecology related issues, and the need for context specific economic theories.

Part III of the book (chapter 22 to 31) covers the sectoral issues and challenges. The sectors covered are: agriculture, industry, banking, and external sector.

Economic Reforms: Growth, Poverty and Inequality

Pulin Nayak in his essay (chapter 3) remarks: "Even till as late as the end of the past century, few analysts anywhere in the world would have predicted that in less than two decades, India would emerge as the fastest growing major economy of the world." This change, however, could not have happened overnight. Certain core policies adopted somewhere during our economic management would have brought in this transformation. While taking the credit of fastest growing economy in the world, we cannot lose sight to the glaring problems of our political economy.

> The performance in terms of job creation is hopelessly poor. There is plenty of evidence to show that inequalities in income and wealth have widened. The ecology is severely degraded. Politically and socially, there appear to be extraordinarily serious strains. Under the present political dispensation, the secular fabric of the country is possibly going through its severest travail that the minorities have known in recent decades. These are not good auguries.

Several of these issues have been discussed in detail in the chapters that follow. Rangarajan (chapter 4) analysing the early thoughts regarding the market failures and role of state, sums up the debate as follows:

> If there is a lesson to be drawn from the development record of the last four decades, it is that there can be both 'government failure' as well as 'market failure', and that the critical issue is not so much the presence or absence of state intervention, as the extent and quality of that intervention.

He is of the view that policymakers in India in the 1950s and 1960s cannot be blamed for the decisions they took as there was no clear model available for accelerating growth in developing countries at that time. However, by early 1970s, it was becoming clear that the model we had chosen was not delivering and that it needed change. But our policymakers refused to recognise this.

The severe economic crisis, triggered by a serious BoPs (balance of payments) problem in the year 1991 is an important landmark in the economic history of India. The crisis was converted into an opportunity to affect some fundamental changes in the content and approach to economic policy, says Rangarajan.

It was Dr Manmohan Singh as Finance Minister who spearheaded the economic reforms, articulated the need for change and provided not only the broad framework but also the details of the reforms, while Prime Minister P.V. Narasimha Rao provided the much needed political support and shield. That the economic reforms undertaken have been on the right track is vindicated by the performance of the economy since the launch of reforms. Continuing this discussion, Pulapre Balakrishnan (chapter 6) says:

> Economic growth in the 10-year period beginning 2005-06 despite the crisis affected year of 2008-2009 was at an average rate of 7.7 per cent. Between 2005-06 and 2007-08, the economy grew at an annual rate of 9.4 per cent. Economic growth slowed down from 2012-13. However, according to the new methodology adopted by Central Statistics Office (CSO), there was a pick-up in growth rate even in 2013-14. It is imperative that we get back to the high growth rate we had seen in the years following 2005-06.

Any discussion on what holds India back focuses on lack of accountability in the administration, inefficiency and corruption, bureaucracy at all levels, lack of coordination, centralisation of power, opaque decision-making, non-delegation to municipalities and *panchayats*, investigation and police systems that are under political control, and the weakened state of the judiciary, to mention only a few. It would be better if we have uniform structures and authorities and if they followed each others' orders to ensure that there is a body of regulatory law and precedents that could enrich the whole business of regulation (S.L. Rao, chapter 19).

Bibek Debroy (chapter 5) poses the question: "Where do we want India to be in 2030? Are we clear about where we want to go? Or, as a country, are we just trundling along, as long as we get somewhere?" In the Preamble to our Constitution, we had promised India's citizens, justice, liberty, equality and dignity. We have not been able to ensure that. "We have failed the Constitution and the Constitutional promise. We have introduced policies that haven't ensured justice, liberty, equality and dignity".

There is an impression that India has changed a lot, particularly after 1991. Indeed it has, and this shows up in all kinds of different indicators. India is described as a young country, with a median age that is around 25 years. There are several external reports that are bullish about India. According to UNDP Human Development Report (HDR), India had a HDI (human development index) value of 0.320 in 1985 placing it in the low human development category. In 2014, this value improved to 0.609, placing it in the medium human development category.

In recent times, HDRs have also introduced a MPI (multi-dimensional poverty index). In addition to standard income or consumption poverty measures, this includes deprivation measured in terms of education, health and other assets. On this basis, 81 per cent of people are multi-dimensionally poor in Bihar—more than any other state. Uttar Pradesh is the home of largest number of poor people—21 per cent of India's poor people live there and

West Bengal is home to the third largest number of poor people. People are poor mostly because even after 70 years of independence, they lack access to physical infrastructure (transport, water, electricity), social infrastructure (education, skills, health), financial products, natural resources, technology, information technology, the judicial system, and markets.

There is also the problem of inequality in access to inputs (physical and social infrastructure, financial products and so on). There is a difference between inequality in access to inputs and inequality in outcomes (income). Everyone would like India to be equitable. The equity should be interpreted in terms of access to inputs and one should be legitimately upset if there is inequity in that. However, why should there be equality in outcomes, remarks Debroy. If there is growth and development, poverty declines. Also, both poverty and inequality are dynamic concepts: they change over time. If there is growth, and poverty declines, there is less resentment about inequality.

Rising inequalities is a concern in many advanced and developing countries of the world. S. Mahendra Dev (chapter 7) has discussed in great detail the dimensions and trends in inequality at the global level and India as well, and how do we tackle rising inequalities at policy level. The focus of his paper is on economic, social and gender inequalities in India, with some discussion at global level. While the governments have implemented policies that unleashed the country's tremendous growth potential, there is urgent need to embark on a process of social transformation that ends discrimination on the basis of caste, class and gender. India has underinvested in human and social capital. Productive employment and quality education for everyone can reduce inequalities significantly. Another issue in the context of India is exclusion of SCs (scheduled castes), STs (scheduled tribes), women and minorities. We need social movements to reduce social exclusion. This happened partially in South India earlier in Kerala and Tamil Nadu, and is now in progress in other parts of the country. But it is still a long way for major social transformations, remarks Mahendra Dev. Process of development must become more socially and economically inclusive. The agenda of inclusiveness and equality has to be given highest priority for broad-based social and economic development.

Regional Inequality in Development

C.H. Hanumantha Rao's paper (chapter 8) is devoted to growing regional inequality in development.

> It is now well established that the inter-state inequality in the growth of GSDP (gross state domestic product) has increased in the post-economic reform period from the early 1990s when compared to the 1980s. In general, the richer states have grown faster than the poorer states. The regional inequality in per capita GSDP growth is even greater because the poorer states have experienced faster growth in population.

Although interstate disparities in per capita GSDP have increased significantly in the post-reform period, the corresponding disparity in HDI has declined from 0.22 in 1981 to 0.19 in 1991 and to 0.16 in 2001. India HDR 2011 shows improvement in HDI for majority of low per capita income states compared to India as a whole. OECD Economic Survey and Economic Survey of India confirm significant reduction in interstate variation in human development indicators. This is a welcome development, says Rao. There is also a silver lining in the experience of recently created smaller states, viz., Chhattisgarh, Jharkhand and Uttaranchal, showing that these states achieved growth rates far exceeding the targets set for the 10th Plan period, whereas the performance of their parent states, viz., Madhya Pradesh, Bihar and Uttar Pradesh fell considerably short of the targets. Apart from releasing the creative energies of the people, viability of smaller states may have contributed to better governance, attracting greater private investment from outside as well as planning and utilising resources more efficiently.

New Challenges and Opportunities

After 25 years of economic reforms, we are witnessing new challenges arising out of recent policy initiatives which according to Y.V. Reddy (chapter 10) are full of promise but not without risks.

Demonetisation, Digitalisation and Beyond

Prime Minister Narendra Modi on 8 November 2016 made the drastic announcement of demonetisation of ₹500 and ₹1,000 notes. What compelled the Prime Minister to take this measure under which 86.4 per cent of the total value of the currency in circulation as of March 2016 became redundant overnight? In seeking public support for demonetisation, he argued it was indispensable to combat: (i) black money, (ii) terrorist financing, and (iii) counterfeit currency. Belated, another rationale emerged: accelerating a shift to a less cash/cashless economy. During the process of implementation of demonetisation, digitalisation of payment transactions accelerated significantly.

> There are downsides to digitalisation, which demand vigilance. Its direct and immediate impact on black money and corruption is negligible as per indications so far. Yet, it is not a mere shock akin to a truckers' strike but has systemic implications for the future (Reddy, chapter 10).

One of the important consequences of the Indian demonetisation experiment according to A. Vasudevan (chapter 11) was that overall demand, especially the retail demand declined, and business investment prospects became somewhat opaque, forcing economic entities to resort to a variety of digital modes of payment. Payments through cheques, credit and debit cards, prepaid cards, e-wallets, online payments and net banking were made by ordinary women and men. A welcome development, this however, gave rise to a number of questions and challenges—the cost of use of different modes—the regulatory framework and how quickly could disputes be settled and about safety, costs and loss of privacy.

According to Vasudevan, while questions relating to transactional modes of digitisation can be resolved with good technology solutions and efficient governance mechanisms, the resolution of the questions would of course take some time. Its effectiveness would depend on the infrastructure and connectivity available for development of technology and easy access for all social and economic classes and for all regions and sub-regions. The costs involved for developing a robust infrastructure including the required skills and innovations in technology as well as sufficient number of sound applications and solutions are phenomenal. Digital systems form a very minor portion of total transactions as of now—the McKinsey Global Institute places them at less than one per cent in a study published in September 2016.

Macroeconomic Policies

To address the challenges that the State faces, the State's macroeconomic policy dynamics, which consist of three major areas, viz., fiscal policy, monetary policy and exchange rate policy as also structural policies such as the industrial policy and contract laws, will have to be geared. Going by the received analytics, it is taken for granted that fiscal and monetary policies should not only be transparent but also led by 'rules' that are supposed to provide domestic economic and monetary stability. More importantly, macroeconomic policies should not contain surprises. They should be devoid of discretion to policymakers (Vasudevan, chapter 11).

A landmark development in macroeconomic management is a new monetary policy framework. The government made a formal commitment to inflation targeting in the budget announcement of 2016. The main features of inflation targeting framework are that there is a single inflation target, viz., inflation and a single instrument used by the central bank, viz., short-term interest rate, and a single objective, viz., price stability. This new framework replaced the multiple indicator approach, the multiple objectives with flexible inter se prioritisation and multiple instruments. With this regime, monetary policy framework is subject to rules and thus constitutes a supplement to the rule based fiscal management established through Fiscal Responsibility and Budget Management (FRBM) Act about 10 years ago. The new framework has several advantages in terms of transparency, focus, accountability, autonomy and predictability (Reddy, chapter 10).

The FRBM review committee was appointed in May 2016, to review FRBM legislation to examine the need and feasibility of having a 'fiscal deficit range' as the target in place of the existing fixed numbers (percentage of GDP) as fiscal deficit target, and to examine the need and feasibility of aligning the fiscal expansion or contraction with credit contraction or expansion respectively in the economy. Indira Rajaraman's paper (chapter 14) tries to capture the state of play in respect of prudential limits on debt and deficits.

The report of the FRBM committee (2017) for India states right at the outset that their approach was to mark a prudential level for general government debt, aggregating across Centre and states, as the anchor to which the fiscal deficit as the operating target would be prescribed. The prudential level was set by them at 60 per cent of GDP, and a draft bill in an annexe to the report accordingly commits the (Central) government to bringing down the national public debt from roughly 70 per cent of GDP at the end of fiscal year 2017 to 60 per cent by 2023. The debt of the Centre is also marked for reduction from 49 per cent to 39 per cent of GDP by 2023. From this it is clear that the heavy lifting in terms of the fairly sharp fiscal correction targeted over the period of 2017 to 2023 is to be done at the Centre; the states essentially are held at the same level of debt as they were in 2017.

The tension between the need for flexibility and the need for firm boundaries so as to rein in political fiscal excesses remains unresolved. The success of fiscal rules, whether rigid or flexible, will be a function of the level of governance in the country. In India, protected as we are from subnational excesses by constitutional guardrails, the fiscal record has been by and large good, with no sovereign defaults. But the governance challenge remains at both Central and state levels. The task of fiscal responsibility lies in so devising the structure that expenditures can be contained at a sustainable deficit over and above revenue, while still maintaining high standards of quality in public service delivery.

GST

The GST, touted as a 'game changer' and the 'reform of the century', was deemed worthy of a launch on the midnight of 30 June 2017 in the Central Hall of the Parliament (Govinda Rao, chapter 12). The enormous publicity that it has received and the great gains spoken about 'one nation, one market, one tax' by both the Government and the captains of industry have raised high expectations and if not realised could lead to disappointments, remarks, Govinda Rao. With multiple rates as it has been introduced, it is not a simple tax and robs much of the benefits from lower administrative, compliance and distortion costs. "There are concerns about the rates of tax, mandated compliances and glitches in transition, and investment activity is virtually at a standstill".

According to Vijay Kelkar (chapter 15), the approach adopted by the authorities robs the GST of its efficiency enhancing potentials because of: (i) multiple rates, (ii) different rates for goods and services, (iii) high rates for retail level and leaving out infrastructure sector such as construction, unworkable assets. Consequently: (i) the growth impact on the economy is estimated to be only one-fourth of its potential impact of what the 13th Finance Commission had estimated, (ii) high compliance cost arising out of different rates and consequent classification of disputes, (iii) lower compliance levels due to the rates going up to as high as 26 per cent at retail level, (iv) potential slackening of tax efforts by the States due to promised 100 per cent compensation of the shortfall. Concluding on the positive note Kelkar remarks:

> I have no doubt that we will eventually move from one nation, one tax to one nation, one tax, one registration and one rate and I am sure this single rate will be closer to 12 per cent. I am reminded by what Sir Winston Churchill said about US as this is relevant to other large democracy such as India. He said, "United States finally does right thing but only after trying all other alternatives".

Fiscal Federalism

Fiscal federalism has been one of the important pillars for the success of our enduring democracy. The subject has been discussed by Vijay Kelkar, M. Govinda Rao and Y.V. Reddy in chapter 15, 17 and 10 respectively. Kelkar has discussed the need to revisit the fiscal federal architecture in contemporary India, the changing political-economic parametric environment calling for commensurate change in the way our fiscal federal setup ought to be conceptualised. He has also suggested some important and innovative policy and fiscal reform proposals for their possible resolution. "While the final resolution of these matters will be attained through a dialectic that will play out in the domain of real politik, it is important that such a process be helped along by evidence based analysis and debate".

According to Govinda Rao, in keeping with the Constitutional arrangement, overwhelming proportions of expenditures on social services are delivered by the State governments and States' share of expenditures on economic services is as much as that of the Union government. This was possible because of the transfer system. Although the States' share in raising revenues is 37 per cent of the total, their share in expenditures is 60 per cent. At the same time, there are large and increasing differences in taxable capacities among the States and the transfer system has not been able to fully offset the revenue disabilities resulting in large and persisting differences in per capita expenditures on social and economic services among the States. Per capita expenditures on social and economic services are positively correlated with per capita GSDP. Per capita development expenditure in the State with the lowest per capita GSDP is less than 50 per cent of the average. The Union government ministries have a number of specific purpose transfers called Centrally Sponsored Schemes (CSS) but it is difficult to link the schemes to outcomes because of the large number of schemes and their spread of resources. Most of the schemes which are close ended and having uniform matching requirements have serious design problems. There have been several attempts to rationalise and consolidate them and yet, the problems continue.

The recommendations of the 14th Finance Commission provided a comprehensive framework for reform of Union-State fiscal relations, and in the process, touched upon some fundamental issues relating to institutional arrangements (Reddy, chapter 10): (i) it eschewed a differentiation between plan and non-plan expenditures, a practice prevalent for decades, (ii) the share of state in taxes from 32 per cent to 42 per cent, thus increasing the fiscal space available to states; and restricting the discretionary fiscal space to Union, (iii) sector specific/ project specific grants-in-aid from the Union to the States eliminated, thus reducing scope for discretion, and (iv) transfers to local bodies were increased and made almost conditions free.

Resulting from the actions taken on the recommendations, according to Reddy, three risks have emerged: (i) increase in the fiscal deficit of states, (ii) fall in the expenditure of Union Government on social sector, and (iii) emboldened the states to announce waiver of loans to farmers.

The 15th Finance Commission due to be appointed before the end of the year, would also indicate the contours of further changes in fiscal federalism in India.

Conditional Cash Transfers

CCTs, targeted at the extremely poor and backward regions are increasingly used in developing countries to improve human development indicators. Their use in improving education and healthcare in poor countries is regarded as a major initiative in promoting investment in human capital among the poor. In the paper by Devendra B. Gupta (chapter 18), an attempt is made to document international experience with CCTs with a view to derive lessons for India. It suggests the need for exploring the possibility of casting schemes in the CCT mould, but before implementing or introducing CCTs on any large scale, as a first step it would be prudent to undertake a pilot study. There are several schemes that could form the basis for such a study: at least two schemes involving cash transfers and one scheme with transfers in kind could be chosen. At least one scheme may be from the area of education and another from the area of health. Another could have a social objective, such as promoting village sanitation, delaying the age at marriage, etc. The pilot study may focus on a couple of districts in at least two or three states. The lessons learnt could then be fine-tuned and refined to adopt CCTs approach on a large scale. International experience with CCTs (Brazil and Bangladesh) with a view to derive lessons for India, have also been documented in the chapter.

Monetary Policy

Deepak Mohanty in his paper (chapter 13) gives a snapshot of monetary policy in India as it evolved over eight decades since the establishment of the Reserve Bank of India (RBI) in 1935. The decades of 1950s and 1960s saw a low level of financial intermediation. This scenario began to change in the 1970s following nationalisation of major banks and consequent expansion of banking. The upward movement in intermediation continued till the mid-1990s. Subsequently, the upward trend in intermediation continued but with a difference: it was accompanied by significant increase in money multiplier emanating from reforms to reduce statutory pre-emptions.

Quoting Mohanty, "With the benefit of hindsight, it is tempting to misjudge history, but developments are best appreciated in the milieu and state of knowledge of the times." Monetary policy evolved alongside the development of the financial sector. Increased financial depth of the Indian economy provided the opportunity for market based reforms in the monetary policy framework. Formulating monetary policy is an ever-evolving process in response to and as a consequence of changes in financial markets and the real economy, and this is a phenomenon we see in India in monetary policy formulation over the eight decades.

Financial Crisis and the Indian Economy

India's management of the 'triple crises'—fiscal, BoP and financial—experienced sequentially between the late-1980s and the mid-1990s, set the stage for India's response to the Asian and, more recently, the 'trans-Atlantic' financial crises (Sanjaya Baru, chapter 16).

> The cumulative impact of the reforms undertaken since 1991 has been to make the Indian economy more resilient to external shocks, even as it has become more open to external flows, enabling India to sustain an acceleration of her economic growth within a more open economy framework.

India's experience with handling the triple economic crises it confronted in the early 1990s has helped put in place a regime of policies that have contributed to an acceleration of economic growth and a strengthening of the Indian economy. This has helped India deal with the current slowdown with a greater degree of confidence, remarks Baru.

While India's reintegration into the world economy in the 1990s has made her more vulnerable to global crises, her pursuit of gradual reform and prudent regulation seem to have helped her minimise the negative impact of the trans-Atlantic financial crisis and the global economic slowdown. From a strategic policy perspective, India can claim that her model of 'gradual' and 'graduated' economic liberalisation, and of risk averse prudential regulation in the banking and financial sector have helped limit her exposure to the Asian and Trans-Atlantic financial crises, and the subsequent global economic slowdown.

The global economic downturn offers an opportunity for the world's largest democracies and market economies to work together to strengthen the foundations of open societies and open economies, by creating a global order that is supportive of India's developmental aspirations and the aspirations of all developing country democracies, like Brazil, Indonesia, and South Africa.

Development and Ecology

India today consists of a society characterised by profound inequality. Multiple stakeholders have emerged with powerful voices in the Indian polity and it is not easy to reconcile their interests. In this kind of set up, is a movement towards thoughtful conservation and development possible? Are we as a nation at all willing to implement policies that ask for some degree of restraint in the exploitation of our natural resources? Or are we going to pursue a pattern of development which concentrates on the maximisation of present gains of the privileged few to the detriment of the interests of vulnerable people and ecologically fragile areas? Kanchan Chopra (chapter 20) has illustrated how we can go about with the help of deliberations and policy formulation with regard to the ecologically sensitive area on a case by case basis, thereby internalising the environmental grass roots learnings and movements into existing institutional structures.

Context-specific Economic Theories

T.C.A. Srinivasa-Raghavan (chapter 21) questions the essential foundations of a discipline of macroeconomics.

> If you keep changing the essential foundations of a discipline, and, most of all, if you can't define its limits, sooner or later you will lose credibility. Nowhere is this truer than in macroeconomics, which is a closed system with about half a dozen or so variables, such as the GDP growth rate, the fiscal deficit, interest rates, the exchange rate,

the current account, capital account, and so on. Economics assumes these variables to be in very tight relationships with each other and arrives at conclusions that go wrong because, in fact, these relationships are very loose.

It is most alarming that under the current framework of macroeconomics, its existing tools have become ineffective for a large variety of reasons, not the least of which is technological change. The author advocates moving away from one size-fits-all economic theory. The 20th century saw two modes of economic thought being universalised: Marshallian analysis at the microeconomic level and Keynesian solutions at the macroeconomic level. Every country needs to develop adaptations of these which are best suited to its context.

Agriculture and Agrarian Distress

In keeping with the importance of agriculture as the mainstay of Indian economy because of its high share of employment and livelihood creation in rural India, agriculture gets its due share in terms of coverage of the subject in this volume. Leading agricultural economists of the country: M.S. Swaminathan, V.S. Vyas, Ashok Gulati, R.S. Deshpande and Ramesh Chand have discussed the problems facing Indian agriculture today. According to Deshpande and Shaha (chapter 23), India's agriculture is stranded at a jagged crossroad for many years now, and not many effective solutions have come forward. This dismal situation is exposed by the agitating farmers throwing their farm produce on the roads, and suicides becoming quite frequent portents of distress besides becoming a tool in the hands of politicians. Farmers are unhappy with the ineffective policies being dished out by the State. The agrarian distress has been highlighted by other authors also: Swaminathan (chapter 22), Ramesh Chand (chapter 24) and Vyas (chapter 26).

"While India was marching ahead in attaining and improving food security and leaving behind the era of food shortage, another crisis started building gradually in the form of agrarian distress. The situation has become particularly bad during the last two years because of two successive failures of monsoon and abnormal rainfall in *Rabi* 2014-15 and highly deficit precipitation in *Rabi* 2015-16. These types of sufferings do not bode well for the country whose economy is growing at more than 7 per cent a year and which plans to be counted as globally powerful nation," remarks Ramesh Chand.

The distress is said to be the cause for some farmers to take the extreme step to end their lives by committing suicides. Ramesh Chand's paper is an attempt to understand the genesis, causes, nature and severity of agrarian distress, and to propose measure and strategy to mitigate and banish agrarian distress in the country. As rightly pointed out by him, agrarian distress cannot be removed by doubling farm subsidies, raising MSP (minimum support price), and expanding MGNREGA, or food subsidies. The sustainable way to address this is to undertake development measures and policy reforms which can lead to fast growth in income per farmer. Swaminathan cautions that in addition to facing the problems of today, we should prepare ourselves for meeting the emerging challenges arising from climate change. He believes that one of the major step needed is to strengthen the ecological foundations for sustainable agriculture—soil, water, biodiversity and climate. The transition from the green to the evergreen revolution requires the mainstreaming of ecological principles in technology development and dissemination. Another problem which needs attention is malnutrition and eradication of hunger.

According to Deshpande, the travelogue of Indian agriculture clearly depicts a staggered approach and lack of any long-term focus. Every phase began to deal with some of the current issues but ended with a few new problems. The fire-fighting approach ended up in dishing out new schemes that did not have any long-term development thinking behind it.

V.S. Vyas (chapter 26) argues, most of the policies of rural development are geared towards making the goods or services cheaper by subsidising them under one plea or the other, be it credit, fertilisers or power. There is ample evidence to show that a large part of these subsidies, with few exceptions, are pre-empted by 'non-poor', and eventually filter back to urban manufacturers, traders or service providers. He continues that to bridge the gap between the rural and the urban sector, we need to look into the policies designed for the rural areas, and also focus on the weakness in the principal rural institutions which are mainly bureaucracy, *panchayats* and cooperatives. Unfortunately, evidence shows that *panchayats* and cooperatives are in state of decay both because of government interference and politicisation. The frequent experimentation in the structure and functioning of the village institutions has yielded very little positive results. There is an urgent need to address the conceptual, structural and technical questions jointly with the villagers who would be the principal beneficiaries, or sufferers, of the changes in these institutions, and to create a consensus for reforms.

Emerging Water Crisis

Ashok Gulati and Pritha Banerjee (chapter 25) highlighting the emerging water crisis say, India is one of the water-stressed countries of the world and is going to become water scarce in due course. Unfortunately, the scarcity of water gets accentuated more by its inefficient use than by its physical availability. Currently, about 78 per cent of water in India is used in agriculture. With rapid urbanisation and industrialisation, water demand for competing uses is going to rise sharply. It is therefore necessary that issues related to water use in agriculture are addressed in time. These issues briefly are: more than half of agricultural area is still dependent on rainfall for production; pricing of irrigation water and power remains woefully low; water use efficiency in irrigation practices is low; the costs of surface irrigation are high; groundwater is depleting fast, and there is total lack of demand side management of water use.

To overcome many of these problems, the authors suggest rationalising water and power charges in sync with improvement in the quality of water and power supplied; direct transfer of irrigation and power subsidies to beneficiaries' accounts instead of subsidising them through price policy; speeding up the process of completing spillover projects in order to avoid further cost escalations; discouraging production of water-intensive crops in water scarce areas and encouraging drip and sprinkler irrigation to improve water use efficiency. It will also be wise to look at best practices in some selected countries that have been more successful in optimising the use of their scarce water supplies, especially by rewarding farmers for frugal use of water and power. Last but not the least, proper extension services are necessary for creating awareness among farmers to ensure optimum use of water. However, the real game changer lies in the hands of our leaders in seeing this crisis situation as an opportunity of introducing some path-breaking reforms in the irrigation sector.

Manufacturing: Growth, Productivity and Job Creation

B.N. Goldar (chapter 27) has analysed growth, productivity and employment generation in Indian manufacturing during 1980-81 to 2014-15, focusing mostly on the organised sector of manufacturing which dominates Indian manufacturing in terms of invested capital, output and value added. The analysis revealed that growth in RVA (real value added) in India's organised manufacturing accelerated significantly since 2003-04. The growth rate in single deflated value added in organised manufacturing was found to be 6.72 per cent per annum during 1980-81 to 2002-03, which increased to 8.93 per cent per annum during 2003-04 to 2014-15. There was a much sharper increase in the growth rate of double deflated value added in organised manufacturing, which is a more satisfactory measure of RVA. The growth rate in double-deflated value added in organised manufacturing was found to be 8.40 per cent per annum during 1980-1981 to 2002-03, which increased to 13.68 per cent per annum during 2003-04 to 2014-15, a hike of about 5.3 percentage points. The analysis of RVA growth in organised manufacturing clearly indicated that the use of single deflation procedure in India's national accounts is leading to an underestimation of manufacturing sector growth, especially for the period from 2003-04.

It was found from the analysis that there was a surge in the growth rates in employment and TFP (total factor productivity) in India's organised manufacturing during the period 2003-04 to 2014-15. While the trend growth rate in employment in organised manufacturing was less than one per cent per annum during 1980-81 to 2002-03, in the subsequent period, 2003-04 to 2014-15, it was more than 4.5 per cent per annum. As regards TFP, the growth rate went up from 3.2 per cent per annum during the period 1980-1981 to 2002-03 to 7.3 per cent per annum during the period 2003-04 to 2014-15 according to one set of TFP estimates, and the increase was from 3.5 per cent per annum during 1980-81 to 2002-03 to 6.01 per cent per annum during 2003-04 to 2014-15, according to an alternate set of TFP estimates. Nearly half of the hike in real (double deflated) value added growth achieved by India's organised manufacturing in the period 2003-04 to 2014-15 was found to be traceable to accelerated TFP growth.

While there was a marked acceleration in employment growth in organised manufacturing since 2003-04, the unorganised manufacturing sector which dominates in terms of the jobs provided by manufacturing, accounting for about 75-80 per cent of total manufacturing employment, experienced a sluggish or negative growth in employment in the 2000s.

According to Y.K. Alagh (chapter 9), there is a connection between employment and poverty. He says that it has been a long journey from 'population problem' to 'demographic dividend', and from 'surplus labour' to 'skill development'. But it would be naïve to pretend that the problématique is not severe any more. Dividends can become losses and there is nothing more frustrating than unrequited skills. There is genuine uncertainty about the future of India's population. When population is poor, hungry, unemployed, or unhealthy, they are certainly not an asset. We need to ensure that our growth process is long-term, holistic, sustainable and all inclusive. It should percolate and trickle down to the lowest strata of the economy. To reap the benefits of demographic dividend, State and society need to work collectively and progressively.

Indian Labour Laws

In a critical review of some recent research on Indian labour laws, Aditya Bhattacharjea (chapter 28) has tried to establish negative economic outcomes for firms exceeding employment levels of 50 and/or 100 workers, supposedly corresponding to the thresholds at which different sections of the Industrial Disputes Act (IDA) become applicable. He has shown in this chapter, that these thresholds are inaccurately mapped from the IDA, and that the classification of factories into the corresponding size classes is also inaccurate because of different methods of calculating employment in the IDA and the Annual Survey of Industries (ASI). The thresholds therefore represent boundaries that are fuzzy rather than sharp.

As the author states, the purpose of his paper is not to argue against quantification, without which economic analysis can make little progress. Rather, what is needed is to be more careful in our understanding of laws and data sources.

Bank Debt and Neoliberal Growth

While India is being lauded for being the fastest growing economy in the world, the government is grappling with a bad debt problem that threatens the solvency of at least some of its banks. A feature of recent Indian development has been the persistence of high growth despite fiscal contraction and the absence of any export boom under neoliberalism in India. But that growth has been accompanied and driven by a credit boom. And a consequence of that credit boom has been the return of large NPAs (non-performing assets) in the banking system, despite reform and recapitalisation and the reduction of NPAs. That is, the early success of banking reform in reducing NPAs was followed by the subsequent dismal failure of reform to keep NPAs from rising once again. The problem is not just the volume of bad assets, but the rapid growth in such assets (Chandrasekhar and Ghosh, chapter 30).

The credit boom of the 2000s was the result of the easy liquidity situation that a surge in capital inflows created. Combined with banking policy liberalisation, this triggered a credit spiral that was based on an expansion of the universe of borrowers that brought in clients who were more prone to default. Unfortunately, the focus of the government and the RBI is on finding ways in which the banks can help large business groups revive, rather than how banks can recover their dues and beef up their balance sheets.

Infrastructure Financing

Nagesh Kumar's paper (chapter 30) reviews the role of NDBs (national development banks) in infrastructure financing in India in the context of need to close wide infrastructure gaps and staggering resource requirements to close them. Starting with the objective of supporting industrialisation, new age NDBs support infrastructure development and sustainable infrastructure investments through a variety of ways and through funds mobilised from diverse domestic and international sources. These NDBs are complemented by a number of NDBs catering to specific infrastructure sectors. The growing focus of the government on harnessing the potential of renewable energy is directing their activities to sustainable infrastructure.

NDBs are helping to address the issue of asset-liability mismatch inherent in bank-lending to infrastructure that continues to provide the bulk of debt to infrastructure investments. NDBs have begun to mobilise large scale longer term resources. They are also relieving the balance sheets of banks through take-out finance and through credit enhancement strategies.

Given the enormity of the infrastructure challenge faced by India requiring mobilisation of nearly $3.5 trillion by 2030, there is need for huge mobilisation of resources. In that context, establishment of new MDBs (multilateral development banks) including NDB of BRICS and Asian Infrastructure Investment Bank (AIIB) is an important development of interest for India. As a founder member of both the institutions, India has much to contribute to their evolution as robust financial institutions equipped to play an important development role complementing the existing MDBs. India has also much to benefit from arrival of the new players on horizon for lending for infrastructure development in developing countries.

Mega Trade Blocs

According to Rajesh Chadha and Devender Pratap (chapter 31), there is need to fill a major gap in India's strategy for moving forward in the era of mega trading blocs. This becomes even more important given the dormant World Trade Organization (WTO). While most of the major economies in the world are busy signing up as members of one or more trading blocs, India has been signing bilateral trade agreements starting 2000s. It is only since 2013 that the discussions on India joining the Regional Comprehensive Economic Partnership (RCEP) have commenced. There has not been a comprehensive ex ante or ex post study to analyse India's preferential trade policy agreements. In a fractured world of trade discipline, India needs to give high priority to undertake policy research on its options for the future.

One of the most important needs today is to generate productive jobs in labour-intensive manufacturing sectors that can absorb the surplus unskilled and semi-skilled labour force in the country. While these sectors can emerge successfully through a better domestic policy regime, external factors are also important. Open trade policies lead to efficient allocation of productive resources. Trade liberalisation is expected to lead to positive outcomes by expanding sectors that produce manufactured goods in which India has a comparative advantage due to its wage rate advantage. The trade opportunities must be exploited through a well-chartered regional trade agreements route along with implementing the right domestic policy regime so as to leverage India's comparative advantage and economic growth along with rapid job creation.

Conclusion

The coming decade is going to be crucial for India. We need to overcome the low growth phase as quickly as possible as growth is the answer to many of our socioeconomic problems, remarks Rangarajan. A large number of schemes have been launched for broadening the base of growth which has been discussed in various chapters in this book. All these programmes have made a substantial demand on public expenditure which has been made possible only because of strong growth witnessed in recent years facilitating raising more resources by the government.

Development is multidimensional. It has to be inclusive. It must be poverty reducing and environment-friendly. We need to incorporate all these elements in the growth process. Growth must benefit all segments of society. It is only strong and balanced growth, which will enable the economy to achieve multiple goals. We cannot take pride in being the fastest growing country if we are not able to ensure a more humane and just world for all the citizens of our great country. Readers will find this message in most of the papers in this volume.

2

The Saga of the Delhi School of Economics

A Sketch

K.L. KRISHNA

Introduction

The Delhi School of Economics (DSE) is an institution of national importance conceived on the eve of Independence and founded in 1949 by the visionary economist, Prof V.K.R.V. Rao. The purpose of this essay is to trace the evolution of DSE, which will soon be completing seven decades of its existence. The original DSE grew out of the Department of Economics of the University of Delhi. In 1959, the departments of Sociology and Human Geography were created on the initiative of the then Vice-Chancellor V.K.R.V. Rao, as constituent units of DSE and located on its campus. This essay deals only with the evolution of the Department of Economics, the original DSE.

Dharma Kumar and Dilip Mookherjee (1995) book covers the departments of Economics and Sociology. It contains 31 essays contributed by some teachers and former students in the two departments. The essays by K.N. Raj, A.L. Nagar, Amartya Sen, Prasanta Pattanaik, Prabhat Patnaik, Ashok Lahiri, Mrinal Datta Chaudhuri, Kaushik Basu and Jean Dreze and by a few students of

---

This essay is prepared in memory of the late Raj Kapila who was a student of V. K.R.V. Rao, B.N. Ganguly and P.N. Dhar in the MA Economics programme at the DSE during 1953-1955. The author of the essay had the privilege of knowing the scholar-entrepreneur Raj Kapila for nearly four decades before his sad demise in August 2016.

Economics provide useful information and fresh insights regarding the academic performance of the department over the years until early 1990s. Some of these assessments will be referred to in the following sections.

The plan of this essay is as follows: Section 2 presents V.K.R.V. Rao's vision for DSE and its actual founding in 1949. Section 3 describes some major developments, namely, the founding of the Institute of Economic Growth (IEG) by transferring the applied economic research sections from DSE in 1958, the creation in 1959 of the departments of Sociology and Human Geography, as constituent units of DSE. Section 4 covering the period 1962 to 1971, depicts how a 'galaxy' of economists attracted to the School contributed to impressive strengthening of the teaching standards and research activities. An 'exodus' occurred around 1970 with several members of the 'galaxy' leaving the School. Section 5 shows how the department coped with the 'exodus' and managed to fill the gaps, and continued to be one of the best departments in the country during the period 1971-1994. The founding of the Centre for Development Economics (CDE) in early 1990s, thanks to the leadership initiative of Kaushik Basu, and the impressive performance of CDE during the past quarter century in raising the research output of the department is outlined in section 6. The student placement project is described in section 7. In section 8, the protagonists of the DSE story, who are no more with us, are remembered, beginning from V.K.R.V. Rao and ending with Suresh Tendulkar. Concluding remarks constitute section 9.

Appendix A-2.1 gives the list of Directors of DSE since 1949, and Appendix A-2.2 gives the list of the Heads of the Department of Economics since 1949.

The Founding of the DSE (1942-1949)

It may be useful to describe briefly the antecedents of Prof V.K.R.V. Rao, the Founder of the DSE.

Vijayendra Kasturi Ranga Varadaraja (V.K.R.V.) Rao (1908-1991) was born at Kancheepuram in Tamil Nadu. His family moved to Mumbai when Rao was 13 years old.

His father, a practising astrologer, identified Rao as the most likely among his four children to change the family fortunes. Rao received preferential nutrition out of the meagre family earnings. English became his medium of instruction. He had a very successful school and college career (see Rao 2002: 2).

Rao did his MA by thesis in 1929 at the University of Bombay, where he was a student of Prof C.N. Vakil, who founded the Bombay School of Economics and Sociology, which enjoyed international reputation. Rao's thesis was published in 1931 with the title Taxation of Income in India and was the first exhaustive study of its kind (see Rao 2002: 4).

Rao pursued higher studies in Cambridge, United Kingdom. At Cambridge, he stood first in the Economics tripos, and won the Adam Smith Prize. He was among the first three PhDs Cambridge produced in Economics, the other two being H.W. Singer and A.K. Cairncross. He caught the attention of J.M. Keynes and became a member of the famous Political Economy Club. Under the influence of Keynes, Rao came to believe that intelligent state intervention would be efficacious in solving economic problems facing developing countries. His PhD thesis was a pioneering exercise of estimating India's national income (Dhar in Rao 2002: vi).

Rao believed in the economic profession playing a major role in public policy for economic development. His conviction was that India needed a first rate teaching and research institution in economics and other social sciences.

After his return to India from Cambridge, in 1937, Rao taught at Andhra University and Karnataka University between 1937 and 1942. He became known for his brilliance, scholarship and debating skills. Maurice Gwyer, Delhi University Vice-Chancellor, appointed Rao as the first professor of Economics in 1942. Rao was also the first professor in the University. At a dinner get together at Dr B.N. Ganguly's residence in 1946, where Dr Ganguly and Prof P.N. Dhar, teachers in Hindu College, were present, Rao declared his plan to establish the DSE on the lines of the London School of Economics (LSE) and sought their help and association with the grand project.

Rao's publications on various problems of the Indian economy around the time of Independence brought him to the notice of Jawaharlal Nehru. Rao was made a member of several important committees set up by the Government of India to examine various economic issues.

As Dhar (1995) notes, Rao's strongly held opinion was that India needed economists who had both technical competence and social awareness. In his first memorandum on the objectives of DSE, he wanted DSE to combine the activities of a department of Economics and an all-India research centre on developmental issues.

For setting up the DSE, Rao worked with singular passion and determination. But the progress was slow. It took him two years to appoint Ganguly as a Reader and Dhar as a Lecturer in the University's Department of Economics. The first major step in establishing the School was the enrolment of students to the MA course in Economics in the academic year 1948-49. The DSE Society with Prime Minister Jawaharlal Nehru as the President got formally registered in 1949, and thus the year of birth of DSE is taken as 1949.

Major Developments during 1949-1962

The expansion of the School began in 1953, after its shifting from barracks to the Arts Faculty building with ample space. Considerable additions were made to the academic and administrative staff. A statistical unit was established and a number of research assistants and research fellows were appointed. The most noteworthy appointment was that of Dr K.N. Raj as Professor of Monetary Economics in 1953. Dr Ganguly was earlier made Professor of International Trade. The school had three professors in 1953, Rao, Ganguly and Raj. Raj came from the Planning Commission after the First Five Year Plan (1951-1956) was finalised. His wide interests, affability, and scholarship endeared him to colleagues and students, as noted by Dhar (1995).

In 1953-54, the School received substantial funding for research on river-valley multipurpose projects, small-scale industries and the process and effects of urbanisation. With heightened research activity and the starting of the journal, *Indian Economic Review*, in 1952, the School became a major centre for research and teaching. Very soon two diploma courses, in Economic Statistics and Economic Administration were introduced, followed by an evening diploma course in Business Management. An orientation centre for foreign technicians was set up with funding from the Ford Foundation.

Rao wanted the School to have its own building and a campus. He secured from the University a nine-acre plot of land which now houses five buildings, in addition to the Department of Economics building (Birla Bhawan).

Thanks to the good offices of Sir V.T. Krishnamachari, Chairman of the Board of Governors, a donation of rupees six lakh from the Birla Educational Trust was obtained for the building. Rao also got one lakh rupees from Lady Ratan Tata for the library. Rao involved Ganguly, Raj and Dhar in drawing up the plans for the building, including the size of the auditorium, the lecture halls, seminar rooms, the number of stacks in the library, etc. He played a domineering role, as only to be expected, consistent with his style of functioning.

A. Dasgupta (Business Management), B.V. Krishnamurty (Economic Theory) and A.M. Khusro (Agriculture and Rural Development) were appointed professors in 1956-57. However, the rapid increase in the number of senior appointments was resented by other University departments.

Dhar notes that with the rapid expansion of the School between 1953 and 1957, its dual character of a University department as well as an autonomous institution of research and training appeared incongruous.

By the beginning of 1957, the pressure to redefine the position of the School vis-à-vis the University reached a critical stage. The School had to choose between being an autonomous institution, with uncertainty of funding or becoming an integral part of the University. Rao stood for autonomy but his colleagues were not in favour and the latter view prevailed. The School returned to its original status of a university department.

Prof V.K.R.V. Rao was appointed Vice-Chancellor of the University of Delhi in 1957. Prof B.N. Ganguly succeeded him as the Director of DSE.

A major institutional transformation in the DSE began in 1958. Prof Rao took steps to set up an institute for applied research in economics and social sciences. This institute was named Institute of Economic Growth (IEG). The applied economics research sections, demography, rural development, urbanisation and orientation centre for technicians located in the DSE building were shifted to the newly founded IEG located adjacent to DSE, and the Department of Economics in the DSE gave up its autonomy to become an integral part of the University of Delhi.

The main building of the DSE, inaugurated in 1956, was donated to the University. P.N. Dhar, A.M. Khusro, Ashish Bose and P.B. Desai and project staff in DSE moved to the IEG in 1958. Agro-Economic Research Centre (AERC) with P.K. Mukherjee as the Chief continued on the DSE Campus, as a separate entity. A couple of years later, AERC moved into its own building on the DSE campus.

In 1959, Prof V.K.R.V. Rao as Vice-Chancellor took the initiative to establish the University departments of Sociology and Human Geography as constituent parts of the DSE. Prof M.N. Srinivas, an eminent sociologist at the University of Baroda, was invited to head the Department of Sociology. A well-known geographer Prof George Kurian was the first head of the Department of Human Geography.

When C.D. Deshmukh became Vice-Chancellor of Delhi University in 1962, he persuaded Prof B.N. Ganguly to be the Pro-Vice-Chancellor. Prof K.N. Raj succeeded Prof Ganguly as the director of DSE in 1962. This was the beginning of a new era in DSE.

Progress towards Academic Excellence (1962-1971)

Prof Raj was Head of the Department of Economics during 1962-1968, and Director of DSE during 1962-1965. Under Raj's young and dynamic leadership, the faculty resources got considerably strengthened, paving the way for the restructuring of courses in mid-1960s and revamping of the PhD programme.

Prof Amartya Sen joined the School in March 1963 as Professor of Economic Theory, the post vacated by Prof V.K.R.V. Rao. With the appointment of Prof Sukhamoy Chakravarty as Professor of Mathematical Economics, Prof Jagdish Bhagwati as Professor of International Trade, succeeding Prof B.N. Ganguly, Dr Tapan Raychaudhuri as Reader in Economic History and Dr A.L. Nagar as Reader in Econometrics, the Department of Economics got considerably strengthened.

I returned to DSE in 1967 after completing my PhD on productivity in Chicago under the guidance of Prof. Zvi Griliches and took active part in teaching newly designed courses in Econometrics at different levels, along with Nagar and a few others. I supervised several theses in different areas of applied economics, to complement the work of Nagar, and other teachers.

Professors Raj and Sen and Dr Nagar in their essays in Kumar and Mookherjee (1995) discuss the major restructuring and strengthening of the MA Programme in economics in the School. The PhD programme too was revamped and reactivated. The high standards of teaching and research achieved after mid-1960s drew worldwide recognition. The School attracted bright students from all parts of India. This was the 'glorious' era for the Department of Economics.

Raj (1995) attributed the fast progress in the Department of Economics of DSE during the subsequent three decades to the "immense strengthening of the teaching and research staff, together with the restructuring of the courses" in the mid-1960s. In his overall assessment of the academic standing of the School in early 1990s, he gives credit to the valuable contributions made by the Department of Sociology in the School and the IEG.

The collaboration between DSE and IEG in the PhD programme for three decades since the inception of IEG in 1958 resulted in significant outcomes. Dharm Narain, C.H Hanumantha Rao, B.B. Bhattacharya, N.S. Siddharthan,

J.B.G. Tilak, Beena Agarwal, S.N. Mishra, and several other prominent economists of the second half of the 20th century were products of this collaboration. Asish Bose completed his PhD at DSE under the supervision of V.K.R.V. Rao around 1958. V. Pandit of DSE and K. Krishnamurty of IEG collaborated in the India World Link Project until Krishnamurty's retirement in mid-1990s. This project is now located in the Centre for Development Economics (CDE): Pami Dua and N.R. Bhanumurthy of National Institute of Public Finance and Policy (NIPFP) are the major actors in this project.

When Prof Bhagwati left for MIT in 1968, Dr Manmohan Singh was invited as Professor of International Trade. In 1970, he moved to the Ministry of Commerce, Government of India. He is still one of the three honorary professors in the Department of Economics along with Prof Amartya Sen and Prof Jean Dreze.

A Small Digression

As an aside, it may be stated that Dr Manmohan Singh has been an ardent well-wisher and benefactor of the School. He was Minister of Finance, Government of India when the CDE was founded in the Department of Economics at the initiative of Prof Kaushik Basu. He was the chief guest at the Golden Jubilee function of the School observed in January 2006. While Pandit Jawaharlal Nehru as Prime Minister inaugurated the main building of the School 50 year ago, Dr Manmohan Singh as the Prime Minister graced the Golden Jubilee function.

Recently, the DSE Annual Day 2015 function was inaugurated by Dr Singh as Honorary Professor and

Former Prime Minster, and Prof C.H. Hanumantha Rao, Chancellor, Central University of Hyderabad was the Chief Guest. It may be noted that Prof Hanumantha Rao was a PhD student in Economics during 1958-1962 at IEG and DSE. Starting as a PhD student in 1958, he rose to the position of Chairman of IEG. Teachers in the three departments of DSE who had retired were felicitated on this occasion.

At the Annual Day 2016 Function, Prof S.L. Rao, a student of DSE in early 1950s and who has held several important positions in the private sector and research institutions (National Council of Applied Economic Research [NCAER] and Institute for Social and Economic Change [ISEC]) was the Chief Guest. Non- academic staff, who retired earlier, teaching staff who retired in the previous year were felicitated at the function.

At the Annual Day 2017, function was presided over by the Vice-Chancellor Prof Yogesh Tyagi. Prof T.N. Srinivasan was the chief guest. He delivered the IER Distinguished Lecture on the "Trends in Morbidity in India: 1944-2014".

Distinguished women alumni of the three departments in DSE were felicitated. The book in honour of (late) Prof Suresh Tendulkar was released by the Vice-Chancellor.[1] Prof Pami Dua, Director DSE, has to be complimented for these initiatives on the Annual Day Functions, 2015, 2016 and 2017.

Returning to the Main Theme

The circumstances at the University level induced Prof Raj to accept the Vice-Chancellorship in 1969. He tried to introduce several institutional reforms in 1969-70. He faced stiff resistance in the decision making bodies of the University. He resigned in disgust in 1970 and returned to the School. In 1971, he accepted the Directorship of the Centre for Development Studies, Trivandrum founded

1. Krishna, K.L., V. Pandit, K. Sundaram and P, Dua (eds.) (2017). *Perspectives on Economic Development and Policy in India: In Honour of Suresh D. Tendulkar.* Singapore: Springer.

with support from the Government of Kerala, and left the School for good.

The departure of Jagdish Bhagwati in 1968, Tapan Raychaudhuri in 1969, Amartya Sen and K.N. Raj in 1971 and Manmohan Singh in 1970 from the School to take up positions elsewhere has been referred to as an exodus. It was like an 'earthquake'. The next section describes how the void was filled and academic standards were maintained.

Teaching and Research Activity Sustained Despite 'Exodus' (1971-1992)

Mrinal Datta Chaudhuri in his essay (Kumar and Mookherkee 1995: 144), notes that the 'exodus' from DSE around 1971 "seemed like an earthquake." The truncated faculty felt "overworked and demoralized". Mrinal himself made up his mind to stay on, got busy with teaching and the organisation of the teaching programme. Other colleagues too worked hard. The students understood the difficulties and became helpful and supportive.

In filling up the vacancies caused by the 'exodus', the then Vice-Chancellor, Sarup Singh, eliminated the bureaucratic delays. Prasanta Pattanaik came over to the School from Oxford in 1971, Pranab Bardhan shifted to the School from Indian Statistical Institute (ISI), Delhi, in the early 1970s, Raj Krishna, who was feeling homesick in the World Bank, joined the School in 1975, and Kaushik Basu joined the School in 1977. He became a Reader in 1978. Pulin Nayak, after getting his PhD at Rochester, was appointed as Reader along with Kaushik Basu. He taught Microeconomics and Public Economics in the following years. V. Pandit returned to DSE in 1971, having obtained his PhD at Pennsylvania under the supervision of Prof Lawrence Klein. He took part in the teaching of Econometrics, Mathematics and Macroeconomics. Former PhD students of the School, Om Prakash, K. Sundaram, J. Krishnamurty, Balvir Singh, Bhaskar Dutta and Ashok Lahiri too helped the department in the teaching arrangements. As a PhD student, Prannoy Roy too participated in teaching. Nirvikar Singh came on a visiting fellowship. Suresh Tendulkar who was in ISI, Delhi, accepted the invitation in 1978 to join the School as Professor and helped in the teaching of the compulsory course, Economic Development and Planning in India (EDPI) in collaboration with Dr K. Sundaram. The Tendulkar-Sundaram duo shared the teaching of the EDPI course for a long time. The willingness and availability of Sukhamoy Chakravarty to teach in spite of his advisory responsibilities in the Planning Commission or the Prime Minister's Economic Advisory Council was appreciated.

However, teaching gaps in some courses could not be filled satisfactorily. This left some students unhappy, as reflected in the essay of Inderjit Kohli of the MA 1980-1982 batch.

Kaushik Basu designed and taught a new elective course, Theoretical Development Economics which was approved by the Department, when Chakravarty supported the proposal. The reservations of some teachers about the desirability of the proposed course made Kaushik unhappy.

The MPhil programme introduced in mid-1970s attracted students from all parts of India. The programme produced many theses of high quality. Some illustrative examples are Nagesh Kumar's work on FDI (foreign direct investment), Adi Bhavani's work on small industry, Shama Gamkhar's work on cotton textile industry. Quite a few PhD Dissertations were completed every year. Nagar and I supervised relatively large number of theses in theoretical econometrics and applied econometrics, respectively. To give some prominent examples, Ashok Lahiri and Aman Ullah worked with Nagar, B.N. Goldar and K.R.G Nair worked with me and Mrinal. Other teachers too played an active part in research supervision. Overall, the output of research scholars did not diminish significantly. The collaboration between DSE and IEG in the doctoral programme was quite successful in the 1970s and 1980s. Several doctoral dissertations written in 1970s and 1980s brought much credit to the department. Some prominent authors are: Bhaskar Dutta, Manimay Sengupta, Sanjay Subrahmanyam, Aman Ullah, Nagesh Kumar, S. Mahendra

Dev and Adi Bhavani. I supervised several PhD and MPhil theses in the department, and extended help to research students of other universities.[2]

The point to make is the department continued to be active in student research in the closing decades of the 20th century. However, the full potential of the department was not exploited. The CDE has helped significantly in upgrading the research infrastructure and in raising and diversifying the research output, as described in the next section.

The tempo of research output of the teachers might have slowed down, because the new recruits took time to settle down. This is particularly true of someone like Kaushik Basu, who states that he was relaxed before his sojourn in Belgium in 1981-82. He adds that he became incredibly productive for the rest of his stay in the School. In 1992, he became the Founder of the CDE before leaving for Cornell University. The Department owes much to him for the initiative he took to establish CDE.

In my assessment, although the Department suffered a great loss due to the adverse effects of the 'exodus', remedial steps were taken to minimise the loss. A new equilibrium was attained. The teaching standards in the department in this post exodus period were still one of the best in the country.

CDE Established and Department Rejuvenated (1992 Onwards)

CDE in the Department of Economics at the DSE founded in August 1992, owes a great deal to the imagination and initiative of Prof Kaushik Basu. After his education in St. Stephens College and LSE, he joined the School in 1977. In *D. School: Reflections on the Delhi*

2. In appreciation of my contributions in research supervision, a three-day Conference was held at DSE on the eve of my retirement in 2000. Some of the papers presented at this Conference were brought out in a volume *India: Industrialisation in a Reforming Economy—Essays for K.L. Krishna* edited by Suresh Tendulkar, Deb Kusum Das, Arup Mitra and K. Narayanan, published by Academic Foundation.

School of Economics, he gives an account of his experiences at the School during 1977-1994, first as reader of economics (1978-1985) and later as professor (1985-1994). I have had the good fortune of knowing him well for the past four decades. He is widely known in India and internationally for his creativity, versatility, and accessibility. At the School, he blossomed in full measure and developed a deep loyalty to the institution. Although the Department of Economics was still one of the best in the country, in terms of teaching standards quantity and quality of research, he seems to have felt that the overall performance was far below the potential. His close associate at that time Jean Dreze gave clear vent to this type of dissatisfaction in his essay in Kumar and Mookherjee (1995).

Kaushik in association with six other teachers in the Department of Economics, namely, Pulin Nayak, Badal Mukherjee, T.C.A. Anant, myself, Ranjan Ray and Sanjay Subrahmanyam formed a formal society and got it registered in early 1990s. The CDE Society obtained funding from the Ministry of Finance, Government of India, and the Ford Foundation for promoting fundamental and policy research in economics.

The council of the CDE comprising Executive Director, Managing Director, Secretary, Treasurer, and three teacher members elected by the General Body of the CDE and the Head of the Department of Economics organise the activities of the Centre. The aims of the CDE are to:

- Promote and disseminate research, by bringing out working papers and supporting the writing of articles and books.
- Sponsor economists from outside Delhi to visit to DSE, give lectures and collaborate with researchers in Delhi.
- Run an annual Winter School where outstanding economists lecture on recent advances in economic theory, econometrics, development economics, economic history and other related subjects.

- Upgrade research infrastructure, including computing and communications at the DSE.

The Winter School annual conference, at which invited lectures by eminent economists from India and abroad, and presentations by scholars on a variety of themes—theoretical, applied, and economic and social policy—are given has become increasingly popular and successful. The quality too has been improving.[3]

CDE has published 23 annual reports. The 23rd Annual Report of CDE was brought out in August 2016.[4] The 24th Annual Report is expected in August 2017.

A couple of years ago, CDE received a supplement to its corpus fund from the Ministry of Finance. The CDE is growing from strength to strength. Its contribution to the revitalisation of the research activity of the faculty and students is indeed significant.

Teachers, Students, Placement Enterprise and Jobs

The Department of Economics runs Master's, MPhil. and PhD programmes. The Master's programme has a

---

3. Winter School 2015: Prof Stephen Morris from Princeton University, Prof Mukhesh Easwaran from British Columbia, Prof Ariel Rubenstein from New York University, and Prof Imran Rasul from University College London, were the invited speakers. A panel discussion on "The Future of Higher Education in India" was also organised. Prof Rudranshu Mukherjee (Ashoka University), Prof Satish Deshpande (Department of Sociology, DSE) and Prof Bhanu Pratap Mehta (Centre for Policy Research [CPR]) were the panelists.
4. The Report provides detailed account of CDE's activities during 2015-16 under different heads:
    - Publications of each CDE member, pages 5 to 11: the total number exceeds 50.
    - Conference and Seminar Talks by each CDE member, pages 12 to 16: total about 40.
    - Working Papers 2015-16 page 17: total 15.
    - Research Projects 2015-16: 13 projects on a variety of themes.
    - Financial Support to Research Students: 9 students were provided financial assistance.
    - Post-Doctoral Fellowship: One from ISI, Delhi, was selected out of 24 applicants.
    - Krishna Raj Travel Fellowships Programme: 10 groups of students from the departments of Economics and Sociology were provided assistance to carry out field surveys during the summer of 2015.
    - Professor Suresh Tendulkar Memorial Scholarships: one for MA (previous) and one from MA (final).

capacity of about 250 students now. Only about 10 per cent of the applicants to the programme get selected. The students come from all parts of India and several from other countries. The programme has acquired the reputation of being one of the best in Asia. It is perhaps the best in India. The programme covers both theoretical and applied economics, with due emphasis on quantitative methods and computational techniques using modern software. It is spread over four semesters in two years, and consists of six compulsory courses and nine electives. The electives cover a wide range of fields. The tutorial system with small groups of students interacting with the tutor for each compulsory course has been the hallmark of the DSE's Master programme since 1960s.

The MPhil and PhD programmes in the department have been revamped, with strict adherence to time limits for the completion of the programme. The programmes are attracting motivated and well-trained candidates. In view of the insistence on high quality in the department, a large proportion MAs in economics even from the Delhi University register for PhD in other departments. The financial assistance in the form of fellowship is however utterly inadequate. This state of affairs is deplorable. PhD students in other leading institutions are much better off in this respect.

At the same time, there is a case for strengthening the course work component of the PhD programme to make it comparable to the best in the world.

Renewal of Faculty Resources

For a student strength of nearly 500 students in the two-year Master's programme, the effective faculty strength is only 25. Some of the teachers at the Assistant Professor level are employed on ad hoc basis for several years.

Bright young economists with diverse specialisations, several of them in emerging areas, have filled the vacancies caused by retirements in the 1990s, 2000s, and 2010s. In alphabetical order the teachers are: T.C.A. Anant (on leave), Sugata Bag, Abhijit Banerjee, Aditya Bhattacharjea (Head of the Department), Mausumi Das, Ashwini Deshpande, Pami Dua (Director-DSE),Deepti Goel (on leave), Parikshit Ghosh, Shreekant Gupta, Sunil Kanwar, Anirban Kar, Surender Kumar, Dipeyndu Maiti, J.V. Meenakshi, Santosh Panda (on leave), Param Jit, Sudhir Shah, Ram Singh, Uday Bhanu Sinha and Rohini Somanathan. Most specialisations are covered, considering the faculty as a whole.

The department was once very strong in Econometrics and Economic History. The faculty resources in these areas need to be replenished without further delay.

In my judgement, the quality of the existing faculty is indeed high and compares favourably with other leading institutions in the country. But the quantum is really inadequate, considering the student strength of nearly 500 at the Master's level. The average quality of the students completing the Master's programme is high while the quality is very uneven across students. This has been so all along. The quality of the student at the lower end may not be very inferior to the average quality of students in most Indian universities. The academic ambience, peer quality, library facilities, training in computational methods, and the placement programme, all help to achieve a minimum level of quality of the Master's student.

The Placement Programme in the Department

The Placement Programme was launched in 1998-1999. In that year, only about 40 per cent of those enrolled were placed. In course of the past 18 years, the Programme has gained considerable momentum. In recent years almost 100 per cent of those enrolled, got placed. Bottomline, the 2016-17 edition of the placement brochure, is a comprehensive documentation of the placement process and its outcomes. About 70 recruiters from the corporate sector, industry, the public sector, and NGOs visited DSE in 2016-17 for selecting suitable students. Business and Risk Analytics (45%) Credit Risk Analytics (18%), Consultation

The Fraternity

Delhi School of Economics

FAREWELL SESSION 1953-54

1st Row Sitting (L to R):	Bimla Goel, N. Nagalakshmi, Promila Uppal, Sunanda Surkund, Tripti B. Sarobar, Kusum Lata, Swaran Kanta, Santosh Puri, (Joint Secy) Inderjeet Shrikant, Praksh Aggarwal, A. Desai, Vimala Raghavan, Bimla Anand, Kamla Rani, Sudha Sarita.
2nd Row Sitting (Chairs):	P.N. Dhar, K.D. Puranik, S.P. Nag, A.B. Ghosh, S.R. Rao, Dr P.K. Mukherji, R.K. Parashar (Vice-President), Dr V.K.R.V. Rao (President), L. Singh (Joint Secretary), S.P.S. Pruthi.
1st Row Standing (L to R):	O.P. Mathur, S.S. Mehta, D.P. Kapil, A. Singh, M.L. Chawla, J.S. Yadav, **R.K. Kapila**, J.K. Kumar, D. Shastri, C.S. Jha, B.L. Jain, P.T. Joseph, S. Krishna Ayyar, S. Padma Kumar, C.C. Pandeya, D.G. Bhave, K.B. Krishnaswamy, R.N. Singh, S.N. Mishra.
2nd Row Standing (L to R):	T. Shreshtha, R.N. Tiwari, M.K. Thavaraj, P.N. Upadhaya, R.K. Diwan, T. Khera, R.N. Mathur, G.N. Yadav, S.S. Ahluwalia, G.V.N. Reddy, O.P. Anand, S.K. Bhattacharya, Kuldip Sehgal, Vir Narayan, A.S. Mehta, B. Nanjundaiya, V. Shri Ram.
3rd Row Standing (L to R):	R.D. Singh, T.K. Bhowmiok, S. Natarajan, C.P. Thakur, V.H. Joshi, J.N. Sharma, S.P. Verma, R.K. Sachdev, Y.M. Sehgal, Dhaneshwar Singh, M.S. Ahluwalia, H.V.S. Prasanna, K.V. Chalapati Rac, A. Premchand, C.V.M. Sharma, Y.R. Rao, D.P. Gupta, B.S. Gupta, K.K. Sehgal.
4th Row Standing (L to R):	E. Njuguna, R.K. Dar, Kanwal Krishan, Jai Krishan, V.N. Vaidyanathan, R. Krishnamurthy, J. Kurian, B.B. Julka, C.M. Khosla, G.P. Srivastava, Ranbir Madan, Y.P. Sharma, Inderjit Marwah, G.S. Ganguli, G.P. Mediratta, M.M. Sethi.

Photograph courtesy: Aditya Bhattac

Raj was Vice-Chancellor of Delhi University during 1969-70. He tried to introduce several major institutional reforms like rotation of the headship of the department. He faced much resistance and resigned in disgust, and returned to DSE in 1970. In 1971, he moved to Trivandrum to set up the CDS. Under the able leadership of Raj, CDS grew fast into a major research and training centre in development studies with formal affiliation to Jawaharlal Nehru University. It is funded by the Government of Kerala and ICSSR.

Raj's own essay and essays by several other contributors in *D. School* highlight Raj's major contributions to DSE, during 1962-1971. Raj (1995) attributed the fast progress in the Department of Economics of DSE during the subsequent three decades to the "immense strengthening of the teaching and research staff, together with the restructuring of the courses" in the mid-1960s. In his overall assessment of the academic standing of the School in early 1990s, he gives credit to the valuable contributions made by the Department of Sociology in the School and the IEG.

Whereas V.K.R.V. Rao founded the DSE in 1949 and established the DSE campus with its main building (Birla Bhawan) and Ratan Tata Library (RTL) in the 1950s, with the active support of B.N. Ganguly and P.N. Dhar and the encouragement received from Prime Minister Jawaharlal Nehru, the leadership of Raj was largely responsible for the academic excellence achieved by the Department of Economics during 1962-1971. In his efforts, Raj received unstinted support and advice from Amartya Sen, Sukhamoy Chakravarty, Jagdish Bhagwati, A.L. Nagar, Tapan Raychaudhuri and several junior colleagues.

It was ironic that Raj was part of the exodus of luminaries from the School in early 1970s. The healthy traditions established in the School since its inception gained further strength during 1960s and stood the School in good stead in subsequent decades.

(in 1963), Minister of Transport and later Minster of Education. In the latter capacity, he established (in 1969) The Indian Council of Social Science Research (ICSSR), which now extends financial support to about 30 institutes in different parts of India. The overall contribution of Rao in institution building, discovering new talent and policy making is immeasurable.

K.N. Raj (1924-2010)

Prof K.N. Raj was born in Thrissur, Kerala, in 1924. He did his Master's in Economics from the Madras Christian College under the University of Madras and his doctorate on the Monetary Policy of Reserve Bank of India (RBI) at the LSE. He joined the RBI in Bombay in 1947. He was invited to be the Assistant Chief of the Economics Division of the Planning Commission when it was set up in 1950. According to K.S. Krishnaswamy, Raj's contemporary and friend, the basic framework of the First Five Year Plan was formulated in the economic division led by J.J. Anjaria and K.N. Raj (see Krishnaswamy in Vaidyanthan and Krishna 2007: xix).

After the First Plan was launched, Raj joined the Delhi School of Economics in 1953 as Professor of Monetary Economics on the invitation of V.K.R.V. Rao. He became Director of DSE and Head of the Department of Economics in 1962, when B.N. Ganguly was appointed as Pro-Vice Chancellor of Delhi University by C.D. Deshmukh. The credit for attracting a galaxy of gifted young economists to DSE, during the period 1963-1971 goes largely to Raj. As noted elsewhere in this essay, this galaxy included Amartya Sen, Sukhamoy Chakravarty, Jagadish Bhagwati, Manmohan Singh, Tapan Raychadhuri, A.L. Nagar and Mrinal Datta Chaudhri. In association with the 'galaxy', Raj effected a major restructuring and modernisation of the Master's programme in economics in mid-1960s. The PhD programme too was revamped. These reforms resulted in the improvement in academic standards. The Master's programme became comparable to the best in the World.

(16%) and Investment Banking (10%) together accounted for nearly 90 per cent of those placed. The highest package was ₹20 lakh per year and the median package was ₹12 lakh per year.

These packages are far more attractive than Assistant Professorship in the public universities and colleges. Thus, only a small proportion of DSE Master's graduates fulfilling the eligibility conditions are available for teaching and research jobs. The dependence on non-DSE eligible candidates has increased over the years, with adverse impact on the quality of teaching in Delhi university colleges. The placement enterprise has been a mixed blessing in a wider perspective.

Remembering the Protagonists

In this section, the life and work (in broad detail) and significant contributions of several late protagonists of DSE are outlined for the benefit of the posterity.

V.K.R.V. Rao (1908-1991)[5]

V.K.R.V. Rao is most famous as the Founder Director of his first creation, the DSE. Although, after 1960 when he gave up the Vice-Chancellorship of Delhi University, he did not take direct interest in DSE, he will always be remembered for his seminal role in founding DSE which has become one of the best centres in Asia for postgraduate teaching and research not only in Economics, but also in Sociology and Geography. The DSE campus a lso houses the Faculty of Management Studies (FMS), Faculty of Commerce, and Agro-Economic Research Centre (AERC).

Rao founded the Institute of Economic Growth in Delhi in 1958, and the Institute for Social and Economic Change in Bangalore in 1972. During his active life time, he came to occupy many important positions: Founder Director of the DSE, IEG and ISEC, Member of Planning Commission

5. This section draws upon: Rao (2012, 2002), Dhar (2000) and Rao et al. (2008), which covers different aspects of V.K.R.V. Rao's multifarious contributions.

A.R. DATT, DELHI

held its Conference in Delhi with Kenneth Arrow as the Chairman. Chakravarty in his capacity as the President of the Indian Econometric Society (TIES) 1983-88, with the encouragement and support of Prof C.R. Rao, who was then the Chairman of TIES, started the *Journal of Quantitative Economics* (JQE) in 1985, with A.L. Nagar as the Editor in Chief, myself as the Managing Editor and Kaushik Basu as the Joint Managing Editor. JQE was published from DSE for 10 years and became one of the leading Indian journals.

Chakravarty and his family lived on the Delhi University campus, even when he was on Government of India advisory assignments. He visited the Ratan Tata Library almost daily. He was accessible to colleagues and students. His continued presence on the University campus and his regular visits to DSE had a salutary impact on the academic ambience of DSE.

Sukhamoy was a highly creative and prodigious scholar,[9] and a voracious reader. He was one of the most outstanding Indian economists of the 20th century with rare social awareness and commitment. His initial interest in high theory and mathematical economics gave way to practical policy analysis of issues relating to the under-privileged. He had put his phenomenal scholarship to continued application in the study of development issues. He left an indelible impression on the intellectual world.

Samuelson and Tinbergen were Chakravarty's life-long admirers. When Chakravarty died his teacher Tinbergen remarked that he had learned more from Chakravarty than Chakravarty learning from him.

A.L. Nagar (1930-2014)

Anirudh Lal Nagar was the most world famous Indian Econometrician. He was among the galaxy of economists who joined the School in the 1960s. After earning his PhD in Econometrics under the guidance of the renowned

9. He had won the Mahalanobis Memorial Medal in 1974 and the V.K.R.V. Rao Prize in Economics in 1978.

Dutch Econometrician Henri Theil in 1959, doing post-doctoral research in Holland and Purdue University he returned to India to join the faculty in Indian Institute of Technology (IIT) Kanpur in 1961. He came to DSE as Reader in Econometrics in 1963 and was appointed to the newly created chair in Econometrics in 1968. He retired in 1995, but continued his academic work till 2011, when he and Mrs Nagar moved to Pune to be with their elder son Ashish. He became the fellow of the Econometric Society in 1971. Nagar held the post of Head of the Department during 1973-1976, Director during 1973-76 and again during 1984-87. He was Pro-Vice-Chancellor during 1990-1995 and acting Vice-Chancellor during 1994-95. He was President of the Indian Econometric Society for three years and Editor-in Chief of the *Journal of Quantitative Economics* from its inception in 1985 until his demise in 2014. I had the good fortune of being the Founder Managing Editor of JQE for 10 years and working with Prof Nagar. In DSE, I shared the teaching of Econometrics at different levels with him from 1967 to 1990.

Nagar was one of the most gifted teachers and active researchers. He was a popular research supervisor in both theoretical econometrics and applied econometrics. His students Nanak Kakwani, Aman Ullah and Ashok Lahiri are the best known among his 20-odd doctoral students. They have brought much credit to DSE.

The School owes a great deal to Late Prof Nagar for his various significant contributions for more than three decades. The continued presence of luminaries like Nagar in the School helped the DSE in maintaining high academic standards and healthy cultural values and traditions.

Mrinal Datta Chaudhri (1934-2015)

MDC, as he was referred to by students and even colleagues, was born in Srigauri in Eastern India in 1934. He was educated at Santiniketan and Presidency College, Calcutta. He was a contemporary of Amartya Sen. They were close friends till MDC's demise in Pune in 2015. His early training was in Statistics. According to him, he became an academic economist almost by accident (See Kumar and Mookherjee 1995: 141).

At the time Pitambar Pant was working on the draft of the Third Five Year Plan, MDC, as member of a small group from ISI, Delhi, assisted Pant and he became a friend of the boss. He went to MIT in 1962 and did his PhD in Economics by 1966 and returned to India. ISI, Delhi, for two years. At the suggestion of Amartya Sen and K.N. Raj, he applied for the Professorship in Transport Economics in DSE and got selected and joined in 1968. Although several of his friends left the School around that time, MDC decided to stay on and he stayed till his retirement in 1999.

When the School was under attack from a group of college teachers in the Academic Council for alleged corruption in student admissions and hiring practices of the Department, he took up the challenge and decided to 'rebuild the School' with the support of the then Vice-Chancellor Dr Sarup Singh (see Kumar and Mookherjee 1995: 143-45).

MDC narrates how Prasanta Pattanaik, then at Oxford, Pranab Bardhan at ISI, Delhi, Raj Krishna with the World Bank, Suresh Tendulkar at ISI, Delhi, came to the school as professors. Badal Mukherjee, Pulin Nayak and Kaushik Basu joined at the level of reader in 1970s. The School's former PhD students K. Sundaram, K. Krishnamurty, Balvir Singh, Bhaskar Dutta, and Ashok Lahiri too helped to fill the vacancies caused by the 'exodus'. MDC, of course, adds that this strengthening of the faculty was the result of the combined effort of the Department.

MDC refers to his bold initiatives for social action during the emergency regime of 1975-1977, in collaboration with Raj Krishna and J.D. Sethi of the department. He gave vent to his sense of achievement and satisfaction as follows:

> For a quarter century it has been a source of great joy for me to belong to an institution which is not only an excellent Centre of teaching research in

social sciences but also a community involved in meaningful social action (See Kumar and Mookherjee 1995: 147).

Mrinal was a brilliant, versatile and well-read economist. He was popular as a teacher and colleague. His presence at departmental seminars had an enlivening impact.

Kaushik Basu, Pulin Nayak and Ranjan Ray, his colleagues at the School, brought out in 2003, a book of essays *Markets and Government* (OUP), in Mrinal's honour. The three editors deserve the compliments of the Department.

I visited Mrinal in Pune on three occasions, after he left Delhi for good. His loneliness in Pune bothered him. He missed the vibrancy of DSE.

Suresh D. Tendulkar (1939-2011)

Suresh Dhondopant Tendulkar was born in Kolhapur, Maharashtra in 1939. During his childhood, his family moved to Pune where he had his early education, before joining the MA Economic Statistics course in DSE in 1960. He passed in the first division in 1962 securing the first rank. I was his teacher in two courses. The teacher and the student became close family friends and the teacher is extremely proud of this illustrious student. Suresh joined Harvard University in 1963 and obtained his PhD degree in 1968 on a Multi-sector Planning Model for India under the supervision of H.S. Houthakkar and H.B. Chenery. On his return to India in 1968, Suresh joined ISI, Delhi, and worked there till 1978. In mid-1970s, Suresh took up an assignment at World Bank, Washington.

In 1978, Suresh accepted an invitation from DSE to be a Professor. He continued in DSE till his retirement in 2004. He was indeed unique in combining three distinctions—a dedicated teacher, a meticulous researcher and a consummate policy advisor.

Suresh in collaboration with K. Sundaram of DSE carried out a thorough job of revamping EDPI course. Both of them together taught the course for many years. They exposed the student to a good deal of up-to-date empirical material on various themes.

Suresh's research on poverty, inequality and employment had few parallels. In his research, he sometimes collaborated with Sundaram or L.R. Jain.

The Suresh Tendulkar Committee Report on the new methodology of poverty measurement submitted to the Government of India a few years before his premature death in 2011 provoked considerable discussion and debate, as is well-known. He defended the approach of the Report single-handedly.

He took considerable interest in issues of improvement of data quality as Chairman or member of several official committees. He was the first chairman of the National Statistical Commission.

He was a member of many expert committees on policy matters. For some time he was Chairman of the Prime Minister's Economic Advisory Council. His publication record was truly impressive.[10]

The School was extremely fortunate in having on i ts faculty a person of such rare distinction, commitment, and humility. His coming to the School after the 'exodus' of early 1970s made a big difference to the maintenance of academic standards and preservation of reputation of the School.

Raj Krishna (1926-1985)

Raj Krishna obtained his MA degree in Economics from Hindu College, Delhi, before DSE was founded. In 1961, he got the PhD degree from the University of Chicago writing his thesis on estimating the price response of farm supply in India and Pakistan.

10. See "Introduction", in Krishna et al. (2017).

As Vijay Krishna (2012) notes, Raj Krishna's writings span from 1946 till his premature death in 1985, on a wide range of themes. He was a footloose scholar with several changes in jobs in India and many international assignments. He was at IEG during 1961-1965, the University of Rajasthan for six years in the late 1960s and early 1970s, and in DSE from 1975 to 1985. He was member of the Planning Commission during the Janata Party government. His work on unemployment in India and the employment guarantee schemes in some states was well received. He popularised applied econometric work in India after his return from Chicago. He had a tendency to avoid administrative responsibilities.

Raj Krishna was a forceful and impressive orator and debater. He coined the phrase 'Hindu Rate of Growth'. He actively participated in political activity against emergency of the 1975-77 period. He was greatly admired by his students and colleagues.[11]

Concluding Remarks

As the title indicates, this paper is a sketch of the development path of the Delhi School of Economics since its inception. DSE is taken to be synonymous with the Department of Economics as initially conceived by

V.K.R.V. Rao in 1940s and most of 1950s. The Department of Sociology and Geography created at the initiative of Rao in 1959 when he was Vice-Chancellor of Delhi University regrettably, are not covered. The Ratan Tata Library (RTL), a vital organ of DSE, is also not covered in this sketch.

The book *D. School* edited by late Dharma Kumar and Dilip Mookherjee in 1995 with contributions from late P.N. Dhar, late K.N. Raj, late A.L. Nagar, late Mrinal Datta Chaudhury, Amartya Sen, Jean Dreze, Prasnatha Pattanaik, late M.N. Srinivas, Andre Beteille, Veena Das, Patricia Uberoi, Ashok Lahiri, Puran Mongia, Sanjay Subrahmanyam, and several former students of DSE is a

11. For a fuller account of Raj Krishna's work, see Krishna (2012).

very rich source of information on the development path of DSE till early 1990s. The social sciences community owes much to the two celebrated editors for their imagination and hard work.

This short essay extends the Kumar-Mookherjee seminal study till 2016, rather superficially, given the time constraint. A more detailed picture of the past quarter century will be very useful.

This paper divides the seventy-five year period ending in 2016 into five sub-periods, 1942-1949, 1949-1962, 1962-1971, 1971-1992 and 1992 onwards. In the last sub-period, the establishment of Centre for Development Economics in 1994 helped the Department of Economics to rejuvenate itself, the credit for this largely goes to Kaushik Basu, and the funding agencies, Ministry of Finance and Ford Foundation. The CDE has acquitted itself very creditably since its inception thanks to the successive Executive Councils and members of the CDE.

The faculty resources are truly rich and get continually renewed. But there is dire need for the increase in size of the faculty, given the student strength of nearly 500.

The Placement enterprise in the Department of Economics, guided by Pami Dua with the active support of the successive Heads of the Department of Economics and the Director of DSE and involving student coordinator of the enterprise, during the past 18 years, has transformed the image of the Department and enhanced the job opportunities for the students completing their studies in the department. With strong preference for lucrative jobs through the placement process the availability of DSE-trained economists for academic jobs and for post-MA research has diminished. This is rather unfortunate.

The founding father of DSE, V.K.R.V. Rao, envisioned an intuition of higher learning and research on socio-economics issues on the lines of the London School of Economics. The seven decade story of the DSE with special focus on the recent quarter century when faculty research output on the theoretical and applied issues has increased manifold would have made V.K.R.V. Rao immensely happy.

DSE is second to none in India in the quality of its products, at the Master's and Doctoral levels. With limited financial resources and infrastructure as compared to several other institutions of higher learning in India, its overall output per faculty member compares very favourably with others.

The healthy traditions and sound cultural values with decentralised and collective decision making inculcated by K.N. Raj, Amartya Sen, Sukhamoy Chakravarty, Jagdish Bhagwati, Dharma Kumar, A.L. Nagar, Mrinal Datta Chaudhuri, Raj Krishna and others are being preserved. DSE has received compliments for avoiding factionalism, intrigue and infighting, and maintaining cohesiveness in spite of differences in perception among the faculty members. As an ardent well-wisher of DSE and long-time participant in the DSE mission, I am optimistic that this healthy image will be sustained in the coming decades and for ever.

References

Balasubrahmanyam, V.N. (2001). *Conversations with Indian Economists.* Palgrave.

Basu, Kaushik (1995). "From a Personal Point of View", in Dharma Kumar and Dilip Mookherjee (eds.), *D. School: Reflections on the Delhi School of Economics.* New Delhi: OUP.

Basu, K. and A. Maertens (eds.) (2012). *The New Oxford Companion to Economics in India.* New Delhi: OUP

Datta Chaudhuri, Mrinal (1995). "The School and I", in Dharma Kumar and Dilip Mookherjee (eds.), *D. School: Reflections on the Delhi School of Economics.* New Delhi: OUP.

Dhar, P. N. (2000). *Indira Gandhi, the Emergency and Indian Democracy.* New Delhi: OUP.

———. (1995). "The Early Years", in Dharma Kumar and Dilip Mookherjee (eds.), *D. School: Reflections on the Delhi School of Economics.* New Delhi: OUP.

Dreze, Jean (1995). "The Delhi School of Economics at the Crossroads", in Dharma Kumar and Dilip Mookherjee (eds.), *D. School: Reflections on the Delhi School of Economics.* New Delhi: OUP.

Kohli, Inderjit (1995). "The D. School: Looking Backwards", in Dharma Kumar and Dilip Mookherjee (eds.), *D. School: Reflections on the Delhi School of Economics.* New Delhi: OUP.

Krishna, K.L., Vishwanath Pandit, K. Sundaram and Pami Dua (2017). "Introduction", in K.L. Krishna, Vishwanath Pandit, K. Sundaram and Pami Dua (eds.), *Perspective on Economic Development and Policy in India. An Honour of Suresh D. Tendulkar.* Singapore: Springer.

Krishna, Vijaya (2012) "Raj Krishna", in K. Basu and A. Maertens (eds.), *The New Oxford Companion to Economics in India*. New Delhi: OUP.

Kumar, Dharma and Dilip Mookherjee (eds.) (1995). *D. School: Reflections on the Delhi School of Economics*. New Delhi: OUP.

Lahiri, Ashok (1995). "Econometrics at the DSE in the 1960s and 1970s", in Dharma Kumar and Dilip Mookherjee (eds.), *D. School: Reflections on the Delhi School of Economics*. New Delhi: OUP.

Nagar, A.L. (1995). "My Experiences at the Delhi School of Economics", in Dharma Kumar and Dilip Mookherjee (eds.), *D. School: Reflections on the Delhi School of Economics*. New Delhi: OUP.

Patnaik, Prabhat (1995). "Delhi School Days", in Dharma Kumar and Dilip Mookherjee (eds.), *D. School: Reflections on the Delhi School of Economics*. New Delhi: OUP.

Pattanaik, Prasanth (1995). "My Years in the School",in Dharma Kumar and Dilip Mookherjee (eds.), *D. School: Reflections on the Delhi School of Economics*. New Delhi: OUP.

Raj, K.N. (1995). "The Delhi School of Economics", in Dharma Kumar and Dilip Mookherjee (eds.), *D. School: Reflections on the Delhi School of Economics*. New Delhi: OUP.

Rao, S.L. (2012). "V.K.R.V. Rao" in K. Basu and A. Maertens (eds.), *The New Oxford Companion to Economics in India*. New Delhi: OUP.

————. (2002). *The Partial Memories of V.K.R.V. Rao*. New Delhi: OUP.

Rao, S.L., N. Jayaram, V.M. Rao, M.V. Nadakarni and R.S. Deshpande (eds.) (2008). *A Passionate Humanitarian V.K.R.V. Rao*. New Delhi: Academic Foundation Association in association with ISEC.

Sen, Amartya (1995). "In the Delhi School", in Dharma Kumar and Dilip Mookherjee (eds.), *D. School: Reflections on the Delhi School of Economics*. New Delhi: OUP.

Somanathan, E. (1995). "An MA at the Delhi School", in Dharma Kumar and Dilip Mookherjee (eds.), *D. School: Reflections on the Delhi School of Economics*. New Delhi: OUP.

Tendulkar, Suresh, Deb Kusum Das, Arup Mitra and K. Narayanan (eds.) (2006). *India: Industrialisation in a Reforming Economy—Essays for K.L. Krishna*. New Delhi: Academic Foundation.

Vaidyanathan, A. and K.L. Krishna (eds.) (2007). *Institutions and Markets in India's Development*. New Delhi: OUP.

Others:

CDE at the Delhi School of Economics (August 2016), *The Twenty Third Annual Report*.

Delhi School of Economics, University of Delhi (2016), *Brochure*.

Department of Economics, Delhi School of Economics, *Bottomline 2016-17*.

Appendix A-2.1

Directors of DSE

Name	*Period*
Prof V.K.R.V. Rao	1949-1957
Prof B.N. Ganguli	1957-1962
Prof K.N. Raj	1962-1965
Prof M. S. A. Rao*	1965-1966
Prof T. Raychaudhuri	1966-1968
Prof A. Das Gupta#	1968-1970
Prof V.L.S. Prakash Rao**	1970-1972
Prof A.B. Ghosh ##	1 972-1973
Prof A.M. Shah*	1973-1975
Prof A.L. Nagar	1975-1977
Prof R. Ramachandran**	1977-1979
Prof Dharma Kumar	1979-1980
Prof K.L. Krishna	1980-1981
Prof Dharma Kumar	1981-1982
Prof K.L. Krishna	1982-1984
Prof A.L. Nagar	1984-1987
Prof Mrinal Datta Chaudhuri	1987-1991
Prof J.P.S. Uberoi*	1991-1992
Prof R.S. Nigam ##	1992-1993
Prof K.L. Krishna	1993-1995
Prof Suresh D. Tendulkar	1995-1998
Prof Badal Mukhopadhyay	1998-2001
Prof Om Prakash	2001-2002
Prof Aneeta A. Minocha*	2002-2003
Prof Badal Mukhopadhyay	2003-2005
Prof Pulin B. Nayak	2005-2008
Prof B.L. Pandit	2008
Prof Partha Sen	2008-2011
Prof Santosh C. Panda	2011-2013
Prof Pami Dua	2013 to date

Note: * Sociology; ** Geography; # Business Management; ## Commerce; Others-Economics.

Appendix A-2.2

Heads of Department of Economics

Name	*Period*
Prof V.K.R.V. Rao	1949-1957
Prof B.N. Ganguli	1957-1962
Prof K.N. Raj	1962-1968
Prof K.A. Naqvi	1968-1969
Prof S. Chakravarty	1969-1971
Prof K.A. Naqvi	1971-1973
Prof A.L. Nagar	1973-1976
Prof Mrinal Datta Chaudhuri	1976-1979
Prof Dharma Kumar	1979-1980
Prof K.L. Krishna	1980-1981
Prof Dharma Kumar	1981-1982
Prof K.L. Krishna	1982-1985
Prof S.B. Gupta	1985-1986
Prof Suresh D. Tendulkar	1986-1989
Prof Om Prakash	1989-1992
Prof Badal Mukhopadhyay	1992-1995
Prof V.N. Pandit	1995-1997
Prof K. Sundaram	1997-2000
Prof Pulin B. Nayak	2000-2003
Prof Partha Sen	2003-2005
Prof Santosh C. Panda	2005-2008
Prof B.L. Pandit	2008-2010
Prof Pami Dua	2010-2014
Prof Aditya Bhattacharjea	2014 to date

Helpful advice and suggestions from Prof Pami Dua, Director, DSE, Prof Aditya Bhattacharjea, Head of the Department of Economics Prof J.V. Meenakshi and Prof V. Pandit are gratefully acknowledged. The author thanks Dr Uma Kapila for providing the opportunity to write about DSE where he has been a teacher since 1958. I wish to thank Dr Sri Hari Naidu of NIPFP, and Rajesh Papnei of CDE for their timely assistance.

II
Macro Issues

3

India's Economic Development

From the Past into the Present

PULIN B. NAYAK

The Past

This year, 2017, marks the 70th year of India's Independence from colonial subjugation. At the stroke of the midnight hour on 15 August 1947, Pandit Nehru had addressed the nation with the stirring words: "Long years ago, we made a tryst with destiny, and now the time comes when we shall redeem our pledge, not wholly or in full measure, but very substantially." Seventy years are possibly a long enough time period: long enough for a human being to have lived a full life and to hope for some years of retirement and reflection. But for a country of sub-continental proportions, seven decades would perhaps constitute a minor span in her rich civilisational history that extends over several millennia. In his *Glimpses of World History,* Nehru (1934-35, 1991) wrote that at the end of 1000 years after Christ,

> The old civilisations of India and China still continue and flourish. Indian culture spreads to Malaysia and Cambodia and brings rich fruit there...trade and learning and the arts flourish; great cities abound; and famous universities attract students from afar (p.179).

By the beginning of the 20th century, India's condition had changed rather dramatically for the worse. After the annexation of large chunks of India by the British East India Company from the 18th century onwards and the gradual subjugation of the entire Indian subcontinent, British imperial policy had ensured greater penetration of British mill goods into the Indian market and the steady decline of Indian home grown cottage and small industry, leading to a general process of 'de-industrialisation'. The grand old man of India, Dadabhai Naoroji (1901), was also able to convincingly demonstrate that there was a massive drain of wealth from India to the colonial master country, Britain.

The rate of growth of the Indian economy during the half century prior to her Independence was under 1 per cent. Famines occurred with regular frequency, the last major one being the great Bengal famine of 1943. Sutherland (1908) points out that during 1800-1880, no less than 18 million Indians perished in various famines. In the very year 1857 when Queen Victoria assumed the title of Empress, five million people in Southern India were starved to death. The British left India with a very low level of per capita income and extremely poor levels of achievement in education and health. To their credit, they had helped set up the rail network, the post and telegraph system, the general administration and the police system and the judiciary, among others, but there is no denying that the average Indian lived a wretched existence.

On taking over the reins of the government in 1947 of a partitioned country, the task before the new ministry under Nehru was nothing short of stupendous. For long, prior to this conjuncture, Nehru had been attracted to the idea of planning. In 1927, he had in fact visited the USSR at the invitation of the Soviet government on the occasion of the 10th anniversary of the October Revolution. The USSR was well on its path of economic development and the Soviets were to embark on their first five year plan in 1928. Nehru was impressed with what he saw and was determined to introduce planning in India as soon as it was politically feasible.

It was Nehru who was called upon by Subhas Chandra Bose, the Congress President, to Chair the National Planning Committee in 1938. It consisted of 15 members plus representatives of provincial governments and such Indian states as chose to collaborate with the Congress Party. "It was a strange assortment of different types and it was not clear how such an odd mixture would work," Nehru (1946) was to write later in the *Discovery of India*. Yet, the group was able to come up with concrete suggestions in respect of agriculture, industry, unemployment, literacy and medical services, among others. It was of course obvious that the country's independence was a prerequisite to the implementation of any of the blueprints.

It is of course well known that Mahatma Gandhi's ideas on development were considerably at variance from the views held by Nehru. In his *Hind Swaraj*, Gandhi (1909) had made a case for self-sufficient village republics. He was against industrialisation and machinery, especially when the latter displaced labour, because he believed that the key to India's economic resurgence lies in removing the massive burden of unemployment. Nehru, in contrast, was for modernisation and industrialisation. He believed that it is this which will ultimately be required to solve the problem of open and disguised unemployment both in the rural and urban areas. Gandhi had tried his best to sort out these differences with Nehru in the mid-1940s, but without any major success, and each held on to his views quite resolutely.

Gandhiji's assassination in January 1948 made Nehru the supreme arbiter of the country's economic management, and true to his long standing conviction, the Planning Commission was set up in 1950. The First Five Year Plan was initiated in 1951 with a fairly balanced allocation of resources between agriculture, industry and the tertiary sectors. It was the Second Five Year Plan (1956-1961), which, following the formulations of the Russian economist Feldman and our physicist statistician Mahalanobis, emphasised the importance of the capital goods sector, relative to the consumption goods sector, in order to bring about a faster rate of growth for the economy. Nehru, too, owned this model, and the idea soon came to be known as the Nehru-Mahalanobis model.

It was in this period that a massive push was given to setting up of the heavy industries sector, and units were set up in Ranchi and Bhopal. The three steel plants in Bhilai, Rourkela and Durgapur were also commissioned at this time. But there were other aspects too. Nehru was conscious of the importance of the building up of human capital in the development of any country and it is during this period that a massive push was given to the growth of higher and professional education by making ample allocations for new universities, the new IITs and IIMs, the AIIMS in Delhi and institutions of fundamental research like the Council of Scientific and Industrial Research (CSIR). Lest one were to conclude that agriculture was left out, it should be mentioned that during this period large allocations were also made for setting up of research centres for rice, wheat and agricultural research generally and institutions like the Indian Council of Agricultural Research (ICAR) came into their own.

Despite the intense debates between Gandhi and Nehru during the mid-1940s regarding the relative importance to be attached to agriculture and industry, it is possible to say that about a decade after the introduction of centralised planning in India, Nehru became more, not less, appreciative of the importance of agriculture and therefore came closer to his mentor's essential position. The formulation of the Third Five Year Plan (1961-1966) was Nehru's last intellectual engagement with the idea of planning. As the Chairman of the Commission, he was known to be always careful about the drafting of the 'approach' document to the plan. At the very beginning of this document, we have:

> In the scheme of development during the Third Plan, the first priority necessarily belongs to agriculture. Experience in the first two Plans, and especially in the Second, has shown that the rate of growth of agricultural production is one of the main limiting factors in the progress of the Indian economy. Agricultural production has, therefore, to be increased to the largest extent feasible, and adequate

resources have to be provided under the Third Plan for realising the agricultural targets (Planning Commission 1961).

The Present Conjuncture

The Indian economy grew at the 'Hindu' rate of about 3.5 to 4.0 per cent during the first three decades of relatively autarkic planning. During Indira Gandhi's second stint of Prime Ministership beginning 1980, there were a lot of pressures to free up the economy as well as to open it up to the external sector. The process continued through the tenure of Rajiv Gandhi as well, and the result was a step up of the GDP (gross domestic product) growth rate in the decade of the 1980s to somewhere in the region of about 5 to 5.5 per cent. This was definitely an improvement over the earlier tepid growth over a long span of three decades. Yet, at the beginning of the last decade of the 20th century poverty was still substantial in large tracts of the country, especially in tribal and drought prone dry areas. There was a strong point of view expressed in several quarters that opportunities had been missed in the early years of Independence, and a strong course correction was needed. Indeed there has been much in the recent media, mistaken and motivated in my view, which puts the blame on all of our present day ills at Nehru's doorstep.

The course correction in economic policy that was brought about in 1991 was the result of the twin crises in the fiscal as well as the foreign trade sectors. During the decade of the 1980s, the hegemony of the old Congress Party was slowly crumbling and a number of regional parties came to the fore. This led to a phase of political populism that had its counterpart in fiscal giveaways. The combined fiscal deficit of the Centre and the states had regularly been in the range of about 10 per cent of GDP, subsidies and loan waivers were the order of the day, and the national debt was mounting. The foreign trade sector had been stressed for a long time with the annual import bill far outstripping our export earnings, and during the brief tenure of Chandra Shekhar as Prime Minister, the reserves of foreign exchange were down to barely two weeks' import bill, which naturally set alarm bells ringing.

It is in this setting that the Congress Party returned to power with a massive mandate after the assassination of Rajiv Gandhi, and the new Prime Minister Narasimha Rao took a call on 'economic reforms', an idea—as Victor Hugo had observed, and as Finance Minister Manmohan Singh very appositely proclaimed in the Lok Sabha—whose time had come. Broad based reforms were introduced in fiscal, monetary and trade sectors, as well as in agriculture and industry. The omniscient role of the state was now underplayed; and the state was now to perform the role more of a facilitator than doer, and the sphere of the market and incentives had now to be widened substantially. A lot of the pent up animal spirits were raring to go in the Indian economy for quite some time, and the results were almost immediate. The growth rate of GDP touched the 6.0 to 6.5 per cent range in the last decade of the 20th century.

As the country was entering into the new millennium, there were two nagging features of the economy that continued to vex our leaders and thinkers, and the issues remain valid concerns even today. The percentage of the population below the poverty line still continued to hover around the 30 per cent range in 2000, too high for comfort, and there was hardly any major addition to jobs in the organised sector, giving rise to the epithet of 'jobless growth'.

It is only in the first decade of this millennium that the growth rate of India's GDP touched the 9 per cent plus range during 2005-2008, a feat that China had perfected over the previous quarter century on a sustained basis. But the realisation now dawned on the Indian policymakers as well as the world media that India's achievement was not simply a one off phenomenon for a single year; it had been sustained over three consecutive years. What had clearly helped was that the gross savings and investment rates of the Indian economy had by now touched the 35 per cent of GDP zone, and with a capital:output ratio of around 4, the crude Harrod-Domar formulation in fact predicted a 9 per cent plus growth rate.

After the onset of the economic reforms of 1991, much of the Indian economy, especially the services sector and IT in particular, had now been operating in a globalised setting, and it was indeed IT that was the key driver of the growth figures. The international financial crisis of 2008 put a serious dampener on the Indian growth rate, and within a few years, by 2013-14, the growth rate had sunk down to the sub 5 per cent level. But luckily the Indian economy was relatively still unscathed when one noted that Europe, North America and Japan were all experiencing even lower growth, in the range of barely 2 to 3 per cent, and, in fact, some economies like those of Brazil and Russia, went through negative growth rates during 2014-15.

The past two years have placed India not only at the high table of the fastest growing major economies of the world, but what is more, India now finds itself at the head of the table. It is a matter of some interest to note that India seems to have even tipped the mighty China. Two years back, India's growth rate was 7.6 per cent and China was at 7.1 per cent. Latest computations of the World Bank suggest that India's GDP is set to grow at 7.2 per cent in 2017-18. The report goes on to say: "India remains the fastest growing economy in the world and it will get a big boost from its approach to GST which will reduce the cost of doing business for firms, reduce logistics costs of moving goods across states, while ensuring no loss in equity" (*Indian Express*, New Delhi, 30 May 2017).

Conclusion

It is now time for us to conclude. Even till as late as the end of the past century, few analysts anywhere in the world would have predicted that in less than two decades, India would emerge as the fastest growing major economy of the world. But this has now happened for at least two years now. Our development process has a lot to answer for, and we shall briefly touch on these presently, but this is no mean achievement. It also goes to show that there must have been certain core policies adopted somewhere during our economic management which has brought us to this happy pass. It would be a no brainer to assert that a country simply does not become the fastest growing country in the world overnight. It is difficult to pinpoint what precisely has brought this about, but one could possibly hazard some hypotheses. First, the emphasis on a large role of the state in promoting education at all stages, and in particular, the growth of the IITs, medical colleges and the university system from the mid 1950s onwards. Second, a large and widely divergent industrial base, as well as a large infrastructure sector, which has received constant push from the policymakers. Third, our commitment to political democracy and a free and active media, which immediately alerts the policymakers when they go wrong. Fourth, a broad consensus that seems to have emerged in the past two decades amongst the major political parties of the country, regardless of their ideological hue, that economic reforms are here to stay and that we would not go back to a purely statist kind of mindset in the coming years.

While giving ourselves encomiums, it would be wrong on our part to ignore some of the glaring problems of our political economy that stare us in the face. While in percentage terms, the poverty ratio has dropped somewhat, the absolute number of poor continue to be staggeringly large. The performance in terms of job creation has been hopelessly poor. And most worryingly, there is plenty of evidence to show that inequalities of income and wealth are getting sharper by the day. The ecology is very severely degraded. Politically and socially, there appear to be extraordinarily serious strains. Under the present political dispensation, the secular fabric of the country is possibly going through its severest travail that the minorities have known in recent decades. These are not good auguries. It is not enough to sit at the head of the high table of the fastest growing countries if we are not able to ensure a more humane and just world for all citizens of this great country of astounding diversity with its rich civilisational past.

References

Dhar, P.N. (1995). "The Early Years", in Dharma Kumar and Dilip Mookherjee (eds.), *D. School: Reflections on the Delhi School of Economics.* New Delhi: Oxford University Press.

Gandhi, Mohandas Karamchand (1909). *Hind Swaraj* (Indian Home Rule). Ahmedabad: Navjivan Publishing House.

Indian Express (2017). "World Bank Pegs India's Economic Growth at 7.2% this Financial Year", *Indian Express* (ENS Economic Bureau), New Delhi, 30 May.

Kapila, Raj (1966). *The Time Demands: A Politico-Economic Analysis of Present-day India.* New Delhi: UBS Publishers.

Naoroji, Dadabhai (1901). *Poverty and Un-British Rule in India.* London: Swan Sonnenschein & Co.

Nehru, Jawaharlal (1934-35, 1991). *Glimpses of World History.* Allahabad: Kitabistan and New Delhi: Oxford University Press.

———. (1946, 1982). *The Discovery of India.* Calcutta: The Signet Press and New Delhi: Oxford University Press.

Planning Commission (1961). *The Third Five Year Plan.* Government of India.

Sutherland, Jabez T. (1908). *The New Nationalist Movement in India.* Washington, D.C.: The Atlantic Monthly.

4

The Journey of India's Economic Reforms

C. RANGARAJAN

It is an honour to write for this volume dedicated to honour Raj Kapila who was one of India's eminent thinkers. He interviewed and interacted with many of India's leading policymakers. He brought out many studies elaborating on the critical issues faced by the Indian economy particularly in the first three decades after India's Independence. His pioneering efforts along with Uma to set up a new publishing house have met with extraordinary success. Academic Foundation can be proud of its record. Its publications include almost all leading Indian economists. Since Raj Kapila was deeply interested in India's 1991 reforms, this article focuses on the genesis and progress of the liberalisation story.[1]

I

The year 1991 is an important landmark in the post-Independence economic history of India. The country faced a severe economic crisis, triggered largely by a serious BoPs (balance of payments) problem. The crisis was converted into an opportunity to effect some fundamental changes in the content and approach to economic policy. The response to the crisis was to put in place a set of policies aimed at stabilisation and structural reform. While the stabilisation polices were aimed at correcting

---

1. This is the text of the Special Lecture delivered at the 99th Annual Conference of Indian Economic Association at Sri Venkateswara University, Tirupati in 2016.

weaknesses that had developed on the fiscal and the BoP fronts, the structural reforms were meant to remove the rigidities that had entered the various segments of the Indian economy.

Early Thoughts

In the 1950s and 1960s, the dominant view in the literature on development economics was that the government had an important role to play, and that it should undertake activities that would compensate for 'market failure'. 'Market failure' was perceived in its inability to optimally allocate resources over time, that is, for investment because of the 'myopic' nature of markets. The literature also emphasised the benefit of a coordinated and consistent set of investment decisions. It is this line of reasoning that led most developing countries, including India, to formulate economy-wide plans. However, four decades of development experience have shown that there can be 'government failure' as well. The regulatory state in many countries has resulted in economic losses not only due to the misallocation of resources arising from faulty investment decisions but also from the diversion of resources to rent-seeking activities because of the very regulations themselves. One of the reasons for the emergence of skepticism regarding the benefits of state intervention has been the growing perception that government failures on account of political factors and bureaucratisation may, in many cases, exceed market failures.

Thus, if there is a lesson to be drawn from the development record of the last four decades, it is that there can be both 'government failure' as well as 'market failure', and that the critical issue is not so much the presence or absence of state intervention, as the extent and quality of that intervention. The new economic policy builds on this experience.

It must be stated at this point that policymakers in India in the 1950s and 1960s cannot be blamed for the decisions they took. At that time, there was no clear model available for accelerating growth in developing countries. State intervention on an extensive scale seemed to be appropriate. However by early 1970s, it was becoming clear that the model we had chosen was not delivering and that it needed change. But our policymakers refused to recognise this. It was at that time, China made a big change.

The New Approach: Break with the Past

There is a common thread running through all the measures introduced since July 1991. The objective is simple: to improve the efficiency of the system. The regulatory mechanism involving multitudes of controls has fragmented capacity and reduced competition even in the private sector. The thrust of the new economic policy is towards creating a more competitive environment in the economy as a means to improving the productivity and efficiency of the system. This is to be achieved by removing the barriers to entry as well as the restrictions on the growth of firms. While the industrial policy seeks to bring about a greater competitive environment domestically, the trade policy seeks to improve international competitiveness, subject to the protection offered by tariffs which are themselves coming down. The private sector is being given a larger space to operate in, as some areas earlier reserved exclusively for the public sector are now also allowed to the private sector. In these areas, the public sector will have to compete with the private sector, even though the public sector may continue to play the dominant role. What is sought to be achieved is an improvement in the functioning of the various entities, whether in the private sector or the public sector, by injecting an element of competition in them. There is, however, nothing in the new economic policy which takes away the role of the state or the public sector in the system. The new economic policy of India has not necessarily diminished the role of state; it has only redefined it, expanding it in some areas and reducing it in others. As has been said, somewhat paradoxically, more market does not mean 'less government' but only 'different government'.

To understand the importance of the changes, we need to go back to the state of the Indian economy in 1990. The sharp rise in crude oil prices as a consequence of the Gulf Crisis in mid 1990 gave a severe jolt to India's BoPs situation which was already under stress. India's CAD (current account deficit) had touched 2.7 per cent of GDP (gross domestic product) even in 1988-89. From the middle of 1990, financing the CAD became an arduous task. Traditional sources of financing started drying up. It became difficult to roll over short-term finance. Non-resident deposits, the inflow of which contributed significantly to bridge the CAD started flowing out. The danger of default was imminent. Along with a high CAD, the fiscal deficit was also high. Centre's deficit was hovering in the region of 7 per cent of GDP for several years. The growth of 1980s was supported by a high fiscal deficit and CADs. This became untenable. Reforms were thus the answer.

This break with the past came in three important directions. The first was to dismantle the complex regime of licenses, permits and controls that dictated almost every facet of production and distribution. Barriers to entry and growth were dismantled. The second change in direction was to reverse the strong bias towards state ownership of means of production and proliferation of public sector enterprises in almost every sphere of economic activity. Areas once reserved exclusively for the state were thrown open to private enterprise. The third change in direction was to abandon the inward looking trade policy. By embracing international trade, India signalled that it was boldly abandoning its export pessimism and was accepting the challenge and opportunity of integrating into the world economy.

Genesis of Reforms

On the genesis of reforms, some interesting questions have been raised. First of all, several people have been curious to know the role of Narasimha Rao in the reform process. Was he an ardent advocate or a reluctant reformer? Second, were the reforms of 1991 a continuation of a process that had already begun in the 1980s or did they constitute really a break? Third, since the leaders and bureaucrats involved in the reform process were themselves part of the earlier control regime, what compelled them to change their approach? How much of the change was influenced by International Monetary Fund (IMF) and other multilateral institutions?

Dr Manmohan Singh as Finance Minister spearheaded the new policy. He articulated the need for change and provided not only the broad framework but also the details of the reforms. It was however Narasimha Rao as Prime Minister who provided the valuable political support and shield which were very much needed. It must be noted that as Prime Minister, Narasimha Rao also held the portfolio of industry which was directly responsible for initiating the changes that led to the dismantling of various types of controls and licenses relating to the industrial sector. This was indeed a key element of the reform programme. The Eighth Five Year Plan in the writing of which I had a role spelt out in some detail the rationale for the reforms. Narasimha Rao as Chairman of Planning Commission had read the draft and approved it fully. However, as a matter of strategy, he couched the reforms in a language which would appeal to the 'old guards' of his own party. He used such expressions as 'middle path' while presiding over a government which initiated far reaching reforms. There is no doubt that reforms could not have moved forward without his solid support and conviction.

The 1980s saw some important changes in economic policy. A number of committees were set up which recommended changes for improving the functioning of the economy. But most of these recommendations were still within the framework of an overall system of controls. What was attempted was only a relaxation of the controls such as raising the threshold for licensing. They were largely incremental in nature. On the other hand, the reforms of 1991 moved away from the control regime and offered a consistent set of measures covering various segments of the economy in line with the new approach.

What changed the mindset of the people who initiated the reforms was the enormity of the crisis of 1991. As mentioned earlier, India's foreign exchange resources had fallen to a level equivalent only to three weeks of imports. The possibility of 'default' loomed large in the horizon. It became obvious that 'business as usual' won't work. We had to move fast and make fundamental changes in our economic policy. It was true that at that time, we were negotiating with IMF and other multilateral institutions. Obviously they had their own bias. They were in favour of a competitive economy with minimal controls. But the decision that we took to introduce reforms was entirely our own. The credit goes fully to our leadership.

Trends in Growth

That the economic reforms India undertook have been on the right track is vindicated by the performance of the economy since the launch of reforms. In the post-reform period beginning 1992-93, the economy has grown at an average rate of 6.8 per cent per annum (Table 4.1), a significant improvement over the pre-reform period.

India's annual growth rate between 1952 and 1980 averaged to 3.5 per cent (Table 4.2). With population growing almost at 2.2 per cent, the average annual growth rate of per capita income was 1.3 per cent. It is true that the Indian economy grew between 1980 and 1990 at 5.6 per cent (Table 4.3). But the economy faced the worst crisis in 1991-92 and the growth rate fell to 1 per cent. It is extremely doubtful if without a change in the strategy of development, growth would have picked up again.

Economic growth in the 10-year period beginning 2005-06 despite the crisis affected year of 2008-09 was at an average rate of 7.7 per cent. Between 2005-06 and 2007-08, the economy grew at an annual rate of 9.4 per cent. Economic growth slowed down from 2012-13.

However, according to the new methodology adopted by Central Statistics Office (CSO), there was a pick-up in growth rate even in 2013-14. For the last few years, the growth rate has been around 7 per cent even though there is continued skepticism about the numbers. It is imperative that we get back to the high growth rate we had seen in the years following 2005-06. All the same, one inescapable fact is that in the post reform period, the growth rate has been distinctly higher. It needs to be added that the BoPs situation was under control except for a hick up in 2013.

Social Development[2]

Growth is not however the only dimension for assessing the performance of the economy. Equally important is the question of who benefits from growth. Obviously, the growth in national income and per capita income is reflected in a number of social performance parameters such as rise in the literacy rate, availability of medical and health facilities and expansion in education. However, as judged by several social indicators the performance of the country is less impressive than on growth front. India ranks low on the HDI (human development index), 130 out of a total 188 countries, even though India is included in the medium human development countries with a value of 0.609. However, growth is a necessary prerequisite for improving the conditions of vulnerable.

Growth leads to improvement in social development. This can happen through two possible routes. As a country grows particularly at a faster rate, there happens the percolation effect and all sections of the society do benefit, even though, perhaps, some sections may benefit more than others. As the saying goes, a rising tide lifts all boats. But the effect may be stronger or weaker depending on the rate of growth and the pattern of growth. Second, in a fast growing economy, more resources are available for the government to provide for various kinds of social

2. For a more detailed analysis, see Rangarajan (2013).

safety nets. Therefore, the ultimate impact depends on the pattern of government expenditures as well.

Growth and Equity

The period 1993-94 to 2011-12 provides some interesting insights into the question of the relationship between growth and reduction in poverty ratio which is taken as a summary indicator of human development. The annual rate of growth in per capita income in the period 1993-94 to 2004-05 was 4.3 per cent and the growth rate for the period 2004-05 to 2011-12 was 6.7 per cent. The annual rate of decline in the poverty ratio in the first period was 0.7 per cent and 2.18 per cent in the second period. This has happened in the backdrop of an unchanged inequality in rural areas and somewhat of an increase in inequality in urban areas (Table 4.4). Perhaps, it is not farfetched to draw the inference that the faster decline in poverty ratio was mainly due to the faster growth of income. It may also be noted that the period 2004-05 to 2011-12 saw a sharp increase in the growth rate of agriculture. The average annual growth rate in agriculture during this period was 3.61 per cent. A state-wise analysis confirms a similar trend. Without exception, in all States the decline in poverty ratio is much stronger in the second period than in the first period.

The impact of higher growth on poverty reduction can also be seen from the decile-wise growth in per capita consumption expenditure. In the period 2004-05 to 2011-2012, an increase in per capita consumption had taken place across all the 10 deciles of the population both in rural and urban areas as compared to the period 1993-94 to 2004-05 (Table 4.5). It is true that the average growth of per capita consumption of the top 5 deciles is more than that of the bottom 5 deciles. However, the ratio of the average growth rates of the two periods is higher for the bottom 5 deciles as compared to the top 5. It implies that the rate of expansion of consumption of the lower deciles of the population was higher than the upper deciles.

Regional Development

Balanced regional development is also an important development objective. There has been a concern that disparities among states is growing. However, a study done by me and few of my colleagues shows that in the recent period, there is strong evidence of 'catching up' by the lower income states. States with lower per capita income in 1993-94 like Assam, Madhya Pradesh (MP), Uttar Pradesh (UP) and Bihar have made significant gains in growth rates in the recent period 2004-05 to 2012-13. Notwithstanding these gains, convergence did not happen mainly because some states, especially Maharashtra, Gujarat, Kerala, Tamil Nadu (TN) and Haryana, which had high initial per capita incomes, also posted high growth rates (in the range of 7% and above). The declining trend in the positive values of the coefficients of divergence points towards increased 'catching up' and greater convergence.[3]

Future Reforms

In the first phase, reforms were introduced in the industrial sector, external trade and investment sectors, exchange rate management, fiscal policy and financial sector. Later, communications and other key infrastructure sectors were covered. We need to extract the full potential of the reforms we have already introduced. However, reforms must form part of a continuing agenda.

Given the favourable impact of reforms on growth, what should be the focus of reforms in the coming years? The objective of reforms is to improve efficiency through enhanced competition. The introduction of GST (goods and services tax) will be a step in the right direction, as it will help to enhance efficiency. 'Acquisition' is against the spirit of competition and the scope of any Land Acquisition Act must therefore be limited. At the same time, we should avoid fixing the price of land. Farmers have become fully conscious of the value of their land. They are unlikely to sell them at throwaway prices. There are still some

---

3. For a full discussion, see Rangarajan et al. (2014).

segments of the industry which are subject to a number of controls of the pre-1991 type. A typical example is the sugar industry. Molasses are subject to a type of control which results in subsiding the liquor industry! The basic principle of liberalisation of creating competitive markets with minimal barriers to entry, should be extended to all sectors. Pricing of natural resources has become an issue. In the absence of competition, transparent mechanisms for fixing the price must be followed which will be fair to producers and end-users. Among the sectors that have remained untouched by reforms, the most important is agriculture. Even as much remains to be done to improve the productivity of agriculture through scientific research and improved dissemination of knowledge, there are areas like marketing where reforms are badly needed. The present marketing arrangements particularly with respect to vegetables are archaic. Barriers to movement of trade across the country must be brought to an end. The other area that demands attention and that will have a big pay-off immediately is the improvement in the administrative structure. Reform of the Government's delivery system not only in terms of the distribution of subsidies but also all other services will have the most immediate impact. Cumbersome rules and procedures must be done away with.

Conclusion

In many ways the coming decade will be crucial for India. If India grows at 8 to 9 per cent per annum, it is estimated that per capita GDP will increase from the current level of US$1,600 to US$8,000 by 2030. Then India will transit from being a low income to a truly middle income country. We need to overcome the low growth phase as quickly as possible, as growth is the answer to many of our socioeconomic problems. In the recent period, we have launched a number of schemes aimed at broadening the base of growth. These include the employment guarantee scheme, universalisation of education, expansion of rural health, and providing food security. All these programmes have made a substantial demand on public expenditure. It has been possible to fund these programmes only because of the strong growth that we have seen in recent years. Growth has facilitated raising more resources by the Government.

Development has many dimensions. It has to be inclusive, it must be poverty reducing, and it must be environment-friendly. We need to incorporate all these elements in the growth process. A strong and balanced growth will enable the economy to achieve multiple goals including reducing poverty. India has to follow a two-fold path of accelerating growth and addressing directly through various schemes the vulnerable and poor groups.

Reforms are not ends in themselves. Even growth is not an end in itself. Ultimately, growth triggered by reforms must benefit all segments of society. Equity and efficiency should not be posed as opposing considerations. They must be weaved together to provide an acceptable pattern of development.

References

Datta K.L. (2014). *Poverty and Development Planning in India.* New Delhi: Concept Publishing Company (P) Ltd. p.470.

Rangarajan, C. (2013). "Economic Growth and Social Development: Synergic or Contradictory?", *Indian Economic Journal* 6(2) July-September.

Rangarajan, C., Padma Iyer Kaul and E.M. Vibeesh (2014). "Convergence: Have the Lower Income States 'Caught Up'?", *Money & Finance* (ICRA Bulletin), February.

Table 4.1

Growth Rate between 1992-93 and 2013-14

Year	*GDP at Factor Cost*	*Per Capita Net National Income*
1992-93	5.4	3.4
1994	5.7	3.7
1995	6.4	4.3
1996	7.3	5.3
1997	8.0	6.2
1998	4.3	2.2
1999	6.7	4.6
2000	8.0	6.0
2001	4.1	1.7
2002	5.4	3.3
2003	3.9	2.3
2004	8.0	6.5
2005	7.1	5.0
2006	9.5	7.8
2007	9.6	7.9
2008	9.3	8.1
2009	6.7	4.7
2010	8.6	6.8
2011	8.9	6.8
2012	6.7	5.1
2013	4.5	2.1
2013-14	4.7	2.7
AVG	6.8	4.8

Source: *Economic Survey 2013-14.*

Table 4.2

Growth Rate between 1951-52 and 1979-80

Year	*GDP at Factor Cost*	*Per Capita Net National Income*
1951-52	2.3	1.2
1953	2.8	1.4
1954	6.1	4.8
1955	4.2	3.6
1956	2.6	0.9
1957	5.7	3.6
1958	-1.2	-3.5
1959	7.6	5.3
1960	2.2	0.0
1961	7.1	5.5
1962	3.1	0.6
1963	2.1	-0.4
1964	5.1	2.8
1965	7.6	5.2
1966	-3.7	-6.5
1967	1.0	-1.4
1968	8.1	5.8
1969	2.6	0.1
1970	6.5	4.3
1971	5.0	2.2
1972	1.0	-1.6
1973	-0.3	-2.9
1974	4.6	2.3
1975	1.2	-1.4
1976	9.0	6.9
1977	1.2	-1.3
1978	7.5	5.5
1979	5.5	3.4
1979-80	-5.2	-8.2
AVG	3.5	1.3

Source: *Economic Survey 2013-14*.

Table 4.3

Growth Rate between 1980-81 and 1990-91

Year	*GDP at Factor Cost*	*Per Capita Net National Income*
1980-81	7.2	5.0
1982	5.6	3.5
1983	2.9	0.0
1984	7.9	5.9
1985	4.0	1.3
1986	4.2	1.7
1987	4.3	1.9
1988	3.5	0.7
1989	10.2	8.1
1990	6.1	3.9
1990-91	5.3	2.7
AVG	5.6	3.2

Source: *Economic Survey 2013-14.*

Table 4.4

Lorenz Ratio of Consumption Distribution

	Rural	*Urban*
1993-94	0.28	0.34
2004-05	0.30	0.37
2011-12	0.30	0.38

Source: Computed from NSSO Data.

Table 4.5

Decile-wise Growth in Per Capita Consumption (Per cent per year, compound)

Decile	*1993-94 to 2004-05*		*2004-05 to 2011-12*	
	Rural	*Urban*	*Rural*	*Urban*
1. First Decile	0.70	0.66	2.91	2.96
2. Second Decile	0.49	0.54	3.00	3.28
3. Third Decile	0.56	0.66	3.15	3.39
4. Fourth Decile	0.55	0.91	3.17	3.42
5. Fifth Decile	0.54	1.00	3.17	3.41
6. Sixth Decile	0.55	1.24	3.30	3.35
7. Seventh Decile	0.52	1.36	3.40	3.30
8. Eighth Decile	0.61	1.35	3.45	3.40
9. Ninth Decile	0.71	1.47	3.48	3.45
10. Tenth Decile	1.61	2.30	3.71	4.52
A. Bottom Five Deciles	0.57	0.75	3.08	3.29
B. Top Five Deciles	0.80	1.54	3.47	3.60

Note: The growth rates are in real terms and derived from URP consumption data.

Source: Computed from NSSO Data and see also Datta (2014).

5

Twenty-Five Years of Economic Reforms and Poverty and Inequality

BIBEK DEBROY[1]

"Alice's Adventures in Wonderland" has a conversation between Alice and the Cheshire cat. "Would you tell me, please, which way I ought to go from here?" "That depends a good deal on where you want to get to," said the Cat. "I don't much care where—" said Alice. "Then it doesn't matter which way you go," said the Cat. "—so long as I get somewhere," Alice added as an explanation. "Oh, you're sure to do that," said the Cat, "if you only walk long enough".

Where do we want India to be in 2030? Are we clear about where we want to go? Or, as a country, are we just trundling along, as long as we get somewhere?

We gave ourselves a Constitution in 1950 and the Preamble promised us a sovereign democratic republic that would ensure, for every citizen, social, economic and political justice; liberty of thought, expression, belief, faith and worship; equality of status and opportunity; and fraternity, assuring the dignity of the individual. The Preamble was subsequently amended through the 42nd Amendment Act of 1976 to make India socialist and secular and to bring in "the integrity of the nation." I will not get into questions about the Preamble being an integral part of the Constitution, or being non-justiciable. That's not terribly pertinent for present purposes. For present purposes, we promised India's citizens justice, liberty,

---

1. The views are personal and not of Niti Aayog.

equality and dignity. We haven't been able to ensure that. We have failed the Constitution and the Constitutional promise. We have introduced policies that haven't ensured justice, liberty, equality and dignity.

It is not quite the case that there have been no successes since 1947, or since 1950. Consider some random figures for 1950-51,[2] life expectancy at birth was 32.1 years. The literacy rate was 18.3 per cent. As shares of GDP (gross domestic product), the savings rate was 8.6 per cent and the investment rate was 8.7 per cent. During the First Plan (1951-1956), the average annual real growth in GNP (gross national product) was 3.7 per cent. But consider also the following quote.

> In the last four or five decades, there has been considerable industrial development in India, accompanied by urbanisation and expansion of commerce. Large towns and cities have grown and transport and communications have developed extensively. The isolation of the village has been broken and the average citizen lives in an environment significantly different from the one in which he lived and worked fifty or sixty years ago. Indian enterprise has made considerable headway, and the country has now considerable experience in the fields of modern business, industry and finance. New economic and social relations have emerged, giving rise in turn to a general desire for more rapid change. But the development that has taken place is partial and limited when judged in terms of the country's needs and potentialities. Industrialism and the use of modern techniques have affected only limited segments of the economy. Agriculture is still the mainstay of the population, and productivity in this sector is exceedingly low. The size of agricultural holdings has progressively diminished; the old cottage and small-scale industries have been decaying, and the rural population suffers from chronic underemployment and low incomes. Population has increased by more than fifty per cent

2. These figures are from *Economic Survey 2010-11*, Department of Economic Affairs, Ministry of Finance, Government of India.

> in the last fifty years, but the growth of alternative occupations either in the rural areas or in the towns has not been on a scale which could absorb this growing population. In the limited spheres which have registered expansion, the level of productivity and the level of incomes have naturally been higher. But, for the community as a whole, the economic development of the last few decades has brought no significant improvement in standards of living and opportunities for employment, and has perhaps accentuated to some extent inequalities of income and wealth.

The Planning Commission was set up in 1950 and the First Five Year Plan was launched in 1951. The Planning Commission has now been succeed by Niti Aayog, which is where I work. This quote isn't from the Twelfth Plan Document or from something Niti Aayog has drafted. This quote is from Chapter 1 of the First Five Year Plan document.[3] A sense of déjà vu is unavoidable. The more things change, the more they seem to remain the same. We are getting somewhere, but we don't seem to care where.

This needs to change. There is an impression that India has changed a lot, particularly after 1991. Indeed it has, and this shows up in all kinds of different indicators. The July 1991 reforms were triggered by a severe BoP (balance of payments) crisis, though there were earlier reforms too, often described as reforms by stealth.[4] When those July 1991 reforms were introduced, few observers would have predicted the kind of changes India has witnessed since 1991. It is no longer a shortage economy, at least in segments where reforms have been introduced. Several news magazines have done stories on 25 years of reforms and they document these changes. But more importantly, it has led to changes in expectations and mindsets. India is described as a young country, with a median age that is around 25 years. This is a generation born after 1991. If not born after 1991, it is a generation that has grown

3. *http://planningcommission.nic.in/plans/planrel/fiveyr/index9.html*

4. See, for example, Panagariya (2008).

up after 1991. It is a generation that is no longer shackled by old mindsets. It is a generation that is impatient. In earlier generations, opportunities for betterment of lives were limited. This new generation may not have benefited entirely from these new opportunities, but it knows these opportunities exist. Thanks to the spread of information, expectations have changed. Policies have to cater to this new generation and the expectations of this new generation. Policies have to cater to the likes of Aastha Arora. Most of us have forgotten who Aastha Arora is. Aastha Arora is the billionth Indian, born on 11 May 2000. She will be 30 in 2030. When she is 30, she is entitled to an India that she is proud of. It should be an India that all Indians are proud of. India is a country that has negative net migration. Net migration is defined as the number of people who leave the country, subtracted from the number of people who enter the country. That is, more people leave India, compared to the number of people who migrate to India. Since all of us left Africa 1000 years ago, human beings have always migrated in search of better economic opportunities, to better their lives. If relatively more people leave India, that is because they perceive better economic opportunities abroad. If we can bring about a prosperous India in 2030, there will be longer queues at Indian missions abroad and shorter queues at Organisation for Economic Co-operation and Development (OECD) missions in India. That's a good outcome, not something that is undesirable.

We are getting there, the question is the speed. When the rupee was devalued in two stages in July 1991, a code was used and that was 'hop, skip and jump'. The devaluation was in two stages, so as to test the waters. That is irrelevant now and is only of historical interest. What is relevant is the phrase 'hop, skip and jump', better known as the triple jump. In a triple jump, each of the three phases is stronger and longer than the preceding one. The hop provides the momentum for the skip and the hop and the skip provide the momentum for the jump. In our reforms, we have hopped. On rare occasions, we have skipped. But we have still not jumped. If this sounds like a strong statement, we should go back and read an official government document that everyone has forgotten about now. It was published in July 1993, two years after the reforms (Ministry of Finance 1993). Among other things, this set out an agenda for future reforms. If we revisit that paper, we will find that many of the reforms that were talked about in July 1993 have still not been implemented. A snide comment is made in comparisons about India and East Asia. "What is the difference between India and East Asia? In East Asia, they do what Indians talk about. And in India, they talk about what East Asia does." We have talked about reforms ad nauseam, but we haven't implemented them. Earlier, pre-1991, Indian economic policy was supposed to have been influenced by Fabian socialism, though it was actually influenced much more by Soviet socialism. The reference to Fabian socialism is a reference to the Fabian Society, established in London in 1884. That kind of socialism was meant to be incremental and creeping, not revolutionary. Hence, the Society consciously adopted the name of Fabius Maximus, the Roman dictator and general during the Second Punic War (218-202 BCE) against Hannibal of Carthage. Fabius didn't take decisive action. He used delaying tactics and was thus named 'Cunctator', the delayer. One need not get into a detailed discussion of Roman history, though we seem to have an obsession with all things Italian. The point is that our economic policy-making lacks decisive action. There is continual resort to delaying tactics. Witness the references to first generation reforms, second generation reforms and third generation reforms. What are these reforms? Since the first generation reforms outlined in 1991, or 1993, weren't implemented, how can we talk about second generation reforms? In any event, what are second generation reforms? Are they reforms that will not be implemented by the present generation, but will have to be implemented by a future generation?

There are several external reports that are bullish about India. The first BRIC (Brazil, Russia, India, China) paper by Goldman Sachs was partly responsible for popularising the idea of India's explosive income and consumption growth potential (Wilson and Purushothaman 2003). But there have been several others since then.[5] What do these reports generally argue? First, the savings rate, as a share of GDP, has increased and will increase further. Second, the investment rate has also increased. Third, the efficiency in the use of capital, measured, say by the ICoR (incremental capital/output ratio), has improved because of competition. Fourth, the share of agriculture and allied activities in GDP is declining, while that of services is increasing. What is pertinent is that the services sector tends to have a lower ICOR, though not invariably. That apart, if agriculture is growing relatively slowly and services are growing relatively fast, the sectoral shift from agriculture to services itself jacks up GDP growth as a statistical inevitability. Fifth, there is the effect of export growth on GDP, though that it is contingent on a global recovery. Sixth, there is the demographic dividend and increase in labour input. Seventh, there is TFP (total factor productivity) growth, after netting out increases in labour and capital inputs. Not every report or study tries to quantify and estimate this, but nevertheless, this is a factor. Eighth, the young population does things to entrepreneurship that is difficult to pin down and make tangible. Ninth and finally, projections are typically in US dollars and if the rupee appreciates against the dollar, there is the impact of exchange rate appreciation.

These reasons are all true. But one should not get carried away. Consider the per capita GDP figures, and not the total GDP. After all, India has, and will continue to have, a large population. An overall GDP figure is spread over many more people. While the precise figure varies across studies, most of them project an Indian per capita GDP of between $2,500 and $3,000 in 2030. This is per capita GDP in today's dollars and is GDP estimated with official exchange rates, the so-called Atlas method. It is not

5. For example, there have been two other BRIC reports, O'Neill et al. (2005) and O'Neill (2007). That apart, there is PricewaterhouseCoopers (PwC) (2006), Deutsche Bank (2005), HSBC (2011), McKinsey (2007) and ADB (2009).

PPP (purchasing power parity) per capita GDP. One can also cite PPP figures, which will increase India's per capita GDP. PPP corrections are based on the idea that goods, and more importantly, services, do not cost the same in developing countries as they do in developed countries. Such items, which cannot be traded, do not necessarily equalise across countries. Because they are relatively lower in developing countries, PPP corrections increase per capita GDP in developing countries and decrease them in developed countries. But that is neither here nor there, since the thrust of the argument remains, whether one is using the Atlas method or PPP. $2,500 to $3,000 will take us to roughly where countries like Ukraine, Congo, Guatemala, Syria, Egypt, Georgia, Iraq and Sri Lanka are today. More than one decade down the line, we will be as prosperous as these countries are today. That's not India Shining by any criterion.

There is no formal definition of a developed country though. The World Bank uses no such term. Instead, it has expressions like high income, upper middle income, lower middle income and low income. The UN has a definition of LDCs (least developed countries). By and large, the OECD economies are regarded as developed countries. And whatever else is left, after taking away the OECD and LDC groups, is loosely called a developing country. Today, the United States (US) has a per capita income of around US $55,000. That is a long, long way off. India is only at around US $1,600. India is what is called a lower middle income country. As of today, to get to upper middle income status, we will need a per capita of US $4,125. We are unlikely to touch that in 2030. High income countries are those that have a per capita income of more than US $12,736. That is an extremely long way off. Many years ago, developing economies were regarded as those that had per capita incomes that were 25 per cent or lower than that of the US. In other words, to cross the developing country status in that loose sense, we need to have a per capita income of US $12,000 and more. In 2030, will we remain in that lower middle income status? Or will we move to upper middle income status? Or can we be more ambitious and move to high income status and attain the status of a developed economy, the latter expression being used in a loose sense? This is one way to pose the question.

It is good to be ambitious. But one shouldn't be widely off the mark. All kinds of things in the world are possible. However, they aren't probable. High income or developed economy status by 2030 has a very low degree of probability. But crossing over to the upper middle income status is eminently doable. If we can get real growth of 9.5 per cent going, even if this does not accelerate to 10 per cent and more, we will cross over to the upper middle income status comfortably. We will have a per capita income of US $6,000 and more.

What will it take to achieve annual real rates of GDP growth of 9.5 per cent and more? No rocket science is involved. At one level, per capita GDP is nothing but the average productivity of India's inhabitants.[6] World Economic Forum's Global Competitiveness Index (GCI) analyses competitiveness on the basis of 12 pillars: (1) institutions; (2) infrastructure; (3) macroeconomic environment; (4) health and primary education; (5) higher education and training; (6) goods market efficiency; (7) labour market efficiency; (8) financial market development; (9) technological readiness; (10) market size; (11) business sophistication; and (12) innovation.[7] As one moves up the development ladder, successive pillars become increasingly important. At India's levels of development, capital and labour inputs are key drivers behind high GDP growth, though technology and innovation also begin to kick in. At an even more simple level, what are we saying? We have got labour, capital, land and other natural resources. Let us use them efficiently. We have entrepreneurship. Let us give people access to market-based opportunities. Let us give them access to physical and social infrastructure. For those

6. Since per capita GDP is GDP divided by population (and not just the working-age population), per capita GDP is more accurately the average productivity of India's working-age population.

7. *http://gcr.weforum.org/gcr2010/*

who are able-bodied, there can be institutional constraints in accessing market-based opportunities. These can be in the form of inadequate access to health, education, skills, technology, information, financial products, land, physical infrastructure (roads, electricity, water) and law and order. Are all these necessarily public goods, in the classic sense? Beyond law and order, it is not obvious that these are public goods. They are often collective private goods. As a follow-up question, are there demonstrated instances of market failure in these segments? One must remember that thanks to possibilities of unbundling and advent of technology, what used to be regarded as an example of market failure in the 1950s is no longer pertinent. Therefore, there are possibilities of private sector provisioning, even if this is backed by public sector financing. Hence, have entry regulations been sufficiently relaxed for private sector entry? To the extent that there are market failures and public sector provisioning is important, how does one improve the efficiency of public expenditure? Other than this, there is the question of direct anti-poverty measures through subsidies, certainly those who aren't able-bodied or in working ages. Direct anti-poverty measures, as opposed to public goods or collective private goods, is a more debatable issue for those who are able-bodied and in working-age groups.

Why do we want growth? That's a good question to ask. Growth of 9.5 per cent and more is not an end in itself. It is a means to an end. First, growth provides additional resources for public expenditure, be it for items that are public or collective private goods, or through direct anti-poverty programmes. If a government doesn't have the resources, how will it spend on such agenda items? Second, growth is correlated with improvements in human development outcomes. As examples, as per capita income increases, so do life expectancy and literacy and assorted other indicators. Infant mortality, gender disparities in access and assorted other indicators show improvements. There is no need to debate the causation right now. It is sufficient to know that there is correlation. So if per capita income goes up, Indians lead better lives. That is precisely what we want for India in 2030. That's precisely what we want the government to do, provide the enabling environment for growth and human development. Indians have plenty of enterprise. They exhibit it when they migrate to other countries. That is not the best solution. They should be able to exhibit enterprise and improve their lives within India.

This is a quote that the 9th Report of the Second Administrative Reforms Commission quoted approvingly, though it didn't include the last part.[8]

> Government control gives rise to fraud, suppression of truth, intensification of the black market and artificial scarcity. Above all, it unmans the people and deprives them of initiative, it undoes the teaching of self-help...I look upon an increase in the power of the State with the greatest fear because, although while apparently doing good by minimising exploitation, it does the greatest harm to mankind by destroying individuality which lies at the heart of all progress.[9]

This was written by Mahatma Gandhi. The reforms were meant to reduce government control and scarcity and increase human initiative.

With that growth angle, let me turn to poverty and inequality. There is often complete confusion about inequality and poverty and what should be done about either. If there is lack of conceptual clarity, is it at all surprising that there should be confusion about policies to address either?

Let us take poverty first. Poverty is a multi-dimensional concept. It is no one's case that a minimum level of income or consumption expenditure is the sole criterion for identifying someone as BPL (below the poverty line) or APL (above the poverty line). However, the use of income or consumption expenditure is customary, because it is

8. *http://arc.gov.in/9threport/ARC_9thReport_preface_contents.pdf*

9. *http://www.gandhiserve.org/cwmg/VOL097.PDF*

easier to get data on income or consumption expenditure. It is not just in India, but also in other countries, that such concepts of a poverty line based on income or expenditure are used. India was one of the earliest countries in the world to formulate and adopt the concept of a poverty line, way back in the 1950s. The methodology has evolved over time, through the Planning Commission. But since the Alagh Committee of 1979, the methodology has been something like the following, and this was also endorsed by the Lakdawala Committee of 1993. Let us fix a per capita daily calorie requirement of 2,400 calories for rural India and a per capita daily calorie requirement of 2,100 calories for urban India. This immediately suggests that the poverty line was primarily dependent on food, though a little bit was thrown in for clothing. In the late 1950s, this made eminent sense, because it was expected that items like education and health were public goods and would be provided by the government. Therefore, they need not figure in private consumption expenditure baskets. We now ask, what is the optimal consumption basket that will guarantee people 2,400 calories per capita per day in rural India and 2,100 calories in urban India? It is a different matter that people, including poor people, need not be 'rational' quite in that sense.[10] Having determined the optimal consumption basket, we next try to figure out how much that consumption basket is going to cost in different States, using State-level prices generated through assorted CPI (consumer price indices), separately for rural and urban India. This converts a calorie-based poverty line into an expenditure-based poverty line. But prices change over time. Therefore, those price indices are again used to adjust the expenditure-based poverty line over time. This was modified in 2005, when the government appointed an Expert Committee chaired by Prof Suresh Tendulkar. Stated simply, this modified the Lakdawala method by using a slightly different kind of indexing. After that, we

10. See Banerjee and Duflo (2011). "Most people living with less than 99 cents a day do not seem to act as if they are starving. If they were, surely they would put every available penny into buying more calories. But they do not."

had another Committee, chaired by Dr C. Rangarajan. I will skip the nitty-gritty details.[11]

Having done all that, one needs data. Data surface through surveys. And that means the National Sample Survey (NSS) Organisation. NSS doesn't collect data on incomes, because data on incomes are felt to be unreliable. NSS collects data on consumption expenditure. Unfortunately, NSS doesn't collect such data every year. More accurately, the larger a sample, the more accurate are the data. And NSS large-samples surface roughly once every five years. We had such large surveys in 1983-84, 1987-88, 1993-94, 1999-2000, 2004-05, 2009-10 and 2011-12. In between, there are thin or small samples and these can't be relied on. Two minor issues should be mentioned. First, as with any household survey, there is underestimation. That is, the aggregate of consumption expenditure collected through a survey like NSS falls short of aggregate consumption expenditure collected through national accounts, Central Statistical Organisation (CSO) in the Indian context. This is not a problem that is typical to India. It happens in every country where surveys are conducted. Second, there is a technical issue of the recall period connected with NSS surveys, namely, the period over which respondents are asked details about their expenditure. Figures are sensitive to the recall period used. However, let us gloss over that.

What's the broad story? If I follow the Tendulkar methodology, in 2011-12, 21.9 per cent of India's population was BPL, 269 million people. There can be immediate shock and outrage. 21.9 per cent of India's population is poor? 269 million Indians are poor? More than 60 years after Independence? That is more than the populations of most countries in the world. True, and the shock and outrage are legitimate. But consider this. There were NSS surveys in 1950-51 and 1977-78. In both those years, the BPL percentage, that is the poverty ratio, was roughly 50 per cent. Therefore, three decades of Fabian

11. Datta (2014) provides an excellent discussion.

cum Soviet policy couldn't make much dent on poverty. Indian growth picked up from the late-1970s, picked up again in the 1990s and then picked up again from 2003. In each of these instances, shackles were eased through reforms and unleashed the growth potential and poverty ratios declined. Thus, the much-maligned trickle-down effect of growth on poverty does work. In general, though not always, rural poverty is higher than urban poverty. Therefore, poverty is fundamentally, though not invariably, a rural phenomenon. We can also see that poverty is concentrated in states like Bihar, Chhattisgarh, Jharkhand, Madhya Pradesh (MP), Orissa, Uttar Pradesh (UP) and Uttarakhand. Therefore, policies need to address deprivation in these States. Clearly, they haven't been that successful yet.

The former Planning Commission faced criticism because of calorie-based norms. Apart from anything else, lifestyles have changed, even in rural India, and even among the poor. You no longer need 2,100 calories per capita per day in urban India and 2,400 calories per capita per day in rural India. For instance, with a switch to LPG (liquefied petroleum gas) for cooking, women no longer have to walk 10 kilometres to fetch firewood. If one sticks to the essentials and does not get into complicated details, the Tendulkar Committee suggested moving away from calorie-based norms. That would ensure that one wasn't bogged down by food items alone. Instead, separately for rural and urban India, let us work out monetary figures on the amount of expenditure required, per person per day and let us recalculate poverty ratios.

As if the waters weren't sufficiently muddied already, internationally, poverty lines of US \$1.90 per day is used. This is at constant, 2005, prices. 21.3 per cent of India's population lives on less than US \$1.90 per day.[12]

Poverty isn't only about income or expenditure poverty. Nor is development only about this. That was part of the reason why the Millennium Development Goal (MDG)

12. *http://povertydata.worldbank.org/poverty/country/IND*

system evolved, with separate targets and indicators. In September 2000, the UN General Assembly agreed to a Millennium Declaration. What was interesting about this declaration, as opposed to several other UN declarations, was that some specific timelines were set out in a section on "Development and Poverty Eradication". In December 2000, the General Assembly asked the Secretary General to prepare a roadmap for implementing this declaration and by September 2001, such a roadmap was available. This not only involved the UN Secretariat and the UN system, but also the International Monetary Fund (IMF), the World Bank and the OECD. Effectively, it is this document[13] that first set out what came to be accepted as the eight MDGs: (1) Eradicate extreme poverty and hunger; (2) Achieve universal primary education; (3) Promote gender equality and empower women: (4) Reduce child mortality: (5) Improve maternal health; (6) Combat HIV/AIDS, malaria, and other diseases; (7) Ensure environmental sustainability; and (8) Develop a global partnership for development. Of these, (1) was directly on poverty and under the MDG system, there was a hierarchy of goals, refined into targets and indicators.

The last Indian country report on MDGs was in February 2015 and this is what it had to say on India's progress towards poverty reduction.[14]

> Target 1: Halve, between 1990 and 2015, the proportion of people whose income is less than one dollar a day. The all India Poverty Head Count Ratio (PHCR) estimate was 47.8% in 1990. In order to meet the target the PHCR level has to be 23.9% by 2015. In 2011-12, the PHCR at all India level is 21.9%, which shows that, India has already achieved the target, well ahead of time. During 2004-05 to 2011-12, the poverty gap ratio reduced both in rural and urban areas. While the rural PGR declined from 9.64 in 2004-05 to 5.05 in 2011-12, in the urban

---

13. General Assembly document, A/56/326.
14. *Millennium Development Goals: India Country Report 2015*, Ministry of Statistics and Programme Implementation, February 2015, *http://mospi.nic.in/Mospi_New/upload/mdg_26feb15.pdf*

areas it declined from 6.08 to 2.70 during the same period. A nearly 50% decline in PGR both in rural and urban areas during 2004-05 to 2011-12 reflects that the conditions of poor have improved both in urban and rural areas. At all India level, the share of the poorest quintile in the total consumption is lower in the urban areas than in rural areas. During 1993-94 to 2011-12, in urban areas, the indicator (URP[15] methodology) showed a decline from 8.0% in 1993-94 to 6.97% in 2009-10, and then showed a slight improvement 7.1% in 2011-12. In rural areas, the share of poorest quintile steadily declined from 9.6% in 1993-94 to 9.1% in 2011-12.

The Sustainable Development Goals (SDGs) have now succeeded the MDGs. But I will refrain from commenting on the SDGs, because the targets and indicators are yet to be firmed up.

Every year, United Nations Development Programme (UNDP) brings out a *Human Development Report* (HDR). Among other things, this has a HDI (Human Development Index). HDI is based on three indicators—education (literacy, gross enrollment ratio), health (life expectancy) and PPP per capita income. The higher the value of HDI, the better it is. In 1985, India had a HDI value of 0.320, placing it in the low human development category. In 2014, India has a HDI value of 0.609, placing it in the medium human development category.[16] There has been steady improvement, primarily driven by income growth. By 2030, India should cross the HDI threshold value of 0.750 and move into the high human development category. Several states have also brought out HDRs and these not only compute HDIs for the individual States, they enable us to pinpoint backward districts and intra-State divergences.

In recent times, HDRs have also introduced a MPI (multi-dimensional poverty index), conceptualised by the Oxford Poverty and Human Development Initiative

15. Uniform recall period.
16. *http://hdr.undp.org/en/countries/profiles/IND*

(OPHDI). In addition to standard income or consumption poverty measures, this includes deprivation measured in terms of education, health and other assets.[17] Thus,

> We see that 81 per cent of people are multi-dimensionally poor in Bihar—more than any other state. Also, poverty in Bihar and Jharkand is most intense—poor people are deprived in 60 per cent of the MPI's weighted indicators. Uttar Pradesh is the home of largest number of poor people—21 per cent of India's poor people live there. West Bengal is home to the third largest number of poor people.

There are other large numbers of poor in Maharashtra and MP. One can refine this further and go down to the level of the districts. After all, State boundaries are administratively determined. Development and deprivation do not follow these administrative boundaries. There are differences within States too. For example, a MPI kind of exercise has been undertaken for 379 of India's districts and the deprived districts are in Assam, Bihar, MP, Odisha, Rajasthan and UP.[18]

This is the right moment to pause and ask several questions. First, are people willingly poor? Do they not wish to better their lives and improve their standards of living? Assuming otherwise is tantamount to a very patronising attitude towards poor people. At best, there can be a qualification for the old and the disabled and households where the head of the household happens to be a woman. These apart, people in working-age groups do not wish to be poor. Income growth and liberalisation will ensure that such people are no longer poor. As a minor statistical point, income and expenditure distributions aren't symmetric. They are log normal, with a thick part towards the left. As soon as this thick part of the distribution passes above the poverty line, however that happens to be defined, there will be sharp drops in poverty. This has already begun to happen for India and will continue, assuming we can ensure that the growth

17. *http://www.ophi.org.uk/wp-content/uploads/Country-Brief-India.pdf*

18. See, Mehta and Bhide (2011).

continues. In States that have grown, there have been such sharp drops in poverty—Punjab, Haryana, Kerala, Tamil Nadu (TN), Gujarat, Andhra Pradesh (AP) and Assam. Second, even if people do not wish to be poor, they may be stuck because they do not have access to education and skills, health services, market information, technology, financial products, roads, electricity, water, sewage and sanitation. But then, the answer is to efficiently provide these public goods or collective private goods. If such people continue to be poor, that is because in more than 65 years, these goods and services haven't been efficiently provided, notwithstanding colossal amounts of public expenditure. People may also be poor because they are stuck in subsistence-level agriculture and have no other employment opportunities. If such people are poor, that is because in more than 65 years, we haven't been able to reform agriculture and the rural sector.

> People can be trapped in poverty, when poverty itself becomes a constraint to growth. This occurs in regions that display characteristics of high conflict, low savings or investment rates, dismal education or health outcomes, poor access to credit or property rights, and incomplete insurance markets which increase the risks of crop failures, floods, and droughts.[19]

Hence, poverty results from lack of integration. Third, we should therefore ask an important question. Are there sections in the Indian Constitution that prevent such integration? For instance, Articles 370 and 371 of the Constitution ensure that certain parts of India will never be integrated and mainstreamed. If that is the case, how can we ensure that people who live in these regions will ever be mainstreamed and become part of the growth process? Fourth, this kind of mindset also ensures that we look at the problem of poverty with a distorted lens. In any table of poverty, there will be categories of SCs (scheduled castes), STs (scheduled tribes), OBCs (other backward classes) and Muslims. But are they deprived because they

---

19. This quote is in the context of all of South Asia. See Ghani (2010).

belong to these collective categories? Or are they deprived because they lack access to the public or collective private goods we have mentioned?

> Indeed, if anything, the data in this volume provide pretty good evidence that the SCs and STs are still particularly disadvantaged in many extraordinary ways. What the numbers do seem to imply are: first, there is a good deal of truth in the old-fashioned story that economic and educational opportunities, more than caste identities, are determinants of access to various goods of poverty (Mehta 2010).[20]

Poverty is an individual household characteristic. By equating it with a collective category like SC, ST or Muslim, we commit a double kind of mistake. We assume that everyone inside this collective category is poor, by virtue of being a member of a collective category. And we also assume that everyone outside this collective category is rich, by virtue of not being a member of this collective category. Neither of these propositions is true.

Fifth, it is plausible to argue that these public or collective private goods aren't going to be efficiently delivered in a hurry. Nor is the rural sector going to be reformed in a hurry. Therefore, in the intervening period, we need to subsidise the poor. And we have been going round and round in circles on this one. In similar vein, there is a great deal of talk about switching from the present system of subsidies (food, fertiliser, petroleum products at the level of the Union) to direct cash transfers. There is no question that this is more efficient. This does not distort resource allocation. It also offers poor consumers the choice. However, technology doesn't solve the problem of identifying BPL. Until the problem of BPL identification is solved, we will continue to go round and round in circles. The simple point is that poverty is a household level characteristic. It has nothing to do with the collective categories that were earlier mentioned, apart from the old and the disabled and women-headed households. Not only do NSS data surface with a time-lag and are available

---

20. Mehta (2010).

only at intervals of five years, there are always question marks about the data, because NSS conducts a survey, not a Census. Poverty has to be based on decentralised and individual household-based identification, an idea that has been floating around since the Ninth Plan (1997-2002). However, this has never properly been implemented. We have been playing around with assorted parameters and centrally-determined templates for surveys.[21] Once we streamline financial flows for development to States and also decentralise within States, why should gram sabhas not determine who is BPL and who is not? Not only does this make better economic sense. It will help dispel the subsidy culture that is rampant.

We now turn to the more controversial question of inequality. Poverty is an absolute concept, while inequality is relative. There is an impression that increases in inequality, real or perceived, are bad. In a paper by Suresh Tendulkar, there is an interesting anecdote about a conference in Bangkok when Manmohan Singh was the Deputy Chairman of the Planning Commission.

> After other delegations presented their experiences in managing a market economy, the Chinese vice minister presented an outline of the Chinese reform program. At the end of the presentation, Manmohan Singh, in his usual gentle but forceful tone, asked, "Would not what you are trying to do result in greater inequality in China? To that the minister replied, with great conviction, "We would certainly hope so!"[22]

There is a difference between inequality in access to inputs (physical and social infrastructure, financial products and so on) and inequality in outcomes (income). Everyone would like India to be equitable. But equity should be interpreted in terms of access to inputs and we should be legitimately upset if there is inequity in that. However, why should there be equality in outcomes? This is a hangover of the socialism introduced in the Preamble

21. See for example, *http://www.pbplanning.gov.in/pdf/BPL16-3-07.pdf*

22. Tendulkar (2010).

to the Constitution, as a result of which, a political party cannot be registered in India unless it abides by the principles of socialism.[23] Socialism is a delightfully vague phrase, which can never be pinned down. As a result of this damage that was done to the Constitution, we have begun to take Article 38 of the Directive Principles too literally. This states:

> The State shall, in particular, strive to minimise the inequalities in income, and endeavour to eliminate inequalities in status, facilities and opportunities, not only amongst individuals but also amongst groups of people residing in different areas or engaged in different vocations.

The second part is fine. But minimising inequalities in income is disastrous. There is a difference between saying that every student should have access to a good school and saying that every student should obtain the same marks. Any period of rapid economic growth results in increased income inequalities. Simon Kuznets (1955) argued this out a long time ago. This should be welcome, not denigrated, while taking care of inequity in access to inputs. For the record, one standard measure of inequality in the distribution of incomes is the Gini coefficient. For the record, India's Gini coefficients, both on income and expenditure, are not that high.

Both on poverty and inequality, we need to be less sanctimonious and hypocritical. We should listen to our brains and not our bleeding hearts. While inequality is a relative concept, poverty is often considered to be absolute. If there is growth and development, poverty declines. Also, both poverty and inequality are dynamic concepts: they change over time. If there is growth and poverty declines, and if one thinks that one's offspring will have a better life, there is less resentment about inequality.

If the general election of 2014 is anything to go by, development, governance, and corruption are the most important issues for Indian voters—though, in such a large

---

23. The Representation of the People Act was amended in 1989.

and diverse country, there is huge variation. What India's citizens want therefore depends on where they happen to reside. Much of India remains outside the mainstream of growth and development. Out of its 676 districts, by any criterion, around 125 still remain deprived, and of 600,000 villages, around 100,000 remain deprived.

To understand this divide, the standard rural/urban lens is not sufficient. In the 2011 Census, 72 per cent of the population was classified as rural and 28 per cent as urban. But this categorisation obscures the fact that, between 2001 and 2011, most urbanisation has occurred in what are known as 'census towns'—that is, the part of India that is between rural and urban. These towns have transcended the rural governance structure of *panchayats* (village-level decision-making bodies), but are not yet municipalities. Dividing India in terms of the neat administrative boundaries of states is also misleading for evaluating development or deprivation. Conventionally, some states have been regarded as backward—for instance, Bihar, Jharkhand, Chhattisgarh, MP, Rajasthan, UP, and Uttarakhand—and others as relatively advanced. But, since 2000, faster growth has occurred in some of these historically backward states, though the base levels of development remain low. In other words, they have caught up. State boundaries can also be misleading because there are intra-state differences. Since economic liberalisation reforms started in 1991, the economic geography story has been one of increasing integration of districts and villages, as the radius of development expands. Many term this 'inclusive development', which emphasises equality in distribution of outcomes, including patterns of income.

More important is the question of why some people are poor. Mostly it is because they lack access to physical infrastructure (transport, water, electricity), social infrastructure (education, skills, health), financial products, natural resources, technology, information technology, the judicial system, and markets. Around 100,000 villages in India have a population of less than 500, and it is difficult to deliver goods and services there because the cost per unit of delivery is much higher. For any government, the priority should be to deliver these goods and services. This is a shared responsibility of subnational governments as well as the Central government. India is a federal country (though, for technical reasons, the word 'federal' isn't used in the Constitution). In May 2014, a new Central, or Union, government was formed in New Delhi. However, many changes can only be implemented by states (under the Constitution, most factor markets are in the State or Concurrent Lists—i.e. the states have the power to legislate on them) and most public goods and services are delivered by local bodies (villages and municipalities). Historically, India has been too centralised. Decentralisation and devolution to the state level, including fiscal devolution, are desirable, and this has started. For instance, land and labour legislation will primarily be reformed at state level. To the extent that Central government legislation is involved, any reform has to wind its way through the democratic processes of parliament.

More importantly, these goods and services have to be financed. There is a clear need to eliminate exemptions and reform subsidies—both on consumption and production. India has a pending agenda of both direct and indirect tax reform. Tax simplification is impossible, in both cases, without the elimination of exemptions. With both Central and State governments included, the tax/GDP ratio is around 18 per cent. Subsidies, both explicit and implicit, amount to 14 per cent of GDP. This can't be sustainable. In addition, total tax exemptions amount to more than 5 per cent of GDP. A lot has been written on the GST (goods and services tax), expected to come into force from 1 April 2017. This is only the beginning of a process to reform indirect taxes, which will take more than 10 years to complete. However, governments at all levels lack the administrative and governance capacity to make the necessary reforms.

India should therefore do three things. First, where there are no clear instances of market failure, governments (at all three levels) need to liberalise entry and allow markets to flourish. This doesn't imply an absence of regulation, but regulation should not be an excuse for excessive government control. This liberalisation can be interpreted as reducing the malign role of government. Some initiatives of the new Central government can be seen in this light, though some areas also fall under states' remit, so it will be necessary to devise means of incentivising states to act. This doesn't mean liberalisation for FDI (foreign direct investment) alone. Yes, FDI is important. But it is only a means to make efficiency gains and not an end in itself. There is much more to the broad canvas of reforming the Indian economy. Nor is liberalisation something to benefit the corporate manufacturing sector alone. Poverty reduction and employment generation are also a function of the form of growth, and, for both, reform of the rural economy is exceedingly important.

Second, the government should cut subsidies. Resources spent on subsidies can't be spent on public goods and services. India is often described as a young society, though this window of demographic transition won't remain open much beyond 2035. Among the young, and especially among villages that have become integrated into the mainstream and in urban and semi-urban India, there is recognition of the 'dole versus development' trade-off. Although one shouldn't oversimplify, and there are pockets where mindsets haven't changed, the preference for economic development over handouts was responsible for part of the electoral success of 2014.

Third, the government can also play a benign role, because in the interim some poor people, suitably identified, will still require subsidies.

India must also deal with five other issues. First, it cannot prosper until its eastern and north-eastern regions develop, and there is the related issue of India's economic integration with neighbouring countries and the need to build transport networks. Second, shortfalls in the workforce's skill base place a significant constraint not only on wages but also on entrepreneurship. Third, female work-participation rates, which are low for a host of reasons, need to increase. Fourth, development must occur without endangering the environment, and ensuring environmental protection is often a function of setting appropriate prices and decentralising public property rights. Fifth, corruption is a key issue, as noted at the beginning of this paper, and has several dimensions. Some types of corruption can be reduced by eliminating shortages, limiting the scope for discretion by officials, and using information technology to oversee interactions.

I have not mentioned the obvious indicators like growth or inflation, because higher growth and lower inflation will follow directly from some of the reforms mentioned here. Irrespective of whether one uses the new or old GDP calculation method, the growth record has improved. Irrespective of which indicator one uses, inflation rates have declined. Other indicators have improved too, but expectations are disproportionately high. Since the legacy of more than six decades is being questioned, the delivery won't happen in the space of a year alone—it will take more than 10.

This government has launched a plan to carry out individual identification of the poor without intermediate layers of administration, and to ensure their inclusion in the financial system by giving them access to bank accounts and transferring subsidies directly to these accounts. That is, even when subsidies are necessary, they can be given through government financing, rather than government performing a service provider role. These three strands form part of the new government's philosophy, sometimes explicitly stated, sometimes less so. The idea is that choice should drive efficiency. Why must healthcare be delivered through primary health centres that don't function well? Why can't the poor obtain subsidised and cashless medical treatment at an institution of their choice, including private hospitals?

However, one must remember that there are political and economic factors driving resistance and that change often takes place at state level. It is therefore going to be a long haul, not an overnight wave of the magic wand. But the silver lining is that much of young India wants what the government in New Delhi wants.

References

ADB (2009). *India 2039: An Affluent Society in One Generation.* ADB and Emerging Markets Forum.

Banerjee, Abhijit V. and Esther Duflo (2011). *Poor Economics: Rethinking Poverty and the Ways to End it.* Random House India.

Datta, K.L. (2014). *Poverty and Development Planning in India.* Concept Publishing.

Deutsche Bank (2005). *India Rising: A Medium-Term Perspective* (by Jennifer Asuncion-Mund). Deutsche Bank Research. May.

Ghani, Ejaz (2010). "The Poor Half Billion in South Asia: An Overview", in Ejaz Ghani (ed). *The Poor Half Billion in South Asia, What is Holding Back Lagging Regions?.* Oxford University Press.

HSBC (2011). The *World in 2050: Quantifying the Shift in the Global Economy.* HSBC Global Research. January.

Kuznets, Simon (1955). "Economic Growth and Income Inequality", *American Economic Review.*

McKinsey (2007). *The Bird of Gold: The Rise of India's Consumer Market.* McKinsey Global Institute. May.

Mehta, Aasha Kapur and Shashanka Bhide (2011). "Poverty: Estimates, Measurement and Profiles", in Aasha Kapur Mehta, Andrew Shepherd, Shashanka Bhide, Amita Shah and Anand Kumar (eds.), *India Chronic Poverty Report, Towards Solutions and New Compacts in a Dynamic Context.* Indian Institute of Public Administration.

Mehta, Pratap Bhanu (2010). "Introduction: Caste, Class and Consumption", in Rajesh Shukla, Sunil Jain and Preeti Kakkar (eds.), *Caste in a Different Mould, Understanding the Discrimination.* NCAER and Business Standard.

Ministry of Finance (1993). "Economic Reforms: Two Years After and the Task Ahead," *Discussion Paper.* Department of Economic Affairs, Government of India. July.

O'Neill, Jim, Dominic Wilson, Roopa Purushothaman and Anna Stupnytska (2005). How Solid are the BRICS?", *Global Economics Paper* No.134. Goldman Sachs. 1 December.

O'Neill, Jim (2007). *BRICs and Beyond.* Goldman Sachs. 23 November.

Panagariya, Arvind (2008). *India: The Emerging Giant.*Oxford University Press.

Pricewaterhouse Coopers (PwC) (2006). *The World in 2050: How Big will the Major Emerging Market Economies get and how can the OECD Compete?* (by John Hawsworth). March.

Tendulkar, Suresh (2010). "Inequality and Equity during Rapid Growth Process", in Shankar Acharya and Rakesh Mohan (eds.), *India's Economy, Performance and Challenges, Essays in Honour of Montek Singh Ahluwalia.* Oxford University Press.

Wilson, Dominic and Roopa Purushothaman (2003). "Dreaming with BRICs: The Path to 2050", *Global Economics Paper* No.99. Goldman Sachs. 1 October.

6

Markets, Growth and Social Opportunity

India since 1991

PULAPRE BALAKRISHNAN

India has by now seen a quarter century of what may be termed market reforms. In 1991, the government had embarked upon an economic reform programme that was largely propelled by an external payments crisis. The focus of the reform, then, was mainly the economy's trade and industrial policy regime. Though widely believed to have been dictated by multilateral agencies (read the International Monetary Fund and World Bank) to which India had to turn for BoP (balance of payments) support, it needs to be remembered that the government had been pursuing a mildly liberalising approach to the economic policy since the 1980s.[1] An impetus to liberalisation other than the immediate BoP crisis was the definitive collapse of the Soviet economic model. This had made it that much more difficult to justify any form of economic restriction.

The structural reforms commencing in 1991 in India may be approached in terms of their focus on the internal and external sectors of the economy. As far as the domestic economy was concerned, the most important change made in 1991 was that industrial licensing was rescinded and private entry permitted in almost all areas of the economy other than the railways, ports, defence, and atomic energy. In subsequent reforms, private investment has been permitted in all areas other than

1. For a discussion of the economics and politics of the regime change in 1991 see P. Balakrishnan (2010).

the last. Though clearly intended to increase competition and productivity—defined widely enough to include also the quality and variety of goods, and therefore believed to potentially benefit mainly the consumer—in the space of entrepreneurial activity, the move may be viewed as contributing to inclusion. After all, investment licensing, irrespective of its motivation, implies a winner-takes-all outcome. Though delicensing is among the rare instances when market liberalisation is per se inclusive, this feature must nevertheless be acknowledged. In academic parlance, it is a move towards a more competitive market structure.

As far as the external sector was concerned, the main changes of 1991 amounted to lowering substantially, if not entirely eliminating, the protection to the domestic industry. A significant across-the-board reduction of the import tariff was implemented. This was staggered over time, with the reduction itself continuing well into the decade, when finally the average rate stabilised at a level far below what it had been, though in some cases yet higher than that in the other non-Organisation for Economic Cooperation and Development (OECD) economies. More than two decades after the onset of the reforms, India is a far more open economy than it was in 1991 even though the rupee is not yet fully convertible on the capital account.

However, the extent of capital-account liberalisation must not be understated either. FDI (foreign direct investment) is encouraged. Portfolio capital flow alone is controlled, that too with an asymmetry, with restrictions placed on domestic investors while international financial institutions and non-resident Indians are permitted to move their capital freely across the border. In particular, quantitative restrictions on trade have disappeared, though this has come about via an international move towards a more open global trade regime under the dispensation of the World Trade Organization (WTO), rather than having been unilaterally administered by India as part of its policy of economic liberalisation. Viewed from the angle of the character of the policy regime, therefore,

India's economy is by now far more integrated with the rest of the world. However, economists remain divided on the question of whether openness is to be judged in terms of the restrictiveness of the trade regime or in terms of outcome indicators such as exports and imports as a share of GDP (gross domestic product). Keeping this in mind, we may point out that trade, that is, exports plus imports, as a share of output has increased very significantly in India since 1991.

Overall, combining the implication of industrial delicensing and the opening up of the economy to global trade flows, market liberalisation has proceeded quite far in India since 1991. As India is increasingly transforming into a major economic entity, at least in terms of its size, we would be interested to know the consequences of this development. The rest of this paper is concerned with two questions. First, it is sought to be known whether the reforms have yielded results in line with the stated objectives of the government. Second, it is investigated whether market liberalisation has spread opportunities evenly across the economy.

Faster Growth, Greater Efficiency

Two goals had motivated the economic reforms as launched in 1991: faster growth and greater efficiency.[2] The precise relationship imagined between the two was not adequately revealed. However, there was the claim that greater competition following market liberalisation would lead to faster productivity growth. Actually, even outside the government and within the wider ambit of the profession itself, for a concept so central to the discourse on economic policy, agreement on a measure of productivity is scarcely found.[3] For instance, what are we to make of productivity growth in the services sector where output is measured by factor payments? This is

---

2. The government's view on the rationale of the reforms may be gathered from the *Economic Survey* of July 1991 and February 1992.

3. For a discussion of the issues involved in the use of the much-used index 'total factor productivity', see Balakrishnan (2010).

particularly relevant for India today, an economy coming to be increasingly dominated by its services sector. For this reason, in this paper, we focus on economic growth, the measurement of which is relatively uncontroversial.

Over the two decades since 1991, the growth rate of the economy has definitely accelerated. For five years from 2003-04, India registered unprecedented high growth rates, though not quite attaining the double-digit bracket aspired to by the policymakers. This phase ended abruptly with the onset of the global financial crisis.[4] However, despite the slowing of growth in India from 2008 onwards, the country is today the fastest growing economy in the world, and this position appears unlikely to change very soon. But, it is the nature of growth in India that is interesting, especially from the point of view of its capacity for spreading opportunity and thus advancing social inclusion. While it is the manufacturing sector that the reforms had focused on, directly in terms of the restructuring of the trade and industrial policy, and indirectly via the financial sector reforms, it is services that have grown the fastest. After 2008, manufacturing has grown tardily. As for the agricultural sector, growth here has not only fluctuated, but in the case of foodgrains, the growth of production has not kept pace with the rate of growth of the population.

For the first time in about five decades, the per capita availability of foodgrains in the country has been declining.[5] While this is a cause for grave concern, there is reason to doubt that the slowing of agricultural growth is related solely to market liberalisation per se. According to an influential line of reasoning, in a two-sector economy, the protection of industry is tantamount to a bias against agriculture. Now, liberalising trade and industrial policy reforms are expected to shift the terms of trade, and

4. For information on the growth of the Indian economy in this period, see *Economic Survey 2009-10*, Government of India, New Delhi.

5. Evidence, based on reports of the Government of India, on the decline of the growth rate in the agricultural sector may be found in Dev (2008). For evidence on foodgrain availability since 1991, see Deaton and Dreze (2002).

thereby income, towards agriculture. This is believed to create the incentives for producers to expand output in this sector.[6]

We now move on to a qualitative assessment of the growth that has taken place in India since market liberalisation. First, though industrial growth has not till well after 1991 shown the marked acceleration that was expected of it, segments within manufacturing have experienced remarkable growth and transformation. Automobiles are a case in point. Here, not only is fast growth evident, but a growing sophistication suggests a potential for India to become a global manufacturing hub. A further development, though not confined to manufacturing, is that of India becoming a preferred international location for research and development, some of it for global manufacturing giants, but even more prominently for information technology firms from IBM to Microsoft. In manufacturing, India is also being seen as a site for both high-end design and reengineering of manufacturing processes.

Some of this is related to the development of cheap international communication networks, including the internet, which has made it possible to leverage the globally competitive skill base built up over the long haul in India, rather than market liberalisation per se. But, it is also true that some of the import liberalisation has helped and that there has been a shift in the understanding of the role of the government.[7] This role has since 1991 got reinterpreted to mean the enabling of business. That this may have taken the form of a relatively greater attention to foreign over domestic investment, and among domestic investors to large corporate houses

6. The view has been articulated in a public lecture by Manmohan Singh, when he was finance minster, see Singh (1995). For an empirical assessment of the relative role of structural factors and the changed policy regime in determining agricultural growth since 1991, which concludes that the former are likely to have been more important, see Balakrishnan et al. (2008).

7. See, Narayana Murthy (2004), though his argument is perhaps more pertinent for software.

over smaller enterprises, cannot be ignored, however. The increased presence of the prominent global firms in India is of course related to the liberalisation of FDI. To conclude this section, it may be said that the map of material production gives the impression of dynamic enclaves within manufacturing and a stagnant hinterland represented by slow-growing agriculture. This is significant from the point of view of inclusive growth as the largest number of India's workers is located in agriculture, even as the sector is shrinking relative to the rest of the economy.

But, what of the 'quality of life', and how may have market liberalisation contributed to its advance in India? This profoundly important issue was not explicitly on the agenda of the government when the reforms were launched in 1991. It would, however, be improper to assume that the government was indifferent to the question, only that it appears to have assumed that growth was what was needed to be focused on. However, the question itself is of essence, as we tend to be interested in economic growth only from the point of view of human well-being.

Nevertheless, in fairness to the policymakers, silence may be related to the understanding that 'the quality of life' must come into our reckoning only after the issue of employment is sorted out; a direct relationship between faster growth and a widespread growth of employment apparently having been assumed. Despite the ambiguity of its definition and the woeful paucity of statistics, we make some effort, here, to assess the contribution of market liberalisation to the quality of life in India.

'Quality of Life' and 'Public Goods'

Casual observation suggests that, in some spaces, the quality of life in India has improved. Thus, there has been a very substantial improvement in the range, quality and availability of manufactured goods produced in the country. This is undoubtedly related to the liberalisation of entry into the sector. Interestingly it appears to have been achieved without much foreign entry, either in the form of FDI or imports. We also see an improvement in the quality of services, notably of air travel and telephony. The mobile phone revolution has swept the country and transformed the opportunities for both business and interpersonal communication. Here, the wherewithal for the hardware had initially come from overseas and the liberalisation of FDI has had a major role to play.

A similar transformation is also to be seen in air travel with direct benefits in the form of reduced cost and greater choice. This owes to the liberalisation of entry into this sector. Interestingly, here, while all the private capital is domestic, some part of the professional services—both of pilots and managers—has on occasion been international. The entry of private players in airlines, telecommunications and banking has had a tangible impact on the quality of services offered to the Indian public. To a lesser extent, this has extended to an improvement in the quality of services rendered by the rival public utilities, which had hitherto been monopolies.

It appears then, that to an extent the assumed strategic role of privatisation, defined broadly to include entry, in India has been borne out. It may safely be assumed though that, except for telecommunications, this improvement in the quality of services is largely confined to the services consumed by the social strata extending from the middle classes and above. This can be inferred by imagining the cohort that uses banking services or relies on the airlines for transportation. Thus, the reforms have certainly ensured that the aspiration of a part of the Indian middle class to global standards in consumption of manufactured goods and access to quality services has, at least to a degree, been satisfied. When flagging this, though, it is important to recognise that even as the numbers may be sizeable, the proportion involved is not so large.

While on the topic of the quality of life, that constitutive of a good life are goods and services beyond banking and the airlines would be agreed on readily. Examples of these range from the courts of law to urban governance and physical infrastructure, from roads to sewerage. Economists refer to these broadly as 'public goods.' They are public in the sense that, given their characteristics of non-rivalrousness and non-excludability in consumption, they have to be publicly provided. There is little evidence of either the quality or quantity of public goods having increased substantially in India since 1991. On the other hand, we have reason to believe that faster growth may have stretched the limits of the meagre infrastructure in existence. Even the most basic awareness of economic theory would remind us that the fixity of public goods in India, despite a more liberal economic regime and indeed faster economic growth, is not a matter of surprise. After all, the goods are referred to as 'public', harbouring the presumption that the market on its own is unlikely to deliver them optimally. We may safely assume, therefore, that their emergence in India in sufficient quantities would require specific interventions beyond the market liberalisation implemented in this country since 1991.

Given the concerns of this note, however, public goods assume an importance that goes beyond their contribution to the quality of life of those already in employment. If the problem of ensuring inclusive growth is to draw much larger numbers into employment, then public goods would be central to inclusive growth. There are instances when agricultural produce rots due to the absence of a road network, or absent irrigation lowers the productive capacity of land. The role of public goods in the sphere of production, as opposed to consumption, has tended to be underestimated in the discourse on growth and development in India.

The first round of reforms in India had, to some extent rightly, focused on incentives for investment or expansion of output, but the time may have come for economic policy to focus aggressively on the factors that enable the production process itself. Where such enabling factors are absent, a favourable incentive structure represented by prices faced by the producer would make little difference. Examples in India range from the water-starved peasantry of Marathwada to the power-short small entrepreneur in

Karnataka.[8] By comparison, with statistics on income, and therefore on poverty, we have no summary statistics on the availability and distribution of public goods and services in India. We must perforce rely on piecemeal reports in the media, and these are not reassuring. The flooding of Chennai in November 2015 is a case in point. Some years prior to this event, the entire electricity grid of northern India melted down temporarily.

Surprises, Pleasant and Unpleasant

While faster growth of the economy has been in accordance with the predictions of the managers of the reform process in India, there have also been some surprises. First, the greater integration of India's economy with the rest of the world has been far smoother than anticipated. Though the BoP in 2009-10 have recorded the largest deficit in six decades, private capital flows have been abundant and the country has been able to finance its payments far more smoothly than was claimed to be ever possible by critics of external liberalisation. Capital inflow poses its own problems for macroeconomic management, but it also reflects a confidence of the rest of the world in the recipient's economy. The fact that India has withstood exposure to both the goods and the capital markets of the world economy speaks of both the inherent resilience of its economy and the quality of its macroeconomic management. In particular, the 25 years since 1991 has been the longest period India has witnessed without experiencing a foreign exchange crisis. Earlier, there had been an acute shortage once in every decade.

The improvement in India's BoP has pleasantly surprised some observers (Chisti 2010). But, there have been unpleasant surprises too. Most unexpected has been the performance of the agricultural sector, where, when growth has not been lacklustre, it has been volatile as it

8. Though water and electricity are not strictly speaking public goods, relieving the environmental constraint and enhancing infrastructure almost inevitably requires an element of what economists refer to as 'collective action', as purely market solutions have limited potential.

has been since 2008. Altogether since 1991, agricultural growth has on average barely kept up with the rate of growth of the population. For an economy with low levels of food consumption per capita by global standards, this is disappointing at a time of high growth of the economy. In fact, a high overall growth rate has masked the failure on the agricultural front.

Evaluations of India's economic performance since market liberalisation have tended to overlook that, over the historian's longue durée, the richest countries of the world are those that have succeeded in making food plentiful and cheap for their populations.[9] An indicator of this is the low share of food in average household expenditure in rich economies. In a cross-country comparison, we would find a strong inverse correlation between the level of GDP per capita and the share of food in household expenditure.[10] At least, from the time of David Ricardo, economists have had an understanding of what underlies this relationship. It represents the mechanism whereby cheaper food releases demand for other goods and services, implying that, at least for poor economies, continuous improvement in agricultural productivity can be an engine of growth at least for a while. In fact, in the absence of international competitiveness in manufacturing, agricultural productivity is the one that holds the most promise.

Contrary to the historical experience of the rich economies of the world, in India not only has the real price of food not declined since 1991, it has actually increased since 2009. Food price inflation has been very high during phases in the last decade and though it has abated more recently, it leads among other factors in contributing to a rising general price level. Persistent food-price inflation is unexpected for a country being hailed by some as a rising economic power.

---

9. See Johnson (2000) for a global history extending over half a millennium.

10. Evident from the United Nation's cross-country data presented at *http://www.data.un.org.*

Of course, higher food prices could well have been more than compensated by rising incomes. Whether this has actually been the case is best answered by looking at the trend in poverty. For this, I draw upon the investigation by Deaton and Drèze (2002). It helps the cause of our enquiry in that the authors take a slightly wider view of what constitutes poverty by focusing on development indicators such as health and education in addition to the standard emphasis on consumption expenditure. Their estimates show that "poverty decline in the 1990s proceeded more or less in line with earlier trends." On development, they conclude that:

> Most indicators have continued to improve in the nineties, but social progress has followed very diverse patterns, ranging from accelerated progress in some fields to slowdown and even regression in others. We find no support for sweeping claims that the nineties have been a period of 'unprecedented improvement' or 'widespread impoverishment' (Deaton and Drèze 2002: 3729).

Alas, there is no comparable study of the progress of living standards in the subsequent decade. Though focusing on the early post-reform phase, the Deaton and Drèze study is particularly relevant to the argument in this paper that accelerated growth per se is unlikely to deliver greater equality. Quite simply, the condition of the poor may not be worsening but the better-off may yet be doing better, thus contributing to widening inequality. We have reason to believe that this characterises India since 1991.

Finally, the government's budgetary policy holds clues as to the section of the population that is gaining from overall economic policy in the era of market reforms. While in the absence of specific empirical investigation, such commentary can only be tentative, it may be observed that much of the Central government's budgetary allocations since 1991 may have disproportionately favoured the middle classes. Note the reduction in the tax rate, the expansion of higher education—especially the new Indian Institutes of Technology and Indian Institutes of

Management—and even the farm-loan waivers. As if to compensate, as it were, governments have targeted the poor via the Mahatma Gandhi National Rural Employment Guarantee Act (MGNREGA).

Economic Reforms and Social Opportunity

Social opportunity refers to the idea that the opportunities available to an individual are circumscribed by her location in the socioeconomic grid. From this vantage point, it would be of interest to know whether the outcome of the reforms is consistent with the spread of opportunity more or less equally across the Indian population.[11] One approach to this question would be to see how the increase in income has been distributed across the various sectors of the economy.

We find that, since 1991, measured in terms of the rate of growth of output, the agricultural sector has performed far less well than the other two sectors, namely, industry and services. However, the greater part of the workforce, that is, over 50 per cent, is concentrated in the agricultural sector. So, agricultural income per worker has grown more slowly than per capita income in the other sectors. Under present trends, a significant section of agricultural workers would have to move to non-agricultural sectors if they are to have an equal opportunity to earn the incomes rising faster in the latter.

This, however, is not a matter of will. Two conditions are entailed here. First, with the exception of manual labour deployed in construction, participating in the non-agricultural sector requires a higher level of education and a certain degree of skilling for the worker contemplating such a move. This is especially true of manufacturing activity, where in a globalised world, firms compete on the basis of labour productivity as the other variable inputs are tradable, implying that firms have equal access to them.

11. Evidence of the concern on the part of India's political class that social justice can no longer be ignored as a criterion by which public policy is to be judged may be seen in the importance given to inclusive growth in the agenda of the United Progressive Alliance-2 and in the proclamation "*sabka saath, sabka vikas*" of the National Democratic Alliance-2.

Immigration controls ensure that labour is national. Now, firms compete on labour cost, which is determined by productivity. The skilling needed for the labour movement envisaged is not acquired costlessly. Either the firms would have to pay for the training of workers or the workers equip themselves with the skill. Historically, by European standards for instance, firms in India have been quite reluctant to train workers. I do not speak of the quality of the training, but the mere willingness to offer it at all. On the other hand, much of the rural landless labour, which is the relevant cohort here, is pretty much destitute and incapable of training itself. It is obvious that under the circumstances, the state would have to step in.

The second factor to reckon with is that the increased non-agricultural production of the migrating labour has to find a market. I digress to place this proposition in perspective. The central insight of the Keynesian Revolution in economic theory, now eclipsed by the reinstallation of Classical economics in the anglophone world, and thus by reflexity in India, was that the demand of labour is a derived one, that is, there is demand for labour only if there is a demand for goods. This implication of the market economy is overlooked by both enthusiasts for the free market economy and their opponents. So, the transfer of workers to the non-agricultural sector cannot merely be wished for. It would have to be dovetailed with developments elsewhere in the economy, to enable which coordination by the state may well be necessary.

In the first instance, the market for expanded non-agricultural production would have to be provided by the growth of agriculture. For, while in principle the demand could come from the rest of the world, a slowing world economy today suggests that external demand cannot be relied upon to enable the desired transition. Does this make me an 'export pessimist', among economists—a taint perhaps more shaming than 'non-nationalist' is in Indian politics today? I believe that it does not! My observation has been made in the light of the fact that in mid-2016, exports from India were still recovering from 17 consecutive months of decline, reflecting the global slowing down. Nevertheless, it is important to not be bound by the present as a guide to action, and everything ought to be done to develop the international competitiveness of Indian enterprises. But, this brings us back to what I have already highlighted as a constraint to achieving it, namely, the skill level of our workforce.

To sum up, I have said that while there are two sources of demand for an economy's goods, namely, the domestic and the external, in the immediate present we would have to rely on the former, and sustained steady agricultural growth is a necessary part of such a strategy. But, if agriculture is to serve as an engine of growth at least for a while, it would have to expand without an increase in the price, for a rise in agricultural prices will stymie the growth of demand for manufactures envisaged in such a strategy. Agricultural expansion without a rise in prices would yet be profitable if there is a concomitant growth of yield. Before I come to the question of what can be done to raise agricultural productivity, I would mention an important reason, beyond the pursuit of equal opportunity, as to why we must reduce overcrowding in agriculture. Indian agriculture is witnessing a progressive decline in the average farm size due to fragmentation. If this were to continue, household income from farming will shrink even if the yield is constant. We would be advised to treat this as an important instance of how our prospects are constrained by natural resources, a possibility yet again scarcely imagined at both ends of the political spectrum.

Increasing agricultural productivity would require at least three interventions by the government. First, an effective physical infrastructure will have to be provided. This can come only from the government. Here, I wish to briefly clarify what I mean by 'effective.' It refers to the actual availability of the input. It has been pointed out that official statistics in India may not reflect the true position with respect to availability. Scepticism has ranged from the data on irrigation statistics to the food stocks of the Government of India.

Second, a far greater agronomic input is required from India's extensive archipelago of agricultural research institutions. Recall that these had been in the forefront of the green revolution in the 1960s and nothing but a governance deficit explains their current dormancy. The reference to the green revolution should also remind us that the last major agricultural thrust in India was made 50 years ago. Finally, education matters not only to manufacturing. Increasing agricultural productivity requires a more educated farmer as farming will have to be increasingly undertaken under conditions of natural resource adversity due to climate change, and economic uncertainty due to the integration of markets.

Conclusions

So, how are we to assess the economic reforms on their 25th anniversary? First, it must be acknowledged that India's BoP constraint has been eased. A payments crisis had triggered the reforms of 1991, and to have strengthened India's external position is a substantial achievement. Next, growth and poverty have continued to accelerate and decline respectively. In this way, the reforms have maintained a trend while providing macroeconomic stability. But, 25 years since, India continues to have an unacceptable level of poverty even as it is measured according to a low international standard. The progress made on this front is disappointing given the claim that the reforms mark a sea change in India. Finally, the spread of opportunity has been uneven going by the fact that the sector containing the largest number of workers has been the one growing the slowest. I have emphasised the importance of far greater dynamism in the agricultural sector if we are to move towards an equalisation of opportunities across the economy. Needless to mention, this would also take the economy closer to the dreamt-of double-digit growth. The importance of agriculture for both poverty reduction and growth is evident to us from both the history of East Asia (Hayami and Godo 2005) and the experience of India's economy during the phase of high growth during 2003-2008.

What can we expect with respect to the spread of opportunity from the economic reforms as practised in more or less similar fashion by the two coalitions that have governed India over the past two decades? Not much, if the present situation is any guide. The analysis in this paper shows us why this must be so. First, there is perhaps excessive focus on the interface of India with the rest of the world, when outward orientation is not going to provide the solution to the most pressing of India's problems today. Historically, countries have solved their problems of agricultural supply shortfall and large-scale physical infrastructure provision on their own. China is perhaps the best example. Second, there is excessive focus on higher education compared to schooling. Finally, the approach to the macroeconomic policy is dogmatic, emphasising fiscal consolidation over capital formation, making it difficult for the state to make a difference via the provision of infrastructure on a significant scale.

Actually, 'Make in India', a flagship programme of the present government, reflects a failure of the reforms to make a serious dent in the very area in which it focused the most, that is, manufacturing. The failure has also to do with the failure to recognise the importance of demand. Much of the focus, it appears, is on the 'ease of doing business.' While this is hardly irrelevant as a consideration, the dramatic decline in manufacturing growth after close to double-digit growth over 2003-2008 suggests that the supply side is unlikely to be the issue.

The wait for a just economy in India could turn out to be long, but we can start by critically engaging with the economic policy encapsulated in the reforms being pursued by both the political formations at the level of the Central government. I hope that this paper has been able to show exactly what needs to be done.

References

Balakrishnan, P. (2010). *Economic Growth in India: History and Prospect*. Delhi: Oxford University Press.

Balakrishnan, P., R. Golait and P. Kumar (2008). "Agricultural Growth in India since 1991", *Development Research Group Study* No 27. Mumbai: Department of Economic Analysis and Policy, Reserve Bank of India.

Chisti, S. (2010). "A Reversal of Fortune: India Lends to the IMF", *Indian Express*, 7 June, viewed on 26 October 2016, *http://archive.indianexpress.comnews/a-reversal-of-fortune-india-lends-to-im-f/630443/*

Deaton, A. and J. Drèze (2002). "Poverty and Inequality in India: A Re-Examination", *Economic & Political Weekly* 37(36): 3729-48.

Dev, S.M. (2008). "Challenges for Revival of Indian Agriculture", First Dayanatha Jha Memorial Lecture (*mimeo*). New Delhi: National Centre for Agricultural Economics and Policy Research.

Hayami, Y. and Y. Godo (2005). *Development Economics: From the Poverty to the Wealth of Nations*. Third Edition. New York: Oxford University Press.

Johnson, D.G. (2000). "Population, Food and Knowledge", *American Economic Review* 90(1): 1-14.

Narayana Murthy, N.R. (2004). "The Impact of Economic Reforms on Industry in India: A Case Study of the Software Industry" in, K. Basu (ed.), *India's Emerging Economy: Performance and Prospects in the 1990s and Beyond* Cambridge, MA: MIT Press. pp.217-22.

Singh, M. (1995). "Inaugural Address", delivered at the *54th Annual Conference of the Indian Society of Agricultural Economics* held at Shivaji University, Kolhapur, Maharashtra, 26 November 1994 [Published in *Indian Journal of Agricultural Economics* 50(1)].

This article originated in a paper written for the Indian Council for Research on International Economic Relations. I am grateful to Rajiv Kumar, its then director, for the invitation to write it and for arranging for four anonymous reviews of the same. Subsequently, it was presented as the first of three lectures on India's economy delivered at the Indian Institute of Advanced Study, Shimla in June 2016 at the invitation of its director, Chetan Singh. Any errors would be my responsibility.

Economic & Political Weekly LII (2), 14 January 2017.

7

The Problem of Inequality

S. MAHENDRA DEV

Introduction

Inequality has been an important issue in development debates. Development can not be discussed without talking about inequality. Theories of income distribution have been in the literature of economics from before Adam Smith to the present day. Ricardo characterises income distribution as the principal problem of economics (Sandmo 2015). Several philosophers and economists have discussed about inequality.[1] In recent years, rising income inequality has attracted the attention of International Monetary Fund (IMF), World Bank, Organisation for Economic Co-operation & Development (OECD) and Davos meetings. Arab Spring and Brexit also brought this issue to the limelight. The number of billionaires is increasing throughout the world with larger share in income and wealth. With the release of the book by French economist Thomas Piketty (2014), there has been more debate on inequality in several parts of the world. European economists have written more about

1. On justice and ethical questions, moral philosophers discussed more as compared to economists although latter also had their foot on this issue. In recent years see, see Rawls (1971) on justice. Economists from classical school (Adam Smith, Karl Marx, J.S. Mill), neoclassical marginalist approach, non-marginalist approach, utilitarians have all discussed about income distribution. See Atkinson and Bourguignon (2015) for a collection of articles on inequality. Kuznets (1957) used statistical approaches for looking at long-term trends in inequality. Also see, Sen (1973).

inequality than American economists although inequality is rising in the US.[2]

First time at global level, a goal on inequality is included in Sustainable Development Goals (SDGs). Goal 10 of SDGs is about reduction in inequality within and among countries. Target 1 of Goal 10 says "By 2030, progressively achieve and sustain income growth of the bottom 40 per cent of the population at a rate higher than the national average." Target 2 tries to achieve much more ambitious one: "By 2030, empower and promote the social, economic and political inclusion of all, irrespective of age, sex, disability, race, ethnicity, origin, religion or economic or other status".

There are two main arguments for reduction in inequality. One is ethical or philosophical argument that equity is important for its own sake (intrinsic value). Second one is reduction in inequality is required for sustainability of growth (instrumental value). The related one is that even if one is concerned only with poverty, inequality can't be ignored as rise in inequality would adversely affect poverty reduction.[3]

It is argued that some degree of inequality may not be a problem if it provides incentives for people to accumulate human capital. Tendulkar (2010) draws a distinction between inequity and inequality. He examines the path breaking work of Simon Kuznets who indicates that inequalities rise with economic growth up to a point and then decline. This is the so called Kuznets inverted 'U' shape curve. Tendulkar says that even if measured inequality increases, there may not be increasing feeling of inequity, as people observe high mobility and can aspire to

2. Apart from Piketty, other Euopean economists like Emmanual Saez (French), Gabriel Zucman (French), Anthony Atkinson (British), Nicholas Bloom (British), Thomas Phillipon (French), Branco Milanovic (Serbian-American) have written on inequality. One reason why American economists are not preoccupied with wealth inequality could be the deep influence of Chicago School. More on this see *http://www.theatlantic.com/business/archive/2016/09/why-so-few-american-economists-are-studying-inequality/499253*

3. See Basu (2006) on globalisation, poverty and inequality.

move upwards like others. In this context, he also reviews the work of economists like Tibor Scitovsky and Albert O. Hirschman who have also discussed the general issue of inequality not leading to inequity. According to Tendulkar, social consensus with respect to social acceptability of a degree of inequality is feasible on the existence of three conditions: (a) the observation of merit based income mobility; (b) the existence of equality of opportunity; (c) improvement in the living conditions of people at the lower end of distribution. He also says that we do need to be mindful about perceived fairness, equality of opportunity, the provision of basic needs, and poverty alleviation.

However, rising inequality can have social costs and lead to reduction in economic growth apart from the normative dimension to equality. It is also useful to distinguish between inequality of outcome and inequality of opportunity. Assets, income or expenditure are generally used for outcomes. Inequality of opportunity is often measured by studying non-income dimensions such as health, education, access to basic services and human development. Individual circumstances are important for examining inequalities in opportunities. The circumstances such as gender, race, ethnicity, or place of birth are outside the control of an individual. However, the outcomes also depend on the efforts the individual makes in education and labour market, given the circumstances (Kanbur et al. 2014).

Economic inequalities co-exist and intersect with many other forms of equally striking social, political and cultural inequalities. Therefore, intersectional inequalities become important (UNDP 2015). In the case of India, caste has a peculiar role that separates it out from the rest of the world (Dreze and Sen 2013). Therefore, inequalities among caste or social groups become important. Similarly, gender inequalities are also high in India.

Against this background, in this paper, we will address two questions:

(a) What are the dimensions and trends in inequality at global level and India?

(b) How do we tackle rising inequalities at policy level?

The focus of the paper will be on economic, social and gender inequalities in India with some discussion at global level.

Dimensions of Inequality at Global Level

Dabla-Norris et al. (2015) study from IMF examines trends in inequality of income and opportunities at global level. The main conclusions of the study on levels and trends are the following: (a) Global inequality is high and ranges from 0.55 to 0.70 depending on the measure used; (b) Inequalities have widened within countries. They have increased substantially in most of the advanced countries. Although inequality remained stable for the group of EMDCs (emerging market developing countries), there are large disparities in levels and trends across countries. Inequality increased in Asia and Eastern Europe while it declined in Latin America although levels are higher in the latter set of countries; (c) In advanced countries, inequality is primarily driven by the growing income share of the top 10 per cent which has income close to nine times to that of the bottom 10 per cent. However, in the case of EMDCs, the rise in inequality is primarily due to shift in incomes from middle class to upper class (e.g. China and South Africa). Gini coefficient in wealth is almost double to that of income in many countries; (d) Inequality in health outcome and access to healthcare is high in developing countries. On the other hand, one notices declining inequality in education in EMDCs. Disparities in access to financial services between advanced countries and EMDCs are high.

A recent World Bank study (2016) examines latest trends in inequalities in income/consumption across the world. Some of the conclusions of the study are the following: (a) Global inequality in per capita income steadily increased from the year 1820 to the 1990s.[4]

4. Here World Bank uses GDP per capita in combination with distributional statistics from household surveys.

Table 7.1

Countries with an Increasing and Decreasing Gini Index and the Average Gini

	Long-run Trend (1993-2008)					
	No. of Countries				*Mean Gini*	
	Increase	*Less Change*	*Decline*	*Total*	*1993*	*2008*
East Asia and Pacific	5	1	3	9	37.8	39.1
Eastern Europe and Central Asia	5	2	6	13	33.9	32.5
Latin America and the Caribbean	8	0	11	19	49.0	47.0
Middle East and North Africa	1	1	3	5	39.8	36.4
South Asia	3	0	1	4	31.0	34.5
Sub-Saharan Africa	8	2	10	20	47.6	45.1
Industrialised Countries	12	4	5	21	31.4	32.6
World	42	10	39	91	40.1	39.3
	Short-run Trend (2008-2013)					
	No. of Countries				*Mean Gini*	
	Increase	*Less Change*	*Decline*	*Total*	*1993*	*2008*
East Asia and Pacific	1	1	5	7	39.2	37.3
Eastern Europe and Central Asia	6	8	9	23	31.9	31.4
Latin America and the Caribbean	3	2	12	17	49.7	48.0
Middle East and North Africa	0	1	1	2	35.3	33.4
South Asia	0	1	2	3	36.7	36.2
Sub-Saharan Africa	3	2	4	9	44.1	43.8
Industrialised Countries	6	6	8	20	32.0	31.8
World	19	21	41	81	37.9	37.1

Source: World Bank (2016).

However, Gini index in recent years fell from 66.8 in 2008 to 62.5 in 2013. This decline in global inequality was due to convergence in average incomes due to rising incomes in populous countries such as China and India. This led to reduction in between country inequality. But within country inequality rose over time; (b) Income/consumption surveys based data shows that inequality increased in 42 countries while it declined in 39 countries for the long period 1993-2008 (Table 7.1). The populous countries where inequality rose include Bangladesh (5 points), China (7 points) and Indonesia (5 points). In the more recent short period (2008-2013), inequality declined in 41 countries while it increased in 19 countries (Table 7.1); (c) The report offers some lessons on the decline in inequality in Brazil (5.5 points), Cambodia (11 points), Mali (6.9 points), Peru (7.1) and Tanzania (2.7 points) in the recent period (2008-2013).

Inequality and Growth: Kuznets Inverted U Shape, U Shape and Kuznets Waves

The story of inequality and growth can be started from Kuznets inverted U shape which shows that inequality increases initially and later falls with economic growth. Piketty's (2014) work on the United States (US) and Europe is well known. The main merit of his book is the massive collection of historical data for several countries. In the 18th and 19th centuries, western European society was highly unequal. But inequality declined and stabilised during 1910-1970. Again income inequality has been rising since then. In contrast to Kuznets inverted U shape curve, Picketty's data indicated U shaped curve. From this history, Piketty develops a grand theory of capital and inequality.

Figure 7.1

Relationship between Income Inequality and Mean Income (The Kuznets Relationship) for the US: 1774-2013

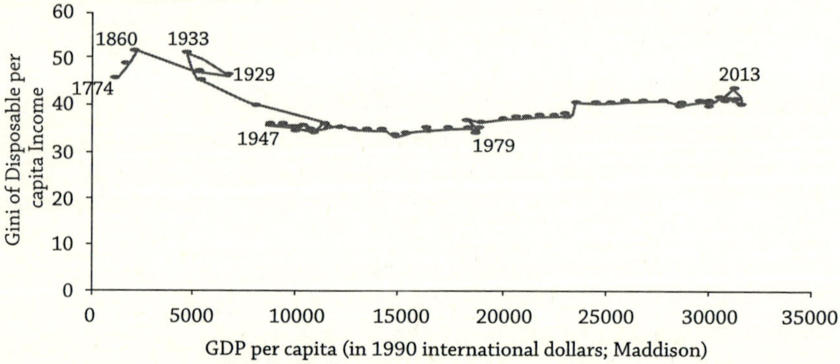

Source: Milanovic (2016).

In a recent book, Milanovic (2016) develops the concept of Kuznets wave or cycle to explain changes in inequality over long period. According to him, Kuznets' approach cannot explain the rising inequality that occurred after 1980. On the other hand, Piketty's theory does not explain if we extend the data further back, into the 18th and 19th centuries.

Milanovic explains Kuznets wave for the US in the following way. Inequality in the US rose between Independence (1774) and the Civil War (1860) and then continued to rise until the early 20th century when it reached peak at slightly over 50 Gini points at an income level of $5,000 per capita (in 1990 prices) (Figure 7.1). After the great depression, it declined steadily until the end of World War II. Inequality remained at a historically low of about 35 Gini points until the trough in 1979. After that it increased steadily, reaching over 40 Gini points by the second decade of 21st century. Kuznet's hypothesis of inverted 'U' shape is consistent up to 1979 but does not explain the rise in inequality in the last 40 years. The concept of Kuznets wave explains the upsurge of inequality since 1980 (Milanovic 2016). The rise in inequality was driven by the second technological revolution.

Inequalities in Asian Countries

Some studies have examined income inequalities in Asian countries. As part of Asian Development Bank (ADB) study, Zhuang et al. (2014) looked at recent trends in inequalities in Asia. According to this study, if we consider Asia as a single unit, its Gini coefficient rose fom 39 in the mid-1990s to 46 in the late 2000s. Gini coefficient increased in 12 of the 30 countries with comparable data. The ratio of top 20 per cent to bottom 20 per cent also increased in these countries. The 12 countries cover 82 per cent of the Asia-Pacific region. Inequality increased for three large countries like China, India, Indonesia. A recent IMF study (Jain-Chandra et al. 2016) also confirms increasing inequalities in Asia. According to this study, on a population-weighted basis, the net Gini coefficient in Asia rose from 37 in 1990 to 48 in 2014, reflecting the sharp rise in inequality in the most populous countries. Of the 22 Asian economies considered in the study,

Gini rose in 15 countries from 1990 to 2013. In China, Gini rose from 33 in 1990 to 53 in 2013. In the ASEAN region, the trends in inequality showed divergent trends with inequalities increasing in Indonesia and declining in Malaysia, Philippines and Thailand. Regarding inequality of opportunity, there is a large gap in access to education and health between the wealthiest quintile of income distribution as compared to the poorest quintile (see Son 2014).

What are the Drivers of Inequality?

Studies at global level show that technological progress, rise in skill premium and the decline of some labour market institutions were responsible for inequality in both advanced economies and EMDCs. Skill premium is associated with rising inequalities in advanced countries while financial deepening has contributed to inequality in EMDCs (Dabla-Norris et al. 2015). The study of Jain-Chandra (2016) shows that financial deepening has been equalising in Asia while surprisingly higher social sector spending, education spending, and capital expenditure are associated with higher inequality in Asia. This is because of weak coverage and disproportionate benefits to non-poor. However, in line with the rest of the world, greater progressive taxation reduces income inequality in Asia.

Dimensions and Trends in Inequality in India

Consumption Inequality

In India, consumer expenditure from National Sample Survey (NSS) is generally used to estimate inequality. Many studies have shown that inequality in consumption increased in the post-reform period.[5] Most of the studies show that inequality increased marginally in rural areas[6] while it rose significantly for urban areas. The numbers in Table 7.2 from Himanshu (2015) show that inequality

5. For example, see Subramanian and Jayaraj (2016), Radhakrishna (2015), Himanshu (2015), Sripad and Vakulabharanam (2013), Dev and Ravi (2008) Sen and Himanshu (2004).
6. May not be statistically significant.

in rural areas increased from 0.26 in 1993-94 to 0.28 in 2004-05 and rose marginally in subsequent years. On the other hand, inequality in urban areas rose from 0.32 in 1993-94 to 0.38 in 2011-12. This study also showed an increase in the consumption shares of top 10 per cent and top 20 per cent along with a corresponding fall in the shares of bottom 20 per cent and bottom 40 per cent. Similarly disparities between urban and rural also increased over time.

Table 7.2

Inequality in India: Gini of Consumption Expenditure

	1983	*1993-94*	*2004-05*	*2009-10*	*2011-12*
Rural	0.271	0.258	0.281	0.284	0.287
Urban	0.314	0.319	0.364	0.381	0.377
All India	0.295	0.300	0.347	0.358	0.359

Note: All estimates are based on MRP (mixed recall period) estimates of consumption expenditure.

Source: Himanshu (2015).

Table 7.3

Annual Growth Rates of Atkinson Inequality

Period	*e =*					
	0.5	*1.5*	*2.0*	*2.5*	*3.0*	*3.5*
Rural						
1983-97 (URP)	-0.17	-0.19	0.39	-0.44	-0.50	-0.51
1993/94-2009/10 (MRP)	1.39***	1.09***	0.95***	0.83***	0.74***	0.65***
Urban						
1983-97 (URP)	1.07*	0.84**	0.75**	0.67**	0.60**	0.55**
1993/94-2009/10 (MRP)	2.17***	1.86***	1.71***	1.58***	1.47***	1.57***

Note: e is the inequality aversion parameter; URP= Uniform Reference Period.

*** significant at 1% level; **significant at 5% level; *significant at 10% level.

Source: Radhakrishna (2015).

Using Atkinson Inequality Index, Radhakrishna (2015) showed positive trend growth in inequalities in rural areas in the post-reform period while pre-reform period did not show any trend. Inequality in urban areas registered a significant positive trend in both the periods and the growth rate was higher in the post-reform period (Table

7.3). The trend growth increases with increase in the value of the inequality aversion parameters in second period in rural areas and both periods in urban areas indicating worsening of inequality. This study also shows worsening of rural-urban disparities over time.

Subramanian and Jayaraj (2016) examine the trends in the shares of bottom quintile population during the period 1983 to 2011-12. The study indicates that on average, the share of bottom quintile in the mean per capita expenditure was around 46 per cent in rural areas and 38 per cent in urban areas. It did not show significant changes in rural areas while it declined from 40 per cent in 1993-1994 to 35 per cent in 2011-12 in urban areas. The bottom quintile expenditure has grown at a compound annual rate of 2.10 per cent per annum in rural and 1.96 per cent per annum in urban over the period 1983 to 2011-12. They say that we should target to have 3 per cent per annum growth in consumption of bottom quintile.

No Trend in Inequality in Consumption Over Long-term

Gini coefficients since 1951 (Figure 7.2) shows that consumption GINI has been stable with few fluctuations. It showed only small increase in the early 1990s.

Figure 7.2

Gini Coefficient in Consumption: All India

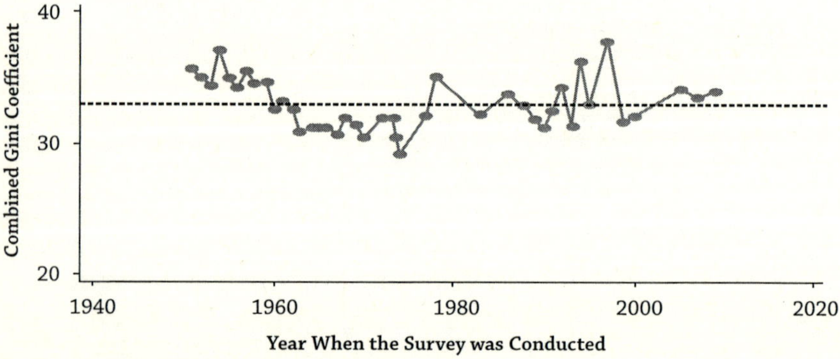

Source: Milanovic 2016.

The Gini in consumption which ranged between mid- and higher-30s, made India's inequality look about the same as in developed countries (Milanovic 2016).[7] It is known that NSS data underestimates the consumption of the rich. This could be one reason for the relatively lower estimates of consumption inequalities in India.

Income Inequality is Higher than Consumption Inequality

The inequality estimates based on consumption are lower than income based inequalities. There are estimates based on income using India Human Development Survey (IHDS). Dubey (2016) shows that Gini coefficient for income is around 0.55 in India as compared to that of consumption at 0.37 (Table 7.4). In other words, income inequality is much higher than expenditure based inequality in India. The income Gini is about 17 to 18 points (nearly 50%) higher than consumption Gini.[8]

Table 7.4

Gini Coefficient for Income and Consumption: All India

	*Income Based (Gini)***		*Consumption Based (Gini)**	
	2004-05	*2011-12*	*2004-05*	*2011-12*
All India	0.52	0.55***	0.35	0.37

Note: * NSS based; ** India Human Development Survey (IHDS); *** IHDS, provisional

Source: Dubey (2016).

Milanovic (2016) says that if we compare India income Gini with other countries that use income surveys, India's Gini is higher than Brazil but lower than only South Africa (Figure 7.3). Even China's inequality is lower than that of India.

7. Using data for 7 years for the period 2001-02 to 2009-10, Srinivasan (2013) showed that there was no trend in Gini coefficients as shown by the confidence intervals.

8. India has made tax data public recently by releasing it for the year 2011-12 (assessment year 2012-13). One can estimate inequality in income from tax data also. Only around 3 per cent of the population filed the returns. Thus, it is very small sample to look at overall income inequalities.

Figure 7.3

Income Inequality in India Compared to Other Countries

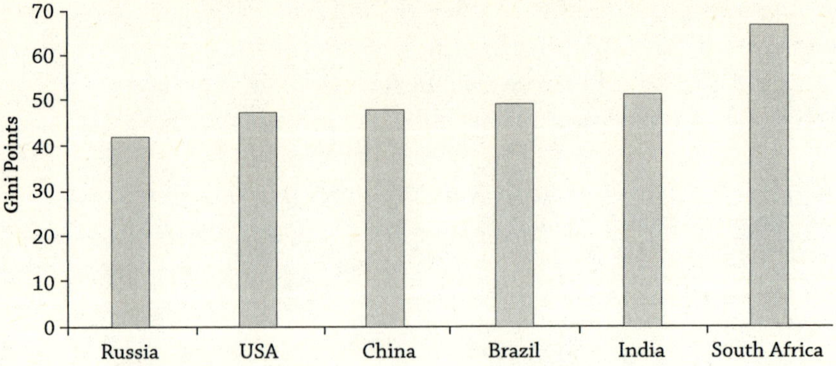

Source: Milanovic (2016).

Inequality in Income of Agricultural Households

One can estimate income inequality for agricultural households based on Situation Assessment Survey of NSS. At the all India level, the income Gini at 0.58 was much higher than consumption Gini at 0.28—around 30 points higher. The estimates at state level also show similar results. The income Gini at state level varies from 0.43 in Chhattisgarh and Gujarat to 0.61 in Bihar. The difference between consumption Gini and income Gini for Bihar is

Table 7.5

Estimates of Inequality (Gini) in Per Capita Income and MPCE for Agricultural Households

States	*Gini Per Capita Income: 2013*	*Gini MPCE 2011-12*	*States*	*Gini Per Capita Income: 2013*	*Gini MPCE 2011-12*
Andhra Pradesh	0.60	0.27	Madhya Pradesh	0.49	0.25
Assam	0.52	0.23	Maharashtra	0.57	0.21
Bihar	0.61	0.22	Odisha	0.53	0.24
Chhattisgarh	0.43	0.22	Punjab	0.53	0.29
Gujarat	0.43	0.23	Rajasthan	0.50	0.27
Haryana	0.51	0.25	Tamil Nadu	0.59	0.28
Jharkhand	0.53	0.28	Uttar Pradesh	0.58	0.28
Karnataka	0.58	0.23	West Bengal	0.53	0.28
Kerala	0.59	0.31	All India	0.58	0.28

Source: Chakravorty *et al.* (2016).

nearly 40 points. The income inequality is higher in South Indian states such as Kerala, Andhra Pradesh (AP) and Tamil Nadu (TN).

Asset Inequalities

Inequalities in assets are quite high in India. Earlier studies show that in 2002, land inequality was 0.73, per capita asset holding was 0.65 and per capita holding of financial assets was 0.99.[9] The inequality in ownership of land was 0.76 in 2003 (Rawal 2008). A study by Rawal (2013) shows that Gini coefficient in oprational holdings in 2011-12 was around 0.78. Credit Suisse report on India reveals that the richest 1 per cent owned 53 per cent of the country's wealth while the share of the top 10 per cent was 76.3 per cent. In other words, 90 per cent of Indians own a less than 25 per cent of the country's wealth.

Inequality across Social Group

One of the important forms of inequality in India relates to disparities across social groups particularly disadvantaged sections like SCs (scheduled castes) and STs (scheduled tribes). One way of looking at this inequality is to examine the poverty ratios across social groups. Poverty declined much faster for all the social groups during the period 2004-05 to 2011-12 as compared to the period 1993-94 to 2004-05. The rate of decline in poverty is the highest for SCs. The decline in poverty for SCs and OBCs (other backward class) exceeded the national average during the period 2004-05 to 2011-12 (Panagariya and More 2013). Poverty decline for STs was more or less similar to that of national average. It looks like SCs, STs and OBCs benefited equally or more in the high growth phase of 2004-05 to 2011-12.

However, the poverty levels are higher for STs and SCs as compared to other groups. Particularly the poverty ratio of STs was two times to that of national average in

9. Himanshu (2015) quoting the study of Jayadev et al. (2007).

2011-12. If we look at the type of household across social groups, the poverty in casual labour in agriculture among SCs (41.3%) and STs (59.7%) was very high compared to other groups (31%) (Table 7.6).

Table 7.6

Incidence of Poverty among Social Groups by Type of Households: 2011-12 (%)

Sector	*SC*	*ST*	*OBC*	*Others*
Rural				
Self-employed in agriculture	28.9	42.2	20.3	13.4
Self-employed in non-agriculture	23.4	28.3	19.1	12.5
Regular wage/salary earnings	12.9	20.8	10.3	7.7
Casual labour in agriculture	41.3	59.7	34.8	31.0
Casual labour in non-agriculture	32.7	54.5	29.7	23.0
Others	27.6	44.3	16.5	8.2
Total	31.5	45.3	22.7	15.5
Urban				
Self-employed	23.0	25.9	17.3	9.4
Regular wage/salary earnings	12.1	9.1	7.1	4.8
Casual labour	37.6	55.7	29.5	28.1
Others	17.9	12.9	9.3	4.5
Total	21.7	24.1	15.4	8.1

Source: Radhakrishna (2015).

Asset distribution also shows that the share of SCs and STs is low in the total assets. Landlessness is high among SC households. Discrimination in labour market and business is also found in some of the studies.[10] Lack of basic necessities such as housing, sanitation, education and health is another problem for these groups.[11] However, income inequality is only one aspect of disparities between upper castes and disadvantaged sections. Discrimination,

10. See Deshpande (2013) on the discrimination in small business.
11. The problem of exclusion in terms of access to basic services also applies to minorities like Muslims.

humiliation and violence against Dalits and *adivasis* are examples of inequalities in non-economic factors.

Regional Inequalities

There have been several studies on convergence and divergence of Indian states. Many studies find no evidence of convergence across states.[12] Inequality across states in Figure 7.4 shows that it was lower during 1980s—coefficient of variation being 0.28 to 0.29. It increased significantly from around 0.32 in 1990-91 to 0.44 in 2008-09 with some fluctuations. It seems to have stabilised in the last few years. As shown in Table 7.7, the share of per capita income in Bihar increased significantly in All India and few developed states. The share of Bihar in All India rose from 33 per cent in 2004-05 to 42 per cent in 2013-14. Similarly, Bihar's share in Punjab increased significantly from 24 per cent to 34 per cent during the same period. There seems to be some catching up by the less developed states in per capita SDP (state domestic product) growth. However, there are significant inequalities within states. This issue is also becoming important.

Table 7.7

Share of Per Capita Income of Bihar in All India and Few Developed States (%)

	Share of Per Capita Income of Bihar in			
	All India	*Maharashtra*	*Punjab*	*Gujarat*
2004-05	32.8	21.9	23.8	24.7
2013-14	41.9	26.6	33.8	29.2

Note: Per Capita Net State Domestic Product is in current prices (2004-05 series).

Source: *Economic Survey 2015*, Ministry of Finance, Government of India.

12. For example, see Ghose et al. (2013). This study shows significant divergence in per capita income across states in the aggregate and sectoral levels for the period 1968-69 to 2008-09. Also see Das et al. (2013) which indicates evidence of conditional convergence for Indian districts but at a rate that is only half of Barro's 'Iron Law'.

Figure 7.4

Inequalities across States: 1980-81 to 2010-11

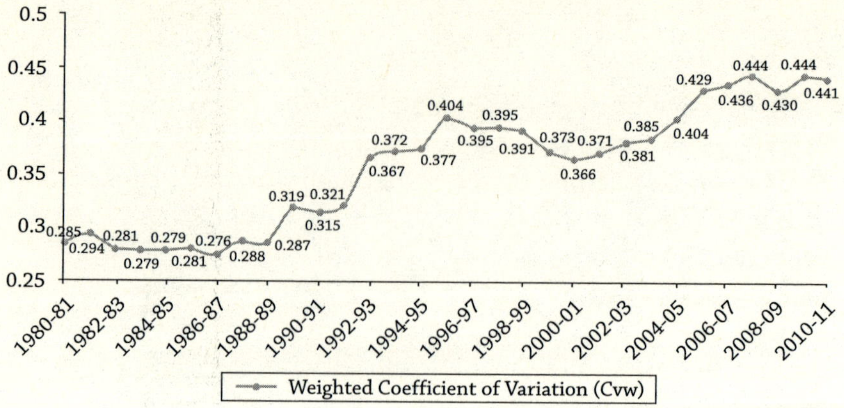

Source: Planning Commission (2012).

Gender Inequalities

Inequality between men and women is an important issue in India. Gender inequality index is the highest for India among the countries listed in Table 7.8. The percentage of 25 plus female population with some secondary education and female participation rates are the lowest among these countries.

Table 7.8

Gender Inequality Index and Other Components for Selected Countries: 2013

Countries	*Gender Inequality Index*		*MMR 2010 (Death per 1 Lakh Life Birth)*	*25+Female Population with at least Some Secondary Education (%)*	*15+ Female Labour Force Participation Rate*
Argentina	0.381	74	77	57.0	47.3
Russian Fed.	0.314	52	34	89.6	57.0
Brazil	0.441	85	56	51.9	59.5
China	0.202	37	37	58.7	63.8
Indonesia	0.500	103	220	39.9	51.3
South Africa	0.461	94	300	72.7	44.2
India	0.563	127	200	26.6	28.8

Source: *HDR 2014* quoted in *Economic Survey 2014-15*, GoI.

Gender discrimination is another form of labour segmentation. As is well known, the wages of women workers are lower than those of men across most employment categories and locations. There are distinct conventionally earmarked spheres of work for women and the entry of women into most male-dominated occupations is constrained. Conventional women's work is characterised by lower wages and earnings and limited upward mobility.

There are many examples of non-economic factors that discriminate women. Decline in child sex ratio (female-male ratio 0-6 years) from 927 in 2001 to 914 in 2011 is one example of 'boy preference'. Rapes and violence against women have been increasing in India. Gender inequality is a major social disparity in Indian society.[13]

Inequality of Opportunity

Equality of opportunity is important for reducing many other forms of inequalities. Access to education is an important indicator of equality of opportunity. Recent NSS 71st Round conducted in 2014 provides NAR (net attendance ratios) by quintiles, social groups and religion. The inequalities in primary education are not high. But inequality increases over the education ladder: secondary, higher secondary and above higher secondary level.

Figure 7.5

Net Attendance Ratio for Higher Secondary Level: All India, 2014

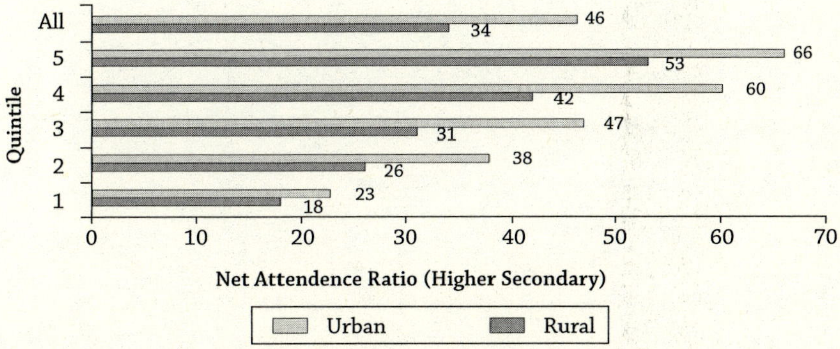

Source: NSS 71st Round, Report No.575 released in 2016.

13. More on gender inequality, see Dreze and Sen (2013).

Figure 7.6

Net Attendance Ratio for Above Higher Secondary Level: All India

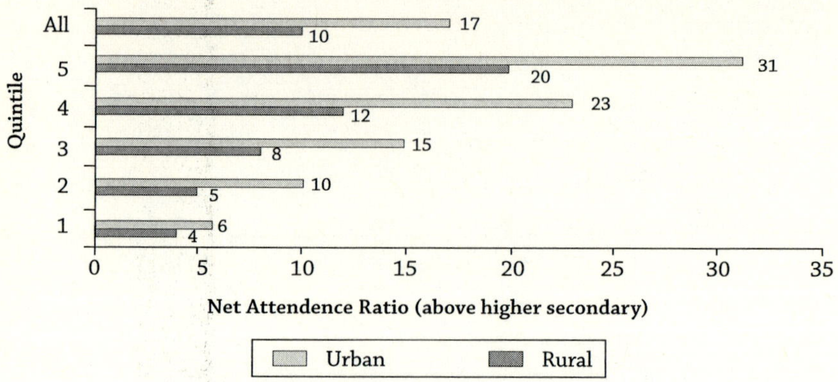

Source: Same as Figure 7.3.

It is known that returns to education are more at higher levels. Figure 7.5 shows that 66 per cent of kids of higher secondary going age of the richest quintile of the population attend school in urban areas (53% for rural) while the proportion drops to 23 per cent for the poorest quintile for urban (18% for rural). In the case of above higher secondary level, only 6 per cent of young people from the bottom quintile of the population attend in urban areas but the proportion is five times higher at 31 per cent for the young people from the richest quintile of the population (Figure 7.6).

Figure 7.7

Net Attendance Ratio by Social Groups: All India, 2014

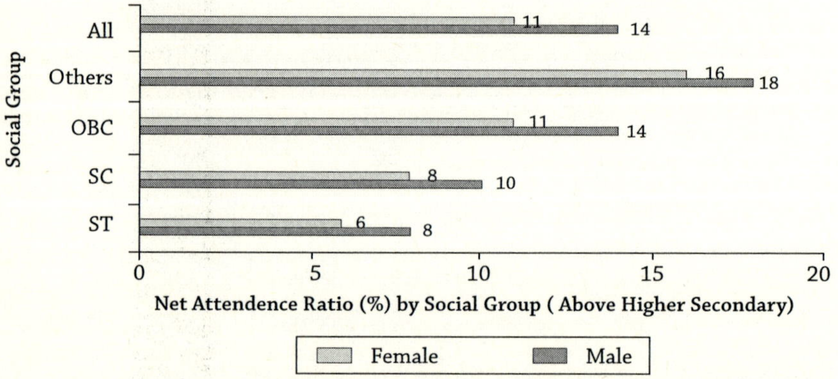

Source: Same as Figure 7.3.

NAR by social group shows that in the case of above higher secondary level, only 6 to 8 per cent of females from ST and SC population attend but the proportion is 11 per cent for OBCs and 16 per cent for other castes (Figure 7.7). Similarly, NAR by religion indicates that only 6 per cent of females from Muslims attend above higher secondary level as compared to 12 per cent for Hindus and 18 per cent for Christians (Figure 7.8). The data shows that inequalities in NAR among quintiles, social groups and religious groups increases with rise in education levels from primary to secondary, higher secondary and above higher secondary.

Figure 7.8

Net Attendance Ratio by Religion: All India, 2014

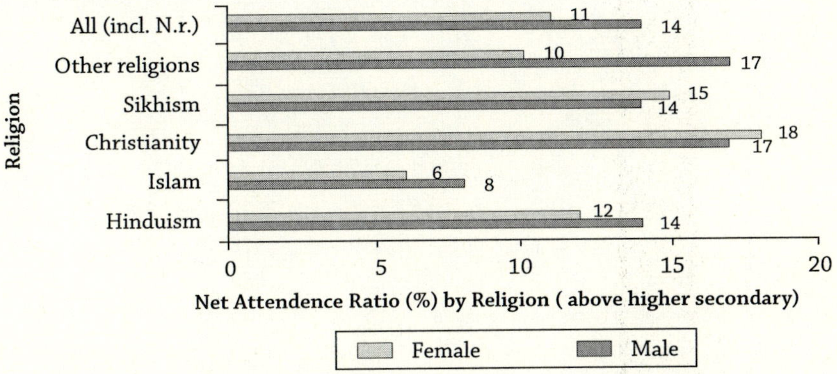

Source: Same as Figure 7.3.

Regional Disparities in Different Types of Courses: Among the students enrolled in higher education, the propensity to be enrolled in technical education is higher for students in South India as compared to other regions (Table 7.9). This is true for both rural and urban areas. So it is not surprising that of all the students enrolled for technical education, the southern states account for the highest share (Table 7.9).

The details about the students enrolled in general education reveal that in rural areas, students from southern states are most likely to study science (38%) or commerce (35%) and less likely to study humanities. This southern pattern is in sharp contrast with all other regions of India where most of the students in rural areas opt for a course in humanities. This is all true for urban areas. Students from western and southern regions are more likely to prefer courses which are skill based or market oriented (Chakravorty et al. 2016). The choice of courses in these regions most likely reflects the expected earnings given their employment prospects. Equality of opportunity in terms of returns to higher education seems to be better in these regions as compared to other regions.

Table 7.9

Distribution of Enrolled Students Over Different Types of Courses, and Regional Distribution of Enrolled Students in Each Type of Course

Region	*Rural*				*Urban*			
	General	*Technical*	*Vocational*	*Total*	*General*	*Technical*	*Vocational*	*Total*
Northern	78.28	19.31	2.4	100	62.86	36.09	1.04	100
	15.35	14.94	37.52	15.49	16.53	14.1	24.13	15.61
North East	88.25	11.24	0.5	100	81.21	17.8	0.99	100
	4.23	2.13	1.92	3.79	3.18	1.03	3.4	2.32
Eastern	84.8	14.36	0.85	100	71.14	28.32	0.54	100
	18.7	12.48	14.92	17.42	16.54	9.78	10.94	13.8
Central	88.02	11.28	0.7	100	67.88	31.19	0.93	100
	34.66	17.51	21.98	31.1	24.83	16.95	29.82	21.72
Western	79.65	19.82	0.53	100	56.82	42.72	0.46	100
	10.27	10.07	5.43	10.18	16.83	18.8	12.1	17.59
Southern	60.18	39.00	0.82	100	45.28	54.26	0.46	100
	16.79	42.88	18.24	22.03	22.09	39.33	19.62	28.97
All India	78.98	20.03	0.99	100	59.37	39.96	0.67	100
	100	100	100	100	100	100	100	100

Notes: For each region, the first row gives the distribution of enrolled students across different types of courses, and the second row gives the share of that region among the students who are enrolled in each type of course.

Source: Chandrasekhar et al. (2016).

Inequality and Human Development: Higher inequality can lead to lower human development. A study by Suryanarana (2013) estimates both HDI (human development index) and inequality adjusted HDI for all India and states (Table 7.10).

The rank of Madhya Pradesh (MP) for inequality adjusted HDI is the lowest while Kerala has the highest rank. The average loss in HDI due to inequality at the All-India level is 32 per cent. It is the highest for MP (36%) and Chhattisgarh (35%) and the lowest for Kerala (17%). The loss due to inequality is the highest with respect to education dimension (43%), followed by health (34%) and income (16%). It shows that inequalities in non-income indicators like education and health are higher than that of income. The analysis also shows that with lower inequalities, HDI would have been much higher.

Table 7.10

IHDI (Inequality Adjusted HDI) and Loss

States	*HDI*	*IHDI*	*Loss (%)*	*Rank HDI*	*Rank IHDI*
AP	0.485	0.332	31.6	19	20
Bihar	0.447	0.303	32.1	26	24
Chhattisgarh	0.458	0.297	35.1	24	25
Gujarat	0.514	0.363	29.5	15	13
Jharkhand	0.470	0.312	33.7	21	21
Karnataka	0.508	0.353	30.5	18	18
Kerala	0.625	0.520	16.8	1	1
MP	0.451	0.290	35.7	25	27
Maharashtra	0.549	0.397	27.8	7	8
Odisha	0.442	0.296	33.1	27	26
Punjab	0.569	0.410	28.0	4	4
Rajasthan	0.468	0.308	34.0	23	22
Tamil Nadu	0.544	0.396	27.3	9	9
UP	0.468	0.307	34.5	22	23
West Bengal	0.509	0.360	29.3	17	14
All India	0.504	0.343	32.0	--	--

Source: Suryanarayana (2013).

Policies for Reduction in Inequality

Global Level

Studies at global level have shown that measures such as fiscal policy, education policy, financial inclusion, well designed labour market and institutions can reduce inequality (Dabla-Norris et al. 2015). Macroeconomic stabilisation through fiscal policy can minimise any financial crisis which hurts the poor. Similarly, fiscal redistribution can improve the share of the poor and middle class. However, there is no-one size fits all policies for tackling inequality. In developed countries, more reliance on wealth and property taxes, progressive income taxation, better targeting of social benefits are needed. In emerging market countries, better access to education and health services, well targeted conditional transfers can reduce inequality (Bastagli et al. 2012).

World Bank (2016) provides some lessons from the experiences of countries such as Brazil, Cambodia, Peru and Tanzania which are best performers in reducing inequalities during 2004-2014 and Mali during 2001-2010. In Brazil, labour market dynamics including a rising minimum wage and expansion of social policies helped in raising incomes of the poor. In fact, these two factors accounted for approximately 80 per cent of inequality in 2003-2013. Some of the lessons for the success of these five countries are prudent macroeconomic policies, strong growth, functioning labour markets and coherent domestic policies focusing on safety nets, human capital, and infrastructure. The report focuses on few policy areas like early childhood development, universal healthcare, universal access to good-quality education, CCTs (conditional cash transfers), investments in new or improved rural roads and electrification, and taxation, mainly on personal income and consumption. These interventions have both efficiency and equity benefits. The report also cautions that universal prescriptions are useful but we need country specific solutions.

It is recognised that reduction in inequality of opportunity is equally or more important than inequality in income. A web-based policymaker's survey carried out by the ADB (Asian Development Bank) shows:

> About 60 per cent of the respondents agree or strongly agree with the statement that it is more important to reduce inequality of opportunity (such

> as access to education, health, and employment services) than to reduce inequality of income; and 84 per cent of the respondents agree or strongly agree with the statement that income inequality is acceptable if it is due to differences in individual efforts and an outcome of fair competition (Kanbur et al. 2014: 4).

Policies for Reduction in Inequality in India

There is a need for several policies for reduction in inequality in India. We concentrate on few policies as it is difficult to cover all in one paper.

As Dreze and Sen (2013) say, the nature of Indian inequality can be distinguished from some of the other countries like China. Aggregate inequality may be similar between India and China. However, the poor in India can't afford even basic necessities. Also access and quality public services in education, healthcare etc. are missing for the poor.

> For both these reasons, inequality in India takes the terrible form of a massive disparity between the privileged and the rest, with a huge deficiency of the basic requirements for a minimally acceptable life for the underdogs of society. The basic facilities of usable school, an accessible hospital, a toilet at home, or two square meals a day, are missing for a huge proportion of the Indian population in a way they are not in, say, China (Dreze and Sen 2013: 280).

Redistribution Measures

There has been a debate on India for a long time on redistribution of assets in favour of the poor to reduce poverty and inequality. Some of the earlier studies have questioned the government's strategy of helping the poor in terms of ad hoc anti-poverty programmes. For example, after analysing some of the studies on government interventions, Kurien (1986: 390) observes,

> What strategies such as target programmes attempt to do is to achieve through administrative

> interventions some redistributions in favour of those who do not have a resource power. The interventionist strategy, therefore, is an attempt to correct structural consequences without altering the structural characteristics.[14]

Land reform in the sense of distribution of land in favour of the poor is largely a failure. Efforts towards redistribution of land and non-land assets have not been successful.

In the context of removal of poverty, in his R.S. Dubhashi Memorial lecture, V.K.R.V. Rao (1978: 17, 18) says the following:

> Unless there is a structural change in property relations in rural India and the poor get an adequate share of productive assets, including land, implements, inputs and credit, any programme of a direct attack on rural poverty is not likely to bring about a reduction either in its magnitude or its intensity. It is not only in respect of productive assets that radical institutional reforms are required to give a better deal to the rural poor. We also need radical institutional reforms to see that the rural poor get a larger and more effective say m the operation of the rural power structure and a more significant and usable share of basic services for human resource development such as housing, education, health etc.

Some advocate measures such as redistribution of assets and wealth in favour of the poor via higher tax rates for the rich. Increasing the income and corporate tax rates may not be the solution. In order to reduce inequalities, richer sections have to pay much more taxes. The tax/GDP ratio has to be raised with a wider tax base and removing exemptions for corporates. The share of direct taxes in total tax revenue has to be raised as indirect taxes are regressive. Fiscal instruments like public investment in physical and social infrastructure can be used to reduce inequality.

---

14. Also see Herring and Edwards (1983) for comments on Employment Guarantee Scheme (EGS) in Maharashtra. They say that there are vested interests in continuing EGS in the state in order to avoid redistributive measures like land reforms.

Agriculture: Increase the Viability of Small and Marginal Farmers

Increase in incomes of farmers particularly those with small holdings is important for reducing inequality in the economy particularly across sectors. In his Radhakrishna Memorial Lectures, Sukhamoy Chakravarty (1987) argued that viability of small and marginal farmers have to be increased for sustainability of agriculture. We are still talking about viability of small farms even after three decades.

Table 7.11 shows that the income of the marginal and small farmers from all sources is only around 1/10th of those of large farmers. The income from agriculture is very low for small farmers. Even if we add the other sources of income, it is not enough to take care of daily consumption and they have to borrow to survive. Small holding farmers have to get part of income from rural non-farm activities. Therefore, promotion of rural non-farm sector is essential for generating incomes for small farmers. Simultaneously, we have to improve the viability of small holdings.

Table 7.11

Monthly Income and Consumption of Agricultural Households, 2013 (₹)

Land Size (ha.)	*Cultivation Income*	*Animals Income*	*Wage Income*	*Non-farm Business*	*Total Income*	*Total Consumption*
<0.01	31	1223	3019	469	4742	5139
0.01-0.40	712	645	2557	482	4396	5402
0.41-1.00	2177	645	2072	477	5371	5979
1.01-2.00	4237	825	1744	599	7405	6430
2.01-4.00	7433	1180	1681	556	10849	7798
4.01-10.00	15547	1501	2067	880	19995	10115
>10.00	35713	2616	1311	1771	41412	14445
All Classes	3194	784	2146	528	6653	6229

Source: *NSS Situation Assessment Survey 2013.*

Small farmers face several challenges in the access to inputs and marketing. They need a level playing field with large farms in terms of accessing land, water, inputs, credit, technology and markets. Small holdings also face new challenges on integration of value chains, liberalisation and globalisation effects, market volatility and other risks and vulnerability, adaptation of climate change etc. (Thapa and Gaiha 2011). There are many technological and institutional innovations which can enable marginal and small farmers to raise agricultural productivity and increase incomes through diversification and high value agriculture.[15] Changes in information technology will help in a big way to improve agri-business and incomes of small farmers. A number of innovative institutional models are emerging and there are many opportunities for small and marginal farmers in India.

Social Protection

The recent theory and evidence "offers a new perspective on social protection policies in poor countries, suggesting that there is a scope for using these policies to compensate for the market failures that perpetuate poverty, particularly in high-inequality settings" (Ravallion 2003). Recent research has shown that risk and vulnerability justification should be added since the poor do not have formal instruments for risk mitigation and coping. Risks and vulnerability are high as more than 90 per cent workers are in the unorganised sector in India. Social protection thus deals with both absolute deprivation and risk and vulnerabilities. Social protection policies play a critical role in realising: (a) the human right to social security for all, (b) reducing poverty and inequality, (c) and supporting inclusive growth—by boosting human capital and productivity, (d) supporting domestic demand and facilitating structural transformation of national economies (ILO 2014).

India has social protection programmes at different levels: (a) Universal Capability Enhancing Programmes

---

15. See Vaidyanathan (2009) for efficiency in investments. See Vyas (2016) for changing role of government in agriculture. See Alagh (2013) for a discussion on future of Indian agriculture.

(e.g. health and education);[16] (b) Targeted programmes for the poor and vulnerable to provide socio-economic security; (c) Infrastructure (rural housing, rural drinking water, Swachh Bharat Mission [Sanitation]); 4. Social protection for the unorganised/informal workers.

The approaches of earlier United Progressive Alliance (UPA) government and that of present National Democratic Alliance (NDA) government on social protection are different. UPA relied mostly on rights based framework: right to education, right to employment, right to food, right to information. However, rights approach alone can't deliver social protection. We need appropriate institutions to implement effectively. The present government is not talking about rights approach but is focusing on some programmes by using approaches like political accountability and good governance. Programmes like Swachh Bharat Abhiyan, focus on housing, financial inclusion (Jan Dhan Yojana) are part of the present strategy on social protection.

Should We Move Towards Universal Basic Income?

Some argue for CCTs and UCTs (unconditional cash transfers). It is advocated that we should move towards DBT (direct benefits transfer) in place of present social protection programmes. There is also a debate on UBI (universal basic income). Recently, there was a proposal in Switzerland to guarantee every adult and long-term citizen 2,500 Swiss Francs per month. However, in a referendum, Swiss voted against this idea of UBI. Some other countries want to experiment on this concept of UBI now. It may be feasible in India if some of the subsidies and tax exemptions are removed.[17] Srinivasan (2016) says that the idea of an assured minimum income was discussed in India as early as 1960s but could not be implemented then on account of certain circumstances.

16. See Rangarajan and Dev (2015) for a discussion on public expenditure on health and education on the poor.
17. On this see Banerjee (2016), Bardhan (2016), Ray (2016).

Focus on Two Areas: Employment and Education

There can be several solutions to reduce inequality.[18] But, let's focus here on two important measures: creating productive employment and providing quality education.

Employment and Skills

There is a feeling that we should have some flagship programmes like Mahatma Gandhi National Rural Employment Guarantee Scheme (MGNREGA) to reduce poverty and inequality. No doubt these programmes are important for protecting the poor. But equitable growth is much broader than this and productive inclusion in terms of generating quality employment should be the focus of any inclusive agenda. We need more diversified agriculture for raising the income of farmers. However, future employment has to be created in manufacturing and services. In this context, the Make in India initiative, focus on start-ups, Mudra, financial inclusion, etc., are steps in the right direction. Equally, service sector employment has to be promoted. Over time, the share of the organised sector has to be raised while simultaneously improving productivity in the unorganised sector. For the new generation, moving to regular wage employment is the aspiration apart from high remunerative self-employment.

Make in India

For improving quality of employment, Make in India campaign is in the right direction. However, the experience of China shows that although the share of manufacturing in GDP rose significantly, the share of employment is low at 16 per cent. Manufacturing today generates less direct employment but more indirect employment in services.[19]

India is an exception to the share of employment in services. The country has high share of services in GDP (gross domestic product) (58.4%) but the share of services

18. See Dev (2008), Ahluwalia (2012), Rao (2009) for the policies on inclusive growth. See Bhagwati and Panagariya (2013) on track II reforms for more effective and inclusive redistribution.

19. Personal correspondence with Ajit Ghose. Also see, Ghose (2016).

in employment is exceptionally low (26.4%). Therefore, the share of employment in services has to be raised. India has the potential to increase the number of workers in manufacturing and the contribution to the sector to overall growth. But its future development path is unlikely to mimic that witnessed in East Asia like Japan, Taiwan or even in China. India has to forge its own path that will rely on both manufacturing and services as growth engines along with emphasis on exports which looks bleak in the short run.

Labour Market Inequalities: Most of the inequalities (economic and social) will have labour market dimension. Some issues on inequality exclusively deal with labour market structures, processes, mechanisms and outcomes while some others are influenced by labour institutions and labour market forces (IHD 2014).

The evidence based current research has shown that there have been significant inequalities in labour markets in India. Inequalities can be found across sectors, wages and earnings, quality of work, labour market access and, between organised and unorganised sector. Labour market segmentation is another important issue regarding inequalities. Wage differentials can't be explained by economic factors alone in spite of increasing occupational and geographical mobility. Segmentation based on occupational skills and consequently industry and sectors is well-known. Reducing labour market inequalities is important for sustainability of growth, rise in human development and reduction in overall inequalities.

Discrimination across Social Groups: According to a study based on the National Sample Survey Organisation (NSSO) data for 2004-05, while chances of securing a regular job were 21.5 per cent in the case of high caste Hindus, they were only 6.7 per cent in the case of STs and 12.4 per cent in the case of those belonging to SCs (Bordia-Das 2010). Another study on newspaper advertisements announcing job vacancies by private sector companies, during 2005-06, revealed that responses significantly vary among Dalit and high caste Hindus and Muslim candidates. Taking high caste Hindu candidate as reference category (1), the probability of a Dalit candidate to be called for interview was 0.67 and that of a Muslim candidate 0.33. Probability for a qualified Dalit candidate was less (0.85) even against an underqualified high caste Hindu candidate (Thorat et al. 2010).

Youth Unemployment and Social Tensions: One of the main problems for the agitations by the people like the Marathas in Maharashtra, Patidars in Gujarat, Jats in Haryana and Kapus in AP relates to youth unemployment and aspirations of these castes to move to quality employment. It is known that youth unemployment in India is three times to that of general unemployment.

Pro-employment Macroeconomic Policies: Appropriate macro policies such as trade, fiscal and monetary policies should promote employment by providing appropriate policies and institutions.[20] Monetary stimulus in advanced countries helped preventing worse outcomes. In response to the global crisis developed countries reduced short term lending rates. These measures prevented a larger fall in employment. However, the extended period of low interest rates and unconventional monetary policy measures seem to have adverse effects on employment by encouraging capital intensive industries (ILO 2014). In other words, monetary policies might have indirectly contributed to observed weaknesses in labour market and increased inequality.

Macro policies that enhance strong aggregate demand, raise productive investment and improve access to finance can have a positive impact of employment prospects. Bardhan (2016) advocates wage subsidies instead of capital subsidies for increasing employment.

Education: Equality of Opportunity

Reduction in inequality of opportunity is important for promoting equity.

---

20. See Nayyar (2013) on macroeconomics and development.

> The distinction between inequality of opportunity and inequality of outcome can be particularly useful in guiding public policy. Equality of opportunity is not only intrinsically important but also a critical condition for a prosperous society. Public policy must be put in place to reduce or eliminate inequality of opportunity. Governments must work hard to promote equality of opportunity and to ensure that everybody has equal opportunity to participate in the growth process and benefit from its fruits. To the extent that inequality of parents' income leads to inequality of opportunity for children, this inequality needs to be overcome by interventions to assure equal access to public services and to markets for all in society. (Kanbur et al. 2014).

Equality of opportunity can reduce the intensity of Kuznets curve. How do you flatten Kuznets curve? Endogenous growth models and capabilities approach or investing in human capital may have some answers. This can reduce the intensity of Kuznets curve. This can be shown in the contrast between East Asia and India/South Asia.

Recently, the Deputy Prime Minister of Singapore cautioned about school education in India. He says "schools are the biggest crisis in India today and have been for a long time. Schools are the biggest gap between India and East Asia. And it is a crisis that cannot be justified."[21]

Equity in quality education is the key for raising human development and reduction in inequalities in labour market. A study by Cain et al. (2014) on India shows that increase in returns to education account for a large part of the increase in urban inequality during 1993-94 to 2004-05. Increase in returns to education has been particularly higher in education intensive services (such as communications, finance, insurance, real estate and other business services) and education intensive occupations (professional/technical, managerial/administrative, and clerical occupations). The study, however, says that raising

---

21. First Lecture of Niti Ayog's 'Transforming India" initiative, 26 August 2016.

productivity in agriculture and expanding manufacturing sector is vital for reducing inequalities.

Education and Affirmative Policies: As shown above, there has been social exclusion and discrimination of some social groups in labour market. There is a need for two types of policies. First one is education and skill improvement for the disadvantaged sections. Education is the key determinant of employment prospects. There is a strong link between educational attainment and employment outcomes, and people with higher levels of education enjoy a competitive advantage in the labour market, including higher wage levels. Education for these groups would reduce the gap with other groups. Second one is affirmative action in education.

Small Things Matter: In their book on *Poor Economics*, Banerjee and Duflo (2011) argue that so much of anti-poverty policy has failed over the years because of an inadequate understanding of poverty. Small changes can have big effects. Several research studies on education have shown strong impact of remedial instruction programmes on learning outcomes. Banerjee et al. (2007) did experimental evaluation of a programme run by PRATHAM targeted at the lower end of the class in public schools in cities of Mumbai and Vadodara. The programme provided an informal teacher (*Balasakhi*) for teaching basic learning in reading arithmetic. For about 2 hours, remedial instruction was given out of the regular classroom. The programme improved student test scores. The gains were more for the lowest performing children.[22] Thus, small changes can make big difference in the lives of the poor.

Gender Disparities

One of the important disparities in gender relates to education. "A Dalit girl from a poor family who dreams of becoming a doctor or engineer may have to struggle not

22. See Muralidharan (2013).

only with a lack of adequate schooling facilities in the neighbourhood and economic penury at home, but also, quite possibly, with indifferent social attitudes towards her education as well as with gender discrimination in the family and society" (Dreze and Sen 2013: 281).

Another issue is gender discrimination in employment. As is well known, the wages of women workers are lower than those of men across most employment categories and locations. The wages of women workers in India are lower by 20 to 50 per cent to male wages across different categories and locations. One question is whether education reduces gender gap. Wage of female worker with no education was 53 per cent of a man's wage in a regular job in rural areas. A graduate degree female received 70 per cent of male's wage in rural areas. In urban areas, gender gap in wages reduces faster with education. In general, education seems to have reduced wage gap between men and women as far as regular jobs were concerned (IHD 2014).

Participation rates of women are low and have declined in India (Table 7.12). Work participation rate for women in India is only 22 per cent compared to 54 per cent for males. In fact in urban areas, women's participation in work is only 15 per cent compared to 55 per cent for men. Recently IMF Chief, Christine Lagarde said increase in women's participation rates would increase 40 per cent GDP in India. Mckinsey report also mentions that GDP could increase by 16 per cent to 60 per cent by the year 2025, with increase in women participation rates. It is true that increase in women's participation is important to reduce gender inequalities.

But, women's 'work' and 'non-work' may be misleading. Time use surveys indicate women's unpaid work as home makers and caregivers is quite high. Some estimates show that if we monetise unpaid work of women, it amounts to around 16 lakh crores per annum (Nandi and Hensman 2015).

Table 7.12

Work Participation Rates of Female and Male

	Rural		*Urban*		*Total*	
	Female	*Male*	*Female*	*Male*	*Female*	*Male*
1983	34.0	54.7	15.1	51.2	29.6	53.9
1993-94	32.8	55.3	15.5	52.1	28.6	54.5
2004-05	32.7	54.6	16.6	54.9	28.7	54.7
2011-12	24.8	54.3	14.7	54.6	21.9	54.4

Source: IHD (2014).

Discrimination against females is practiced throughout the life cycle. It starts from the womb with sex determination tests and it goes on with discrimination in education and employment. Crimes against women are much more visible and increasing now than before. Legal route is important to address the problems faced by women. However, economic and social empowerment of women is important. Similarly, change in society attitudes and mindset of men are also essential to stop gender discrimination.

Corruption and Inequality

Good governance is important for promoting equity. Corruption is one of the obstacles for good governance. There have been studies linking corruption to inequality. IMF (2016) examines the costs of corruption and mitigating strategies as corruption can seriously undermine inclusive economic growth. It can adversely affect the determinants of economic performance that include macro financial stability, investment, human capital accumulation and total factor productivity. It can also have devastating economic and social consequences due to violence, civil strife and conflict. According to the study, anti-corruption strategy include transparency, rule of law, reforms to eliminate excessive regulation and effective institutions. Using cross country regressions for the period 1980-1997, Gupta et al. (1998) show that a worsening in the corruption index of a country by one standard deviation is associated with the same increase in the Gini coefficient as a reduction in average secondary schooling of 2.3 years. The study says that corruption raises inequality and poverty through lower economic growth, biased tax system in favour of rich, poor targeting of social programmes, lobbying the government by the rich for favourable policies which perpetuate inequality in asset ownership, unequal access in education and lower social spending.

India: Determinants and Root Causes of Corruption

Different Types of Corruption: There are different types of corruption even within the definition of misusing public office for private gain.[23] Sridharan (2014) discusses three types of corruption in India. First one is petty bureaucratic corruption at the level of traffic police, judicial services, land administration, education, tax, health services. Second one is big ticket corruption involving politicians, business people, and bureaucrats, the so called crony capitalism involving huge bribes on major government contracts, particularly on large infrastructure contracts, allocation of natural resources, such as minerals, telecom spectrum. These are controlled by politicians in certain key economic ministries. A third form of corruption is directly diverting government funds from development programmes, irrigation projects, roads, from social and anti-poverty programmes from publicly funded loans to the poor.

Democracy and Corruption: Liberal democracies with free press tend to have less corruption. It varies across countries regarding democracy and corruption (Treisman 2007). Scandinavian countries like Denmark, Sweden, Norway etc. have very low corruption. But some of the low income countries with democracy have high corruption. While democracy is commonly believed to reduce corruption, there are obvious endogeneity problems in measuring the impact of democracy on corruption. Of course, there are different types of democracy. For

23. On different types of corruption, see Bardhan (2005), Das-Gupta (2007), Basu (2011).

example, Indian democracy may be different from some other countries. It is important to ask and identify which features of democracy can reduce corruption and which features enhance corruption. Some democracies may have features which reduce while some have which increase corruption.

Elections and Corruption: One of the main root causes for corruption in India is election funding. This is the main cause for big ticket corruption. Most of the party funds are from corrupt payments in return for contracts or clearances according to politicians across parties as well as bureaucrats. Real estate developers have reportedly become the single top source of funds for parties and politicians (Sridharan 2014). Therefore, election funding is the root cause of corruption in countries like India.

Economic Reforms and Corruption: Economic reforms are supposed to reduce corruption. However, corruption is widespread and pervasive in countries like India even after economic liberalisation. One can say that there are two key sources of corruption in India. First, that economic liberalisation has not ended the discretionary powers of the government over resource-allocation in several fields. Second one is election funding for political parties mentioned above. Despite 25 years of economic liberalisation, there still remain plenty of government clearances at central and state levels which remains highly discretionary rather than transparently rule based.

The correlation between corruption and economic reforms, positive or negative, is however, no means clear. Think of China with its combination of institutionalised corruption and economic reforms and high growth rates. China is ranked lower (83) than India (76) in transparency international global perceptions index but much higher than India in World Bank's Ease of Doing Business Index.

Women in Government and Corruption: Women's participation in government is supposed to reduce corruption. For example, more women in Parliament can improve things. Women's participation in local councils like *panchayats* seems to have improved the performance compared to men.

What are the measures needed for reducing corruption in India? First, we have to find out the solution for the major source of corruption which is party finances for election funding. Otherwise, the corruption problem in India can't be solved. Other measures include transparency, rule of law and economic reforms with rule based than discretions. Addressing the corruption issue requires effective institutions. Of course administrative, legal reforms are also part of the strategy. As some people argue, Jan Lokpal like the Anna Hazare movement can solve problems of corruption.

Some scholars like Avinash Dixit and Kaushik Basu also mention that without waiting, actions from the government, the business community, civil society and media can take a lead on reducing corruption. Dixit (2016) discusses demand and supply sides of corruption. He shifts the focus to the supply side viz., firms. He proposes that business community itself could set a norm of 'no bribes' and enforce it through ostracism such as 'not doing business with those firms who give bribes'. Dixit suggests that largest firms could potentially take the lead as they may be better able to withstand initial losses till the norm takes roots. But to be fair to Avinash Dixit (2016: 58), he says that:

> Even within its limited domain, my proposal will not achieve anywhere close to 100 per cent success. It is not a panacea; there are no panaceas. But the problem of corruption is sufficiently important and urgent to justify exploring all potential solutions and starting with imperfect ones. Waiting for a 100 per cent solution to emerge only guarantees getting 0 per cent.

Finally, use of technology can be a game changer for some forms of corruption. There are many examples in India where use of technology reduced corruption.

Thus, we need multipronged strategy to reduce corruption in India. Inequalities are expected to reduce with decline in corruption as it affects the poor and vulnerable adversely.

Conclusion

Rising inequalities is a concern in many advanced and developing countries of the world. Inclusive approach is needed for several reasons. In the context of ethics and humanism, equality is important for its own sake. Inequality reduction is also required for sustainability of growth. If we reduce personal, social, gender, rural-urban and regional disparities, both the objectives of ethics and growth of equality will be achieved. Lower inequalities would result in higher demand from bottom deciles, vulnerable and disadvantaged sections and lead to higher growth. If we define equity in terms of empowerment and increase in participation of the poor, there is no trade-off between growth and equity. Reduction in corruption can help in improvement of equality.

One issue that we have not touched explicitly in the paper is environmental sustainability. Climate change is already having impact on the lives of the people, particularly the poor.

India should be concerned about this problem. There are two types of inequalities regarding environmental sustainability. First one is the inequality in consumption patterns between advanced countries and developing countries. Second one is inequalities in consumption patterns between rich and poor in India. The consumption of the rich in India is more or less equal to the rich of the advanced countries. There is a need for reduction of unsustainable consumption pattern of the developed countries and those of rich in India.

Equality of opportunity is important. While the governments have implemented policies that unleashed the country's tremendous growth potential, it should also embark on a process of social transformation that ends discrimination on the basis of caste, class and gender. More attention has to be paid for providing clean water, sanitation, access to healthcare and education. India has under invested in human and social capital. Productive employment and quality education for everyone can reduce inequalities significantly.

Another issue in the context of India is exclusion of SCs, STs, women and minorities. Here economics alone will not help inclusion. Social and political factors are important apart from economic factors. Growth with redistribution efforts will not affect social behaviour without social transformation. We need social movements to reduce social exclusion. This happened partially in South India earlier in Kerala and TN and is happening in other parts of the country now.[24] It is still a long way for major social transformations.

There are limits to economic analysis regarding equity and inclusive approach. Non-economic factors like norms, culture, and beliefs can also influence the level of inclusion/exclusion. Inequalities are much more than economic disparities. The ideas of equality and inequality also have non-economic dimension. The idea of citizenship is one such example. Democratic countries have expanded the domain of citizenship by institutionalising universal rights and entitlements in the spheres of education, healthcare and housing.[25]

Politically, for having a stable and democratic society, one needs to have equitable approach. Large sections of the society can't be ignored. It is increasingly clear that the process of development must become more socially and economically inclusive. If we do not have tolerant and inclusive society, it can generate severe social tensions. Thus, there are strong social, political and economic reasons for reducing inequalities. The agenda of inclusiveness and equality has to be given highest priority for broad-based social and economic development.

---

24. On social movements in different parts of the country, see Baviskar (2015).
25. See Jodhka and Vaid (2015).

Acknowledgement: This is the Malcolm Adiseshaiah Memorial Award lecture delivered by the author.

References

Ahluwalia, Montek (2012). "Prospects and Policy Challenges in the Twelfth Plan", *Economic and Political Weekly* 46(21).

Alagh, Y.K. (2013). *Future of Indian Agriculture.* New Delhi: National Book Trust of India.

Atkison, A.B. and F. Bourguignon (2015). *Hand Book of Economics.* Vol. 2A and 2B. North-Holland, U.K.; Elsevier.

Banerjee, Abhijit and Esther Duflo (2011). *Poor Economics: A Radical Thinking of the Way to fight Global Poverty.* New York: Public Affairs.

Banerjee, Abhijit (2016). "The Best way to Welfare", *Indian Express,* June 18.

Bardhan, P.K. (2005). "The Economists Approach to the Problem of Corruption", *World Development* 34(2).

Bardhan, P. (2016), "Lack of Adequate Jobs Serious Problem... Caste War Possible", *Interview in Indian Express*, 14 April.

———. (2016a). *Basic Income in a Poor Country.* Ideas for India. *www.ideasforindia.in*

Bastagli, F.D. Coady, and S. Gupta (2012). "Income Inequality and Fiscal Policy", *IMF Staff Discussion Note* 12/08, International Monetary Fund, Washington.

Basu, K. (2006). "Globalisation, Poverty and Inequality: What is the Relationship? What can be done?, *World Development* 34(8).

———. (2011). *Why, for a Class of Bribes, the Act of Giving a Bribe should be Treated as Legal.* Ministry of Finance, Government of India.

Baviskar, Amita (2015). "Regional Dimensions of Social Movement in India", in *India Rural Development Report 2013/14.* IDFC Rural Development Network and Orient Blackswan.

Bhagwati, J. and A. Panagariya (2013). *Why Growth Matters: How Economic Growth in India Reduced Poverty and the Lessons for other Developing Countries.* New York: Public Affairs.

Bordia-Das, Maitreyi (2010). "Minority Status and Labour Market, Outcomes: Does India Have Minority Enclaves?", in Sukhadeo Thorat and Katherine S. Newman (eds.), *Blocked by Caste: Economic Discrimination in Modern India.* New Delhi: Oxford University Press.

Cain, J.S., R. Hasan, R. Magsombol and Ajay Tandon (2014). "Accounting for Inequality in India: Evidence from Household Expenditures", in R. Kanbur, C. Rhee, and J. Zhuang (eds.), *Inequality in Asia and the Pacific.* Asian Development Bank and Routledge.

Chandrasekhar, S.P., Geetha Rani and S. Sahoo (2016). "Estimates of Household Expenditure on Higher Education and Borrowing for Higher Education: What do Recent Data have to say?". (*mimeo*). Mumbai: Indira Gandhi Institute of Development Research.

Chakravarty, Sukhamoy (1987). *Development Planning: Indian Experience.* Oxford: Clarendon Press.

Chakravorty, S., S. Chandrasekhar and K. Naraparaju (2016). "Income Inequality in India's Agricultural Sector: New Estimates and Explanations". (*mimeo*). Mumbai: Indira Gandhi Institute of Development Research.

Dabla-Norris, K. Kocchar, N. Suphaphiphat, F. Ricka, E. Tsounta (2015). "Causes and Consequences of Income inequality: A Global Perspective", *IMF Staff Discussion Note.* Washington D.C.: IMF.

Das, S. Chetan Ghate and Peter E. Robertson (n.d.). "Remoteness and Unbalanced Growth: Understanding Divergence Across Indian Districts", *Working Paper* no. 268.New Delhi; ICRIER.

Das-Gupta, Arindam (2007). "Corruption", in K. Basu (ed.), *Oxford Companion to Economics in India*. New Delhi: Oxford University Press.

Deshpande, Ashwini (2013). "Entrepreneurship or Survival? Caste and Gender in Small Business in India", *Economic and Political Weekly* 48(28).

Dev, S. Mahendra (2008). *Inclusive Growth in India: Agriculture, Poverty and Human Development*. New Delhi: Oxford University Press.

Dev, S. Mahendra and C. Ravi (2008). "Poverty and Inequality: All India and States, 1983-2005", *Economic and Political Weekly* 43(10).

Dixit, Avinash K. (2016). "Corruption: Supply side and Demand side Solutions", in S. Mahendra Dev and P.G. Babu (ed.), *Development in India: Micro and Macro Perspectives*. New Delhi: Springer.

Dreze, J. and Amartya Sen (2013). *An Uncertain Glory: India and its Contradictions*. Princeton University Press.

Dubey, Amaresh (2016). *Growth, Poverty and Inequality in India*. PowerPoint presentation. GIGA, Hamburg, Germany.

Ghose, Ajit (2016). *India Employment Report 2016*. Oxford University Press.

Ghosh, M., A. Ghoshray and I. Malki (2013). "Regional Divergence and Club Convergence in India", *Economic Modelling* 30(1): 733-742.

Himanshu (2015). "Inequality in India", *Seminar* 672, August.

Herring, R.J. and Rex M. Edwards (1983). "Guaranteeing Employment to the Rural Poor: Social Functions and Class Interests in the Employment Guarantee Scheme in Western India", *World Development* 11(7): 575-92.

Institute for Human Development (IHD) (2014). *India: Labour and Employment Report 2014*. Delhi.

International Labour Organization (ILO) (2014). *Global Employment Trends 2014: Risk of Jobless Recovery*. Geneva.

Jain-Chandra, S., T. Kinda, K. Kocchar, S. Piao and J. Schauer (2016). *Sharing the Growth Dividend: Analysis of Inequality in Asia*.

Jodka, S.S. and D. Vaid (2015). "The Problem", posed in Seminar magazine symposium on "Emerging Patterns of Social Inequality in India", *Seminar* 672. New Delhi.

Kanbur, R., C. Rhee, and J. Zhuang (2014). "Introduction", in R. Kanbur, C. Rhee, and J. Zhuang (eds.), *Inequality in Asia and the Pacific*. Asian Development Bank and Routledge.

Kanbur, R., C. Rhee, and J. Zhuang (eds.) (2014). *Inequality in Asia and the Pacific*. Asian Development Bank and Routledge.

Kuznets, S. (1955). "Economic Growth and Income Inequality", *American Economic Review* 95(1).

Kurien, C.T. (1986). 'Reconciling Growth and Social Justice: Strategies vs. Structure", in M.L. Dantwala et al. (eds.), *Asian Seminar on Rural Development: The Indian Experience*. New Delhi: Oxford & IBH Publishing Co Pvt. Ltd.

Milanovic, Branko (2016). *Global Inequality: A New Approach for the Age of Globalization*. The Belknap Press of Harvard University Press.

Motiram, Sripad and V. Vakulabharanam (2013). "Indian Inequality: Patterns and Changes, 1993-2010", in S. Mahendra Dev (ed.), *India Development Report 2012-13*. New Delhi: Oxford University Press.

Muralidharan, Kartik (2013). "Priorities for Primary education Policy in India's 12th Five Year Plan", *India Policy Forum 2013*. New Delhi: NCAER-Brookings.

Nandy, Amrita and Rohini Hensman (2015). "The Work Women Do", *Indian Express*, 7 November.

Nayyar, Deepak (ed.) (2013). *Macroeconomics and Human Development*. London: Taylor and Francis.

Panagariya, Arvind and Vishal More (2013). "Poverty by Social, Religious & Economic Groups in India and its Large States: 1993-94 to 2011-12", *Working Paper* No.2013-02. USA: Columbia University, Program on Indian Economic Policies.

Piketty, Thomas (2014). *Capital in the Twenty-First Century*. London: The Belknap Press of Harvard University Press.

Planning Commission (2012). *Twelfth Five Year Plan*. Government of India.

Radhakrishna, R. (2015). "Well-being, Inequality, Poverty and Pathways Out of Poverty in India", *Economic and Political Weekly* 50(41).

Rangarajan, C. and S. Mahendra Dev (2016). "A Higher Well Being", *Indian Express*, 29 April.

Rao, C.H. Hanumantha (2009). "Inclusive Growth: Recent Experiences and Challenges Ahead", *Economic and Political Weekly* 44(13).

Rao, V.K.R.V. (1978). "Has Rural Poverty Increased in India", *R.S. Dubhashi Memorial Lecture*. 19 January. University of Poona, Pune.

Ravallion, M.(2003). "The Debate on Globalisation, Poverty & Inequality: Why Measurement Matters", *World Bank Policy Research Working Paper* 3038.

Rawal, Vikas (2008). "Ownership of Land in Rural India: Putting the Record Straight", *Economic and Political Weekly* 43(10).

———. (2013). "Changes in the Distribution of Operational land holdings in Rural India: A Study of National Sample Survey Data", *Review of Agrarian Studies* 3(2). July 2013-January 2014.

Rawls, John (1971). *A Theory of Justice*. Cambridge, MA: Harvard University Press.

Ray, Debraj (2016). *Universal Basic Share*. Ideas for India. *www.ideasforindia.in*

Sandimo, Agnar (2015). "The Principal Problem in Political Economy: Income Distribution in the History of Economic Thought", in A.B. Atkinson, A.B. and F. Bourguignon (ed), *Hand Book of Economics*. Vol. 2A and 2B. North-Holland, U.K.; Elsevier.

Sen, Amartya (1973). *On Economic Inequality*. Oxford: Oxford University Press.

Sen, Abhijit and Himanshu (2004). "Poverty and Inequality in India", *Economic and Political Weekly* 39(38, 39).

Son, H.H. (2014). "Inequality of human opportunities in developing Asia", in R. Kanbur, C. Rhee, and J. Zhuang (eds.), *Inequality in Asia and the Pacific*. Asian Development Bank and Routledge.

Sridharan, Eswaran (2014). "India: Democracy and Corruption", *Democracy Works Conference Paper*. A project of Legatum Institute, London and Centre for Development and Enterprise, South Africa.

Srinivasan, T.N. (2013). "Planning, Poverty and Political Economy of Reforms: A Tribute to Suresh Tendulkar", *Indian Economic Review* (Special Issue on "Perspectives on Economic Development and Policy") XLVIII(1): 167-88.

———. (2016). *Minimum Standard of Living for All Indian. www.ideasforindia.in*

Subramanian, S. and D. Jayaraj (2016). "The Quintile Income Statistic, Money-metric Poverty, and Disequalising Growth in India: 1983 to 2011-12", *Economic and Political Weekly* 51(5).

Suryanarayana, M.H. (2013). "Promoting Human Development In India", in S. Mahendra Dev (ed.), *India Development Report, 2012-13*. New Delhi: Oxford University Press.

Tendulkar, S.D. (2010). "Inequality and Equity during Rapid Growth Process", in Shankar Acharya and Rakesh Mohan. *Indian Economy: Performances and Challenges: Essays in Honour of Montek Singh Ahluwalia*. New Delhi: Oxford University Press.

Thapa, G. and R. Gaiha (2011). "Smallholder Farming in Asia and the Pacific: Challenges and Opportunities", Paper presented at the *Conference on New Directions for Small holder Agriculture*, 24-25 January, Rome, IFAD

Thorat, Sukhadeo and Paul Attewell (2010). 'The Legacy of Social Exclusion: A Correspondence Study of Job Discrimination in India's Urban Private Sector", in Sukhadeo Thorat and Katherine S. Newman (eds.), *Blocked by Caste: Economic Discrimination in Modern India*. New Delhi: Oxford University Press.

Triesman, D. (2007). "What have we Learned about the Causes of Corruption from Ten Years of Cross-National Empirical Research?", *Annual Review of Political Science* 10: 211-244.

UNDP (2015). *Round Table: Intersectional Inequality, Perspectives from South Asia, Summary of Discussions*. February. New Delhi.

Vaidyanathan, A. (2009). *Role of Technology, Incentives and Institutions*. Oxford University Press.

Vyas, V.S. (2016). "Changing Role of Government in Indian Agriculture", L.S. *Venkataraman Lecture*, Institute for Social and Economic Change, Bangalore.

World Bank (2016). "Taking on Inequality", *Poverty and Shared Poverty 2016*. Washington DC.

Zhuang, J. R. Kanbur and C. Rhee (2014). "What Drives Asia's Rising Inequality?", in R. Kanbur, C. Rhee, and J. Zhuang (eds.), *Inequality in Asia and the Pacific*. Asian Development Bank and Routledge.

8

Growing Regional Inequality in Development in India

Recent Experience and the Way Forward

C.H. HANUMANTHA RAO

Shri Raj Kapila had an excellent training in the Delhi School of Economics under the guidance of some of the leading economists in the country. His intellectual interests were wide-ranging, but his interest in economic policy issues was foremost and abiding among them. He was independent-minded in his thinking as well as articulation. This perhaps explains why he could not stay for long with his assignments in the government or the private sector. He subsequently got into economic journalism on his own which gave him full freedom of thought and expression. This, combined with his academic interests, culminated in the birth of Academic Foundation which, under his leadership and the diligent work of the cohesive family that he nurtured, has grown into a premier publisher of books in social sciences, particularly in economics, in the country with the leading authorities on the subject availing this opportunity. This paper is an humble tribute to the memory of a long-standing and genial friend.

I

Growing Regional Inequality in Development

It is now well established that the inter-state inequality in the growth of GSDP (gross state domestic product) has increased in the post-economic reform period beginning from the early 1990s when compared to the 1980s. In general, the richer states have grown faster than the poorer states (Ahluwalia 2000, Dev and Ravi 2003, Bhattacharya and Sakthivel 2004). The regional inequality in per capita GSDP growth is even greater because the poorer states in general have experienced a faster growth in population. The exercise on regional equality presented by the Planning Commission in the Twelfth Plan confirms this position, notwithstanding the recent acceleration in the GSDP growth rates of some poorer states, including especially Bihar, and rise in the ratio of their average growth rates to the All India average growth rate (Planning Commission 2012). This position is also confirmed by the GoI's latest *Economic Survey 2016-17* (Government of India 2017) as well as *OECD Economic Survey for India* (OECD February 2017).

Although these disparities have accentuated in the post-reform period, they have been building up in the pre-reform period itself. For example, according to Central Statistics Office (CSO) data, in the early 1960s, the per capita GSDP of the richer states like Punjab, Maharashtra and Gujarat was, on an average, about 80 per cent higher than the average per capita GSDP of the bottom four states viz., Bihar, Uttar Pradesh (UP), Orissa and Madhya Pradesh (MP). This disparity increased to 125 per cent by the early 1970s (Rao 2005), was contained at a little over 100 per cent during the 1980s, but escalated steeply to 156 per cent towards the mid-1990s (1993-1996), and further to 176 per cent during 2007-2010.

States whose per capita GSDP is below the national average together account for over 60 per cent of the country's population and as high as 75 per cent of the country's population below the poverty line. Further, these states account for nearly 60 per cent of the population belonging to the socio-economically disadvantaged sections like SCs (scheduled castes) and STs (scheduled tribes). There is thus a large potential for growth waiting to be harnessed for sustaining development in the country over a long period, and for improving regional and social equity.

Whereas inter-state disparities in per capita GSDP have increased significantly in the post-reform period, the corresponding disparity in HDI (human development index) has declined. The coefficient of variation in HDI declined from 0.22 in 1981 to 0.19 in 1991 and to 0.16 in 2001. The rise in public expenditure in these sectors was very slow in the poorer states in the post-reform decade (Dev and Mooij 2003). This is reflected in the slower decline in regional disparities in HDI in the post-reform decade.

The estimates from the *India Human Development Report 2011*, show that the coefficient of variation of the HDI for states has fallen sharply between 2000 and 2008, the improvement in HDI for majority of low per capita income states being greater than for India as a whole (Planning Commission 2012). The latest *Economic Survey* as well as the *OECD Economic Survey for India* confirm significant reduction in interstate variation in human development indicators. Therefore, policies towards strengthening this convergence in HDI can be expected to stimulate GSDP growth in the lagging regions in course of time and have a softening impact on regional disparities in per capita GSDP (Ghani 2010).

Causal Factors

Investment

Planning and Public Investment

Investment in physical and human capital, technical change and institutions, including those of governance, are the three key variables usually invoked for explaining the growth performance. A glaring feature of the investment scene in the post-reform period is the steady decline in the rate of public investment and a steep rise in the share of private investment. According to the estimates by the CSO, gross capital formation by the public and private sectors were roughly equal at around 10 per cent of GDP (gross domestic product) each in the early 1980s. But between 2005-06 and 2007-08, public sector investment constituted 8.4 per cent of GDP, while that by the private corporate sector rose to 15.1 per cent and by households to 11.4 per cent (Reserve Bank of India, *Annual Report 2011-12*).

The decline in public investment is even more glaring at the state level where bulk of the public expenditure on irrigation, power and social sectors is incurred. This is indicated by the fact that the share of the states declined from around 50 per cent of total plan expenditure in the country in the 1980s to 40 per cent towards the close of the 1990s.

Within the states, the per capita plan outlays of the poorer states have always been much lower than those of the better-off states. These disparities have widened in the post-reform period. For instance, during the Sixth Plan period (1980-1985), the actual per capita plan expenditure for the poorest four states, on an average, was a little over half of the average per capita plan expenditure of the better-off states like Gujarat, Maharashtra and Punjab. But during the Ninth Plan period (1997-2002), this proportion came down to around 40 per cent.

Central assistance for state plans (including assistance for externally aided projects), which is a major component of state plan resources, has been progressive in that the per capita assistance for the poorer states has been higher than for the richer states. The poorer states have been handicapped basically by their own weaker resource position. The per capita own plan resources of the poorer states, including market borrowing, constituted around 40 per cent of own per capita plan resources of some of the better-off states, viz., Punjab, Maharashtra, Haryana and Kerala during the Sixth Plan period. This ratio deteriorated to 28 per cent in 2003-04 and further to less than 20 per cent in 2004-05.

An important factor responsible for this deterioration in the financial position of the poorer states is the decline in the tax-GDP ratio of the Centre for quite some time in the post-reform period and the consequent decline in the transfers to the states through devolution as recommended by the Finance Commissions. The loss to the states, that is, the difference between the devolution estimated by the Finance Commissions and the actual devolution, amounted to ₹100,000 crore for the decade 1995 to 2005 (Reddy 2005). The decline in per capita transfers to the poorer states was even greater because the formula for devolution by the Finance Commissions is quite progressive. Therefore, the 12th Finance Commission had done well by raising the tax devolution by 1 percentage point (Government of India 2004).

Among states, the correlation between per capita GSDP growth rate in the post-reform period of the 1990s and the index of social and economic infrastructure in 1995 as well as 2000 is positive and significant. Clearly, therefore, the states whose initial or pre-reform conditions were favourable in respect of infrastructure, could benefit more from the opportunities opened up, especially in the service sector, by economic reforms and register higher growth rates in GSDP (Rao and Dev 2003). In the subsequent period, the rank correlation between infrastructure index and per capita income of states was quite high, rising from 0.79 in 1999-2000 to 0.86 and 0.85 in 2007-08 and 2008-2009 respectively (Planning Commission 2012).

Private Investment

Private investment has been higher in high income states where per capita plan outlays have been higher and where, therefore, infrastructure is well developed. For example, according to the IDBI data, the per capita cumulative disbursements by the All India financial institutions up to March 2004, were ₹15 lakh for Maharashtra, ₹14 lakh for Gujarat and ₹7 lakh for Tamil Nadu (TN), as against less than ₹3 lakh for MP, less than ₹2 lakh for UP, and less than half a lakh for Bihar. Similarly, in March 2011, investment plus credit-deposit ratios of SCBs (scheduled commercial banks) (as per utilisation) were high for the Northern (88%), Western (78%) and Southern (106%) regions, and low for the Eastern (61%), Central (57%), and North-Eastern (45%) regions. As to the amount of FDI (foreign direct investment) and FTC (foreign technical cases) approved from August 1991 to December 2006, a few advanced states, viz., Maharashtra, Gujarat, TN, Karnataka and Delhi together accounted for half the share as against the combined share of less than 10 per cent by the four poorest states, viz., Bihar, MP, Orissa and UP (Government of India 2007).

Technical Change

The issue of technical change does not seem to figure prominently in the debate on regional disparities in development in India. This could be partly because much of the technology is embodied in capital equipment and hence is highly correlated with such investment. Also, this may be attributed to the speedy diffusion of frontier technologies like biotechnology and IT (information technology) across regions and even among income groups with large differences in asset endowments, when adequate support services are provided. The success of green revolution in India provides a classic illustration of this process. After the initial success with wheat in the north-western India for a decade beginning from the mid-1960s, it soon spread to different parts of the country by the 1980s covering rice even in the poorer eastern Gangetic plains because of its inherent profitability and relatively low investment requirements.

The experience so far with IT is equally encouraging and holds the prospect for raising productivity enormously in millions of farms and factories of varying sizes and the government offices throughout the country. This experience underlines the need to exploit the potential offered by these emerging technologies as well as human development for giving a fillip to the catching-up process in the less developed areas of the country.

Institutions

Historically, the developed states were, in general, characterised by progressive land tenures like the *Ryotwari* or the *Mahalwari* systems, whereas most of the less developed states were under the exploitative tenures like the *Zamindari* and the *Jagirdari* systems. Many of these areas were under the princely states for a long period. The social structure evolved under progressive land tenures has been conducive to the growth of enterprise and generated incentives for work, whereas the social structure perpetuated by the exploitative land tenures has been inimical to enterprise and bred apathy.

For understanding the causes of backwardness, and for formulating appropriate development strategies, one has to go deeper into the history. For example, for over a century and half before independence, the rate of taxation was very high in the eastern zone and the extraction of surplus was much higher than in many other parts of the country. We know that there has been a significant drain of resources from the country in the colonial period. But there was also a significant inter-regional flow of resources within the country. There was a large net outflow of resources from the eastern region which was partly frittered away in conspicuous consumption and partly invested in other regions in infrastructure like irrigation and transport (Rao 2005). This is how the less developed regions inherited poor infrastructure and outmoded institutions at the time of independence.

Even after independence, the per capita transfer of resources from the Finance Commission as well as the Planning Commission were lower for many of the less developed states for at least two decades when the cost of creating infrastructure was relatively low (Rao 2005). The transfer of resources, especially from the Finance Commissions, have become progressive only after the 1970s. But in a federal democratic polity, there are limits to such statutory transfers, particularly because many of our 'developed' states too are poor in absolute terms.

The role of exploitative or extractive institutions in perpetuating underdevelopment and backwardness, and that of inclusive or progressive institutions in triggering-off sustainable development in countries—otherwise similarly placed geographically and culturally—has been highlighted recently in an insightful and path-breaking work (Acemoglu and Robinson 2012). According to this work, inclusive institutions which promote innovation and enterprise can thrive only under freedom and democracy with opportunities for wider participation of stakeholders in decision-making as well as implementation. Differences in the existing political systems explain the coexistence of backwardness in some countries with development in some others.

The Way Ahead

There is a silver lining in the experience of recently created smaller states, viz., Chhattisgarh, Jharkhand and Uttaranchal, showing that these states achieved growth rates far exceeding the targets set for the Tenth Plan period whereas the performance of their parent states, viz., MP, Bihar and UP fell considerably short of the targets (Planning Commission 2008). Of late, Bihar too has been growing faster because, among other things, it has become smaller and viable following the creation of Jharkhand. Apart from releasing the creative energies of the people, viability of smaller states may have contributed to better governance, attracting greater private investment from outside as well as planning and utilising resources more efficiently (World Bank 2007).

It is clear from the foregoing discussion that for reducing regional disparities in development, improving social and economic infrastructure in the backward regions through greater public investment needs to be given the highest priority in the development strategy. The other two areas of priority action for these regions are: speeding up social transformation through the empowerment of the common people and measures for good governance. The Twelfth Plan proposals on improving governance are promising as they centre round the need for empowering people, strengthening the accountability mechanisms, better coordination between various departments, and enhancing the capabilities at the grass roots level, among other things, by involving voluntary agencies.

In this paper, I have chosen to focus mainly on the interstate disparities in levels of development. However, growing regional disparities within certain states, especially the bigger ones, is a matter of equal concern. For example, the Twelfth Plan in its chapter on Regional Equality noted that:

> Though Maharashtra, Karnataka, and Andhra Pradesh are regarded as rapidly developing States, the fact of the matter is that there are a few pockets within these States which, due to their better physical and social infrastructure, have been able to attract large investments and register a faster rate of economic growth. State-level analysis does not reveal anything about what might be taking place in different regions within States. In fact, intra-state disparities are as much a cause of concern as inter-state disparities (Planning Commission 2012).

It is clear from the development experience and the simmering unrest in several less developed parts of the country that without major initiatives at the national level, the regional disparities in development may accentuate further to crisis proportions threatening social harmony and national integrity, apart from depriving the nation of the opportunities for higher, equitable and sustainable development.

The current debate on 'good governance' in India is largely divorced from the nature of the prevailing social structure and the need to generate socioeconomic impulses for its transformation. As such, it comes out essentially with technocratic prescriptions regarding good governance in the poorer states as a prerequisite for attracting greater investment flows and for stepping up growth through the efficient use of resources. It underplays the role of factors like investment in infrastructure, technical change for raising the profitability of investment and making governance accountable to the people by empowering them through the PRIs (panchayati raj institutions) for triggering-off the desirable changes in the prevailing socio-economic structure, which is the root cause of poor governance and inefficient delivery systems in the less developed areas.

Governance is not simply a matter of particular administrative arrangements, procedures, monitoring, etc. In view of the all-pervading influence of the prevailing social structure on decision-making as well as implementation processes, governance has to be shaped in the context of ongoing social change through the functioning of our democratic system. It is wrong to attribute the existing deficiencies in decision-making and tardiness in implementation to the prevailing democratic system as such. Rather, they can be traced to the way the functioning of our democracy has been twisted and moulded by the pulls and pressures from the vested interests. Unlike in mature western democracies where democratic institutions evolved in the course of radical social transformation over a long period, in India the institutions of democracy were adopted even as the traditional and iniquitous social structure remained largely intact. In our situation, therefore, democracy and state power have to become instruments for social transformation. This requires broadening and deepening of our democracy by effectively extending it to the grass roots.

Experience has amply demonstrated that participatory or inclusive governance is indispensable for achieving inclusive growth. This is woefully lacking at the grass root levels where the formulation of schemes is not quite in keeping with the local needs and circumstances, and administration is not accountable to the people. It is precisely to cope with such challenges that *panchayati raj* was visualised by the late Prime Minister Rajiv Gandhi.

Thanks to the 73rd and 74th amendments to the Constitution, elected *panchayats* have been in place. But they are deprived of necessary functions, finances and functionaries. No serious effort has been made so far to devolve such powers, not to speak of any effort to build up local capabilities by training the elected functionaries. On the other hand, certain state governments have been active in pursuing top-down development and governance by floating numerous schemes and parallel implementation structures which cut at the very root of PRIs. This is explained solely by the resistance from the entrenched interests to part with their powers. Therefore, the change in attitudes has necessarily to be driven by the political process.

It is naïve to expect a genuinely inclusive governance without inclusive politics or empowerment of social groups hitherto not having access to political power at different levels. The recent decision of the Central government to enhance reservation for women in local bodies to 50 per cent and the ongoing efforts to provide 33 per cent reservation for women in parliament and state legislative bodies, when successful, should go a long way towards ensuring inclusive growth through inclusive politics and governance.

References

Acemoglu, Daron and James A. Robinson (2012). *Why Nations Fail: The Origins of Power, Prosperity and Poverty.* London; Profile Books Ltd.

Ahluwalia, Montek S. (2000). "Economic Performance of States in Post-Reform Period', *Economic and Political Weekly*, 6 May.

Bhattacharya, B.B. and S. Sakthivel (2004). "Regional Growth and Disparity in India: Comparison of Pre- and Post-Reform Decades", *Economic and Political Weekly* 29(10), 6 March.

Dev, S.M. and C. Ravi (2003). "Macroeconomic Scene: Performance and Policies", in C.H.H. Rao and S. Mahendra Dev (eds.), *Andhra Pradesh Development: Economic Reforms and Challenges Ahead.* Hyderabad: Centre for Economic and Social Studies.

Dev, S.M. and Jos Mooij (2003). "Patterns in Social Sector Expenditure: Pre- and Post-Reform Period". (*mimeo*). Hyerabad; Centre for Economic and Social Studies.

Ghani, Ejaz (ed.) (2010). *The Poor Half Billion in South Asia: What is Holding Back Lagging Regions?* New Delhi: The World Bank and Oxford University Press.

Government of India (2017). *Economic Survey 2016-17*. Ministry of Finance.

———. (2007). *Handbook of Industrial Policy and Statistics, 2006-07*. Department of Industrial Policy and Promotion

———. (2004). *Report of the Twelfth Finance Commission (2005-10)*.

OECD (2017). *OECD Economic Surveys: India 2017*. New Delhi; Academic Foundation.

Planning Commission (2012). *Twelfth Five Year Plan (2012-2017)*. Government of India.

———. (2008). *Eleventh Five Year Plan (2007-2012)*. Vols. I & III. Government of India.

Rao, C.H.H. (2005). *Essays on Development Strategy, Regional Disparities and Centre-State Financial Relations in India*. New Delhi: Academic Foundation.

Rao, C.H.H. and S. Mahendra Dev (2003). "Economic Reforms and Challenges Ahead: An Overview", in C.H.H. Rao and S. Mahendra Dev (eds.), *Andhra Pradesh Development: Economic Reforms and Challenges Ahead*. Hyderabad; Centre for Economic and Social Studies.

Reddy, G.R. (2005). "Twelfth Finance Commission and Backward States", *Economic and Political Weekly* XLI(32), 12-18 August 2006.

World Bank (2007). *Jharkhand: Addressing the Challenges of Inclusive Development*. Rural Poverty and Economic Management, India Country Management Unit, South Asia.

9

Leveraging the Demographic Dividend

YOGINDER K. ALAGH

I am happy that a volume is being brought out in the memory of my friend Raj Kapila. Decades of academic experience had taught him the need to make knowledge available to generations of students, researchers and college teachers. He knew that dated information in Economics was losing interest. At the same time, good ideas persisted with tenacity. He developed the skills of product differentiation in the knowledge market and of course was eminently successful. He made the reputation of many scholars and in turn they stood by him.

Introduction

It has been a long journey from 'population problem' to 'demographic dividend', and from 'surplus labour' to 'skill development'. Some of us have not changed the vision and have always held that mouths are also born with hands and capabilities latent to be developed. But it would be naïve to pretend that the problématique is not severe any more. Dividends can become losses and there is nothing more frustrating than unrequited skills. The fact that planning has been abolished means that population studies are now on the back burner.

There is a connection between employment and poverty, and poverty has definitely gone down. Yet, a point we had made in the late 1980s, while setting up the Lakdawala Committee, that poverty debate has to shift from the so called Official Poverty Line (OPL),[1] is still on the agenda including in a recent report by Arvind Panagriya.[2] This however needs remedying. What we need is a new definition of the minimum requirements of the '*aam aadmi*'.

Population Projections

Now that planning has been abolished, there seems to be no urgency in making population projections. Although, the Expert Group of the Registrar General of the Census is working on it, the results are not yet here. The Eleventh Fiver-year Plan did not have a separate population projection exercise, but in one of its sections the numbers were given which are provided in Table 9.1

Table 9.1

Population Projections in the Eleventh Five-Year Plan

Year	*Population*
2011-12	1,208 million
2016-17	1,283 million

Source: GoI (2008). *Eleventh Plan.* Volume 1. New Delhi: Planning Commission. p.75.

As compared to these estimates, India's most distinguished and experienced demographer, P.N. Marie Bhat, estimated that the growth rate of population would go down from 1.52 per cent per annum during the decade 2001-2011 to 1.25 per cent per annum during 2011-2021. This would imply a population level of 1.345.38 million by 2020, which is higher. Demographer Tim Dyson, who has been working on India's demography, estimates India's population at 1,271 million in 2020 in his standard projection, and his (high) projection is close to the figures estimated by Bhat (Dyson 2003a, 2003b). These alternate estimates suggest that population and therefore the future demand projections have a degree of uncertainty

1. The term OPL was designed in the 1970s by a Task Force with an emphasis on calorie intake. OPL is sometimes described as the Alagh Poverty Line also.
2. Government appointed task force headed by NITI Aayog Vice-Chairman Arvind Panagariya to prepare a road map for elimination of poverty.

attached to them. However, it needs to be noted that India's humongous population is now seen as an asset—demographic dividend—in its growth process (Alagh 2006b). As compared to our official figures, certain FAO publications have recently used slightly higher projections (see Table 9.2).

Table 9.2

FAO Population Projections

Year	*Population (in billions)*
2000	1.0
2015	1.2
2030	1.4

Source: FAO (2006) as quoted in FAO (2008: 24).

There is genuine uncertainty about the future of India's population. As compared to the past (Alagh 1991), our policies now do not have much interest in the so-called 'long term' matters.

Demographic Dividend

The sections on demographic dividends in the Eleventh and Twelfth Five-year Plan, and the Economic Survey were professionally disappointing. A part of the problem was that these plans did not have perspectives and long term vision. As Kirit Parikh said in an official history of plan modeling, we now rely on the private sector for future studies. Following this to a logical conclusion, planning has been abolished by the National Democratic Alliance (NDA) government.

In the early work on demographic dividends, Goldman Sachs and their then brand ambassador, Roopa Purshotama (2003), told the World that not only was India growing but its population was an asset. They were right, but not necessarily for the right reasons. Growth needs to be long-term, holistic, sustainable and all inclusive. It should percolate and trickle down to the lowest strata of the economy. When population is poor, hungry, unemployed, or unhealthy, they are certainly not an asset.

P.N. Marie Bhat had shown that where labour force grows faster than population, dependency ratio goes down, savings rise, women participation in workforce increases as fertility rates go down. Historically, we have known that population growth is associated with economic growth and we were keen to model population into our development plans. These earlier lessons were however, forgotten.

> The integration of population factors into the technical work of development planning in Indian context can be considered at two levels. The first level is the integration of population factors explicitly into development planning models. The second level is the integration of population factors into the planning of social services. In research studies and in official statements relating to population policies reflecting socio-political aspirations, the integration of population factors into development policy in an interactive framework has been strongly urged. But in formal planning work, population factors generally enter explicitly exogenously. Recently, interesting experimental studies have been done, however, in which the relationship between population planning and socio-economic factors has been estimated in some level of detail. The pursuit of such work would finally lead to the use of population factors in an endogenous framework in development planning models....Population projections play an important role at the macro level and in sectoral plans at the national level...population estimates have an important impact on the commodity planning for sectors such as food-grains, edible oils and clothing. The Indian estimates for the consumption sectors are made separately for the rural and urban population and integrated into the national plan models. Such population projections, therefore, play an important role in projections of demand for consumer goods..... Based on data collected through both the Census and also sample surveys conducted by the National Sample Survey Organisation, labour force participation rates are estimated and used for the national planning framework.... In the Indian federal policy population projections play a very important

> role for estimating the demand for social services at the state (provincial or regional level) and district (sub-regional level) planning. Such projections are important for education and health targets. They have also been used for estimating water supply and sanitation programmes and the need for welfare programmes. The national Programme of Minimum Needs is dependent on the population projections, particularly in critical areas such as primary education and health planning (Alagh 1980 quoted in UN 1981: 119-120).

It can be shown that some consequences of demographic variables are truisms. But even these vary depending on parameter values taken. Others depend on assumptions, which have hidden policies behind them. Projection models, particularly of the BRICSAM[3] variety, derive demographic dividends from 'inevitable' consequences of fertility patterns, age structure of populations and labour force and savings consequences. Results are striking. These projections are becoming fashionable and it is important to assess which of the results are robust and why? Some consequences may turn out correct, but for wrong reasons. Future is not inevitable; dividends will be garnered by the brave who have an operating strategic vision of human resource development.

Future Possibilities

Some analysis of the possibilities arising from the changing age structure of the population will be useful. The differences between say India and rest of the world are large. We can infer from Table 9.2 that retirees are thrice more than workers (also children) in Japan/Spain as compared to India, consequently 4.4 workers would support a retiree in India as compared to 1.4 in Japan/ Spain. The difference in savings and demand led growth will obviously create large imbalances. Econometrics, however, also teaches us the frailty of long term projections. Even if output per worker does not change, output per capita

3. BRICSAM countries: Brazil, Russia, India, Indonesia, China, South Africa and Mexico.

would grow if the growth rate of workers exceeds the growth rate of total population (the difference between the two growth rates being critical). This is the substantial demographic dividend and its robustness comes from the fact that it takes place even if workers' productivity growth does not rise.

Table 9.3

Possibilities? Scenarios 2050

Country	Dependency Ratio	Support Ratio	Ageing Index	Growth Rate %
India	22.6	4.4	105.1	0.4
US	34.6	2.9	144.9	0.5
UK	73.3	2.1	226.7	(0.3)
Japan	71.3	1.4	338.2	(0.6)
Singapore	50.0	2.0	258.8	(0.6)
Spain	73.8	1.4	386.4	(0.6)
China	37.2	2.7	183.3	(0.3)

Table 9.4

Projected Difference in the Growth Rate of Population Aged 15-64 and Growth Rate of Total Population, 1991 to 2031

Decade	1991-01	2001-11	2011-21	2021-31
All-India	0.35	0.56	0.43	0.07

The difference between the growth rate of working-age population (15-64) and the growth rate of total population as worked out by Marie Bhat can be seen in Figure 9.1.

There is also the effect on the saving ratio because of changing dependency burden. If the dependency ratio is low, the savings rate would rise and therefore the growth rate. For measuring this, the relation $\Delta s = -\Delta d(1-s)/(1+d)$, is derived where s is the savings rate and d is the dependency ratio. However, societies are known to have increased savings rates even when the dependency burden is rising, Therefore, the relationship is possibly more complex, and factors like joint families and estate motives also need to be studied.

Figure 9.1

Growth Rate of Total Population Under Optimistic and Realistic Scenarios: 1955-2055

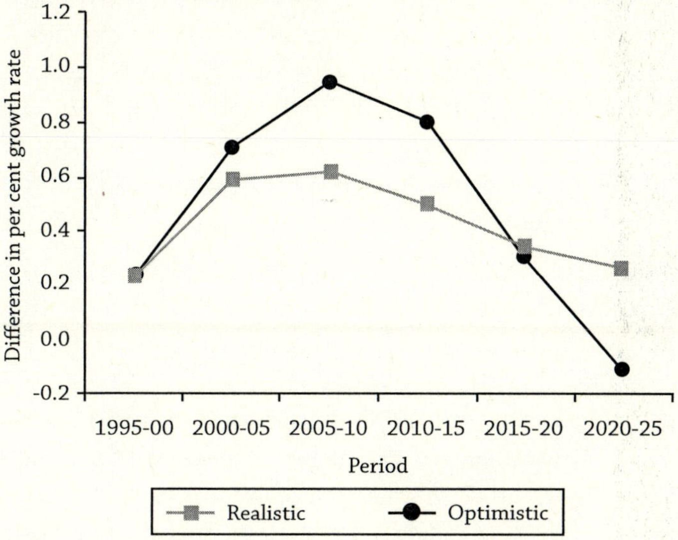

Figure 9.2

Relationship between Dependency and Savings Ratios in India

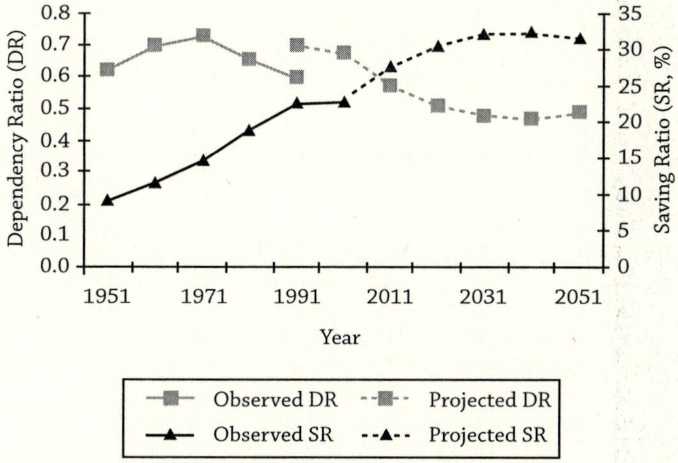

To summarise, demographic dividend[4] will not be achieved on its own. If we misuse land, water and energy,

4. For the author's technical assessment of demographic dividend models for India, see his invited paper in the IMF/ADB/Bank Indonesia volume on Global Imbalances (Alagh 2006a, Simongarkir 2008).

and do not generate sufficient employment, the growing population will not be a bonus. Take the case of women participation in the labour force. When demographic transition nears completion in India, the age at first birth would be 21-22 years (less than 20 now) and the age at last birth would be around 28 years (38 now). Women could then be expected to enter the labour force in large numbers. This structural change in the composition of labour force due to the changing age structure will neither happen automatically nor will it be easy to achieve in our highly dominant patriarchal society.

Mazumdar and Sarkar (2006) estimated that contrasted from the 1980s when employment went up, "the employment loss in subsidiary employment for females between 1993/94 and 2000 is 4.88 million just in cereal growing." If we mess up agriculture, we will be faced with negative dividend of women withdrawing from the labor force. But societies respond to crisis. In fact the latest NSS data show subsidiary employment of women rising in agriculture during the period 1999/2000 to 2004/05, presumably reflecting the improvement of the agricultural growth rate and its diversification. To reap the benefits of demographic dividend, State and society needs to work collectively and progressively.

References and Readings

Alagh.Yoginder K. (2006). "India 2020", *Journal of Quantitative Economics* (New Series) 4(1): 1-14, January.

———. (2006a). "Demographic Dividend: Possibilities and Realities", Presented at *Seminar on Global Imbalances and their Impacts on Emerging Economies.* Reprinted in Iskandar Simorangkir (ed.) (2008). *Global Imbalances and their Impacts on Emerging Market Economies.* Denpasaar, Bali; IMF, ADB and Bank of Indonesia. pp.310-16

———. (2005). "Development Policy and Governance", *Indian Economic Journal*: 3-13, April.

———. (2004). "Poverty, Food Security and Human Security", in Bibek Debroy and Rahul Mukherji (ed.), *India: The Political Economy of Reforms.* New Delhi: Rajiv Gandhi Institute of Contemporary Studies. pp.159-84.

———. (1995). "Development Models: The Next Phase", *Sankhya Series A, Indian Journal of Pure and Applied Mathematics* 26(6). Reprinted in B.L.S. Prakasa Rao (ed.) (1996), *Statistics and its Applications: Essays in Honour of P.C. Mahalanobis.* New Delhi: Indian National Science Academy.

———. (1991). "Population and Development Planning", *Anvesak* 21(2): 53-98, December.

———. (1979). *The Importance of Integrating Population Components into Development Models.* UN, DIESA. pp.119-22.

Bhat, P.N. Marie (1998). "Demographic Estimates for Post Independence India: A New Integration", *Demography India* 27(1): 23-57.

———. (2000). *General Growth Balance Method as an Integrated Procedure for Evaluation of Completeness of Censuses and Registration Systems: A Case Study of India 1971-1991.* Delhi: Institute of Economic Growth

Bloom, David E. and Jeffery G. Williamson (1998). "Demographic Transitions and Economic Miracles in Emerging Asia", *The World Bank Economic Review* 12(3): 419-55.

Datta, K.L. (2006). "The Debate on the Poverty Estimates of 1999-2000", *Working Paper* No.188. Delhi: ICRIER.

Dyson, T. (2003a). "New Population Projections for India", *Wellcome Trust India Project Paper* No.1. London: London School of Economics.

———. (2003b). "India's Population: The Future", in T. Dyson, R. Cassen and L. Visaria (ed.), *Population, Environment and Human Development*, Oxford: OUP.

Dyson, T., R. Cassen and L. Visaria (ed.) (2003). *Population, Environment and Human Development*, Oxford: OUP.

Government of India (1979). *Report of The Task Force on Projections of Minimum Needs and Effective Consumption Demand.* New Delhi, Perspective Planning Division, Planning Commission.

Lakadawala, D.T. (1977). "Presidential Address", to the Indian Labour Economics Conference, Tirupati.

Mazumdar D. and Sandip Sarkar (2006). *Accounting for the Decline in Labor Supply in the Nineties: Meeting the Employment Challenge*, New Delhi: Institute for Human Development and World Bank, India. July.

NITI Aayog (2016) "Eliminating Poverty: Creating Jobs and Strengthening Social Programs", *Occasional Paper* No. 2. Government of India.

Subramanian, S. (2005). "Unravelling a Conceptual Muddle: India's Poverty Statistics in the Light of Basic Demand Theory", *Economic and Political Weekly*; 57-66, 1 January.

United Nations (1981). "Population and Development Modelling: Proceedings of the United Nations/UNFPA Expert Group Meeting", *Population Studies* No. 73. New York: Department of International Economic and Social Affairs.

Wilson, D. and Roopa Purshottaman (2003). "Dreaming With BRICs: The Path to 2050", *Global Economics Paper* 99. New York: Goldman Sachs.

Wold, H., and L. Jureen (1953). *Demand Analysis.* Amsterdam, North Holland.

10

Indian Economy

New Challenges and Opportunities

Y.V. REDDY[1]

Raj Kapila has done a service to the academia and policy making, by conceptualising and launching successfully the Academic Foundation. It is a testimony to his vision, his devotion to the causes he believed in and his capacity to build an institution. Raj along with Uma, Rituraj and Sanu, have demonstrated what a family means in our tradition. Having contributed several pieces for publications by Kapilas as author and being a reader of some of the literature from Academic Foundation, I am happy to write this paper as a tribute to commemorate the lasting memory of Raj Kapila.

Raj Kapila founded Academic Foundation in 1990, the year which witnessed the beginning of balance of payments crisis leading to reform in 1991. After 25 years, we are witnessing new challenges arising out of the recent policy initiatives that are full of promise but not without risks. The impressive policy initiatives since mid-2014 are: demonetisation; fiscal-monetary policy interface; fiscal federalism; banking sector and external sector.

As a prelude to the analysis of each of the new policies, it is useful to recognise the persisting challenges which continue to be important, and should always be kept in mind.

---

1. The author acknowledges the valuable assistance of Mr Pradeep Kamble of Centre for Economic and Social Studies (CESS), Hyderabad.

Persisting Challenges

Macroeconomic indicators since reform of 1990s are a source of comfort, but in qualitative terms there are continuing concerns in other areas. The human development indicators which are important, even if not the only indicators of well-being, show that we rank very low in the world (Table 10.1). The coverage of health facilities and the quality of education are dismal by all accounts, though there are islands of excellence. Our physical infrastructure is by all accounts closer to the poorer developing countries, than middle income countries. On matters relating to energy and water, shortages persist. The inequalities among the regions and between various segments of population continue to widen. Disturbing factors that are extremely difficult to reverse even in the long term are environmental degradation and collapse of educational system. Above all, the capacities of public institutions seem to be deteriorating. The size of the government has shrunk since reform while the quality of governance appears to be deteriorating.

We should be equally aware of the advantages that we have (Table 10.2). These include a robust political system; a strong private sector; and high level of household savings. Demographic transition is taking place in different parts of the country at different periods of time, and hence the demographic transition is likely to be smoother for us than for other countries. There is a widespread recognition that to take advantage of our strengths and overcome persistent challenges, the capacity of the government to govern should be enhanced while addressing issues relating to corruption and black money.

Demonetisation and Beyond: 2016

Demonetisation is essentially the process by which currency of specified denomination or series are declared to be no longer a legal tender and are replaced by new currency. Demonetisation of 2016 went beyond the normal objectives and sought to curb black money and corruption. The process covered a large segment of the currency in circulation, lasted several weeks and affected the whole population. During the process of implementation of demonetisation, digitalisation of payment transactions accelerated significantly. The unintended consequence is a quantum jump in digitalisation which was reinforced by policies of government. There are downsides to digitalisation, which demand vigilance, but they do not deter its benign impact on modernisation of our economy mainly by formalising semi-informal sector and reducing transaction costs. An unintended and incidental consequence of demonetisation is the new age digital economy of India.

The short term economic impact of demonetisation has been negligible as per data available so far. Its direct and immediate impact on black money and corruption is similarly negligible as per indications so far. Yet, it is not a mere shock akin to a truckers' strike but has systemic implications for the future.

First, as mentioned, there is an irreversible quantum jump in digitalisation.

Second, there is a massive popular mandate in the form of no protest from people at the inconvenience caused by it to the Government to fight corruption and black money. This should have impact on behaviour of the people associated with such nefarious activities.

Third, demonetisation was in a way continuation of a package of measures relating to *benami* transactions, black money, and money stashed abroad. The follow-up in the recent budget has strengthened the regulatory powers of tax-administration.

Finally, there is a strong and massive support for reforms that address these systemic problems that were at one time considered intractable.

Way forward, there are three important sources of risk.

First, there is an asymmetry in the treatment of the parties to generation of black money. Black money is generated when some citizens violate the law; the governmental agencies, especially tax authorities are less than effective and related agencies involved in governance, such as bankers, auditors, and corporate lawyers collude in the process. If punitive action is directed at one of the parties, namely, the citizen, the other players gain strength in the game. In that case, their relative shares in the illegal gains may change, but the game and illegal gains will not end.

Second, evidence so far with enactments like Foreign Exchange Regulation Act, shows that severity of punishment by itself does not serve the intended purpose. Often, it is counter-productive and even jeopardises genuine economic activity. Administering punishment is not cost free and the intended benefits of punishment are often overestimated. The net result could undermine genuine market forces by promoting arbitrariness rather than rule of law.

Third, approach to black money or corruption would be appealing to the masses if it were in the nature of severe punishment, but it will be effective only if it addresses the causes of generation of black money and its perpetuation. The causes range from unrealistic laws (such as prohibition of gold imports and restrictions on trading in gold) to petty corruption for rendering services that a citizen is entitled to, since there is no reliable recourse to redressal. In the absence of fundamental changes in governance that would enhance efficiency and integrity of governmental machinery, there is a serious risk of loss of credibility of the fight against black money and corruption.

Fiscal Monetary Interface

A landmark development in macroeconomic management is a new monetary policy framework. The government made a formal commitment to inflation targetting in the budget announcement of 2016. The main features of inflation targetting framework are that there is a single target, viz., inflation, and a single instrument used by the central bank, viz., short term interest rate, and a single objective, viz., price stability. This new framework replaced the multiple indicator approach, the multiple objectives with flexible inter se prioritisation and multiple instruments.

A Monetary Policy Committee (MPC) has been constituted as part of new framework, which is entrusted with the task of deciding on the benchmark policy rate (repo rate) required to contain inflation within the specified target level. This replaces the earlier arrangement whereby the Governor under the overall guidance of the Central Board of Reserve Bank of India (RBI) determined the policy measures in consultation with a Technical Advisory Committee on Monetary Policy, voluntarily constituted by the Governor. In some ways, the MPC is continuation of Technical Advisory Committee on Monetary Policy and the inflation targetting framework is a continuation of the self-imposed inflation target of the past. However, the new arrangements provide for a greater transparency, better focus and firm commitment to price stability.

With this regime, monetary policy framework is subject to rules and thus constitutes a supplement to the rule based fiscal management established through Fiscal Responsibility and Budget Management (FRBM) Act about 10 years ago. The new framework has several advantages in terms of transparency, focus, accountability, autonomy and predictability.

At the same time, it has risks that arise out of the complexities in the actual conduct of policy in Indian conditions.

Firstly, there is a risk of neglect of other objectives which may be crucial for macroeconomic management in our country. Experience has shown that for decades our policy space was constrained by scarcity of foreign exchange. Experience has also shown that external sector balance is very critical to us. There is also a temptation to contain inflation by allowing overvalued exchange rate. The stability in terms of external sector is a matter in which RBI, more than any other institution, has focus, expertise and capacity.

Secondly, regulation of banks has traditionally been closely aligned and coordinated with the monetary policy measures. The new framework does not guarantee or envisage such coordination.

Thirdly, there is a potential risk of loss of credibility of the RBI since the tools at its disposal are grossly inadequate to deliver the targets. For example, major components of consumer price inflation are food and fuel. However, a change in the prices of both food and fuel are significantly influenced by the decision of the government on subsidies and taxes in the context of fiscal management. In other words, the prices of these two commodities are virtually determined by the fiscal authorities. Further, the transmission of monetary policy through interest rates has to take place essentially through the banking system. A large part of the banking system is owned by the Government. It does not necessarily respond to the policy instruments operating through impact on balance sheets. Further, the moral suasion in regard to banking system is generally the prerogative of the Central bank, but in our case, this happens essentially through the government.

In order to give effect to inflation targetting frameworks, an institutional arrangement for the new framework, namely, MPC has been established through amendments to the RBI Act. Currently, monetary policies take pride of place in terms of functioning of the RBI. A committee constituted by the Government either with Governor/Deputy Governor concerned, and the members of the committee appointed, is answerable to the Government.

Prime facie, a committee approach has significant advantages over reliance of an individual for monetary policy operations, but much would depend on the manner in which the committee is constituted and the procedures adopted by the committee as well as the arrangements of accountability. These vary among countries and there is no set model. It is therefore necessary to keep a careful watch on the manner in which the committee functions.

As of now, fortunately it has members who command confidence of the system.

There are, however, some issues that arise with this arrangement. The institutional identity of the RBI has become less clear than before. It has been functioning essentially as a full service central bank performing several functions with monetary policy as one of the functions. The new arrangement creates uncertainties about the role of RBI as a monetary authority and the RBI in regard to other functions.

Secondly, the Governor has to be concerned whether he is being assessed by the Government solely with reference to his performance on price front or in regard to other activities of the RBI also. Similarly, the Government will have to take a view on the role of the Governor vis-á-vis the Central Board which, in fact, is vested with running the affairs of the RBI.

Finally, the stature of Governor has been changed since in the new institutional arrangement, he is a member of a Committee presided over by a Government functionary, viz., Cabinet Secretary for selection of members of MPC.

The fiscal policy framework under the FRBM deals with fiscal indicators of Union Government. The state governments, however, account for a significant percentage of the public debt of fiscal deficit every year. Monetary policy is concerned with general government debt and not debt of Union Government alone. In actual operations, the new framework will have to incorporate the fiscal factors of the state governments, in addition to that of Union Governments.

Fiscal-Federalism

The recommendations of the 14th Finance Commission provided a comprehensive framework for reform of Union-State fiscal relations, and in the process, touched upon some fundamental issues relating to institutional arrangements.

First, it eschewed a differentiation between plan and non-plan expenditures, a practice prevalent for decades.

Second, it increased share of state in taxes from 32 per cent to 42 per cent, thus increasing the fiscal space available to states; and correspondingly restricting the discretionary fiscal space to Union. Acceptance of these recommendations meant virtual elimination of process of planning as was understood till then.

Third, sector specific or project specific grants-in-aid from the Union to the States have been eliminated, thus reducing scope for discretion.

Finally, transfers to local bodies were increased and made almost totally free of imposition of conditions.

Three risks have emerged so far partly as a result of the actions taken on the recommendations.

First, the State governments have increased the fiscal deficit, though most of it is attributable to Government of India's indulgence to some States to take care of the problem of power sector. The indulgence to accommodate losses of states on account of power sector is not new and this is third time in 20 years that it is happening.

Second, expenditures of Union Government in regard to social sector have fallen mainly because of the change in burden sharing in regard to central sector schemes between Union and States. The expenditure of Union Government on social sector programme has decreased but that by the States has, from evidence available so far, correspondingly increased.

Third, the recommendations emboldened the states to announce waiver of loans to farmers. No doubt, these states followed example of Union Government's loan waiver of 2008.

The 15th Finance Commission is due to be appointed before the end of the year. The terms of reference of the Commission would also indicate the contours of further changes in fiscal federalism in India.

A historic development is the introduction of Goods and Services Tax (GST) in 2017. This was first mooted in 2007. It enables a common market for India, eliminates cascading effect of multiple taxes, and improves the ease of doing business. The potential benefits of reducing the transaction costs in the system are huge.

GST has been in the making for several years, and it is perhaps the most significant structural reform so far in the economy of India. It changes the very nature of fiscal federalism, since so far the tax jurisdictions of Union and States were distinct and separate. Now, the Union and States, have to jointly decide on the design, structure, and rates of indirect taxes. The introduction of GST constitutes the biggest sacrifice of powers by states in broader national interest.

There are several risks to the successful implementation, and each one of them should be recognised and managed.

First, building of administrative, technological and logistical base for a unified system from 30, if not more, of the systems in India is daunting, but well within reach.

Second, convergence towards one rate is desirable but may not take place unless the goal is specified and multiple rates treated as temporary exceptions.

Third, the positive consequences of GST will be unevenly distributed with more developed states growing faster than the underdeveloped states. But, any dilution of GST in implementation will adversely impact both the sets of states. Hence, the distributional consequences of GST, both among sections of society and among states need to be considered by the Union, perhaps, outside of GST regime.

Fourth, there is a need to moderate the expectations of short-term benefits and focus on the difficult tasks ahead. As my former colleague Dr V. Bhasker wrote, these include continuing trust between Union and States, especially the responsibility of the former, repeated assertion of common goals, and ensuring credible commitments through actual performance. These are in the domain of political economy, but are critical for success of this great reform.

Fifth, the compensation mechanism does not provide incentives to States to be efficient in the immediate future, while the recourse to cesses available to Union gives easy option to fund its obligations.

Finally, the current dispensation has the potential to a levy of an aggregate (Union and States) tax of 40 per cent as against 28 per cent that has been assured.

Banking Sector: Concentration of Risks

Banking sector, in particular PSBs (public sector banks) is, perhaps, the most complex problem facing the economy now. There are two inter-related issues that the Government is trying to address simultaneously, namely, the structural aspects of governance and recapitalisation to make the system function viably soon and work better in future; and the legacy problems of NPAs (non-performing assets).

On the governance, the Government created Banks Board Bureau as an autonomous body of Union Government of India tasked to improve the governance of PSBs, business strategies, capital raising plans and also recommend selection of chiefs of Government owned banks. The effort is to depoliticise and professionalise the working of PSBs. It is headed by a person of expertise and eminence and thus commands credibility. It is in the nature of an arrangement that advises the Government and guides the banks. This is certainly an improvement over the past, though the underlying structural and incentives issues in PSBs remain the same.

There are some risks in this arrangement. First, the office of the Bureau is located in the main building of RBI. The relationship between the regulator and owner (Government) of regulated unit gets blurred.

Second, it has a potential to undermine the boards of PSBs. It also has the potential to adversely affect or excessively reward minority shareholders in PSBs.

In brief, as an immediate response to the problem, this arrangement has much to commend itself.

Recently, an ordinance has been promulgated on bad debt resolution with the objective of expediting resolution through restructuring or insolvency. The ordinance amending RBI Act empowers the Government to direct the RBI to ensure expeditious resolution by the banks. This move has lopsided incentives built-in, accompanied by potential reputational risk to RBI. The extraordinary measure will hopefully be time bound.

Recapitalisation is a requirement demanded by the regulator, and the demand applies to individual banks. Each PSB has both Government and private shareholders, including FIIs (foreign institutional investors). It should be the responsibility of all shareholders, not the government alone to recapitalise the banks. Unilateral support to recapitalise by the majority owner, namely, Government, may give windfall gains to the private shareholders.

The tax-payers interests are thus involved in any recapitalisation. Whatever be the accounting mechanism, recapitalisation by the Government which has a fiscal deficit means that it is borrowing and investing in risk capital of banks—thus assuming risks and expecting reward for future. It appears that major private sector banks do not have problem of capital adequacy despite NPAs.

A proposal to recapitalise banks with use of reserves with Reserve Bank has been made. From the regulatory perspective, it means that the regulator is providing capital to the regulated to ensure capital adequacy—an odd situation. It also means, essentially, creation of money for government for specific purpose, by the central bank. No doubt, all transactions are within public sector, except that PSBs are partly owned by private shareholders. This does make a difference to the respective balance sheets.

The magnitudes of NPAs has created bottlenecks in flow of credit, and stalling of projects, especially infrastructure. Several ideas have been considered and are under examination to address the problem, but the real issue is tackling the legacy problem in a way that such requirements do not arise in future. Solution to legacy problems range from writing-off the non-performing loans to punishing the defaulters. The former amounts to a bonanza to the borrower and the latter may in some cases hurt the progress of the project implementation, if done indiscriminately.

It is also necessary to reorganise that NPAs that are not entirely on account of fraud by the borrower. It may be due to lending without good appraisal, high leverage, business cycle in the industry, unanticipated legal and administrative bottlenecks, etc.

The major problem with the NPAs on account of infra projects is that government has a direct stake in such projects in multiple ways—as a customer and as a partner—and in addition indirect stake as owner of banks that lent to the venture. There is concentration of risks on the government, whichever way they are resolved.

Way forward, there is a danger that banks would hesitate to lend to infrastructure; and in that case alternative means have to be found. RBI has recently mooted a proposal to licence wholesale banks. The experience with DFI's (development finance institutions) in the past, and two other institutions promoted by government for the purpose in recent years, Infrastructure Development Finance Company (IDFC) and India Infrastructure Finance Company Ltd. (IIFCL) has not been satisfactory either. There is a risk that progress in financing of infrastructure projects in future will be hampered unless these are resolved.

External Sector

A noteworthy policy initiative recently is India's decision to renegotiate its investment agreements on the basis of a new Model BIT (bilateral investment treaty), which is based on our experience. It is significant for several reasons. First, the fear of losing the confidence of foreign investors was overcome. Second, we produced a Model agreement which became the anchor and thus introduced assertion of our interests. Third, many of these treaties give more protection to foreign investments than to domestic investments. Dispute settlement is not governed by our laws. Finally, there is no empirical evidence that such treaties attract more investment, quantitatively or qualitatively.

There are no indications of downside risks of the decision, so far. In any case, the prospects for external sector are bright and hence we are in a position to manage such risks.

Since global financial crisis, there has been an effort to regain policy space for national authorities in the face of relentless globalisation. Our approach to bilateral treaties is in line with global trend.

More generally, our external sector will be affected by the recent developments mainly in the United States (US), especially in regard to export of services. This shock can be absorbed smoothly provided the oil prices do not escalate. On capital account also, despite our heavy dependence on portfolio flows, and deterioration in net investment position, we should expect normal capital flows to meet our current account deficits.

Risks would, however, arise if our exchange rate does not ensure a sustainable current account deficit, and the policy does not manage the excess volatility well.

Reform and Reform Process

There are large elements of continuity in the substance and direction of reform, but there could be some elements of a change in the process.

First, reform since 1990s was considered a process and it was taken step by step; as a result, many people commented that in India, there is a strong consensus for weak economic reforms. In the recent years, however, there is evidence of an accelerated reform relative to the past. Now it is agenda led more than consensus determined reform.

Second, reforms in the past were focussed on deregulation and were supplementary to institutions that existed while some new regulatory systems were put in place. In recent years, some established institutions have been dismantled or replaced, going beyond supplementing. There is no hesitation to create new institutions, such as NITI Aayog and have a regulator for railways.

Third, legislative measures of systemic importance such as bankruptcy code and prohibition of *benami* transactions and land acquisition have been undertaken. States were also given flexibility to pass laws in the Concurrent List that could prevail over Union laws by liberally extending consent of President.

Fourth, till recently the reforms at State level were incidental to reforms at Union level, and were focussed on energy, environment and fiscal consolidation. Currently, states are integral to the process of reform.

Finally, there are large elements of continuity also, in the reform. The GST is a prime example of long pending reform. The legislation relating to *benami* transactions is another example of expeditious action on pending reforms. The noticeable feature is that such languishing legislative measures were brought to fruition on a priority basis.

The recent policy initiatives do indicate a new era in the process of reform characterised by new opportunities and new challenges.

Table 10.1

Comparison among the Emerging G20 Countries with respect to Different Social Indicators

	Poverty Head Count Ratio[1]	Literacy Rate (in per cent)	Life Expectancy at Birth (in years)	Maternal Mortality Ratio (MMR)	Infant Mortality Rate (IMR)	Under Five Mortality Rate	% of Households without Access to Sanitation
Argentina	1.7	98	76.3	32.4	11.1	12.5	96.4
	(2015)	(2015)	(2015)	(2013)	(2015)	(2015)	(2015)
Brazil	3.7	92.6	74.7	58.2	14.6	16.4	82.8
	(2014)	(2015)	(2015)	(2012)	(2015)	(2015)	(2015)
China	1.9	96.4	76.0	23.2	9.2	10.7	76.5
	(2013)	(2015)	(2015)	(2013)	(2015)	(2015)	(2015)
India	21.2	72.2	68.3	170	37.9	47.7	39.6
	(2011)	(2015)	(2015)	(2013)	(2015)	(2015)	(2015)
Indonesia	8.3	95.4	69.1	313	22.8	27.2	60.8
	(2014)	(2015)	(2015)	(2012)	(2015)	(2015)	(2015)
Republic of Korea	NA	97.97	82.2	11.0	2.9	3.4	100
		(2008)[2]	(2015)	(2015)	(2015)	(2015)	(2015)
Mexico	3.0	94.5	76.9	38.2	11.3	13.2	85.2
	(2014)	(2015)	(2015)	(2013)	(2015)	(2015)	(2015)

Russia	0.0	99.7	70.9	11.5	8.2	9.6	72.2
	(2012)	(2015)	(2015)	(2012)	(2015)	(2015)	(2015)
Saudi Arabia	NA	94.8	74.5	12	12.5	14.5	100
		(2015)	(2015)	(2015)	(2015)	(2015)	(2015)
South Africa	16.6	94.6	57.4	200	33.6	40.5	66.4
	(2011)	(2015)	(2015)	(2013)	(2015)	(2015)	(2015)
Turkey	0.3	95.7	75.4	16.0	11.6	13.5	94.9
	(2013)	(2015)	(2015)	(2015)	(2015)	(2015)	(2015)

Note: 1. Poverty headcount ratio at $1.90 a day (2011 PPP) (% of population).
2. Poverty headcount ratio for Republic of Korea: UNESCO Institute for Statistics.

Sources: Poverty Head Count Ratio: Millennium Development Goals, Data Bank, The World Bank.

Literacy rate, life expectancy at birth, MMR, IMR, Under five mortality rate, Percentage of households without access to sanitation: *World Development Indicators*, Data Bank, The World Bank.

Table 10.2

Real GDP Growth

	Real GDP Growth Base: 2004-05	*WPI Annual Variation Base: 1993-94*	*Gross Fiscal Deficit Base: 2004-05*	*CAD/GDP*	*Reserves (US$ Bn)*	*SCBs' Credit Growth Rate*
Year	*Per Cent*	*All Commodities*	*% of GDP*			*Per Cent*
2000-01	4.3	7.2	5.46	-1.0	38.0	17.3
2001-02	5.5	3.6	5.98	-0.6	42.3	15.3
2002-03	4.0	3.4	5.72	0.7	54.1	23.7
2003-04	8.1	5.5	4.34	1.3	76.1	15.3
2004-05	7.0	6.5	3.88	2.3	113.0	30.9
	Base: 2004-05					
2005-06	9.5	4.4	3.96	-0.3	141.5	30.8
2006-07	9.6	6.6	3.32	-1.2	151.6	28.1
2007-08	9.3	4.7	2.54	-1.0	199.2	22.3
2008-09	6.7	8.1	5.99	-1.3	309.7	17.5
2009-10	8.6	3.8	6.46	-2.3	252.0	16.9
2010-11	8.9	9.6	4.80	-2.8	279.1	21.5
2011-12	6.7	8.9	5.91	-2.8	304.8	17.0
	Base: 2011-12					
2012-13	5.4	7.4	4.93	-4.2	294.4	14.1
2013-14	6.3	6.0	4.46	-4.8	292.0	13.9
2014-15	7.1	2.0	4.09	-1.7	304.2	9.0
2015-16	7.2	-2.5	3.94	-1.3	341.6	10.9
2016-17	NA	NA	3.54	-1.1	360.2	NA

Notes:

1. The Ministry of Statistics & Programme Implementation has released the new series of national accounts, revising the base year from 2004-05 to 2011-12. Base year revisions differ from annual revisions in National Accounts primarily because of nature of changes. In annual revisions, changes are made only on the basis of updated data becoming available without making any changes in the conceptual framework or using any new data source, to ensure strict comparison over years. In case of base year revisions, apart from a shift in the reference year for measuring the real growth, conceptual changes, as recommended by the international guidelines, are incorporated. Further, statistical changes like revisions in the methodology of compilation, adoption of latest classification systems, and, inclusion of new and recent data sources are also made. Changes are also made in the presentation of estimates to improve ease of understanding for analysis and facilitate international comparability.
2. SCBs: Scheduled Commercial Banks.
3. Real GDP growth rate or the real economic growth rate is a more useful measure than the nominal GDP growth rate due to the fact that it takes into account the effect that inflation has on economic data. The real economic growth rate is a 'constant Rupee' figure, and therefore provides a consistent measure, one that is not subject to being distorted by periods of extreme inflation or deflation.
4. WPI (wholesale price index) measures and tracks the changes in the price of goods in the stages before the retail level. WPI shows the average price change of goods included in the index and is often expressed

as a ratio or percentage, and the change is one indicator of a country's level of inflation.

5. Household Financial Savings: The investment in financial saving comprises currency, net deposits, shares and debentures, net claims on government in the form of small saving, investment in central and state government securities, life insurance funds and provident & pension funds.
6. Fiscal Deficit: The difference between total revenue and total expenditure of the government is termed as fiscal deficit. It is an indication of the total borrowings needed by the government. While calculating the total revenue, borrowings are not included. The GFD (gross fiscal deficit) is the excess of total expenditure including loans net of recovery over revenue receipts (including external grants) and non-debt capital receipts. The net fiscal deficit is the GFD less net lending of the Central government.
7. CAD (current account deficit) is a measurement of a country's trade where the value of the goods and services it imports exceeds the value of the goods and services it exports. The current account also includes net income, such as interest and dividends, as well as transfers, such as foreign aid, though these components make up only a small percentage of the current account when compared to exports and imports.
8. Reserves are defined as external assets that are readily available to and controlled by monetary authorities for direct financing of external payments imbalances, for indirectly regulating the magnitudes of such imbalances through intervention in exchange markets to affect the currency exchange rate, and/or for other purposes.

Sources: Poverty Head Count Ratio: *Millennium Development Goals*, Data Bank, The World Bank. *http://databank.worldbank.org/data/reports.aspx?source=millennium-development-goals*

Literacy Rate, Life Expectancy at Birth, Maternal Mortality Ratio, Infant Mortality Rate, Under Five Mortality Rate, Percentage of households without access to sanitation: *World Development Indicators*, Data Bank, The World Bank. *http://databank.worldbank.org/data/reports.aspx?source=world-development-indicators*

11

Some Notes on Digitisation, Demonetisation and Macroeconomic Policies

A. VASUDEVAN*

Introduction

Digitisation as an idea is a technical one but has over time become a critical component in the understanding of many physical and social sciences. Digitisation in its broad sense requires one to have information, computing ability and communication vehicles/channels. Digitisation would help reduce opaqueness in the understanding of the principles of business and economics. Since the emergence of econometrics and mathematical economics as special subjects within the broad area of economics in the 1950s, digitisation has helped to quantify variables associated with different economic phenomena and measure the impact of economic policies on the economy. From these special subjects arose models and forecasting skills. These developments have been facilitated further by new IT (information technology) and infrastructures including net connectivity since about the beginning of the 1990s.

---

* This paper is essentially a tribute to late Shri Raj Kapila whose interest in macroeconomic and structural issues and for propagation of economic literacy with the help of digital solutions is demonstrated by the establishment and promotion of an important publication outlet, Academic Foundation for scholars in social sciences.

Digitisation and Demonetisation

Digitisation has gained enormous boost in the context of the recent Indian experiment with demonetisation of two HDNs (high denomination notes) from 8 November 2016. The Indian experiment is distinctly unique. It is not like (i) the general demonetisation of all currency note denominations that is often undertaken due to high inflation and depreciated external value of a national currency, and (ii) the demonetisation of HDNs in a gradual fashion over a fairly long time-period, of say, 18-24 months or even more. The famous example of general demonetisation due to hyper-inflation and highly depreciated currency is the German one of the 1920s (Brescini-Turroni 2003). Confidence in the then existing German currency, the Papier Mark, was lost, requiring the Government to demonetise it by issuing in its place a new currency called the Renten Mark. One million Papier Mark was made equal to 1 Renten Mark on October 1923. It stabilised the external value of the currency to some extent but quickly the Renten Mark too began to depreciate. The German authorities issued in August 1924 a new currency called Reichen Mark with terms of exchange between Papier Mark and Reichen Mark remaining the same. This action gave confidence to people that the authorities are serious about controlling inflation and stabilising the exchange rate.

Economic literature shows that inflation could be due to demand pull as Bent Hansen (1951)[1] had so famously shown or supply shocks or structural factors at play as the Latin American experiences in late 1950s and 1960s (Furtado 1967)[2] has shown. In general, in many EDEs (emerging and developing economies), all the three factors could act to lead to inflation pressures. While demand and supply factors could be influenced by macroeconomic policies, especially fiscal and monetary policies, structural

1. This is a most authentic study of demand pull inflation.
2. This is the most cited interpretation of structural problems facing EDEs.

reforms would be needed to address structural rigidities in the economies.

The well-known example of the second type of demonetisation was the one announced by the US on 19 July 1969 when US $500, $1,000, $5,000 and $10,000 which appeared first in the 1940s, were recalled. It is best to recognise that this may not be, strictly speaking, referred to as demonetisation. These denominations thus are still legal tender and are largely held by collectors of coins and currency notes and by the US museums. The US also issued $100,000 notes in the form of 1934 gold certificate and are used only for internal Government transactions.

In Japan, Yen 10,000 (equivalent of US $100) notes form about 90 per cent of cash holding. There is a proposal to demonetise this denomination note. The European Central Bank (ECB) has gone further. It has announced in May 2016 that the HDNs, Euro 500 (equivalent of US $100) note would be phased out by the end of 2018. These examples form part of the second type of demonetisation.

The Indian experiment with demonetisation of HDNs which accounted for 86 per cent of the total currency notes issued, is however, a different sort.[3] For want of a better term, the Indian demonetisation could well be called SD ('sectional' demonetisation). SD has been strewn with a number of constraints, the important ones being those that relate to the number and amounts of withdrawals of money from banks and ATMs and ban on conversions into legal tender currency before end-December 2016. Those who held demonetised HDNs could deposit them with banks before the end of the year 2016. NRIs (non-resident Indians) could submit at the specified offices of the Reserve Bank of India (RBI), the demonetised notes and park them into their bank accounts in India after providing

3. Please compare the Indian issuance of HDNs with those in the US and Japan. US $100 notes account for 80 per cent of total cash supply. In the case of Japan, Yen 10,000 notes account for 90 per cent of cash holdings. This trend is visible in almost all the countries.

documents that clearly prove that they could not convert the demonetised notes within the given time period of end December 2016 because they were outside the country. The facility to NRIs, however, would be available only up to the end of March 2017.

One of the important consequences of the Indian demonetisation experiment was that overall demand, especially the retail demand, declined and business investment prospects became somewhat opaque, forcing economic entities to resort to a variety of digital modes of payment. Payments through cheques, credit and debit cards, prepaid cards, e-wallets and net banking were made by ordinary women and men. Many of these modes were made at retail vendors and with vendors that had facilities to handle such operations. There has also been an increase in online payments of utility bills and taxes. The sudden upsurge of such payments showed that use of cash could over time be reduced. This is a welcome development. It however, gave rise to a number of questions and challenges. A few of them may be mentioned here. Would there be a tectonic shift in the behavioural responses of people to transactional payments and receipts from the use of hard cash to digital modes on a more or less permanent basis? Would the whole area of digital transactions be easily comprehensive to all individuals of different educational qualifications and simple to operate with certainty and confidence-providing privacy? Could the transactions be conducted on different technology platforms and on different types of gadgets? Will the wide range of transactions be amenable to payments through digital modes? What about the cost of use of different modes? What about the regulatory framework and how quickly could disputes be settled should there be questions about safety, costs and loss of privacy?

These questions relating to transactional modes of digitisation can be resolved with good technology solutions and efficient governance mechanisms. Quite clearly, resolution of the questions will take some time even if new innovative digital solutions are made available.[4] Digitisation however, goes beyond transactional modes. It has to handle issues of personal as well as economy-wide data, measurement of impacts of macroeconomic and structural policy actions, surveys and forecasting, to name a few, without causing unemployment or displacement of labour and with cost effectiveness and social and financial inclusion. Its effectiveness would depend on the infrastructure and connectivity available for development of technology and easy access for all social and economic classes and for all regions and sub-regions as also on innovativeness.

The costs involved for developing a robust infrastructure including the required skills and innovations in technology as well as sufficient number of sound applications and solutions are phenomenal. It is doubtful that such costs could be borne only by the private sector. The Government has to in any case have a share in the ownership of infrastructure in EDEs. The Government has to, however, have an arms-length relationship with regulators of the digital economy. It has to be transparent and accountable. This is essential, given the concerns of the ordinary public about the fees and other levies that service providers levy for use of digital modes and more importantly about the use of private information for purposes that could harm the interests of the main owners of information. It is therefore important for the State to play a major part in this area in EDEs like India where payment infrastructure is not as yet fully developed and stabilised.

Clearly, the challenges that the State faces are humungous. India however falls in a category of its own with a large adult population of over 915 million of which little less than 70 per cent belong to rural areas. Around 350 million individuals would have to be newly included in the financial system. Digital systems form a very minor

4. One of the interesting developments in recent times is the evolution of a number of applications on mobile phones that help to take care of transactional mode of payments. The mobile phones need not have Android base. In India too, such initiatives are coming up and it is expected that consumers will take recourse to them.

portion of total transactions as of now: the McKinsey Global Institute places them at less than one per cent in a study published in September 2016. This study also reveals through surveys that mobile technology penetration and access to credit and mobile money accounts have to grow by leaps and bounds, beyond the existing position. This provides an important means by which all transactions are traceable and wealth accumulation of households over time is based on foundations of moral credibility.

Macroeconomic Policies

To address the challenges that the State faces, the State's macroeconomic policy dynamics, which consist of three major areas, viz., the fiscal policy, monetary policy and exchange rate policy as also structural policies such as the industrial policy and contract laws, will have to be geared. Going by the received analytics, it is taken for granted that fiscal and monetary policies should not only be transparent but also led by 'rules' that are supposed to provide domestic economic and monetary stability. The received premise about monetary stability is simple. Exchange rates should not be volatile and should be stable within a predictable range. Payments under such an analytical premise should be certain, timely and without loss of privacy. More importantly, macroeconomic policies should not contain surprises. They should be devoid of discretion to policymakers.

Assuming that structural and legal matters are quickly settled, there would still be question about the current state of macroeconomics which forms the basis for macroeconomic policies. Unfortunately, macroeconomics at the moment is in disarray and is drifting, notwithstanding some stray voices to the contrary. Look at the recent writings/blogs of well-known economists such as Olivier Blanchard, Ben Bernanke, Simon Wren-Lewis, Paul Krugman, Larry Summers, Joseph Stiglitz, Willem

Buiter, Bill White, and more recently Paul Romer (2016).[5] Some of these economists are critical of the models and forecasting that macroeconomists have come out in recent years. At Harvard University of the US, students demanded that macroeconomists teach the subject on the basis of the ground realities. The same situation was seen at the Manchester University in the UK.[6] Should one still believe after the GFC (global financial crisis) experience (since 2008) that markets are perfect and are led by an invisible hand that promotes an end which is no part of its contention? Should DSGE (dynamic stochastic general equilibrium) models, so much used in many central banks, be relied upon as the most realistic portrayal of the economic situation? Would the markets always have inherent self-correcting mechanisms? There is also little appreciation among macroeconomists for the ideas that have been emanating in the area of behavioural economics. How the employment and social security conditions could be improved with the received macroeconomic analytics, when the growing number of senior citizens and unemployed youth with little or no vocational training or skills are not even enabled to be self-employed with dignity and without loss of 'identity'?

As it happens, a mix of macroeconomic policies was used to counter recessionary and unemployment conditions when the GFC occurred, but the situation has not improved much even after eight years of the mix policy

5. Romer highlighted the troubles that macroeconomics faces because of the assumptions and premises that are widely perceived to be not realistic.

6. Ever since the GFC, the teaching of macroeconomics has been the subject of attention of students at various universities in the US and in Europe. In 2011, a group of 70 students walked out of Gregory Mankiw's Introductory Economics course at Harvard University. The group felt that the module is biased towards promotion of conservative economic policies. In UK, the student movement at the University of Manchester, at around the same time led to some rethinking on the teaching of macroeconomics. Student movements were also there in Germany and France. In general the student movements show that it is important for students to know the philosophy of economics, the history of economic thought, complexity economics and post-Keynesian economics. They also indicate some antipathy to the use of highly sophisticated mathematics in the teaching of economics. They also object to large scale models that do not take into account the countries' economic conditions and aspirations.

experiment. However, the faith in such a mix has not weakened. It is inspired in part by John Maynard Keynes' advocacy for fiscal stimulus to address the challenges of the Great Depression of the 1930s. In the world of Keynes, however, fiscal policy would have a dominant role with monetary and exchange rate policies having only a muted supportive roles to play. Later day macroeconomics turned to market oriented explanations of economic phenomena with reduced importance attached to fiscal policies and more active role for monetary policy to exert. The resultant proliferation of monetarist, rational, new classical and new Keynesian theories is extraordinary in terms of the number of books and articles that have appeared since the 1950s. These schools of thought became powerful in the way that they have influenced the thinking of the international financial institutions such as the International Monetary Fund (IMF) and World Bank and the thinking of many economists in EDEs who received training abroad. The GFC gave the first knock to the entire analytical architecture of the post-Keynesian paradigms because they were found to be ineffective in explaining how and why markets behave as they did. The severity of the GFC is such that even now AEs (advanced economies) as a group have not registered any significant increase in growth rate. Unemployment rates have been high and have not shown any evidence of perceptible decline. Inflation rates on the other hand have been low and have not gone up despite the huge expansionary macro-economic policies. On the other hand, fiscal sustainability has become a matter of concern in many AEs. Income inequalities have increased. There is high uncertain future in almost all AEs. There is not much hope that in the near to medium term, AEs would recover well and lead the world economic recovery. EDEs are seen as critical for ensuring that the world economic growth would move up in the medium term.[7]

What is surprising and somewhat disconcerting is that economic thinkers in India have shown little

---

7. *World Economic Outlook* publications of the IMF clearly demonstrate the fact that the EDEs are leading the world economic performance and prospects.

enthusiasm to be part of the debate on the current state of macroeconomics as it is presently taught at universities and business schools and as it is used by policymakers. The near silence on the part of economic thinkers in EDEs is forbiddingly loud despite the growing need for improving the infrastructure for digitisation and for fostering financial inclusion. Digitisation costs on infrastructure include costs on account of regulation and governance, apart from the costs that have to be incurred on account of R&D efforts. They could be large and when superimposed on the need to incur expenditure for development of general infrastructure, social welfare schemes, defence and security could be humungous and could well question the sanctity of the fiscal rule that places GFD (gross fiscal deficit) at 3 per cent of GDP for India.[8]

The fiscal rule has many implications. It is said to be based on calculations of fiscal sustainability which in its turn can be realised only by following fiscal dynamic policies and strong fiscal governance. This suggests that given the institutional arrangements, a flexible fiscal rule would be greatly helpful. At least one needs to have escape clauses from the application of a rigid fiscal rule. For example, when overall economic activity slumps, fiscal stimulus could be given either by tax cuts or expenditure boost or by a combination of both. A similar solution could become pertinent where an export dependent economy finds a sudden sharp decline in external demand or in the external value of nation's exports of goods and services. This has been a reality about the beginning of 2015 for oil exporting countries.[9]

It is not only the fiscal rule that needs to be used with a modicum of flexibility. Monetary policy as well as

8. The fiscal rule was passed through an Act of Parliament in India in 2002 called the Fiscal Responsibility and Budget Management Act. One of the principal economists behind this initiative is Dr Vijay Kelkar.

9. Nigeria presents a classic example of a country that is facing recession due to low international prices of crude oil. In general, all oil exporting countries where fiscal and external payments positions crucially depend on international crude oil prices have been recording low growth rates since 2015.

exchange rate policies need to be undertaken in line with the obtained fiscal and structural policies. Coordination of macroeconomic and structural policies has to be the watchword of modern day policymaking. This however is easier said than done. A non-synchronous and uncoordinated policy set would place a question mark on the authorities' economic governance capability. For example, in EDEs where supply and institutional constraints exist, the limitations of stimulus of all macroeconomic policies could pose serious threats to macro stability and loss of confidence in future economic prospects. How does one optimise high growth, low unemployment, price and exchange rate stability depends on how economists and policymakers in EDEs would have to resolve optimisation problem with facts and with a desired institutional arrangement.

This is a tall order. But the alternative to the critique of macroeconomics is not necessarily to cut it off in the curricula of universities and business schools and to replace it with microeconomics where firms strategise for optimal resource allocation and profit maximisation. Such an approach may not yield desired results. For, firms do not operate in vacuum. They would depend on a host of fiscal, monetary and external sector variables and actions as much as on endogenously determined plans for heightened competitiveness and productivity growth. Also, actions of firms may not be necessarily synchronous or harmonious and could produce overall dysfunctional economic systems. One of the lessons of the recent economic history is the simple fact that firms have participated in the generation of economic cycles, financial instability, economic inequities and social and economic exclusions. This is amply demonstrated by the emergence of the GFC due to firms not observing financial and corporate discipline and internationally accepted standards and codes.

Final Remarks

Economists and policy wonks would need to revisit the existing economic and financial models and the realism that is embedded in the assumptions underlying them. In matters of policymaking, facts alone would not play a part: judgements too help to address the challenges. Digital economy can facilitate this process if social scientists undertake this project with a sense zeal and urgency to ensure that India's GDP gets a boost by at least 5 per cent more within the next 10 years.

References

Brescini-Turroni, C. (2003). *The Economics of Inflation: A Study of Currency Depreciation in Post-war Germany*. Oxford, UK: Routledge Publications. (Original English edition, 1937, George Allen & Unwin Ltd.)

Furtado, Celso (1967). *Development and Underdevelopment*. USA: University of California Press (originally published in 1964).

Hansen, Bent (1951). *The Theory of Inflation*. London: George Allen and Unwin.

Romer, Paul (2016). *The Trouble with Macroeconomics*. Stern School of Business/New York University. 14 September.

12

Entering the Age of GST

Celebrate with Caution

M. GOVINDA RAO

Introduction

After years of confabulation, hesitancy, controversy and indecision, the Government has, at last, implemented the Goods and Services Tax (GST) from 1 July 2017. The reform, touted as a 'game changer' and the 'reform of the century', was deemed worthy of a launch on the midnight of 30 June in the Central Hall of the Parliament. Indeed, one is reminded of the famous speech by Pandit Jawaharlal Nehru on the midnight of 14-15 August 1947. He spoke of a "tryst with destiny", of "redeeming the pledge" and referred to India waking up to life and freedom when the whole world slept. Now, the economy will face the tryst with GST, and there is much hope that the 'one nation, one market, one tax' will bring freedom from tax tyranny. Taxes and death are inevitable, but the attempt always should be to make them less painful. Given the fanfare with which unveiling of the GST reform has been done, it seems to be a reform with consequences never before seen in the country.

The enormous publicity that it has received and the great gains spoken about the 'one nation, one market, one tax' by both the Government and the captains of industry have raised high expectations. However, there is palpable nervousness at both Government and industry levels. There is the fear of unknown and the nervousness of transition to the new system.

Prelude to GST

The country has waited for the reform for long, and I had once described implementation of the GST as the "bullock cart stuck in the mud". The discussion on the reform has spanned more than a decade and half, and the then Finance Minister, P. Chidambaram, in his Budget of 2007 spoke of implementing the tax from April 2010. Suddenly the mud seems to have dried and the bullock cart seems to have been powered with a Rolls-Royce engine!

It was Lord Keynes who stated, "...Ultimately, it is ideas, not vested interests that are dangerous for good or evil," and GST implementation is clearly the triumph of ideas. There is a long list of those who contributed to erecting the building blocks. The L.K. Jha committee recommended the conversion of excise duties into a manufacturing stage VAT (value-added tax) in 1976 (Chelliah, a member of the Jha committee used to mention that when he mooted the idea, Jha commented that he only knew about VAT 69 and was not aware of this new intoxicant!). Chelliah dealt with the issue of VAT at length in his Tax Reforms Commission reports in 1991-92. The LTFP (long-term fiscal policy) authored by Shankar Acharya, then Economic Adviser in the Ministry of Finance recommended the need to have a nation-wide VAT. Amaresh Bagchi, in the seminal report, *Reform of Domestic Trade Taxes in India*, recommended the conversion—cascading type—sales taxes into a VAT, and in this, Satya Poddar's contribution—having earlier worked on the Canadian GST reform—was significant. The taxation of services was introduced for the first time by Manmohan Singh on non-life insurance, stock brokerage and telecommunication in the 1994 Budget at the advice of Chelliah. Over the years, the coverage of the tax was expanded and a specific entry (92B) was inserted in the Union List after the 88th amendment in Constitution in 2004. The Expert Group on Taxation of Services chaired by Govinda Rao recommended the taxing on all services with a small negative list and integrating it with the excise duty by unifying the tax rates and giving input tax credit for goods against services and vice versa in 2001. It also recommended giving concurrent powers to levy the service tax to the states to enable them to levy the VAT on goods and services. I was called upon to make a presentation to the Task Force on Indirect Taxes chaired by Vijay Kelkar, which made the recommendation on the GST on similar lines. When a separate entry for levying service tax was inserted in 2004 in the Union List, the task Force on FRBM chaired by Kelkar recommended the retail stage GST by both Union and state governments. The report of the 13th Finance Commission chaired by Kelkar advocated a broad based GST to include all goods and services including real estate transactions and having a single rate GST capped at 12 per cent. It also recommended that if any State were to violate this structure that would not be eligible for compensation. This actually created a setback as the States were unwilling to settle for such a 'flawless' GST. Greater setback was when the Union government refused to pay compensation for the loss of revenue for the reduction in CST (central sales tax) after 2010, as according to the understanding, the CST was to be reduced to 2 per cent and the compensation was to be paid until 2010 when the GST was to come into play. However, the GST could not be implemented and the refusal to pay compensation was seen as a breach of trust. Within the Empowered Committee where the reform process was discussed, there was a logjam. There were also problems of arriving at a consensus on the structure of the tax in the Empowered Committee with the States of Gujarat and Madhya Pradesh not agreeing to go with the rest. The rest of the history is well-known.

Celebrate GST with a Caution

GST is a major tax harmonisation exercise and will significantly reduce the transaction-cost of doing business in India. It will unify multiple taxes into a single tax and reduce compliance and administrative costs in the long-term and do away with levies like octroi and ensure a more unified market. It will reduce cascading on account of levies like octroi, purchase tax and central sales tax and make the economy more export-competitive. More importantly, it might see a significant increase in revenue productivity of income tax as the seeding of PAN (permanent account number) in GST number will make it difficult for the businessmen to evade the tax. All these could contribute to greater compliance, improved revenue productivity, reduced cascading and acceleration in growth. To know when that will happen, we will have to wait and keep our fingers crossed.

However, there is palpable unease in the air, felt by all—the investors, traders, consumers and even governments. The fanfare with which it is implemented has created considerable over-optimism on its favourable impact on productivity and revenue gains. This has built high expectations and if not realised, could lead to disappointments. The journey towards 'one nation, one tax and one market' has just begun, and there is considerable distance to traverse. It must be noted that non-inclusion of petroleum products in the base of GST will cause considerable cascading. The revenue from petroleum products contribute to 35-40 per cent of indirect taxes in the country, and the cost escalation on that account could be considerable. The multiple rates of tax have robbed its simplicity. It will not only enhance administrative and compliance costs but will also alter the relative prices in unintended ways. This could also lead to arbitrary interpretations and classification disputes. There are concerns about the anti-profiteering clause as well. Moreover, multiple rates are a sure invitation for lobbying. Despite the assurances given, there is considerable anxiety about the load bearing capacity of the technology. Above all, there can be disruptions on account of transition to the new system. It is therefore, important to ensure that the transitional problems are minimised. It is thus, desirable to see the reform as a work in progress rather than a game changer.

With multiple rates, it is not a simple tax and robs much of the benefits from lower administrative, compliance and distortion costs. There will be classification disputes, and many of them will end up in courts. Having multiple rates is a sure invitation for lobbying. This also puts additional burden on administration, increases the compliance cost and the load-bearing capacity of technology needed for providing input tax credit with multiple rates by matching every invoice. Requiring the regular GST dealers to file 37 returns in a year raises anxiety, given an untested technology platform. Despite the assurances given, the anti-profiteering clause creates considerable apprehension. The requirement of e-way bills for interstate movements has also been a cause of concern. Above all, there is a palpable fear of the unknown, given the recent disruptive experience with demonetisation. Indeed, any major tax reform could lead to disruption, and the complexity of the structure and the untested technology platform adds to the fear. Of course, a majority of retail traders, who buy and sell commodities and services within a State and have a turnover of less than ₹75 lakh, will come under the compounding system. They will pay a simplified tax at 1-2 per cent on the turnover without the facility of availing or according input tax credit, and submit only quarterly returns.

How 'Short' is the Short-term?

It is clear that the GST reform will lead to significant disruption in the economy in the short- term. How short is the short-term depends on how well the transition is planned, and how fast the economic agents will adjust to the new normal. The disruptions caused by demonetisation continue to haunt large parts of the unorganised economy even as the economy had been substantially remonetised. It is very difficult to predict the impact of such disruptions and the discontent they create. The power loom sector has considerably suffered on account of one disruption, and with different tax rates proposed to be levied on yarn, fabrics and ready-made garments, Tamil Nadu manufacturers are at war. Transporters will soon find that the tax paid on fuel cannot be credited against the GST payable on the transportation services rendered by them. The GDP estimates for the last quarter of 2016-2017 show that the construction sector has decelerated sharply to record a negative growth. There are concerns about the rates of tax, mandated compliances and glitches in transition, and investment activity is virtually at a standstill, with everyone waiting to see how the reform pans. Even as the tax is about to be unveiled, old decisions are changed and new decisions are taken by the GST Council, and there is hardly any time to internalise them. The Government could have used the time until September to provide greater clarity and test the technology through some dry runs to ensure a smoother transition.

Instead of viewing the GST as a game changer, it is useful to see it merely as the next stage of consumption tax reform in the country. To be sure, there will be disruptions which may slowdown the economy in the short-term. The much-wanted growth acceleration may happen only in the long-term when the transaction cost of businesses comes down. The statement by the Union Finance Minister that there could be short-term pains for long-term gains is very appropriate. The Revenue Secretary too has stated that this is a work in progress, and that is refreshing. Hopefully, his statement that the tax will be unified eventually to have one or two rates will be achieved sooner than later. The objective of including real estate within a reasonable time period is welcome because besides expanding the tax base, this will help in fighting black money. It would be useful to simultaneously include petroleum products within the ambit of the GST, for the expanded base could offset the revenue loss due to the prevailing high rates on petroleum products.

Conclusion

The GST reform is an important reform. It is a major tax harmonisation exercise and will significantly reduce the transaction cost of doing business in India. It will unify multiple taxes into a single tax and reduce compliance and administrative cost in the long-term, do away with levies like octroi and ensure a more unified market. It will reduce cascading on account of levies like octroi, purchase tax and CST and make the economy more export-competitive.

More importantly, it might see a significant increase in revenue productivity of income tax as the seeding of PAN in GST registration will make it difficult for businessmen to evade the tax. All these could contribute to acceleration in growth. To know how and when that will happen, we will have to wait and keep the fingers crossed.

The paper is an expanded version of the articles, "Entering the Age of GST", in *The Hindu*, 1 July 2017 and "GST Implementation: Here is Why We Should Celebrate with Caution", in *Financial Express*, 4 July 2017.

13

Eight Decades of Monetary Policy in India

DEEPAK MOHANTY[1]

Raj Kapila was a multifaceted personality—an economist, literature enthusiast, an author and editor. He was passionate about publication, and the publishing house of Academic Foundation is a testimony to that. Raj spent a lifetime of learning and making that knowledge accessible. It is a privilege for me to be contributing to this volume in his honour.

Introduction

In this paper, I give a snapshot of monetary policy in India as it evolved over eight decades since the establishment of the Reserve Bank of India (RBI) in 1935. With the benefit of hindsight, it is tempting to misjudge history, but developments are best appreciated in the milieu and state of knowledge of the times. I begin with a general reference to the objectives of central banks, review the evolution of monetary policy in India in phases marked by important events and conclude with a few financial indicators which mirror the progression of policy and economic outcome.

Objective of Central Banks

Central banks around the world were established to preserve monetary and financial stability. They also had several other functions such as issuance of currency and

1. The views expressed in this paper are the personal views of the author.

management of public debt, but monetary and financial stability have remained the core objective of central banks. The functions of central banks were written into law to empower them to deliver on their mandate effectively. Notwithstanding the intended objectives, the mandate was often couched in general terms, at least in the central bank legislations of earlier vintage. This could be because: first, the state of knowledge continued to evolve backed by economic theory and empirical evidence; second, quantification of objectives that may seem appropriate in a particular period may not hold true in another period as the structure of the economy undergoes change. Let me illustrate. Price stability may mean different things to different people, including economists.

There is reasonable theoretical foundation that 'zero' rate of inflation can be considered as the optimal level of inflation. But as we know from the experience of the Great Depression of 1929 and the Great Recession of 2008 that a very low inflation prompting excessive risk taking can impose significant costs on the economy. In practice, therefore, an annual rate of consumer price inflation of 2.0 per cent is considered the metric for price stability in AEs (advanced economies), and somewhat higher around 4.0 per cent for EMEs (emerging market economies). These inflation figures are also empirically validated as threshold levels of inflation that are considered as growth optimising. It is not clear that the current consensus on the inflation rate that corresponds to price stability will endure in the years to come, given the recent debate on this issue as the policy rates hit zero lower bound in AEs, where traditional monetary policy tools are considered ineffective (Ball 2014).

As regards the other major objective of central banks, it is difficult to define financial stability, let alone quantify it. Nevertheless, central banks have been assigned a pivotal role in financial stability. As in monetary policy, central banks' role as a LoLR (lender of last resort) has been written into the statute of many central banks. This was a response to frequent financial panic in the 18th and 19th century, which necessitated an institution to safeguard financial stability. The idea of LoLR was buttressed by the powerful insight by the 19th century economist and the first editor of the iconic *Economist* magazine, Walter Bagehot (1873) that "in a crisis a central bank should lend freely against good collateral at a penal rate." This is considered as the single most important tool in a financial crisis.

In the recent global financial crisis, the provision of LoLR was put to its severest test by a number of AE central banks. The swift response of the Federal Reserve in the United States of America (US Fed) was attributed to its wider invocation of LoLR provision in the US Fed statute, section 13. Apparently slower response to euro crisis in the euro area was partly attributed to lack of adequate empowerment in the statute of the European Central Bank (ECB).[2] As regards India, sections 17 and 18 of the RBI Act provide for LoLR operations.

However, critics of unfettered application of LoLR provision allege central bank overreach, particularly in the context of the recent global financial crisis, demanding curbing their activity (Paul 2009). Here again the jury is still out on what is an appropriate level of engagement. At the same time, there are initiatives under way to limit the LoLR function of the central bank and/or to make the governance framework broad-based with the participation of the government and other regulators. Another important aspect is that, 'transparency' is not considered so much of a virtue in the extension of LoLR facility unlike in the case of monetary policy. The thought goes like this: if a financial entity gets the comfort that the central bank is standing behind it solidly with liquidity support, it could engender reckless lending practices leading to financial instability. Hence, 'constructive ambiguity', meaning a surprise element and/or lack of clear commitment, is considered a virtue.

What the above brief discussion suggests is that the core of central bank objectives of price and financial

2. De Grauwe (2011), Winkler (2014).

stability has remained unchanged over the centuries of central bank existence, while the relative emphasis in its application and quantification has changed from time to time. Both these objectives may not, however, always be in harmony. There are synergies and trade-offs: as monetary policy is conducted in the financial market, a stable financial system contributes to the efficacy of monetary policy transmission; similarly, disproportionate emphasis on financial stability may at times underplay the price stability objective of monetary policy leading to sub-optimal growth and macroeconomic imbalances. There is also the issue of accountability with multiple objectives needing greater clarity on the framework. Such dilemmas become all the more compelling for EMEs such as India.

The Reserve Bank was instituted at a time when the world was in the throes of the Great Depression in the early 1930s. The preamble to the Reserve Bank of India (RBI) Act, 1934 delineated the basic functions of the Reserve Bank as,

> To regulate the issue of Bank notes and keeping of reserves with a view to securing monetary stability in India and generally to operate the currency and credit system of the country to its advantage.

Interestingly, the question of monetary standard best suited to the country was left open in the preamble, and the then existing monetary system was considered as a temporary provision given the unsettled international monetary systems, leaving the question of a suitable monetary framework open for later consideration. The objectives of monetary policy evolved from this broad guideline as the country transitioned from a British colony to an independent nation, and a predominantly agrarian economy transformed into a diversified one and the financial markets developed.

Subsequently, the RBI Act was amended several times reflecting the dictates of the evolving economy and financial structure. But the preamble, considered temporary by the framers of the statute, endured for over eight decades. In a momentous change, the preamble of the RBI Act was amended in 2016 to put in place a modern monetary framework "whereas the primary objective of monetary policy is to maintain price stability while keeping in mind the objective of growth".

Thus, price stability got clearly defined in terms of an inflation target based on the CPI (consumer price index). The numerical inflation target would be determined by the Government in consultation with the RBI. The first such inflation target that was announced starting from the financial year 2016-17 was 4 per cent with a band of +/-2 per cent.

Evolution of Monetary Policy[3]

The evolution of monetary policy in India can be conveniently seen in six phases: (i) sterling parity (1935-1949), (ii) developmental years (1949-1969), (iii) credit planning (1969-1985), (iv) monetary targeting (1985-1998), (v) multiple indicators (1998-2015), and (vi) flexible inflation targeting (2015 onwards). A chronology of key events having a bearing on inflation and monetary policy is given in the Annexure Table A-13.1.

Sterling Parity (1935-1949)

In the early years of 1935-1949, the primary task of monetary policy was to maintain a fixed exchange rate in terms of a sterling-rupee parity. In modern parlance, it could be said that exchange rate was the nominal anchor for monetary policy. In order to manage the consequent changes in money supply, the RBI was equipped with three monetary tools: the bank rate, OMOs (open market operations) and the CRR (cash reserve ratio).The CRR was to be used in exigencies rather than as an active instrument of credit control. The RBI first announced its official policy rate, the bank rate, at 3.5 per cent in July 1935, which was the same rate as was maintained by its predecessor, the Imperial Bank of India. Liquidity was plentiful and inflation was low due to worldwide depression, which

---

3. I draw upon four volumes of *RBI History, RBI Annual Reports* and some of my earlier papers.

prompted the RBI to reduce the bank rate to 3.0 per cent in November 1935, despite the Government's strong reservations on its adverse implication for rupee-sterling exchange rate.

The down-trend in prices was reversed as war was declared in September 1939. The 1940s witnessed an upsurge in inflation emanating from the impact of the Second World War coupled with the disastrous Bengal famines in 1943. With the partition of the country in 1947, India lost a predominantly agrarian province, which had consequences for inflation. Civil unrest stifled industry. Relief and rehabilitation measures strained the government budget. Deficit financing increased money supply. In order to discourage tax evasion, rupee notes of denomination of ₹500 and above were demonetised in 1946. On the face of a supply shock, monetary policy was ineffective in controlling inflation. The government resorted to price control measures and rationing of essential commodities. Instruments of selective credit control and moral suasion were deployed by the RBI to restrain banks from extending credit for speculative purposes.

In view of rising external imbalance and to match the devaluation of the pound-sterling against the US dollar, the rupee was devalued in September 1949 by 30.5 per cent. The exchange rate between pound-sterling and the rupee, however, remained unchanged. In the formative years during 1935-1949, the bank rate and CRR remained unchanged. The focus of monetary policy was on regulating liquidity in the system through OMO—by buying and selling of government securities—so as to maintain exchange rate parity. During this period, annual inflation rate showed considerable volatility in the range of (-) 18.4 per cent to 86.7 per cent. Inflation was particularly severe during 1941-1944 and again in 1947-1949.

Developmental Years (1949-1969)

The year 1949 marked a paradigm shift in central banking in India. In line with the trend around the world, the government nationalised the RBI on 1 January 1949. Another important development in 1949 was the enactment of the Banking Regulation Act for sound development of the banking sector. The Act also required banks to maintain SLR (statutory liquidity ratio) of 20 per cent of their NDTL (net demand and time liabilities) with the RBI in the form of cash, gold or approved securities. This provided a secured source for government borrowings besides an additional instrument of monetary and liquidity management to the RBI. These developments coupled with government's embarkation of planned economic development marked a definitive switch in the conduct of monetary and financial policy.

Monetary policy had to move in sync with the national five-year plans to bridge the resource gap, though the inflation risk of deficit financing was always there. Orderly development of the banking sector, greater institutional provision of credit and mobilisation of saving was expected to ameliorate resource constraint. A number of steps were taken to reduce government expenditure and boost food supplies by giving greater emphasis on agriculture in the first five-year plan. The bank rate was raised in November 1951. These measures had a sobering effect, and inflation moderated during the first half of the 1950s.

Starting from the second five-year plan, the need for supporting plan financing through accommodation of government deficit by the RBI began to significantly influence the conduct of monetary policy. The SLR (statutory liquidity ratio) was raised to 25 per cent of the NDTL of banks in 1964. Border conflict with China in 1962-63, Pakistan aggression of 1965, two successive droughts in Bihar in 1966-67 accentuated inflationary pressures. External imbalance developed with CAD (current account deficit) of BoP (balance of payments) expanding to 3.7 per cent of GDP (gross domestic product) in 1966-67. This led to devaluation of the rupee by 36.5 per cent vis-à-vis the US dollar in June 1966.

In the 1960s, inflation was considered to be structural and inflation volatility primarily caused by agricultural failures, so there was greater reliance on selective credit controls. This led to the introduction of several quantitative control measures to contain inflationary pressures while ensuring credit to preferred sectors. The quota-slab system, which determined the cost of credit from RBI to commercial banks, was replaced by a measure of NLR (net liquidity ratio). Besides selective credit control, a CAS (credit authorisation scheme) aimed at aligning credit policy more closely with the requirement of the five-year plans was introduced. Barring the period 1964-1968, inflation mostly remained moderate.

Credit Planning (1969-1985)

Nationalisation of major banks in 1969 marked another phase in monetary and financial policy. The period 1969-1985 was characterised by greater 'social control' of credit and fiscal dominance. The focus of monetary policy was on credit planning. India fought a war with Pakistan in 1971, encountered two droughts in 1973 and 1979 coinciding with two oil price shocks. There was also breakdown of Bretton-Woods system of global exchange rate arrangements in 1973. These developments had severe inflationary consequences. Inflation mounted from 10 per cent in 1972-73 to 20 per cent in 1973-74 and 25 per cent by 1974-75. The 1980s began with elevated inflation and a BoP crisis necessitating recourse to a loan of SDR 5 billion from the International Monetary Fund (IMF).

The dominance of fiscal policy over monetary policy accentuated. The system of ad hoc treasury bills which had begun in 1956, for temporary financial accommodation to the government from the RBI, became the dominant instrument of automatic monetisation of budgetary deficit. Additionally, to raise resources from banks for the government, the SLR was progressively increased from the statutory minimum then of 25 per cent of banks' NDTL in 1969 to 37 per cent by July 1985. And to neutralise the inflationary impact of deficit financing, CRR was gradually raised from its statutory minimum then of 3 per cent to 10 per cent of NDTL during the period. The bank rate had also risen from 5 per cent to 10 per cent. Average inflation during this period rose sharply to 8.2 per cent per annum.

Monetary Targeting (1985-1998)

The period 1985-1998 can be characterised as monetary targeting period where the focus shifted to inflation management through control of money supply. The monetary targeting framework was based on the recommendations of the Chakravarty Committee (1985). Under this framework, reserve money (M0) was used as the operating target, and broad money (M3) as an intermediate target. However, it was not a strict form of constant rate of M3 growth. Monetary targeting was flexible to accommodate changes in real GDP growth. In practice, it was an indicative monetary targeting framework with a feedback from real economic activity. Nevertheless, this framework provided a nominal anchor in terms of desired rate of growth of M3 for the conduct of monetary policy.

A number of money market instruments such as IBPCs (interbank participation certificates), CDs (certificates of deposit) and CP (commercial paper) were introduced based on the recommendations of the Vaghul Committee (1987).

In 1985, the government set out a LTP (long-term fiscal policy). But fiscal dominance continued in terms of large government borrowings. The statutory pre-emption of bank resources through CRR and SLR had peaked to 53.5 per cent of banks' NDTL by 1990. The macro-balance had turned adverse, and the Gulf War of 1990 precipitated a BoP crisis. India had to turn to the IMF for financing. The exchange rate of the rupee was adjusted downwards by 18.7 per cent vis-à-vis the US dollar. Most importantly, the BoP crisis of 1991 triggered wide ranging reforms unshackling the Indian economy. As they say the rest is history.

Structural reforms and financial liberalisation in the 1990s led to a shift in the financing paradigm for the government and commercial sectors with increasingly market-determined interest and exchange rate. Automatic monetisation of government budget deficit was eschewed in 1997. The CRR and SLR were brought down to 9.5 per cent and 25 per cent of banks' NDTL by 1997. By the second half of the 1990s, the RBI was able to move away from direct instruments to indirect market-based instruments in its liquidity management operations.

During the monetary targeting period, inflation remained in single digit except for the period 1990-1993 and 1994-95. In the 13-years of monetary targeting during 1985-1998, the real GDP increased at the rate of 5.4 per cent per annum, wholesale price inflation increased by 8.0 per cent per annum and consumer price inflation increased by 9.1 per cent per annum.

Multiple Indicators (1998-2015)

In 1997-98, the Indian economy had to contend with the spillover effects of the Southeast Asian crisis. The bank rate had to be raised sharply by 200 basis points to 11.0 per cent to fend off capital outflows. While stability could be restored in the financial markets, real GDP growth slowed. Subsequently the bank rate was reduced three times to 9.0 per cent by April 1998. From a monetary policy perspective, 1997-98 was a watershed year as it marked the activation of interest rate as a tool of monetary policy. This was evident from the fact that between April 1997 and April 1998, the bank rate was changed seven times. Prior to this, the bank rate was changed only twice in 1991 in the wake of the BoP crisis.

On account of measures undertaken during the 1990s for developing various segments of the financial market, there was a discernible deepening of the financial sector. This significantly improved the effectiveness in the transmission of policy signals through indirect instruments such as interest rates. Recognising the challenges posed by financial liberalisation and the growing complexities of monetary management, the Reserve Bank switched to a multiple indicators approach in 1998-99.

The *RBI Annual Report* for 1999-2000 summed up the rationale for such an approach:

> The flexibility to conduct monetary management in India was recognised and strengthened by the analytical work of the Reserve Bank's Working Group on Money Supply (1998). The Group reported that monetary policy exclusively based on monetary targets set by estimates of money demand could lack precision because while the money demand function exhibited parametric stability, predictive stability was less certain. The gradual emergence of rate variables such as interest rates with their growing sensitivity to financial developments and economic activity has contributed to the information content of quantity variables. Rate variables together with quantity variables would thus need to be used in the framework of multiple indicators to optimise management goals.

Under the multiple indicators approach, while broad money (M3) continued to remain an information variable, greater emphasis was placed on rate channels for formulating monetary policy. A host of macroeconomic indicators including interest rates or rates of return in different segments of financial markets, along with other indicators on currency, credit by banks and financial institutions, fiscal position, trade, capital flows, inflation rate, exchange rate, refinancing and transactions in foreign exchange available on a high frequency basis were juxtaposed with output data for drawing implications for forming monetary policy.

As a result, monetary policy operations became more broad-based on diverse sets of information and provided flexibility in the conduct of monetary management. The multiple indicators approach continued to evolve and was further augmented by forward-looking indicators and a panel of parsimonious time series models. The forward-looking indicators were drawn from the Reserve Bank's industrial outlook survey, capacity utilisation survey, professional forecasters' survey, and inflation expectations survey. The assessment from these indicators and models fed into the projection of growth and inflation.

In 1998-99, despite a variety of domestic and international uncertainties, the economy performed reasonably well. The year also marked the introduction of a liquidity management strategy through an active use of fixed rate repo operations. In order to influence the long-term interest rate, the bank rate was revised downward thrice, from 10.5 per cent in March 1998 to 8.0 per cent by end-March 1999. In 1999-2000, despite a number of difficult domestic and international developments, such as the Kargil conflict and the sharp increase in oil prices, the Indian economy registered a higher real GDP growth.

Monetary and financial conditions continued to remain stable in 2001-02. The monetary and credit policy for 2002-03 was reinforced by favourable developments in the form of low inflation, ample liquidity in financial markets, continuing capital inflows and a substantial build-up of foreign exchange reserves The return to high growth in 2003-04 brought with it renewed business optimism and consumer confidence in the near-term outlook for the economy and a wider appreciation regarding India's potential for growth.

Interestingly the RBI also recognised the impact of global developments on domestic monetary policy:

> With the growing financial integration across borders, the conduct of monetary policy is becoming increasingly complex. It is not a coincidence that most of the uncertainties facing monetary policy at the present juncture are essentially international in character. The path of inflation is governed not only by domestic economic activity, but also by the extent of liquidity emanating from capital flows and the movements in international commodity prices.[4]

The unveiling of the LAF (liquidity adjustment facility) with repo auctions in June 2000, as an operating aid to manage liquidity and influence the rate variables, gained importance. With a view to managing liquidity pressures emanating from large and persistent capital flows, sterilisation operations were undertaken through the LAF

---

4. "The Economy: Review and Prospects", *RBI Annual Report* for the Year July 2003 to 30 June 2004, Part I, 30 August 2004.

(liquidity adjustment facility) and open market operations, supported by the Market Stabilisation Scheme (MSS).

With increasing globalisation of the Indian economy and greater integration of the financial markets, it was becoming apparent that the frequency of monetary policy making twice a year was becoming inadequate. While the RBI had the flexibility to announce monetary policy actions any time during the year, it was not the same as more frequent structured communication practiced by major central banks. The RBI, therefore, announced major changes in its monetary policy formulation process.

With a view to further strengthening the consultative process in monetary policy, the Reserve Bank, in July 2005, set up a Technical Advisory Committee on Monetary Policy (TACMP) with external experts in the areas of monetary economics, central banking, financial markets and public finance. The Committee was expected to meet at least once in a quarter to review macroeconomic and monetary developments and advise the Reserve Bank on the stance of monetary policy. Concomitantly, the Reserve Bank switched to a quarterly announcement of monetary policy while retaining the flexibility to take specific measures as the evolving circumstances warrant. The First Quarter Review, the first in the series, was released in July 2005.

The Indian economy recorded a strong growth of 8.6 per cent per annum during the four-year period ended 2006-2007. Underlying inflationary pressures were also rising in parts because of faster growth and occasional supply shocks emanating from food and crude oil prices. This prompted the RBI not only to reiterate its self-imposed medium-term ceiling on WPI headline inflation at 5.0 per cent but also to set a more ambitious target on inflation:

> In recognition of India's evolving integration with the global economy and societal preferences in this regard, the resolve, going forward, would be to condition policy and expectations for inflation in the range of 4.0-4.5 per cent. This would help

> in maintaining self-accelerating growth over the medium-term, keeping in view the desirability of inflation at around 3 per cent to ensure India's smooth global integration.[5]

The RBI also recognised the challenges of conducting monetary policy in absence of a representative consumer price index:

> In the context of inflation, it may be noted that, globally, consumer price inflation is the preferred indicator of central banks for assessing inflationary conditions. On the other hand, in India, wholesale price inflation has emerged as the key measure of assessing inflationary pressures, partly due to its availability on a higher frequency (weekly basis) and partly due to the absence of a comprehensive measure of consumer price inflation in the country.[6]

Global financial markets witnessed turbulent conditions during the most part of 2007-08 as losses on US sub-prime mortgage loans escalated into widespread financial stress, raising fears about stability of banks and other financial institutions. The crisis in the sub-prime mortgage market gradually deepened and spilled over to markets for other assets.

The Indian economy continued to perform well during 2007-08, with a GDP growth rate of 9 per cent but an upsurge in inflation in India occurred at a time when global commodity prices were volatile and at historically elevated levels. Net capital flows to India increased sharply to US$ 108.0 billion (or 9.2% of GDP) during 2007-08, which were 2.4 times higher than the level in 2006-07. Large net capital flows, which were significantly higher than the CAD, led to an accretion of foreign exchange reserves, placing continued pressure on monetary management. Ratio of net foreign exchange assets of RBI to reserve

---

5. "RBI Releases Annual Report for 2006-07", Press Release, Reserve Bank of India, 30 August 2007.

6. "II. Assessment and Prospects", *Annual Report for 2005-06*, Reserve Bank of India, 30 August 2006.

money (M0) peaked to 157 per cent in 2007-08 from only 9 per cent in 1989-90.

In view of the progressive build-up of underlying inflationary pressures, monetary policy recognised the need to smoothen and enable the adjustment of demand on an economy-wide basis so that inflation expectations were contained. Accordingly, the Reserve Bank continued taking monetary tightening measures. The CRR was increased by 300 basis points in phases from 6.0 per cent in March 2007 to 9.0 per cent by August 2008. The repo rate under the LAF was increased in phases by 150 basis points from 7.5 per cent in March 2007 to 9 per cent by July 2008.

As the global economy veered towards recession, commodity prices fell sharply. This was reflected in a decline in headline WPI inflation to under 1.0 per cent by end March 2009 from the peak of about 13 per cent in August 2008. However, this was cold comfort as consumer price inflation remained high. The divergent trends in inflation as measured by the WPI and CPI once again brought out the measurement issues as well as the choice of an appropriate price index for monitoring changes in price levels at the national level that could be used as the reference indicator for conduct of policies.

As a response to global crisis, the Reserve Bank had lowered the repo rate by 425 basis points, the reverse repo rate by 275 basis points and the CRR by 400 basis points over a period of about seven months between October 2008 and April 2009. The overall provision of potential liquidity through conventional as well as several non-conventional liquidity windows was close to ₹5.6 trillion, or equivalent of about 9.0 per cent of GDP.

In 2009-10, the focus of macroeconomic policy shifted from containing the contagion of the global crisis to management of recovery. Nevertheless the reform process continued to make the financial system more responsive. With a view to imparting transparency to the loan pricing process, and improving the assessment of monetary policy transmission and promoting competition in the credit market, the Reserve Bank introduced a new system of 'base rate' for banks in July 2010, which replaced the earlier BPLR (benchmark prime lending rate) system.

Even as growth reverted to its trend, new challenges emerged. First, the headline inflation accelerated from the negative levels in mid-2009 to double digits during March-July of 2010. The year 2010-11 was marked by inflation persistence, with headline inflation averaging 9.6 per cent. The Reserve Bank responded to the inflation challenge through calibrated monetary policy normalisation. It raised repo rate seven times during the year by 25 bps (basis points) each. Despite these actions, inflation remained elevated due to both newer supply-side shocks and demand factors. As input costs rose and were passed on substantially amidst strong consumption demand, inflation became generalised.

The year 2012-13 was marked by slowing growth, lingering inflation, large fiscal and current account gaps and deteriorating asset quality. Thus, monetary policy was faced with a Hobson's choice. With growth decelerating, ordinarily the policy response would have been accommodative. At the same time, there were worries that consumer price inflation was hurting people and that the Reserve Bank was not able to subdue inflation. Persisting inflation was eroding the competitive efficiency of the economy and lowering the financial savings of households with its adverse consequences for the CAD, investment and long-term growth.

The year 2013-14 began with upheaval in global financial markets. The indication by the US Federal Reserve (US Fed) that it would unwind a part of the monetary stimulus earlier than anticipated led to severe tightening in financial conditions. Currencies of the EMEs depreciated speedily. This, in turn, led to a decline in equity prices as portfolio shifts occurred from EMEs to the US markets. Political unrest in parts of the Middle East also put upward pressure on global oil prices.

The economy had to face serious challenges to stability in 2013-14 emanating from exchange rate pressures amid capital outflows, persistence of near double digit inflation, fiscal imbalances and a decline in investment. This prompted the Reserve Bank and the government to take several measures to stabilise the economy. A combination of favourable factors such as the collapse of international commodity prices, particularly of crude, and loss of pricing power among corporates due to weakening demand as well as pro-active supply management and deregulation of key fuel prices worked in alignment with a disinflationary monetary policy stance to moderate inflation significantly in 2014-15. WPI inflation declined to 1.3 per cent, whereas CPI inflation fell to 5.8 per cent from earlier higher levels.

In a longer perspective, during 16-year period of a multiple indicators approach (1998-2015), GDP increased at a rate of 6.9 per cent per annum, wholesale price inflation was 5.6 per cent per annum and consumer price inflation was to 7.1 per cent per annum. The period of the multiple indicators approach also encompassed a period of very high growth and even lower inflation. During the 5-year period 2003-2008, GDP growth averaged 8.7 per cent per annum, wholesale price inflation averaged 5.5 per cent per annum and consumer price inflation was even lower at 5.0 per cent per annum. These growth-inflation outcomes underscore the importance of price stability for securing higher growth. The credit for good performance cannot be attributed to monetary policy alone. The period 2003-2008 witnessed considerable fiscal consolidation which opened up the space for monetary policy to address the credit needs of the private sector. If fiscal and monetary policies work in tandem, the economic outcome can certainly be better.

Flexible Inflation Targeting (2015 Onwards)

In the backdrop of inflationary pressures and persistent divergence between wholesale price and consumer price inflation, the RBI moved to review its monetary policy framework. With the annual average consumer price inflation touching double digits for six years, establishing a credible nominal anchor to rein in inflation and anchor inflation expectations was important. Against this backdrop, the Reserve Bank constituted an Expert Committee to Revise and Strengthen the Monetary Policy Framework (Chairman: Dr Urjit R. Patel). Following the Expert Committee's recommendation, the Reserve Bank adopted a glide path to bring consumer price inflation down to 6 per cent by January 2016. Following an agreement with the government and subsequent amendment to the RBI Act, a formal FIT (flexible inflation targeting) framework with consumer price inflation target of 4 per cent with a band of +/- 2 per cent was adopted from the financial year 2016-17. Not only that the RBI could successfully execute the glide path, the inflation target for 2016-17 was met. The average consumer price inflation declined to 4.9 per cent in 2015-16 and 4.5 per cent in 2016-17.

Financial Stability

Let me now turn to the interface between monetary policy and financial stability. As mentioned earlier, the evolution of monetary policy was influenced not only by the changing paradigm in monetary economics but also by the developments in the financial market and macroeconomic outcomes. In the event of adverse developments, adequacy of extant economic policies is put to test as was during the recent global financial crisis. Crises are not desirable but they are unavoidable. They, however, provide an opportunity for assessing various tenets of the extant policy framework.

Even before the crisis, institutional arrangement in the financial sector was already in place for inter-regulatory coordination for monitoring financial stability in the economy. A High Level Coordination Committee on Financial Markets (HLCCFM) was set up in 1992 with the Governor of the Reserve Bank as its Chairman, and the chiefs of the Securities and Exchange Board of India (SEBI), the Insurance Regulatory and Development Authority of India (IRDAI) and the Pension Fund Regulatory and Development Authority (PFRDA), and the

Finance Secretary to Government of India as members. However, post-crisis, the collegial approach to financial stability was further strengthened by constituting the Financial Stability and Development Council (FSDC).

FSDC, headed by the Finance Minister, was set up in December 2010 in the wake of the global financial crisis with a specific mandate, inter alia, for systemic financial stability. FSDC is expected to deal with issues relating to financial stability, developing the financial sector, inter-regulatory coordination and macro-prudential supervision of the economy including the functioning of large financial conglomerates. A sub-committee of FSDC, headed by the Governor of the Reserve Bank, replaced the HLCCFM and is the primary operating arm of the FSDC. This sub-committee has also set up a dedicated crisis management framework.

In addition, various committees of the Reserve Bank's central board monitor financial stability issues: the Board for Financial Supervision reviews the Reserve Bank's supervisory and regulatory initiatives and the Board for Payment and Settlement Systems oversees the overall functioning of the payment system. Another development signifying the Reserve Bank's role in the context of financial stability is the setting up of a Financial Stability Unit in the RBI in July 2009 with a mandate of conducting an effective macro-prudential surveillance of the financial system on an ongoing basis and enabling early detection of any incipient signs of instability. The RBI also brings out biannual financial stability reports.

The RBI is one of those central banks which explicitly recognises financial stability as one of its objectives which was vindicated by the crisis with an increasing number of central banks, giving greater attention to financial stability. While there is broad consensus that financial stability should be an objective of central banks, it is not clear if it should be a direct objective of monetary policy. Multiple objectives call for multiple instruments. In this context, macro-prudential instruments of risk weights and provisioning are considered better suited to financial stability than the interest rate, a key element of monetary policy.

Conclusion

Monetary policy evolved alongside the development of the financial sector. Various financial ratios[7] would suggest broadly three phases since 1950-51 (Figure 13.1). The decades of 1950s and 1960s saw a low level of financial intermediation. The ratio of broad money (M3) to currency remained in the range of 1.7-2.3 suggesting limited banking facility. The money multiplier, was also in the range of 1.6-2.1 reflecting low secondary expansion of money supply. The ratio of broad money (M3) to GDP stagnated around 20 per cent reflecting lower monetisation of the economy.

This scenario began to change in the 1970s following nationalisation of major banks and consequent expansion of banking. The upward movement in intermediation continued till the mid-1990s when the ratio of M3 to GDP crossed the 45 per cent mark. During this period, increase in money multiplier though was subdued suggesting an element of financial repression through large pre-emption of resource from the banking sector, particularly through high CRR. Subsequently, the upward trend in intermediation continued but with a difference: it was accompanied by significant increase in money multiplier emanating from reforms to reduce statutory pre-emptions. By 2014-15, M3 to GDP ratio had risen to over 80 per cent from about 20 per cent in 1950-51. Increased financial depth of the Indian economy provided the opportunity for market based reforms in the monetary policy framework.

Over 80 years of inflation, trend since 1935 would suggest that inflation remained volatile in earlier years, partly reflecting the nature of agrarian economy (Figure 13.2 and Table 13.1). For example, in 1950-51, the share

---

7. In simple terms reserve money (M0) ≡ currency + banks' deposits with RBI; broad money (M3) ≡ currency with the public + bank deposits; money multiplier = M3/M0; and a measure of financial depth is the ratio of M3 to GDP at current market price.

of agriculture and allied sector was around 53 per cent of GDP and over one-half of GDP growth was accounted for by this sector. Hence, crop failure had an adverse impact on both growth and inflation. The country also had to endure periodic wars, oil price shocks and external imbalances leading to devaluation of currency, all of which had inflationary implications.

As the economy became more diversified, inflation volatility reduced from the mid-1980s. On the demand side, large government borrowings and automatic monetisation of budget deficit till the late 1990s added to price pressures. With reforms which included discontinuation of automatic monetisation of budget deficit and move towards rule-based fiscal policy and reduction of statutory pre-emption of resources that reduced crowding out of private investment, inflation generally trended down since the late 1990s except for a period following the global financial crisis in 2008. The uptrend in inflation has since been reversed with a firmer commitment to a rule based monetary policy with the adoption of flexible inflation targeting, coupled with moderation in global commodity prices.

Formulating monetary policy is an ever-evolving process both in response to and as a consequence of changes in financial markets and the real economy. This is a phenomenon we see in India in monetary policy formulation over the eight decades.

References

Bagehot, Walter (1873). *Lombard Street: A Description of the Money Market*. London: H.S. King.

Ball, Laurence (2014). "The Case for Long-Run Inflation Target of Four Percent", *IMF Working Paper* WP/14/92.

De Grauwe, Paul (2011). *The European Central Bank as a Lender of Last Resort*.

Paul, Ron (2009). *End the Fed*. New York: Grand Central Publishing.

Winkler, Adalbert (2014). "The ECB as Lender of Last Resort: Banks versus Government", *LSE Financial Markets Group, Special Paper* 228.

Figure 13.1

Select Financial Indicators

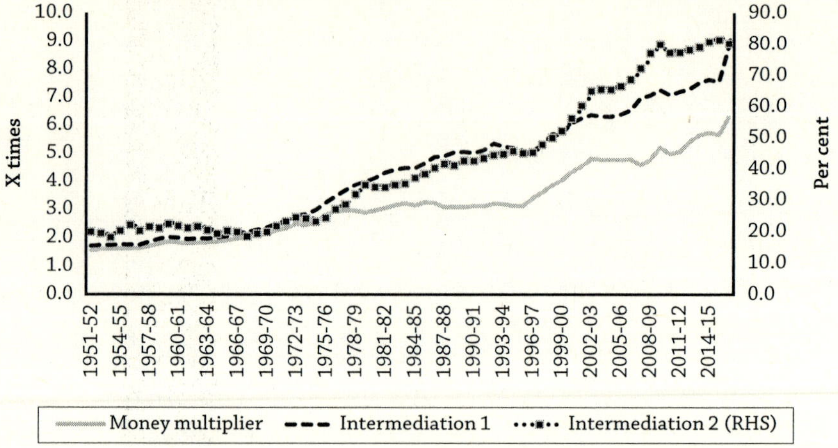

Note: 1. Money multiplier is defined as ratio of broad money to reserve money.

2. Intermediation 1 is defined as ratio of broad money to currency with the public.

3. Intermediation 2 is defined as ratio of broad money to nominal GDP (in per cent).

Figure 13.2

Inflation and Bank Rate since 1935-36

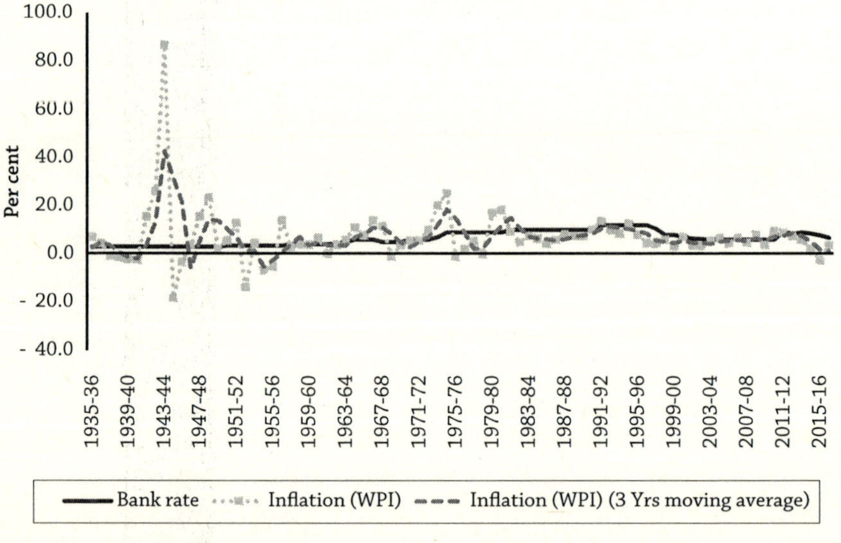

Table 13.1

Inflation, Interest Rate, Money and Output

(In per cent)

Indicators/Years	*1935-1952*	*1952-1969*	*1969-1985*	*1985-1998*	*1998-2015*	*1952-2015*
Inflation Rate						
A	9.9	3.7	8.2	8.0	5.6	6.4
L	-18.4	-13.9	-1.1	4.4	2.0	-13.9
H	86.7	13.9	25.2	13.7	9.6	25.2
Bank Rate						
A	3.1	4.4	8.1	10.9	7.2	7.5
L	3.0	3.5	5.0	10.0	6.0	3.5
H	3.5	6.0	10.0	12.0	10.5	12.0
Broad Money Growth						
A	16.1	7.8	16.6	17.3	16.5	14.4
L	0.4	-4.4	10.7	15.6	11.9	-4.4
H	68.0	12.0	20.4	19.8	22.1	22.1
Narrow Money Growth						
A	—	6.6	12.5	16.2	13.6	12.0
L	—	-6.5	-5.9	11.8	5.8	-6.5
H	—	12.0	19.0	24.1	19.8	24.1
Reserve Money Growth						
A	—	6.0	13.7	16.4	13.3	12.1
L	—	-7.1	3.2	6.3	6.0	-7.1
H	—	10.6	22.9	22.9	27.5	27.5
Real GDP Growth						
A	2.8	3.9	3.9	5.4	6.9	5.1
L	-5.6	-2.6	-5.2	1.1	3.8	-5.2
H	11.5	7.8	9.1	9.6	10.3	10.3

Notes: A: Average, L: Low, H: High; —: Not Available.

Inflation: Variations in wholesale price index (WPI).

Bank Rate: Interest rate announced by RBI.

Broad Money: Currency with the public and bank deposits.

Narrow Money: Currency with the public and demand deposits with banks.

Reserve Money: Currency in circulation and banks' deposits with RBI.

Real GDP: GDP at constant market price.

Figures for 1935-1952 are not comparable with that of 1952-2015 because of difference in coverage and definition. Real GDP growth for 1935-1952 is proxied by industrial production and broad money by money supply.

Source: *Handbook of Statistics on Indian Economy*, RBI.

History of the Reserve Bank of India, Volume 1 (1935-1951), RBI.

Annexure Table A-13.1

Key Events Impacting Monetary Policy: 1935-2016

Year	Events
1935	RBI instituted; official Bank Rate 3.5 per cent
1943	Bengal Famine
1946	Rupee notes of denomination ≥₹500 demonetised
1947	Partition & independence of India
1949	Rupee was devalued by 30.5% vis-à-vis pound-sterling; Banking Regulation Act enacted; RBI was nationalised
1951	First Five-year Plan
1956	System of ad hoc treasury bills for government introduced
1962	Border conflict with China
1964	Net Liquidity Ratio (NLR) for commercial banks introduced
1965	Pakistan Aggression; Credit Authorisation Scheme (CAS) introduced
1966	Rupee devalued by 36.5% vis-à-vis US dollar
1969	Nationalisation of major commercial banks
1971	Indo-Pak war
1973	First oil price shock; drought
1976	Monetary projection replaces credit budgeting
1981	Policy focus shifts to broad money (M3); recourse to IMF loan of US $ 5 billion
1986	Introduction of monetary targeting policy framework with M3 as the intermediate target
1989	Peak pre-emption through CRR and SLR at 53% of banks' NDTL
1990	Gulf war hastens Balance of Payments (BoP) crisis
1991	BoP crisis and initiation of far reaching reforms; Rupee devalued by 18.7% vis-à-vis US dollar
1993	Switch to fully market determined exchange rate system
1997	Automatic monetisation government budget deficit discontinued; South-East Asian crisis; Pokhran nuclear test and economic sanctions and consequent pressure on BoP
1998	Multiple Indicators Framework for monetary policy introduced
2000	Liquidity Adjustment Facility (LAF) introduced; launch of India Millennium Deposits (IMD)
2004	Ratio of Net Foreign Assets (NFA) to reserve money rises to 125%, Market Stabilisation Scheme (MSS) bonds introduced as instrument of sterilisation
2005	Technical Advisory Committee on Monetary Policy (TACMP) set up; macro-prudential tools of higher risk-weight, loan to value (LTV) introduced
2006	Ceiling and floor restriction for CRR removed empowering RBI to determine the level of CRR
2007	The floor rate of 25% for SLR removed empowering RBI to determine SLR level
2011	New monetary operating procedure introduced with repo rate as the single policy rate with other rates linked to it in a corridor for interest rate determination
2015	A flexible inflation targeting framework for monetary policy introduced
2016	The preamble of RBI Act amended clearly assigning price stability as the objective of monetary policy; a voting Monetary Policy Committee (MPC) was set up to take monetary policy decision

14

Prudential Levels of Public Debt

INDIRA RAJARAMAN

Introduction

If all students trained in Economics had looped back into teaching Economics, the subject would have lived in a self-contained bubble and had no impact on the world. It is because of students like Raj Kapila, who took a Master's degree from the Delhi School of Economics, and then moved out into a career as an economist with Government at Central and state levels and with industry associations, interspersed with spells as an economic journalist, that we see the impact of that training on the functioning of the world. He took early retirement and used his savings to set up Academic Foundation, which has grown into a pre-eminent publishing house in India. In this venture, Raj Kapila was ably partnered by his wife Uma Kapila, my revered teacher as an undergraduate at Miranda House, Delhi University, and later a senior colleague in the same department. Academic Foundation covers a very wide range, but is known in particular for advancing discourse on public policy in India by making available scholarly writings and official reports in reasonably priced, high quality publications. In this way, it has created widespread understanding of policy issues, and public participation in the process of formulating policy.

To honour Raj Kapila's life and memory, I decided to write on public debt sustainability, which came back into policy focus in the year of his passing, with the establishment of a Governmental committee in May 2016 to review Fiscal Responsibility and Budget Management (FRBM) legislation.

This paper tries to capture the present state of play in respect of prudential limits on debt and deficits.

Borrowing by governments to fund the fiscal deficit, when public expenditure requirements exceed total current revenue, is not new. Such fiscal deficits build up a stock of public debt. A government can run a fiscal deficit only as long as there is a counterparty willing to lend, since borrowing is always voluntary unlike taxation.[1] So the ability of a government to borrow is subject to its reputation for fiscal responsibility.

Fiscal deficits became sanctified by John Keynes in the 1930s, as a way by which to boost aggregate demand and pull economies out of a slump in economic activity, of the kind that happened during the Great Depression. Keynesian thinking revolutionised macroeconomics and in particular public economics—the study and practice of governmental expenditure on provision of public goods, and the financing of that expenditure through taxation and other means. Prior to Keynes, governments did borrow for financing unusual expenditure, such as on wars, or for financing large infrastructure projects like rail networks, through the issue of bonds or loans from private moneylenders or banks. It was Keynes who justified the idea of general purpose borrowing, for no targeted intent other than the need to pump-prime the economy through public expenditure.[2] These borrowings would be backed not by the promise of payback through collections from an

---

1. India has had a SLR (statutory liquidity ratio), whereby banks are required to invest a stipulated per cent of their funds in government securities, which creates a captive market and could in a sense be termed involuntary lending to government. The SLR is presently 20.5 per cent of deposit and time liabilities of banks.

2. In a developing country however, there is the larger need of ensuring that the expenditure creates capital assets as a secure foundation for long-term growth. This requirement underlies the tension within the Mahatma Gandhi National Rural Employment Guarantee Scheme (MNREGA), a workfare programme in India legislated in 2005, between the immediate purpose of placing purchasing power in the hands of the rural poor, and the need of the country for productivity-enhancing capital assets in rural areas, like drains and wells and roads.

infrastructure project, but by the status of governments as responsible entities who would not default on their promise to service and eventually redeem the loans they take. And indeed, although there have been defaults by sovereign governments from time to time, people all over the world still willingly buy government securities on the strength of their faith in the borrowing government.

Over the 1980s and 1990s, there developed a fear that Keynesian thinking could move economies to licentious fiscal conduct, and thereby endanger the economic health of all countries in a financially interconnected world. This was despite the rise of rating agencies, which gave sovereign governments risk ratings, with the risk premium getting built into the interest payable on the bond. Governmental expenditure programmes can develop an internal persistence and survive well beyond the immediate need, such as a Keynesian stimulus, which gave birth to them at the time of an economic slump. Similarly, tax cuts introduced at such times to stimulate private demand for goods and services are difficult to reverse when the economy has recovered. There also arose a reinforcing recognition that government is not the benevolent agent assumed in much of public economics, but an elected body (in democratic systems) which is interested principally in holding on to political power, and not so much in what is good for the country over the longer term, except where voters are sufficiently discerning as to reject short term gains in favour of more enduring benefits. Empirical work on the term of office of elected governments established that fiscal deficits do spike upwards as elections approach,[3] as the government in power seeks to find favour with the electorate by loosening on both expenditure and tax fronts. It became clear that the political cycle was if anything more influential than the business cycle in dictating the path of fiscal deficits.

3. In India over the 55 years 1950-2005, there was an upward spike in the primary fiscal deficit of between 0.5-0.6 per cent of GDP in every year preceding a general election (Rajaraman 2008). The introduction of fiscal responsibility legislation in 2003 was intended to bank down such spikes, although the call for a global fiscal stimulus in 2008-09 threw off that restraint before the general election of 2009.

By the 1990s, the need to legislatively enact fiscal targets so as to contain these naturally inherent political incentives in the system had become a fairly routine element of advice rendered by the multilateral agencies to countries emerging from socialist rule, and those in the developing world. The adoption of the Maastricht treaty targets in 1992 whereby member countries of the European Union agreed to limit public debt at 60 per cent of GDP (gross domestic product), and fiscal deficits at 3 per cent of GDP, acted also as an aspirational example of self-imposed fiscal responsibility.

In India, the first FRBM Act enacted by the Central Government in 2003 ran from 2004-2009.[4] Although, as in the Indian case, there is no real legislative penalty for a government which fails to keep to its fiscal targets, the watch kept by rating agencies acts as a powerful reinforcement to adhere to legislated targets, since the sovereign rating affects borrowing rates and the willingness of foreign capital to enter the country.

After the global crisis of September 2008, the move towards inviolable legislated fiscal targets took a back seat again, as the G-20 issued a call for a concerted macroeconomic stimulus across its member countries. The last year, 2008-09, of the fiscal correction horizon under the Central FRBM Act of 2003 was overshadowed by the fiscal stimulus call.[5] During that and subsequent years, the fiscal deficit at the Central level of the Indian federal system ballooned out of control, and borrowing limits for states were also enhanced.

This experience of runaway public debt, shared by other G-20 countries who followed the global stimulus call, gave rise to post-stimulus realisation of the natural tendency of the fiscal system to spin out of control, and

4. State governments also enacted fiscal responsibility legislation, a few unilaterally even before 2003, but most of them in response to the incentives offered by the 12th Finance Commission (2005-2010), followed on by incentives offered by the 13th Finance Commission (2010-2015).

5. There were reinforcing domestic considerations, such as the introduction of higher salary scales for civil servants by the 6th Pay Commission, which were implemented that year.

the need to curb it. Even so, calls for fiscal austerity were fiercely contested, in the United States (US) as well as in the Eurozone, from those who saw no harm in continuing fiscal laxity in view of slow global recovery. Those who argued against fiscal flexibility to combat the business cycle saw the need to have curbs in place at all times on natural political tendencies, cutting across ideologies and parties. The term in office of any government ranges typically between 4 to 5 years. During this time, a politically embattled government will have a natural preference for fiscal profligacy, so as to broaden its appeal to the electorate. If it loses the next election, the painful task of restoring fiscal order—cutting expenditures and raising taxes—devolves on the victorious party elected to office. That painful task may lose the victor his popularity with the electorate. And so it could go, endless political turbulence resulting from failure to enact limits on deficits and public debt. The gradual acceptance of this point of view led to what might be termed the second birth of inflexible fiscal targets.

A follow-on FRBM was accordingly enacted in India by the Central government, which ran from 2013 to 2018. But by 2016, the tide in India had turned again in favour of flexibility, in response to the macroeconomic slowdown that was becoming apparent. It was in this context that the FRBM review committee was appointed in May 2016. Their report submitted in January 2017 in four volumes was released in mid-April 2017.

Volume 1 of the report, which will be the principal focus of attention here, carries the key recommendations of the committee, along with a note of dissent by the Chief Economic Advisor, a member of the committee.[6] From the terms of reference given to the Committee, it is clear that fiscal flexibility was foremost among the tasks assigned to it. The relevant extract given in the report reads as follows:

6. Volumes 2 and 4 carry papers and presentations submitted to the committee by national and international experts and multilateral agencies. They are a rich source of information on international practice in respect of fiscal control legislation. Volume 3 carries the official responses of state governments to a questionnaire sent to all states by the committee.

- To examine the need and feasibility of having a 'fiscal deficit range' as the target in place of the existing fixed numbers (percentage of GDP) as fiscal deficit target; if so, the specific recommendations of the Committee thereon; and
- To examine the need and feasibility of aligning the fiscal expansion or contraction with credit contraction or expansion respectively in the economy.

In what follows, the next section on public debt, deficits and fiscal flexibility will look at the targets set by the FRBM Committee, in the context of the analytics of debt and deficits. The committee chose a six year horizon for fiscal correction going upto 2023.[7] What the committee had in mind for the period beyond 2023 was unclear, and was among the issues raised in the dissent note of the CEA (chief economic adviser). It will also examine the recommendations of the Committee on the issue of fiscal flexibility.

The section following, on parastatal debt and other fiscal worries, will focus on the pile-up of debt taken by state-level parastatal entities, with or without formal guarantees from the State government in whose jurisdiction they fall. The problem of debt taken by parastatals at state-level, particularly in the power sector, was so acute that an Ujwal Debt Assurance Yojana (UDAY) scheme was formulated in November 2015, specifically to address this problem. States were given permission to borrow additionally, over and above their routine entitlements as approved by the Centre under Article 293(3) of the Constitution,[8] to give

7. On the grounds that six years is the standard projection horizon of the World Economic Outlook, the annual publication of the International Monetary Fund.

8. State borrowing is subject to the approval of the Central government for states carrying any outstanding debt to the Centre, which until now has included all states; a time may come in the future when one or more states may be freed from this constraint if they have paid off all loans to the Centre. Central control over sub-national borrowing has been a positive feature of the Indian federation, enabling retention of control of overall public borrowing at national level.

them the wherewithal with which to take over power sector debt. Unfortunately, the FRBM Report says very little about UDAY, even though it provides the template for a one-time resolution of all parastatal debt. The section also covers two other fiscal phenomena peculiar to India. The first is that of Pay Commissions, which are appointed by the Central government roughly every 10 years or so, to revise the pay scales of civil servants (defined to include government employees in all categories, and not just those in the elite services). These scales then become almost mandatorily payable to officials appointed by state governments, and increasingly, to officials at the third tier of government—municipal bodies and *panchayats*—as well. When the further burden of upgrading teachers in state-supported institutions, schools, universities and other institutions of higher learning are added on, the initial expenditure spike to the public finances of the system becomes magnified several fold. The other is the concern that fiscal deficit restraints should not cramp capital expenditure, which is critical for growth in a country still starved of physical infrastructure in essential public services like roads, and sanitation and sewerage networks. This has been sought to be protected by having limits on current expenditure through something called a RD (revenue deficit) in addition to the FD (fiscal deficit). The issue of whether there should be a limit on the RD will be covered in this section as well, as it is dealt with in the FRBM report, and in the CEA's dissent.

Public Debt, Deficits and Fiscal Flexibility

The FD measures the net[9] new borrowing every year, and is the annual flow addition to the stock of public debt outstanding. An FD time-table is the most usual form taken by fiscal responsibility legislation. However every such time-table, even if specified only in terms of the operating deficit target, has in mind a desired level of public debt which is judged sustainable. All fiscal

9. Net of repayments; the stock is the aggregate face value of outstanding borrowings.

targets, whether for deficits or the stock of debt, are specified as percentages of current nominal GDP rather than as absolute magnitudes, so as to enable comparison over time.[10] Therefore, the dynamics of the relationship between debts and deficits is mediated by the growth rate in nominal GDP, which is roughly the real growth rate plus the inflation rate.[11]

The formal link between fiscal targets for debts and deficits, is worked out and illustrated in a table in the Appendix A-14.1. The Maastricht treaty explicitly stated the operating target for the FD at 3 per cent of GDP, and also stated the steady state debt target to be approached through this operating target, at 60 per cent of GDP. The implicit growth rate from the ratio of the debt to the FD target (20 in this case) is 5.26 per cent, which was clearly judged feasible for the member countries of the EU.

The report of the FRBM committee for India states right at the outset that their approach was to mark a prudential level for general government debt, aggregating across Centre and states, as the anchor to which the fiscal deficit as the operating target would be prescribed. The prudential level was set by them at 60 per cent of GDP, and a draft bill in an annexe to the report accordingly commits the (Central) government to bringing down the national public debt from roughly 70 per cent of GDP at the end of fiscal year 2017[12] to 60 per cent by 2023. The debt of the Centre is also marked for reduction from 49 per cent to 39 per cent[13] of GDP by 2023. From this it is clear that the heavy lifting in terms of the fairly sharp fiscal correction targeted over the period to 2017-2023 is to be done at the

10. The US is a major exception, where the federal debt limit is prescribed as an absolute amount in dollars, currently approximately $19.9 trillion. The limit can only be raised by Congress, as an amendment to a 1917 law. President Obama struck a deal with Congress to suspend the debt ceiling, but the suspension expired on 15 March 2017. So as of that date, total debt is frozen at the absolute dollar limit.

11. That is just the summation approximation to the true value, obtained by multiplication of the relevant factors.

12. *FRBM Review Committee Report 2017*: Chapter 4, p.63.

13. The summary of the report rounds this off to 40 per cent.

Centre; the states essentially are held at the same level of debt as they were in 2017. The FD at the Centre is marked for a front-loaded reduction of 0.5 per cent of GDP to 3.0 per cent in 2017-18, and thereafter to an eventual level of 2.5 per cent of GDP in 2022-23.

Among the points of dissent raised by the CEA, a member of the committee, is that he does not see the need for such precipitate fiscal correction over so short a period. Fiscal targets are legislated typically in situations where the debt level is either too high, or rising dangerously, calling for an immediate correction through the FD. The general government debt level has actually declined sharply in India since 2005-06, and is not the highest in a league table of comparator countries.[14]

Another point of dissent raised by the CEA is that the report is not very clear as to what will happen after the correction period is over. The bill commits to holding the debt level reached by 2023 as a ceiling indefinitely thereafter. But the steady state destination for public debt is left unspecified, other than that it will lie below the ceiling. The steady state level will be a function of the operating target for the general government FD. But since the bill prescribes the FD path only for the Centre, and only up to 2022-23, it does not in fact carry a fiscal vision for general government going beyond six years.

The FRBM committee's target for the general government FD, not stated in the bill but specified in Chapter 4 of the report, is set at 5 per cent of GDP.[15] The nominal GDP growth rate assumed is 11.5 per cent obtained as a summation approximation of a plausible projection of 7.0 per cent for annual real GDP growth, and inflation at 4.5 per cent, just above the mid-point of the inflation targeting range committed to in the

14. *FRBM Review Committee Report 2017*: Chapter 4, Figures 4 and 5.

15. There is some confusion about how the FD target will be split between Centre and states, with Chapter 4 saying 2.5 per cent each, but Chapter 5 suggesting states will go down to 2.0 per cent of GDP by 2022-23, and to 1.7 per cent of GDP by 2024-25.

new monetary policy framework.[16] Staying with general government for the moment, an FD held steady at 5 per cent will move the economy at that nominal GDP growth rate towards a steady state debt level of 48.5 per cent of GDP (see table in Appendix A-14.1). But that is at odds with Chapter 4, which strenuously strives to establish 60 per cent as the prudent level for debt—as a target, not just as a ceiling. For the economy to move towards a steady state target for debt at 60 per cent, the required general government FD at a nominal growth rate of 11.5 per cent works out to 6.2 per cent, not 5.0 per cent (marked as an alternative to the FRBM path in the table of Appendix A-14.1).

The CEA also questions why the FD target of 5 per cent for general government had to be obtained through a back-of-the-envelope calculation first used by the 12th Finance Commission, based on very uncertain estimates of the household financial savings rate. If, as the report claims, their entire exercise was anchored on choosing a prudential debt target, and if they had a projected nominal GDP growth rate, their required FD would have emerged automatically out of the relevant equation. As the CEA argues in his dissenting note, there was no need whatever for arriving independently at an FD target. The consistency requirement between debt and deficit targets for the medium term has to be formally upheld, since debt is the accumulation of fiscal deficits over time, mediated by the nominal rate of GDP growth.

On the key term of reference given, to look into the possibility of prescribing a FD range rather than a single number, the committee has this to say:

> The Committee, however, unanimously ruled this out for three reasons. First, consultation with domain experts, particularly in the context of Parliamentary

---

16. The correct nominal GDP growth rate at those real growth and inflation factors works out to 11.8 per cent. The new monetary policy framework, contained in an amendment to the RBI Act effected through the Finance Act 2016, states that an inflation target will be determined once every five years. The inflation target as announced in a gazette notification dated 5 August 2016 for the period until 31 March 2021, is 4 per cent, with a +/- band of 2 per cent on either side.

> democracies, suggests that a range for the fiscal deficit more often than not tends to get operationalised at the upper end of the range. Second, some amount of flexibility is automatically built in the proposed framework, if fiscal deficit targets are fixed to one decimal, which allows for some space for changes within the decimal point. Finally, the Committee agreed that fixed targets rather than a range can make fiscal policy more predictable, and therefore enhance investor confidence (Volume 1, Chapter 1, pp.10-11).

What the committee proposes instead, to deal with the need for countercyclicality in fiscal targets, is an escape clause which can be triggered when growth departs (in either direction) by 3 percentage points or more from its latest four-quarter average. Even though the committee prescribes a departure of no more than 0.5 per cent of GDP from the FD target in such an event, and an immediate return the next year to the routine path, the growth trigger is so large as to make it a low probability event. This too is a point of dissent raised by the CEA, although clearly he was a party to the unanimous decision not to specify a range.

A fiscal design which enables countercyclical adjustment in a timely way so as to smooth normal slowdowns or overheating requires calibration to departures of growth indicators from the expected trend. That is admittedly difficult to do, given the somewhat brittle state of GDP estimates in India, and the proclivity to fairly radical revision of GDP estimates. The further problem is that it can carry perverse policy incentives, if the permissible relaxations are not clearly calibrated to exogenous shocks.

The larger issue remains, of how flexibility in fiscal targets can be attained, even in the best of data situations. Fiscal relaxation can be achieved through either tax relief, or expenditure enhancements. Tax relief has an adhesive quality—reversal of a rate reduction attracts hostility from tax payers. Expenditure enhancements in productive directions requires a shelf of shovel-ready projects that can be instantly started in the event of fiscal need. Since that is not feasible, expenditure stimuli typically consist of handouts, like writing off farm loans (an episodic occurrence in India).[17] Likewise, fiscal tightening at a time of overheating whether in the form of tax rate enhancements, or expenditure reductions faces hostility, and therefore tends to penalise segments that are most vulnerable and least able to protest, or to take a non-transparent form, such as delays in payments of student scholarships, or of wages on workfare schemes. The purpose of including flexibility as a key element in the terms of reference given to the FRBM committee was so as to systematise countercyclical adjustments in place of ad hoc and possibly capricious adjustments.

The tension between the need for flexibility and the need for firm boundaries so as to rein in political fiscal excesses, remains unresolved. There can be no question about the enormous need for physical infrastructure in India, particularly for water conservation and for processing of waste water. The water crisis staring at us happens to have come starkly to the fore with the drought in Tamil Nadu and neighbouring states during the summer of 2017. Unless resolved in a permanent manner, this will cause human distress on an unparalleled scale, not to mention the growth cost in a dynamic region of the country. Fiscal relaxations to permit a major onslaught on the capital structures required, not just in Tamil Nadu but all over the country, will add to deficits and debt. If well implemented, they will give a growth impetus that will, most of all, be sustainable, and provide the GDP denominator on which a sharp subsequent reduction in debt will be enabled. If badly implemented, the resulting disaster will have both financial and real dimensions.

---

17. During the press conference following the first bi-monthly monetary policy statement on 6 April 2017, the RBI Governor in response to a question about a recent farm loan waiver announced by a State government, was critical of such schemes for undermining credit discipline, and for impacting public debt and the cost of borrowing (*https://rbi.org.in/Scripts/bs_viewcontent.aspx?Id=3334*; accessed on 6 May 2017). Farm loan waivers have also in the past been announced by the Central government, and are not exclusively a State government giveaway.

At the end of the day, the success of fiscal rules, whether rigid or flexible, will be a function of the level of governance in the country. In India, protected as we are from subnational excesses by constitutional guardrails, the fiscal record has been by and large good, with no sovereign defaults. But the governance challenge remains at both Central and state levels.

Parastatal Debt and Other Fiscal Worries

The FD of states in aggregate is recorded in the FRBM review report as having risen alarmingly in recent years. Aggregate figures for states suffer from a greater reporting time-lag than for the Centre, but subject to that, there does not seem to have been a general rise so much as a spike to 2.9 per cent in 2014-15, from 2.2 per cent the previous year.[18] Two points are worth noting here. First, the FD limits for states are set in accordance with their FRBM time paths as recommended by Finance Commissions, and in general target a prudential 3.0 per cent of the state-level GVA (gross value added). The 3.0 per cent limit is similar to the Central FRBM fiscal deficit target, but because the GVA of states in aggregate is necessarily lower than the GDP, the targeted limit for states works out to roughly 2.7 per cent of GDP.[19] Second, since market borrowings of states are subject to overall approval by the Centre under Article 293(3) of the Constitution,[20] any observed increase crossing 2.7 per cent has to have had the prior approval of the Centre.

Since 2015-16, there has been a sanctioned increase in state debt, beyond approved limits under the 14th Finance Commission provisions, under the UDAY scheme for a one-

18. There was a fall again by the budget estimates to 2.5 per cent by 2015-16 (*FRBM Committee Report 2017*: Chapter 5, Table 1).

19. Actually, it would be a little lower, because the national GVA aggregate is higher than the aggregate GVA of states, on account of Union Territories being included with the Central Government. The 2.7 per cent equivalence has been calculated from the ratio of GDP to GVA at current prices by the latest figures from the Central Statistical Organisation for the triennium 2014-2017.

20. See footnote 8.

time rationalisation of debt incurred by State government owned power distribution companies (DISCOMs), announced on 5 November 2015. The scheme permitted a one-time transfer onto the explicit outstanding debt stock of states of DISCOM debt, over a two-year window—50 per cent in 2015-16 and 25 per cent in 2016-17. Over several years, these companies have dived into ever deeper debt on account of inability to recover payments from users and failure of state governments to set power tariffs at levels compatible with full cost recovery, supplemented by distribution losses. The willingness of banks to lend to DISCOMs beyond prudential limits was undoubtedly because the debt carried either an explicit or implicit State government guarantee. State-level fiscal responsibility legislation, in force since 2005, carries limits on contingent debt (debt underwritten by the state government), precisely to limit the risk to the exchequer from these kinds of debt build-ups. But whether these limits are adhered to is a function of the effectiveness of the state auditor. Outstanding debt of DISCOMs was estimated in the press release announcing the scheme at around 3.5 per cent of GDP. The Financial Stability Reports of the RBI do not report sectoral default ratios in the banking sector for DISCOMs as a group. DISCOMs are packaged into the infrastructure group, which covers telecommunications and transport along with power. The latest report dated December 2016 with figures for September 2016, shows the stressed advances ratio of scheduled commercial banks for the infrastructure group at 18.6 per cent, as against 12.3 per cent across all sectors.[21]

Participation in the UDAY scheme was optional. The new debt replacement securities issued by states were outside the SLR (statutory liquidity ratio) obligations of banks, which was reasonable since the DISCOM debt being replaced was not included in the SLR. At the same time, there was a compulsion on banks to convert DISCOM debt not taken over by the state government into loans

21. RBI, *Financial Stability Report No. 14*: para 2.3 and chart 2.2g.

or bonds at interest rates not exceeding the bank's base rate plus 0.1 per cent. The scheme also committed states to directly funding the losses of DISCOMs over the period 2017-2021 in a graded manner (5; 10; 25; 50%). This latter provision was undoubtedly intended to incentivise states to rationalise the tariff structure, to remove political obstacles from recovery of revenues from users, and to enable the efficiency of DISCOM functioning. The scheme provided for additional grant funding from the Centre through which states could fund these additional expenditures.

The FRBM review committee does not give any sense of how many states had opted to participate in UDAY by the time of finalisation of their report. Experience with the UDAY scheme is important, because it provides a possible template for resolution of a malpractice reported in the FRBM report, whereby state governments contract debt through parastatals, which therefore does not get recorded as state debt, but service the debt through the budget. These kinds of violations of both contingent liability limits as set in FRBM legislation, as well as acceptable accounting practices, reflects a shocking failure on the part of state auditors. Unless these past deals are cleaned up through a one-time UDAY-like transfer to official state debt, the basic transparency requirement for public debt is not met. The FRBM report gives no sense of the impact such a resolution of parastatal debt will have on aggregate state debt, and without that, its projection of holding states at their starting level of debt (at 21% of GDP) is not adequately underpinned.

The committee does not also address the problem of state governments having to face the impact of Central Government Pay Commission salary hikes every 10 years. These commissions periodically hike the salaries of civil servants on the Central payroll, but there is an immediate demand by state government employees for the revised pay scales. This then ripples out in concentric circles to include employees in state assisted health and education facilities. Pay Commissions over the years have interpreted their task to mean quantifying salary scales at parity with those in the private sector at comparable levels of skill. But because the disparity in pay within government employment cannot be very wide, this has come to mean that employees at lower skill levels are paid vastly more than what their equivalent skill levels command in private employment. This has therefore perpetuated the desperate rush to get into government employment at lower skill levels, and the concomitant practices of paying bribes to political leaders to get in. Pay Commissions should instead have paid attention to the task of transforming governance, but have unfortunately failed to do so (Rajaraman 2015).

For state governments, the decadal Pay Commission salary hikes are equivalent to an unfunded mandate, since there is no central assistance for a decision taken at the Centre but with incremental expenditure implications for them. However, since this is a predictable external shock, states can build up a reserve fund over a 10-year period to draw down at the time of the shock. The issue of Pay Commission shocks was considered by the 13th Finance Commission. The report recommends that the shock can be ameliorated by making the pay award commence from the date on which the recommendations are accepted by the government, thus doing away with the need for arrears.[22]

Finally, the issue of having a separate limit for the fiscal deficit on the current account (called a RD), has been a part of Indian practice with respect to fiscal legislation right from the start. In a developing country like India, functioning at seriously deprived levels of capital structures for basic transportation, sanitation and sewerage, and law and order, there is a need to protect capital expenditure from being compressed on account of fiscal deficit caps. The tendency of current expenditures on salary and perquisites to grow over time is inherent in any governmental system, and a separate limit on the deficit

---

22. *Report of the 13th Finance Commission 2009*: Volume I, para 9.64.

on current account has been the traditional mechanism through which this is done in India. The difference between the targeted FD and RD yields the level of protection given to capital expenditure, as a per cent of GDP.

The very first Central FRBM of 2003 targeted an RD at zero, so that capital expenditure would be protected at the full extent of the targeted cap on FD (3% of GDP). In fact, the RD target was the only one actually included in the bill; all the other targets were relegated to the rules accompanying the act. The rules can be changed just through an administrative notification. But the RD target could not be altered without actually amending the act (which was done, when the initial act was extended in the Finance Bill of 2012).

Increasingly, setting the RD at zero has been under fire for two reasons. One is that expenditures booked in the current account can be in the form of grants flowing to lower levels of government in the federal structure, which may have high capital expenditure content. Accordingly the amendment to the Central FRBM in 2012 introduced the idea of an effective RD, defined as the RD minus the capital content of current expenditures. The effective RD was targeted as zero in the amended act, corresponding to an RD of 2 per cent, thus yielding from the difference the computed capital content of current expenditure.

The second reason for criticism of the RD is that current expenditure on health and education is no less desirable than expenditure on physical capital, for the development of the country. The issue however, and the reason why it has gained traction in recent years, is that both health and education are salary intensive expenditures. With Pay Commission salary increases, a limit on current expenditure crowds out non-salary components, with the widely reported consequence of public health centres without medicines, and primary schools without books and other consumables like chalk and blackboards.

This really gets back to the issue of Pay Commissions, and points to how their blind salary increases without any attention to performance or outcomes, has exerted pressure on effective delivery of public services. There can be no question of the need for limits on FDs and RDs, as components of prudential financial management of the fiscal resources of government. Wherever those limits are drawn, ultimately there will be pressure on the deficit if the salary cost of providing those services is notched up every 10 years with no concomitant improvement in service delivery. It is this failure to improve the structure of governance that is at the heart of the dispute over whether there should be an RD in addition to an FD.

There is also the necessity for maintenance of capital structures, which has been seriously underfunded in India. This has led to the other common occurrence in India, of dangerously crumbling structures like bridges and rail tracks, endangering the lives of all citizens. Maintenance provisions are made on the current (revenue) account, and unless they fully accommodate the requirements of keeping capital structures in safe working order, the productivity of capital expenditures made in the past will be lost over time.

In this connection, an extract from the report of the 13th Finance Commission, is relevant:

> We recommend that all capital expenditure proposals for inclusion in the Government of India Budget are accompanied by a statement of the Revenue Consequences of Capital Expenditure (RCCE) for the lifetime of the proposed projects. RCCE statements should be annually modified to take into account price and other changes. The RCCE statements should be used to calculate revenue expenditure requirements in the years covered by the MTFP such that revenue expenditure projections are consistent with the RCCE statements (Report of the 13th Finance Commission, Volume I, para 9.45.).

Clearly therefore, the link between revenue and capital expenditure, and thereby the link between the RD and the FD, are at the heart of fiscal rectitude, which is not just a matter of targeting the RD at 0.8 per cent of GDP (as the

FRBM Committee prescribes), or not targeting it at all, as the CEA argues in his dissent note.

Finally, any deficit target defines the limits of expenditure over and above revenue raised. Therefore attention to fair collection of taxes from the entire tax base, and not just a portion of it, lies at the heart of fiscal responsibility. Then when it comes to expenditure, there has to be a partitioning while prescribing fiscal rules between committed expenditures like interest, salaries and pensions, and the residual—the compressible components of expenditure which can be subordinated to fiscal rules. Capital expenditure is an element in this compressible residual, and that is the reason why in India we have an RD so as to shift the burden of compressibility from the capital account to the revenue account.

The task of fiscal responsibility lies in so devising the structure that expenditures can be contained at a sustainable deficit over and above revenue, while still maintaining high standards of quality in public service delivery.

Acknowledgements: Thanks are due to Promila Rajvanshi for enabling access to the FRBM Review Committee Report in hard copy.

Appendix A-14.1

The Stock of Public Debt in the Steady State

If D is the absolute quantum of the debt stock, F is the absolute net new borrowing (net of repayments) to cover the fiscal deficit in any year, and the year to which these magnitudes refer is denoted by subscript t, then:

$$D_t = D_{t-1} + F_t$$

If these absolute magnitudes normalised by GDP in their respective years are denoted by the corresponding lower case for each, and the nominal rate of GDP growth between the years t and (t-1) by n, we have:

$$d_t = [d_{t-1}/(1+n)] + f_t$$

When normalised debt stabilises, we have $d_t = d_{t-1} = d$

If the FD is held constant at the level f in an economy growing steadily at the rate n, it can easily be shown that debt will stabilise at a level given by:

$$d/f = \left((1+n)/n\right)$$

Alternatively, the rate of nominal growth of GDP required for consistency between a debt target and an operating target for the fiscal deficit is given by:

$$n = 1/[\frac{d}{f} - 1]$$

In the case of the Maastricht treaty targets, where the ratio between the debt target at 60 per cent of GDP and the fiscal target at 3 per cent of GDP is 20, the implicit rate of GDP growth is given by $\left(\frac{1}{19}\right)$=5.26 per cent.

% of GDP	*d*	*n*	*f*
Maastricht	Target: 60	Implicit: 5.26	Target: 3
FRBM Review Committee path	Implicit: 48.5	Assumed: 11.25	Target: 5
Alternative FRBM path	Target: 60	Assumed: 11.25	Required: 6.2

References

FRBM Review Committee (2017). *FRBM Review Committee Report*, Volumes I-IV. New Delhi.

Rajaraman, Indira (2008). "The Political Economy of the Indian Fiscal Federation," *India Policy Forum* 4: 1–51.

———. (2015). "Governance and the Seventh Pay Commission", *Mint*, 4 December.

Reserve Bank of India (2016). *Financial Stability Report*, Issue No. 14. December. Mumbai.

Thirteenth Finance Commission (2009). *Report of the Thirteenth Finance Commission*, Volume I. New Delhi.

15

Fiscal Reforms in a Federal Framework

VIJAY KELKAR

By all accounts, Indian economy today is on a growth turnpike, not very different from the growth miracles experienced by Asian tigers as well as China in earlier decades. India has consistently accelerated its growth rate over the last three decades. Indian economy experienced an upward structural break in the mid-1980s. This was followed by growth story originated due to the initial push given by Rajiv Gandhi, Narasimha Rao and Manmohan Singh reforms of 1991 and subsequent reforms by Shri Atal Bihari Vajpayee and the United Progressive Alliance (UPA) government. Consequently, our country has not looked back ever since.

The deep determinants of this remarkable growth experience of ours have been institutions, demographic transition, modern technology and accumulation of both human and physical capital. In my view, the most important of these factors has been our democratic framework, a key foundational institution. Our democracy has proved to be sine qua non for effectively formulating key economic policies and conducting policy reforms in a country that is so diverse.

In a country as beautifully diverse as ours, federalism as an organising principle is clearly the only way to succeed. In the analytical literature, 'coming together' and 'holding together' are the recognised forms of federalism. United States (US) is the classic illustration of the first whereas the erstwhile Pakistan or Yugoslavia perhaps could be seen as illustrating the second.

Our approach to federalism is idiosyncratic. Distinguished jurist Nariman calls it 'quasi federalism'. I think it is better described as 'cooperative federalism', where governance has a multi-level form with evolving relations between different levels of government. 'Co-operative federalism' as a phrase was perhaps first used by the great Sanjeevi Guhan. As an aside, I may mention here that some people also talk about competitive federalism. I have considerable hesitation in deploying this term as I fear that it can only lead to race to the bottom via competitive populism. Ours is essentially a union of States consequently a unitary State, but with clearly demarcated rights and responsibilities at different levels of the government. Our model of cooperative federalism also offers flexibility for creatively responding to evolving structural changes. An example perhaps is the unique feature of concurrent list in our Constitution.

I want to argue that fiscal federalism has been one of the most important pillars for the success of our enduring democracy. Fiscal federalism has been the oxygen for the unique cooperative federal model of ours. The fiscal federalism mainly comprises allocation of rights and duties related to taxation and expenditure responsibilities and system of transfers between the different jurisdictions/levels of government such as Centre, State and local governments.

In the framework of fiscal federalism, federations all over have tried to tackle two important issues i.e., vertical imbalance and horizontal imbalance.

Vertical imbalance essentially arises due to the fiscal asymmetry in powers of taxation vested with the different levels of government in relation to their expenditure responsibilities prescribed by the Constitution. In India the Central government has far greater or larger domain where it may tax e.g., income taxes personal or corporate, taxing foreign transactions (exports/imports) or indeed the taxes on services are exclusively reserved for the Central government. In contrast, the State governments may only tax manufacturing and agricultural incomes, while the local or the third tier has even more limited power to tax being largely confined to property tax. Consequently, the Central government collects around 60 per cent while its expenditure responsibility for carrying out its constitutionally mandated responsibility such as defence is only to the tune of 40 per cent of the total public expenditure. Thus arises the vertical imbalance.

Horizontal imbalance arises because of the differential capacity to tax amongst the States as against the expenditures required for providing public goods of comparable quantity and quality to those residing in their States. This in turn arises because of the vast regional imbalances in terms of per capita incomes, physical and social capital endowments, natural resources availability such as water, mineral resources and geographical differences such as hilly terrain or desert area. The unevenness of developmental outcomes of course get further compounded by the differences in the levels of effective governance.

Both these imbalances if not satisfactorily resolved have the potential to provide the seeds for political discontent that could threaten the very democratic fabric and hence the national security and integrity.

In our county, unlike the other developed federal or quasi federal economies such as the US, Canada, Australia, and the European Union (EU) the regional disparities in terms of per capita incomes is much sharper due to yet another imbalance i.e. 'development or growth imbalance'. For instance, in developed countries the ratio of per capita incomes between the most and least developed regions seldom exceeds 2, whereas in our case it can be a high 5 to 6. This is accounted by differences in growth rates between States over a period of time, i.e., due to 'growth imbalance'. This differential growth rates could be due to several reasons as I have mentioned earlier but there is yet an additional important reason. Increased supply of both physical and social infrastructure is one of the major source for accelerating growth. The stock of infrastructure that gets accumulated over a period of time and lends a character of path dependency to this process. This in turn affects the growth going forward via the economics of agglomeration. This underlines the fact that when it comes to accelerating growth, it's not just geography and physical and natural resources but indeed, history matters! This issue too if kept unresolved can lead to a serious threat to Indian integrity. This is thus a fit case for serious fiscal policy intervention.

Our Constitution and creative democratic politics addressed these issues by creating two institutions viz., Finance Commission and Planning Commission. The Finance Commission derives its *raison de etre* from Articles 275, 280 and their sub-clauses to meet horizontal and vertical imbalance, whereas our political process leveraged Article 282 to create the Planning Commission. These institutions were used to carry out systematic fiscal transfers in the nature of devolution or conditional ones. This arrangement or framework of fiscal federalism in India served well in maintaining the general well-being and integrity of our country. I may add that many thoughtful analysts have argued that lack of such instrumentalities have led to break ups in many other federations.

Over the years, successive FCs (finance commissions) played important role towards strengthening fiscal federalism. Let me take the example of the more recent ones. The 10th FC chaired by K.C. Pant combined all the taxes into one combined pool for the purpose of devolution rather than doing it based on tax sources. This paved the way for important tariff reforms. Earlier to this, the Central government had no incentive to undertake such reforms as import duties were not shareable. The 12th FC under the Chairmanship of Dr Rangarajan enhanced the fiscal stability of the states by linking grants conditional upon observable fiscal discipline by the States. These conditional grants were in addition to the statutory unconditional/untied devolution of funds. This was very effective in improving the fiscal health of the States. The 13th FC opened up the possibility of formulaic tax devolution to the third tier in order to strengthen and empower democratic decentralisation process, through an interesting/innovative mechanism. This provided much needed "revenue buoyancy" to the local governments. The 14th FC gave a sharp increase in the percentage share of taxes devolved to the States whilst virtually in effect eliminating conditional transfers via the Planning Commission grants or grants under Central sector/ sponsored schemes. This along with the replacement of Planning Commission by NITI Aayog is considered by some to be a major reform for our cooperative federalism. I have a somewhat different perspective in this regard to which I will now turn.

In the present scheme of things, the collapsing of two different sources of transfers, aimed at differing objectives, is deeply problematic. Let me step back here for a bit and recall the different types of imbalances that I talked about. Each of these imbalances is important and needs to be rectified. One has to do with the differing levels of per capita consumption of basic public goods and services. The other has to do with the differing levels of stock of infrastructure leading the differential growth accelerating potential. These are two distinct policy goals and following Tinbergen Principle warrants two distinct policy instruments. Eliminating the Planning Commission and replacing this with NITI Aayog merely as a thinktank leaves us with only one instrument, namely Finance Commission. This approach if not reviewed can lead to a serious problem of increasing regional and sub-regional inequities.

I would therefore argue strongly that there is deep analytical foundation for a case where the NITI Aayog gets significant levels of resources for allocating to different States. These resource transfers will be aimed at mitigating growth imbalances by promoting accelerated growth of lagging States and sub-regions. Given our political economy, these grants need to be conditional and formulaic. The purpose of these grants would be to enable the lagging States to build capacities in infrastructure sectors such as roads, ports, railways and digital connectivity, supply of power, access to credit and improving governance. This will serve the objective of helping the lagging States and regions to attain growth acceleration and the reduction in developmental gap. Planning Commission as is well known, has been using the various forms of the famous Gadgil formula and later the Gadgil-Mukherjea formula for allocating plan grants. Although they did serve the needs of the time, given the acuteness of challenges posed by growing inequalities between States and regions. I believe we need to reinvent the formula by using somewhat different variables and emphasis, while being mindful of macroeconomic conjuncture and structural needs.

It is possible to suggest that such allocation of capital grants be administered by the Ministry of Finance. But, by nature of its mandate the Ministry of Finance is primarily concerned not with structural transformation but rather with the issues related to short/medium term macroeconomic stability including managing balance of payments, inflation and business cycle. Once gain invoking the Tinbergen's assignment principle viz., number of objectives matching the number of instruments, it is desirable that a functionally distinct entity such as the NITI Aayog be put to use to do the job at hand related to the structural problems including removal of regional imbalances in the economy as I have outlined above.

This would mean that NITI Aayog will be responsible for allocating development or transformational capital grants to the States. Given the overall resource constraints, what this would mean is that the future FCs, as against what has been done by the 14th FC, will have to revert to the modest percentages income in their devolution formula as was indeed the historical trend. This of course does not mean an overall reduction in the overall transfers but only in their composition and their source. I dare say that such an approach will help in strengthening the cooperative federalism as an acceleration of lagging regions will lead to higher growth in all the regions. A rigorous study by Prof Bhanumurthy, currently with National Institute of

Public Finance and Policy (NIPFF) demonstrates how such an outcome happens. Needless to say the overall levels of such transfers will be determined by the Ministry of Finance keeping in mind the FRBM regime in place.

Let me hasten to add that I am not suggesting for a moment that NITI Aayog should take the form of the old Planning Commission. On the contrary, it should take care to eschew yesteryears micro-management vis-à-vis Central Ministries and the State governments via excessive bureaucratisation. It should rather strive to be a think tank albeit with financial muscle and devote its energies to outline coherent medium and long term vision and strategy for transforming India.

I may also point out that such issues are increasingly arising at the State level due to emerging intra state/ regional disparities. I would recall the approach we suggested in the recent report of High Powered Committee in Maharashtra that I had chaired. We essentially adopted a two track approach, one related to equalisation of universal access to basic public goods and services in a benchmarked and per capita manner. The second track looks at the initial conditions and leverages the comparative advantage of a particular region and provides resources in an equitable fashion. This will lead to growth acceleration in the lagging regions. Similarly in the initial context, FC would be taking care of the first track and the second track, which is very important in the context of the correcting growth imbalance, and should be the primary focus of the empowered NITI Aayog along the lines of what I have suggested. I need to mention here that the key conditionality for the success of this approach that we recommended was an effective democratic decentralisation via empowerment of ULBs (urban local bodies) and PRIs (panchayati raj institutions) as envisaged by the letter and the spirit of 73rd and 74th Constitutional amendment/acts. I hope that NITI Aayog will find sufficient merit and adopt such an approach in its new suggested avatar.

Let me now turn to the final but to my mind the most important reform in the Indian fiscal federal framework.

This relates to the successful implementation of the flawless GST (goods and services tax). I must say that the recent passage of the GST Constitutional Amendment with unanimity in the Parliament, the notification, the ratification by 17 States and the Presidential nod all of this must surely gladden the heart of every right thinking citizen. This has demonstrated the ability of our political parties to be bi- partisan and almost statesman like to come together when fundamental national interests are involved.

In effect, this is also a 'grand bargain' with the Centre undertaking to implement a commonly agreed GST which would be done through a joint GST council. The GST council so created by the constitutional amendment is a landmark event in the history of India's fiscal federalism. The Centre and the States from being good fiscal neighbours now will become equal fiscal partners in sharing a common indirect tax base. To enable a successful and a smoother implementation of GST, the Centre has also agreed to compensate the states for any loss of revenue for a period of five years. While this is by no means a perfect grand bargain—electricity duties and taxes on real estate continue to be outside the purview of GST—it embodies the desired reform with the objective of creating a single Indian market in substantive measure. And yet this is only the beginning and a lot remains to be done. In this endeavour, the newly created GST council will indeed be decisive.

A mature engagement of all stakeholders with the GST council and laying down its rules of procedure and protocols will be the first order of the day. Fixing the exemptions as well as the rate structure will impact all the stakeholders and hence will entail much debate and technicalities. It would perhaps be prudent to follow the empowered committee system to sort such things out in a time bound manner outside the full council.

Whereas compensation to the States for five years is now a done deal, there is scope to decide the extent of compensation. A full compensation will create a perverse incentive for the States and lead to their not exerting enough to collect the tax revenues in an efficient fashion. To avoid such an adverse outcome, a tapered form of less than full compensation is the way forward.

Yet another issue that needs to be decided upon upfront has to do with the precise form and content that will comprise the delegated legislation. Whereas delegation may solve some specific problems for some States, it will be at the cost of the very national character of the GST. The council needs to ensure that as far as possible, there is a convergence of incentives amongst States which further means that there is consensus on the right compensation formula and minimising delegated legislation.

As the GST roll out happens, we need to keep in mind that taxation policy has to be transparent, predictable and inclusive. This alone can maximise the favourable impact of the GST on investment and growth. There are sweeping powers vested with the GST council not unlike a regulator who also arbitrates. This makes it even more essential that the changes and deliberations are put out as discussion papers and real consultations with the public take place. And then there is an important issue of capacity building. Let us ensure that the GST council will be a 21st century institution with digital empowerment and digital processes. Can we hope that it will be our first paperless institution? This council will need human resources as well as technical facility of high order. Having such capabilities should be GST councils' first priority.

The commitment to a shared tax structure across the Indian union, the end of cascading, the institutional approach to taxing the consumption of Indian citizens commonly wherever they reside are all features of a truly national single market that will bind the federation by removal of manmade barriers to the consumption of goods and services across the country. This will of course bring improvements in efficiency but will also promote inclusive and equalising growth.

The Central government has outlined its proposal for the GST rate structure. To me the approach outlined by the authorities signals a disappointing beginning which could have been otherwise; a thundering take off to shock and awe the domestic and international community and capital markets. I feel that this approach adopted by the authorities robs the GST of its efficiency enhancing potentials. This is due to several reasons:

1. Multiple rates varying from 4 per cent to 26 per cent.
2. Different rates for goods and services.
3. High rates for retail level.
4. Leaving out infrastructure sector such as construction, petroleum and electricity.

Consequently,

- The growth impact on the economy is estimated to be only one-fourth of its potential impact of what the 13th FC had estimated.
- High compliance cost arising out of different rates and consequent classification of disputes.
- Lower compliance levels due to the rates going up to as high as 26 per cent at retail level.
- Potential slackening of tax efforts by the States due to promised 100 per cent compensation of the shortfall.

I am afraid that all these difficulties may surface rather sooner than the later. Growing adverse reactions due to the unfolding of these problems will, I am sure, persuade the authorities to change its approach and follow a path more like the one outlined by the 13th FC.

I have no doubt that we will eventually move from one nation one tax to one nation, one tax, one registration and one rate and I am sure this single rate will be closer to 12 per cent. I am reminded by what Sir Winston Churchill said about US as this is relevant to other large democracy such as India. He said, "United States finally does right thing but only after trying all other alternatives".

In conclusion, I have discussed the issue of the need to revisit the fiscal federal architecture in contemporary India. Briefly tracing the origin of arrangement in contemporary history, I have attempted to point out the changing political-economic parametric environment calling for commensurate change in the way our fiscal federal setup ought to be conceptualised, here and now. In doing this, I have identified some of the important issues that arise as we move forward as well as suggested some important and innovative policy and fiscal reform proposals for their possible resolution. While the final resolution of these matters will be attained through a dialectic that will play out in the domain of real politik, it is important that such a process be helped along by evidence based analysis and debate.

This article draws upon the Shankar Aiyar Memorial Lecture on "Fiscal Reforms in a federal framework" delivered by Vijay Kelkar in Chennai on 21 October 2016.

16

The Geo-economics of the Trans-Atlantic Financial Crisis and the Indian Economy

SANJAYA BARU

The fiscal, trade, industrial, financial and banking sector reform that India undertook in the early 1990s helped her weather the consequences of the 'Asian financial crisis' in the late 1990s. India undertook further reforms and economic policy initiatives to overcome the impact of economic sanctions imposed on it by some developed countries in response to the nuclear tests conducted in the summer of 1998, following which India declared itself a 'nuclear weapons power'. Consequently, India's economic growth rate did not decline as sharply as that of the East and South-east Asian economies in the late 1990s (See Figure 16.1)

While India survived the initial impact of the trans-Atlantic financial crisis in 2008-09 despite being a more open and globally integrated economy, it did finally feel the impact of the global slowdown.

The Indian economy is on a long-term path of accelerating economic growth. Maddison's (2001) OECD-funded study of historical trends in the national income of major world economies shows that at the beginning of the 18th century Europe, China and India had more or less equal shares of world GDP (gross domestic product) and the two Asian economies have been recovering their lost space, albeit at a different pace, over the past half century (Figure 16.2).

Figure 16.1

Impact of Asian Financial Crisis on India's Real GDP Growth

Real Growth Rates of Selected Asian Economies

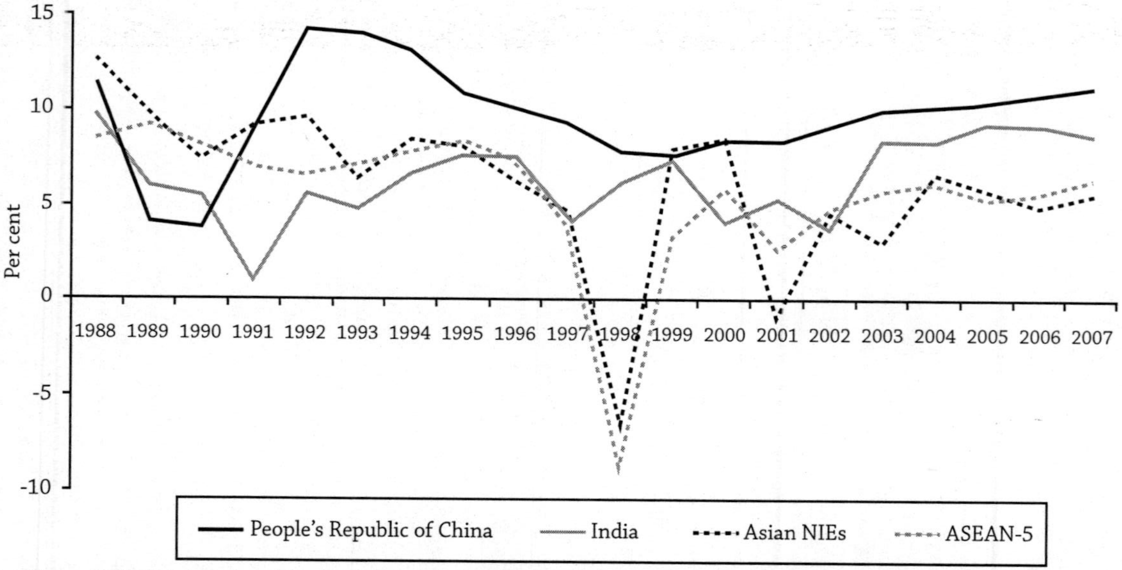

Notes: ASEAN= Association of Southeast Asian Nations, NIE= newly industrialising economy. Asian NIEs include Hong Kong, China, Republic of Korea, Singapore, and Taiwan, China.

Source: Asian Development Bank (ADB) (2008a; 2008b).

Figure 16.2

Historical Trends in Distribution of World Income: Percentage of World GDP (last 500 years)

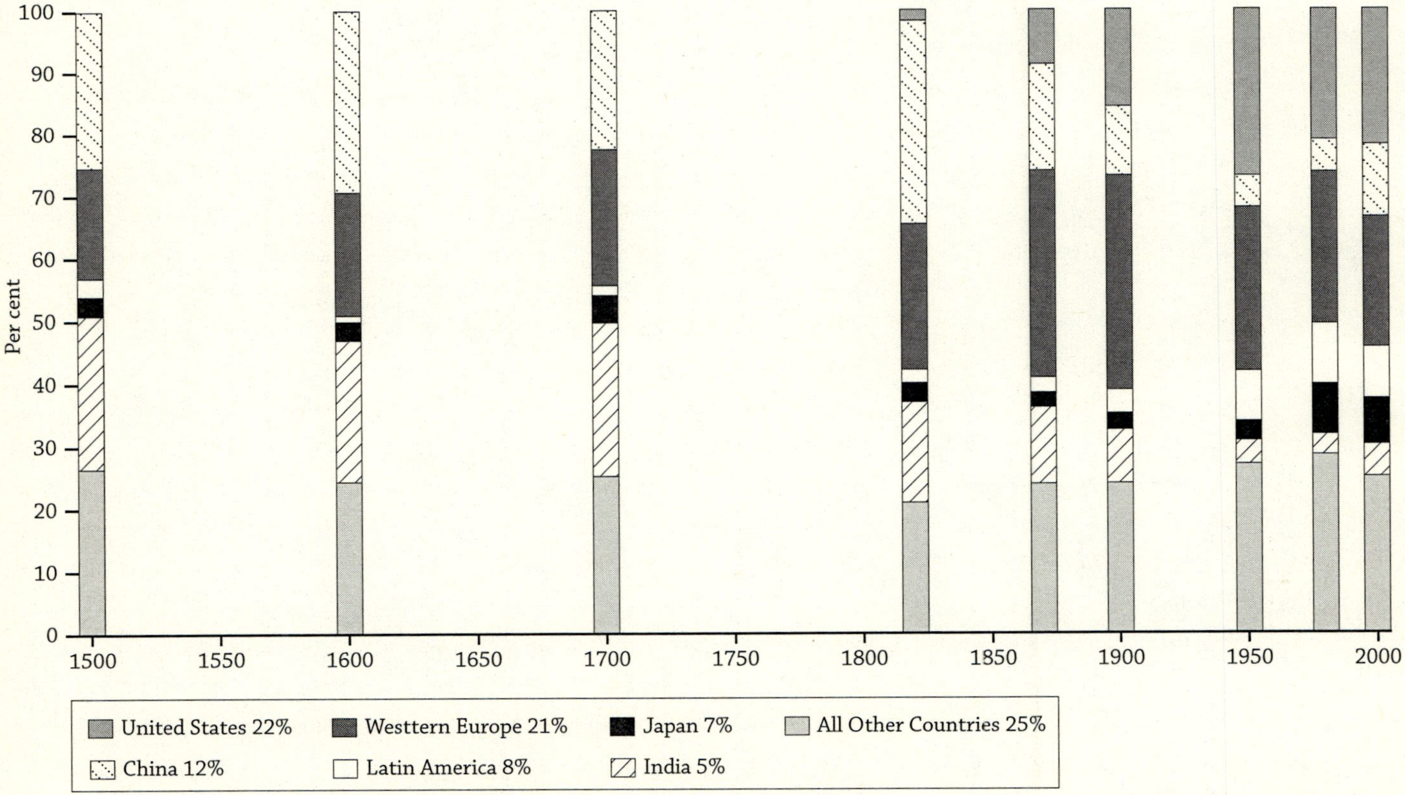

Source: Maddison (2001); *http://www.visualizingeconomics.com/category/angusmaddison/*

Figure 16.3

Trends in GDP Growth: 1952-2009

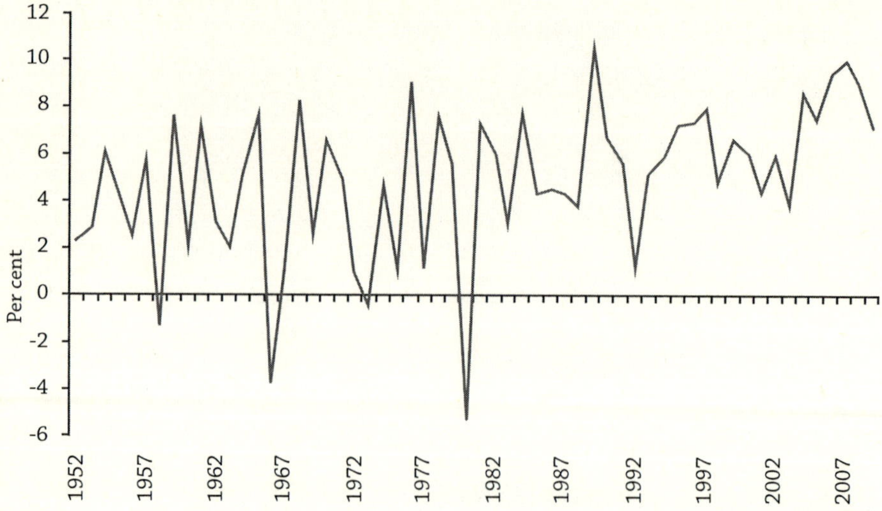

Source: Economic Advisory Council to Prime Minister, Government of India, March 2009.

The Indian economy has grown at an annual average of 3.5 per cent in 1950-80, close to 6.0 per cent in 1980-2004 and at close to 9.0 per cent since 2004 (Figure 16.3). India's more recent growth acceleration, since the early 1990s, has followed a shift in the macro-economic policy framework, with greater external and internal economic liberalisation. India's economic rise, as a 'free market democracy', and her reintegration into the global economy, creating new relationships of interdependence both globally and regionally, has shaped her strategic and foreign policies.[1]

Policy Impact of the Triple Crises of the 1990s

India's management of the 'triple crises'—fiscal, BoP (balance of payments) and financial crises—experienced sequentially between the late-1980s and the mid-1990s, set the stage for India's response to the Asian and, more recently, the 'trans-Atlantic' financial crises.

1. Baru 2006.

First came the 'fiscal crises of the 1990s. Responding to an unsustainable rise in budgetary and fiscal deficits, India adopted a fiscal stabilisation programme, subsequently enacting a Fiscal Responsibility and Budget Management (FRBM) Act, ensuring a reduction in revenue and fiscal deficits. However, the recent fiscal stimulus packages put in place in response to the current slowdown have forced the Government to breach the provisions of the FRBM Act.

Second came an external payments crisis in 1991. India has since undertaken transformative changes in her trade, tariffs and foreign investment policies. These have helped improve India's external economic profile, including a reduction in external debt to GDP ratios, an increase in trade/GDP and foreign investment/GDP ratios, and, most importantly, enabled India to accumulate foreign currency reserves. India's increased openness to global trade and capital flows has, however, increased her vulnerability to global crises and recession.

Third came the financial sector crisis of the early 1990s, which included a stock market crash and problems in the banking sector. India has since undertaken comprehensive financial sector reforms, put in place a world class regulatory and supervisory system for the equities market and the financial and banking sectors, recapitalised banks and improved their asset position.

While undertaking these internal reforms, India opted for gradualism in external sector liberalisation, adopting full currency convertibility only on the current account and eschewing it on the capital account. The cumulative impact of the reforms undertaken since 1991 has been to make the Indian economy more resilient to external shocks, even as it has become more open to external flows, enabling India to sustain an acceleration of her economic growth within a more open economy framework.

India's low inflation tolerance (the average rate of inflation for 50 years, 1950-2000, has been around 8.0%) has meant that fiscal and monetary policies have been largely conservative, with brief episodes of high inflation and fiscal laxity. It was the easing up of this fiscal conservatism that contributed to the 1990 crisis. Though India returned to a more conservative approach in fiscal policy, the current crisis has forced the government to adopt a liberal fiscal stance.[2]

In his authoritative review of India's new economic policies Panagariya concludes, "India has had a history of maintaining a relatively stable macroeconomic environment....,"[3] and says of India's external sector management in recent years: "The judicious handling of the monetary and exchange rate policies must be largely credited with price stability in the domestic market and a broadly competitive exchange rate that facilitated a healthy growth of international trade."[4]

In short, India's experience with handling the triple economic crises it confronted in the early 1990s has helped put in place a regime of policies that have contributed to an acceleration of economic growth and a strengthening of the Indian economy. This has helped India deal with the current slowdown with a greater degree of confidence.

Closing the Two Gaps

In the past, India's growth process has been constrained by what economists referred to as the 'two gaps'—a domestic savings gap and an external financing gap. Rising domestic savings and increased inflow of foreign capital have helped bridge both gaps, contributing to higher growth. For a long time India's savings rate was below 20 per cent, even as East and South-east Asian economies saw their savings rates exceed 30 per cent. In the 1990s India caught up. India's more recent growth acceleration has been facilitated by a sharp rise in the savings and investment rates (See Table 16.1).

Traditionally India had bridged the 'external gap' through foreign aid and concessional debt. However, after

2. See Joshi and Little (1994).
3. Panagariya (2008): xxiv.
4. Ibid.: 207.

1991, India reduced its dependence on aid and debt flows, and has allowed private capital flows to bridge the gap. The share of foreign investment in India's GDP has gone up (See Table 16.2 and 16.3) and foreign capital inflows have increased on account of higher remittances from overseas Indians.

Table 16.1

Growth Rate of GDP, Investment and Savings Rates

Financial Year	*GDP Growth (%)*	*Investment/GDP (%)*	*Savings/GDP (%)*
2000-01	4.4	24.3	23.7
2001-02	5.8	22.8	23.5
2002-03	3.8	25.2	26.3
2003-04	8.5	28.2	29.8
2004-05	7.5	32.2	31.7
2005-06	9.5	35.5	34.3
2006-07	9.7	35.9	35.6
2007-08 QE	9.0	37.4	37.8
2008-09 AE	7.1	35.5	35.9

Note: QE = quick estimate; AE = advance estimate.

Source: Prime Minister's Economic Advisory Council, Government of India, 2009.

Table 16.2

External Economy Indicators

Year	*Foreign Investment/GDP (%)*	*Foreign Investment/ Exports (%)*	*Import Cover of Foreign Exchange Reserves (Months)*
1990-91	0.0	0.6	2.5
1995-96	1.4	14.9	6.0
2000-01	1.5	14.9	8.8
2005-06	2.6	20.3	11.6
2007-08	5.2	38.8	15.0

Source: Reserve Bank of India Database.

Following the Asian financial crisis and, more importantly, after facing economic sanctions in the wake of the 1998 nuclear tests, imposed among others by the United States (US) and Japan, India chose to accumulate foreign exchange reserves as a hedge against risk of currency shortage. This explains the sustained rise in foreign currency assets since 2000 (Table 16.3).

Table 16.3

Foreign Investment and Income Flows into India

Year	Foreign Direct Investment (US$Mn)	Portfolio Investment (US$Mn)	Total Foreign Investment (US$Mn)	Net Private Income Transfers (US$ Bn)	Foreign Currency Assets (US$Bn)
1990-91	97	6	103	2.07	2.24
1995-96	2144	2748	4892	8.51	20.81
2000-01	4029	2760	6789	12.85	39.55
2005-06	8961	12492	21453	24.46	145.11
2007-08P	32435	29395	61830	40.78	299.23

Note: P = Provisional.

Source: Reserve Bank of India Database.

Table 16.4

Trends in External Debt Indicators

Financial Year	Debt Stock- GDP Ratio	Debt-Service Ratio	Short-term Debt to Total Debt Ratio
1990-91	28.7	35.3	10.3
1995-96	27.1	24.3	5.2
1999-00	22.0	16.0	4.1
2005-06	17.2	9.9	14.1
2007-08	18.8	5.4	20.0

Source: Reserve Bank of India Database at *www.rbi.org.in*

Table 16.5

Trends in Trade/GDP Ratio

Year	Exports/GDP	Imports/GDP	X+M/GDP
1980-81	6.2	9.8	16.0
1985-86	5.6	8.5	14.1
1990-91	7.3	9.9	17.2
1995-96	11.2	14.5	25.7
2000-01	13.0	14.7	27.7
2007-08	13.5	21.2	34.7

The share of external trade in India's national income has doubled since 1991 (Table 16.5). India's trade/GDP ratio, at over 33 per cent, is higher than that of the US (around 25%). While increased trade dependence has made India more vulnerable to external shocks, her relatively low export dependence compared to other newly industrialising economies in Asia (China's trade/GDP ratio is close to 80%) has helped to limit the negative impact of a global slowdown.

The policy of ensuring reduced dependence on external debt flows has, therefore, been accompanied by a policy of increased openness to investment and income inflows (Table 16.4) In response to the current global slowdown, India has further liberalised her foreign investment rules to attract increased capital flows. Inward remittances of income earned by Indian workers abroad, especially in the Persian Gulf region, have increased in importance as a source of foreign currency earnings for India. Nearly 3.5 million Indians work in the member-countries of the Gulf Cooperation Council (GCC). They send home monthly remittances which constitute a bulk of the US$40 billion that India received in 2007-08 (in 2008-09 it was US$ 55 billion) (Table 16.6). The slowdown of economic activity in the Middle East could result in a decline in such repatriated incomes. This is an important concern for India's BoP management.

India is also concerned about a decline in the number of H1B visa holders in the US, since many of them would also be repatriating some part of their income to families based in India. The downside of the high profile skilled manpower and services exports from India is increased exposure to the risk of a global slowdown in demand.

Increased openness and external integration have made the Indian economy more efficient, increasing India's share in world trade from 0.5 per cent in 1991 to over 1.0 per cent by 2008. India has also been able to draw on foreign savings. However, for these very reasons, the current global slowdown could be expected to have a higher negative impact on India's economic growth compared to the Asian crisis of 1997-98 or earlier episodes of global recession.

Already India's trade deficit and current account deficit have gone up, and India has had to draw down its

Table 16.6

India's Balance of Payments

Unit: US$ billion

	2004/05 (R)	*2005/06 (PR)*	*2006/07 (P)*	*2007/08 (P)*	*2008/09*		
					H1	*H2*	*Year*
Merchandise Exports	85.2	105.2	127.1	158.5	96.7	86.1	182.9
Merchandise Imports	118.9	157.0	192.0	248.5	165.9	137.7	303.6
Merchandise Trade Balance	-33.7	-51.8	-64.9	-90.1	-69.2	-51.6	-120.7
	-4.8%	-6.4%	-7.1%	-7.7%	-11.5%	-8.6%	-10.1%
Net Invisibles	31.2	42.7	55.3	72.7	46.9	51.1	97.9
o/w Software & BPO	14.7	24.6	31.2	37.0	22.2	25.0	47.2
Private Remittances	20.5	24.1	27.9	40.8	25.8	29.5	55.3
Investment Income	-4.1	-4.9	-6.0	-5.2	-1.6	-4.5	-6.1
Current Account Balance	-2.5	-9.2	-9.6	-17.40	-22.3	-0.5	-22.9
	-0.4%	-1.1%	-1.0%	-1.5%	-3.7%	-0.1%	-1.9%
Foreign Investment	13.0	17.2	15.5	44.8	9.0	2.7	11.8
o/w FDI (net)	3.7	4.7	8.5	15.5	14.6	3.0	17.6
Portfolio Capital	9.3	12.5	7.1	29.3	-5.5	-0.3	-5.8
Loans	10.9	6.1	24.5	42.0	7.3	-14.3	-6.9
Banking Capital	3.9	1.4	1.9	11.8	4.8	-0.4	4.4
Capital Account Balance	28	23.4	45.8	108.0	19.9	-9.9	10.0
	4.0%	2.9%	5.0%	9.2%	-3.3%	-1.7%	0.7%
Errors & Omissions	0.6	0.8	0.6	1.5	-0.1	0.0	-0.1
Accretion to Reserves	26.2	15.1	36.6	92.2	-2.5	-10.5	-13.0
	3.7%	1.9%	4.0%	7.9%	-0.4%	-1.7%	-1.1%

Note: BPO=business process outsourcing; P=Provisional; Figures in italics denote percentage of GDP.

Source: Economic Advisory Council to Prime Minister (2009).

foreign exchange reserves defending the rupee, which has depreciated against the dollar by close to 30 per cent in the past year, with a sharp fall in February 2009.

From a national security perspective, it is relevant to note that India's policy of external economic liberalisation after 1991 has focused on increasing non-debt inflows, including foreign equity and inward private remittances. India has never pursued a mercantilist trade policy. Rather, it has always run a trade deficit that has been financed by inflows on the capital account. These inflows have contributed to an accumulation of foreign currency reserves.

Popular resistance to approaching the International Monetary Fund (IMF), as in much of the developing world, has encouraged India to shift its source of external financing away from debt and aid flows, including multilateral and bilateral aid and official development assistance, to increased trade and private equity flows.

Figure 16.4

Nominal Exchange Rate of Indian Rupee

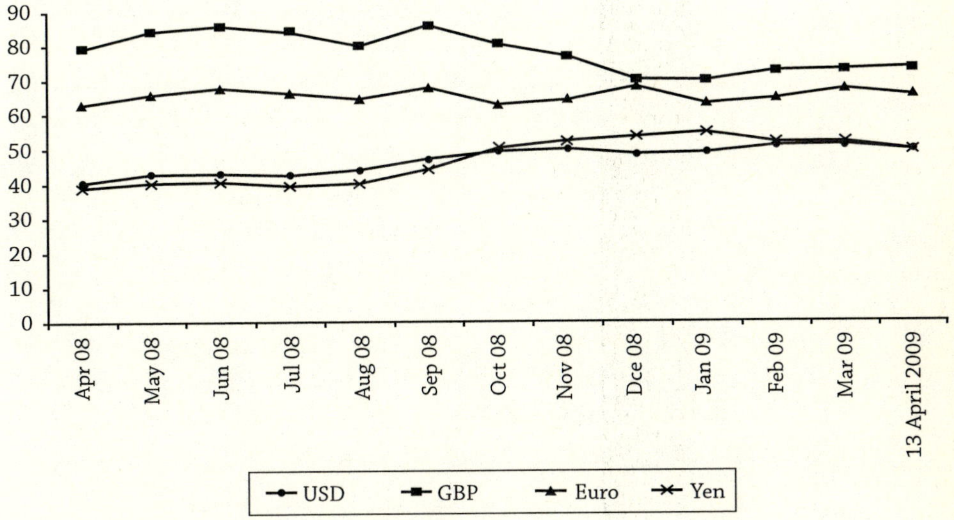

Source: Reserve Bank of India Bulletins, Various Issues.

Banking and Finance

The 'third' dimension of India's reform and stabilisation programme has been financial and banking sector reform. A stock market 'scam' in the early 1990s, that brought issues of banking supervision and use of bank funds in the equities market into focus, kick-started the first phase of banking and equities market reform. The Asian financial crisis and the Government's decision to prepare a roadmap for capital account convertibility defined the second phase of banking and financial sector reform in the late 1990s. A third wave of financial sector reform was initiated by the bursting of dotcom bubble and its impact on the Indian stock market.

India's decision to attract foreign currency inflows through the capital market by opening up the stock market to foreign institutional investors also forced the authorities to undertake institutional reform. Consequently, India put in place a more efficient and transparent regulatory system for the equities market and the banking and financial sectors.[5] The relatively high standards of governance and institutional credibility of the Reserve Bank of India (RBI) and the Securities and Exchange Board of India (SEBI) have helped.

It has been widely commented that India's banking sector has not been impacted by the banking and financial sector crises of 2008, that preceded the global slowdown.[6] D. Subba Rao has claimed that, "The Indian banking system has had no direct exposure to the sub-prime mortgage assets or to the failed institutions. It has very limited off-balance sheet activities or securitised assets."[7] The RBI has been credited with taking pre-emptive action that has minimised the vulnerability of Indian banks to the ripple effects of the US sub-prime crisis and the crisis in the equities market. In fact, in an early public statement on this, former RBI Governor, Y.V. Reddy claimed:

> Financial stability in India has been achieved through perseverance of prudential policies which prevent institutions from excessive risk taking, and financial markets from becoming extremely volatile and turbulent. As a result, while there are orderly conditions in financial markets, the financial

5. See Reddy (2004).
6. Mohan (2008).
7. Rao (2009).

institutions, especially banks, reflect strength and resilience. While supervision is exercised by a quasi-independent Board carved out of the RBI Board, the interface between regulation and supervision is close in respect of banks and financial institutions, and on market regulation, a close coordination with other regulators exists.[8]

The RBI also took counter-cyclical and precautionary measures to limit the exposure of banks to high risk lending, especially in real estate and housing. According to Reddy:

> In the year 2000, the Reserve Bank of India (RBI) conducted a stress test of the banks' investment portfolio in an increasing interest rate scenario, when the general trend then was decreasing interest rates. At that time, banks in India were maintaining a surrogate capital charge for market risk, which was at a variance from the Basel norms.
>
> On the basis of the findings, in order to equip the banking system to be better positioned to meet the adverse impact of interest rate risk, banks were advised in January 2002 to build up an Investment Fluctuation Reserve (IFR) within a period of five years. The prudential target for the IFR was 5 per cent of their investments in 'Held for Trading' (HFT) and 'Available for Sale' (AFS) categories. Banks were encouraged to build up a higher percentage of IFR up to 10 per cent of their AFS and HFT investments. This counter-cyclical prudential requirement enabled banks to absorb some of the adverse impact when interest rates began moving in the opposite direction in late 2004. Banks have been maintaining capital charge for market risk as envisaged under the Basel norms since end-March 2006.[9]

Fiscal Policy

Higher economic growth had enabled India to reduce its budgetary and fiscal deficits over the past decade. This had

8. Reddy (2008a).
9. Ibid.

also created the fiscal space for increased public investment in infrastructure development, defence modernisation and the development of strategic capabilities, including maritime. The current slowdown will undoubtedly exert a fiscal pressure on such strategic investments. The Government has pursued a counter-cyclical fiscal policy and provided a fiscal stimulus, variously estimated to be between 3 per cent and 4 per cent of GDP during 2008-09. However, a large part of such spending would naturally go into counter-cyclical safety nets and employment generation programmes. This would reduce the funds available for defence and strategic modernisation.

The Indian government can view some of the defence spending as part of the fiscal stimulus. However, given the high import intensity of defence spending in India, and the capital intensive nature of defence modernisation, there are limits to how much defence spending can be a counter-cyclical activity.

To sum up, while India's reintegration into the world economy in the 1990s has made her more vulnerable to global crises, her pursuit of gradual reform and prudent regulation seem to have helped her minimise the negative impact of the trans-Atlantic financial crisis and the global economic slowdown. From a strategic policy perspective, therefore, India can claim that her model of 'gradual' and 'graduated' economic liberalisation, and of risk averse prudential regulation in the banking and financial sector have helped limit her exposure to the Asian and Trans-Atlantic financial crises and the subsequent global economic slowdown.

While India still lags behind China, in terms of her share of world trade and capital flows as well as her share of global currency reserves, her strategy of gradual re-integration into the world economy has yielded strategic dividends. India has been able to increase its share of world income, trade and capital flows, emerging as a participant at the 'G-7 plus' forums, along with China, Brazil and South Africa, and a member of the G-20 Summit. India has also increased its economic linkages with East and South-east Asia, and is a founder-member of the East Asian Summit. Finally, the improved economic performance has enabled India to find resources for defence modernisation and to upgrade her maritime and strategic capabilities. Slower growth will exert a fiscal pressure that would adversely affect investments in these areas.

India and the Global Slowdown: New Vulnerabilities

In underscoring the new 'post-reform' resilience of the economy, we do take account of new vulnerabilities that could hurt the growth process. First, the higher trade/GDP ratio and the consequent increased dependence on the global market in both goods and services. Second, the increased importance of foreign capital inflows—portfolio, direct investment, ECB (external commercial borrowing) of Indian private corporate sector and private remittances by overseas Indians. While India's recent growth acceleration benefitted from this external connectivity, the global crisis would hurt economic growth in the near term on account of the importance of these linkages[10] (See Figure 16.5).

In a candid rejection of the so-called 'decoupling thesis', namely that higher growth based on domestic savings and investment, and the greater reliance on domestic demand has 'decoupled' the Indian economy from the global economy, D. Subba Rao told the Confederation of Indian Industry (c 11):

> The reason India has been hit by the crisis, despite mitigating factors, is clearly India's rapid and growing integration into the global economy. The contagion of the crisis has spread to India through all the channels—the financial channel, the real channel, and importantly, as happens in all financial crises, the confidence channel.[11]

10. Kumar et al. (2009).
11. Rao (2009b).

Figure 16.5

India's Increasing Global Linkages

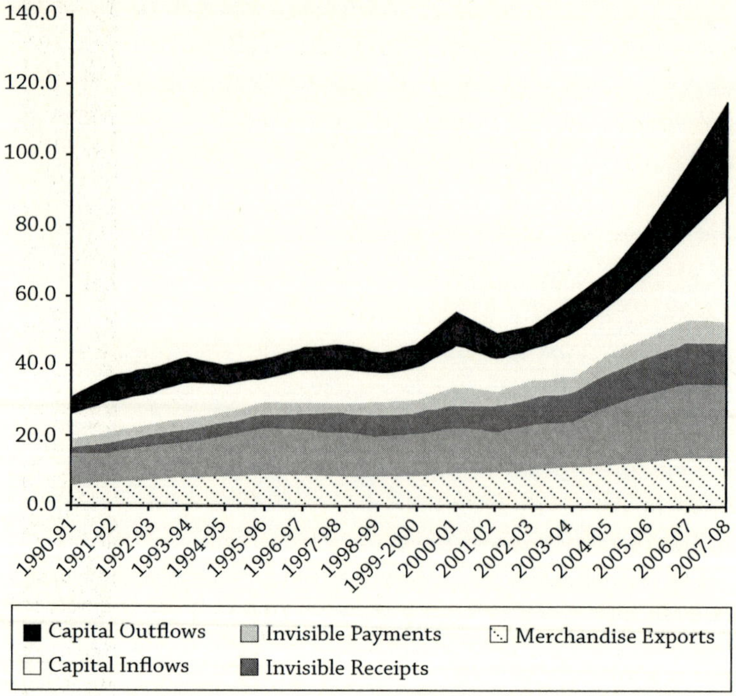

Source: Kumar et al. (2009).

Both public and private sector companies in India have become more dependent on the capital market for securing equity and debt finance, and India's equity market is fully integrated with global markets. Though the debt market is not. Indian companies are estimated to have raised US$41 billion (net of repayment) as overseas debt through ECB and fully convertible commercial debentures.[12] Even in the period October to December 2008, Indian companies were able to raise a total of US$4.5 billion from global debt markets. But these flows are expected to weaken, given increased risk aversion in global markets. The decline in global merchandise trade has also slowed down growth of India's exports, and for the first time in seven years export growth has been negative in the first quarter of 2009.

12. *Money & Finance*, ICRA Bulletin, March 2009. New Delhi.

Apart from these macro linkages and the overall increase in the trade/GDP ratio, the changes in the geographical pattern of trade also points to increased vulnerability to a slowdown. The depreciation of the Rupee is a reflection of these external vulnerabilities. India has had to draw down its foreign exchange reserves through the last quarter of 2008 and the first quarter of 2009 largely in defence of the Rupee. While India's reserves are denominated in a basket of currencies, the US dollar is the principle foreign currency in which India's external transactions are denominated. The US and European Union still account for over a third of India's exports, but Asia's share has increased in recent years. The share of Japan and Russia has gone down, but that of China, South Korea and ASEAN economies has increased (Table 16.7). Each of these economies has experienced a slowdown in growth and a consequent decline in trade.

Table 16.7

Geographical Direction of India's Exports

Region	*1960-61*	*1970-71*	*1980-81*	*1990-91*	*2000-01*	*2006-07*
EU	36.2	18.4	21.6	27.5	22.7	21.3
US	16.0	13.5	11.1	14.7	20.9	14.0
Africa	6.3	8.4	5.2	2.1	3.2	6.7
L. America	1.6	0.7	0.5	0.4	2.1	3.4
USSR	4.5	13.7	18.3	16.1	2.0	1.0
- Russia						0.7
Asia (non-Oil)	6.9	10.8	13.4	14.3	21.4	31.6
Asia (incl Oil)						49.8
OPEC	4.1	6.4	11.1	5.6	10.9	--
Japan	5.5	13.3	8.9	9.3	4.9	2.2
ASEAN				3.0	7.5	10.0
China					1.0	6.6
S. Asia						5.1

Source: *Economic Survey* (various issues), Ministry of Finance, Government of India.

Tables 16.5 and 16.7 refer to merchandise exports. The growth of inward remittances from expatriate Indian workers, especially in the Persian Gulf region, and earnings from IT (information technology) and software services exports has increased the importance of services exports to India's BoPs management. While low-skilled manpower exports are mainly to the OPEC[13] member countries of the Persian Gulf and Middle East, high skilled services exports are mainly to the US and other OECD economies. In 2008-09, inward remittances amounted to US$55 billion, while export earnings from IT and BPO business was estimated to be US$47 billion.

The IT, IT services and BPO industry is now estimated to account for almost 6.0 per cent of India's GDP. Two-thirds of the US$72 billion business is accounted for by exports, mainly to trans-Atlantic economies. While spokespersons of the National Association of Software Services Companies in India (NASSCOM), have expressed optimism that their exports would not be hurt if developed economies do not resort to protectionist measures, since firms in OECD economies would increase their demand for lower cost Indian software services in a downturn, NASSCOM has forecast a reduction in export earnings in 2009-10.[14] Growth in IT enabled services exports is expected to be around 15 per cent in 2009-10, compared to annual growth rates of around 25 per cent in recent years.

Speaking at the London Summit of the G-20, former Prime Minister Manmohan Singh summed up the official thinking in India on the impact of the trans-Atlantic financial crisis and the global economic slowdown in these words:

> We in India have been fortunate in having weathered the global downturn better than many others. Our growth rate, which was close to 9% in the previous 5 years, will fall below 7% in 2008-09. Like other countries, we have made aggressive use of both monetary and fiscal policy, with a total fiscal stimulus or expansion of the fiscal deficit above the

13. OPEC: Organization of the Petroleum Exporting Countries.
14. NASSCOM (2010).

> planned level of almost 4 percentage points of GDP in 2008-09. We hope to be able to achieve a similar growth rate in 2009-10, with continuing reliance on monetary and fiscal policy. We recognize the importance of fiscal sustainability and it is our firm intention to return to a fiscally sustainable path after 2010. The additional fiscal stimulus we have undertaken will raise our debt to GDP ratio by a few percentage points above what it would otherwise have been, but this is relatively modest compared to what would have happened had our banks suffered a financial crisis. Effective regulation of the banking system has gained us much more than any additional strain imposed by temporary fiscal expansion. Besides, since most of the fiscal stimulus will be directed to increased investment in infrastructure, it will in the medium term contribute to growth and thus help reduce the debt ratio automatically.
>
> Expansionary policy at home in an environment where exports are weak and private capital flows have dried up would normally lead to pressure on the balance of payments. In our case this has been partly offset by the fall in oil prices, but even so, India's current account deficit in 2009-10, is likely to be about 1.4. per cent of GDP. We expect to be able to finance this without difficulty and in any case, our strong foreign exchange reserves position enables us to cope with any shortfall in capital flows we may experience.[15]

This sense of optimism is based on India's growth experience in the past decade. In the period 2002-2008, the global economic environment was benign for India. By 2003, Bimal Jalan, was declaring that "there is no longer any external constraint on growth."[16] This marked a turning point in Indian thinking about globalisation and external dependence.

---

15. Singh (2009).
16. Interview with RBI Governor Bimal Jalan, *The Financial Express*, Mumbai, 18 August 2003. Available at: *http://www.financialexpress.com/news/there-is-no-longer-an-external-constraint-to-growth/90535/0*

Jalan's view was shared by Singh who often spoke of how India had overcome external constraints on growth and that the remaining constraints are essentially domestic.[17] Singh saw this as symbolising the success of India's economic openness and globalisation. Even as recently as in March 2007 he told *The Economist Roundtable*:

> An important strength of the Indian economy today is that we no longer face any insurmountable external constraint on growth. The global environment, both political and economic, is largely benign from our point of view. There are, of course, issues and trends that cause concern but these are generally applicable to most countries. For example, we are all concerned with high energy prices and uncertainty in the oil-producing regions of the world. We are all equally concerned about terrorism and threats to global peace and stability. Finally, we are all equally concerned about global warming and climate change. We are also concerned about the growth of protectionism in major developed countries. But these are global challenges and merit a global response.[18]

While this optimism about future growth prospects has been dented by recent events, there is as yet no anti-globalisation or protectionist sentiment in India. However, such protectionism in the OECD economies, and the pursuit of 'beggar-my-neighbour' policies by her economic partners may make India less sanguine about globalisation, given the new external vulnerabilities.[19]

---

17. "I have often said that there are no external constraints to our growth. The world wants India to do well. The global community will be happy to see us participate more actively in the global exchange of goods, services, ideas and people. If at all there is a constraint, it is at home. The constraint of illiteracy, ill-health, low incomes, poverty, poor infrastructure—in short, the constraint of inadequate investment in people and in their capabilities", Prime Minister Manmohan Singh, India International Trade Fair, New Delhi, 14 November 2005. Available at: *http://pmindia.nic.in/speech/content.asp?id=220*

18. Available at: *http://pmindia.nic.in/speech/content.asp?id=510*

19. It is significant that the election manifestos of all the major mainstream political parties in the 2009 elections to the Indian Parliament do not adopt a protectionist stance. In fact the global crisis and slowdown has not encouraged a protectionist sentiment at home, even though there is increased awareness of and concern with China's rising global profile.

Globalisation, Geopolitics and India's Grand Strategy

India's economic rise and the success of its gradual outward-orientation have brought economics to the centre of its strategic thinking, influencing India's grand strategy. In the early years after its Independence, India did see its economic rise as key to its re-emergence as a great power.[20] However, the Cold War interregnum, and India's relatively unimpressive economic performance during that period, saw high politics displace economics in the conceptualisation of India's grand strategy. Bringing the economy to the centre of India's strategic *weltanschauung*, former Prime Minister Manmohan Singh told a Commanders Conference in 2005:

> Our strategy has to be based on three broad pillars. First, to strengthen ourselves economically and technologically; Second, to acquire adequate defence capability to counter and rebut threats to our security, and third, to seek partnerships both on the strategic front and on the economic and technological front to widen our policy and developmental options...
>
> In the *Arthashastra*, Kautilya wrote that a healthy economy is a sound foundation for well-funded armed forces. "From the strength of the treasury", he said "the army is born". But it is not only for fiscal reasons that the health of our economy is important for our national security. A healthy, growing and stable economy in itself enhances security. New notions of "Comprehensive National Power" give high weightage to economic, social, scientific, technological, educational and cultural aspects of power. Military strength alone no longer guarantees a nation's security. Knowledge, power and economic capabilities are equally important.[21]

---

20. In his first major foreign policy speech to the Indian Constituent Assembly, in December 1947, India's first Prime Minister Jawaharlal Nehru said: "Talking about foreign policies, the House must remember that these are not just empty struggles on a chess board. Behind them lie all manner of things. Ultimately, foreign policy is the outcome of economic policy." See Baru (2006: 58), Chapter 2.

21. Manmohan Singh, Address to Combined Commanders Conference, New Delhi, 20 October 2005. Available at: *http://www.pmindia.nic.in/speeches.htm*

This view of India's grand strategy firmly embeds it on the foundations of her economic performance. It is only as a 'growing and globalising economy' that India can be a 'rising power'. Hence, safeguarding the environment for economic growth, albeit as a 'free market democracy', is critical to India's reemergence as a 'great power'.[22]

China's rise as a 'socialist market economy', globally and regionally integrated with major industrial and newly industrialising economies, has only added urgency to India's efforts to boost domestic economic growth and build economic bridges with the rest of the world.

Improved economic performance has also enabled India to become more globally and regionally integrated with her Asian neighbours. In the 1990s, India had launched a 'Look East Policy' aimed at closer economic integration with East and South-east Asia. A decade later India felt confident enough to seek a free trade agreement with ASEAN. This was preceded by an India-Sri Lanka Free Trade Agreement (FTA) and the launch of negotiations for a South Asian Free Trade Agreement (SAFTA). India launched a series of FTA negotiations with her other Asian neighbours (Table 16.8).

The geopolitical dimension to these trade agreements is obvious. Nevertheless, in defending the India-ASEAN FTA against domestic criticism, that it may hurt Indian farmers, Prime Minister Manmohan Singh pointedly drew attention to its geopolitical dimension. Writing to Congress President Sonia Gandhi on the merits of the India-ASEAN FTA, Manmohan Singh said,

> Our approach to regional trade agreements, in general, and FTAs, in particular, has been evolved after careful consideration of our geo-political as

---

22. In an official banquet speech on his visit to Tokyo, Prime Minister Manmohan Singh told his Japanese hosts: "India and Japan share a proud civilisational heritage and a common Asian identity. Our two nations have converging long-term political, economic and strategic interests. We have a common commitment to democracy, human rights, the rule of law and a free market economy. India and Japan are thus natural partners with a mutual stake in each other's progress and prosperity" (15 December 2006, available at: *http://pmindia.nic.in/visits/content.asp?id=149)*

well as economic interests. Although India has a large domestic market, our experience with earlier relatively insular policies, as also the global experience in this regard, clearly bring out the growth potential of trade and economic cooperation with the global economy.[23]

Table 16.8

Preferential, Free and Regional Trade Agreements and Comprehensive Economic Cooperation/Partnership Agreements being Pursued by India

Mauritius–CEPA*	SAARC–FTA*/CECA
South Africa Customs Union - PTA	Gulf Coop Council–FTA
Africa–PTA/CECA	New Zealand–FTA
Australia–FTA	Japan–CEPA
Chile–PTA	Israel–FTA
South Korea–CEC/PA	BIMSTEC–FTA
India, Brazil S Africa–CECA	Mercosur–PTA
South Korea–CEPA	ASEAN–FTA/ CECA
Singapore–FTA*/CECA	Sri Lanka–FTA*/CECA
China–FTA	Russia–CECA
Malaysia–CECA	EU–FTA
Egypt–PTA	Thailand–FTA

Note: *: indicates concluded; PTA: Preferential Trade Agreement; CECA: Comprehensive Economic Cooperation Agreement; CEPA: Comprehensive Economic Partnership Agreement.

Source: *Annual Report*, Ministry of Commerce, Government of India, 2008.

Even the India-Sri lanka FTA was sealed at the highest political level in the face of opposition from farm and business lobbies. Such opposition was muted in the past since the Indian economy has been performing well. Any economic slowdown can intensify such opposition to external liberalisation, with consequent geopolitical implications in an increasingly integrated economic region.[24]

23. See Baru (2008a).

24. This has already delayed finalisation of the India-ASEAN FTA, though the official reason given is that the summit meeting has been postponed due to the situation in Thailand and that India is now into election season. It is possible that the global slowdown may have encouraged both sides to go slow on the FTA.

The strategic significance of being actively engaged in the processes of Asian economic integration cannot be over-emphasised. India's improved economic performance since 1990, and especially since 2003, helped ensure that the imperatives of globalisation worked in tandem with the logic of geopolitics. As a 'rising power', India felt more confident dealing with a 'rising China' and was able to mentally 'dehyphenate' itself from slow-growing Pakistan. It also felt encouraged to participate more actively in the processes of East and South-east Asian regionalism. India's membership of the ASEAN Regional Forum (ARF) was a stepping stone to closer strategic engagement with the region. Closer economic relations with countries of the region has enabled India to participate in the East Asia Summit and the regional community building efforts.

China's rise and globalisation has encouraged India's own policy transition. China has emerged as a key economic partner for most Asian economies, including Japan and South Korea. It has overtaken India as an economic partner of South and Central Asian economies as well, and is well on its way to emerging as a major economic partner for Africa.

While India's share of global trade, merchandise and services, has doubled in the past decade, it still lags way behind China's. In 2007, India's share of world merchandise trade was around 1.2 per cent and of commercial services trade it was estimated to be around 2.5 per cent. While respective shares for China were 8.0 per cent and 3.5 per cent respectively. But India's lower level of global integration has in fact made it less vulnerable to the global downturn than China.

Hence, there are two ways of viewing the implications of globalisation for national power. On the one hand, it creates new relationships of global interdependence that add to a country's global influence and power; on the other hand, this also creates new vulnerabilities that less globally integrated economies do not face. For India, sustaining her recent growth acceleration and increasing the competitiveness of the Indian economy remain vital strategic objectives, but the gradualism of India's globalisation has yielded dividends in dealing with a global economic downturn. Given that India's growth acceleration has also helped alter her global and regional profile, sustaining this process is vital to its grand strategy.

The Re-hyphenation with Pakistan

In the past decade, an important perceptional gain for India in strategic terms was its 'de-hyphenation' from Pakistan and a new 're-hyphenation' with China in the popular and intellectual imagination, especially in the West. Rather than view India only as a 'South Asian' economy, western investors and analysts began viewing her in the context of Asia's rise. In recent years, the idea of '*Chindia*'—a joint assessment of the rise of China and India—had gained currency.[25] This new 'hyphenation' with China, and 'de-hyphenation' with Pakistan was firmly embedded in the relative economic performance of each of the three countries. The period since 1991 has been a turning point for India in terms of global appreciation of her economic prospects relative to China, Pakistan, South-east and other South Asian economies.

Till the 1980s, Pakistan had a relatively superior record in economic performance compared to India. This shaped her self-image as well. But the 1990s saw India not only overtaking, but also breaking ranks. Changing economic performance has had its impact on changing strategic perceptions about the two neighbours, both within the region and outside (See Table 16.9).

The overall deceleration in Pakistan's growth comes through even more sharply when we compare per capita income growth. Pakistan's higher population growth rate and the deceleration of India's population growth has widened per capita income disparity between the two South Asian neighbours.

---

25. The word 'Chindia' got 177,000 hits on google. A selection of 'Chindia' books includes: Ramesh (2005), Sheth (2007), Meredith (2008). Winters and Yusuf (2007), Engardio (2006), Smith (2007), Emmott (2008).

In more recent years, Pakistan has been able to improve its economic performance due to a huge infusion of aid from the US and multilateral financial institutions. However, the overall deterioration in Pakistan's security environment has meant that this marginal improvement in her economic performance has not yet altered the changed perceptions of the economic weight and performance of India and Pakistan. This could well be one reason why *jehadi* terrorists with links to Pakistan have specifically targeted important economic centres in India like Mumbai, Delhi, Hyderabad and Bangalore.[26]

Table 16.9

Average Real GDP Growth

Period	*Pakistan*	*India*
1954-1958	2.01	
1953-1960	3.80	3.7
1959-1971	3.90	
1961-1970	3.35	3.3
1971-1980	4.81	3.5
1981-1990	6.19	5.4
1991-2000	3.96	6.2
2000-2005	4.98	7.0

Source: Razmi (2007); *Economic Survey* (various issues), Ministry of Finance, Government of India.

Table 16.10

Growth Rate of Per Capita National Income

(Percentage/Year)

Country/Period	*1975-1990*	*1990-2003*
India	2.8	3.8
Pakistan	3.4	1.4

Source: Ahmed (2006).

26. Speaking in Parliament on the 26 November 2008 terrorist attacks in Mumbai, Prime Minister Manmohan Singh drew pointed attention to the targetting of India's economy: "As far as Mumbai is concerned, it was a very calculated and sinister attack, intended to cause widespread terror and damage to the image of India. The forces behind these attacks wanted to destabilize our secular polity, create communal discord and undermine our country's economic and social progress" (Lok Sabha, 11 December 2008, available at: *http://www.pmindia.nic.in/speeches.htm).*

India's superior economic performance in the 1990s had the effect of subduing Pakistani bravado, on the one hand, and encouraged India to adopt a more accommodative stance towards Pakistan, and its other South Asian neighbours. This is reflected in India's policy of 'asymmetric liberalisation' within the South Asian Association for Regional Cooperation (SAARC) region. At the Dhaka, Delhi and Colombo Summits of the SAARC, India proposed a series of initiatives to boost regional economic cooperation.[27]

An economically stronger and stable India has felt encouraged to pursue a policy of 'asymmetric' or non-reciprocal liberalisation in South Asia, offering duty free access to less developed countries. This policy would also be reassessed as a consequence of the economic slowdown. On the other hand, if Pakistan feels emboldened by the renewed injection of economic and military assistance and aid from the West, it may spur new adventurism within the military leadership. Any slowing down of the Indian economy would only encourage such adventurist elements in Pakistan.

Pakistan is the source of India's biggest security problem—*jehadi* terrorism. However, India faces a strategic dilemma. It is in India's interests that Pakistan should stabilise as a nation, a society and an economy. It is in India's interest that Pakistan economy should do well, a moderate and peace-loving middle class and business class gains ascendance and that democratic institutions take root. However, if improved economic performance, aided by US assistance, emboldens Pakistan to return to adventurist tactics vis-à-vis India, the security environment in the region would only deteriorate.

The impact of the slowdown on the US economy and politics, and the challenge of US budget management, could also shape the US response to the challenge of terrorism in South Asia. If domestic economic and political pressures encourage the US Administration to pursue a so-called

27. See Baru , (2008b).

'AfPak' strategy that is not in line with Indian security perceptions, India would be constrained to develop its own response to the threat of regional instability. How the US policy response to the global economic crisis influences its policy on *jehadi* terrorism in South Asia would, therefore, have a direct bearing on India's strategic environment.

India and Least Developed Countries

India's growth acceleration since 2003 has also enabled it to adopt a more liberal stance towards other LDCs (least developed countries) in Asia and Africa. The policy of non-reciprocal trade liberalisation involving duty free access was extended to all African LDCs at the India-Africa Summit in New Delhi in April 2008, and to the so-called 'CMLV' countries in South-east Asia (Cambodia, Myanmar, Laos and Vietnam). There are clearly two distinct strands of Indian strategic policy defining these initiatives. On the one hand, India's traditional policy of building bridges with other developing countries and promoting South-South cooperation; on the other hand, the need to keep pace with China in providing aid and assistance to other developing countries, especially LDCs.

Liberal unilateral trade concessions, even if to LDCs, would come under attack from producers' lobbies and politicians in a slow growing India. For example, India's trade concessions to Vietnam, a friendly country, in commodities such as coffee have already come in for sharp attack from even the Communist Party led State government of Kerala, where coffee growers have political clout. Apart from unilateral trade concessions, India has also stepped up aid and technical assistance to other developing countries. Indian external aid budget has increased substantially in recent years, with a significant share of it going to Afghanistan and Bhutan[28] (Table 16.11).

While strategic interests in South Asia and traditional commitment to South-South cooperation drive India's aid

28. See Chanana (2009).

budget, competition for influence with China, both within South Asia and in the developing world as a whole, is also a major driver. India's growth acceleration in the past decade has enabled her to find the resources for such aid. Any deceleration in growth and consequent fiscal pressures would impose constraints. This would most certainly be an adverse strategic consequence of the extant economic slowdown.

Table 16.11

Budget Allocations for External Aid Financing

(In Indian Rupees)

	2008-09	*1998-09*
Foreign grants	192,643	5,604
Foreign loans	1,386	2,730
Total grants and loans	2064,950	8,334
Of which, MEA budget for ITEC	650	
Africa	800	110
Afghanistan	4,450	
Bhutan	8,184	4,500
Nepal	1,400	700
Myanmar	560	510
Contributions to IOs	3,531	1,621
Allocations to IFIs	171	-
Of which, AfDB	144	
Exim Bank interest equalisation subsidy	2,320	
Total estimated foreign aid	266,712	9,955
Exim Bank loans and guarantees	350,039	21,013

Source: Chanana (2009).

The G-2 Challenge

The bigger challenge for India, however, is to ensure that the current global economic slowdown does not constrain it from catching up with China. Without doubt, the rise of China is India's main long-term strategic challenge. Already China's influence in Asia is rising. China had long overtaken India as the main business partner of many South Asian economies, not to mention East and South-east Asia.[29] China has also emerged as a major source of external financial support through its contribution to the Chiang Mai Initiative and direct financial assistance to various countries.[30]

The two Asian giants are already engaged in a race for resources and markets in Asia and Africa, with China far ahead of India. A deceleration in China's growth could blunt the edge of this competition. But it will not go away. Rather, it is likely to accentuate as India catches up in the growth race. As a consequence of the current global slowdown, we can conjecture three alternative scenarios of regional growth.

First, India is able to recover more easily than China, due to its lower dependence on global markets and lower exposure to the US economy; *Second,* India is unable to regain its growth momentum, while China does; *Third,* no relative change in the status of India and China in the world economy.

How the global slowdown impacts this bilateral relationship will shape the overall strategy of both the Asian powers. It will also impact on their relations with other Asian economies as well as Western powers. It will shape the process of institution building in Asia, and the structure of regional economic and security architecture. The resolution of the problem of the savings-consumption imbalance between China and the US will have a profound impact on the emerging global strategic balance. A US-China 'condominium' could alter India's strategic environment and options.

The idea of such a condominium was first proposed by Fred Bergsten, who called for a US-China 'G-2' working together to deal with the challenge of global imbalances and other issues like climate change and the completion of Doha Round negotiations.[31] The idea of 'Chimerica' captured popular imagination in the western media on

29. See Baru (2006), Chapter 38.
30. See Henning (2009).
31. Bergsten (2008).

the eve of the London Summit of the G-20, but Chinese commentators have so far reacted cautiously.[32]

A US-China condominium could go beyond the management of global imbalances and crises. If it encapsulates multilateral trade negotiations and discussions on global warming and climate change, it would have an even greater impact on India's strategic environment. India seeks a benign global environment for trade and investment that will enable it to sustain higher rates of economic growth.

The US offered such a 'benign' economic environment for the reconstruction of post-War western Europe and East Asia. Its' policies also facilitated the rise of China. How open the US remains towards India, keeping her markets open, being liberal with H1-B visas, being supportive in multilateral economic institutions, will have a bearing on India's growth process.

India's strategic perspective on trade and climate change negotiations has been defined in the framework of economic development, employment generation and poverty eradication. So far India and China have been able to work together on these issues. If China breaks ranks and arrives at an understanding with the US that does not meet India's needs, India would have no option but to join ranks with other developing countries and other powers to secure its own interests. Here too the US could adopt a supportive stance towards India or adopt postures that would revive old North-South divisions on global economic issues.

The global economic slowdown has increased the salience of trade and climate change negotiations since the outcomes of these negotiations will shape the overall environment for India's economic development. India has often been portrayed as a 'spoiler' both in the Doha Round and in the climate change negotiations. This is

32. The phrase 'Chimerica' was first popularised by Ferguson and Moritz Schularick (2007). However, Ferguson (2008) has himself since expressed skepticism about the idea. Also see Economy and Segal (2009).

not true. India has a 'strategic stake' in multilateralism on both counts. However, its priority lies in defending the environment for economic growth and poverty eradication. Without a 'development' dimension to the trade and climate change negotiations, India would be hard put to join a multilateral agreement.

A US-China condominium, with its attendant implications for relations with Pakistan, would force India to rethink its own strategy of global engagement. It would certainly strengthen anti-US and anti-China sentiment in India. It would encourage India to return to its leadership role in the developing world, imparting new momentum to the India-Brazil-South Africa (IBSA) forum and to its relations with other powers like Russia, the European Union and Japan. Indeed, if the G-20 gets reduced to a G-2, then IBSA could become the core of a new G-77, the developing country forum. It remains to be seen if China would risk yielding the leadership space in the developing world to India.

The management of the global economic crisis has forced the pace of events with respect to the reform of institutions of global economic governance. The G-7 have realised the need to bring China, India and other major developing economies into the institutions of global governance like the IMF and the Financial Stability Board. For India the challenge would be to ensure that China does not once again steal a march over it, as it did in the creation of the UN Security Council, in the anticipated reform of global institutions and the creation of new regional institutions.

Finally, India would want to see how the changing relationship between the US and China would shape global negotiations on trade, finance and climate change, and impact on dealing with the challenges of food and energy security. The US and India have a shared stake in reducing their dependence on imported petroleum and natural gas, and in the development of nuclear and non-conventional energy. Given India's low per capita, domestic availability of energy and other natural resources, ensuring access to these resources is vital to India's development process and national security.

Crisis Management, Regional Stability and Implications for India-US relations

It is an appreciation of the strategic importance of sustained growth of a free market democracy in the developing world, and the assurance of energy security for it, that helped define an improvement in India-US relations in recent years, especially during the Bush Administration. The US came to appreciate that India's economic success within the framework of a secular and plural democracy is of strategic importance to all open societies and open economies.

Condoleezza Rice best articulated this view when she wrote,

> India stands on the front lines of globalisation. This democratic nation promises to become a global power and an ally in shaping an international order rooted in freedom and the rule of law..... the United States has a vital stake in India's rise to global power and prosperity, and relations between the two countries have never been stronger or broader. It will take continued work, but this is a dramatic breakthrough for both our strategic interests and our values.[33]

Responding to this supportive stance of the US and seeking long term US commitment to both democracy and development in India, former Prime Minister Manmohan Singh told the US Congress in July 2005:

> Democracy is one part of our national endeavour. Development is the other. Openness will not gain popular support if an open society is not a prosperous society. This is especially so in developing countries, where a large number of people leave legitimate material expectations which must be met. That is why we must transform India's economy, to raise the standard of living of all our people and in the process eliminate poverty.

---

33. Rice (2008). Also see, Tellis (2005).

> India's aspirations in the respect are not different from those of other developing countries. But we are unique in one respect. There is no other country of a billion people, with our tremendous cultural, linguistic and religious diversity, that has tried to modernise its society and transform its economy within the framework of a functioning democracy. To attempt this at our modest levels of per capita income is a major challenge. We are determined to succeed in this effort.[34]

President Obama's first important statement on US-India relations, conveyed through a letter written when he was still a candidate in the presidential elections, to Prime Minister Manmohan Singh, adopted a forward looking and supportive position on US-India relations, underscoring the importance of India's democratic development. Obama said:

> I strongly support civil nuclear cooperation, because I believe it will enhance our partnership and deepen our cooperation on a whole range of matters. Importantly, it will help India to meet its growing electricity demands while aiding in the important effort to combat global warming. But I see this agreement only as a beginning of a much closer relationship between our two great countries. I would like to see US-India relations grow across the board to reflect our shared interests, shared values, shared sense of threats and ever-burgeoning ties between our two economies and societies.
>
> As a starting point, our common strategic interests call for redoubling US-Indian military, intelligence and law enforcement cooperation. The recent bombings remind us that we are both victims of terrorist attacks on our soil, and we share a common goal of defeating these forces of extremism. India and America should similarly work together to promote our democratic values and strengthen legal institutions in South Asia and beyond. We also should be working hand-in-hand to tap into

34. Prime Minister Manmohan Singh's Address to the Joint Session of the US Congress, Washington DC, 19 July 2005. Available at: *http://www.pmindia.nic.in/speeches.htm*

the creativity and dynamism of our entrepreneurs, engineers and scientists to promote development of alternative sources of clean energy. Imagine our two democracies in action: Indian laboratories and industry collaborating with American laboratories and industry to discover innovative solutions to today's energy problems. That is the kind of new partnership I would like to build with India as President.[35]

However, the Obama Administration has so far not shown strong and visible commitment to this vision of US-India relations. It is instructive to remember that the September letter was written when the financial crisis was just unfolding and few had foreseen the depths of the impending global economic downturn. In the months following this statement, not only has the economic crisis become worse but the situation in Afghanistan and Pakistan has sharply deteriorated.

In dealing with the economic crisis, the US has moved closer to China, in dealing with terrorism it has become more dependent on Pakistan. It is, therefore, possible that these remarks do not any longer fully reflect the worldview of President Obama. The Obama Administration's outreach to China, on the one hand, and its so-called 'AfPak' strategy in South Asia, on the other, have not been viewed favourably in India.[36]

Any dilution of the focus on shared democratic values could make US policy excessively transactional and less value-based in Asia. US-India relations have been defined both by "ideals and interests", to use a phrase used by Rice, and "principles and pragmatism", to use a phrase used by Singh.[37]

35. Letter of President Barack Obama to Prime Minister Manmohan Singh, 23 September 2008. Available at: *http://en.wikisource.org/wiki/Barack_Obama's_Letter_to_Prime_Minister_Manmohan_Singh*

36. The Obama administration's 'AfPak' strategy has come in for critical comments in India and experts are already expressing doubts about the durability of the 'strategic partnership' that President Bush and Prime Minister Singh sought. See for example Sibal (2009).

37. Rice (2008); Manmohan Singh *op. cit.* no. 34.

Faced with an economic deceleration, India's priority would be to regain the growth momentum of the past decade. US strategy in Asia will shape the strategic environment within which India is trying to improve her economic prospects. Stabilising the economy is also vital for India to deal with the instability of her neighbourhood. Apart from Pakistan, Sri Lanka too is in turmoil and both Nepal and Bangladesh remain potentially unstable polities. In each of these countries, we see China's growing influence and interest. China has also arrived in the Indian Ocean with its naval fleet and is once again flexing its muscles on the status of Arunachal Pradesh. Its influence is growing in Pakistan, Nepal, Sri Lanka, Myanmar and Bangladesh. Chinese leaders have visited the Indian Ocean islands of Seychelles and Mauritius, and China is probing the newly democratic Bhutan.

Against the background of a rising China that is increasingly influential in her troubled neighbourhood, India cannot afford to see a weakening of its own growth process that underpins her strategic capabilities.

The global economic crisis has reopened a debate that many thought was buried by the debris of the collapse of the Soviet Union and the end of the Cold War. The debate about 'State versus Market' and the pros and cons of a free market democracy.[38] The debate is significant for the future of policy in developing country democracies around the world, as China's success increases the appeal of its model of single party based Statist rule. India's worldview, of the importance of a developing country becoming economically better off within the framework of a democracy, is losing salience as that of China's 'socialist market economy' gains ground.

The issue at stake is not the extent of government intervention in markets and State support for private enterprise. Most economies are 'mixed economies' anyway. The issue is the political basis of governance. Has democracy been devalued by the economic crisis?

38. Bremmer (2009).

India, like the US, has a strategic stake in ensuring that democratic institutions are not so delegitimised.

How nations and peoples respond to the current global economic crisis will determine the ideological and political foundations of the world order in the 21st century. Many in East Asia are already suggesting that China's model of the 'development state', based on benign authoritarianism, is more relevant to developing countries than western models of multi-party democracy that are handicapped by internal political dissent. Claims are being made that a 'Beijing Consensus' on economic policy is replacing the disgraced 'Washington Consensus' (a phrase used to describe policies that defined IMF conditionality in the past two decades).[39]

There was much that was wrong with the policies of the so-called 'Washington Consensus'. But the answer for a democracy like India cannot be the economics of a 'Beijing Consensus'. India has a strategic stake in the success of its model of a liberal democracy and a mixed economy—a 'New Delhi Consensus', if you like. The Great Depression of the 1930s gave rise to non-democratic political movements in the wake of popular resentment against the failure of democratic governments to deal with the challenge of an economic downturn. The US and India have the opportunity to work together in ensuring that the current recession does not encourage non-democratic political movements and systems. Rather, the global economic downturn offers an opportunity for the world's largest democracies and market economies to work together to strengthen the foundations of open societies and open economies, by creating a global order that is supportive of India's developmental aspirations and the aspirations of all developing country democracies, like Brazil, Indonesia, and South Africa.

---

39. "It is very possible that the Beijing Consensus can replace the Washington Consensus," said Cui Zhiyuan, a professor of public policy at Tsinghua University who edited a recent book on the subject. "Since the crisis, the world doesn't have as much confidence in the U.S. economic model as before" (Cha 2009).

References

Ahmed, Sadiq (2006). *Explaining South Asia's Development Success*. The World Bank.

Asian Development Bank (ADB) (2008a). *The Statistical Database System*. Available: *https://sdbs.adb.org/sdbs/index.jsp* (accessed on April 2008).

———. (2008b). *Emerging Asian Regionalism: A Partnership for Shared Prosperity*, 2008. Figure 2.4. p.36. Available at: *http://www.adb.org/Documents/Books/Emerging-Asian- Regionalism/chapter02.pdf*

Baru, Sanjaya (2008a). "India and the World: Economics and Politics of the Manmohan Singh Doctrine in Foreign Policy", *Working Paper* No. 53. Singapore: Institute of South Asian Studies. November. Available at: *http://www.isasnus.org/events/workingpapers/52.pdf*

———. (2008b). "India and the World: Economics and Politics of 'The Manmohan Singh Doctrine in Foreign Policy", *ISAS Working Paper* No. 53, November. Available at: *http://www.isasnus.org/events/workingpapers/52.pdf*

———. (2006). *Strategic Consequences of India's Economic Performance. New Delhi;* Academic Foundation.

Bergsten, Fred C. (2008). "A Partnership of Equals: How Washington Should Respond to China's Economic Challenge", *Foreign Affairs*, July-August. Available at: *http://www.foreignaffairs.com/articles/64448/c-fred-bergsten/a-partnership-of-equals*

Bremmer, Ian (2009). "State Capitalism Comes of Age: The End of the Free Market?", *Foreign Affairs*, May-June. Available at: *http://www.foreignaffairs.com/articles/64948/ian-bremmer/state-capitalism-comes-of-age*

Cha, Ariana Eunjung (2009). "China Uses Global Crisis to Assert Its Influence: Along With Aid to Other Nations, Beijing Offers Up Criticism of the West", *The Washington Post*, 23 April. Available at: *http://www.washingtonpost.com/wp-dyn/content/article/2009/04/22/AR2009042203823.html?wpisrc=newsletter*

Chanana, Dweep (2009). "India as an Emerging Donor", *Economic and Political Weekly*, 21 March. Available at: *http://www.epw.in/uploads/articles/13314.pdf*

Economic Advisory Council to Prime Minister (2009). *Review of the Economy, 2008-09*. Government of India. March.

Economy, Elizabeth C. and Adam Segal (2009). "The G-2 Mirage", *Foreign Affairs*, May-June. Available at: *http://www.foreignaffairs.com/issues/2009/88/3*

Emmott, Bill (2008). *Rivals: How the Power Struggle Between China, India and Japan Will Shape Our Next Decade*. London: Harcourt.

Engardio, Pete (ed.) (2006). *Chindia: How China and India are Revolutionizing Global Business*. New York: McGraw Hill.

Ferguson, Niall and Moritz Schularick (2007). "Chimerica and Global Asset Markets", *International Finance* 10.3 (Winter): 215-39.

Ferguson, Niall (2008). "The End of Chimerica", *StandPoint*, September. Available at: *http://www.standpointmag.co.uk/the-end-of-chimerica-september*

Henning, C. Randall (2009). *The Future of the Chiang Mai Initiative: An Asian Monetary Fund?*. Available at: *http://www.iie.com/publications/pb/pb09-5.pdf*

Joshi, Vijay and I.M.D. Little (1994). *India: Macroeconomics and Political Economy, 1964-1991*. New Delhi: Oxford University Press.

Kumar, Rajiv, Mathew Joseph, Dony Alex, Pankaj Vashisht and Debosree Banerjee (2009). "Indian Economic Outlook, 2008-09 and 2009-10", *ICRIER Working Paper* No. 234. March. Available at: *www.icrier.res.in*

Maddison, Angus (2001). *The World Economy: A Millennial Perspective*. Paris: OECD.

Meredith, Robyn (2008). *The Elephant and the Dragon: The Rise of India and China and What it Means for All of Us.* New York: W.W. Norton & Company.

Mohan, Rakesh (2008). "Global Financial Crisis and Key Risks: Impact on India and Asia", Remarks prepared for *IMF-FSF High-Level Meeting on the Recent Financial Turmoil and Policy Responses* at Washington D.C., 9 October. Available at *www.rbi.org.in*

NASSCOM (2010). *Report on IT Software and Services: Performance and Prospects, 2009.* Available at: *www.nasscom.in & http://www.nasscom.in/upload/60387/Key_Highlights.pdf*

Panagariya, Arvind (2008). *India: The Emerging Giant.* New Delhi: Oxford University Press. p.xxiv.

Ramesh, Jairam (2005). *Making Sense of Chindia: Reflections on China and India.* New Delhi: India Research Press.

Rao, D. Subba (2009a). "Impact of the Global Financial Crisis on India: Collateral Damage and Response", Speech delivered at the Symposium on *The Global Economic Crisis and Challenges for the Asian Economy in a Changing World.* Institute for International Monetary Affairs, Tokyo, 18 February. Available at: *www.rbi.org.in*

———. (2009b). *India: Managing the Impact of the Global Financial Crisis.* Reserve Bank of India. 29 March. Available at: *http://www.rbi.org.in/scripts/BS_SpeechesView.aspx?Id=413*

Razmi, Arslan (2007). "Analyzing Pakistan's Economic Prospects in an Increasingly Integrated World: External Constraints on Sustainable Growth", *ISAS Working Paper*, March. Available at: *http://www.isasnus.org/2007MaySymposium/Panel%20Three%20-%20Presentation%20Paper%20-%20Dr%20Arslan%20Razmi.pdf*

Reddy, Y.V. (2004). "Monetary and Financial Sector Reforms in India: A Practitioner's Perspective", in Kaushik Basu (ed.) *India's Emerging Economy.* Oxford University Press.

———. (2008a). *Global Financial Turbulence and Financial Sector in India: A Practitioner's Perspective.* Reserve Bank of India. July. Available at: *http://rbidocs.rbi.org.in/rdocs/Speeches/PDFs/85529.pdf*

Rice, Condoleezza (2008). "Rethinking the National Interest: American Realism for a New World", *Foreign Affairs*, July- August. Available at: *http://www.foreignaffairs.com/articles/64445/condoleezza-rice/rethinking-the-national-interest?page=show*

Sheth, Jagdish N. (2007). *Chindia Rising.* New Delhi: McGraw Hill India.

Sibal, Kanwal (2009). "Promise of Indo-US Ties Diluted by Obama", *Mail Today* (New Delhi), 21 April.

Singh, Manmohan (2009). *Statement at G-20 Summit*, London 2 April. Available at: *http://www.pmindia.nic.in/lspeech.asp?id=784*

Smith, David (2007). *The Dragon and the Elephant: China, India and the New World Order.* London: Profile Books.

Tellis, Ashley (2005). "Indo-US Relations Headed for a Grand Transformation?", *YaleGlobal Online*, July, Available at: *http://yaleglobal.yale.edu/display.article?id=5999*

Winters, Alan and Shahid Yusuf (eds.) (2007). *Dancing with Giants: China, India, and the Global Economy.* World Bank.

17

Expenditure Decentralisation in India

Institutions and Policy

M. GOVINDA RAO

Introduction

The Constitution describes India as a "Union of States" and a "Sovereign, Secular, Socialist, Democratic Republic" established to secure justice, liberty, and equality. It is the largest democratic federal republic, inhabited by 1.3 billion people over an area of 3.29 million square kilometres. India is a developing country federation having an average per capita GDP (gross domestic product) (PPP) of USD 5,855 in 2015. Indian economy registered an annual average growth rate of 3.5 per cent during 1950-1980, increased to 5.8 per cent during 1980-2000 and further accelerated to 7.8 per cent since 2001-02. The acceleration in the growth rate coincided with economic reforms.

India attained Independence in 1947, the Constitution was adopted in 1950. The country evolved as a two-tier federation during the first 40 years of Independence. In 1992, with Amendments 73 and 74 to the Constitution, the third tier of government—urban and rural local bodies—was given the constitutional status, though there has hardly been much progress in terms of devolution of functions and finances to the third tier.

An important feature of the Indian economy is its marked diversity. People of several races and religions and speaking 114 languages (18 of which are included in the schedule), coexist peacefully with a strong bond of history and culture. Hindi is the official language, but as people in large parts of southern and eastern India do not speak this language, English continues to be a major language of official communication. State legislatures may adopt additional languages for official business. The country is predominantly rural, according to the 2001 Census, 72 per cent of the population live in rural areas.

The country has a three-tier federal structure with governments at the Union, regional, and local levels. At the regional level there are 29 States and 7 centrally administered territories—2 of which have legislatures. Below the state governments, in urban areas there are 96 municipal corporations, 1,494 municipalities, and 2,092 smaller municipalities (called *Nagar Panchayats*). There are 247,033 rural local bodies, of which 515 are at the district level, 5,930 at the block level, and 240,588 at the village level.

There are wide variations in size and economic structure among the States. In 2011-12 Uttar Pradesh (UP), at 200 million people, was the largest state, and Sikkim, with 0.6 million, was the smallest. The average per capita GSDP (gross state domestic product) for 2013-14, at ₹224,138 was the highest in Goa, a small state on the western coast. It was lowest in Bihar, at ₹31,199, the second largest state in the Gangetic plains in northern India. Due to their small size, low economic base, and strategic location, 11 small, mountainous States are categorised as 'special-category states.'

India is a Parliamentary democracy with a bicameral legislature. The Seventh Schedule to the Constitution divides legislative, executive, and judicial functions in terms of Union,[1] State, and concurrent lists. The members of Parliament at the Union and the legislatures in the States are directly elected. The upper house of the Parliament—*Rajya Sabha*—is the Council of States, and the members are elected through the electoral college

1. I use the terms 'Union' and 'Centre' interchangeably.

from each of the States. The Constitution also requires the president of India to appoint a finance commission every five years to review the finances of the Union and the States and to recommend devolution of divisible Union taxes and grants to be given to the States for the ensuing five years.

This paper deals with expenditure decentralisation in India. The principles of fiscal federalism and intergovernmental transfers are discussed in section 2. The assignment of revenues and expenditures to the Union and States and their revenue and expenditure shares are discussed in section 3. In financing subnational expenditures, given their limited availability of resources, intergovernmental transfers are inevitable and they themselves impact the level and pattern of expenditures across States. Section 4 analyses the intergovernmental transfers. In section 5, pattern of expenditures at the State level is examined. This also analyses the intrusion of the Union government in changing the priorities of the States through specific purpose transfers. The last section summarises the major conclusions.

Principles of Fiscal Federalism and Intergovernmental Transfers

Alexis de Tocqueville in his celebrated book, *Democracy in America* stated, "The federal system was created with the intention of combining the different advantages which result from the magnitude and littleness of nations." Thus, the major objective of fiscal federalism is to provide public services to match varying preferences of people living in different jurisdictions while reaping the economies of scale. The principles of fiscal federalism state that while macroeconomic stabilisation and redistribution are predominantly a function of the Union governments, subnational governments play a very important role in carrying out the allocative function.

The Union government's predominance in ensuring macroeconomic stabilisation and redistribution does not mean that the subnational governments do not have a role. The latter can and do undertake functions to generate employment and control prices within their jurisdictions and even when the Union government undertakes employment programmes or measures to stabilise prices, it can involve the subnational governments as agencies to carry out implementation (Inman and Rubinfeld 1997). Similarly, while the financing of programmes to alleviate poverty will have to come from the Union government through redistributive taxes, the implementation of the programmes will have to be undertaken by the subnational governments to minimise the transaction cost. If financing of these programmes is left to the subnational governments, they will have no interest in undertaking these programmes. Every state would prefer to attract more capital and rich taxpayers and not the poor. However, the information and search costs of implementing the anti-poverty interventions are lower at subnational levels. It is easier to get information as to who the poor are, why they are poor and what are the appropriate policy interventions that would alleviate poverty at the local level. Thus, assignment according to comparative advantage will result in a system where the design and implementation of anti-poverty interventions should be left to the subnational governments while the funding will have to come from the Union government.

From the above, it follows that the principles of efficiency in expenditure assignment system states that subnational governments, besides providing regional and local public and merit goods, will have to carry out the functions of stabilisation and redistribution, albeit in a limited manner as assigned to them in the spirit of cooperative federalism. In carrying out some of these functions, they would have unfettered autonomy. At the same time, the Union government can and often do assign some programmes to implement. In particular, the objective of such programmes is to ensure minimum standards of public service delivery in respect of the services chosen across the country. These are carried out by subnational governments essentially as agencies of the Union government and the extent of autonomy and flexibility in the design and implementation of the programmes is limited.

Assigning macroeconomic stabilisation and redistribution functions predominantly with the Union government implies that all broad based taxes, borrowing powers and money supply lie with it. At the same time, assigning the allocation function predominantly to the States imposes heavy expenditure responsibilities on them. This asymmetry between revenue and expenditure assignments results in the vertical fiscal imbalance. Furthermore, as the taxable capacities and unit cost of providing public services are different between the States, there are horizontal fiscal imbalances. Resolving vertical and horizontal imbalances call for designing intergovernmental transfers. Thus, general purpose (unconditional) transfers are given to the States to enable them to provide comparable levels of services at comparable tax rates. In addition, the Union government may consider some services as meritorious and of national importance and therefore, also design specific purpose transfers to ensure given normative levels of public services throughout the country requiring the States to make matching contributions.

The Assignment System and Revenue and Expenditure Shares of the Union and States

Historical factors have played an important role in the adoption of a federal Constitution with high centripetal bias. Although, the vast diversity of the country required considerable decentralisation at the time of independence, the need to unify a large number of small principalities resulted in the adoption of a highly centralised and yet a federal Constitution. The centralisation inherent in the constitutional assignments was strengthened with the adoption of a planned development strategy, nationalisation of the major banks and encroachment of States' legislative domains through various national programmes by the Central government called the CSS (centrally sponsored schemes).

The political architecture of the country has undergone four important changes, with significant implications for fiscal federalism. The first is the end of a single-party dominance and emergence of coalition governments at the Union level. Second, the emergence of regional parties as ruling parties in many of the States. The two factors mentioned above have necessitated the need to have effective mechanisms for intergovernmental consultation, bargaining and conflict resolution. Third, even as the regional parties dominate the political landscape in many States, their strategic alliance as pivotal members of the coalition at the Union has led to asymmetric arrangements in the functioning of fiscal federalism. Finally, the declining time horizon of political parties and politicians has led to the adoption of populist policies for short-term political gains—'competitive populism'—to the detriment of the medium- and longer-term developmental agenda.

The Assignment System

The Seventh Schedule to the Constitution specifies the legislative, executive, and fiscal domains of the Union and State governments in terms of Union, State, and Concurrent lists. There are 97 items in the Union list, 67 items under the State list, and 47 items under the Concurrent list. Both Union and State governments have powers to deal with the areas in the Concurrent List, but in the event of a conflict, the views of the Union government will prevail. The residual powers are assigned to the Union. The assignment of tax powers follows the principle of separation: they are assigned either to the Union or to the State governments. However, the assignment according to the principle of separation does not always result in the clear separation of tax powers. For example, the power to tax personal incomes is divided between the Union and the States, the jurisdiction of the former is confined to non-agricultural incomes and wealth and the latter is given the power to tax agricultural incomes and wealth. Similarly, the power to levy sales tax on goods is assigned to the States, but the Union can levy excise duty on all goods produced and manufactured, which in effect, is the sales tax at the manufacturing/production sage. Taxes on services are leviable only by the Union government.

The functions relating to the protection of the country from external aggression, those relating to international affairs and trade, macroeconomy, functions having trans-state scope and those with significant scale economies are assigned to the Union government. Thus, the Union List includes defence, external relations, international trade and commerce, national highways, air transport, maritime shipping, railways, post and telecommunications, broadcasting, railways and air travel, space, atomic energy, interstate matters, and external borrowing. The State List includes maintenance of law and order, agriculture, animal husbandry, fisheries, irrigation, urban development, public health, water supply and sanitation, intrastate trade, and local self-government. The concurrent subjects include education, environment (including forestry), electricity, economic and social planning, and all residual matters not included in either the Union or the State lists.

Although there is no specific Article in the Constitution, macroeconomic management of the economy is the responsibility of the Union. The affairs relating to Reserve Bank of India (RBI) is placed in the Union List. The RBI Act assigns it the tasks of the responsibility to conduct monetary policy, exchange rate determination, banking sector regulation and supervision, and public debt management of the Union government. The matters relating to, money supply, foreign trade, domestic and international borrowing are placed in the Union List. The States can borrow domestically, but cannot borrow from external sources. Even in regard to domestic borrowing, if the States are indebted to the Union government, the latter's permission is required. All States are indebted to the Union government; and therefore, each year, States' borrowing limits are determined by the Union government.

The functions with benefits spanning the regional boundaries are placed either in the State or placed in the Concurrent List. The State List includes activities such as public order, police, prisons and reformatories, High Courts and subordinate courts, public health, agriculture and allied activities, rural development, urban development, water supply and sanitation, local (below the State level) governments shipping and navigation and regulation of mines and mineral development except major minerals. The entries in the Concurrent List include criminal law and procedures, marriage and divorce, transfer of property except agricultural property (State List), education, forests and environment, bankruptcy and solvency, economic and social planning, welfare of labour, displaced persons, charitable institutions, ports except those declared under law by Parliament, electricity, industry, trade and commerce and consumer protection.

The tax assignment is made on the basis of the principle of separation. A particular tax is assigned either to the Union or the States in the legal sense. Responsibility for most broad-based and progressive tax handles is assigned to the Union. The Union also has residual tax powers. The major Union taxes comprise personal income tax on non-agricultural incomes, corporation tax customs duty, excise duty on tobacco and non-alcoholic products and tax on services. The assignment to the States include land revenue, tax on agricultural incomes, tax on sale and purchase of goods, excise duty on alcohol, tax on motor vehicles, tax on passengers and goods transported by motor vehicles, profession tax, entertainment tax and electricity duty, entry tax and octroi. However, from the viewpoint of revenue productivity, only the sales tax is important.

On the basis of the principle of separation, tax powers are assigned exclusively either to the Union or to the States. However, exclusivity is only in the legal sense, and this has given rise to anomalous situations. Thus, the Union can levy taxes on production (excise duties), but States can levy taxes on the sale of goods. Similarly, taxes on agricultural income and wealth are in the States'

Table 17.1

States' Share in Revenues and Expenditure

Years	Total Revenue (Union+States)	Total Expenditure (Union+States)	States' Share in Revenues			States' Share in Expenditures		
	Per cent of GDP	Per cent of GDP	Tax Revenue	Non-Tax Revenue	Total Revenue	Current Expenditure	Capital Expenditure	Total Expenditure
1990-91	17.4	26.7	34.4	44.9	35.9	55.2	44.5	53.6
2000-01	16.7	25.8	38.2	40.8	39.1	56.0	57.0	56.5
2005-06	18.9	24.9	37.7	34.7	36.8	55.2	59.4	56.7
2007-08	20.2	24.4	31.9	38.5	32.9	53.5	53.1	54.7
2008-09	18.7	25.7	33.9	40.5	34.7	49.3	64.2	53.8
2009-10	18.2	27.2	37.6	39.6	37.5	51.2	61.5	54.3
2010-11	19.9	26.4	37.6	23.8	35.0	51.3	53.7	53.1
2011-12	18.4	26.8	38.9	38.3	34.0	53.7	60.9	55.8
2012-13	19.1	26.1	39.2	40.8	39.0	54.9	59.6	54.9
2013-14	20.4	27.6	40.3	35.7	37.3	56.0	62.4	56.9
2014-15	20.5	27.3	39.0	37.3	37.3	62.2	56.9	60.7

Source: *Indian Public Finance Statistics*, Ministry of Finance, Government of India.

domain, whereas the tax on non-agricultural income is a Union prerogative.

Trends in Fiscal Imbalances and the Transfer System

The constitutional assignment and developments over the years have caused a high degree of vertical fiscal imbalance. The state governments in 2014-15 collected only 37 per cent of total current revenues, but their share in total current expenditure was 61 per cent (Table 17.1). From the revenue sources assigned to them, they could finance only 60 per cent of their current expenditures. In other words, the States depend on Union transfers to finance about 40 per cent of their current expenditures.

There is considerable variation among the States on their fiscal dependence on the Union government. There are 17 relatively homogenous general-category States, but even these have wide differences in size, revenue-raising capacities and efforts, expenditure levels, and fiscal dependence on the Union government. In addition, in terms of economic characteristics, the 11 mountainous States in the north and northeast differ markedly from the rest and, therefore, are designated as 'special-category' States. Of the 28, 3 States have recently been carved out of 3 large States.[2]

Analysis of the fiscal indicators of different States presented in Table 17.2 brings out important features. First, there are wide interstate variations in revenues in both per capita terms and as a ratio of GSDP. Second, these variations indicate differences in revenue capacity as well as differences in effort. Third, the tax-GSDP ratios in the special-category States are lower in the general-category States, even when their per capita GSDP is higher. This is because, in these States, there is not much economic activity other than that derived from the government

2. The state of Telengana was carved out of Andhra Pradesh (AP) in 2014 and with this the number of general category States are 19. As firm fiscal data for the two new States of AP and Telengana are yet to be available, in this study the interstate analysis includes the composite state of AP.

and given their hilly terrain, there is considerable cost disabilities in them. Fourth, although the revenue bases in the special-category States are low, their average per capita current expenditure in 2013-14 was ₹201,817 which was almost twice that of general category States at ₹14,245. Fifth, in the case of general-category States, the fiscal dependence on the Union is high and varies inversely with per capita income. Thus, large differences in per capita expenditures have persisted despite equalisation.

Interstate disparities in India, even among the general-category States, are not only high but are also increasing. In 1980-81, the per capita GSDP of the richest state, Punjab (₹2,674), was about 2.9 times that of the poorest, Bihar (₹919). In 2013-14 however, the difference between the lowest per capita income even if the small state of Goa is not taken into account, the difference increased to 4.3 times with the per capita GSDP of the poorest state Bihar, at ₹31,199 and in Haryana the highest per capita income state excluding the small state of Goa was ₹133,427.

There are wide variations in the ratio of revenues to GSDP and this represents the differences among the States in both revenue raising capacity and efforts capacity to raise revenues. The revenue—GSDP ratio among the general-category States in 2013-14 varied from 5.8 per cent in West Bengal to 11.2 in Karnataka. Although the revenue ratio has a high correlation with per capita GSDP, there are instances of States with lower per capita GSDP having a higher revenue—GSDP ratio and vice versa. West Bengal, for example, is a middle income state, but has the lowest revenue—GSDP ratio. Haryana, Maharashtra and Punjab, although have higher per capita GSDP than Karnataka, Kerala and Tamil Nadu, have much lower revenue GSDP ratios.

Per capita developmental as well as total expenditures in the States are highly correlated with per capita GSDP. A careful analysis shows that Bihar, which has the lowest per capita GSDP has the lowest development expenditure as well. In fact, Bihar's per capita development expenditure is 56 per cent of average development expenditure of the general-category States and just 42 per cent of that of the highest (leaving aside Goa). The differences in per capita total expenditures too are similar. The per capita expenditure in Bihar was 63 per cent of the average of general category States and 50 per cent of that in Haryana. When there are no differences in the unit cost of providing public services, differences in per capita expenditures between the States result in the differences in the levels of services provided in them. The differences in per capita development expenditures are of particular concern as these will result in significant differences in physical and social infrastructures and will accentuate interstate differences in development. The persistence of such large differences in per capita expenditures, and more particularly development expenditures shows the inability of the federal transfer system to offset the revenue disabilities of the States.

The Transfer System in India

The Constitution recognises that the States' tax powers are inadequate to meet their expenditure needs and therefore provides for the sharing of revenues from Union taxes. Until 1999-2000, the Constitution provided only for the sharing of personal income tax and Union excise duties. However, the Constitution was amended in 2000 (80th amendment) to enable sharing of the net proceeds of all the Union taxes. In addition to tax devolution, the Constitution provides for grants to aid the States (Article 275). The responsibility for determining the tax shares between the Union and States and the shares of individual States as well as the grants in aid of revenues has to be determined by an independent body—the Finance Commission.

Article 280 of the Constitution provides for the appointment of the Finance Commission by the President of India every five years. The Commission has a Chairman and four other members whose qualification for appointment is laid down in the Finance Commission Act passed by the Parliament. The ToR (terms of reference)

Table 17.2

Inter-State Differences in Per Capita GSDP and Fiscal Variables, 2013-14

States	Population	Per Capita GSDP	Own Rev/ GSDP	Exp/ GSDP	PC Revenues	PC Dev. Exp.	Pc Tot. Exp.
General Category States	**1115000**	**82806**	**9.2**	**17.2**	**7618**	**9440**	**14243**
Andhra Pradesh	84666	87234	10.2	17.3	8898	11253	15091
Bihar	103805	31199	6.7	28.7	2090	5241	8954
Chhattisgarh	25540	58547	11.6	23	6791	12119	13466
Goa	1458	224138	11	18.2	24655	35190	40793
Gujarat	60384	106831	8.8	13.2	9401	9935	14102
Haryana	25353	133427	8.1	13.5	10808	12409	18013
Jharkhand	32966	46131	8.3	20.8	3829	6781	9595
Karnataka	61131	89545	11.2	19.3	10029	12357	17282
Kerala	33387	103820	10.4	16.9	10797	10071	17546
Madhya Pradesh	72597	51798	9.7	19.8	5024	8132	10256
Maharashtra	112373	117091	8.3	12.4	9719	9250	14519
Odisha	41947	52559	9	21.9	4730	6833	11510
Punjab	27704	92350	9.5	15.5	8773	9327	14314
Rajasthan	68621	65974	9.2	18.4	6070	8313	12139
Tamil Nadu	72139	112664	10.7	15.9	12055	11379	17914
Uttar Pradesh	199581	36250	9.8	22.8	3553	5184	8265
West Bengal	91348	70059	5.8	14.5	4063	6025	10159
Special Category States	**75111**	**64251**	**7.8**	**32.4**	**5012**	**13621**	**20817**
Arunachal Pradesh	1383	85468	7.7	71	6581	22564	60682
Assam	31169	44263	7.6	30.7	3364	8897	13589
Himachal Pradesh	6857	92300	7.6	24.8	7015	14768	22890
Jammu and Kashmir	12549	59279	11.7	39.2	6936	16539	23237
Manipur	2722	41573	6.5	58.7	2702	19207	24403
Meghalaya	2964	61548	6.3	41.6	3878	21788	25604
Mizoram	1091	76420	4.7	69.1	3592	30797	52806
Nagaland	1980	77529	3	43.6	2326	23646	33803
Sikkim	608	176491	12.2	43.9	21532	51535	77480
Tripura	3671	69205	5.8	34.5	4014	14671	23876
Uttarakhand	10117	103716	6.9	19.8	7156	13172	20536

Source: 1. Finance Accounts of State Governments, Comptroller and Auditor General, Government of India.
2. *Economic Survey, 2015-16*, Ministry of Finance, Government of India.

of the Commissions are: (i) the distribution of the net proceeds of Union taxes between the Union and States and among the States inter-se; (ii) grant in aid of revenues to be given to the States; (iii) measures to augment the consolidated funds of the States to supplement the resources of rural and urban local governments in the States based on the recommendations of the States' finance commissions; and (iv) any other matter referred to the Commission by the President in the interest of sound finance. Under the last item, a number of tasks have been assigned to the Commission such as setting the fiscal rules and targets for the Union and States, measures to be taken for sustainable development and the protection of ecology and environment, rescheduling and writing off of States' loans and incentivising the States to undertake tax reforms. So far 14 Finance Commissions have submitted their report. Interestingly, the Finance Commissions are well regarded and their major recommendations have always been accepted and implemented by the Union government.

The adoption of planned development strategy and the creation of Planning Commission to design and implement development plans led to the Commission taking over the task of giving grants for planned development of the States. This was done by eroding the powers of the Finance Commission by restricting its scope of review to the non-plan expenditure requirements of the States in the ToR issued to the Commissions. However, the 14th Finance Commission's ToR did not restrict its scope to non-plan requirements and the Commission made recommendations to cover the entire general purpose transfers. Thus, the abolition of Planning Commission in August 2014, did not create any discontinuity.

Another source of grants is given by various Union ministries to the respective State ministries for specific purposes under the CSS. These grants are meant to ensure minimum standards in respect of public services considered to be meritorious with nation-wide externalities. These are specific purpose matching grants. There were 147 grants prior to their consolidation into 66 in 2012 and the new government has further consolidated them in 28 this year.

After the 14th Finance Commission made the recommendations, the entire architecture of grants got changed. The Commission assessed expenditure requirements of the States in their revenue (current) accounts without making a distinction between plan and non-plan, and recommended tax devolution and grants to cover their total current requirements. In effect, this subsumed the grants given by the Planning Commission earlier. The Finance Commission's recommendations came into effect in 2015-16 and subsequently, the plan grants are essentially specific purpose grants given by various Union ministries for CSS.

The extent to which the fiscal disabilities are offset through the transfer system can be seen from Figure 17.1. The indices of per capita own revenues and per capita revenues accruing to each of the States is plotted against per capita GSDP of the States. It is seen that both the indices show an upward trend as the per capita GSDP increases. The slope of the revenue accrual curve is flatter and the difference between own revenues and revenue accruals represents the extent to which the revenue disabilities are offset. It is seen that even after the transfers are given, the per capita revenue accruals are significantly higher in States with higher per capita GSDP.

The analysis of special-category states shows that many of the fiscal variables are influenced by the high weight of the large States namely, Assam, Himachal Pradesh and Uttarakhand. The revenues in other States are much lower and they are dependent on the Union government grants for financing overwhelming proportion of their expenditures. In some of the states like Arunachal Pradesh, Mizoram, Nagaland and Sikkim, both per capita development and aggregate expenditures are very high and in some ways it represents high unit cost of providing public services in these States due to the hilly terrain, sparsity of population and large forest area.

Table 17.3

Intergovernmental Transfers in India

	2013-14	2014-15 BE	2014-15 RE	2015-16 BE
Percentage of Transfers to GDP				
Tax Devolution	2.78	3.02	2.67	3.71
Non-plan Grants	0.53	0.55	0.63	0.77
Plan Grants	1.93	2.61	2.15	1.39
Total Transfers	5.24	6.19	5.45	5.88
Percentage of Transfers to Gross Union Tax Revenue				
Tax Devolution	27.95	28.01	26.99	36.15
Non-plan Grants	5.32	5.13	6.42	7.49
Plan Grants	19.35	24.24	21.71	13.57
Total Transfers	52.62	57.38	55.13	57.22
Percentage of Transfers to Gross Union Revenues				
Tax Devolution	23.87	24.31	23.07	31.46
Non-plan Grants	4.55	4.45	5.49	6.52
Plan Grants	16.53	21.04	18.56	11.81
Total Transfers	44.95	49.81	47.12	49.79

Source: Budget Documents of the Union Government, Ministry of Finance, Government of India

Figure 17.1

Progressivity of the Transfer System

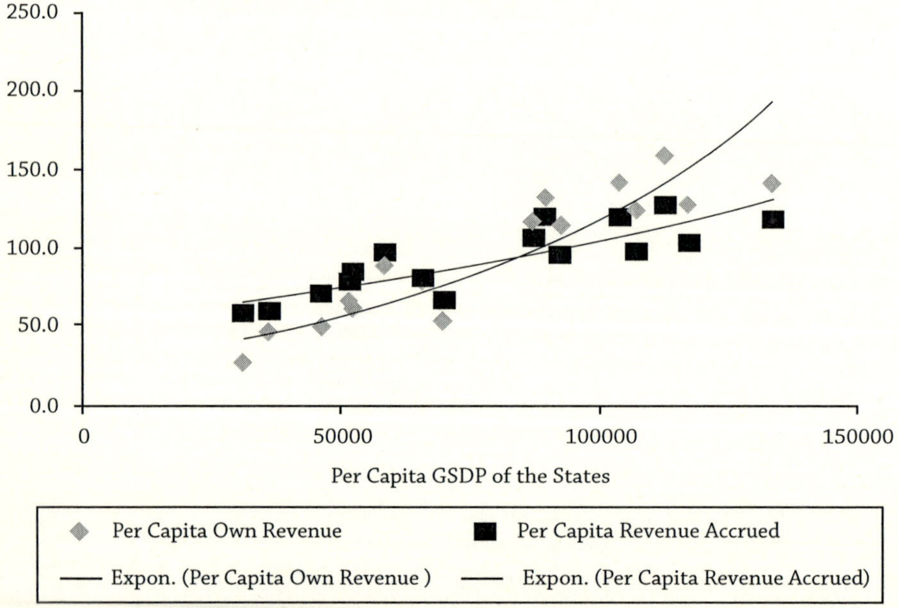

Note: The vertical axis represents indices of own revenues and total revenues with the States' average set at 100. The differences in the slopes represent the progressivity of the transfer system.

Considering the wide variations in per capita GSDP among the States with the richest state having more than five times the per capita GSDP of the poorest, completely offsetting the fiscal disabilities to enable the low income states to equalise their per capita expenditures, may neither be desirable nor feasible. First, in the prevailing fiscal environment where the Union government does not have fiscal space to meet its own obligations, to assume any significant increase in the transfers is unrealistic. Second, the standards of services provided even by high per capita GSDP states are not very high and they too need to spend large amounts on developmental heads. Therefore, there is a clamour for higher transfers from all the states. Third, there are arguments that equitable transfers may reduce the overall growth of the economy which, in the long run may prove inimical to the interests of the poorer states themselves.[3]

The adverse effect on efficiency and accountability from transfers arise mainly by softening budget constraints of States. It is also argued that equalisation may actually impede the development of backward regions by preventing the inter-regional mobility of resources, particularly labour (McKinnon 1997). It is argued that the transfers given to offset fiscal disadvantages can interfere with the normal process of income convergence seen in the process of economic growth which occurs due to migration of labour and capital from places with lower productivity to those with higher productivity. They also create 'transfer dependency' (Weingast 1995), which undermines fiscal discipline.

---

3. There is considerable discussion in the literature on whether or not equitable transfers have a trade off in terms of lower growth. Buchanan (1950) argues that as the transfers are made to States with low capital-labour ratio, given the high marginal productivity, it will increase the growth rate. In contrast, Scott (1950, 1964) argues that the low incomes in the poorer states is the result of lower marginal productivity of capital and transfer of resources to these states necessarily entails a cost in terms of lower growth of GDP. The debate is inconclusive as the issue is essentially empirical. If the transfers to poorer States are used to augment infrastructure which, in turn enhances their productivity, it may not result in equity–growth trade off. See Rao and Singh (2005) for detailed discussion of these issues.

In any case, the volume of transfers and its distribution among the States is, to a considerable degree is determined by various socio-political factors and are remarkably stable over time. This implies that in the short and medium term, increasing per capita expenditures on developmental services in low income States will have to significantly depend on their mobilising additional resources

Decentralising Expenditures: Important Issues

Table 17.4 brings out the salient features of public expenditure in India. First, the aggretate level of public expenditure in India is remarkably stable at about 26-

Table 17.4

Expenditure Decentralisation in India

	1990-91	*2000-01*	*2010-11*	*2011-12*	*2012-13*	*2013-14*	*2014-15*
About 84 per cent General Services	12.50	14.30	12.86	12.57	12.18	12.81	12.80
Social Services: of which	5.44	5.42	6.35	6.68	6.61	7.04	6.82
Education	3.29	3.23	3.42	3.54	3.17	3.34	3.18
Healthcare	1.28	1.29	1.31	1.31	1.19	1.34	1.37
Economic Services	6.78	5.15	6.50	6.88	6.86	7.27	7.25
Total Expenditure	26.65	25.82	26.35	26.83	26.21	27.76	27.37
Ratio of State Government Expenditure to GDP							
General Services	4.64	6.15	5.31	5.41	5.11	5.56	5.57
Social Services of which	4.56	4.45	4.83	4.85	5.18	5.75	6.12
Education	2.76	2.70	2.55	2.53	2.45	2.75	2.93
Healthcare	1.02	1.13	0.93	0.91	0.93	1.04	1.21
Economic Services	4.14	3.56	3.47	3.50	3.74	4.17	4.77
Total Expenditure	13.34	14.16	13.61	13.76	14.04	15.48	16.46
Share of the States in Total Expenditure							
General Services	37.14	42.99	41.32	43.04	41.96	43.40	43.50
Social Services of which	83.78	82.07	75.99	72.52	78.49	81.76	89.72
Education	83.97	83.58	74.51	71.33	77.49	82.54	92.23
Healthcare	79.75	87.26	70.83	69.19	78.29	77.85	88.50
Economic Services	61.09	69.11	53.32	50.87	54.52	57.44	65.83
Total Expenditure	50.05	54.83	51.63	51.27	53.57	55.78	60.13

Source: *Indian Public Finance Statistics* (various issues), Ministry of Finance, Government of India.

27 per cent of GDP. This is also true of expenditures on general and economic services though, the spending on social services shows some increase. Within the social services, spending on education and healthcare actually shows a marginal decline since 2010-11. The increase in social services was mainly on account of social security and welfare, a predominant proportion of which is in the form of transfers to the people.

While the aggregate public expenditure has been remarkably stable over 25 years, beginning 1990-91 expenditures incurred at the State level have shown a steady increase from 13.3 per cent in 1990-91 to 14.2 per cent in 2001-02 and further to 16.5 per cent in 2014-15. Thus, the share of States in total expenditures increased from 50 per cent in 1990-91 to 55 per cent in 2001-02 to 60 per cent in 2014-15. This however, does not mean that the States' discretion over expenditures has increased commensurately. In fact, a significant portion of the increase is due to the Union government's specific purpose transfers on various CSS. In fact, this has curtailed States' expenditure autonomy as they are required to making matching contributions to avail the central grants.

Notably, expenditure on social services is predominantly undertaken at the State level. The share of States in social service expenditures is almost 90 per cent in 2014-15 and throughout the period from 1990-91, it has been over 70 per cent. This is particularly true of spending on education and healthcare where the States have a predominant role. Interestingly, the time series data on the share of the States in social services expenditures shows a steady decline from about 84 per cent in 1990-91 to 72 per cent in 2011-12 and sudden increase in the last two years. This in fact, represents a policy change. In the initial years, all the specific purpose grants to the States on major social services including education and healthcare were made to the consolidated funds of the States. However, after 2003-2004, the grants were directly transferred from the Central government to implementing agencies bypassing the States. Thus, in these years, the central grants were shown as Central expenditures rather than State expenditures. The policy was reversed in 2014-15 after the High Level Committee on Expenditure Efficiency recommended that the funds should be routed through the States to ensure greater accountability. This also indicates that although in respect of providing social services, the States have a predominant role, the Union government exerts considerable influence through specific purpose grants to them.

This brings us to the role of specific purpose grants in India. Such grants are given in most federations to ensure minimum standards in respect of public services considered meritorious with nation-wide externalities. Ideally, such grants should be limited in number and open-ended to ensure outcomes. Given the objective of ensuring minimum standards, ideally, the matching ratios required to be paid by the States should vary depending on how far away they are from the minimum standards. The changing ratios are advocated also for the reason that the responsiveness of the States to transfers vary and uniform matching ratio will not provide them adequate incentives to access the grants for achieving the required level of spending.

In India, the CSS is the major instrument through which the Union Ministries seek to change the allocations by the States. Indeed some schemes on anti-poverty interventions, education, water supply and sanitation are important as these are meritorious services of national importance and therefore, ensuring minimum standards of services throughout the country is important. Even here, it is important to design the transfers carefully to stimulate the States to increase outlay rather than substitute their own spending for central grants.[4]

An important precondition for the success of the specific purpose grants is that the funding should be adequate to meet the specified minimum standards. In

4. Rao and Choudhury (2012) show that the grants given to augment health expenditures actually are entirely substituted by the States.

India, there were 147 schemes in 2013 and these were consolidated into 66 in 2014. The recent rationalisation by the Committee appointed by the Government reduced the number to 19. But a careful perusal of the list shows that most of the schemes are retained as sub-schemes and almost all of them are placed as either core of the core or core with the States having to make matching contribution of 30 per cent and 40 per cent for the two categories. All these are closed ended and the funding is not related to minimum standards of public services and therefore, there is no linking of the outlays to outcomes. The matching ratio is uniform and therefore, the funds are given irrespective of the responsiveness. Most low income states end up not availing the assistance for many of the schemes due to their lack of fiscal space to making matching contributions and when such non-availed funds are redistributed to those states that avail them, it defeats the very purpose of giving such transfers. The schemes seem to have been drawn to meet the political purpose of the Union government intervening in essential public services to claim its role for electoral gains.

Concluding Remarks

Like most other large, diverse countries, expenditure decentralisation in India is important. The Constitution assigns the States with predominant powers to deliver social services and co-equal responsibility in providing economic services. At the same time, the revenue bases assigned to the States is inadequate to provide the services assigned to them satisfactorily and therefore, the Constitution also provides for the appointment of the Finance Commission by the President, an independent body to make recommendations on the devolution of Union taxes and grants in aid to be given to the States.

In keeping with the Constitutional assignment, overwhelming proportions of expenditures on social services are delivered by the State governments and States' share of expenditures on economic services is as much as that of the Union government. This was possible because of the transfer system. Although the States' share in raising revenues is 37 per cent of the total, their share in expenditures is 60 per cent. At the same time, there are large and increasing differences in taxable capacities among the States and the transfer system has not been able to fully offset the revenue disabilities. The consequence of this has been the large and persisting differences in per capita expenditures on social and economic services among the States. Per capita expenditures on social and economic services are positively correlated with per capita GSDP. Per capita development expenditure in the State with the lowest per capita GSDP is less than 50 per cent of the average.

The Union government Ministries have a number of specific purpose transfers called CSS. The analysis shows that the large number of schemes and thin spread of resources makes it difficult to link the schemes to outcomes. Most of the schemes which are closed ended and having uniform matching requirements have serious design problems. There have been several attempts to rationalise and consolidate them and yet, the problems continue.

References

Buchanan, James, M. (1950). "Federalism and Fiscal Equity", *American Economic Review* 40(4): 583-99.

Inman, Robert P. and Daniel Rubinfeld (1997). "Rethinking Federalism", *Journal of Economic Perspectives* 11: 43-64.

McKinnon, Ronald L. (1997). "Market Preserving Fiscal federalism in the American Monetary Union", in Mario Blejer and Teresa Ter-Minassian (eds.), *Macroeconomic Dimensions of Public Finance: Essays in Honor of Vito Tanzi.* London and New York: Routledge. pp.73-93.

Rao, M. Govinda and Mita Choudhury (2012). "Healthcare Financing Reform in India's Decentralized Healthcare System", in Benedict Clements, David Cody and Sanjeev Gupta (eds.), *The Economics of Public Healthcare Reform in Advanced and Developing Economies.* Washington D.C.: International Monetary Fund.

Rao, M. Govinda and Nirvikar Singh (2005). *Political Economy of Federalism in India.* New Delhi: Oxford University Press.

Scott, Anthony (1964). "The Economic Goals of Federal Finance", *Public Finance/ Finances Publiques* 13(3): 241-88.

Scott, S.D (1950). "A Note on Grants to Federal Countries", *Economica* 17: 416-22.

Weinghast, B.R. (1995). "The Economic Role of Political Institutions: Market Preserving Federalism and Economic Development", *Journal of Law and Economics* 11(1): 1-18.

18

Conditional Cash Transfers and Behaviour Change in India*

DEVENDRA B. GUPTA

Introduction

CCTs (conditional cash transfers), targeted at the extremely poor and backward regions are increasingly used in developing countries to improve human development indicators. Their use in improving education and health care in poor countries is regarded as a major initiative in promoting investment in human capital among the poor. These transfers impose a behavioural condition on the recipient of a cash transfer that transforms the payment from an income effect (unconditional) to a price effect (subsidy) on the required condition. The underlying justification for the condition is to reduce market failures due to positive externalities from investments in human capital, while transferring money to the poor. It must, however, be noted that in addition to the demand-side action, supply-side action needs attention, and a balance between the two is required, as often the poor quality and uncertainty of service provision deters people from accessing such services. For instance, in situations of high absenteeism of teachers and poor quality teaching, there

---

* This paper is specifically contributed in the memory of our good friend Shri Raj Kapila whom I had known since he was a student of the Delhi School of Economics in mid-1950s of the last century. We undertook the same course largely inspired by Prof V.K.R.V. Rao's vision to undertake evidence based policy research. To this end he had set up erstwhile programme in Economic Statistics at the postgraduate level. Both Raj and I were students of the same course, although he was my senior. The present work in some ways represent inspiration from friends like Raj.

is little motivation for parents to send their children to school, leading to premature withdrawal. Similarly, in the case of primary healthcare, poor services may result in low utilisation. However, the poor and socially excluded experience other barriers to access, such as costs of transport, medicines, uniforms, textbooks, etc. In the case of working children, enrolling in school would mean a loss in earnings. Transfers, whether in kind or in cash, attempt to address these demand-related barriers, especially when school attendance and/or use of preventive health services are conditions for payment.

In this paper, an attempt is made to document international experience with CCTs with a view to derive lessons for India. It also provides a brief review of select, relevant government programmes and schemes targeted at women, children and poor communities and regions. The findings from this review are supplemented with actual workings of key child-related programmes in Meerut, a district in one of the most populous and poorest states of India, namely Uttar Pradesh (UP). The paper is organised as follows: section 2 brings out the relevance of CCTs to India. Section 3 contains a brief description of the experience with the working of CCTs in select countries, indicating the lessons learnt. Section 4 is devoted to a review of select incentive schemes of the Central and state governments aimed at improving development indices/behaviour change through providing incentives in cash or in kind; the underlying motive being to assess how close are the features of these schemes to the ones adopted under the CCT approach. Inter alia the lessons learnt from the review are briefly outlined. We use the results of an earlier study of select incentive schemes in Meerut district in UP to validate the lessons learnt from the literature review of incentive schemes. The findings are presented in section 5. Section 6 summarises the evidence emerging from literature review and case study. Section 7 is concerned with highlighting the main issues emerging from a detailed analysis of key incentive schemes with a view to draw lessons for the application of CCTs as a policy tool in the country.

The Context and Relevance of Conditional Cash Transfers in India

India has a very large pool of children below 14 years of age, and the number is expected to increase substantially over the coming years. Table 18.1 gives an idea of the dimension of the challenge in the coming years.

Most of these children belong to households living in abject poverty, generally with low levels of literacy, especially among females. Most of them are in poor health as well and indicators like infant mortality, child mortality and maternal mortality are well below the levels of other developing countries. Within India, there are specific regions and states, and within these specific communities, the development indicators are well below the country average. Table 18.2 provides an overview of the current human development indicators for India and for the state of UP.

Table 18.1

Child Population by Age Group, India, 2001-2016

Age (in years)		*2001*	*2006*	*2011*	*2016*
<1 (infants)	No. (million)	21.706	24.855	24.294	24.918
	%	2.14	2.27	2.06	1.97
1-2 (toddlers)	No. (million)	43.084	45.865	48.177	49.357
	%	4.26	4.19	4.09	3.91
3-5 (pre-school)	No. (million)	66.065	63.731	70.034	72.498
	%	6.53	5.82	5.94	5.74
6-10 (primary school)	No. (million)	118.256	106.945	109.131	115.801
	%	11.68	9.77	9.26	9.16
11-13 (middle school)	No. (million)	74.468	69.364	62.520	66.398
	%	7.36	6.34	5.30	5.25
14-15 (high school)	No. (million)	47.269	48.397	43.607	42.51
	%	4.67	4.42	3.70	3.36

Notes: Figures are based on projections made by the Technical Group on Population Projections. Percentages have been calculated from the total population.

Source: *Census of India: Population Projections for India and States 1996-2016*, Registrar General, India, for figures from 2001 onwards.

Table 18.2

Socioeconomic and Demographic Indicators

Indicator	*Reference Period*	*Uttar Pradesh*	*India*
Poverty ratio	1999-2000	31.20%	26.10%
Child population	2001	50.50%	45.10%
Child population as per cent of national	2001	18.10%	
Infant mortality rate (IMR)	2004	72	58
Maternal mortality ratio (MMR)	SRS 1998	707	540
Under-five mortality rate (U5MR)	1998-99	122.5	94.5
Underweight children >3 yr	1998-99	51.70%	47.00%
GER (I-VIII) in age group 6-14 yr	2003-04	78.16	84.19
Literacy—overall	2001	56.3	64.8
Literacy—female	2001	42.2	53.7
Net domestic product (₹ per capita)	2001-02	9,753	17,947

Source: Various Central and State government reports/documents including those of India's Planning Commission.

The above indicators clearly underline the need to boost investment in child health and education for achieving the Millennium Development Goals (MDGs).

Over the period, Central and state governments have initiated numerous welfare schemes and programmes targeting women, children and other disadvantaged groups to improve these indicators and tackle poverty.[1] These are generally focused on the provision of incentives in cash and/or kind in the areas of health, education and nutrition. Free primary healthcare through a highly developed network of health infrastructure, especially in the rural areas, free elementary education, and mid-day meals (MDM) to school children, supplementary nutrition to children less than 6 years and ante- and post-natal care to pregnant and lactating women are some of the benefits provided to the poor. In addition, many welfare services are highly subsidised. It may be noted here that most of these benefits/incentives are directed at individuals, and

1. For detailed review of government welfare schemes for children in India, including public spending see Gupta (2003a) and Gupta (2003). Also see, World Bank (2004).

the household per se is seldom targeted. A number of studies assessing the benefits of these schemes suggest that most public expenditure tends to provide greater benefits to the relatively less poor households.[2] As a first step, an attempt is made to assess how effectively some of these schemes function internationally and nationally.

Lessons from International Experience[3]

Countries that have experimented with CCTs such as Brazil and Bangladesh are known to have benefited from these transfers, and it is not surprising that the interest in and the scope of CCT programmes have grown enormously over the past 10-12 years. Along with the rise in the number of countries with CCT programmes, there is a simultaneous increase in the size of some programmes. Brazil's Bolsa Escolar began in 1995 as a small-scale programme to pay mothers for sending to school as many as three children. From 1995 to 2004, the federal government distributed money to each municipality based on poverty indices and a national census. School records were reviewed by local officials, for compliance. Mothers whose children attended school on a regular basis—and promised not to work—received as much as $18 a month. While the programme operated:

- Incomes of participating families in Brazil rose by 20 to 30 per cent and drop-out rates declined.
- Among participating families, less than 1.0 per cent of girls and boys dropped out, against a drop-out rate of 5.6 per cent for non-participating families.

Children in Bolsa Escolar were more likely than non-participating classmates in similarly poor families, to start school at the appropriate age and to be promoted to the next grade on time. Since its success, Bolsa Escola's CCT programme has been replicated by several local

2. Mahal et al. (2002) and Gupta (2003b).
3. For an excellent summary of the impact of CCTs on school enrolment and attendance and health centre visits by children, refer to Tables 4 and 5 in Fiszbein and Schady (2009: 17-20).

governments, followed by formulation of sector-specific federal programmes, and then their unification and reform.

Bangladesh's Food for Education programme has achieved similar impressive results. The programme emphasised educational performance in school; a school could be temporarily suspended from the programme if random inspection revealed a less than 60 per cent attendance. Participating families received a monthly allotment of about 12-15 kg of wheat or rice if the children attended school at least 85 per cent of the time. In 1997-98, 2.10 million households benefited from the programme. The cost per beneficiary family was small, about USD 40 per year or roughly 60 cents per month per person. Among the benefits are:

- In the very poor families that participated in the programme, monthly calorie consumption increased by about 9 per cent.
- In participating schools, enrollment increased by 44 per cent for girls and 28 per cent for boys compared to a 2.5 per cent increase in enrollments nationally.
- Only about 6 per cent of beneficiary students dropped out, compared to 15 per cent of non-beneficiary students.

It may however be noted that the costs of large-scale implementation of a CCT programme could prove prohibitive. For example, it is estimated that expanding the cash-for-education programme worldwide to South Asia and Sub-Saharan Africa would cost about USD 10 billion and cover 170 million children. Excluding the Middle East and North Africa for which data was lacking, a global programme to pay poor families to keep their children in school would cost about USD 12.5 billion per year.[4]

There are several positive effects of CCT programmes on the incomes of poor households and backward regions,

4. Morley and Coody (2003).

as well as on empowerment of and accountability to the poor. de Janvry (2006) lists these as:

- Cash transfers create an immediate income effect for the beneficiary household, reducing poverty and inequality.
- The condition creates a price effect on the demand for child human capital, which can increase the future autonomous income capacity of the child.
- The transfer can insure the asset (child human capital) against shocks, and be targeted to provide this insurance coverage to vulnerable and transitory poor households.
- The transfer can be done in a way that increases empowerment of and accountability to the poor.

A review of existing international evidence suggests that for CCT programmes to be efficient, caution needs to be exercised. First, it concerns the rule for selecting the poor. This implies a means test, defined in terms of a maximum household income level below which households are eligible (or perhaps some similar eligibility conditions, for example, belonging to a socially excluded section of society like the SCs (scheduled castes) or STs (scheduled tribes) in India to receive the benefit. The second aspect of CCT is behavioral conditionality, which requires a recipient household, apart from satisfying the income eligibility criterion, to regularly undertake some pre-specified action. Such a requirement could be enrolment and actual attendance in school for children or in the case of pregnant and lactating women, it may be regular visits to health facilities for antenatal and postnatal care. There is also the issue of calibration of transfers, particularly when there are constraints on funds to provide universal transfers.

Review of Some of the Incentive Schemes in India

We now review the working of some key incentive schemes of the Central and state governments aimed at improving development indices/behaviour change through providing incentives in cash or kind.[5] Some of these provide scholarships and school lunches as a way of increasing school enrolment by subsidising the costs of schooling, and improving attendance and retention rates as well as the health status of children. This, in turn, is likely to lead to enhanced productivity, and higher incomes as adult workers. Many of these incentives are targeted towards the poorer and disadvantaged sections of the society.

As a rule, student numbers increase substantially when there is a substantial cut in the cost of education. Education grants in the form of subsidies, school funds, education vouchers, and scholarships also bring more children into schools. In order to offer greater incentives for attendance and to ensure that children remain in school, additional supplementary facilities such as medical care and school meals are provided. A school meal or food ration to take home can be a critical factor in motivating parents to send their children to school. Several studies in India have revealed that school attendance, especially of girls, increases substantially when children are provided with meals. In fact, if the food rations are substantial, parents generally tend to regard them as the child's income.

There is also a campaign worldwide, including India, to make school attendance a main activity for all children. India's Central government has taken several initiatives including the setting up of National Child Labour Projects (NCLP) in different parts of the country to rehabilitate child labour. A major activity under the NCLP is the establishment of special schools to provide non-formal education, vocational training, supplementary nutrition, and so on, to children withdrawn from employment. Under a Supreme Court order, while an offending employer must make a contribution of ₹20,000 to a welfare fund

5. See Appendix Table A-18.1 for a matrix of some incentive schemes of the Central government. We may mention that we have not included some of the more recent schemes initiated post mid-2014 as not much information is yet available in public domain.

established for the purpose, the state government is expected to provide employment to one adult member of the family of the child so withdrawn, or a contribution of ₹5,000 to the welfare fund. Financial assistance is provided to families out of the interest on the corpus of ₹20,000-25,000 deposited in the welfare fund, as long as the child is actually sent to school. In Brazil too, families with children have been given income support through a nation-wide programme, if each child attends at least 90 per cent of classes. Efforts have been made through various incentives—financial and in kind—to promote gender equality in primary education. Many children in various regions of the country, especially in the Empowered Action Group (EAG) states[6] and remote areas of India (particularly, the SC/ST and those belonging to backward communities) do not attend school. In order to increase enrolment and improve retention rates of children in these areas, incentives such as hostels and *ashram* schools have been provided, besides provision of adequate schooling facilities.

In the context of CCT, it is crucial to assess the extent to which incentives have contributed to achieving the stated objectives, and the factors responsible for below par performance of some key schemes. To begin, we provide a brief description of the working of some major incentive schemes and evaluate their impact on the behaviour of the target population. The choice is largely dictated by availability of relevant studies.[7] The schemes are grouped into three categories: the MDM scheme (transfers in kind); other educational incentives, including scholarships, textbooks, uniforms, etc. (transfers in kind and cash), and the *ashram* schools.

---

6. The Government of India had appointed an EAG to identify such states that needed special attention for their development. These states are now called the EAG states.

7. It may be noted that while a large number of existing evaluations have focused on the MDM programme, these studies have inter alia examined the impact of other incentives such as scholarships and stipends, free textbooks, uniforms, stationery, etc., and free tuition, although these have received relatively less attention in the evaluations.

The Mid Day Meal Scheme

The MDM programme was launched in August 1995 by the Central government to boost school enrolment and attendance, while providing nutritional support to children. The scheme was to provide 3 kg of foodgrains (dry rations) per student every month, subject to a minimum attendance of 80 per cent, until (within two years) cooked or processed food could be given. It now extends to all children in primary classes in government, local body, and government-aided schools in 5,400 blocks of 507 districts.

The impact of dry rations on retention levels in schools was found to be generally short-lived with students enrolling in large numbers only to drop-out after receiving the incentive (Education Research Unit: 2003). The teachers did not think that rations for poor children ensured food security at home or prevented them from taking on extra work.

The provision of actual MDMs (which is only foodgrains in all the study states, except Odisha) has helped enhance enrolment. Parents insist on enrolling even under-age children to get the incentive. The nation-wide norm requiring 80 per cent attendance to be eligible for foodgrains, is not followed anywhere; despite low attendance rates, teachers have to distribute grain to all parents of enrolled children because of the fear of pressure from parents. In Sidhi (a district in Madhya Pradesh [MP]), some teachers calibrate the amount of foodgrains in proportion to actual attendance. Clearly, the MDM has not been able to ensure regular attendance of children. Delays and corruption were reported as well. Several parents at different places complained about receiving much less than the prescribed norm. In Bihar and Assam, the scheme was non-functional for a long time and has only recently been resumed.

Another study[8] shows that the benefits in terms of nutritional status are probably not perceptible. In a comparison of children in MDM schools against those in non-MDM schools showed that improvement, if any, was only marginal in terms of distribution of weight for age and Waterlow's classification in the former. The MDM programme seems however to have achieved educational rather than nutritional benefits as indicated by lower drop-out rates and higher retention rates. However, another study (Devadas and Prem Kumari 1978) had observed significant nutritional and educational impacts of the MDM programme.

Another evaluation of the scheme[9] showed an increase in enrolment in the first year, followed by a decline. The trends in attendance showed the proportion of children with attendance over 80 per cent dropping sharply from 53 per cent in the pre-scheme period to 45 per cent in the post-scheme period, although an increase of 9 per cent was indicated for children with attendance between 70 and 79 per cent. For other children, no marked difference was visible.

A cohort analysis was undertaken for the pre-scheme period to examine the impact of the scheme on retention rates.[10] It showed an increase in the drop-out rate from 20 per cent in the pre-scheme period to 25 per cent after the MDM was introduced. The results are surprising, as typically one would have expected a decline in the dropout-rate. One possible reason is that initially there is a spurt in

8. This study is an impact assessment (1992-93) of the Applied Nutrition Programme in Karnataka on enrolment, attendance, drop-out and retention rates in schools, and on nutritional status and school performance. For this, 2,694 primary school children (1,361children in MDM schools and 1,333 in non-MDM schools) from 60 schools were surveyed (Laxmaniah 1999).

9. This was conducted by the Operations Research Group in selected blocks of four districts—Guna, Raisen, Rajnadgaon and Rewa—in MP, and it documented enrolment, attendance and retention rates for the pre- and post-programme periods.

10. The study evaluated 814 students from class I in the pre-scheme period (1992-93) and 1,078 children in class I during the post-scheme period.

enrolment on account of a particular incentive, but some children enrolling to gain from the incentives may not continue, and drop out. Thus for incentive programmes to be effective and sustainable, additional efforts are needed.

Table 18.3

Schools Providing Incentives (%)

Incentive	*Per cent*
Free textbooks	86
Mid-day meals	100
Free stationery	2
Free uniforms	31
Scholarships	63
Free bags	-

Source: Operations Research Group Survey of primary schools in four districts—Guna, Raisen, Rajnadgaon, and Rewa—in Madhya Pradesh.

A scrutiny of schools providing various incentives would reveal that the offer of transfers to generate a demand for schooling among child labour is not a sufficient condition. It may be mentioned here that free stationery and uniforms have not had much of an effect on parents' decision to enroll their children to school, as the expenditure incurred on these is low enough that even relatively poor parents can meet the costs. This suggests the need to search for other factors which would bring working children and out-of-school children to school and help them to stay there (a la Bangladesh's Food for Education Programme and Brazil's Bolsa Escolar, referred to earlier).

Other Education Incentives

A study (Indicus Analytics 2006) in the tribal blocks of Bajna (project block) and Sailana (control block) in Ratlam district in MP, found that these incentives are largely reaching their intended beneficiaries. Over 90 per cent of parents reported their children as having received free textbooks, though the Sailana block recorded a slightly lower percentage. Almost 85 per cent of the schools reported health checkups of students, with schools in the

Sailana block faring better. In the case of scholarships, around 50 per cent of the parents reported their wards receiving scholarships. It is interesting to see that most schools did not face any problem with funds.

Based on the UNICEF field survey for 1999, Panchmukhi (2006) found that about 13 out of every 100 children in the state received some sort of incentive. The percentage of children receiving incentives was higher for rural areas (20%) than for urban ones (7.3%). As expected, the availability of incentives for SCs, STs and OBCs was much higher (18 to 26%) than for others (12%) in rural areas. In urban areas, for the less-developed communities, the availability of incentives is 7 to 9 per cent, while for others it is about 6 per cent. By and large, the incentives seem to be properly distributed among children considering their social background, household income, parents' education and occupational status. While the UNICEF survey-based study for MP has not per se assessed the impact of various incentives, enrolment seems to have risen, although marginally, and drop-out rates have also fallen marginally.

FGDs (focus group discussions) seem to suggest (in view of the high opportunity costs of elementary education), the need for monetary incentives to encourage parents to send their children to schools and to ensure they complete their education. The findings also suggest exploring the possibility of replacing current systems of multiple incentives by a single monetary incentive system. The high incidence of complaints against the present incentive system in MP underlines the dire need for evolving a regime of strict monitoring and serious implementation of the incentive system.

Based on the UNICEF survey, Tilak and Nalla Gounden (2006) find that more than 90 per cent of the children in rural areas, from grades I-VIII, get free or subsidised books; more than 70 per cent receive free uniforms; and 2 per cent receive scholarships. In urban areas, about 50 per cent receive books and about 40 per cent uniforms. A breakdown of benefits (free textbooks) by social classes in urban areas shows that the percentage of the

Table 18.4

Children in Primary Grades Receiving Incentives (%)

	Books			*Mid-day Meal*			*Scholarship*			*Attendance Money*		
	Boys	*Girls*	*Total*	*Boys*	*Girls*	*Total*	*Boys*	*Girls*	*Total*	*Boys*	*Girls*	*Total*
Rural												
ST+SC	6.76	5.26	9.16	9.46	7.02	8.40	52.70	68.42	59.54	35.14	38.60	36.64
OBC	3.15	1.52	2.59	1.57	9.09	4.15	4.72	9.09	6.22	37.01	31.82	35.23
Others	3.08	3.81	3.40	5.38	7.62	6.38	6.15	8.57	7.23	28.46	25.71	27.23
All	3.93	5.26	4.47	4.83	7.89	6.08	16.01	23.68	19.14	33.23	30.70	32.20
Urban												
ST+SC	0.00	0.00	0.00	10.77	16.67	13.45	29.23	29.63	29.41	18.46	12.96	15.97
OBC	0.00	1.61	0.69	1.20	8.06	4.14	14.46	8.06	11.72	12.05	6.45	9.66
Others	0.00	0.00	0.00	0.00	0.00	0.00	8.57	11.11	9.86	0.00	8.33	4.23
All	0.00	0.66	0.30	4.37	9.21	6.57	18.58	16.45	17.61	12.02	9.21	10.75

Source: UNICEF (1999).

disadvantaged groups is higher, their percentages being 76 per cent for SC children, 53 per cent for OBC and only 30 per for other category children.

The same survey also shows that in UP, specific incentives offered to students include tuition waivers (free-ships), stipends or scholarships, free textbooks and stationery, free meals, and free uniforms and shoes. Since 1995-96, the distribution of incentives has steadily expanded. The UNICEF survey reports an improved coverage under one scheme (scholarships), principally for SC/ST students (Table 18.4).

Both household interviews and FGDs revealed a high degree of dissatisfaction among parents and the community regarding the distribution of incentives. Table 18.5 details their perceptions regarding scholarships and other incentives (MDMs, textbooks, etc.). The table shows that while scholarships are available regularly to a large number of recepients, a large share of households in both the rural and urban areas was dissatisfied with the quality of other incentives. Only 13 per cent of the village FGDs reported satisfaction regarding the distribution of incentives, while 87 per cent reported the situation to be unsatisfactory or very unsatisfactory.

Thus, although incentives do play an important role in off-setting opportunity costs and motivating parents to

Table 18.5

Households Reporting Satisfaction/Dissatisfaction with Incentives (%)

Caste	*Rural*				*Urban*			
	Is the scholarship available regularly		*Are you satisfied with the quality of incentives*		*Is the scholarship available regularly*		*Are you satisfied with the quality of incentives*	
	Yes	*No*	*Yes*	*No*	*Yes*	*No*	*Yes*	*No*
SC+ST	87.16	12.84	34.57	65.43	90.91	9.09	58.14	41.86
OBC	42.86	57.14	15.12	84.88	64.00	36.00	41.38	58.62
Others	45.16	54.84	5.81	94.19	69.23	30.77	33.33	66.67
Total	73.29	26.71	18.18	81.82	80.65	19.35	48.81	51.19

Source: UNICEF (1999).

send children to school, the state of affairs regarding their distribution is far from satisfactory.

A World Bank-commissioned study (Economic Research Unit 2003) in UP found that students enrolling because of incentives are regular in attendance only prior to distribution. In regard to scholarships as an incentive for dealing with problems of drop-out and irregular attendance, most teachers felt that they would be effective only if provided at the end of the academic session to ensure children did not drop-out mid-term or attend classes at whim. They also indicated that the scholarship money was used by the family to meet household needs. Regarding other incentives like textbooks, uniforms and scholarships, the implementation was reportedly poor with persistent delays in distribution. The study found that in UP the practice of substituting textbooks with guide-books begins from class I, and teachers and parents blamed each other for it (World Bank 2004).

In rural Assam, 87.5 per cent of students benefit from free textbooks at the primary, upper primary and elementary levels. Scholarships do not exist at the primary level, but cover 2 per cent of children at upper-primary and 1 per cent at the elementary levels, with the beneficiaries mainly SC boys. In urban Assam, textbooks are distributed to 45.5 per cent, 40 per cent and 42.5 per cent boys, and 52.5 per cent, 29.6 per cent and 41.7 per cent girls at the primary, upper primary and elementary levels, respectively. The distribution of free textbooks and uniforms is supposed to help reduce household expenditures, but such incentives as provided by the state are inadequate, ill-targeted and least responsive to their objectives.

Another assessment[11] shows that the coverage of incentives is extremely limited (Table 18.6). Specific incentive schemes such as the attendance scholarship or free uniform are for children who belong to SC or ST

11. Jhingran and Jha (2002) in a survey of selected urban and rural districts in 15 states assessed the coverage of four types of incentive schemes.

families, but in practice do not cover all the children from these groups, in fact, very few children from these groups receive them. The survey results indicate mismanagement, delays and corruption in the delivery of these incentives. Schools in Araria (Bihar), Palamu (Jharkhand) and Sidhi (MP) faced the longest delays.

Table 18.6

Common Incentives and their Coverage

Incentive Schemes	*Coverage of Children (% of total enrolment)**
Attendance scholarship	8.0
Free textbooks	50.0
Free uniform (ever received)	16.0
Exercise books	7.7

Note: *The percentage of children who have received the particular incentive (e.g. uniforms) at least once in the past two years unless otherwise specified.

Source: Mehrotra (2006).

Delays can defeat the very purpose of the scheme: for instance, the purpose of the attendance scholarship is to provide a monetary incentive at the end of the day or month to motivate parents to send their children to school regularly. When this is received as a lump-sum several months after the actual period for which it is meant, it loses its meaning and relevance. Free textbooks are to be supplied to all SC and ST children, and to all girls in districts where the District Primary Education Programme (DPEP) is operational. However, schools do not receive these books in time and often in insufficient quantities for all the eligible children.

Ashram Schools

Ashram schools generally admit children living at least 6-8 km away from the school; if children of nearby villages are given admission, they are not provided with lodging. Thus, children from the local villages were not enrolled in the Ashram schools in Mahal in Dangs district (in Gujarat) and in the Kathkuiyan Kala in Shravasti district (in UP). Of all the villages in the study, the highest number of children in Ashram schools was in Wakarya village, Dangs district. One reason is that the village had no local primary school till 1999.

Many parents in Jharkand, Odisha and Gujarat showed a preference for the Ashram schools, because they provided 'free food, clothing and lodging'. Unlike other places in the study, parents at Wakarya also felt that the education imparted at an Ashram school was more relevant to their lives. Village reports suggest that the curriculum of Ashram schools includes agriculture and other life-skills, in addition to general subjects, only in Gujarat, but not in other states like Odisha, UP or Karnataka. Parents at Wakarya and at Bharwa Munda felt that since the schools were residential, their children's education did not suffer because of seasonal migration. However, with very limited seats, it is not easy to get admission in Ashram schools and people complained of interference and nepotism by influential persons in getting admission.

The availability of residential Ashram schools has helped in increasing the participation rates in areas where seasonal family migration is common, e.g., Bharwa Munda (Odisha) and Wakarya (Gujarat). Although the rate of enrolment was low at Bharwa Munda, 5 out of 6 enrolled children were in an Ashram school. At Wakarya until two years ago, there was no local school and all enrolled children attended Ashram schools. The demand for Ashram schools was evident at many places, especially because it did not involve any direct costs and parents were free from responsibilities of the child. However, the demand was visible mainly among parents with some exposure to education and the outside world. School participation rates are higher in well-connected and developed areas where better employment avenues are available. Also, a higher level of literacy in the village has a positive impact on school participation (Jhingran and Jha 2002).

Lessons Learnt

To summarise, in the delivery of incentive programmes, there appears to be considerable differences among districts within the same state and among schools within the same district. These differences cannot be fully explained by differences in caste composition. Both teachers and parents are uncertain about who is entitled to incentives and who actually receives them. There appears to be some resentment that the eligibility criteria are caste-based, rather than poverty-based, and distribution schedules are somewhat erratic.

There are substantial differences between the number of children who benefit from the schemes as recorded in school records and as acknowledged by parents. In addition, there are accusations that school records inflate the number of SC and ST children to increase receipts from the scheme components. Attendance allowances, in particular, are perceived to be inadequately distributed. There is also evidence that schools do not receive all the supplies for which they qualify. One result is that textbooks sets are divided up, or alternatively, not distributed at all because the excess demand would lead to disharmony in the classroom.

The effectiveness of incentive schemes in increasing enrollment and attendance and in reducing drop-out rates has not emerged very clearly from the analysis. School enrollment records are too unreliable to use and, in any case, show no clear pattern. Detailed follow-up studies over three years indicate that drop-out rates among those who receive incentives are at least as high as rates for those who do not. Although the rates may have been even higher in the absence of incentives, any impact appears to be muted. Far more important factors impacting enrollment and retention appear to be problems specific to the locality and school, such as the functioning of the village *panchayat* and the quality and commitment of teachers.

What level of incentive programmes would be required to bring children to school? To what extent do existing programmes influence current enrollments? The surveys shed little light on these important issues. While poor families welcome any additional income, it is unlikely that attendance allowances are leading to higher enrollments and retention. Of the incentives that do appear to have an effect and that may require strengthening, the textbooks scheme appears to be most favoured by teachers, parents and the community.

One study that throws some light on the issue considers the effects of costs and subsidies (incentives) on child school decisions controlling for individual, household and community factors.[12] The study indicates that an increase in the value of subsidies increases the probability of enrollment in primary schools. Further, as expected, an increase in school fees significantly reduces school enrolment rates. An interesting and significant conclusion of Duraiswamy's study in the context of CCTs is the significant role of all indicators of school quality on child enrolment rates. In the context of decisions on enrolment by SCs/STs and OBCs, however, no significant difference is indicated.

The Case of Meerut

As a validation (or otherwise) of the findings of the literature review in the preceding sections, we undertook a field visit to Meerut to assess the workings of a few child-related schemes. While there are number of welfare schemes, both centrally sponsored as well as those initiated by the state government[13] operating in Meerut district, the field study confined itself to assessing the workings of a few select schemes, namely, the Kanya Vidya Dhan, MDM scheme, and supplementary nutrition at AWCs (anganwadi centres).

Kanya Vidya Dhan

This is a state government scheme for girls who have passed the intermediate examination and whose parents'

12. In a recent study, Duraiswamy (2003) analysed the impact of government incentives—MDMs, free uniforms, books, and transport and scholarships on school enrolment and attainment in Tamil Nadu. One of the objectives of the study was to identify which incentives would result in increased enrolment in primary and secondary schools, particularly that of girls.

13. See Appendix Table A-18.2 for some of the child welfare schemes and their allocations in UP.

income does not exceed a prescribed limit, namely, ₹19,884 per annum for rural areas and ₹25,546 per annum for urban areas. The scheme aims to allow girls to pursue higher education opportunities. While the scheme was well-conceived in design, various malpractices have reportedly emerged in its functioning: specifically in the selection of target beneficiaries, as some of the most deserving girls were left out because of lack of awareness of procedures and application dates; fake certificates of eligibility are accepted; intermediaries will, for a consideration (which could be as much as ₹1,500) arrange for an eligibility certificate as well as ensure the incentive amount is received. There was general skepticism about the success of the scheme, which many regarded as politically motivated, though some felt that it was too premature to make a judgement about its working.

A recent CAG review of the scheme confirmed the findings from the field visit. According to its report, no survey was undertaken to identify the beneficiaries. Almost 7,400 girls from families that were not BPL (below the poverty line) received incentive money, while eligible beneficiaries from BPL families were left out. The review also found that income certificates of eligible beneficiaries were not scrutinised for verification.

Mid-day Meal Scheme

Another incentive programme taken for the field visit was the MDM programme (benefits in kind). During the unannounced field visits to some primary schools, we witnessed the serving of the MDM prepared by a NGO (non-governmental organisation). The meals looked appetising and the children were seen to be enjoying their food. Most children were present, but some teachers were missing (reportedly on polio duty). Teachers stated that MDMs helped in improving attendance and almost all children remained in school after the meal. Teachers were unsure whether the MDM worked as an incentive for higher enrolment and felt most children would continue in school irrespective of school meals. This could have been because the schools were located in urban areas. Most children looked clean and they washed their own utensils after the meal. Of course, MDMs are an additional burden on teachers as teaching time is lost despite the fact that food is prepared and served by the NGO.

In a unpublished paper, Ajwad (2006) while evaluating the grain distribution and cooked meal distribution scheme, has confirmed a lower quality of foodgrains than officially designated. His evaluation has found stocks being kept in classrooms because of lack of storage, and misreporting of student beneficiaries to facilitate grain theft. His study also reported caste prejudices, but at the same time indicated that sitting together and eating food has to some extent broken caste barriers. He also confirmed the disruption to the school schedule due to MDMs.

Supplementary Nutrition at Anganwadi Centres

In our review of the supplementary nutrition and other components of the Integrated Child Development Scheme (ICDS), we found that RTE (ready-to-eat) food in the form of panjiri was not popular with the children and the quality of this food was generally poor. There was no proper system of monitoring; supervisors were more interested in their transport allowance, which was often supplemented by the sale of part of the rations supplied to the anganwadi workers. On the plus side, the growth-monitoring activity was generally satisfactory. As anganwadis are now often located within the premises of a primary school, certain externalities are becoming evident. A major benefit is that more and more children coming out of the AWC after six years enrol in primary school, compared to children who attend anganwadis still located in separate premises. Similar conclusions emerged from a nationwide survey of anganwadis (Gupta et al. 2002).

Other School Incentives

In the schools visited, while textbooks were provided free to all, uniforms and stationery were not provided in some cases. It may, however, be mentioned that girls in elementary schools classified as Abhinav schools received free uniforms. While tuition fees were not charged, there was a nominal 25 paisa charge for sports for SC children, while non-SC children were charged ₹1.25 (25 paisa for sports and ₹1 as development charges). All children, whose parents' income was less than certain specified amount (₹24,000 per annum according to our information), received an annual scholarship of ₹300, paid in a lump sum amount at the beginning of the school session. To overcome problems connected with obtaining income certificates, ward representatives were authorised to issue such certificates.

Although scholarships are meant to be disbursed prior to the session, schools visited in September had not received funds. Reportedly, scholarship amounts were released every year, although delays are common. It was also felt that such delays are not altogether detrimental, as students who may have dropped out after receiving the money, have to continue attending classes till the scholarship is disbursed. In fact, once the scholarship amount is released, 10-15 per cent of students stop coming to school. Sometimes, a child even collects a scholarship from more than one school!

Attendance was reportedly very high before the scholarship is released, but following disbursement attendance rates tend to decline and settle at 65 to 70 per cent. A significant point relevant to the design of the scholarship scheme (Ajwad 2006) is that the scholarship money on average amounted to about 1.37 per cent of the household's per capita expenditure. Thus, the overall impact of the transfer is trivial from the perspective of the household.

Lessons from Meerut Visit

The Kanya Vidya Dhan Yojana for girls has many features similar to those of a CCT programme and can serve as a possible scheme for a pilot. To ensure better targeting, the state government needs to ensure proper identification of beneficiaries. The other issue relates to the option of transfers in kind versus the transfers in cash. In the latter case, the evidence is that a considerable amount of such transfers are likely to be lost before they reach the target beneficiaries. However, transfers in kind raise issues of quality and also the possibility of a large part of the transfer being diverted to other functionaries.

Another implementation issue is that benefits, such as textbooks and scholarship money, not reaching in time can lose their impact. The benefit-incidence analysis for UP clearly shows that public expenditure on child health and education does not fully reach the poor, with most of the funds or benefits being cornered by relatively better-off economic groups.

There are problems in the design of schemes as well. One such example is the disbursement of the entire scholarship at the beginning of the session. No conditions are imposed, thus making the scholarship a free gift! Also, even when conditions are imposed, as in the case of dry rations which require 80 per cent attendance, these are seldom adhered to. What is needed is a unified monitoring machinery to ensure the successful implementation of incentive schemes. What is more important, when such transfers in the form of incentives are envisaged, is to ensure there is a fundamental change in behaviour in respect to the targeted parameter.

Summary of Evidence

The above discussion focused on outlining some salient features of child-related schemes in the country and examining their impact through a literature review and field visit. While the evidence is mixed, the findings of most studies indicate a positive impact on the utilisation of education and health services, indicated by higher enrolment, reduced drop-out rates, and an improvement in school attendance. However, no significant improvement in scholastic achievement was indicated, although the evidence is limited. Where improvements have been dramatic, as in the case of school enrolment, they are often short-lived. This was clear from the Meerut case study where scholarship money was paid as a lump sum at the start of the school session.

A major drawback to effectiveness appears to be poor implementation capacity and weak monitoring. For instance, the condition of 80 per cent school attendance in the erstwhile MDM programme was seldom adhered to. States which had strong commitment from the government and its functionaries, proper implementation and a competent monitoring authority, show superior results (for instance, the Tamil Nadu Integrated Nutrition Programme, which has became a model for the rest of the country).

None of the studies reviewed tells us enough about the eventual outcome of a particular programme or scheme. When the objective of targeting the poor is to effect improvements in human development indicators, the reviews fail to deliver. However, a study by Foster and Rosenzweig (1995) has demonstrated that spending on elementary education has external effects through improved efficiency. They have demonstrated this effect "in the case of agriculture, where educated farmers tend to help increase the yield of their neighbouring farms, at least in periods of changing technology".

Their study does, however, demonstrate equity effects from primary education. The first column of Table 18.7 shows the proportion of primary school age students from each income group. Children from families in the poorest 20 per cent of the population of Maharashtra represent 24 per cent of all students in contrast to 16 per cent from families in the richest fifth of income. Subsidies to primary school students are quite progressive due to the tendency of poorer families to have more children. Higher-income groups have virtually all their children in school, thus children not in school are disproportionately from poor families.

Finally, enrolments respond to greater resources devoted to primary education. Even very crude measures

Table 18.7

Current and Marginal Entrants to Schools by Income Groups: Maharashtra (%)

		1	2	3	4
		Primary School		*Secondary School*	
Quintile	*Quintile*	*Current Share of Students*	*Share of New Entrants*	*Current Share of Students*	*Share of New Entrants*
Poorest	1	0.24	0.4	0.14	0.13
	2	0.23	0.32	0.17	0.18
	3	0.19	0.18	0.18	0.18
	4	0.18	0.08	0.19	0.19
Richest	5	0.16	0.02	0.29	0.31

Source: Foster and Rosenzweig (1995).

of quality such as better teacher-student ratios in any one year are shown to positively influence primary school enrolments in subsequent years. This indicates that quality improvements paid for by reducing commercial subsidies could contribute substantially to achieving full enrolment and better educational outcomes.

Another class of issues relates to the quality of education. There is enough evidence to show that no amount of incentives will work in the long run, when supply-side factors are ignored. People expect good teachers and good school infrastructure to attract students. When it comes to evaluating which works better, transfers in kind or cash, evidence from cash transfers in the area of industry and housing has shown diversion and misappropriation of funds; the experience with transfers in kind is slightly better. Regarding the appropriate identification of the intended beneficiary, available evidence suggests that benefits are not fully reaching targeted beneficiaries and are cornered by the less needy. Part of the reason could be low levels of awareness of schemes by the intended beneficiaries.

Issues and Implications for CCTs

In conclusion, we highlight the main issues emerging from preceding analysis of select child-related incentive schemes in India to derive lessons for the application of CCTs as a policy tool in the country. The issues are both of a general nature and also specific issues arising from the field visit.

General Issues

Concept and Design of Incentives

Schemes which carry conditions are likely to be more effective in achieving their stated objectives than those that have no conditions. For example, the post-metric scholarship scheme for girls, known to be a success in Haryana, is linked to performance—the scholarship is subject to the recipient not failing in the examination more than once in a particular class. The other aspect concerns framing of realistic financial norms. For instance, a trivial sum of ₹10 per annum per beneficiary for stationery, given current price levels, makes little sense as an incentive.

Then there is also the problem of the mode and frequency of payment. When the entire stipend or scholarship for the year is paid to students at the beginning of the session, there is no incentive to attend classes, and many students drop-out soon after receipt of the scholarship. Thus while scholarship as an incentive causes enrolment to increase, attendance rates are found to go down and drop-out rates to increase. Clearly, if the scholarships/stipends were paid on a monthly basis, one could avoid high drop-out rates and ensure better attendance.

In the case of scholarships and related schemes, cash transfers should have some relationship with the prevailing prices. If incentives are not sufficiently attractive, there may not be many takers. This calls for a constant review of the monetary benefits provided by the schemes. Quality issues are also very important in schemes where benefits are in kind (e.g., MDM or ICDS). If the quality of food is poor, as is generally observed, intended beneficiaries will not participate in the scheme.

Targeting: A major issue in the context of CCT relates to targeting. While the incentives or transfers of the schemes are generally targeted at persons living BPL, disadvantaged sections like the SCs and STs, poor and uncovered geographical regions (e.g., tribal areas, northeastern states, the EAG states, etc.), and so on, the reality reveals numerous instances where benefits have been extended to the less needy and general population, as well: non-targeted children are allowed to participate in supplementary nutrition schemes, and the general population are provided stipends under the Kanya Vidya Dhan as girls from APL households are allowed to participate in the scheme if enough applications are not received from the targeted group. While a large proportion of vulnerable groups benefit from the ICDS, there is substantial programme capture by the less needy—possibly at the expense of more vulnerable children. Attendance by lower castes is relatively high, but there is still scope to attract a larger proportion of this group.

The criterion of caste or tribe membership as the basis for targeting is also questionable. The reason being that over the years a large section of SC, ST and OBC populations have already derived benefits under various incentive-based schemes and programmes and continue to do so, in fact, with greater vigour because they are better informed and have greater awareness about the existence of the schemes. To improve targeting, additional means criteria may become necessary. Given the current status of girls and women, to achieve gender parity it is important that incentive schemes continue to target girl-children and women. Certain areas in the country, especially the north-eastern region, the Hindi-speaking belt of the EAG states, and tribal areas which are known to have poor socio-economic indicators, may continue to be targeted.

Underfunding: Another basic lacuna in the design of these schemes is underfunding. While incentives may be attractive, funds allocated, released and utilised are usually inadequate to cover the intended target populations. An examination of the functioning of the post-matric scholarship, provision of textbooks to all, and so on show that funds provided are generally lower than required to cover all the intended beneficiaries. In the Total Sanitation Campaign, for example, there is a specific provision for IEC (information education and communication) activities, but it is common knowledge that neither are IEC activities properly designed, nor are the funds adequate for the purpose. Successful implementation of any cash or in-kind transfer programmes depends crucially on sensitising target populations on various parameters of the schemes, and sufficient funds should be provided for this.

Implementation Arrangements

The review of the workings of various incentives has indicated sluggishness in the implementation of most schemes, and a hesitation in implementing the required conditions to avail of the benefits. These findings clearly highlight the need for a proper implementation plan, which would ensure adherence to the conditions attached to the transfer. This is critical to ensure behaviour change in the beneficiaries, and achieve the intended objective of the CCT.

A related but important consideration for the success of any CCT scheme is the capacity of the institution implementing the programme. The review revealed the involvement of several key departments and ministries associated directly or indirectly with the formulation and implementation of programmes. There are also PTAs (parent-teacher associations), PRIs (panchayati raj institutions), women's groups, self-help groups, NGOs, etc., involved in the planning and implementation process. Two factors need to be kept in mind: the capacity of the institution to implement the programme, and the need for effective coordination among the major sectors and departments. For example, in the implementation of the ICDS programme, both the Ministry of Women and Child Development and the Ministry of Health and Family Welfare are involved; in addition, PRIs and PTAs are key stakeholders. Clearly they need to work together to achieve optimal results. In India to date, there has been little attempt to involve the private sector in any aspect of these schemes. There is a clear case for public-private partnerships (or outsourcing), given the distinct advantage that the private sector may have in terms of capacity.

Monitoring

A major reason for the poor functioning of many schemes relates to weak monitoring arrangements. The real issue is having the right institutional arrangement to monitor each scheme. This study has shown that hardly any of the existing arrangements for monitoring are satisfactory. There was much expectation from PRIs, but field visits, especially to districts in MP, have revealed their weaknesses in undertaking this important work. The rivalry between alternative factions deters PRIs from being objective, and they admitted to playing safe, essentially to ensure re-election. PTAs too have vested interests, apart from being generally weak in capacity and lacking objectivity. They are also generally unwilling to confront teachers and other key functionaries when the need arises. To bring objectivity and to reduce the role of vested interests, one may consider the involvement of members of civil society representing various interests from more than one village.

In conclusion apart from the demand-side factors, the supply-side factors influencing incentive schemes need to be emphasised, because of strong complementarities between the two for optimising the benefits from every rupee spent on a programme. Poor infrastructure—physical and human resources—would ensure the failure of any incentive scheme. What is important is to create demand and ensure that the supply-side factors keep pace with the emerging demand. The strategy should be to swiftly adjust to meeting the newly created demand.

Specific Issues

Monthly versus One-Shot Transfers: As the review of studies has shown both approaches can be defended.

In certain situations, one-shot transfers are preferred, as in the case of the Janani Suraksha Yojana (JSS) for women and newly born children after receiving all the prescribed immunisations, as a pre-condition.[14] However, scholarships/stipends should be paid on a monthly basis to ensure that children continue attending classes regularly. The Meerut field visit has shown that a one-shot payment of scholarships in advance resulted in many students dropping out. Moreover, a lump sum in such situations tends to get used for other family needs.

Corruption in Selecting Beneficiaries and in Transfer of Funds: Many schemes have their origins in election promises, and are rarely piloted, before their implementation on a large scale. The result is that the gaps in implementation lead to their misapplication. It is important first to fully work out the parameters of a scheme. There is very little effective monitoring of programmes; the formation of local monitoring committees with due representation from all key stakeholders including primary stakeholder groups and civil society, could contribute significantly to reducing corruption and nepotism. While schemes should leave no gaps in design for people to take advantage of loopholes; at the same time, procedures should be simple and easily understood by poor and illiterate groups. Lack of awareness also contributes to some people taking advantage of other people's ignorance.

Targeting Poor Areas or only the Poor in all Areas: The decision should not be based on one versus the other, but should depend on the needs and costs involved. In India, both models have been in operation, but no review of cost effectiveness has been carried out to answer this question. This may be an area which requires dedicated work. Sometimes, it is cost-effective to target only the poor areas, such as the EAG states and north-eastern states with

14. JSS is an incentive scheme of the Government of India under National Rural Health Mission (NRHM) to promote institutional deliveries with a view to reducing maternal mortality. The cash incentives are provided to the pregnant woman for hospital delivery as well as to the motivator.

tribal populations. However, within the poor areas there is further targeting of the poor and the disadvantaged

In addition to the cost-effectiveness aspect, there is also the political aspect. Most decision makers weigh the political losses and gains. Here again, civil society and the media could play an important role in sensitising the masses to the issues.

Concluding Remarks

The above review, especially the international experience with CCTs, suggests the need for exploring the possibility of casting schemes in the CCT mould. But before implementing or introducing CCTs on any large scale, as a first step it would be prudent to undertake a pilot study. There are several schemes that could form the basis for such a study: at least two schemes involving cash transfers and one scheme with transfers in kind could be chosen. One scheme from within the cash transfer category should involve one-shot transfers, and the other one should have periodic payments. At least one scheme may be from the area of education and another from the area of health. Another could have a social objective, such as promoting village sanitation, delaying the age at marriage, etc. The pilot study may focus on a couple of districts in at least two or three states. The lessons learnt could then be fine-tuned and refined to adopt CCTs approach on a large scale.

References

Ajwad, M. Ihsan (2006). "Anti-poverty Programs in Uttar Pradesh". Washington DC:World Bank (*mimeo*)

Bose, A.B. (2003). *The State of Children in India: Promises to Keep.* New Delhi: Manohar Publishers and Distributors.

Centre for Budget & Governance Accountability (2006). *Child Budget Analysis of Union and State Budgets (1993-94 to 2006-07).* New Delhi,

de Janvry, Alain (2006). Key note address: "Conditional Cash Transfer Programs in the Bigger Picture of Social Policy", *Third International Conference on Conditional Cash Transfers*, Istanbul, Turkey, 26-30 June.

Devadas, R.P. and S. Prem Kumari (1978). "Nutritional Impact of School Lunch Programme on Children Over a Period of Five Years", *Indian J. Nutr Diet* 15: 257-63

Duraiswamy, Malathy (2003). "Effectiveness of Incentives in School Enrolment and Attainment". (*mimeo*).

Education Research Unit (2003). *Synthesis Report on Factors Facilitating/Impeding Successful Primary School completion* (Draft-28 February 2003), Study Commissioned by the World Bank , New Delhi.

Fiszbein, Ariel and Norbert Schady (2009). *Conditional Cash Transfers: Reducing Present and Future Poverty.* Washington D.C.: The World Bank.

Foster, A. and Mark Rosenzweig (1995). "Learning by Doing and Learning from Others: Human Capital and Technological Change in Agriculture", *Journal of Political Economy* 103: 1176-209

Government of India (2006). *Annual Report 2005-06.* New Delhi: Ministry of Women and Child Development.

———. (2002). *Tenth Five Year Plan (2002-2007).* New Delhi: Planning Commission.

———. (2001). *Census of India: Population Projections for India and States 1996-2016*. New Delhi: Registrar General, India.

———. (2000). *Integrated Child Development Services Programme.* Report No. 2 and 3 (Civil) of 2000. New Delhi, Comptroller and Auditor General of India.

Goyal, Nirupam and Sangeeta Goyal (2004). "Primary Education: Low Coverage, Poor Quality", in *Business Line,* 6 September.

Gupta, D. B. et al. (2002). "Nation-wide Evaluation of Integrated Child Development Services Scheme". New Delhi: National Council of Applied Economic Research. (*mimeo*).

Gupta, D.B. (2003). "Public Spending on Child Development". New Delhi: The World Bank. (*mimeo*).

———. (2003a). "Study of Existing Policies and Related Provisions/Schemes Promoting the Developmental and Educational Needs of Children in the Age Group 0-11 Years". New Delhi: The World Bank. (*mimeo*).

———. (2003b). "Benefit Incidence Analysis in the Context of Health Spending in Bihar", A Background Note for the World Bank Report *Bihar: Towards a Development Strategy.* (*mimeo*)

Indicus Analytics (2006). "Monitoring and Evaluation of the Pilot Study in Integrated Child Development Scheme in Madhya Pradesh". New Delhi. (*mimeo*).

Jha, Jyotsna and Dhir Jhingran (2002). *Elementary Education for the Poorest and Other Deprived Groups: The Real Challenge of Universalisation.* New Delhi: Centre for Policy Research.

Kumar, Pushpendra and Tanushree Sood (2005). "Report of the Midday Meal Survey in Champaran and Supaul Districts of Bihar". September. (*mimeo*).

Laxmaniah, A., K.V. Rameshwar Sarma, D. Hanumantha Rao, Ch. Gal Reddy, M. Ravindranath, M. Vishnuvardhan Rao and K. Vijayaraghvan (1999). "Impact of Mid-day Meal Program on Educational and Nutritional Status of School Children in Karnataka", *Indian Pediatrics* 36: 1221-28.

Mahal, Ajay, Janmejaya Singh, Farzana Afridi and Vikram Lamba (2002). *Who Benefits from Public Sector Health Spending in India.* New Delhi: National Council of Applied Economic Research.

Mehrotra, Santosh (2006). The *Economics of Elementary Education in India: The Challenge of Public Finance, Private Provision and Household Costs.* New Delhi: SAGE Publications.

Morley, Samuel and David Coodey (2003). *Making it Pay to Stay in School.* Washington D.C.: Centre for Global Development (CGD) and International Food Policy Research Institute (IFPRI).

New Concept (1995) "Evidence from Haryana and Maharashtra, New Delhi". The World Bank. (*mimeo*).

Panchamukhi, P.R. (2006). "Universalising Elementary Education in Madhya Pradesh: Can the Successes of Decentralised Governance Offset the Problems of Public Finance, Private Cost!", in Santosh Mehrotra (ed.), *The Economics of Elementary Education in India: The Challenge of Public Finance, Private Provision and Household Costs.* New Delhi: SAGE Publications.

Subba Rao, K. (1989). "Improving Nutrition in India: Policies and Programmes and their Impact", *World Bank Discussion Paper* Number 49. Washington D.C: The World Bank.

The PROBE Team (1999). *Public Report on Primary Education in India.* New Delhi: Oxford University Press.

Thorat, Sukhdeo and Joel Lee (2005). "Caste Discrimination and Food Security Programmes", *Economic and Political Weekly* 40(39), 24 September,

Tilak, J.B.G. and A. Nalla Gounden (2006). "Private Costs and Public Financing of Elementary Education in a High-achiever State: Tamil Nadu", in Santosh Mehrotra (ed.), *The Economics of Elementary Education in India: The Challenge of Public Finance, Private Provision and Household Costs.* New Delhi: SAGE Publications.

UNICEF Survey (1999). *Survey of Elementary Education in Various Indian States.* New Delhi: New Concept.

World Bank (2004). *Reaching Out to the Child: An Integrated Approach to Child Development.* New Delhi: World Bank and Oxford University Press.

———. (2004a). "Snakes and Ladders", *World Bank Report* Number 8. South Asia Human Development Series. New Delhi: World Bank and Oxford University Press.

———. (2002). *India: Poverty in India—The Challenge of Uttar Pradesh.* Report number 22323-IN.

This paper is based on a study report prepared earlier for UNICEF, India Office.

Appendix Table A-18.1

Major Central Government Incentive Schemes (in percentage)

Scheme/Programme	*2001-02*	*2002-03*	*2003-04*	*2004-05*	*2005-06*	*2006-07*	*Rating*	*Remarks*
Balika Smridhi Yojana	16.00	1.8	0.01	48.0	0.03	0.03	*	Lack of commitment from Central and state governments
Janani Suraksha Yojana	72.0	65.0	40.0	50.0	100.0*		**	New scheme under NHRM as the earlier NMB scheme had inadequate funds
Pre-metric scholarship for children in unclean professions (BE)		13.98	13.55	14.11	16.00	16.00	**1/2	Inadequate awareness
Actual expenditure		4..94	13.66	8.82				
PMS for SC allocation	154.63	268.00	260.00				***	Working reasonably well, but scheme not publicised enough
Funds released	159.27	153.05	264.99					
Funds utilised	156.57	103.07	191.26					
PMS for ST allocation	63.00	66.00	54.00	82.50	230.65	189.78	***	Awareness levels low
Funds released	66.78	51.59	NA	101.38	184.12	NA		
Funds utilised	65.42	38.83	NA	NA	NA	NA		

Total Sanitation Scheme allocation	63.00	66.00	54.00	82.50	230.65	189.78	**1/2	IEC activities not adequate
Amount released	66.78	51.59	NA	101.38	184.12	NA		
Amount utilised	65.42	38.83	NA	NA	NA	NA		
MDM Scheme BE	930.00	1,057.50	1,175.00	1,675.00	3,010.00	2,915.00	***1/2	Cooked meals not always palatable
ICDS Scheme—Funds released		1,504.98	1,458.68	17,265.49	1,963.65	4,795.85	****	SNP supplies irregular, non-targeted beneficiaries taking advantage, immunisation efforts for children inadequate
Expenditure reported by state		1,386.56	1,735.43	1,795.25				
Ashram schools in TSP Areas BE		13.50	13.09	12.35	6.00	16.00	**	Not many takers because of poor infrastructure of Ashram schools
Actual expenditure		9.16	6.05	5.29				
Textbooks/stationery/uniforms, transportation allowance							***1/2	Few students worry about textbooks, and prefer guide books.

Appendix Table A-18.2

Funds Allocated Under Various Schemes in Uttar Pradesh (in million rupees)

Scheme	*State Allocation*	*Centre's Allocation*	*Total Allocation*
Kanya Vidya Dhan	6,000.0	-	6,000.0
Unemployment allowance	4,000.0	-	4,000.0
Pension for the destitute	349.5	-	349.5
Old-age pension	2,464.0	-	2,464.0
Family Benefit Scheme	250.0	-	250.0
Pre-metric scholarships	6,910.9	75.0	6,985.9
Post-metric scholarships	2,765.6	1,910.0	4,675.6
Financial assistance for girl's marriage and sick ST/OBC girls	300.0	-	300.0
Pre-metric scholarship for children of persons in unclean professions	11.8	11.9	23.7
Financial assistance for persons afflicted with disability	80.0	80.0	160.0
Financial assistance for the marriage and sickness of SC girls	1.5	-	1.5
Assistance for disabled	1,033.3	-	1,033.3

19

Statutory Regulation and Self-Regulation

S.L. RAO

Any discussion on what holds India back focuses on lack of accountability in the administration, inefficiency and corruption, bureaucracy at all levels, lack of coordination, centralisation of power, opaque decision-making, non-delegation to municipalities and *panchayats*, investigation and police systems that are under political control, and the weakened state of the judiciary, to mention only a few.

Our executive system provides policy inputs to the political class, and also implements policies. To ensure that legislative intentions are carried out, constitutional and statutory bodies also have the responsibility of regulating certain fields. For example, constitutional bodies like Comptroller and Auditor General (CAG), Union Public Service Commission (UPSC), Election Commission; and statutory bodies like Telecom Regulatory Authority of India (TRAI), Central and state electricity regulatory commissions, and others.

Both constitutional and statutory bodies are expected to be independent of government, and to function within the laws that created them. However, the constitutional bodies have been more effective as being independent of government. They are invariably autonomous, independent and are not expected to report to any government functionary.

Post liberalisation, mostly after 1991, the government transferred (Centre for purely central subjects like telecom, licensing, tariff setting and also state governments when it was a concurrent subject like electricity) some of these regulatory powers to non-elected statutory regulatory bodies (created by legislation) with the aim to ensuring competitive markets. This was done for reasons as listed below:

- The technical nature of the subject under regulation.
- The need for clarity and transparency since large sums of money are involved in tariffs setting and to prevent its misuse.
- The need for a judicial process so that there is a balanced approach that takes all factors into account.
- Due to pressure from international financing institutions that felt that the Indian system of infrastructure licensing, operations and pricing, was opaque and subject to misuse. International investment that India wanted badly demanded greater transparency.
- The entry of the private sector after 1991 into many areas and particularly infrastructure, demanded more transparency.

For such regulatory bodies, their jurisdiction, the extent of their powers, the manner of exercising them, penal powers and so on, are laid down by the statutes that created them. They might be bodies with national or individual state jurisdictions depending on the constitutional allocation of subjects.

None of the statutory regulatory agencies have been a model for the others. Each has been created by the concerned Ministry. Thus, the TRAI is a recommendatory body. The electricity commissions are still trying to get authority over some aspects like forward markets from the Forward Markets Commission (FMC). Many state regulators are submissive to government desires that electricity tariffs be low, resulting in massive losses to the distributing companies. Penal powers to regulators over non-compliance are weak in most cases except for the Securities and Exchange Board of India (SEBI) and the Competition Commission of India (CCI). The appellate tribunals who deal with appeals however, tend to undercut the penalties imposed by the SEBI or the CCI.

Majority of these bodies were created in 1991 after economic liberalisation. A few of these bodies however, were created earlier like the FMC (in 1952), the Reserve Bank of India (RBI) (in 1935), the Institute of Chartered Accountants of India (ICAI) (in 1949).

There is little research on the comparative powers and performance of regulatory bodies. On a rough count, the following regulatory agencies are in place today:

1. Transportation—4: including waterways, highways and the Airports Economic Regulatory Authority.
2. Energy—27: the Central Electricity Regulatory Commission (CERC), 25 state electricity regulatory commissions (one for each state), and the Petroleum and Natural Gas Regulatory Board.
3. Communications—1: TRAI.
4. Markets—3: the FMC; the Warehousing Development and Regulatory Authority (WDRA), and the Cotton Corporation of India.
5. Finance—4: the Reserve Bank of India RBI), SEBI, the Insurance Regulatory and Development Authority (IRDA), and the Pension Fund Regulatory and Development Authority (PFRDA).

In addition to above, there are:

6. Education—2: the University Grants Commission (UGC), and the All India Council for Technical Education (AICTE).
7. Food—1: the Food Safety and Standards Authority of India (FSSAI).

Over and above, 24 self-regulated bodies have been created under the legislative charter:

8. For sports, there is the Indian Olympic Association, the All India Tennis Association, the Board of Control for Cricket in India, and others.
9. Other self-regulated bodies include the Medical Council of India (MCI), the Institute of Chartered Accountants of India (ICAI), the Institute of Cost Accountants of India, the Indian Institute of Architects, and the Bar Council of India.

It is generally accepted that the self-regulated institutions do not implement their rules satisfactorily. There are allegations of malfeasance against almost all of them. The professional bodies (like the ICAI or the MCI) are not known to take stringent actions against violators. The sports organisations tend to have people running them almost for lifetimes and there are doubts about their financial integrity.

In the cases of electricity, telecommunications, competition, securities, the appeals against the orders of the concerned commissions are made to appellate tribunals, and not directly to the high courts. This was expected to speed the process of appeal and develop expertise in technical areas. This has often led to dilution of the original intent of the orders of the commissions. This is particularly the case with competition. In cases where CCI imposed heavy penalties, the Tribunal either stayed the orders for long or heavily diluted the penalty. Effectively, the purpose of sending strong signal to others that they should not violate the rules was defeated. TRAI is always subject to being overruled by the ministry since it is only a recommendatory body.

With such extensive powers over their sectors, one would expect that government departments would have diminished greatly in size. This has not happened. They continue to influence most regulatory bodies and monitor them closely for their consonance with government policies.

Indeed, the government departments in many cases, particularly state governments, are able to influence the regulatory commissions to act according to their wishes curbing their independence and efficacy.

> In India, sector regulators have been mandated with independence though such autonomy is limited in various aspects. Moreover, there is a difference between mandated and delegated independence with the latter much lower than the former due to control exercised by the executive. Functional independence is often curbed by the dependence of regulators on concerned line ministries for budgetary allocations and sanctioning of staff appointments as well as the need for the former to report to the latter.[1]

The issue of independence of regulators is important as the government holds a major share in operations leading to the problem of independence and accountability; properties that are required for good regulatory governance. A prominent reason for this is the selection process of chairmen and members of the regulatory bodies. The selection committees (as specified in the legislation) are invariably composed of administrators, many from the concerned ministry. Invariably, a retired government servant is selected. Many times they come from the same ministry in the sector which they are to regulate. Thus, they bring to the regulatory assignments the baggage of the administrative mindsets of their years in administration, and the procedures and rules that go with them. They are usually over 60 years of age, and many do not exercise the independence that the law has given them, nor do they have the courage to do so. They have little commercial or management aptitude. Their decisions are often pedestrian and do not include an articulation of desired outcomes, provisions for closely monitoring achievement, ordering mid-term corrections, and evaluating the enterprise's performance. Hence, the sectors function under orders that are taken arbitrarily without weighing the pros and the cons.

---

1. *Regulatory Management and Reform in India: Background Paper for OECD.* Prepared by Vijay Vir Singh and Siddhartha Mitra.

With most regulatory bodies, the staff on deputation from other government departments do not regard themselves as having a career in regulation. Few, if any, rise to become members or chairmen of the regulatory bodies.

The regulatory bodies are invariably subservient to their ministries and follow their diktats affecting their regulatory effectiveness, efficiency, transparency and accountability. Thus, none of the state electricity regulatory commission has ever objected to the free power given to agriculture and other select vote blocs. These loss-making supplies have to be met by cross-subsidies, that is, higher tariffs to other consumers. This has led to distortions in the cropping patterns, depletion of groundwater and growing salinity of land. The Electricity Act mandates open access in order to optimise use of available electricity in the country. State governments prefer to get the supply from local electricity generators. No regulatory commission has protested against the prevention of open access of electricity between states.

There is no possibility of codification of regulatory order into precedents for future use. This is because many orders do not enunciate principles.

> A recent development towards obtaining better regulatory governance in the Indian financial sector is in the report of the Financial Sector Legislative Reforms Commission (FSLRC), headed by Justice Shri B.N. Srikrishna. The FSLRC has proposed the Indian Financial Code (IFC), a consolidated draft law for the financial sector. Non-legislative elements of the draft Code have been culled out into the Handbook on adoption of governance enhancing and non-legislative elements of the draft IFC (Handbook). The Handbook lays down international best practices on regulatory governance and lists the procedures that the Indian regulators should follow to achieve better governance in regulation making.[2]

---

2. *https://ajayshahblog.blogspot.in/2015/09/regulatory-governance-problems-in.html*

There are of course regulatory bodies like the RBI and the SEBI that have had much impact on the economy due to their independent decisions. Most regulatory bodies are content with submitting to state government desires.

Has the statutory regulatory process been successful? I would say that it has not done what was expected from it, namely create transparency and clarity in licensing, tariff setting, and so on. This is mainly owing to the key positions in these bodies becoming post-retirement perquisites for retiring bureaucrats and government servants and resulting in little independence, courage or expertise in regulating the concerned sectors. However, there is now more transparency than when decisions were made in closed government offices and not in open courtrooms.

Where appellate tribunals have been created, they might have been better replaced by special benches in the high courts which would focus on law and leave ascertaining facts to the commissions.

It would have been better if all the commissions had uniform structures and authorities and if they followed each others' orders to ensure that there is a body of regulatory law and precedents that could enrich the whole business of regulation.

20

Transforming Socioeconomic Systems for an Ecologically Safe Operating Space[1]

KANCHAN CHOPRA

The understanding that our economic and social system is nested in a larger ecological or ecosystem is well accepted now. That there exist limits within which our economic activity can expand and enlarge itself has been reiterated time and again by natural scientists, most recently in two widely quoted papers indicating "a safe operating space for humanity" (See Rockstorm et al. 2009 and Steffen et al. 2015). The planet earth stated by the astronomer, Carl Sagan, to look from outer space like "a mote of dust suspended on a sunbeam" is indeed, in some areas, reaching the limits of its natural bounty. This paper aims to analyse, whether as social scientists, opinion leaders and decision makers, we take cognizance of this threat to the environment around us. If not, how can we move in a direction which does so.

The Indian Agenda on the Environment

The Indian agenda on environment stands at a cross roads. Two kinds of influences are determining this agenda, albeit they operate at different scales. The first is an awareness and understanding of the impending environmental crises of different kinds among sections of society. The recognition of the urgent need to regulate

1. This paper is a revised version of my Boulding Award lecture delivered on 27 June 2016 at the Conference of the International Society for Ecological Economics held at Washington DC.

some aspects of economic activity in the interest of conservation and to build social norms to assist such regulation exists. Judicial intervention and slowly evolving legal codes, pushed ahead often by grass roots conflicts and their documentation, also illustrate an intention to take note and introduce regulation of environment-damaging economic activity.

However, other elements in the system, moving at a much faster pace, demand faster economic growth in the shorter run. These elements are driven by unconstrained market forces, irresponsible industrialisation and urbanisation. As it happens, the dominant political economy discourse often stresses development, employment and more jobs, often at the cost of longer run sustainability. This discourse urges that projects need to be cleared fast. Bureaucratic delays are not accepted as readily as they were in the past and there is cause for concern that this accent on speed may be at the cost of the environment. Some of these changes have been documented by an editorial in the *Economic & Political Weekly*.[2] It seems that in several cases, compromises are being made to ensure fast implementation of projects, overruling earlier advice on caution. Such compromises could refer to a range of issues such as implementation of the Forest Rights Act, moratorium on industry in heavily polluted areas or wetlands regulation acts. Which way will the balance tilt? Will a judicial mix of development and environmental protection, of speed and caution, be possible?

In such a divisive environment, it is useful to examine some of the reasons why the issues relating to the environment are critical for planet earth and its human and non-human inhabitants. Boulding, in a seminal paper published in 1966 (Boulding 1966),[3] made a few points

2. See Editorial "Choosing Speed Over Diligence," *Economic & Political Weekly* LI (23), 4 June 2016.

3. First presented by Kenneth Ewart Boulding at the Sixth Resources for the Future Forum on Environmental Quality in a Growing Economy in Washington, D.C. on 8 March 1966.

which deserve reiteration in such a policy context. These points also encapsulate the directions towards which research has since then tried to move policy.

The 'Cowboy Economy' and 'the Spaceship Economy'

Boulding emphasised the difference between ways in which economies could be organised in terms of a striking metaphor of the difference between 'the cowboy economy' and 'the spaceship economy'. In the former, there always exist new frontiers to explore, new resources to exploit and so on. Note his words "the cowboy being symbolic of the illimitable plains and also associated with reckless, exploitative, romantic, and violent behaviour, which is characteristic of open societies...... The economy of the future might similarly be called the 'spaceman' economy, in which the earth has become a single spaceship, without unlimited reservoirs of anything, either for extraction or for pollution." In the 'spaceman economy', the earth is likened to a spaceship where stocks of resources are fixed. So, one functions always with an eye on the stock. In such an economy, consumption and production are desirable but only within limits. Note, further, the following:

> The essential measure of the success of the economy is not production and consumption at all, but the nature, extent, quality, and complexity of the total capital stock, including in this the state of the human bodies and minds which form a part of the system. In the spaceman economy, what we are primarily concerned with is stock maintenance, and any technological change which results in the maintenance of a given total stock with a lessened throughput is clearly a gain. This idea that both production and consumption are (at times) bad things rather than good things is very strange to economists, who have been obsessed with the income-flow concepts to the exclusion, almost, of capital-stock concepts.

It might be more accurate to say that the notions of maintaining a constant stock of capital, intrinsic to all measurements of income flows in national income accounting, has somehow taken a back seat. More so the notion of maintaining stocks of natural capital intact. However, in recent years since, there has emerged a school of thought which maintains that changes in wealth, rather than in the availability of goods and services measure human well-being. In other words, that we need to focus on stock, rather than flows of production and consumption. Further, 'comprehensive wealth' and 'inclusive wealth' have been defined to include human capital and natural capital, in addition to the usual reproducible capital (Arrow et al. 2012).[4] With endorsement from United Nations (UN) agencies, these concepts have now started making a dent, albeit a small one, on the national accounts of nations. The work is an attempt to use theoretical developments defining 'sustainable income' starting with constancy of stocks into a System of Environmental Economic Accounting (SEEA). The UN presented SEEA as a starting point in 2003.

Parallely, 'genuine savings', a concept which accounts for depletion in natural capital, is one of the most documented macro parameters in this context. Estimates from the World Bank indicate that for India, the number for 'genuine savings' is 26.64 per cent for 2008 and 24.56 per cent for 2009 as against net savings of 29.68 per cent and 26.60 per cent (all per cent of the GDP).[5] Though these estimates are partial, they provide the way forward with respect to the SEEA framework, and provide ample testimony for the relevance of Boulding's legacy today.

A few initiatives were taken in India to bring the national statistical and planning systems in line with these developments. One of these took the form of an Expert Group report. The Green Accounting Committee Report submitted by the Expert Group (chaired by Partha Dasgupta) to the Government of India (2013) attempted to introduce alternative wealth based concepts of welfare into the national statistical system. Another was the

4. See Arrow et al. (2012). Also, UNU-IHDP/UNEP (2012).

5. See World Bank (2010, 2011).

Planning Commission Report (2014) on low carbon growth.[6] Alternative scenarios were studied to provide the nature of trade-offs if a 'green growth' path was to be followed. But no follow-up on either of these two report seems to have taken place since then.

Why Think of the Future? After me, the Deluge?

Another question asked by Boulding in that paper and which continues to engage both academics and policymakers across the world is: " Why should we not maximise the welfare of this generation at the cost of posterity? After all, 'after me, the deluge' has been the motto of not insignificant numbers of human societies. Boulding had said,

> The only answer to this, as far as I can see, is to point out that the welfare of the individual depends on the extent to which he can identify himself with others, and that the most satisfactory individual identity is that which identifies...with a community extending over time from the past into the future. If this kind of identity is recognised as desirable, then posterity has a voice.

However, even if posterity has a voice, the question of time discounting remains and we could hold the view that let the future take care of itself. Discounting the future has been a part of economists' toolkit for long now. Projects are approved and planning conducted on the basis of this article of faith.

In spite of this article of faith, "the future has a bad habit of becoming the present", as someone has stated. And the problems of the future manifest themselves soon enough, sometimes in our own lifetimes. Some had already started manifesting themselves when Boulding wrote (in 1966) perhaps more in the context of pollution than in that of resource scarcity. In the world of today, the pollution of outer space which he referred to has become a living reality as climate change hovers over us,

6. See Government of India (2013, 2014).

challenging humanity to find an internationally negotiated solution. The science is pretty well established. Successive reports of the IPCC from 1988 onwards have ensured this. However, there exist almost insurmountable political challenges to arriving at an internationally negotiated way ahead of dealing with it. We find a schism between science practice and policy which is proving difficult to bridge. The transformation we seek requires that the state of knowledge, the framing of policy and practice on the ground move in sync. I shall argue that different steps need to be taken at the local, national and international levels of governance to ensure that this takes place. These steps would fall under the category of 'crafting new institutional frameworks', institutions being interpreted as 'rules of the game'.

In self-sufficient resource based economies (for example fishing communities), crafting new institutions internalising new knowledge was simple. New knowledge came from replicated practical experience which was used as the basis for defining institution structures with rules about times for fishing, for abstaining from it and the number of boats to go to sea.

However, the specialised economic and financial systems of today are far removed from natural ecosystem realities. Generation of knowledge itself is within specialised disciplines, each of which impinge on the natural ecosystems.

The challenge lies in being able to transform social and ecological systems in line with new knowledge. 'Transformation' can be interpreted as change, a makeover or a revolution. It implies going from an undesirable situation to one more desirable. And desirable by what indicators? Maybe ecological indicators are what we have in mind in this context.

Further, the word 'transformation' also, more often than not, suggests a huge change, not an incremental one. How do we achieve it?

Drivers of Change: Technology

Change in social-ecological systems begins with the so-called propellers or drivers. For example, technology could be the driver of transformation from one state of the system to the next: say with reference to food or water. More often than not, at the time when such a transformation driven by technology is taking place, we rarely know whether a certain change is 'good' from the ecological perspective: is it something which ecosystems will absorb, without affecting their functioning capability, or their long term 'resilience'. The state of knowledge at that point of time may not be able to establish this issue one way or the other in a conclusive manner.

With reference to production of food, take the example of the green revolution of the 1960s and 70s in India. It was heralded as path breaking when it happened: it transformed traditional agriculture and fed the millions. And so policy interventions to encourage the spread of the new technology were put in place. With better knowledge now, there is universal acceptance of the fact that this technology/revolution has also degraded the soil and led to overexploitation of ground water; in other words, undermined the capability of the natural capital in the long run.

But, truly, in hindsight, was it feasible not to accept that change? Those familiar with the agricultural economy of India of that time (and the country's 'ship to mouth' existence) will agree it was not.

With reference to water, at one point of time, big dams were heralded as the harbingers of prosperity. Now, we know better, and scientific evidence points in the direction of minimising structural interventions across rivers . But meanwhile, society and the institutions that leverage political decision-making are all aligned to reproduce structural interventions (such as big dams and interlinking of rivers) in many parts of the world.

Another kind of situation exists in the context of climate change in the world of today. The science is pretty well established. Successive reports of the IPCC from 1988 onwards have ensured this. However, there exist almost insurmountable political challenges to arriving at an internationally negotiated way ahead of dealing with it. Again we find a schism between science practice and policy of another kind.

Change through Laws and Social Norms and the Role of Ethical Positions

A second mode of bringing about change or transformation in systems is through legal and social norms. At the national level, an overarching set of laws that encourage protection of vulnerable ecosystems and people could be put in place. Instruments such as law and social norms, which reflect the larger ethical concerns of humans, have a significant role to play. Many a time, these larger ethical concerns viewed from the perspective of 'an ecologically safe operating space for humanity' are at odds with human aspirations. And the individualistically oriented market ethic treats preferences as sacrosanct. Creating formal and informal institutions to achieve other ends conflicts with the model of liberal individualism. One could ask whether the implementation of policies that deliberately aim at shaping people's preferences is desirable. Where the aim is societal transformation to pro-environmental behaviour, the question becomes merely rhetorical. In the standard behavioural model, there is no option but to change what motivates choice (e.g., attitudes, norms). It is these choices expressed in the rapidly growing economic system through markets which drive consumption (and overconsumption) in all major countries of the world today. Overconsumption in turn drives excessive resource use and violates the boundaries of the safe operating space for humanity.

Internationally, future progress in designing appropriate policy responses to the climate change issue will have to address these ethical underpinnings squarely. Among several others, Stern (2006) starts his review of climate change by noting these ethical concerns, which at times have entered the literature through a discussion of the issue of appropriate social rates of discount for future consumption. He has called for immediate decisive action to stabilise greenhouse gases because "the benefits of strong early action on climate change outweigh the costs." The Stern Review, also points towards the danger of extending the principles of economics to the analysis of problems of critical import for the existence of life on earth. While Stern does so in the context of climate change, the same conclusions could be reached through an analysis of critical ecosystem services and 'biodiversity'. The National Oceanic Atmospheric Administration (NOAA) Panel in the US, way back in the 1990s, also opted for use of the precautionary principle in a large gamut of issues where the limits to human understanding posed significant questions. The limits of economic analysis are perhaps best understood by the most authentic of its practitioners.

Human values then are at the core of all major transformations. How do norms which reflect these values change? And how can they be influenced? Answers vary from a paternalistic top down approach to 'unconscious behavioural influences' to 'nudging' (as some policy practitioners choose to call it). But transformations will not take place by themselves, it depends on the choices we make, particularly at certain critical points in history.

Multiple Stakeholders and the Making of Choices in an Unequal World

Choices made depend on the stakeholders involved in decision-making. India today consists of a society characterised by profound inequality. Clearly, multiple stakeholders have emerged with powerful voices in the Indian polity and it is not easy to reconcile their interests. The question that inevitably arises can be posed as follows: is a movement towards thoughtful conservation and development possible? Are we as a nation at all willing to implement policies that ask for some degree of restraint in the exploitation of our natural resources? Or are we going to pursue a pattern of development which concentrates on the maximisation of present gains of the privileged few to the detriment of the interests of vulnerable people and ecologically fragile areas?

It can be argued that 'transformations' take time and social norms change slowly. Meanwhile can we go ahead in formulating laws on a case by case basis, thereby internalising the learnings of environmental grass roots learnings and movements into existing institutional structures. In this way, we can identify critical ecosystems and ecological services as also vulnerable populations and say that we value their continued and dynamic resilience more than that of others. In other words, the ordering principle is based on extending, first and foremost, the choice sets of vulnerable people and ensure that critical ecosystems are kept away from threshold changes in their state and functioning. Vulnerable people and vulnerable places need to be identified and protected. Such an approach can probably be illustrated best in the context of specific issues and regions. We illustrate below with the help of deliberations and policy formulation with regard to the ecologically sensitive Western Ghats.

Can a Process of Gradual, Law-driven Change be Envisaged? The Case of the Western Ghats

By the first decade of the 21st century, there existed a dominant public opinion in the country that ESAs (ecologically sensitive areas), including those in the Western Ghats, needed to be protected. Successive pieces of legislation in the preceding years had also endorsed such an understanding. It seemed that the motivation to conserve at the cost of reckless development existed in several quarters. It was in this vein that the Western Ghats Ecology Experts Panel (WGEEP), chaired by the eminent ecologist, Madhav Gadgil, was set up by the Ministry of Environment and Forests (MoEF) in March 2010. The committee, after due diligence, submitted its report in August 2011. For some time after this, there was complete silence on the part of the MoEF, which had set up the

Committee in the first instance. The report seemed to have been forgotten by the Ministry and was made public only in May 2012 after a High Court injunction asking for the same. The reasons for this unwarranted delay can only be conjectured. Perhaps some of its recommendations, tilting towards conservation and local-level decision-making which had not found favour with the powers that be or with other dominant stakeholders such as industry.

The story took another turn with the constitution of a second committee called the High Level Working Group (HLWG) under the chairmanship of K. Kasturirangan.[7] The HLWG (popularly referred to as the Kasturirangan Committee) was mandated to examine the implementation of the Gadgil Committee report with a view to holistic development. In a carefully nuanced report, the HLWG recommended that the area to be conserved as ecologically fragile be somewhat smaller than that recommended by the WGEEP earlier. However, it recommended a complete ban on mining, quarrying and sand mining, 'red' category industry, thermal power projects and large urban developments within this area. The committee mandated that in these ESAs, all projects were to be undertaken after prior informed consent of the villagers. Further, a set of economic incentives were to be set in place for movement towards green growth and sustainable agriculture. In other words, the report envisaged a moving together of the five state governments in the region in pursuance of some common goals in relation to the Western Ghats.

In the wake of the submission of this report, almost all government, civil society, and media attention was focused on the identification of ESAs and the bans imposed therein. Other aspects of the recommendations were completely overlooked. Also, there was criticism from both sides of the spectrum of stakeholders. To begin with, restive voices in civil society immediately claimed that the case for conservation had been compromised, both with regard to the extent of the ESAs and the primacy of

---

7. For a detailed comparative analysis of the two reports, see Chopra (2014).

local-level decision-making. These voices from civil society completely overlooked the recommendation that *gram sabhas* were to be the drivers of development in ESAs.

State governments responded negatively to the restrictions and bans on some activities within ESAs. These, predictably, related to industries and urban development projects. The restrictions were dubbed as 'anti-development'. And this, when all the report was asking for was an alternative paradigm of development for some parts of the Western Ghats. The Centre, through the Ministry of Environment, Forests and Climate Change (MoEFCC) continued its parleys with state governments. A second draft notification was issued in September 2015 for marking out an area of 56,825 sq kms as ESA, down from 60,000 sq kms of the KR Committee and 77,000 kms of the Gadgil Committee. Meanwhile, Kerala had set up its own Committee superceding the Central committees. The matter continues to hang fire.

Quo Vadis: Where are We Going?

Many other instances of policy moving too slowly or in wrong directions exist. Water policy for large urban conglomerations is another glaring example. Media reports talk about drying urban water bodies, both lakes and ponds in Delhi, where 30 per cent of household water demand at one time came from recharged groundwater. With wetlands of the Yamuna also being destroyed by wanton construction, water for Delhi has to be transferred from Himachal Pradesh, where the construction of the Renuka dam is being subsidised for the same purpose. This construction will submerge land, including forest land and impact local livelihoods. Where indeed is ecological planning in this melee?

Where a few steps are taken in the right direction, consequent developments negate all that was done. The Forest Rights Act of 2006 was hailed at that time as the correction of a historical injustice. But today, very few forest communities are aware of it. Mining companies find it a dispensable hurdle and the state has the mining industry as its priority in the race for higher rates of growth.[8]

And so we move on, as one would in "the cowboy economy" envisaged by Boulding. Till local and national catastrophes alert us and then we adopt quick fix solutions and move on nevertheless? Any suggestions for caution or a considered slow down are waylaid or ignored. One wonders how long this will continue.[9]

References

Arrow, K.J., P. Dasgupta, L.H. Goulder, K. Mumford and K. Oleson (2012). "Sustainability and the Measurement of Wealth", *Environment and Development Economics* 17(3): 317-53.

Boulding, Kenneth E. (1966). "The Economics of the Coming Spaceship Earth", in H. Jarrett (ed.), *Environmental Quality in a Growing Economy.* Baltimore, MD: Resources for the Future/Johns Hopkins University Press. pp.3-14.

Chopra, Kanchan (2017). "Development and Environmental Policy in India: The Last Few Decades", *Springer Briefs in Economics.* Springer.

———. (2014). "Conservation and Development in the Western Ghats: A Tale of Two Committees and More", *Economic & Political Weekly* XLIX(11): 12-14, 15 March.

Government of India (2013). *Green Accounting in India: Report of the Expert Group.* Central Statistical Office.

———. (2014). *Final Report of the Expert Group on Low Carbon Strategies for India.* Planning Commission.

Rockstorm, J., Will Steffen, Kevin Noone et al. (2009). "A Safe Operating Space for Humanity", *Nature* 461: 472-75.

Steffen, W., K. Richardson, J. Rockstorm et al. (2015). "Planetary Boundaries: Guiding Human Development on a Changing Planet", *Science* 347. doi.http://dx.doi.org/10.1126/science 1259855

Stern, Nicholas (2006). *Stern Review on the Economics of Climate Change.* Cambridge University Press.

UNU-IHDP/UNEP (2012). *Inclusive Wealth Report 2012: Measuring Progress towards Sustainability.* Cambridge: Cambridge University Press.

World Bank (2011). *World Development Indicators.*

———. (2010). *World Development Indicators.*

8. Samantara, winner of the Goldman Environment Prize, reportedly stated "the state has a history of not honouring legal protection of indigenous people in the Constitution, the mining industry has become the priority of the government, Forest rights are not known to them".
9. For an analysis of environmental policy and the different effects on it in India in the last few decades, see Chopra (2017).

21

Why We Need Context-Specific Economic Theories*

T.C.A. SRINIVASA-RAGHAVAN

Between 1970 and 1972 when I was studying for my Master's degree at the Delhi School of Economics, I often felt two conflicting emotions. One was of persistent elation that I was registered in the crème de la crème of the courses that Delhi University had to offer. The other was of deep depression arising from the growing suspicion that we were being taught nonsense, especially in economic theory.

That was a time when economic theory still held sway and when econometrics had just begun to come into its own. Little did anyone know that by the time the 1970s ended empiricism, supported by the ever increasing robustness of econometrics, would replace theory as the core of modern economics. The demand for better data from governments and other donors on the one hand, and the increasing supply of data on the other, had made this possible. One result is that, as the years have gone by and computing power has grown, economics is no longer a discipline requiring great intellect. A robot with a powerful laptop is usually just as good.

I have often wondered if this is something worth mourning. On balance, yes, it is. But we must also keep in

* The ideas in this paper first appeared in a series of articles I wrote for the *Hindu Business Line* in 2009. They were distilled over the previous 10 years when I wrote a weekly column for the *Business Standard* on economics research. I stopped that column in September 2008.

mind that the theorists had overplayed their hands. The foundations of economic theory were based on patently absurd assumptions. Altogether too often to 'prove' a theory, the theorists would assume the equivalent of, say, water does not boil at 100 degrees centigrade under normal atmospheric pressure.

However, in social sciences, thanks to the intellectual inertia of adherents, the decline of orthodox methods and the resulting wisdom tends to be very gradual. Usually it needs a shock of gigantic proportions to deliver the coup de grace. The Great Depression of the 1930s ended the sway of classical economics which had assumed that markets adjusted instantaneously. The oil shock of the 1970s created a demand for empirical proof backed by reliable data, rather than arcane theories based on advanced mathematics. And in 2008, the global financial crash sent economists to meditation rooms to figure out where even empiricism had gone wrong. A discipline which had been preening like a peacock in the monsoon was now in total disarray.

Meanwhile the triumph of mindless empiricism has seen the advent of a menace called the policy economist. This tribe is to economics what 'non-state actors' are to security. The trouble with empiricists, as opposed to empiricism whose importance can't be denied, is that they can't tell the difference between correlation and causality. I once wrote an article showing how every change of party of government in the United States (US) after 1945 has been accompanied by a recession.

The mere existence of a data set has enabled an entire generation of economists to postulate things that do not fit comfortably into a composite theory. Often, they fall prey to the post hoc, ergo propter hoc (after this, therefore resulting from it) mistake.

The correlation was easy to establish but causation, in either direction, is another kettle of fish altogether. Even after having been advised early not to fall prey to it, they make the classic post hoc fallacy. Governments, in particular, are very prone to making this type of mistake.

Overall, the swings between the two extremes—of economics posturing as physics so that it can use advanced mathematics, and data-based vacuity which has no roots in politics, custom, institutions, law, etc—have led the discipline into a state of meaningless debate and argument amongst economists—*tarka* and *vitarka*—where scoring petty points is mistaken for scholarship and where debate becomes an end in itself.

Oscar Wilde, who said that an economist is a person who knows the price of everything but the value of none, was wrong. Today, it is the other way round.

***

The story of how demand for post-war economics was created is fascinating, not least because its roots lie in the struggle for ideological supremacy during the Cold War. The key intellectual challenge posed by communism to capitalism was that markets always delivered socially inferior outcomes. Implicit in this ideology was an even more devastating belief: that often markets did not exist at all.

For the West, then, it became something of an intellectual obsession to prove the opposite, namely, that not only that markets always exist for everything but also that they always deliver socially superior outcomes. It was not enough for the people to know this instinctively and see it daily in front of their eyes. It had to be proved to the satisfaction of the intellectuals, in an intellectually acceptable manner and garb.

This led to a proliferation of 'theorems', 'lemmas' and the like. Simple common sense was dressed up in mathematical finery. A new prize was created in 1969. Its real name is the Bank of Sweden Prize in Economics but it was projected as the Nobel Prize. No other social science was hyped in this manner.

Through clever research funding, economists were persuaded to ask questions that had no real answers. Growth theory and development economics—both now very passe—were excellent examples of this. Indeed, almost all of economics were like this. To give it all a garb of science, a battery of tools from advanced mathematics was employed as economists chose to believe that economics mimicked physics in many important ways.

But, as in Newton's Third Law, for every explanation there has been an equal and opposite explanation. In fact, there has been more than one. And it is not just the simultaneous presence of multiple and equally valid explanations that was a problem. It was also the refusal by economists to acknowledge that, beyond a point, this was a pointless pursuit because it was never going to yield any definitive answers.

Take for instance, quite randomly, the famous Turnpike Theorem which led to a huge number of reputations being established. Turnpike is old English for a highway which connects two places by the shortest distance. Using this analogy, economists asked if you want to accelerate your country's long-run growth, think of your economy as being on a side road. You now have to decide whether to get on to the highway or not. This wasn't a terribly hard problem to solve but it acquired huge intellectual momentum in the 1960s.

Politically, the new growth theory involved giving distribution and distributive justice a much lower priority than growth. But India discovered in 1967—when the all-powerful Congress party was given a beating on the elections—that this was not very clever if you were a democracy. The reaction to the electoral disasters that followed came in the 1970s when India decided to over-compensate in terms of distribution. In contrast China, without a democracy, has done well out of the Turnpike Theorem. Amazingly, it had been tried by the USSR first and then Mao Zedong as well, but had failed to work for them. But it worked for Deng Xiaoping because the US, in order to bring down the USSR, decided to cooperate with China and not refuse to buy things from it.

The Turnpike theory thus had very little to do with China's success. Suffice it to say that growth theory has been an awful waste of time and effort because it has suffered from the key deficiency of economics: it has not been able to establish causality beyond reasonable doubt.

***

As mentioned earlier, assumptions are central to any discipline of structured thought. Thus psychologists assume that everyone is a little crazy; historians automatically assume that the historical material they use is true merely because it is old; social anthropologies assume that what is true of a part is also true of the whole. And so on.

Economics differs from these disciplines in one very important respect. It makes more assumptions than any other discipline. One of these is (or used to be) that people and societies act rationally, where rationality consists mostly of consistency. But after more than a century of using this assumption as the bedrock of their theories, economists have now begun to abandon it in order to justify the discipline's inability to come up with explanations that stand the test of time.

They are not saying that people don't behave rationally but only that there can be no standard yardstick by which to judge an action as rational. Thus, even though suicide bombing is regarded as completely irrational behaviour, to the bomber himself it appears to be the most rational thing to do if the reward is 72 virgins in heaven. The result is a complete overturning of the rationality assumption. What is left of the old economic theory then?

The abandonment of rational behaviour, without acknowledging that rationality has to be judged in a given context, was honoured with a Nobel in 2002. Daniel Kahneman who is now regarded as the father of behavioural economics, was awarded the prize. But his explanations were rooted in psychology, not context.

Kahneman and his colleague Amos Tversky basically said that you could not wholly disregard intuition. They "explored the psychology of intuitive beliefs and choices and examined their bounded rationality." They conducted experiments using individuals and groups to validate their theories.

Bounded rationality? What in heaven is that? No one really knows who invented the term but it is most widely attributed to another Nobel Prize winner, Herbert Simon. People, he said, don't have the brains to handle complex situations, so they often act in ways that are not consistent with total rationality. In other words, people are rational only some of the time.

But the question that needs asking but which no one is asking is: by diluting the rationality requirement, has the subject gained or lost? Having thought about it a lot during the last two decades, I would say that one way or another, it has not made any difference.

Therein lies the real tragedy of modern economics. Nothing, or very little, that went before has made a difference.

***

In any decent university, one of the first warnings given to students of economics pertains to the problem of causality. If, say, the demand curve for something shifts upwards, how do you know which of the following caused it: an upward shift in per capita incomes, a change in tastes and preferences, or simply a generational change?

Economists, with their certitudes, often carry on as if they know for sure. The truth, however, is that there is simply no way of telling. The volume of intellectual effort that has gone into the problem of analysing causality in economics is staggering. But the discipline is no further along the road to establishing rules for causality now than it was five decades ago.

In spite of having been warned early, economists also often fall prey to the oldest fallacy that haunts causation, not just in economics but in all subjects: erroneously assuming that if X happens after Y had happened, X happened because Y happened.

A British nutritionist once referred me to the famous British medical statistician who laid down seven conditions that had to be fulfilled before association in medicine could be viewed as being causal. These were strength, consistency, biological gradient (the more the causal factor, the more the disease), temporal pattern, specificity, biological plausibility, and the coherence of the evidence.

Now how many of the causalities in economics would fulfil such rigorous criteria? Not one, I would venture to suggest. This is because many of the so-called causal factors in economics are related in both directions: A causes B but B also causes A. In medicine this is the equivalent of saying smoking causes cancer but cancer also causes smoking!

Superstition, it is easy to see from this, is purely a result of the post hoc, ergo propter hoc fallacy. Economic theory was more-or-less the same.

***

If you keep changing the essential foundations of a discipline, and, most of all, if you can't define its limits, sooner or later you will lose credibility. Nowhere is this truer than in macroeconomics, which is a closed system with about half a dozen or so variables, such as the GDP growth rate, the fiscal deficit, interest rates, the exchange rate, the current account, capital account, and so on. Economics assumes these variables to be in very tight relationships with each other and arrives at conclusions that go wrong because, in fact, these relationships are very loose.

Also, at the intellectual level, macroeconomics consists of a series of conditional—if this, then that—statements. Thus, if governments borrow more, interest rates will go up. But by how much, no one can tell. If interest rates go up, bond prices will go down. But by how much, no one knows. And so on. The result is that anyone can, and does, become a macroeconomist and everyone can claim to be right all the time without actually being so.

There is another problem which professional economists will not even begin to admit. In a way it is the central problem of macroeconomics. This is that it rests on very weak logical foundations because it uses what logicians call induction—its chief means of drawing an inference.

But induction as a valid method of logical inference was discredited when macroeconomics was growing up, that is, in the 1940s.

It was Karl Popper who first asked the question that Nissim Taleb of the *Black Swan* fame asked half a century later: does the fact that all the swans you have seen are white mean that all swans are white? That is, could it not be that there is at least one swan that you have not seen, and that it is not white? When you apply this to economics, its problem becomes clear: does the fact that all fiscal deficits that, say, International Monetary Fund (IMF) economists have seen were associated with major crises mean that all fiscal deficits always lead to crises?

The realisation that swans are not always white is what has led the US to adopt diametrically opposite policies for itself in the current financial crisis to what its handmaiden, the IMF, had proposed for East Asia in 1997. This shows how macroeconomics and its policy prescriptions make a giant leap from a few observed particulars to a universally valid generalisation.

But using inductive logic is not the only flaw in macroeconomics. Even the logical structure of theoretical macroeconomics is deeply flawed because it is tautological in that it makes a series of self-evident statements such as "let us bifurcate this into two" or "income-tax is a tax on income". The best example of a tautology is the famous Keynesian identity, which he developed to explain how the economy worked, mainly to the UK's Conservative politicians. It was a deliberate gross over-simplification to explain a very complex phenomenon.

But from it have followed a set of standard prescriptions that are appropriate only 25 per cent of the time. Can you imagine such a high failure rate in real science? Yet, economics calls itself a science.

***

It is most alarming that under the current framework of macroeconomics, its existing tools have become ineffective for a large variety of reasons, not the least of which are technological change, the removal of an upper bound on how much currency the US can print, and the slow disappearance of the 20th century employment model wherein income was smoothened for the working life of a worker. Theoreticians need to address this issue, especially in regard to the role of G in the identity. The old prime the pump approach is now only a way of increasing inflation and/or debt, as the Chinese economy has so ably demonstrated.

For the last few years, I have been arguing that Keynesian solutions in a democracy are a recipe for disaster in a globalised economy, especially when both labour and capital are in excess supply. A month after Lehman's crash in September 2008, I had written all this in an article for the *Hindu Business Line* in which I had pointed out that Keynes had "essentially provided an intellectual basis and, therefore, political respectability, to support a policy of government spending designed to prop up sagging economies. This was a new idea. Until then, markets were supposed to equilibrate the economy while the government looked on hopefully or helplessly depending on the context".

But massive unemployment increased the Communist threat and the governments of the Western hemisphere needed to be more pro-active to prevent Communist ideas from taking deeper root. Keynes, with his immortal identity, provided the economic rationale for convincing the politicians. Basically, said Keynes, the controlling variable for the level of economic activity in a country would be the level of government expenditure. Keynes thus quietly smuggled politics into economics. He said the only way to keep the economy on even keel was for the government to 'prime the pump' when aggregate demand fell below the level needed to keep employment at some notional equilibrium level.

His theory was accepted by a frightened British political class. After all, Hitler, with his massive re-armament programme of Germany, had already proved that the idea worked. Roosevelt had done the same thing in the US. So by the time the Second World War ended in 1945, Keynesian theory had become the received wisdom. Governments had moved centre stage which meant politicians now wrote the script.

My argument in 2014 was that the role of G in the Keynesian identity had undergone the most fundamental change imaginable. Instead of governments intervening to stabilise the real sector—Keynes' famous let them dig holes and fill them dictum—they had intervened to stabilise the financial sector. Government spending, from once being something that sought to boost investment and activate the employment multiplier, had become the grease in the wheels of finance. It is my submission that Keynesian theory needs an upgrade. But none seems to be forthcoming because now Keynes has ceased to be the property of economics and has become an indispensable instrument of politics.

***

So where do we go from here? I think we need to discard the Western mode of economic thought which is based, at its core, on legitimising the third deadly sin of Christianity, greed. The fancy name for it is maximising utility—at the level of the individual—and maximising profit, at the firm level. The system seeks to incorporate greed into an intellectual system and, when things get out of hand, to regulate it.

Even then, in the first instance, the regulation is left to the markets and when those fail, to state intervention. The premise that it is perfectly all right for greed to drive economic activity has never been questioned. Its natural consequence has been environmental depredation, climate change and the now fashionable calls for 'sustainable' development.

If this is accepted, it becomes necessary to move away from one size-fits-all economic theory. The 20th century saw two modes of economic thought being universalised: Marshallian analysis at the microeconomic level and Keynesian solutions at the macroeconomic level. Every country needs to develop adaptations of these which are best suited to its context. That is, a 'socialism with Chinese characteristics' sort of approach is needed.

In their own ways, both Marx and Gandhi had pointed this out but both lost out because neither was able to go beyond appeals to human nature. A more robust intellectual framework is needed. This is not going to happen overnight but some Indian economists need to start thinking about these issues.

III
Sectoral Issues

22

Biodiversity, Biotechnology, Food and Nutrition Security

M.S. SWAMINATHAN

It was in 1990 that the unique couple Raj and Uma Kapila established the Academic Foundation. Since then it has become the flagship of quality, excellence and relevance of printed books and other publications. Through hard and determined work, Raj Kapila ably assisted by his wife Umaji, has made the Academic Foundation the leading publishing house of India. I have had the personal privilege of getting several of my books printed and distributed by the Academic Foundation.

Academic Foundation has become a highly valued source of credible information. I am therefore happy that a special publication is being brought out to pay tribute to the life and work of Raj Kapila. I also wish to pay a tribute to Dr Uma Kapila and her two sons Rituraj Kapila and Sanu Kapila. In this paper dedicated to the memory of Raj Kapila, I wish to deal with a few issues in the areas of biodiversity, biotechnology and food and nutrition security.

Biodiversity and Food and Nutrition Security

In all areas of human endeavour, the past, present and future constitute a continuum. The history of agriculture and biodiversity conservation teaches us many lessons. First of all, about 10,000 years ago, when men went out hunting for food, women started gathering seeds and cultivating crops. This was the origin of agriculture or early settled civilisations. The evolution of agriculture was based on selections from naturally occurring genetic variability. Thus, there is a strong relationship between cultural, culinary and curative diversity and biodiversity.

It has been an act of foresight on the part of the Food and Agriculture Organization (FAO) to initiate a programme for recognising Globally Important Agricultural Heritage Systems (GIAHS) by FAO member countries and rewarding smallholders, family farmers and indigenous communities who have created and maintained such outstanding systems for present and future generations. Small-scale farmers, family farmers and indigenous communities produce the bulk of global food and are the largest number of stewards of the environment and its services especially biodiversity. Many small-scale farms and traditional agricultural systems that still form the majority of landscapes of developing countries can be part of the solution. The diversity of these systems, and the creativity and knowledge of family farmers and indigenous communities are assets of great value for solving the daunting problems affecting agriculture in the 21st century. Higher and sustainable productivity increase at their level will have a major impact on poverty reduction, economic growth and climate change mitigation and adaptation. With the right policies, investments and political will to reach into poor communities, we can meet the formidable challenges of our century.

A GIAHS Partnership Initiative was formally launched at the UN Conference on Sustainable Development held in Johannesburg in 2002. I attended the launching ceremony and pointed out the importance of these systems for agro-biodiversity conservation and sustainable use in an era of climate change, which I have also done in an editorial in *Science* journal (31 July 2009) in the following words:

> The bicentenary of Charles Darwin's life and work reminds us that the great biodiversity on earth underlies natural selection, selective breeding, and the biotechnology required to provide humanity with food, fibre, fodder and fuels. In particular, biodiversity affords the development of plant

> varieties with novel genetic combinations, which will be required to meet the challenges arising from adverse alterations in temperature, precipitation, sea level, and the frequency of drought and floods—all of which are anticipated from human-induced climate change. The loss of each gene and species therefore limits our options for the future.

Thus, GIAHS represent not only a celebration of the achievements of our ancestors, but also a guide to achieving sustainable food and nutrition security amidst climate change. GIAHS raises awareness among the young generations of the glory of past agricultural innovations and stimulates them to make their own contributions to our agricultural legacy. Above all, it recognises the role of the women in the origin and development of crop diversification and animal husbandry, fisheries and forestry.

Some years ago, I published the book entitled: *Towards an Era of Bio Happiness* (Swaminathan 2011). This particular book shows how we can convert—and by we I mean local communities mostly made up of women and men living in remote areas—bioresources into job opportunities and income growth on a foundation of environmental sustainability and social equity. The biodiversity-rich areas in our world also tend to be characterised by poverty and hunger. This is ironic because although the communities in these areas are the ones primarily conserving nature for the public good, most of them remain poor in today's globalised market.

How can we disengage or separate poverty among the world's primary conservationists from the prosperity of nature? How can we additionally help them prosper by using nature's resources in an equitable and sustainable manner? The answer begins with recognising and safeguarding the world's most tried and tested agricultural heritage systems. They show us the way forward—how from the distant past up until today, many local communities have conserved natural resources and managed them sustainably. Whether we look to the people of Koraput in India, the Island of Chiloé in Chile, the Andean corridors, the great rice terraces of the Philippines and China or countless other splendid examples of agriculture heritage throughout the world for inspiration, we can find veritable models of sustainable agriculture.

Achieving the Zero Hunger Challenge

Ban Ki-moon, Secretary General of the United Nations (UN), launched the Zero Hunger Challenge at the Rio+20 Conference on Sustainable Development held in Brazil in June 2012. At a high level consultation held in Madrid in April 2013, it was agreed that the global community should commit to a common vision that hunger, food insecurity and malnutrition should be ended by 2025. At these meetings, governments were requested to pay concurrent attention to the following five pillars of the Zero Hunger Challenge:

- 100 per cent access to adequate food all year round;
- zero stunted children less than two years of age;
- all food systems made sustainable;
- 100 per cent increase in smallholder productivity and income; and
- zero loss or waste of food.

Each one of these pillars is relevant to the rice-growing regions of Asia. Taking food losses and food waste alone, it has been estimated that one-third of food production is lost or wasted globally, i.e., about 1.3 billion tonnes per year. In India, 100 per cent access to adequate food all year round can be achieved if the legal entitlements under the National Food Security Act reach those needing social protection against hunger. In spite of all the technological progress made, FAO estimates that 531 million people still suffer from chronic hunger in the Asia-Pacific region. This implies that about two-thirds of those who are hungry live in India. In addition, 100 million children under the age of 5 (or 28% of the world total) were stunted in 2010 in the Asia-Pacific region. It is in this context that the role of rice farming systems in achieving the zero hunger goals has to be considered.

The world will require 50 per cent more rice in 2030 than in 2015 with approximately 30 per cent less arable land than now. It has been estimated that an additional 100 million tonnes will be required by 2035 in the Asia-Pacific region. The total production of rice in 2013 was 718 million tonnes. How can these challenges be met in countries where rice is the main staple?

First, in all irrigated areas the major emphasis should be on increasing yield per units of land and water. Hybrid rice can help increase yield by about 20 per cent. If ongoing research to convert rice into a new photosynthetic pathway is successful, the yield potential can be further increased by about 20 per cent. Fertiliser is the most effective, and at the same time most expensive, of the market-purchased inputs used by farmers. However, in spite of the high cost of urea and other fertilisers, efficiency of use is poor. It is now clear that efficiency can be increased by about 50 per cent through the use of new techniques like deep placement using prilled urea. Suitable implements are available for this purpose, and Bangladesh has been able to improve very significantly the efficiency of fertiliser use with the help of the International Fertilizer Development Centre.

The yield of the rice crop is also affected by several pests and diseases. IPM (integrated pest management) could help control pests in an environmentally sustainable manner. Since the average farm size is usually one hectare and below, there are logistic problems in adopting ecofriendly pest management methods. Such methods require an area approach with all farm families in a village cooperating in pest management. Scientific water management as well as the control of the triple alliance of weeds, pests and pathogens require group cooperation through social engineering. Providing the power of scale to small producers is emerging as a major challenge. If the services sector can be strengthened through the involvement of young educated farmers in taking up the responsibility of pest-proofing entire villages, pests can be eliminated and the cost of plant protection can be considerably brought down as well.

The evergreen revolution pathway of production, which involves improvement of productivity in perpetuity without associated ecological harm, has to be popularised (Swaminathan 2010). In addition to the production phase of rice farming, post-harvest management requires urgent attention. Post-harvest management should not only consider rice grains, but also pay attention to value addition to rice straw, bran and husk. For this purpose, MS Swaminathan Research Foundation (MSSRF) is establishing a Rice BioPark at Nay Pyi Taw in Myanmar on behalf of the Ministry of External Affairs, Government of India. The major aim of the Rice Bio Park is the conversion of the entire rice biomass into value-added products, thereby increasing opportunities for non-farm employment and income.

Rice farming systems should include a grain or fodder legume in the rotation so that soil fertility can be enhanced through biological nitrogen fixation. Unfortunately, scientific crop rotations are being threatened. For example, in Punjab there has been controversy about the ecological consequences of the rice-wheat rotation. Such rotation is now providing considerable income to small farmers since they take to the cultivation of high-yielding basmati varieties of rice such as Pusa Basmati 1121 and Pusa Basmati 1509. It is estimated that these varieties have helped the country earn over USD 5 billion in foreign exchange and have added nearly ₹28,000 crore to the income of farmers. Therefore, the suggestion by some experts that the Punjab/Haryana region should give up rice cultivation is not a wise one. What India needs is 'do ecology' to show how to do things right rather than 'don't ecology'. Through water harvesting during the *kharif* season and the introduction of legumes in the rotation, it will be possible to promote an evergreen revolution in both rice and wheat in the Punjab/Haryana region, which is the heartland of the Green Revolution.

In addition to facing the problems of today, we should prepare ourselves for meeting the emerging challenges arising from climate change. More frequent drought and floods as well as a rise in sea level will be some of the consequences of global warming. By adopting the fertiliser management techniques described earlier, the role of rice in adding to greenhouse gases in the atmosphere can be minimised. Fortunately, genes are available today for developing rice varieties, which can withstand flood as well as drought.

Another problem, which needs attention is the malnutrition associated with the lack of diversity in food in rice-growing and consuming areas. Through bio-fortification, rice varieties rich in iron and zinc have been developed by breeders. Bangladesh has already released for cultivation a high-zinc rice variety. In India also, rice varieties rich in vitamin A and iron have been developed. Thus, agricultural remedies can be introduced for nutritional maladies.

National Policy for Farmers: Ten Years Later

Both during colonial times and after independence, no commission has been set up to look at the problems of farm families with special emphasis on the human dimension of this ancient profession. The most important commission set up in the days of the British headed by Lord Linlithgow was the Royal Commission on Agriculture. An important statement made by this Commission is:

> However efficient the organisation which is built up for demonstration and propaganda be, unless that organisation is based on the solid foundation provided by research, it will be merely a house built on sand.

This assessment of the need for scientific backstopping of extension advice lead to the birth of the Indian Council of Agriculture Research in 1928, which was given concurrent responsibilities in the field of research, extension and education. In spite of the steps taken from time to time to make farming profitable and save farmers from undue economic distress, the agrarian crisis continues and India has become known for the widespread occurrence of farmer's suicides. The size of landholding is also getting smaller and water resources are becoming scarce. It is under these conditions, the then Minister for Agriculture Rajnath Singh and the then Prime Minister Atul Bihari Vajpayee decided to set up a National Commission on Farmers (NCF) under the chairmanship of Sompal on 10 February 2004. This is the first time a Commission for farmers has been set up since the mandate for all the earlier commissions was to look at the problems of agriculture and not specifically of farmers. After the change in government, I was appointed as Chairman of the NCF on 18 November 2004. The other Members of the Commission were Dr R.B. Singh, Y.C. Nanda, Atul Sinha, Atul Kumar Anjan, Jagadish Pradhan, R.L. Pitale and Chanda Nimbakar. The Committee work hard and submitted its report on 4 October 2006 within the prescribed time limit. To facilitate speedy government action, the report was submitted in parts making a total of five reports. In addition NCF prepared a Draft National Policy for Farmers based on the recommendations contained in the five reports. The National Policy for Farmers form the basis of the discussion with state governments and the final policy was placed in Parliament in October 2007.

It is 10 years now since NCF presented its reports as a Draft National Policy for Farmers. Today, the main issue seems to be one of total lack of implementation. Meanwhile several new issues have emerged which also need careful consideration in relation to farmers' economic and ecological survival. Some of these are:

1. Local climatic variability has been rising, but cropping choices and patterns are not adapting at the same pace, leading to greater seasonal vulnerability, nutrition levels and enhanced migration due to distress.
2. Market mechanisms have penetrated even deeper into the rural areas, signalling types of crops to be

grown, with the purpose of economic gain, even if not appropriate for soil and water conditions (e.g. sugarcane in Maharashtra).

3. While research exists, mechanisms for sharing public sector research knowledge have virtually collapsed.

The crisis in Indian agriculture is due to many reasons some of which are the following:

- Growth rate of agriculture sector declined from 3.69 per cent per annum during 1990-1996 to 1.65 per cent per annum during 1996 to 2005.
- Net sown area, gross cropped area, gross irrigated area, fertiliser use, electricity consumption—all have declined.
- Growth rate of terms of trade for agriculture declined from 0.95 per cent per annum during 1990-1996 to (-) 1.63 per cent per annum 1996-2005.
- The plight of farmers will be evident from the fact that the Punjab farmers with an average farm size of 3.79 ha, growing wheat and rice are able to earn an income which is less than the starting salary of a class IV employee in Government.

The main emphasis of the draft policy presented by us was therefore the following:

> Do not measure agricultural progress merely in statistical terms, but mainstream the human dimension in all agricultural programmes and strategies and use increase in farmers' real income as the measure of progress.

Among the goals of the National Policy for Farmers recommended by NCF, the following are important:

1. To improve the economic viability of farming by substantially increasing the net income of farmers and to ensure that agricultural progress is measured by advances made in their income.

2. To provide opportunities in adequate measure for non-farm employment for the farm households.
3. To introduce measures which can help to attract and retain youth in farming.

Also, NCF had recommended the renaming of the Ministry of Agriculture as Ministry of Agriculture and Farmers Welfare in order to emphasise that an important responsibility of the ministry is to ensure the economic and social well-being of farm families. This has since been done. We also laid much emphasis on the gender dimensions of farming. In fact the very first volume starts with a chapter on Women and Agriculture. I later followed it up with introducing in Rajya Sabha a Private Member's Bill on the Women Farmers' Empowerment. Unfortunately, no action has been taken so far on the gender specific recommendations. An urgent need is access to credit and to the Kisan Credit Cards issued by National Bank for Agriculture and Rural Development (NABARD). Unfortunately, credit availability to women farmers depends very much on title to land.

As I mentioned earlier, this is the first commission which was entrusted with the responsibility of attending to the needs of farmers as citizens and fellow human beings. Therefore, we wanted to make our report the voice of farming families. Considering the fact that there is widespread demand from farmers for the implementation of the NCF recommendations, I can say that we have been somewhat successful in voicing the voiceless.

The NCF reports and the draft policy for farmers placed considerable emphasis on enhancing the income of farmers and ensuring income security. The 2016-17 Union Budget has indicated that government will try to help farmers double their income in five years.

Doubling the Income of Farmers in Five Years

Giving an income orientation to farming is probably the most significant announcement made by the Finance Minister. He has said that the aim of government will be to double the income of farmers in five years. The Economic Survey however points out that the contribution of agriculture and allied sectors has been declining. It is in this context that the emphasis on income becomes urgent. For achieving income enhancement, we need in my view, at least five major steps. These are, first, higher productivity of small farms leading to larger marketable surplus; second, knowledge, skill, credit and land ownership empowerment of women farmers, who carry out over 60 per cent of farm work; third, substitution of low value crops with high value ones like fruits, vegetables and flowers as well as animal products; four, promotion of biomass utilisation so that every part of the plant is utilised for preparing value added products through initiatives like Rice BioPark and finally, the procurement price should be based on the NCF proposal namely, C2 (total cost of production) plus 50 per cent. An important need is concurrent attention to on-farm and non-farm employment.

The total outlay of agriculture and farmers' welfare is ₹35,985 crore. The schemes already announced like those relating to irrigation, including groundwater utilisation, efficient fertiliser use, improved soil healthcare, better post-harvest technology and a more comprehensive agricultural insurance policy are being backed up by enhancing financial provision. A long-term irrigation fund will be created in NABARD. Emphasis has been placed on greater investment in the food processing industry. Also, 100 per cent FDI (foreign direct investment) will be allowed for marketing food products made in India. The year 2016 is the International Year of pulses and we will be importing nearly 10 million tonnes of pulses to bridge the gap between demand and supply. It is therefore appropriate that the Finance Minister has provided ₹500 crore for a special pulses mission. The Mahatma Gandhi National Rural Employment Guarantee Act (MGNREGA) will also be reoriented to meet the needs of agriculture like soil conservation, watershed management and groundwater harvesting. In a significant move, 0.5 per cent Krishi Kalyan Cess on all taxable services will be utilised for farmers' welfare, for increasing their social protection and for providing them with minimum needs for a better quality of life. This is appropriate since the Finance Minister even at the very outset emphasised that agriculture and farmers' welfare will be the first among the 9 pillars of the Budget. The budget places emphasis on organic farming. Paramparagat Krishi Vikas Yojana for bringing 5 lakh acres under organic farming, as well as the proposal for organic value chain development in the north-east region are welcome measures in this decade of sustainable development. The introduction of technology and e-platforms for regulating agricultural markets are forward looking steps. Taking into account the high risk nature of farming, the credit allocation for this sector has been increased to ₹9 lakh crore.

In order for the MSP (minimum support price) benefit to reach farmers, it is proposed to decentralise procurement, promote online procurement through Food Corporation of India (FCI) and effective arrangements for the procurement of pulses at an attractive MSP. Also, four new dairy programmes namely, animal health card, advanced breeding technology, e-market portal and the establishment of a National Centre for Indigenous Breeds with an allocation of ₹850 crore are timely, since we have nearly a billion farm animals.

An allocation of ₹80 lakh per *Gram Panchayat* will now be available to villages for filling infrastructure gaps. As recommended by the NCF at least ₹20 lakh out of this amount should be reserved for meeting the gender specific needs of women. Facilities will be created for an additional storage of ₹97 lakh metric tonnes of foodgrains. Rural infrastructure will be improved by the allocation of ₹19,000 crore for the Pradhan Mantri Gram Sadak Yojana. The adverse impact of natural calamities will be minimised through increased agricultural credit and improved insurance. A sum of ₹5,500 crore has been provided for an enlarged crop insurance scheme. On the whole, the budget has tried to be as pro-farmer as possible subject to the limitation of resources. Seeds have been sown for agricultural transformation and for attracting and retaining youth in farming. Another area relevant to income announcement is the technological upgrading of small scale farming. Fortunately, many new technologies have become available and many of them originate from the private sector to ensure that the new IPR (intellectual property rights) policy does not lead to a denial of improve technologies to small scale farming.

New IPR Policy

Union Minister Nirmala Sitharaman has rightly mentioned that the new IPR Policy will provide stimulus to R&D innovations. This is the rationale behind IPR policies since a reward and recognition system for innovations helps to attract more financial investment and professional engagement. One question which is always to be kept in view, is the impact of an efficient IPR system from making scientific discoveries more exclusive in terms of access. For example, vaccines covered by patents may not be easily available to those who need them, unless government takes special steps. Therefore, while safeguarding the interest of the innovators and discoverers, we should ensure that patent rights do not come in the way of the economically and socially underprivileged sections of the society benefitting from the discovery. An interesting model was developed in Switzerland to promote concurrently innovation and social access. This was related to the golden rice characterised by high vitamin A content. To ensure that the original scientists who developed golden rice are not deprived of reward for their scientific genius, the Government of Switzerland along with a few private foundations like Syngenta, initiated a Humanitarian Trust. This Trust was intended to buy the relevant patent and make it available to those suffering from vitamin A deficiency at very low cost or even free. In a country like ours with gross social and economic inequity, we should ensure that those who benefit from a discovery are enabled to do so, through initiatives like the Humanitarian Trust. MSSRF which holds patents for genes for salinity tolerance and drought resistance adopts a pre-breeding cum participatory breeding policy, i.e. the genes for abiotic resistance developed through molecular genetics are available to farmers for breeding location specific strains. This falls under defensive patenting.

Insulating Farmers from Financial Collapse Through Effective Crop Insurance

The Prime Minister has announced a new crop insurance scheme which attempts simultaneously to keep the insurance cost affordable and farmers insulated from financial distress as a result of crop losses due to reasons beyond their control. The NCF also emphasised the critical need for a small farmer friendly insurance policy. In addition to the welcome steps already taken by the government to address the real needs of small farmers, the following four measures need consideration. First, there should be a system of group insurance according to both location and farming system, so that the transaction cost can be brought down. Secondly, seed companies which sell hybrid seeds at high costs should provide at their cost an insurance policy to small farmers. For example, this year, Bt Cotton became a victim to white fly thereby, causing heavy losses. Third, we should perfect remote sensing technologies which can provide speedily reliable information on crop losses due to unfavourable meteorological conditions. This would assist in greatly reducing the time taken to settle claims. Finally, women farmers who constitute nearly 50 per cent of farm families do not become eligible to credit since they lack title to land and are thereby deprived of insurance facilities. This situation should be corrected and Mahila Kisans should be eligible both for credit and insurance.

Safeguarding Farmer's Welfare

Our Prime Minister announced in his Independence Day Speech on 15 August 2015 that hereafter the Ministry of Agriculture will assume the additional responsibility of safeguarding the welfare of our farm families. Ultimately success in agriculture depends on our ability to help farm men and women to help the country. In spite of difficulties arising from unfavourable trends in the monsoon and market behaviour, our farmers are working hard to protect our food security. The steps needed to promote the well-being of farm families who constitute over 60 per cent of the rural population are described in the five reports of NCF and in the Draft National Policy for Farmers. At the national level, the share of agriculture to GDP has come down to 13 per cent. However, the onus of providing employment rests with the farm sector which caters to the livelihood security of nearly 75 per cent of population in rural India. The NCF has made detailed recommendation on how to serve farmers and thereby save farming. Even in Punjab, nearly 80 per cent of farmers do not want their sons to be agriculturists. The immediate implementation of NCF recommendations in their totality will help. Meanwhile, to minimise the incidence of farmers' suicides, there is need for establishing of Agrarian Distress Counselling Centres wherever feasible in Krishi Vigyan Kendras. I hope that the responsibility of safeguarding farmer's welfare given to the Union Ministry of Agriculture will help to improve the livelihood security of rural families and thereby save their lives and livelihoods.

Online Trading Platform for Farm Goods

The launch of a National Agriculture Market portal (e-NAM) by the Government of India is a welcome and timely step. It will help to increase the bargaining power of farmers provided they are trained in the effective use of this technology. Assured and remunerative marketing is the best way of stimulating and sustaining high productivity. In addition to this initiative, there is an urgent need for implementing the recommendations of the NCF in the chapter dealing with the establishment of an Indian single market. This will help to avoid constraints in the movement of grains and also will help to establish an Indian Trade Organisation (ITO) which will function at the National Level in the same way at World Trade Organisation (WTO) at the global level. The agriculture market reform has begun and it should now be taken to its logical end namely a strong farmer centric single market covering the country as a whole.

Attention to Women Farmers: A Private Members' Bill

As mentioned earlier, there is an urgent need to recogonise, emphasise and protect the gender specific needs and rights of women farmers. The Women Farmers' Entitlements Bill, 2011 (introduced in Rajya Sabha on 11 May 2012) aims to:

> Provide for the gender specific needs of women farmers, to protect their legitimate needs and entitlements and to empower them, with a view to carrying out the aforesaid purposes, of establishing mechanisms, authorities, powers and functions relating thereto and for matters connected therewith.

'Woman farmer' means and includes, irrespective of marital status or ownership of land, any woman who is a farmer which includes:

- engaged in agriculture directly or through the supervision of others; or
- contributes to conservation or preservation of agriculture related varieties or seeds; or contributes through traditional knowledge to any type of innovation, conservation or to propagation of new agricultural varieties or to agricultural cultivation methods or practices; or
- any woman living in rural area and primarily engaged in agricultural activity, though occasionally engaged in non-agricultural activity; or
- any woman living in urban or semi-urban areas and engaged in agriculture; or any tribal women directly or indirectly engaged in agriculture or shifting cultivation or in the collection, use and sale of minor or non-timber forest produce by virtue of usufructory rights.

Context of the Bill

- Increasing feminisation of agriculture: Women constitute
  - more than 50 per cent of Indian farmers.
  - 60 per cent of the workforce in farming sector.
- India being party to the Convention on the Elimination of All Forms of Discrimination against Women (CEDAW) 1979
  - which calls for elimination of discrimination against women by ensuring equal access to agricultural services and technologies.
- Fourth World Conference on Women in September, 1995, in which India participated, called for legislative and administrative reforms to give women equal rights with men to economic resources.
- The Government of India has recognised the special needs of women farmers by initiating a "Mahila Kisan Sashaktikaran Pariyojana" programme under the National Rural Livelihoods Mission.
- It is considered necessary to implement the decisions aforesaid under Article 253 of the Constitution of India in so far as they relate to the women farmers' entitlements.

Provisions under the Bill

- *Land Rights*: Every woman shall have equal ownership and inheritance rights over agricultural land in her husband's family.
- *Water Rights*: A woman farmer shall have equal right, as enjoyed by male farmers, to all water rights connected with the agricultural land to which she is the owner, shareholder, possessor or uses for farming activity and shall have access to water, water resources and irrigation facilities for carrying out agricultural activities as defined in this Act.

- Legal access to credit, insurance, technology and other agricultural inputs.
- Fund for support services to women farmers.

From Agrarian Crisis to Agrarian Prosperity

As mentioned earlier, the Government of India has re-designated the Ministry of Agriculture as the Ministry of Agriculture and Farmers' Welfare, as suggested by NCF. Such a change in name should also be accompanied by a change in the outlook towards farm families. For example, farming is a life giving profession, the fact that farmers take their own lives is indicative of the serious problems confronting farming and farmers. During the period NCF was developing its report, agrarian distress and farmers' suicides became serious issues. It is sad that those who practice a life giving profession like agriculture should be forced to take their own lives. NCF therefore gave very serious consideration to methods of overcoming agrarian crisis and making the problem of farmer suicides a problem of the past. One of the major step needed to overcome the problem is to strengthen the Ecological foundations for sustainable agriculture. These are soil, water, biodiversity and climate. It may be worthwhile recalling in this context, what the Chinese philosopher Confucius said long ago:

> Despite the many accomplishments of mankind, we owe our existence to a six-inch layer of topsoil and the fact that it rains.

The transition from the green to the evergreen revolution requires the mainstreaming of ecological principles in technology development and dissemination. Among the major recommendations of NCF in this area are:

1. Issue of SHC (soil health card) to every farmer giving information on the management of the physics, chemistry, microbiology and hydrolic conductivity of the soil. The SHC will be the important tool for farmers to benefit from government support in the form of nutrient based subsidy rather than product based ones.

2. The second area relates to all aspects of water security with concurrent attention to demand management and supply augmentation. Water quality also requires attention. Water harvesting, watershed management and the efficient use of water should all become priority areas in the agrarian distress free agricultural technology. Rain water harvesting should be made mandatory in farms and homes.
3. The third area that requires attention is technology. Ecotechnologies which can help to improve productivity in perpetuity should be developed and introduced.
4. The fourth area relates to credit and insurance. The NCF had recommended that credit should be available at an interest rate of 4 per cent or less. Most of the banks are now providing to farmers who pay back their loan promptly, credit at 4 per cent interest. In fact some banks in Surat, have gone to the extent of providing loans at zero per cent interest.
5. Insurance, as already mentioned, is vital for insulating farmers from risks beyond their control. We should also accompany a risk minimisation fund as the one recommended for plantation crops like natural rubber.

Managing Price Volatility

A couple of months ago I had written about the hardship caused to the growers of natural rubber in Kerala as a result of low price. Currently, rubber farmers are experiencing considerable price improvement. But unfortunately their hopes for higher production will depend upon monsoon behaviour. Extreme heat and drought will reduce the production of latex. In this context, we should take two steps to achieve price stability. First, as suggested by me in a report about 10 years ago, the Governments of Kerala and India, should jointly establish a price stabilisation fund. Secondly, drought tolerant and climate smart clones should be planted, while taking up new plantings. The Rubber Research Institute of India (RRII) at Kottayam has developed drought tolerant strains of natural rubber through genetic modification. Because of their GMO origin, they have not been approved for field trials. We should permit field trials since such clones can be of immense value in an era of climate change. Also, the area under natural rubber can be increased in north-east India with such clones. Natural rubber is one of our greatest assets and through a combination of technology and public policy, we should be able to achieve sustainable production and price stabilisation.

Implementing the Food Security Act

I am happy that the Public Accounts Committee (PAC) of Parliament has decided to prepare a report on the implementation of the Food Security Act. The National Food Security Act is a unique one and make our farmers proud since they were mainly responsible for taking our country from the days of the Bengal Famine to the time we can confer the legal right to food with home grown food. This transition is probably unique in the world history. I would suggest that the following unique features of the Bill should be examined in the context of implementation:

- The Bill provides for a whole life cycle approach in terms of food security. This will require particular attention to the first thousand days of a child's life which are critical for brain development and later cognitive abilities.
- The senior most woman in the household will be designated the head of the household from the point of view of food entitlements.
- Enlargement of the food basket by including nutri-millets and other neglected crops in the PDS (public distribution system).
- The pricing, procurement and PDS should involve millets, including *jowar*, *bajra* and *ragi*. It will also

be appropriate to redesignate the so called coarse grains as nutri-rich climate smart cereals.

I hope PAC will also take into consideration the good features enshrined in the Chhattisgarh Act such as provision of pulses, and biofortified salt, so that protein hunger and micronutrient malnutrition can also be addressed simultaneously. The review by PAC provides a unique opportunity for strengthening the Bill and improving its administration and delivery systems, so that we can achieve the Zero Hunger Target soon.

Food Security and Eradication of Hunger

Food security is a multidimensional problem. We really want to overcome hunger. It is not just a problem of providing the calories, although undernourishment is the cause of malnutrition in many cases. Cereal-based diets help in meeting a part of protein and micronutrient requirements too. In Africa and other places, where diets are tuber-based, like cassava, staple food does not provide as much of proteins and micronutrients.

Hidden hunger is one of the most serious parts of hunger because you require a very small quantity of micronutrients. But if these are absent, they can seriously impair functioning of the human body. Very small quantities of micronutrients make a large impact in the quality of life of an individual. Also, micronutrient deficiencies are much more widespread than deprivation in terms of calories. For example, while nearly 800 million people suffer from undernourishment or calorie deprivation, about 2 billion suffer from iron deficiency. Prevalence of micronutrient deficiencies is particularly high among pregnant women and children. A large number of children go blind because of vitamin A deficiency.

The earlier approach to eradication of hidden hunger was primarily based on chemical fortification. Even today, for example, salt can be fortified with iron, iodine, vitamin A and many other micronutrients. And everybody consumes salt. There are good and inexpensive methods of using salt as a carrier. Similarly, earlier, people thought wheat should be fortified. Chemical fortification was considered to be the approach.

The next approach was the genetic fortification. Starting with genetic fortification of rice—what is called the 'Golden Rice'—with a high content of beta-carotene. Of course, that became controversial because of genetic modification.

But nature provides a wide range of naturally bio-fortified foods. A simple plant like moringa has almost all the micronutrients you need. Sweet potato is very rich in vitamin A. There are varieties of pearl millet, commonly consumed in India, which are very rich in iron. There are varieties of sorghum, which are very rich in zinc. So, our approach should be to take naturally biofortified foods and introduce them in the farming system. Agricultural remedies for nutritional maladies can be easily found. They are the simplest and least expensive. In other words, we must promote nutrition sensitive farming system.

Some of the traditional culinary practices are based on knowledge of nutritional value of different food items and how to bring together plants or animal products that can provide mutually reinforcing nutrients. In Europe, combining egg and chips, or fish and chips, is based on the fact that egg and fish, and potato chips, have complementary amino acid profiles. When you take them together, one amino acid which is missing in one food is provided by the other.

How do we marry nutrition and agriculture together in such a way that many of our choices of crops are based both on the market as well as on the nutritional content of the crop? Department for International Development (DFID) is supporting a large project called Leveraging Agriculture for Nutrition in South Asia (LANSA). The CGIAR calls it HarvestPlus. You harvest something but you have a bonus there in terms of nutrition. The HarvestPlus programme is doing a good job. Earlier they were thinking of mostly genetically modified crops. But, now we know, it is not necessary. There is enough variability in nature in terms of micronutrients. All that you need is to cultivate them and have a good yield.

We are at the threshold of a nutrition revolution based on agriculture. There is much more understanding today of the importance of using agricultural remedies for nutritional maladies.

Consumption, with an Emphasis on Diversification of Diets

Consumption is an area where FAO, in my view, should make more contribution in widening the food basket. With commercialisation of agriculture, particularly with large multinationals engaging in grain trade, you find that the grain trade has become very narrow and is limited to four or five crops like wheat, rice, corn and soybean. FAO has so many diagrams to show that in the past we had a very large number of crops in the food base. We must revive the earlier culinary traditions, which involved a large number of crops. That is why the declaration of 2013 as the Year of Quinoa is very important. People need to know that there is a crop like this. I have been suggesting we should have an International Year of Orphan and Underutilised Crops.

With great difficulty, I got the Indian Food Security Act to include, apart from wheat and rice, the traditional two crops in the PDS, the whole set of millets in the basket of commodities that will be provided. The consumption pattern and the culinary diversity must be enlarged in relation to consumption of grains because many of these crops are also much more climate resilient. They do not require so much water. Unfortunately, if you see the GIAHS, you will find many of them grew crops that are either extinct or which farmers are not growing any more.

Commerce, with Emphasis on Protection of Small Farmers

The challenge in this area is, how do you protect the small farmers and ensure that they get a fair price in the market? Because all said and done, progress towards a right to food can only be possible if farmers—in particular, small farmers—are provided an assured and remunerative procurement price, and a commitment to procure what they produce at that price. In trade, of course, WTO is there. But we have to ensure that there is no conflict between WTO rules and the goal of food security and overcoming hunger. The Zero Hunger Vision should be the bottom-line of WTO policies on foodgrains.

Role of Public and Private Sectors in Agricultural Research

The pros and cons of the role of public and private sectors have to be analysed very carefully. In countries like India, China and Brazil, public good research is still the dominant form of research. For example, over 80 per cent of the investment in agricultural research in India comes from the Government of India. Rest of the 20 per cent is accounted for by various types of private investment including by seed companies and companies producing farm machinery. But predominantly, public good research is still the dominant form of research. It may change in future.

The private sector is unlikely to invest in areas where returns are low. For example, take the public health issue—private companies are not going to produce a vaccine for leprosy because leprosy-affected people are poor and cannot pay for it. So there are areas—in health, agriculture or even industry—where public-sector research is crucial. There are also other differences between public research and for-profit research. For example, historically, farmers are used to keeping their own seeds. But, in promoting new varieties of seeds, a private company may prefer a hybrid seed because farmers will have to buy seeds every year.

I do not approve of IPR for technologies that can help the small farmers produce more. It is important that both options—preserving their own seeds and buying new seeds—are available to farmers. Many farmers will not be able to buy seeds. I have also been arguing that, when companies sell expensive seeds, they should also provide insurance. In areas like Vidarbha in Central India, there is a continuing incidence of a large number of suicides by farmers because they take to high cost technology without the ability to cope with the loss, which often occurs for reasons beyond their control. Every country will have to strike a balance between public good research to ensure availability of appropriate technologies to resource-poor farmers and private research for high-value agriculture and horticulture for resource-rich farmers producing for niche and export markets. We must ensure that in the science policy of a country, there is adequate provision to ensure that technological solutions for problems of the poorer sections of the population are researched and that technology is available free to them, without IPR restrictions.

The bottom line should be the well-being of the poorer sections of the community. Mahatma Gandhi used to talk about *antyodaya*, well-being of the worst-off person: look at whether your actions are going to benefit the poorest person. That is the test we should use for public funding. If it is going to do something good for the poor, you should go ahead and do it. So, I think that has to be the policy in a country with a lot of economic disparities, where there is a lot of human suffering, and a lot of people are living at or below the subsistence level.

Food Self-sufficiency in the Era of Globalisation

Globalisation has its advantages but it should not result in undermining sovereignty in the area of food. A country has to ensure that it has the minimum amount of food that is needed.

Globalisation's benefits are seen, for example, in diffusion of information technology, which has benefited everyone, including the poor. But it is important to protect areas where globalisation would result in job losses. Job-led growth should be the most important priority. Also, people have diverse preferences of what they would like to do. Globalisation should not undermine that diversity.

Price volatility in international markets is very high. With a country of 1.2 billion in India, we can't afford to depend on imported food for managing our food security. Our Food Security Act cannot be managed on the basis of imported food. If big countries like India or China buy large quantities of grain from the international markets, this would drive international prices up.

So, I think, in areas like food or drinking water, which are fundamental requirements of human beings, national governments have the primary responsibility. They should ensure that their sovereignty is protected. Food sovereignty is important because people cannot live without food. And hence, I would say in such cases, a more balanced approach should be adopted.

We had the same problem when we introduced the Protection of Plant Varieties and Farmers' Rights Act in India. The International Union for the Protection of New Varieties of Plants established by the UPOV convention in Geneva along with the World Intellectual Property Organization (WIPO) said that we could not protect farmers' rights. I said, what is the purpose of breeders if there are no farmers? Farmers are the primary conservers and we insisted that their rights must be protected.

I think that the first and foremost duty of any government is to eradicate hunger. Mahatma Gandhi said, "to the millions who have to go without two meals a day... God can only appear as bread... this God of bread must be available to every home and hut in an independent India." It is after a long time, after more than 60 years of independence, we have been able to redeem this pledge. We all need to realise that we are all humans, and it is important that we think of humanity rather than some petty regulations.

References

Swaminathan, M.S. (2009). "Gene Banks for a Warming Planet", *Science* 325: 517.

———. (2010). *From Green to Evergreen Revolution: Indian Agriculture—Performance and Challenges.* New Delhi: Academic Foundation p.410.

———. (2011). *Towards an Era of Biohappiness: Biodiversity and Food, Health and Livelihood Security.* Singapore: World Scientific. 170 pages.

———. (2015). *In conversation with Nitya Rao: From Reflections on my Life to the Ethics and Politics of Science.* New Delhi: Academic Foundation. 227 pages.

Swaminathan, M.S., Prasun Kumar Das and R.V. Bhavani (2014). "A Farming System Model to Leverage Agriculture for Nutritional Outcomes", *Agric Res.* DOI 10.1007/s40003-014-0119-5.

Others:

5 *Reports of the National Commission on Farmers*, Ministry of Agriculture, Government of India, New Delhi.

Serving Farmers and Saving Farming Jai Kisan: Revised Draft National Policy for Farmers, National Commission on Farmers, Ministry of Agriculture, Government of India, New Delhi.

23

Stranded at Jagged Crossroads

Agricultural Sector of India

R.S. DESHPANDE and KHALIL MUSA SHAHA

An Eclectic View

India's agriculture is stranded at a crossroads[1] for many years now and not many effective solutions have come forward. Agricultural sector is trapped at the same place where we began a few decades ago. And the dismal situation is exposed by the agitating farmers throwing their farm produce on the roads, and suicides becoming quite frequent portents of distress besides becoming a tool in the hands of politicians. The situation is turning from bad to evil. Farmers are truly quite unhappy with the ineffective policies dished out by the State. Most of the analysts begin their analyses with the retrogression of Indian agriculture suffered during British rule. This colonial hangover theory continues as an explanation of retrogression in our academic writings, even after seven decades of independence and of 'systematic' economic planning.

Most of the analysts of Indian agriculture proverbially look into three phases of development. The first phase begins immediately after independence and ends at 1964, to mark the two years of turmoil in Indian agriculture due to drought and reflected in the growth of the economy.

1. There are more than half a dozen writers who have used this title at various time points and this includes renowned Indian geneticist Prof M.S. Swaminathan. See, Krishna and Swaminathan 1980, Swaminathan 1982, 2015, Green Peace 2009 and IAASTD Report 2016.

The period after the technological change during mid-1960s is termed as the phase of 'Green Revolution' marked with achieving food security and then straight away analysts jump to the period of liberalisation of the Indian economy. There is one analytical problem in this kind of 'phasing' wherein we miss a large number of nuances of Indian agriculture and changes that have taken place during the intermittent periods. Recognising fully that Indian agriculture must be analysed from the perspective of political economy, it would be essential to look at these phases from the viewpoint of political economy.[2]

Table 23.1

Travelogue of Indian Agriculture

Phase	*Period*	*Economic Pursuits*	*Agriculture*
I	1947-1959	Colonial Hangover	Primacy to Food Policy
II	1960-1965	Groping for a Developmental Model	Mixed Economy Tangles
III	1965-1968	Negotiating External & Internal Issues	Food & Institutions
IV	1968-1973	Ideological entangles	Settling Green Revolution
V	1975-1982	Strengthening home Industry linkage	Travails of Green Revolution
VI	1982-1990	Reaffirming Democracy	Relative Neglect of Agriculture
VII	1990-2001	Decade of Swift Changes	Taking on the World Market New Equations
VIII	2001-2016	Staggered Tryst with Reforms	Farm Sector Distress

Source: Based on the presidential address delivered at Indian Society of Agricultural Economics Platinum Jubilee Conference 2015, Punjab Agricultural University, Ludhiana.

There are three axis on which one must analyse the transformations of Indian agriculture. First being the trends in the growth of the agricultural economy whereas, the second axis relates to the broad policy interventions. Along with these two, the third axis in determining these phases is the then prevailing political domain that wields a significant influence. Therefore in this analysis of changing scenario, we shall take help from these phases that I have delineated during the Presidential address. We have quite

2. I had attempted this in my Presidential address given to the Platinum Jubilee Conference of the Indian Society of Agricultural Economics held at Ludhiana, Punjab, in 2015 (Deshpande 2015).

a few studies analysing the scenario of agriculture in the post-independence period and hence I am taking a different path altogether (see Table 23.1).

The travelogue of Indian agriculture is marked with cyclical phases after the independence (Sawant 1983). We began with a strong colonial hangover and the major problem was of food scarcity that needed to be tackled with the policy instruments. India did not have the required policy arsenal to substantially enhance agricultural production quickly. At the same time, in an infant nation, Indian policy wizards were engaged with the homework to search a suitable development model. Two international ideological pulls were quite strong on the policy makers. On one side, the capitalist development model was quite celebrated in the world, and on the other the Socialist blocks' centralised planning model demonstrated good results. These two were quite dominant ideologies dictating economic policies. The choice was tricky and difficult, and Prime Minister Pandit Jawaharlal Nehru preferred mixed economy, possibly taking the best out of the two models. Planning began in the economy with the first plan unfolding a model of investment in rural areas. Bhalla and Singh (2001) take a full view of the developments during that period and in later years. Agricultural sector was moving at its natural pace with some policy tinkering in the form of community development and village level schemes. The drought of 1965-66, and the subsequent year brought agriculture sector to a grinding speed and consequently policy need was invoked. The foodgrain availability in the economy had touched the lowest minimum in the economy. Agriculture sector did not show the required promise to meet that huge obligation of foodgrains within the economy. Added to that the war with Pakistan had crippled the macroeconomic strong holds. Domestic political stability was a given advantage. Those were the days when internationally 'politics of aid' was strong on the cards along with the simmering 'Cold War' between the international giants. India with certain conditionality imported huge amount of foodgrains but at the same time, a decision was taken to usher in a technological revolution in agriculture through the new varieties of wheat and paddy. Dr B.P. Pal, the then Director General of Indian Council of Agricultural Research (ICAR) led the policy from front and Dr Challam, a seed breeder at Indian Agricultural Research Institute (IARI) brought in the first few kilos of new seeds. A decision to import significant amount of new seeds of paddy and wheat was taken at the Cabinet level. The decision was pushed forward by the then Minister for Agriculture Dr C. Subramanyan and supported by the Prime Minister. Things started moving in agriculture significantly. Foodgrains production and productivity experienced a quantum jump during the years and India was ushered in with the Green Revolution.

The fourth phase in the travelogue of Indian agriculture was dominated by the accommodation with the Green Revolution and a political instability in the mid-1970s. The political instability also inflicted significant negative externality on the growth of the sector. Large number of externalities were surfacing and deceleration in growth was experienced in the early 1980s (Deshpande et al. 2004). The environmental effect of the Green Revolution as also the economic fallouts were quite significant. The following are a few among the noted fallouts:

(a) skewed income distribution effect in the farm sector,

(b) increased regional disparities,

(c) higher crop specialisations,

(d) reduced emphasis on the traditional crops like millets,

(e) slow-growth experienced by a few crop groups like oil seeds and pulses,

(f) increased cost of cultivation due to higher usage of purchased inputs, and

(g) shrinking of the net income out of agriculture (Deshpande et al. 2004).

Early 1980s saw emergence of new focus on industries and it was in 1982 that a deliberate policy decision was taken to allow joint manufacturing in the country. FDI (foreign direct investment) in certain sectors was allowed and we could see the transition from the old Bajaj, Vespa or Lambretta scooters to many new two wheelers and vehicles like Hero-Honda, Kawasaki-Bajaj coming into the market with collaborative manufacturing. The television and telecom revolution also began but along with this there was a relative neglect of agricultural sector. All this was on the background of a politically unstable state and no firm agricultural policy could be made. The macroeconomic crisis of 1990-91, shook the country and that changed the course of history. The economy and along with agriculture moved towards market centralism. New roads, new equations were being drawn and the decades of 1990s and 2000 saw significant political changes along with policy. First time, in the year 1999, India had an Agricultural Policy document. As usual that remained in the shelves of the Ministry of Agriculture for the coming decades. These two decades also saw the emergence of international trade as a central policy initiative. By mid-1990s, World Trade Organization (WTO) agreement was signed and India became a prominent member of WTO. International trade became one of the central points in our discussions on agriculture and QR (quantitative restriction) was quite a troublesome area to deal with (Deshpande and Thippaiah 2005). Willy-nilly the sector had to participate in the international trade even though the institutional backup was absolutely fragile. A few farmers (white collared farmers) could graduate to this new environment and participated in international trade. Agricultural trade (imports plus exports) increased from ₹9,284 crore (TE [triennium ending] 1992-93) to ₹46,331 crore (TE 2002-03) and further to ₹2,62,299 crore (TE 2012-13) and ₹3,55,684 crore (TE 2015-16).

India was poised to take on the world market but this situation was confined to a few regions, a few crops and only some groups of farmers. As a result there were farmers with significantly high income and at the same time many had to manage livelihood on really meagre income (Deshpande and Prabhu 2005). Many authors have concluded that the real net income of the farmers has not increased and largely remained stagnant during last two decades. The climatic conditions as well as inefficiency in the markets also played havoc with the farmers. The signs of distress in the farm sector were visible during late 1990s and aggravated further. The inequality increased significantly so also the distress across the country. The unrest among the farmers engulfed the entire country. It is now that we are negotiating to usher in a new agricultural policy with possibly a very fragile slogan of doubling the farmers' income. Often we are viewing India's dream of reaching a two-digit growth rate and possibly this ambition assumed the participation of agriculture naturally with its ongoing stagnation. The 11th Plan envisaged a four per cent growth for agriculture and that could not be achieved despite the vibrant scheme like Rashtriya Krishi Vikas Yojana (RKVY). In every discussion on agricultural sector we centralise growth, and that has eluded us for many years. In this paper, we attempt to document the rapids through which Indian agriculture navigated the path during last seven decades. We do not prefer to go chronologically and shall focus on only major points of discussions.

Is Agriculture Growing?

Growth in Indian agriculture has been analysed by many that included Bhalla and Singh 2001, Alagh 2013, Deokar and Shetty 2014. We have been talking about the growth performance of Indian agriculture in the recent past and ambitions about a double-digit rate of growth. Dandekar (1994) gives a good historical and authoritative account of the developments. There has been a good amount of discussion about the feasibility of such ambition in the literature. Subsequently, the NITI (National Institution for Transforming India) Aayog came out with a new game of doubling the farmers' income. The desire to achieve such a noble destination is most welcome but one needs to look at the scaffolding to be made ready for this purpose. Our experience of long-term growth will surely bother us in this new experiment as historically we have often failed to get to the set goals. Here, it is not really the growth alone that would suffice to double the farmers' income but on priority imperfections in the markets have to be removed. Our contribution of agriculture sector to GDP (gross domestic product) has been the lowest across sectors, and we hope to reach about 4 per cent rate of growth in agriculture and 8.2 per cent during the 12th Plan. This was the target of the plan, which was aborted after closure of the Planning Commission. The ground situation however, betray these ambitions by far margins.

Table 23.2

Growth Performance of Sectors across the Periods (Based on 2004-05 Prices)

(Average Annual Compound Growth Rates [%])

Sl No	*Growth Periods*	*Agriculture*	*Industry*	*Services*	*GDP*
1	1950-51 to 1968-69	2.01	6.48	4.60	3.67
2	1968-69 to 1975-76	2.19	2.75	4.07	3.07
3	1975-76 to 1988-89	2.74	4.89	5.80	4.30
4	1988-89 to 1995-96	2.69	5.59	6.38	5.06
5	1995-96 to 2004-05	2.23	5.57	7.87	5.92
6	2004-05 to 2016-17	3.19	6.41	8.89	7.29

Note: Phase I: Pre-green revolution period (PGR)—1960-61 to 1968-69; (ii) Phase II: Early green revolution period (EGR))—1968-69 to 1975-76; (iii) Phase III: Period of wider technology dissemination (WTD)—1975-76 to 1988-89; (iv) Phase IV: Period of diversification (DIV)—1988-89 to 1995-96; (v) Phase V: Post-reform period (PR)—1995-96 to 2004-05; (vi) Phase VI: Period of recovery (REC)—2004-05 to 2016-17.

The growth rates presented in Table 23.2 are based on the traditional methodology across the phases. These growth rates are based on the data from National Accounts Statistics and the GDP contributed by the sectors at constant prices. Chand and Parappurathu (2012) used similar periods and found that the growth trajectory has shifted from less than 1 per cent to about 3 per cent. It is quite clear that till 2004-05 we could not cross the 3 per cent barrier of growth in the agricultural sector even though the aggregate economy progressed quite well. The overall GDP grew at a rate above 5 per cent and reached to almost 8 per cent but the contribution of agriculture to this overall growth has always stayed a point of worry. It is only during the period 2004-05 to 2016-17 that agriculture sector could marginally cross the 3 per cent barrier and posted a growth rate of about 3.19 per cent per annum.

In the Indian agricultural economics fraternity, growth rates are usually calculated either in terms of year-to-year changes or based on the exponential trend estimated through a regression equation. After a long discussion in the workshop organised at Lonawala by the Indian Society of Agricultural Economics in 1980, it was concluded that both methods are misleading (Dandekar 1980). At the seminar Prof Dandekar concluded about truly representative growth rates:

> The research worker who explores the statistical method for quantitative economic analysis and hopes to obtain meaningful results should bear in mind the limitations of his data and keep his expectations modest lest he might give up the whole analytical effort in unwarranted scepticism (Dandekar 1980: 12).

This exposes the significance and limitations of growth analyses in the presence of weather responding to fluctuations. A decade back a controversy emerged in Karnataka about the growth performance of agriculture. The state government had confronted a ticklish issue: 'when monsoon and all other parameters were normal, how come the State Economic Survey reported negative growth for agricultural sector?' Government of Karnataka (2009) constituted a Committee under my Chairmanship, to look into the matter and it was found that the growth rates reported in the State Economic Survey (or for that matter in all Government publications) were only the 'percent change over last year'. In my report, I had pointed the inherent mistake committed in any growth analysis—the assumption of 'exponential growth behaviour in agriculture', an unpardonable folly. Performance of the agricultural sector has built-in fluctuations with troughs and peaks alternating due to weather fluctuations. In the earlier attempt, Rao et al. (1980) tried to work out growth rates excluding fluctuations. It involved throwing out some data and that was not a very welcome idea. Growth rates should bring out the intrinsic behaviour in the series by using all the data and not throwing out any observations. This brought forth the fallacy of using the traditional growth rates as policy tool.

Figure 23.1

Five Years Rolling Growth Rates of Agricultural and Allied Sector GDP and Production of Foodgrain and Non-Foodgrains in India

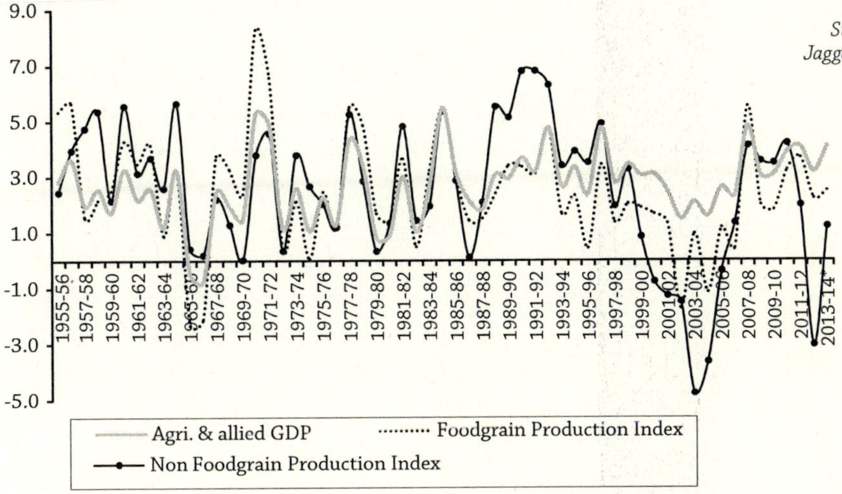

Following this, I took a close look at the data and 'year-to-year' changes. It became clear that in agricultural sector, we needed to define a new measurement of growth. I named it as "Rolling Growth Rate", computed on a moving five year series. The justification for rolling over five years is that the 'probability of bad/bumper year' arriving from a long time series is about 20 per cent and that would mean once in five years, we have an extreme observation. Therefore, a rolling five year growth rate provided the inherent movement of the growth. We suggested a five year rolling growth rate to be used as a policy tool which, irons out the fluctuations. In Figure 23.1, we have presented such five year rolling growth rates based on rolling five years periods. The five year rolling growth rates and the results match with the ground realities. The figure shows a lot of fluctuations but no specific trend.

It is quite clear from Figure 23.1 that foodgrains and non-food grains series in production have always been under the 3.15 per cent barrier. Over a long time series, agricultural sector showed a sticky behaviour with this threshold of 3.15 per cent. Albeit there are a few peaks which can be observed but equal number of troughs are visible. Especially the performance of the sector has not been quite encouraging between 1996-97 and 2007-08. Among the major reasons for the constrained growth at 3.15 per cent is the large share of rain fed agriculture, the technological fatigue, fluctuating weather conditions that sets back the clock etc. More than 50 per cent of the gross cropped area is at the mercy of monsoon rains. Even the area under irrigation also fluctuates according to the moods of the monsoon. In a drought year we cannot expect irrigation support to be dependable. Besides, even though the technology has been supportive it is mainly confined to wheat, paddy and a few more crops. We began with per hectare yield of 541 kgs in foodgrains in the TE 1952-53 and today in the TE 2015-16, the use of foodgrains has crossed 2,000 kgs per hectare.

Table 23.3

Source-wise Irrigation in India
(in million ha; percentage share in brackets)

Sources	*1950-51*	*1960-61*	*1970-71*	*1980-81*	*1990-91*	*2000-01*	*2010-11*	*2013-14*
Canal	8.3	10.4	12.8	15.3	17.5	16.0	15.4	16.3
	(39.7)	(42.1)	(41.2)	(39.4)	(36.5)	(29.0)	(25.3)	(23.9)
Tanks	3.6	4.6	4.1	3.2	2.9	2.5	2.0	1.8
	(17.2)	(18.6)	(13.2)	(8.2)	(6.0)	(4.5)	(3.3)	(2.7)
Wells & Tube Wells	6.0	7.3	11.9	17.7	24.69	33.8	35.9	42.4
	(28.7)	(29.6)	(38.3)	(45.6)	(51.4)	(61.3)	(58.9)	(62.3)
Other Sources	3.0	2.4	2.3	2.6	2.9	2.9	7.6	7.5
	(14.4)	(9.7)	(7.4)	(6.7)	(6.0)	(5.3)	(12.5)	(11.1)
	20.9	24.7	31.1	38.8	48.0	55.1	60.9	68.1
GIA	22.6	27.9	38.2	49.8	63.2	76.6	85.8	93.1*

Note: Figures in bracket are in percentage to total net irrigated area;
*: Estimated based on trend.

Source: Directorate of Economics and Statistics, Ministry of Agriculture website.

A large share of this increase in the productivity can be assigned to the increments in yield of rice and wheat only, the rest of the foodgrains have experienced stagnation in yield per hectare or at the most a marginal increment. Irrigation has been a critical determinant of growth and one does not have to get into any in-depth computations to prove that irrigation is the critical deciding factor of growth in the last decade. The support of irrigation has been increasing and the increase was quite sharp during 1980-1990 and after that the yield growth has slowed down. Most of the increment in yield came out of increased irrigated area, fertiliser use and new varieties (Evenson et al. 1999). They commented that the "estimated effect of irrigation on TFP is strongly positive, indicating that irrigation does influence productivity above and beyond its value as an input" (p.51). The share of NIA (net irrigated area) to NSA (net sown area) has increased by about six per cent per decade and this growth seem to have enhanced during the last two decades.

Table 23.4

Prospects of Growth as Envisaged by NITI Aayog

Sl No	*Source*	*Scope*	*Incremental Contribution*		*Remarks*
			7 Years	10 Years	
1	Crop productivity (70% seg)	3.1	16.7	25.0	Same as 2001-2013 for crop sector (70% seg)
2	Livestock value added (30% seg)	4.5	10.8	16.6	Same as in 2004 to 2014
3	Improvement in resource use efficiency	2.26	16.7	25.0	Same as in 2005 to 2012
4	Crop intensity (70% seg)	1 percent-age point	3.4	4.9	Same as during 2001 to 2012
5	Crop diversification (70% seg) area: increase by 3.13%, elasticity 0.319	3.13%	5.0	7.3	
6	Better price realisation (crops only)	13.0%	9.1	9.1	Implemented in 7 or 10 years
7	Shift to non-farm occupation	1.81%	13.4	19.6	Same as in 2005 to 2012
8	Total		75.1	107.5	

Source: Ramesh Chand (2017: 19, Table 5.1).

Certainly during this phase the resource intensity has also increased and consumption of fertilisers' has gone up from about 15 kg per hectare to above 138 kg per hectare (see Annexure Table A-23.1). Similar growth is seen in the distribution of certified quality seeds. In the TE 1982-83 the distribution of certified quality seeds was 44 lakh quintal. It has now come up to 295 lakh quintal in TE 2015-16 (see Annexure Table A-23.1). But these increments in the resource use did not get translated in increment in productivity proportionately. In fact, real net income of the farmer has almost stagnated over years (Sen and Bhatia 2004, Deshpande and Prabhu 2005, Narayanamoorthy 2013). The expressions of distress are loud and clear, getting acute over time. It needs to be seen why the increment in the productivity is minuscule as against the growth in resource use, unfortunately from the broad data trends this seems to have not taken place and that has also not been translated in the net income generated for the farmers.

Table 23.5

Sources of Growth in Farm Income: The Required Growth Rates

Sl No	*Source*	*Recent Achievements*		*Required Growth Rate for DFI*	*Increment Required (%)*
		Period	*Growth Rate/Change*		
1	Crop productivity (70% segment)	2001-2013	3.1	4.1	32.2
2	Livestock value added (30% segment)	2005-2014	4.5	6.0	33
3	Improvement in resource use efficiency	2005-2012	2.26	3.0	33
4	Crop intensity (70% segment)	2001-2012	1 percentage	1.3	33
5	Crop diversification towards fruits and vegetables (70% segment)	2003-2014	3.89	5.17	33
6	Better price realisation: Crops	Karnataka experience, Reforms	13% total (in real term)	17.0	31
7	Shift to non-farm occupation	2005-2012	1.81	2.4	33

Note: DFI: Doubling the Farm Income

Source: NITI Aayog 2017: 20.

In the recent past, we have been talking about a newer craze of doubling agricultural income in the coming five years.[3] This strategy seems to be quite simple of

3. See the excellent paper Chand (2017) prepared for the Niti Aayog.

manoeuvring seven parameters threefold (Table 23.5). The table (reproduced from Chand 2017) gives us the component wise prospects of growth and contributing elements. NITI Aayog envisages seven factors that will impact potential growth. These include crop productivity, livestock, resource use efficiency, crop intensity, crop diversification, better price realisation and shift to non-farm occupation. Table 23.4 gives the scope for growth of these factors and their contribution in the coming 7 years and 10 years respectively. It is presumed that if the factors underlying growth is at the same rate as experience between 2001 and 2014 farmer's income will rise by 66 per cent in 2022-23.

It is however, not certain that each of these factors will have the expected secular growth. Our experience of seven decades is not that. Further, in order to double the farmers income the NITI Aayog envisages increments in the seven factors and incidentally these do not include animal husbandry, market behaviour and prices, sericulture and other allied activities in agriculture. Table 23.4 from the paper shows the base level of the factors and the targeted value for 2022-23. Chand (2017: 28) stated:

> Doubling farmers' income by 2022 is quite challenging but it is needed and is attainable. Three pronged strategy focused on: (i) development initiatives,(ii) technology and (iii) policy reforms in agriculture is needed to double farmers income. The rate of increase in the sources underlying growth in output need to be accelerated by 33% to meet the goal.

The explanation for this 33 per cent magic increments is desired. The question remains about the magic number of 33 per cent for every factor that promotes growth in short run as also in long run (See Table 23.5). The targets indicated in Table 23.6, seem to be more imaginary than real and non-achievable with the current infrastructure. The increments indicated in the last column of the Table 23.6 are to be achieved in about 7 to 10 years' time, and history of development of these factors for seven decades indicated clear non-feasibility of these levels. Further, there has to be massive investment to get to these levels and above all the question remains if the increase in production and productivity will get translated into increased income to the farmer. The regional differences in the responses to policy are absolutely forgotten. Besides, it is also important to ask if enough room is made for accommodating time fluctuations, which is hallmark of Indian agriculture. It is therefore, clear that if Indian agriculture has to be competent, the sole emphasis needs to be on market corrections and reducing the market inefficiencies. Only than the farmers get prices closer to the price at which the commodities are sold to the final consumers in the market. The farmers share in the consumer's rupee has to be enhanced and that will create a built-in incentive for the farmer to go ahead. When we accepted a liberalised market system, the distortion correcting institutions got placed in the market itself. Our experiment with the Agricultural Produce Market Committee (APMC) Act of the late 1960s did more harm than good, and the model act was implemented half-heartedly. Highhandedness in directing the market from outside is detrimental to the growth and is resented causing higher distress.

Changing Structure of Agricultural Economy

Any structural change in an economy is a product of culture, society, income generation and the aggregate policy framework. The structural change in Indian agriculture began almost immediately after independence. It is well-known that culturally agriculture was considered as inferior to the urban based work and so also the farmer. This culturally imposed inferiority on the profession as also on the sector had a telling effect on the foregoing structural changes. Its reflection could be seen on the policy front too, and for a long we did not have any policy blueprint for the development of the sector. Not many farmers preferred to stay in agriculture nor their children. The lure and attraction of urbane goods and services steadily eroded the emphasis on the policy towards agriculture.

It is not a big secret, that large number of the graduates from agricultural universities do not practice agriculture after completion of their education in agriculture. They prefer white collared jobs in the urban locations rather than soiling their hands in agriculture. As a result, the proportion of workforce in agriculture was going down, which is usually justified in development economics as an usual indicator of development trend, but the speed at which the sectors' contribution is shrinking as against the workforce causes an alarm.

The structure of population dependent on agriculture and the cultivators as also labourers working in the agriculture sector are undergoing significant changes over decades. These are usual observations but something unusual is also happening in the sector that needs attention. It can be seen from Table 23.7 that the share of rural population started declining from 1971 onwards and the decline was quite sharp between 2001 and 2011,

Table 23.6

Base Level and Target for Development Initiatives to Double the Farmers' Income (As Envisaged by NITI Aayog)

Sl No	*Inputs*	*Unit*	*Base Level (2014-15)*	*Target for 2022-23*	*Increment Expected@*	*Increment Expected#*	*Increment Achieved per Decade in the Last 30 Years#*
1	Quality seeds (Distribution)	Million Tonnes	3.03	7.97	4.94	4.94	0.85
2	Fertilisers (NPK) consumption	Million Tonnes	25.58	36.24	10.66	10.66	5.77
3	Irrigation (Gross)	Million Hectares	*92.58	110.40	17.82	13.94	13.97
4	Electricity for agri. purpose	1000 GWh	*147.48	307.39	159.91	138.43	49.3
5	Area under more than one crop	Percent to NSA	*40.0	53.00	13.00	11.45	5.47
6	Area under fruits & vegetables	Million Hectares	**16.17	26.38	9.63	16.40	1.41
7	Area under HYV	Percent	69.30	90.00	20.70	20.70	3.5

Notes: *: 2012-13; **: 2013-14; @: Revised on common base year 2014-15; #: column computed by the authors.

Source: Chand (2017: 21).

coinciding with the decade of liberalisation. Initially, the decline was about 2 to 4 per cent (1951 to 1991), and suddenly it jumped to above 6 per cent in the last decade. This cannot be brushed aside as a normal trend, but there is a clear evidence of de-ruralisation after 2001. This sharp decline during 2001 to 2011 is a matter of anxiety.

Table 23.7

Population, Cultivators and Agricultural Labourers in India (in million)

Year	*Growth in General Population*			*Growth in Agricultural Workers***			*Total Workers*
	Total Population	*ACGR (%) Total Pop.*	*Rural Population*	*Cultivators*	*Agri. Labourers*	*Agricultural Workers*	
1951	361.1	1.25	298.6	69.9	27.3	97.2	139.5
			(82.7)*	(50.1)	(19.1)	(69.7)	(100.0)
1961	439.2	1.96	360.3	99.6	31.5	188.7	188.7
			(82.0)*	(52.8)	(16.7)	(69.5)	(100.0)
1971	548.2	2.22	439	78.2	47.5	180.4	180.4
			(80.1)*	(43.3)	(26.3)	(69.7)	(100.0)
1981	683.3	2.20	523.9	92.5	55.5	244.6	244.6
			(76.7)*	(37.8)	(22.7)	60.5)	(100.0)
1991	846.4	2.14	642.6	110.7	74.6	185.3	314.1
			(74.3)*	(35.2)	(23.8)	(59.0)	(100.0)
2001	1028.7	1.95	742.6	127.3	106.8	234.1	402.2
			(72.2)*	(31.7)	(26.6)	(58.2)	(100.0)
2011	1210.8	1.50	833.7	118.8	144.3	263.1	481.7
			(68.9)*	(24.7)	(30.0)	(54.6)	(100.0)

Note: Figures in parenthesis represent percentage. *: Percentage to total population. **: includes main and marginal workers.

Source: Agricultural Statistics at a Glance 2015, Ministry of Agriculture, Govt. of India.

There can be two implications of this to the overall structural change in the Indian economy. First, the rural workers are finding better work environment elsewhere (non-rural locations), and they are shifting out of agriculture (a Lewisian shift) in search of better income sources attracted by those new emerging vocations. But this cannot be compared strictly with Lewisian transfer, as it is happening more out of 'push effect' than 'pull effect'. Agriculturists as well as a large portion of rural population does not find it economical to stay in rural areas or in the agriculture sector and hence they prefer to move out of the sector. Second, it can be observed from Table 23.7 that there is secular decline in the percentage of cultivators to total agricultural workers. The changing composition of the rural workforce is more due to economic compulsions than the natural development process. The share of cultivators came down from 53 per cent in 1961 to 31 per cent in 2001. Except in the first decade, till 2001 the waning in the share of cultivators has been about 4 per cent per decade but suddenly between 2001 and 2011 the decline is very sharp of about 7 per cent of the total workforce. This is alarming indicator of de-peasantisation of the agrarian economy.

At the same time the share of agricultural labourers in the total agricultural workers has been increasing at about 3 per cent per decade. In any case, it is a fact that agriculturists are preferring to leave agriculture leaving agricultural labour behind. This process indicates economic marginalisation of workers in rural areas and their degeneration in the status from cultivators to agricultural labourers. The decline of the poverty ratio therefore, should be credited to the availability of that proverbial ₹26 (poverty line arrived at by the Planning Commission on 19 March 2012, that was subsequently pushed forward to ₹32 [Rangrajan Committee in July 2014]) to remain above the line of poverty but probably just on it so that the poor sinks down at the slightest economic jerk. The disappearing cultivator is a matter of concern. We can see from Table 23.7 that as per 1991 Census, India had 1,246.8 lakh workers recorded as cultivators and this number has come down by 59.9 lakh by 2011. This change in two decades means almost 3 lakh cultivators disappearing from the fields every year. They may get into the fold of 'other workers' or become agricultural labourer'. The increase in the number of agricultural workers is also substantial and there are enough reasons to believe that the cultivators would have moved as agricultural labourers. The process of de-pesantisation is setting in the rural areas.

Figure 23.2

Number of Operational Holdings (in lakh) and Area Operated (in ha)

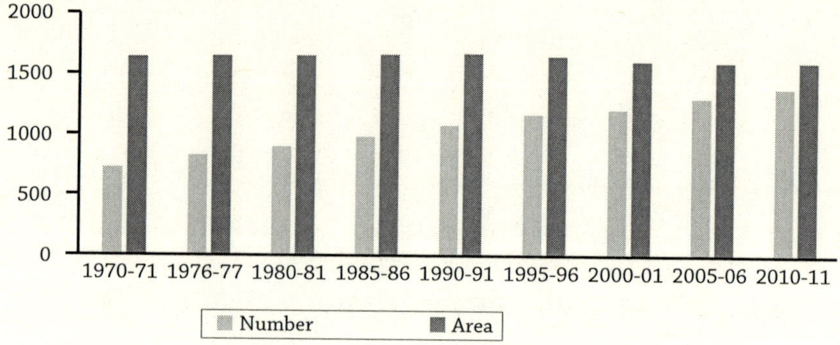

Source: *Report of Agricultural Censuses* (various years), Ministry of Agriculture and Cooperation, Government of India.

This fact can also be corroborated with the agricultural census data. Figure 23.2 shows that there was some increase in the area under operational holding till Agricultural Census of 1990-91 but there is a slight decline after that till the recent Agricultural Census. Across the agricultural censuses, the area operated has also changed substantially. According to 1970-71 Agricultural Census, the number of marginal and small holdings were 49.6 million, this has increased to 117.1 million. The area operated by the marginal and small holdings increased by 36.8 million hectares and the area under the medium and large holdings has reduced by 39.6 million hectares. As a result 31.38 lakh hectares seem to have gone out of agriculture. This fact needs to be read with the decline in the number of cultivators that have reduced in the population census and the decline in the poverty ratio as seen from the Planning Commission data. There are only three possibilities to reach this situation. First, the agricultural income per hectare must increase as a result of increase in the number of farmers despite marginalisation of the size of holding, and because many should have crossed the poverty barrier. That means farming should have become highly remunerative, by now. Alas, this was true! Second, if the farming is not remunerative, as indicated by the NSSO 59th Round and other sources of data (Deshpande and Nagesh Prabhu 2005), then the increase in agricultural wages or the availability of other employment opportunities could have helped the farmers/ agricultural workers to stay above the poverty line. Real wages must have increased in this situation. Third, there is a possibility of rural poor just crossing the official poverty line but staying in the very close neighbourhood of that income threshold with the help of many ongoing schemes like Mahatma Gandhi National Rural Employment Guarantee Scheme (MGNREGS). This is the most probable reason explaining the clustering of persons just 'above poverty line', but not well above the poverty line or totally out of poverty. The result is therefore deceptive and the dependence culture (continuous dependence on the Government schemes) in the farm sector continues to haunt the sector. This view point finds empirical corroboration through NSSO Situation Assessment Survey (2003). This round of NSSO (2005) brought out clearly that about 40 per cent of the farmers would like to leave agriculture either as the profession is non-remunerative or it involves drudgery.

Table 23.8

Changes in Structural Distribution of Economy and Employment

Sl No	*Year*	*Percentage Share in GDP*				*Percentage Share in Total Workers*		
		Agriculture & Allied	*Agriculture*	*Industry*	*Services*	*Agriculture & Allied*	*Industry*	*Services*
1	1950-51	51.9	41.8	16.2	29.5	72.1	10.7	17.2
2	1960-61	47.6	39.4	20.1	30.2	71.8	12.2	16.0
3	1970-71	41.7	34.2	23.6	33.3	72.1	11.2	16.7
4	1980-81	35.3	29.6	26.2	37.5	68.5	13.5	17.7
5	1990-91	29.5	24.9	27.6	42.5	66.9	11.9	19.2
6	2000-01	22.3	18.8	27.3	50.4	56.9	16.9	25.8
7	2010-11	14.6	12.4	27.9	57.5	54.6	45.4	
8	2016-17	11.6	9.9	25.8	62.7	-	-	-

Source: *Economic Survey* of the respective years.

In western theories of development economics it is well accepted that development is the one where economy undergoes a transition from agriculture to non-agriculture.

Therefore, this transition could be seen in the per cent of GDP generated from agriculture and workforce in agriculture sector. In Table 23.8, we have presented these changes in the structure of the economy as reflected from the share of GDP and the workforce across sectors.

The share of GDP has been declining continuously over the period of six and half decades, so also the share of workforce. This has been observed in many studies and noted that the share of agriculture & allied activities in the GDP has come down from about 52 per cent to end at 12 per cent in 2016-17. Interestingly, this share declined sharply during 2000-01 and 2010-11 by about 8 per cent. Similar decline is seen in the share of workforce for the period 1990-91 to 2000-01. It is quite clear that this was the phase of liberalisation and possibly large of rural population shifting to urban locations. It can be inferred that liberalisation has drawn out workforce from agriculture and rural India, but it has failed to increase the GDP generated in the sector proportionately. This is actually the residual of earlier policies and therefore, one can expect larger percolation of growth to the rural area if liberalisation has to be a successful policy.

The growth performance of various sub-sectors and allied agricultural sectors indicate a strong structural change witnessed in the agricultural sector under the force of new economic policies. Even though in the crop sector we do not see any substantial changes until 1990s. But certainly GDP originating from agriculture & allied sector at constant prices has increased substantially after 2004-05 as also ToT (terms of trade) (Shaha 2015). It was contributed significantly by the allied sectors which include animal husbandry and livestock economy. Net agricultural output at constant prices from 1980 onwards increased by more than 3 per cent per annum and the growth was quite substantial during the last two decades. One of the important observations here is that agriculture is no more getting restricted only to crop economy sector, but has been contributed largely by horticulture, animal husbandry and other allied activities. This clearly shows

Table 23.9

Growth Performance of Production and Agricultural Output and Input in India across Different Decades and Phases

Periods	*Production*		*Agriculture & Allied Sector GDP# (2004-05 Constant prices)*	*Output and Input (2004-05 Constant Prices)*			
	Foodgrain	*Non-Foodgrain*		*Crop Output*	*Livestock output*	*Agri* Inputs*	*Net Agri Output***
Decades							
1950s	4.25	3.66	2.71	3.06	1.42	2.00	2.91
1960s	1.85	1.49	1.51	1.70	0.41	2.34	1.25
1970s	2.07	2.17	1.74	1.79	3.92	3.27	1.88
1980s	2.73	3.77	2.97	2.24	4.91	1.96	3.11
1990s	2.09	2.67	3.34	3.02	3.79	2.58	3.40
2000-01 to 2013-14	2.52	1.18	3.41	3.17	4.52	3.46	3.57
Phases							
1950-51 to 1965-66	2.96	3.60	2.27	2.47	1.22	1.90	2.31
1966-67 to 1990-91	2.84	2.96	2.62	2.75	4.16	3.90	2.80
1991-92 to 2013-14	1.70	0.55	3.02	2.67	4.00	2.84	3.09

Note: # GDP at factor cost; * Crop and Livestock; ** output minus inputs

Source: Based on various issues of National Account Statistics, MoSPI, GoI and *Agricultural Statistics at a Glance*, Ministry of Agriculture, GoI

the move towards integrated farming, about which there used to be policy discussions two decades ago (see Table 23.9). We need to revive the impetus in order to step up the growth of agriculture as also incomes of the farmers.

Another important structural change that has occurred in agriculture is marginalisation of the farmers. The process of marginalisation can be understood from two different angles. First, as usually understood by agricultural economists that demographic pressure and non-viability of the land results into fragmentation of holdings. Thus, we have strong proliferation of small and marginal holdings across the country (see Table 23.10). Substantial increase in the marginal holdings makes it difficult for the cultivators to adopt new technology or new inputs. This brings down the productivity at aggregate level due to high density of marginal and small farmers. Despite their best efforts they cannot bring the productivity to the levels promised by the technology due to the cash intensive technology. On an aggregate, more than 80 per cent of the farmers have holding less than 1 hectare and about 11 per cent have holdings between 1 and 2 ha. This would mean a large number of farmers cannot even think of reaching the doorstep of the expensive technologies let alone adopting these to the fullest extent.

Table 23.10

Distribution of Household Owning Land and Area Owned by Size of Holdings in Rural Areas of India

	Size of Holdings	*1953-54*	*1961-62*	*1971-72*	*1982*	*1992*	*2003*	*2013*
I	Landless Households (%)	23.09	11.69	9.60	11.30	11.30	10.00	7.41
II	Percentage to All Rural Households							
1	Marginal (≤1.0 ha)	61.24	66.06	62.62	66.64	71.88	79.60	81.45
2	Small (1.01 – 2.0 ha)	13.49	9.16	15.49	14.70	13.42	10.80	10.80
	Sub-Total	74.73	75.22	78.11	81.34	85.30	90.40	92.25
3	Semi-Medium (2.01 – 4.0 ha)	12.50	12.86	11.94	10.78	9.28	6.00	5.41
4	Medium (4.01- 10.0 ha)	9.17	9.07	7.83	6.45	4.54	3.00	2.08
5	Large (10.01 ha & above)	3.60	2.85	2.12	1.42	0.88	0.60	0.26
III	Percentage to Total Area Owned							
1	Marginal (≤1.0 ha)	6.23	7.59	9.76	12.22	16.93	23.02	29.76
2	Small (1.01 – 2.0 ha)	10.09	12.40	14.68	16.49	18.59	20.38	23.53
	Sub-Total	16.32	19.99	24.44	28.71	35.52	43.40	53.29
3	Semi-Medium (2.01 – 4.0 ha)	18.40	20.54	21.92	23.38	24.58	21.97	22.07
4	Medium (4.01- 10.0 ha)	29.11	31.23	30.73	29.83	26.07	23.08	18.83
5	Large (10.01 ha & above)	36.17	28.24	22.91	18.08	13.83	11.55	5.81

Source: 1) Government of India (1968), Tables with Notes on Some Aspects of Landholdings in Rural Areas(States and All India Estimates), Report No. 144, New Delhi: NSSO, 2) Government of India (2006 & 2016), Household Ownership Holdings in India, 2003 & 2013, Report No. 491 & 571, NSS 59th Round and 71st Round respectively, New Delhi: NSSO.

The small farm based cultivation further marginalises the farmers in economic terms by providing them only frugal income and increasing their dependence on the state agencies as also the private money lenders and land sharks. This process of marginalisation has increased very sharply between 1992 and 2003. Between these two years, we can see that the increment in the share of marginal holdings is about 8 per cent which is unprecedented high as compared to the earlier increments in the share of marginal holdings.

Figure 23.3

Distribution of Landholdings across Rural Households Landowners in India: 1953-54 to 2013

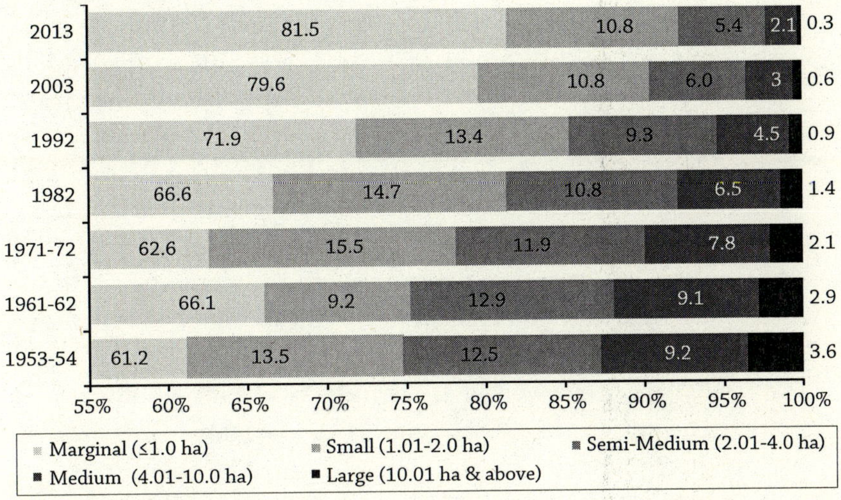

Source: Agricultural Census Data.

There are a few important pickups from the foregoing analysis that we should not miss for reading the changing agrarian structure of India. First, the share of GDP originating from agriculture & allied sector has been declining and this decline is quite sharp during the phase of liberalisation. This could be both due to the sharp increase in growth of GDP originating from non-agriculture sector or owing to the deceleration of growth in agriculture & allied sectors. On the safer side, we can assume that this decline in the share is mainly attributable to high incremental growth in the non-agricultural sector. But when we look at the relative shares of GVO (gross value of output) from agriculture, it is problematic that the share of crop sector is almost stagnant in real terms almost for the two decades. Second, it was observed that the share of rural population as well as cultivators in the total workforce is declining. It is well-known that the farmers do not prefer farming as their main vocation both due to lower dignity assigned to the profession by the society as well as low income generation and dependence on state or financial institutions (formal or informal) even for bare survival. The Population Census data from 1991 and 2011 indicates that about 50 lakh cultivators have changed their profession from cultivation. As a result the number of cultivators indicated in the Population Census has declined by 50 lakh and the operational land has gone down by more than 31 lakh hectares. This would clearly mean that either they have changed their profession to agricultural labour, or migrated to urban areas in search of work in any of the available vocations in cities and abandoned cultivation of 31 lakh hectares. At the same time, we also observed that the share of agricultural labour has increased substantially during that period. Third, the marginalisation of the farmers both in terms of size of landholding as well as on the economic front could be clearly observed in rural India and that is manifested in the agitations we see in most of the states. This process of marginalisation and loss of dignity to the profession has sparked the agitations among farmers. This change has intensified quite significantly during the last three decades.

Liberalisation and Crop Commercialisation

There is no doubt that Indian agriculture is undergoing transition from subsistence agriculture to a market friendly agricultural sector. The role of market started increasing in the agricultural sector way back in 1950s and strengthened during 1960s. The APMC Act was passed in late 1960s and the role of market increased in the sector. The pace of commercialisation also increased after we achieved the arithmetic food self-sufficiency by 1970 and farmers started moving towards commercial crops away from food crops. Commercialisation has been slowly stalking agricultural sector since then. With the increased cash requirement in the cost of cultivation as also the income requirement for incremental lifestyle based on the urban consumption patterns, it was natural that farmers would move to commercial crops. Punjab farmers being the first rank rice traders came from this change in the market structure and commercialisation. The process of liberalisation ushered in during 1990s played a critical role in increasing the velocity of this process. The agricultural sector became trade friendly as export of agricultural commodities increased significantly. We have taken six indicators to understand the pace of commercialisation and these include: i) share of core commercial crops in the total crop output; ii) share of horticultural crops output in the GVO; iii) share of foodgrains in the GVO; iv) area share of core commercial crops in GCA; v) area share of horticultural crops; vi) area share of total foodgrains in the GCA. All these indicators depict six different faces of commercialisation and increase in the process or time.

Figure 23.4

Pace of Commercialisation in Indian Agriculture

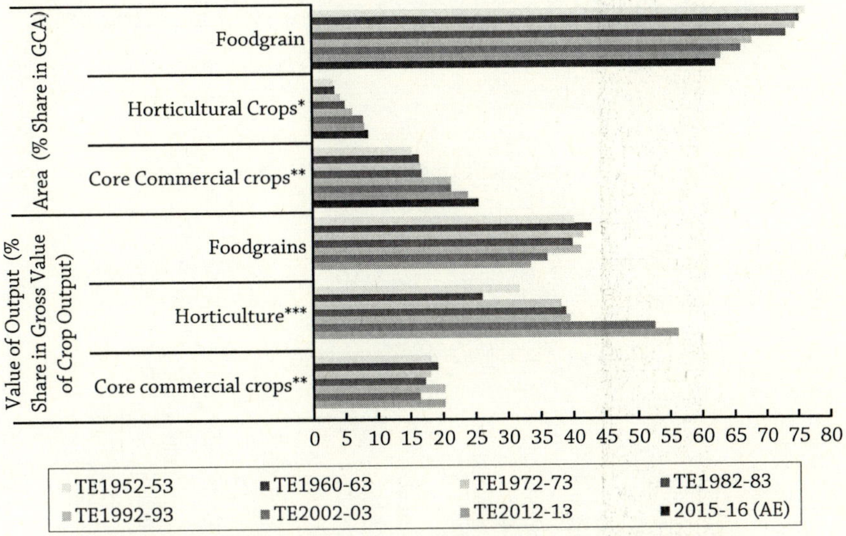

Note: 1) *: Condiments & Spices, Fruits & Vegetables, Plantation crops; **: Total Oilseeds, Sugarcane, Total Fibre and Tobacco; ***; Condiments & Spices, Fruits & Vegeatables, Plantation and Floriculture & other horticulture crops; 2) light to dark shades indicate periodic progression beginning from TE 1952-53 to 2015-16; 3) Value of crop output 2004-05 series.

Source: Authors' depiction based on data from Land Use Statistics, DE&S, Government of India, Ministry of Agriculture Website and National Account Statistics 2004-05 Back Series and 2013 and 2013, CSO, New Delhi: MoSPI.

It is clear from the Figure 23.4 that commercialisation has increased at a slower pace till TE 1992 to 1993, but the pace increased sharply after that. This however, should not be construed as higher income increments in the agricultural sector. In fact, the process of commercialisation possibly has injected some new sort of inequality in the agricultural sector. The possibility to graduate to commercial agriculture was largely available to the resource rich farmers who had good access to state initiated schemes and water resources. Therefore, those farmers who did not have access to these facilities remained in the lower income bracket and the lucky ones graduated to higher income bracket. This new source of inequality was injected in the agriculture sector during the process of liberalisation.

The new economic reforms increased the pace of India's participation in international trade. Initially from 1990-1991 to 2000-01 the pace of trade was slow and we did not achieve high export growth. The trade balance also was not that unfavourable, but the pace of exports increased after 2010-11. This has brought in new avenues of sources of income to the Indian agriculturists.

Figure 23.5

Performance of Agricultural Trade in Different Phases: 2001 to 2013

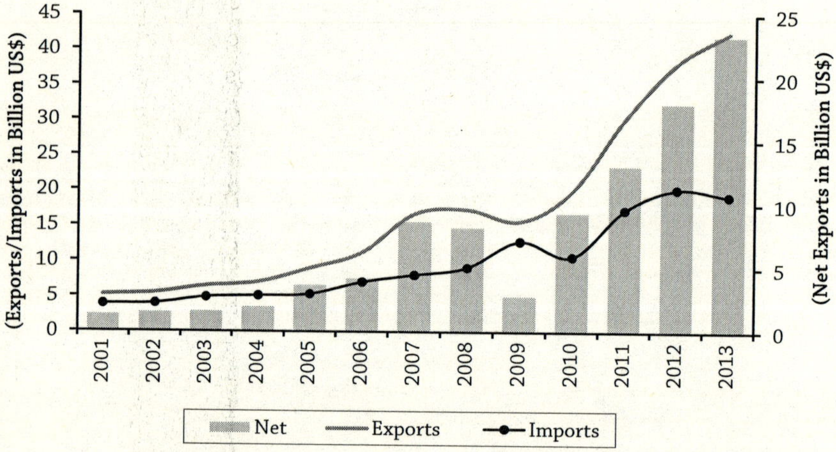

Source: *Economic Survey* (various years), Ministry of Finance, Government of India.

In the process of liberalisation, opening up of the economy for international trade as also our active participation in WTO, are quite welcome steps. Given the pace of commercialisation in Indian agriculture there are good hopes that agriculture can positively enter into international trade arena. However, can international trade become an engine of growth and instrument to enhance farmers' income to the expected level is a question that remains unanswered. Given the structural composition of agriculture sector, we have a strong proliferation of marginal and small farmers. The marketable as also exportable surplus does not generate largely from this group. More than that as density of holdings, the marginal and small farmers are predominant. The income of this group is the real crux of the story to increment income in agricultural sector. Therefore, we cannot expect income of the marginal and small farmers to have a quantum jump with the help of international trade. Commercialisation of agriculture sector should however be participated by this group very aggressively. This will surely change the prospects and if the group farming approach as advocated by Beena Agarwal (2008, 2011) is followed, possibly the small and marginal farmers will have chance to achieve better income levels.

Vanishing Villages

In our textbooks, during college, we were taught that India lives in its villages. Keeping in view the experience of post-1990s, the rural population is shrinking very fast. Deepankar Gupta (2005) and many others question if we are losing our villages. Indian sociologists as well as Indian agricultural economists grew on the information collected from villages to understand the village economy and Indian society. Strangely, most of the experts writing on village India grew in urban sophisticated settings and inferred about Indian villages based on their 'participant observation method'. Beginning with Slater's villages in the Madras Presidency and going through Harold Mann, G.S. Ghurye, A.M. Shah, Andre Betele, M.N. Srinivas,

Dipankar Gupta to Surinder Jodhka, we understood India's villages from different angles. Jodhka (2012: 5) calls it as three views namely,

> While Gandhi saw it as a site of 'authenticity', for Nehru the village was the source and site of India's 'backwardness'. For Ambedkar village was a site of 'oppression', where the institution of caste presented itself in the most brutal and inhuman form.

For an agricultural economist, village is an epicentre where the culture of agriculture changes gradually and decides the fate of the sector. It is essential to understand Indian agriculture through Indian villages and with that intention the Agro-Economic Research Centres were started in the entire country across the regions. These centres made significant attempts to document the culture of agriculture in the villages across India. No attempt however was made to weave these studies together to make a collage of changing Indian villages. There are three important currents in the literature on understanding villages. The first stream is that of the initial authors who tried to understand the villages and most of them belonged to a different socio-cultural environment altogether. Slater's villages come under this category as well as many of the Indian authors who entered the village after having born and brought up in a pure urban influenced sophisticated environment. For them, many things in the villages were strange and therefore, theorising on these important issues was the task they assigned to themselves. In 1955, M.N. Srinivas edited a book titled: *India's Villages*, consisting of the essays on villages published in *Economic Weekly* which brought together many authors and their understanding. Almost in the same year Marriott (1955) brought out another book titled: *Villages India* and then Majumdar's (1955) first volume of studies on *Rural Profiles* came out. The study by S.C. Dube (1955) titled: *Indian Village* was also on the stands in the same year. Interestingly, these studies incorporated a lot of information about structure and processes in the Indian villages across many regions of India. Many concepts and processes not known to the outside world were documented and many of these enhanced rich research material.

The second stream of studies were conducted under Agro-Economic Research Centres in an attempt to understand agrarian economy prevailing in the villages. This was provoked by Dr Gadgil and his study of Wai taluka undertaken by Gokhale Institute of Politics and Economics during 1931, which got down to see the economics of the agriculturists. These studies conducted all over the country, and probably most of them remained unpublished, focused on the structure of landholding and organisation of agriculture in the villages of India. Harold Mann's study on Pimple Saudagar and a resurvey of that by P.D. Diskalkar are quite incisive to understand the village changing structures.

The third stream of studies on the villages incorporated specific purpose studies beginning with the studies on *Bhdan* movement, Community Development Programme, rural development initiatives, evaluation of various interventions by the government's and finding new initiatives towards development in the villages. These studies also touched on the structure and processes in the villages and therefore, that became the common thread across the three streams.

Our interest in the villages as an epicentre of the changes in the culture of agriculture begins from understanding of these studies. It is now well accepted that Indian villages are changing significantly. Dipankar Gupta (2005) feels that the Indian villages have come out of the twin shackles namely caste and agriculture. He surmised that these no longer exercise their vigorous hold on the Indian villagers. Any person who has been born and brought up in a village and has been constantly in touch with the villagers may not accept this urban centric view of the villages. True that the villages are changing and the core culture in the village is undergoing metamorphosis. It is not however in the fashion in which Gupta has felt. His observation however about the preference for agriculture as a vocation is correct. He writes,

> Rarely would a villager today the want to be a farmer if given an opportunity elsewhere. Indeed, there are few rural institutions that have not been mauled severely from within (Gupta 2005: 752).

It is true that rural India is losing its identity and personality very fast. McKim Marriot (1955) indicated that during mid-1950s Indian villages were not little republics as visualised by many. This observation as well as that of many authors who studied Indian villages during 1950s and 1960s come from their urbane background. The influence of cities was observed by many and has been taken as one of the explanations for changing rural culture. The influence of urban development on the village culture actually stems out of the misconstrued perspective of development in India. Every village dweller dreams to be an urbanite after earning some money and would like to shift out of the rural environs. Therefore, the villagers did not change on their own but buckled under the influence of understanding of development as urbanisation.

There were earlier studies of village India by many authors including Slator, Ghurye, Gadgil, Srinivas, Shah, Betille, McKim Marriot. These and other studies are very succinctly analysed and collated in the volume edited by Jodhka (2012). Change is an integral part of human development and therefore changes in the village society is not an unexpected outcome. However, tracking the path of change and its externalities is an important analytical issue. Historically, villages as described by many authors was an independent, self-sufficient organisation of production and incorporated its own cultural ethos. Villages used to have socio-cultural axis with the towns in the region, however, the influences were not so sharp to alter process of production. Development was rather inclusive and depended on the resources available in the vicinity of the village borrowing both knowledge and technology from the closest town nearby. Village had its own administrative structure which was caste ridden and exploitative in nature. Most of these village offices were represented by a certain caste such as Patil, Gowda,

Karnam, Kulkarni, Deshmukh, Deshpande, Kotwal, Bhaldar, Bangar etc. Each caste also lived in its own closed periphery. The division of labour was across the class lines as well as caste which played an important role. The system of agriculture production was primitive but openness predominated in the context of technology and change. This picture of the village provided an inclusive economic picture possibly with a low level technology. As the technology of agriculture production was tradition bound, growth in agriculture sector was slow but the village was largely self-sufficient and operated at low-level equilibrium.

After independence, rapid changes took place in the villages spearheaded by the policy interventions. In every five year plan, development of villages and the schemes leading to such development where discussed and implemented. The core of such schemes as well as the philosophy of development was more to convert villages initially into small towns and if possible connect to the urban locations. The meaning of development itself provided to the villages was to follow the consumption pattern of the urban population. One of the examples of this philosophy of development was to consider coarse cereals and small millets as food of the poor. Culturally, the millets and coarse cereals were degraded by not using them as food in festivals and religious functions. As a result, the cropping pattern in the villages changed in favour of paddy, wheat and pulses, and the crafts usually preferred for consumption by the urban elites. Villages thus were now more dependent on the nearest towns and followed the consumption pattern of the urban locale. This dependence on the town economy was mutually perpetuated by using town as a market for village products and utilising the new commodities and services available in the towns. Ambitions were increasing as there was an immediate effect of the consumption pattern of the towns with desires climbing steadily to reach that consumption pattern. Decentralised democratisation reached the villages albeit superimposed on the class and caste structure of the village. New forms of exploitation and new expressions of the ugly caste system started emerging. The culture of agriculture was changing fast with the availability of new technology, equipment, inputs and seeds. Education played a very critical role in changing the age composition of the cultivators and agricultural labourers residing in the villages. Largely, elderly persons remained in the village and youngsters found either seasonal or permanent migration as better choice. Shrinking labour availability in the villages and higher average age of the cultivator changed the culture of agriculture. The farmers preferred either commercial crops or going out of agriculture in search of work at the nearby town.

The Agricultural Census as well as the Population Census of India brings out two important observations. Agriculture Census clearly shows that the sector is being proliferated by small and marginal farmers resulting in to low viability of the farm. As a consequence, large number of farmers who were pushed into non-viable agriculture now either sold out their land or rented it out to the large landholders. Villages today have large number of tenants on whose land the land owners are working as labourers. The signal of this change was given by Prof Dantwala (1952) and he named it as 'reverse tenancy'. On the one side, we find that the village lands are going out of cultivation and for other uses whereas, on the other the number of cultivators has been declining as shown by the Population Census. Vintage villages are certainly disappearing from the scene, and what is left behind is commercial agglomeration of individuals with caste, class and commercially oriented agricultural operations. Technology has not been able to positively change the course of social development.

Whither the Farmer Distress

Distress in the farm sector culminating into farmer suicides has become an important area of discussion in Indian agriculture for the last decade. This genesis of distress has been traced back to the technological change of mid-1960s, which has caused the demand for cash inputs and brought into new seeds along with it. It had also ushered in a new culture of technological change and that is believed to be one of the starting points of the distress. During the last three decades the situation has aggravated both due to policy fatigue (Narayanamoorthy 2007) and the successive droughts. Prices did not pick up even in the event of low production and the net income of the farmers was shrinking. The recent demonstrations of the farmers in many parts of the country stand as a testimony of increasing distress. The situation was quite alarming in Karnataka, Andhra Pradesh and Maharashtra. The spate of farmers' suicides that surfaced in these states was naturally associated with the performance of the sector, along with the other factors that were prominent including advent of WTO, GM varieties, price collapses, and spurious inputs. Agricultural production in these states always had significant fluctuations, the prices also did not increase despite supply stress. This brought down the gross income flow to the farmer. On the other side, the cash component in the cost of cultivation has been increasing. Farmer would borrow to meet the increased cost of cultivation or for irrigation (well and pump sets). Declining net income did not allow the payment of debts and as a result, the farmer households faced increased indebtedness. The accumulation of unpaid debts created a cascading effect and it became impossible for the farmer to pay after a few years. By this time, the farmers have exhausted all the avenues of borrowing from institutional and non-institutional sources. As a result farmers are compelled to press for loan waivers. Distress among the farmers in the country is genuine and the situation is quite depressing in Andhra Pradesh, Karnataka, Maharashtra, Rajasthan, Odisha and Assam. Though one cannot draw any 'one to one' correspondence between distress in the farm sector and the present spate of suicides in some of the states, but the farm and farm related activities have the largest stake in explaining the unfortunate occurrences.

A recent study by Manjunath and Ramappa (2017) conducted across all the states in the country revealed quite a few interesting results. According to them, suicides are largely concentrated in five states namely, Maharashtra, Karnataka, Madhya Pradesh, Telangana and Chhattisgarh. The study concludes that suicide is largely committed by farmers under various stress among which financial stress is one of the significant reason. Largely density of suicides is high among small and medium size of holdings and specially among farmers cultivating one or the other commercial crop. The rate of suicides has come down from 2012 and 2013, but that does not mean that the distress has mollified in the farm sector.

Figure 23.6

Farmer Suicides in India

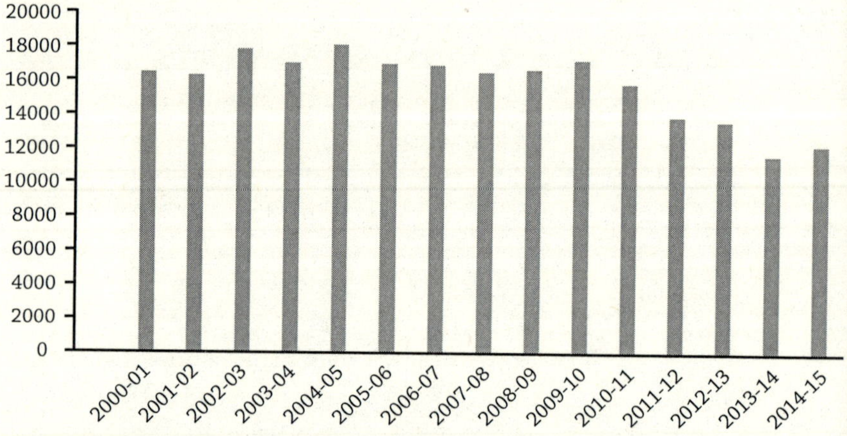

Source: Data from Manjunath and Ramappa (2017).

Among many issues analysed in the study referred above, it was found that suicides are committed due to multiple reasons, and indebtedness is one of the prominent among them. In the recent past, we have seen that across states there is a spate of loan waivers and this is considered as one of the important alleviatory measure. It is also argued that due to the frequent loan waivers the credit discipline in the rural credit structure gets totally disturbed and large NPAs (non-performing assets) accumulate with the expectation of the next loan waiver. It is essential to build a proper safety net programme as well as insurance cover for the farmers and their loans. However, there has not been significant policy thinking on this front.

One of the earlier studies (Deshpande and Arora 2010), suggested a plethora of measures to alleviate the possible distress in the agricultural sector. Similarly, Reddy and Mishra (2009) suggested quite a few policy interventions. However, the Government decided to focus only on short term solutions rather than getting into long-term policy alternatives. Farm sector distress in Indian agriculture is not a sudden phenomenon. The genesis goes back to the planning and implementation of the policies leading to green revolution during the mid-1960s. The externalities emerging after the Green Revolution culminated into the simmering crisis of 1970s. This manifested into the farmers' movements as it remained unattended. At the same time, the agrarian changes in the farm sector were reaching a crescendo by weakening the livelihood base of the farmers. Tiny farm sizes and marginalised farmers became a hallmark of 1990s, with the farmers facing increasing non-viability both due to the size and contents of the agricultural technology. Market imperfections both in factor and product markets added to the intensity. Therefore, attention now should be more on the policy corrections rather than analysing the causation. Mitigation must take precedence over causation and explanation. Treatment of the maladies is always better than the post-mortem approach, and this calls for a long term policy formulation.

Price the Achilles Heel

Farmers' agitations pertaining to prices have erupted quite significantly during the last four decades. The tools and methodology of the agricultural price policy came under severe scrutiny and have been commented upon by many. Evolving long-term price policy was one of the major recommendations of Jha committee (Government of India 1965a) during mid-1960s. Raj Krishna was one of the important crusader of putting in place right price policy and hence Jha committee recommended besides establishment of a commission, interventions in the product markets. Prof M.L. Dantwala headed the first Agricultural Prices Commission (APC) and in its report, in 1965, the Commission suggested the MSP (minimum support price) for paddy. The focus of the emerging price policy of India was also made clear in the report. The Preamble of the report states:

> The Agricultural Prices Commission was set up in January 1965 to advise Government on price policy for agricultural commodities, with a view to evolving a balanced and integrated price structure in the perspective of the overall needs of the economy and with due regard to the interests of the producer and the consumer (Government of India 1965b).

The emphasis of the price policy was to protect the interests of the producers and consumers besides looking into the overall needs of the economy. The terms of reference of the APC were quite clear from the beginning, but were possibly blurred during the process of implementation. It states:

> (i) To provide incentive to the producer for adopting technology and for maximising production; (ii) to ensure rational utilisation of land and other production resources; (iii) to keep in view the likely effect of the price policy on the rest of the economy, particularly on the cost of living, level of wages, industrial cost structure, etc.; (iv) to recommend from time to time, in respect of different commodities, measures necessary to make the price policy effective; (v) to examine, where necessary, the prevailing methods and cost of marketing of agricultural commodities in different regions, suggest measures to reduce costs of marketing and recommend fair price margins for different stages of marketing; (vi) to keep under review the developing price situation and to make appropriate recommendations, as and when necessary, within the framework of the overall price policy; (vii) to keep under review studies relating to the price policy and arrangements for collection of information regarding agricultural prices and other related data and suggest improvements in the same; (vii) to advise on any problems relating to agricultural prices and production that may be referred to it by Government from time to time (Government of India 1965b: 47-48).

One does not need great research to find that the APC as well as its new incarnation in the form of Commission on Agricultural Costs and Prices (CACP) did not keep pace with the set objectives. Surprisingly, India has had only one Agricultural Price Policy document which was published in 1986 (Government of India 1986), but it never made out of the shelves of the Ministry of Agriculture or the CACP. In fact all through the years, CACP has been totally engaged only in competitions and declaration of MSP. The irony of the situation is that the MSP declared by CACP and the final support prices announced by the Government of India or the state governments are not the same. Therefore, the entire so-called scientific exercise of arriving at the cost of cultivation through cost accounting data across the country and declaring the prices based on various factors does not make any sense. The committee headed by Dr S.R. Sen during 1979 submitted its report in 1980 (Government of India 1980) suggesting many improvements in the entire methodology of declaring the support prices. The methodology underwent quite a few changes over time. The committee headed by Prof Abhijit Sen on "Long-Term Grain Policy' (GoI 2002) recommended that the scheme of MSP be continued with some corrections and these include:

> (i) the CACP should be made an empowered statutory body; (ii) CACP should act directly on the basis of C2 cost of production; (iii) CACP should also indicate a system of imputing family labour cost; (iv) CACP should recommend only one price for Paddy for the country as a whole; (v) All the procurement agencies and Public Grain Management Institutions should be legally bound by the MSP Policy; (vi) Central government should under-write open purchase of grains under MSP; (vii) FCI should be the buyer of last resort. FCI should withdraw from states like Punjab and Haryana and concentrate on other states (Mentioned in the detailed recommendations given by the Committee, GoI 2002: 9-10).

The initial role of MSP was not only to protect the farmers but also to incentivise them to adopt new technology. In this context, Prof Dantwala who was one of the founding architects of India's price policy, stated that:

> Though no rigid formula has been accepted to determine the levels of floor prices, the criterion followed is that *progressive farmers should find these levels adequate to encourage enterprise and investment to augment production through the adoption of improved technology with all its risk and uncertainty* (emphasis added) (Dantwala 1996: 213 originally published in 1967).

MSP is now viewed as a form of market intervention on the part of the State and also as one of the supportive measures (safety nets) to the agricultural producers. Even though it is perfectly WTO compatible (GoI 2002) eyebrows are raised about its continuance and effectiveness to deal with the objectives set by its architects. The issues that dominated the current debate include reasons for continuation of the price support scheme, its effectiveness in terms of the objectives set forth in the 1986 document, and support price vis-à-vis remunerative price approach. After an experience of a quarter of century, in the implementation of the market intervention scheme Prof Dantwala wrote again during early 1990s clearly recognising the changing role of MSP and the interventions. He wrote,

> *Likewise, intervention has to be selective. Its need must be clearly established and its effectiveness should be constantly under review. The real problem is not simply to establish the legitimacy of intervention, but that of ensuring its effective and judicious implementation* (emphasis added) (Dantwala 1996: 292, originally published in 1993).

It is therefore, imperative to revisit the entire agricultural price policy in the context of three important parameters. First, we are strongly entering into the international trade arena and therefore, our farm sector must become competitive with our farm products deriving better comparative advantageous compared with other competing countries. Second, it has been brought out by many studies that market imperfections actually mar the economic interests of the farmers. For almost two decades we have been thinking of revising the APMC Act, without any success. The market imperfections both at the village markets as also in the APMCs play havoc with the farmers. And therefore, the price policy statement should be more protective in nature for the farmers as producers. The implementation of MSP in the country as a whole is a well-known failure. Plugging the loopholes causing such failure is not a difficult task and hence that becomes the third and the most important priority on the policy front. It is well-known that actual root causes of farmer's agitations have been failure in the markets and the state not taking note of the welfare loss to the farmers due to such failures. It is high time that the Government of India works on a long-term price policy keeping in view the commitment to international trade, plugging the market inadequacies, incentivising the farmers and putting in place institutions that will ensure farmers welfare in the market (See Deshpande 2008, 2013).

Policy on Horizons

India's experience in framing its own agricultural policies has been not less than pathetic. Right from the independence we have had a few reports that could be termed as attempts towards building up of a policy, but no sooner these came in public domain the thrust was totally lost. The policies were always laid down in response to meet the ensuing crisis and hence could be called as a riverine experience—like a river, whose flow is dictated by the obstacles coming in the way and the smoothness offered by the neat slopes. Our concerns about policy studies are precisely directed at trying to improve the ability of a society and its governance to confront the issues with the well tested policy tools. It involves changing over the pattern of past policies to the present one and analyse the impact of these changes. In the process of current trade-led growth, where international trade serves as the engine of growth, the trade related decisions are likely to be at the centre stage. Most of the trade related decisions are taken by the Ministry of Commerce in the Union Government and the welfare implications of these decisions essentially befall on the sub-national governments. In this context, the nations with federal constitution will be placed in a tricky situation. Therefore, in such situation, a clear design of the policy is an essential prerequisite at the sub-national level.

Policymaking in agriculture at sub-national level inevitably passes through difficult contours. One can list at least five bold reasons entailing such difficulties. First, agriculture is an unorganised sector and, therefore, policy responses could not be predicted *a priori* with objective probabilities. Second, the information flow to agricultural sector is not as quick as it takes place in other sectors. The information asymmetry in the absence of objective probabilities about outcomes virtually authenticates to formulate disjointed policies in isolation, without detailed homework or mostly arbitrarily. Third, the sector in most of the agro-climatic regions has strong proverbial weather dependence and thus a quick firefighting job is usually the core of the policy. Fourth, the significant factor is level of income and asset distribution in the sector that has always been a point in question. This is further complicated by variations, a mark of the peculiar sector. The policies framed need to keep these variations in view. Last, the sector has a strong link with consumers and other industries. The growth of the aggregate economy of any country is sensitive to the fluctuations in the sector. Therefore, agricultural policies in India as well as many other countries have a strong State dependence.

Our experience of policy formulation in India is largely from two sources namely the Five-year Plans and various schemes initiated by the concerned development departments. There is a general lack of awareness about the theory of policymaking and, therefore, to a significant extent the policy is understood often as the problem solving steps taken in the context of severity of the issue and/or a common denominator of various programmes.

> A policy aims at specific, often quantifiable, objectives, deploys an array of instruments to achieve them and operates according to a pre-

planned time frame for implementation. It lends itself to standardised monitoring and evaluation procedures to assess the outcome and to identify those responsible for the success/failure of the policy. (Rao 1998: 1).

In India we have totally neglected the theory and practice of policymaking and largely the policies are made in a firefighting mode through hurriedly planned and erroneously implemented schemes (Lasswell 1956, Hall 1993, Deshpande and Raju 2009). Elsewhere, I have attempted to deliberate on the process of policymaking in India, initially through a theoretical perspective on policymaking, followed by the experience of agricultural policy during the last seven decades. This is followed by an empirical study of policymaking across the states in the Deccan Plateau region. We have chosen these states with a particular purpose. First, agriculture being a State subject any exercise at policymaking has to be at state level. Second, the challenge of policymaking in the states on Deccan Plateau is unique due to typically similar constraints and differential experience. Third, these are the states that are hotspots of agrarian distress as also rapid commercialisation and differential experience. Therefore, these are typical cases that pose challenge for policymaking (see Deshpande and Prachitha 2006).

In India, we had sporadic attempts at making agricultural policy, but none of these attempts culminated into any long-term policy document. These include: Gregory Committee 1943, Thakurdas Committee 1947, Maitra Committee 1950, Mehta Committee 1957, Vekatappaiah Committee 1966, High Power Committee (Bhanu Pratap Singh Committee) 1990a, policy document under the prime ministership of Deve Gowda (Government of India 1999), and the draft agricultural policy document prepared by Sharad Joshi (Government of India 1990b). Most of these documents focused on the current problems and little was done to allow long-term thinking. The agricultural policy document of 2000 (Government of India 2002) was the first complete attempt towards formulating a long-term policy for the sector. The NAP (2000) seeks to realise by 2020:

(a) vast untapped growth potential of Indian agriculture;

(b) strengthen rural infrastructure to support faster agricultural development;

(c) promote value addition;

(d) accelerate the growth of agro-business;

(e) create employment in rural areas;

(f) secure a fair standard of living for the farmers and agricultural workers and their families;

(g) discourage migration to urban areas and face the challenges arising out of economic liberalisation and globalisation.

The policy aims stated in the document to achieve these are:

(a) a growth rate of 4 per cent per annum;

(b) efficient use of natural resources and bio-diversity;

(c) growth with equity;

(d) protect from economic liberalisation and globalisation by demand driven growth and catering to domestic markets and maximise agricultural exports;

(e) environmentally, technologically and economically sustainable growth.

However, the document is rather a collection and compilation of all the niches in the literature and does not attempt any phased or properly directed programme.

A holistic approach to the development of the farm sector was brought out by the National Policy for Farmers in 2007. The broad focus areas of the policy included:

- Economic well-being of the farmers in addition to production and productivity.
- Building skill sets of farm households by ensuring

that each farmer household in villages either possesses or have access to a productive asset or a marketable skill.

- Maximise the use of irrigation water in all crop production programmes with stress on awareness and efficiency on water use.
- Encouraging new technologies like biotechnology, ICT, renewable energy, space applications and nano-technology for improving productivity of land and water use.
- Establishing National Agricultural Bio-security system.
- Issuing of soil health passbook to farmers and supply of quality seeds and disease free planting material for ensuring seed and soil health.
- Funding of support services for women working in fields like crèches, childcare centres and adequate nutrition.
- Galvanising the financial services of credit and insurance for timely, adequate and easy reach to the farmers at reasonable rates of interest.
- Effective implementation of MSP mechanism to ensure remunerative prices for agricultural produce.
- Enlarging of food security basket to include nutritious millets like *bajra, jowar, ragi* etc.

Notwithstanding this, it must be clear that largely our policy statements for the sector emerge from the Five-year Plan documents and thus the genesis and process can also be traced through these. In the absence of a long-term policy paper, the experience based on the impact on ground gives us a fair idea about the policy directives. Therefore, we need to review the policy experience over the last five decades to understand the direction.

India's agricultural sector is presently at a crossroads with the advent of the forces of new economic policy. The sensitivity of aggregate growth of the economy to the fluctuations in growth trends of agricultural sector is undisputable. Thus, the onus of maintaining a good tempo of growth, provision of food security to the millions below poverty line, contributing to the overall development scenario and participating in the global trade are among the major expectations from the sector. The performance of agricultural sector during the 1990s has not failed these expectations. However, there are quite a few questions of specific nature, which have to be looked into while analysing the performance of the sector. First of all it is necessary to review the question of sustainability of the process of growth in a medium-term perspective and the food security question in the background of performance during the last five decades. Any such analysis will require a long-term understanding of growth process of the agricultural sector in India. Secondly, the growth performance has to be viewed from two distinct perspectives, namely the resource use and institutional perspective. Thirdly, under the Indian Constitution, agriculture is a subject assigned to provincial governments (State governments) for the purpose of policy. Therefore, the policy has to be viewed from the perspective of the states.

Conclusions

Indian agriculture has undergone many changes during the last century. Initially, it was the hangover of colonial policies that were predominantly drawn from the British model of development and superimposed in India, when Gandhian village inclusivity was the dominant development philosophy. We did not significantly change the organisation of our administration and followed the British systems. Keeping away the capitalistic or socialistic development alternatives, India took the path of a mixed economy with the Planning Commission at the helm, taking control as a policy think tank. Initial two decades after 1947, were invested in correcting the aberrations caused due to the mismanagement of food sector in the pre-independence years. The food availability was even far below the medically determined minimum needs. Distribution of food was a problem and shortages of commodities dominated the markets. We confronted seven major constrictions in the agricultural sector among many other. First, the food production was quite insufficient with the given population pressure. Productivity of most of the crops was dismally low and the crop pattern was subsistence oriented dominated with low value low density crops. Second, irrigation and water resources were not well developed, and except in a few pockets, India was largely monsoon dependent. Third, land distribution was extremely skewed and land relations were refractory in nature (Thorner and Thorner 1958).[4] Fourth, the institutional support to agriculture was awfully dismal and the research and teaching institutions were in embryonic stage. This had an impact on the level of literacy and was a hurdle for getting into the new vocations. Fifth, the technology was primitive in nature and provided very low yields per hectare. There were no avenues to develop the technology too. Sixth, market imperfections infested the agriculture produce markets as also factor markets. Farmers remained at the receiving end in both markets and were harshly exploited by the market operators. Last, there was no clear blueprint available with the Government in the form a long run agricultural development policy nor were there any attempts to get one.

Indian agriculture took upon its journey with these heavy constraints. In 1947, Jawaharlal Nehru said the famous quote, with loaded passion that, "everything else can wait, but not agriculture." History however, tells us that in reality it turned out to be the other way round till 1966-67, everything else was taken care on the policy front except agriculture. Indian agriculturists had to wait till 1999 to get an independent exclusive policy statement. Planning Commission and other think tanks undertook only the firefighting through ad hoc schemes.

During the last 65 years, the share of agricultural sector to the total GDP has come down from 52.6 per

4. Land reforms were strongly recommended by the sub-committee of the Congress Working Committee (1949), which was headed by Dr J.C. Kumarappa.

cent in TE 1952-53 to 11.8 per cent in TE 2015-16. This decline of 41 per cent points is not very secular and marked with fluctuations. The share of agricultural sector to the total GDP declined by about 5-6 per cent points, in every triennium till 1990s, and suddenly this decline between TE 1992-93 and TE 2002-03 was double, reaching an all-time record of 8 per cent. This was indeed an unprecedented decline in the share of GDP. Similar fall was noticed, though at slower rate, in the share of agricultural workforce out of the total workforce. Initially, this decline was of the order of 1 to 4 per cent in every TE, but again during the period TE 1992-93 and TE 2002-03, the decline in the share of agricultural workforce to total workers was 10 per cent points. This clearly marks a structural break in the Indian agriculture during 1992-93 and 2002-03. The change in the structure of agriculture was quite significant and gets reflected in many other indicators also. Clearly, this was the decade that brought down the primacy of agriculture in the Indian economy. Indian economy and so also the agriculture entered into international trade arena without proper ground preparations.

The travelogue of Indian agriculture clearly depicts a staggered approach and lack of any long term focus. Every phase began to deal with some of the current issues but ended with a few new problems. As a result, we were stranded on crossroads for decades with very little positive movements. The challenging ground conditions are really arduous and getting worst over time. The Commission appointed by UPA Government under the independent evaluation authority of the Planning Commission remarked:

> Since the Planning Commission has defied attempts to reform it, to bring it in line with the needs of a modern economy and the trend of empowering the States, it is proposed that the Planning Commission be abolished (GoI 2014: 10).

The failure of policy to read these conditions and their inter-play have been enhancing the difficulties. No clear developmental model emerged out of our efforts in the agriculture sector and rather policy got defined as a problem solving instrument. The firefighting approach ended up in dishing out new schemes that did not have any long term development thinking behind it.

The agrarian distress prevailing in India since late 1990s and continuing over the last two decades raises quite a few questions. Are the farmers really unhappy and have we been doing sufficient for the farm sector and the incomes of the farmers? A full review of the picture does not give very satisfactory answers. Even the question has the growth taking place in the economy percolated down to the agriculture sector, opens up a dreadful reality.

The Government of Karnataka in 2009 had taken steps to revisit the methodology of computing growth on a five-year rolling growth model. It comes out clearly that we have not crossed the 3.2 per cent barrier for long in the agricultural sector. Besides, the structure of agriculture in the country has been changing fast. The culture of agriculture itself is coming under shadow and changing fast towards mutated new commercial culture unsuitable to the given institutional setup. The changes in the agriculture sector have taken sharp turns during the last two decades with the process of liberalisation. According to the Population Census 1991 and 2011, 50 lakh cultivators have disappeared and the agricultural labourers have increased. Villages are changing rapidly as hinterlands of the urban economy. The reverse dependence has become prominent and commercialisation is the vehicle through which this is strengthened. Farm sector distress is visible in every region of the country and is being responded by the policy in the form of packages rather than addressing the root of the problem. Loan waivers and incidental help to the farm sector have overshadowed any long term policy thinking. Since 1986, India does not have any price policy to guide us in the agricultural market or price fixation. It is here that the problem of distress begins as also ends. The cascading effect is quite strong and ironically the farmer has become more a political coin than an important economic entity in the country contributing towards its development. The lack of long-term policy and understanding of making of the agricultural policy is causing strong negative externalities. We need to deal with these foundations that are the root cause for the jagged texture of the crossroads. Dealing with this phenomena is the major challenge.

References

Agarwal, Bina (2011). *Working Group on Disadvantaged Farmers Including Women, Twelfth Five Year Plan.* New Delhi: Planning Commission.

———. (2008). "Rethinking Collectives: Institutional Innovations in Group Farming, Community Forestry and Strategic Alliances", *Occasional Paper.* New Delhi; Centre for Study of Developing Societies.

All India Congress Committee (1949). *Report of the Congress on Agrarian Reform Committee* (Chairman: J.C. Kumarappa). New Delhi

Alagh, Yoginder K. (2013). *The Future of Indian Agriculture.* New Delhi: National Book Trust of India.

Balakrishnan, P., R. Golait and P. Kumar (2008) "Agricultural Growth in India since1991", *Development Study Group Study* No. 27. Mumbai: Reserve Bank of India.

Bhalla, G.S and Gurmail Singh (2001). *Indian Agriculture: Four Decades of Development.* New Delhi; Sage.

Chand, Ramesh and Shinoj Parppurathu (2012). "Temporal and Spatial Variations in Agricultural Growth and its Determinants", *Economic and Political Weekly* 47(26-27): 55-64.

Chand, Ramesh (2017). "Doubling Farmers' Income: Rationale, Strategy, Prospects and Action Plan", *NITI Policy Paper* No. 1/2017. New Delhi: National Institution for Transforming India (NITI Aayog). Available at: *http://niti.gov.in/writereaddata/files/document_publication/DOUBLING%20FARMERS%20INCOME.pdf*

Dandekar, V.M. (1980). "Introduction to the Seminar on Data Base and Methodology for the Study of Growth Rates in Agriculture" *in Indian Journal of Agricultural Economics*, Vol. 35, No. 2, April-June.

Dandekar, V.M. (1994). *The Indian Economy 1947-92.* New Delhi: Sage.

Dantwala, M.L. (1996). *Dilemmas of Growth: The Indian Experience.* New Delhi: Sage Publications.

———. (eds.) (1991). *Indian Agricultural Development since Independence: A Collection of Essays.* Delhi: Oxford and IBH Publishing.

———. (1986). "Agrarian Structure and Agrarian relations in India", in M.L. Dantwala (ed.), *Indian Agricultural Development since Independence: A Collection of Essays.* Second (Revised) Edition, 1991. New Delhi: Oxford & IBH Publishing Co. Pvt. Ltd.

———. (1952). "Bombay Tenancy: Promise and Performance", *Economic and Political Weekly* 4(35).

Deokar, Bipin and S.L. Shetty (2014). "Growth in Indian Agriculture", *Economic and Political Weekly* XLIX(26), June.

Deshpande, R.S. (2015). "State, Agriculture and Policymaking", *Presidential Address* to the Platinum Jubilee Conference of the Indian Society of Agricultural Economics, Ludhiana.

———. (2013). "Under the Shadow: Pricing and Marketing in Indian Agriculture in Globalisation", in Sarmila Banerjee and Anjan Chakrabarti (eds.), *Development and Sustainability: India in a Global Perspective*. Delhi: Springer.

———. (2008). "Price Policy and Minimum Support Prices in the Changing Agricultural Economy", in Shankar Kumar Bhaumik (ed.), *Reforming Indian Agriculture: Towards Employment Generation and Poverty Reduction*. New Delhi; Sage.

Deshpande R.S., M.J. Bhende, P. Thippaiah and M. Vivekananda (2004). "Crops and Cultivation", Volume 9 of the *State of the Indian Farmer: A Millennium Study*. New Delhi: Academic Foundation.

Deshpande R.S. and Saroj Arora (eds.) (2010). *Agrarian Crisis and Farmer Suicides*. New Delhi: Sage Publications.

Deshpande R.S. and K.V. Raju (2009). "Making of Agricultural Policy", in Surjit Singh and Ratna Reddy (eds.), *Changing Contours of Asian Agriculture: Policies, Performance and Challenges*. New Delhi: Academic Foundation.

Deshpande, R.S. and J. Prachitha (2006). *Agricultural Policy in India: Towards a Policy Matrix in a Federal System*. Research Project Report. Bangalore: Institute for Social and Economic Change.

Deshpande, R.S. and Nagesh Prabhu (2005). "Farmers Distress: Proof Beyond Doubt", *Economic and Political Weekly*, 29 October.

Deshpande, R.S. and P. Thippaiah (2005). "Impact of Removal of Quantitative Restrictions in the Globalised Economy of India: A Critical Analysis", *Agricultural Situation in India* LXII(5). New Delhi: Ministry of Agriculture, Government of India.

Dube, S.C. (1955). *Indian Village*. London: Routledge and Kegan Paul.

Evenson, Robert E., Carl Pray and Mark W. Rosengrant (1999). "Agricultural Research and Productivity Growth in India", *IFPRI Research Report* No 109. Washington DC: International Food Policy Research Institute.

Government of India (2014). *Reforming the Planning Commission :An Assessment by Independent Evaluation Office* (Ajay Chhibber). New Delhi: Planning Commission, Govt of India.

———. (2006). *Serving Farmers and Saving Farming: Report No V.* National Commission on Farmers (Chairman: M S Swaminathan). New Delhi: Ministry of Agriculture, Govt of India.

———. (2002). *Report of the High Level Committee on Long Term Grain Policy* (Chairman: Abhijit Sen). New Delhi: Department of Public Distribution, Government of India. July.

———. (2000). *National Agricultural Policy.* Department of Agricultural and Cooperative, Ministry of Agricultural Government of India. July.

———. (1999). *Imperatives for Agricultural and Rural Development in India.* A memorandum submitted to Prime Minister of India by H.D. Deve Gowda, 17 February.

———. (1990a). *Agricultural Policies and Programmes: Report of the High Powered Committee* (Chairman: Shri Bhanu Pratap Singh). July .

———. (1990b). *National Agricultural Policy Resolution: Comment by Standing Advisory Committee* (Chairman: Sharad Joshi). New Delhi: Ministry of Agriculture.

———. (1986). *Agricultural Price Policy: A Long Term Perspective.* New Delhi: Ministry of Agriculture. November.

———. (1980). *Report of the Special Expert Committee on Cost of Production Estimates* (Chairman: S.R. Sen). New Delhi: Ministry of Agriculture, Department of Agriculture and Cooperation, Govt of India.

———. (1965a). *Government Resolution on the Terms of Reference of the Agricultural Prices, Agricultural Prices Commission*. New Delhi: Ministry of Food and Agriculture. 8 January.

———. (1965b). *Report of the Agricultural Prices Commission* (M.L. Dantwala, Raj Krishna, S.C. Chaudhri). New Delhi: Ministry of Food and Agriculture.

———. (1947). *Interim Report-Foodgrains Policy Committee* (Purushottamdas Thakurdas Committee). New Delhi: Manger of Publications, Government of India.

Government of Karnataka (2009). *Report of the Expert Group on Growth Rates in Agriculture* (Chairman: R.S. Deshpande). Bangalore: Office of the Development Commissioner, Government of Karnataka.

Gregory, Sir Theodore (1943). *Report of the Foodgrains Policy Committee*. New Delhi: Government of India.

Green Peace (2009). *Agriculture at Crossroads: Food for Survival*. Amsterdam: Green Peace International.

Gupta, Dipankar (2005). "Whither the Indian Village: Culture and Agriculture in 'Rural' India", *Economic and Political Weekly* 40(8): 751-58, February.

Hall, P.A. (1993). "Policy Paradigms, Social learning, and the State: The Case of Economic Policymaking in Britain", *Comparative Politics:* 275-96.

IAASTD (2016). *Agriculture at Crossroads*. Berlin: International Assessment of Agricultural Knowledge, Science and Technology for Development (IAASTD).

Jodhka, Surinder S. (eds) (2012). *Village Society*. Hyderabad: Orient Black Swan.

Krishna, D. and F.B. Swaminathan (1980). *Indian Farmer at Crossroad*. New Delhi: Swan Publishers .

Lasswell, Harold (1956). *The Decision Process*. Maryland: University of Maryland.

Maitra, Laxmikanta (1950). *Report of the Foodgrains Investigation Committee*. New Delhi: Government of India.

Majunath A.V. and K.B. Ramappa (2017), *Farmer Suicides: An All India Study*. Bangalore: ADRTC, Institute for Social and Economic Change.

Marriot, McKim (1955). *Village India: Studies in the Little Community*. Chicago: Chicago University Press.

Mehta, Ashok (1957). *Report of the Foodgrains Enquiry Committee*. New Delhi: Ministry of Food and Agriculture, Government of India.

Mujumdar D.N. (ed) (1955). *Rural Profiles*. Lucknow: The Ethnographic and Folk Culture Society.

Narayanamoorthy, A. (2007). "Deceleration in Agricultural Growth Technology Fatigue or Policy Fatigue?" *Economic and Political Weekly* 42(25): 2376-79.

———. (2013). "Profitability in Crop Cultivation in India: Some Evidence from Cost of Cultivation Survey Data", *Indian Journal of Agricultural Economics* 68(1), Jan-March.

NSSO (2005). *Situation Assessment Survey of Farmers Report No 496: Some Aspects of Farming*. New Delhi: National Sample Survey Organisation, Ministry of Statistics and Programme Implementation, Government of India.

Rao, V.M, M.V. Nadkarni and R.S. Deshpande (1980). "Measurement of Growth and Fluctuations in Crop Output: An Approach Based on the Concept of Non-systematic Component", *Indian Journal of Agricultural Economics* 35(2), April-June.

Rao, V.M. (1998). "Policymaking for Agricultural Development: Why it Misses the Poor", *V.B. Singh Memorial Lecture* delivered during the 40th Conference of the Indian Society of Labour Economics, Hyderabad (Later published in the *Indian Journal of Labour Economics* 42(1), 1999).

Reddy, D.N. and Srijit Mishra (2009). *Agrarian Crisis in India.* New Delhi: Oxford University Press.

Sawant S.D. (1983). "Investigation of the Hypothesis of Deceleration in Indian Agriculture", *Indian Journal of Agricultural Economics* 38(4): 475-96

Sen, Abhijit and M.S. Bhatia (2004). "Cost of Cultivation and Farm Income", Volume 14 of the *State of the Indian Farmer: A Millennium Study.* New Delhi: Academic Foundation.

Singh, A. and Suresh Pal (2011). *Public Investments in Indian Agriculture: Recent Trends and Implications for Growth.* Presented in Workshop organised jointly by IGIDR, Mumbai and IHD, New Delhi on Policy Options and Investment Priorities for Accelerating Agricultural Productivity and Development in India, at India International Centre, New Delhi. 10-11 November.

Shaha, Khalil M. (2015). *Terms of Trade for the Agricultural Sector in India: A State Level Analysis.* PhD Thesis. Dr. Babasaheb Ambedkar Marathwada University, Aurangabad.

Srinivas, M.N. (ed) (1955). *Indian Villages.* Bombay: Asia Publishing House.

Swaminathan, M.S. (1982). "Indian Agriculture at Cross Roads", *Current Science* 51(1), 5 January.

———. (2015). "Indian Agriculture at Cross Roads", *Business Standard,* 11 May.

Thorner, Daniel and Alice Thorner (1958). *Land and Labour in India.* Delhi: Asia Publishing House.

Venkatappaiah, B. (1966). *Report of the Foodgrains Policy Committee.* New Delhi: Department of Food, Ministry of Food and Agriculture, Government of India.

Annexure Table A-23.1

Major Indicators of Performance of Indian Agricultural Sector

		Unit	TE 1952-53	TE 1960-63	TE 1972-73	TE 1982-83	TE 1992-93	TE 2002-03	TE 2012-13	TE 2015-16 (AE)
1	Share of Agricultural Sector in GDP	%	51.6	46.1	40.2	35.1	29.0	21.6	15.0	11.8
2	Share of Agricultural Workers in Total Workers~	%	72.1	71.8	72.1	68.5	66.9	56.9	54.6	-
3	Foodgrain Production	Million Tonnes	54.0	81.6	103.5	130.8	174.8	194.8	253.6	252.22
4	Foodgrain Yield	Kg/ha	541.1	698.4	847.8	1030.2	1406.3	1631.7	2045.7	2056.0
5	Cropping Intensity	%	111.4	115.0	118.0	123.4	129.6	132.2	139.1	$142.0
6	Irrigation Intensity	%	109.6	114.2	122.4	127.6	132.0	137.1	139.8	$140.6
7	Gross Irrigated Area to GCA	%	17.1	18.4	23.5	29.3	35.3	41.6	46.5	$ 47.7
8	Net Irrigated Area to NSA	%	17.4	18.6	22.6	28.3	34.7	40.1	46.3	$48.1
9	Area Share of Foodgrain to GCA	%	76.3	75.4	74.8	73.3	67.9	66.2	63.1	$62.3
10	Area Share of Horticultural Crops* to GCA	%	3.3	3.5	4.3	5.1	6.3	7.9	8.1	$8.7
11	Area Share of Core Commercial Crops** to GCA	%	15.4	16.5	16.7	16.9	21.4	21.4	24.0	$25.6
12	Share of Foodgrains in Total Crop Output	% (2004-05 prices)	40.3	42.9	41.7	40.0	41.3	36.1	33.6	-
13	Share of Horticulture*** in Total Crop Output	% (2004-05 prices)	31.9	26.1	38.2	38.9	39.6	52.7	56.3	-
14	Share of Core Commercial Crops** in Total Crop Output	% (2004-05 prices)	18.2	19.2	18.1	17.3	20.3	16.5	20.3	-

15	Consumption of Pesticides (Technical Grade Material)	1000 MT	2.5	8.6	29.7	47.3	72.7	46.3	51.4	50.4
16	Consumption of Fertilisers (NPK)	Kg per Ha	0.5	2.3	15.4	34.4	67.6	90.7	138.5	130.7
17	Distribution of Certified/Quality Seeds	Lakhs qtles	-	-	-	44.2	58.1	92.0	295.2	304.4
18	Electricity Consumption for Agricultural Purposes	Gwh	-	-	-	17812	57402	83629	^133668	168913
19	Tractors /Pump sets per ha (respectively)	Per '000 ha	-	0.03/5	-	3.7/49	8.6/79	13/111	-	-
20	Gross Capital Formation as % to Agricultural GDP	% (current prices)	3.9	4.8	5.9	8.1	7.4	11.8	16.3	$15.8
21	Gross Capital Formation as % to GDP	% (current prices)	2.0	2.0	2.4	2.8	2.2	2.6	2.90	$2.40
22	Trade in Agricultural Commodities (Exports & Imports)	₹ crore	-	-	-	-	9484	46331	262299	355684
23	Exports of agricultural Commodities	₹ crore	-	-	-	-	7630	31013	179045	215396
24	Public Expenditure on Agricultural Research and Extension@@	% GDP	-	0.30	0.23	0.50	0.55	0.65	^^0.65 (0.73)	0.070

Note: *: Condiments & Spices, Fruits & Vegetable, Plantation Crops; **: Total Oilseeds, Sugarcane, Total Fibre and Tobacco; ***: Condiments & Spices, Fruits & Vegetables, Plantation and Floriculture & other horticulture crops; @: allied sector excluded forestry and fisheries output; ~: Census years; ^: TE2011-12; $: 2013-14; @@ & ^^: TE 2005-06 from Balakrishnan et al. (2008). Figures in bracket for TE 2010-11 (Source: Singh and Pal 2011).

24

Addressing Agrarian Distress

RAMESH CHAND

India is facing the second major challenge in agriculture in the post independence period. The first major challenge was experienced during mid 1960s when per capita foodgrain production dropped to very low level (150 kg) and the country faced serious shortage of staple food. This left the country hugely dependent on food import and food aid. The shortage of food was so severe that the Prime Minister Lal Bahadur Shastri had to appeal to the countrymen to observe fast and miss one meal once a week to cope with the shortage of food. The country then decided to adopt and promote new high yielding varieties of wheat and paddy, known as green revolution technology, which were dwarf and much more responsive to fertiliser and other inputs as compared to the traditional varieties. The adoption of green revolution technology produced quick results. Despite its adoption in limited area, India was able to come out of crisis situation of shortage of staple food in less than a decade. Since the onset of green revolution, growth rate in production of all type of food group except pulses remained higher than population growth in most of the period. During the last half a century (1965 to 2015) total food production, including cereals, pulses, oilseeds, vegetable, fruits and livestock products, became 3.7 times while population rose to 2.55 times. The net result has been a 45 per cent increase in per person food production, which has made India not only food self-sufficient at aggregate level but a net food exporting country.

While India was marching ahead in attaining and improving food security and leaving behind the era of food shortage, another crisis started building gradually in the form of agrarian distress. The distress turned serious during the early 1990s, though it started developing a few years earlier. Initially severe distress was confined to some pockets with poor resource endowments but gradually spread to many parts of the country. Incidents of farmers distress are reported even from agriculturally developed states like Punjab, Haryana and Kerala. The situation has become particularly bad during the last two years because of two successive failures of monsoon and abnormal rainfall in *Rabi* 2014-15 and highly deficit precipitation in *Rabi* 2015-16. These types of sufferings do not bode well for the country whose economy is growing at more than 7 per cent a year and which plans to be counted as globally powerful nation.

The distress is said to be the cause for some farmers to take the extreme step to end their lives by committing suicides.[1] This kind of incidents further worsens the suffering of such families. The distress paints a very dismal picture of Indian agriculture. It threatens the future of agriculture sector and also reflects poor state of large population of farming community in the country. This paper is an attempt to understand the genesis, causes, nature and severity of agrarian distress and to propose measure and strategy to mitigate and banish agrarian distress in the country.

Genesis and Symptoms

It is ironical that despite so much concern about the agrarian distress in the country, there is no clear description of what is agrarian distress. Thus, before proceeding further, it is important to discuss what is agrarian distress. According to us agrarian distress is

1. Though financial stress is identified as the main reason for suicides, some analysts attribute suicides to psychological factors rather than economic factors (Guruswamy 2017). This line of argument cites comparison of suicides in India with rich countries and suicides in farming and other professions to dismiss link of suicides with income or farming profession.

manifest at two levels: (i) sectoral or macro level, and (ii) household or farm level. Further, the distress could be absolute or it could be relative. The absolute agrarian distress characterises a situation of agriculture production becoming economically unviable or highly vulnerable. The relative agrarian distress implies rise in gap in performance of agriculture relative to rest of the economy. Agrarian distress at household level refer to a situation when the income of a agricultural household is not adequate to meet family and business obligations. The symptoms of agrarian distress are:

- Rising debt, loan default.
- Networth turning negative.
- Forced migration.
- Rise in hunger.
- Sale of productive assets like land, bullock, tractor, machinery to meet family expenditure.
- Sale of family assets to meet family expenditure.
- Adoption of untested and risky ventures.
- Dissatisfaction with the profession.
- Rise in tragedies like suicides.

The genesis of agrarian distress, at aggregate level, is rooted in structural imbalance in Indian economy which is reflected in two important indicators. The first one is the mismatch in the share of agriculture in national income vis-à-vis its share in workforce and the second one is ratio of per worker income in agriculture vis-à-vis non-agriculture. At the time of onset of green revolution (1970-1971), agriculture employed 69 per cent of workforce and shared about 42 per cent of national income (Table 24.1). As the green revolution progressed and spread, a sizeable proportion of labour force shifted from agriculture to non-agriculture sectors. Agriculture growth created backward and forward linkages leading to growth in employment in non-farm rural as well as urban sectors (Mellor and Lele 1973, Chadha 1986). However, the shift in labour force almost stopped somewhere between 1980-81 and 1990-1991. During 1980-81 to 2000-01, there was negligible shift in labour force from agriculture to non-agriculture whereas share of agriculture in national income reduced by one third.

The decline in share of agriculture in national income resulted from a faster rate of growth in non-agriculture, which is considered natural in the development process, but it did not translate into creation of jobs in non-agriculture sector to pull workforce from agriculture sector after 1980-81. The situation started worsening with the beginning of economic reforms in 1991. The economic reforms resulted in acceleration in growth rate of non-agriculture sector but growth rate in agriculture sector did not follow a secular trend (Figure 24.1). Only for some brief spell, the growth rate went high which was soon followed by a spell of low growth.

Table 24.1

Share of Agriculture and Non-agriculture Sectors in National Income and Workforce (%)

Year	*Share in National Income*		*Share in Workforce*	
	Agriculture	*Non-Agriculture*	*Agriculture*	*Non-Agriculture*
1950-51	51.81	48.19	68.85	31.15
1960-61	42.56	57.44	69.41	30.59
1970-71	41.95	58.05	69.36	30.64
1980-81	35.39	64.61	59.02	40.98
1990-91	29.02	70.98	58.38	41.62
2000-01	23.02	76.98	58.20	41.80
2010-11	18.21	81.79	54.59	45.41

Sources of basic data: 1. *National Accounts Statistics*, CSO, GoI. 2. *Agricultural Statistics at a Glance 2016*, Ministry of Agriculture and Farmers Welfare, GoI.

Disparities in Agricultural and Non-agricultural Income

A worker in agriculture sector earned one third of income of a worker in non-agriculture sector at the time of onset of green revolution. The ratio increased to 38 per cent in the initial phase of green revolution. However

Figure 24.1

Average Annual Growth Rate in Five Years Period in Agriculture and Non-agriculture Sectors at Constant Prices

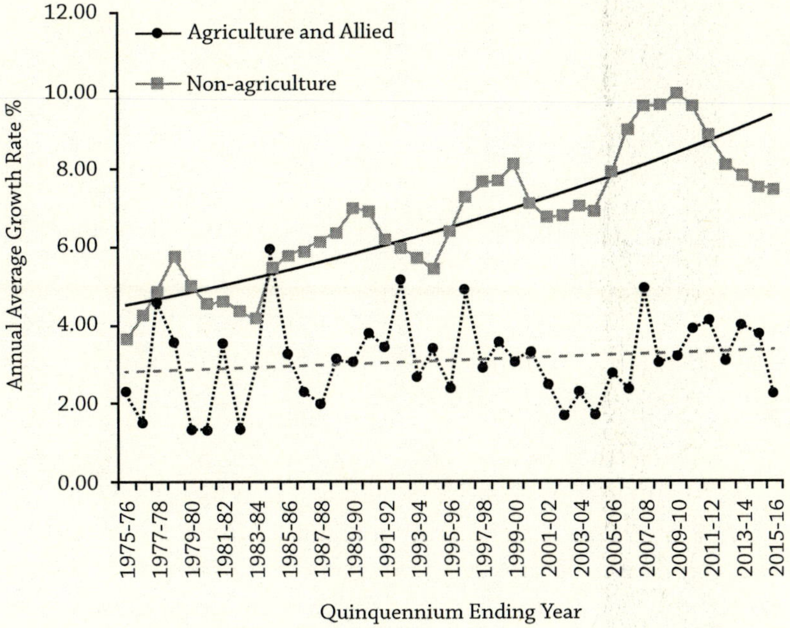

Source: National Accounts Statistics, CSO, GoI.

this trend of decline in disparity in sectoral income reversed somewhere during 1980s and income earned by an agriculture worker fell to just 29 per cent of non-agriculture worker by 1990-91. This has been the starting point for the beginning of agrarian distress in the country. The disparities between agriculture and non-agriculture income further worsened during 1990s (Figure 24.2).

The rise in income of non-agriculture workers put strong pressure on those working in agriculture sector to catch up with the standard of living of former and thus put pressure to raise consumption expenditure without commensurate increase in income. It is also important to note that in non-agriculture sector, the number and scale of production unit has risen sharply but the scale of agriculture production unit only got divided and became smaller.

Figure 24.2

Ratio of Income per Worker in Agriculture and Non-agriculture Sector at Current Prices

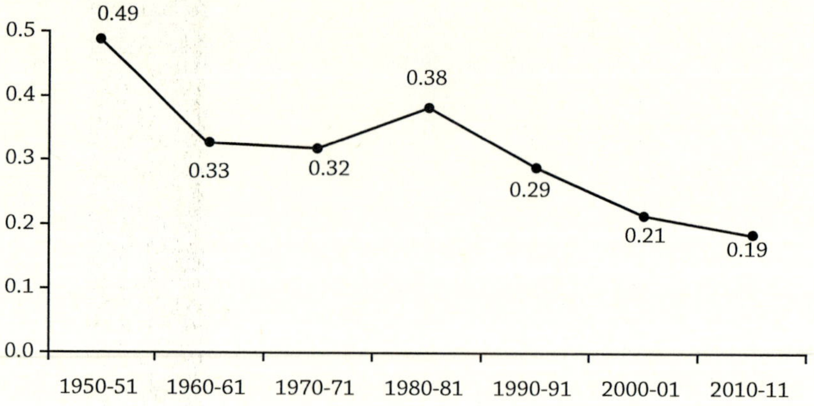

Source: National Accounts Statistics, CSO, GoI.

The terms of trade between sectors is another important factor in affecting welfare of farmers. Liberalisation and globalisation started during 1990s led to increase in integration of domestic prices with global prices which contributed strongly towards decline in terms of trade for agriculture during late 1990s and early 2000s.

Reforms and Sectoral Growth

One would like to know the reasons for acceleration in growth rate of non-agriculture sector and trendless and cyclical growth trajectory in agriculture. The reason for this is that a series of economic reforms were undertaken beginning 1991 to remove various types of controls, liberalise economy, attract private investments and promote globalisation. Some of these reforms, particularly globalisation and liberalisation of external trade subjected agriculture to international competition but the domestic reforms in agriculture remained patchy and piecemeal. After lot of pressure from researchers and thinkers, some reforms were undertaken during the years 2002 to 2004 which imparted some strength to Indian agriculture. These include:

1. Removal of (Licensing Requirements, Stock

Limits and Movement Restrictions) on Specified Foodstuffs Order, 2002 and 2003. As per this order wheat, paddy/rice, coarse grains, sugar, edible oilseeds and edible oils, pulses, *gur*, wheat products and hydrogenated vegetable oil or *vanaspathi* were removed from the list of Essential Commodities Act (ECA) (1955) and they shall not require a permit or licence for their trading, storage and movement.

2. Milk and Milk Product Order (MMPO) of 2002 modified MMPO of 1992 and removed restrictions on setting up of new capacity in milk processing and to do away with the concept of milkshed.
3. Removal of prohibition on futures trading in any commodity, in year 2003.

These reforms attracted much needed investments by private sector in dairy sector and in agricultural marketing. By the year 2005, 10 big corporate players entered into the system of agricultural marketing. This resulted in considerable increase in competition in agricultural market and farmers were able to get higher market price than MSP (minimum support price) for wheat and paddy in some states, where farm harvest prices often remained lower than MSP. This competition in primary market raised wholesale and retail prices of wheat followed by rice in the country. Increase in global prices and sharp shortfall in wheat output in the country in two successive years (2004-05 and 2005-06) also pulled domestic prices up. Ignoring these facts, it was argued by the officials in Ministry of Food that entry of private corporate players and grain stocked by them was the cause for surge in wheat prices. On this ground, reforms in Essential Commodities Act (ECA) to liberalise agriculture marketing were rolled back during 2006-2008 leading to exit of most of the big players from grain market (Chand 2013). So the situation of agri marketing was back to 2002 level and prices received by farmers in the grain markets was left to be determined with limited competition among traditional section of traders.

While some reforms were attempted in agricultural trade, they did not include reforms in agricultural marketing or transactions of farmers produce. One reason for this was that agricultural marketing is a state subject—it required reform by respective states. However, measures were initiated by the Central government to bring reforms in the system of agricultural market in states. A Model Act called the State Agricultural Produce Marketing (Development & Regulation) Act, 2003, was prepared and shared with all the states for implementation. Some incentives were also offered to states to adopt the Model Act to improve competitiveness of primary markets. The ground reality has been that except in states like Karnataka, various reforms have been considerably diluted and only partly implemented at state level. In some cases, new conditions were attached to reforms which defeated the very goal of reforms. Thus, while non agriculture sector was getting more and more competitive and getting benefits of new innovations in trade and commerce, agricultural marketing remained stuck in the old mould with farmers getting depressed prices in harvest season. The effect of this discriminatory approach of reforms towards agriculture became visible towards late 1990s which saw increase in number of farmers' suicides and it got quite serious in the beginning of 21st century.

Another, often less talked reason for build up of agrarian distress is ecological degradation and unsustainable use of water resources. To cope up with these stresses, farmers have been adopting more resource and capital intensive production. As the ecological limits cannot be stretched too far, the unsustainable use of natural resource system has been manifesting in various forms becoming more serious over time. Drying of water bodies, reduced flow of water in streams and rivers, declining groundwater level, frequent failure of bore wells in some parts of the country, are forcing more investment in irrigation, changes in crop pattern, and affecting yield. These changes ultimately affect farm income; in some cases shrinking natural resources destroy livelihood options.

Indicators of Agrarian Distress

It looks strange that despite so much discussion and writings on agrarian distress, quantitative indicators to assess the distress have not been developed. P. Sainath used the information on farmers suicides to draw attention of the country to the plight of farmers and farming. The data on suicides committed by various socio-economic groups and by gender are published regularly by National Crime Record Bureau since 1995. This data shows that number of farmers suicides followed a rising trend during 1995 to 2004. In these nine years, suicides committed by farmers (cultivators and agricultural labourers) increased by 70 per cent—from 10,720 to 18,241 (Figure 24.3). After peaking in year 2004, the number of farmers suicides started declining. The declining trend continued till year 2013 and shows a small increase during 2014. It will be interesting to find out how the trend in farmers suicides is associated with changes in agriculture sector.

Based on the information available in various studies and anecdotal evidence, it is observed that agrarian distress is closely associated with the level and growth of farm income. Further, the level and growth of farm income is determined by growth in value added in agriculture

Figure 24.3

Number of Farmers (Cultivators + Agri Labourers) Suicides according to NCRB Data

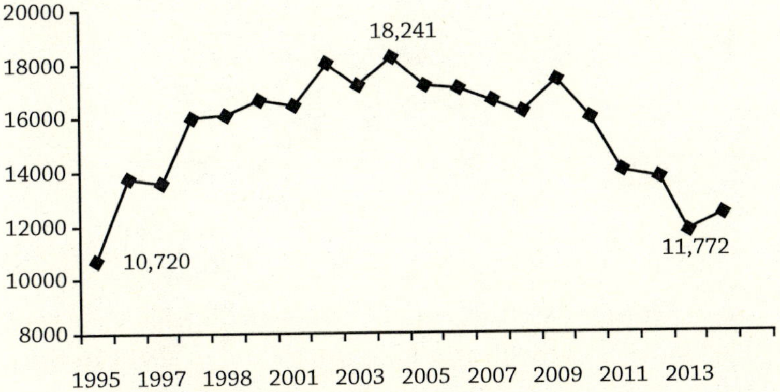

Source: Accidental Deaths and Suicides in India, National Crime Records Bureau, Ministry of Home Affairs, GOI, various Issues.

Figure 24.4

Five Yearly Moving Average of Annual Growth Rate in GDP Agriculture at Constant Prices of Year 2004-05

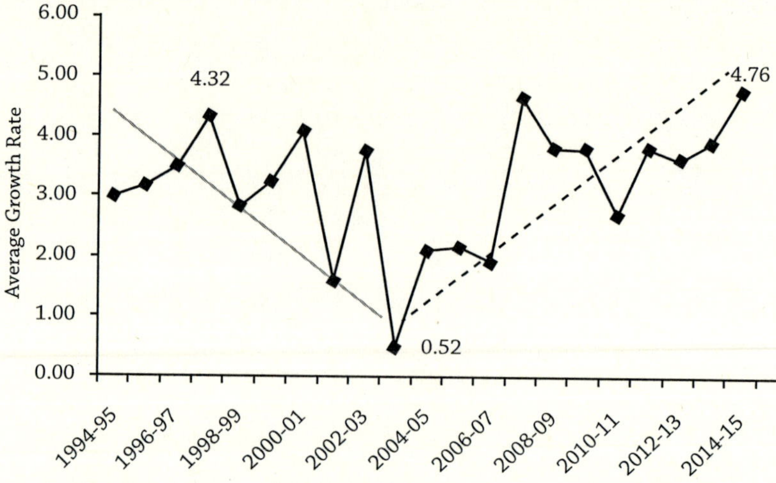

Source: *National Accounts Statistics*, CSO, GoI.

Figure 24.5

Terms of Trade: Prices Paid and Received by Agriculture Old and New Series

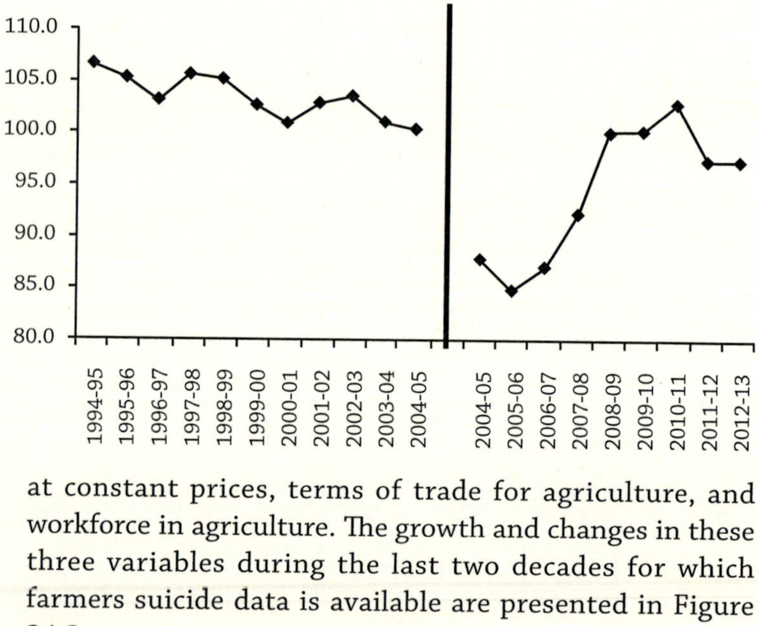

at constant prices, terms of trade for agriculture, and workforce in agriculture. The growth and changes in these three variables during the last two decades for which farmers suicide data is available are presented in Figure 24.3.

Figure 24.6

Workforce in Agriculture

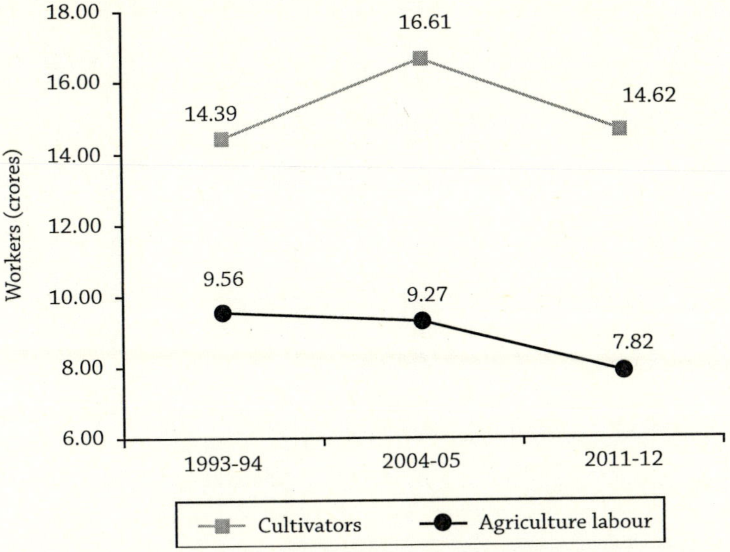

It comes out clearly from Figure 24.3, 24.4, 24.5 and 25.6 that: (i) farmers suicides increased when agriculture growth slowed down and declined when the growth rate went up (ii) suicides increased when terms of trade for agriculture deteriorated (1994-95 to 2004-05) and declined with the increase in relative prices of agricultural produce (2004-2005 to 2013-14) and (iii) farmers suicides increased when there was increase in workforce in agriculture and declined with the decrease in workforce. These three factors, which are moving closely with rise and fall in farmers suicides, are the three components of agricultural income (Chand et al. 2015). The net effect of changes in agriculture growth, terms of trade for agriculture and workers dependent on agriculture on income from agriculture is presented in Table 24.2. Income of agricultural labourers and farmers at current prices, deflated by CPIAL (consumer price index for agriculture labourers) increased at the rate of 2.76 per cent per year during 1994-95 to 2004-05 and then accelerated to 4.74 per cent per year during 2004-05 to 2013-14. This evidence confirms that income is crucial to alleviate agrarian distress. Therefore, all factors which contribute to rise in income should be rigorously followed to address agrarian distress.

Table 24.2

Growth Rate in Real Agriculture Income during the Rising and Falling Phase of Agrarian Distress

Period	Total Sectoral Income	Income Per Worker
1993-94 to 2004-05	2.76	2.24
2004-05 to 2013-14	4.74	7.25
2014-15	-1.68	--

Distress at Household Level

At household level, agrarian distress develops and worsens under two types of circumstances. One, when the income of a farmer is chronically lower than his family expenditure and a farmer borrows money from some source to meet the gap. Expenditure on social ceremonies and illness of family members, which is not part of regular household expenditure, are also important reasons to borrow money, particularly from non-institutional sources, and to fall under debt. The accumulated debt in such situations becomes so large that it becomes impossible to repay it from the household income. Some farmers are forced to sell a part or whole of farm land and other household assets to repay the loan and to meet the expenditure on social ceremonies. Some of the farmers, who do not find any way to get out of this situation, are forced to undergo humiliation as a defaulter and are unable to face their family and society. The loss of honour due to default to repay the loan and the sensitivity towards the ensuing humiliation, push some farmers to the extreme step of ending their life.

The second situation involves a sudden loss in income due to failure of crop, or, price crash for the major income earning crops grown by a farmer, making it difficult to run the household affairs. In the absence of crop insurance or adequate relief, crop failure can have a devastating effect on farm income. Further, there is no mechanism to escape effect of price crash. Any loss of income of severe nature on account of crop failure or market failure becomes a source of distress and frustration, in some cases leading to the extreme step. This is more pertinent in the case of high value commercial crops. A year or two of high prices attract many farmers to put excessive resources under risky commercial crops. The sudden increase in supply is often met with violent price crash. Without risk coverage, which is unknown to most of the Indian farmers, the price volatility can have a killing effect on farm income and farmers.

Another factor that leads to household level distress is consumption expenditure. As it is well known, consumption basket is expanding and expenditure on items of social consumption such as education and health is rising. There is also a big increase in expenditure on social ceremonies. Some farmers spend on such ceremonies beyond their means. Strong culture is growing in rural area towards profligate expenditure on social ceremonies and conspicuous consumption. As agriculture income often falls short of meeting such expenditure, farmers are forced to borrow money from private sources at exhorbitant interest rate.

Strategy

The response as well as demand to address agrarian distress focus mainly on treating the symptoms and not doing much for curing the situation. The efforts to address this depressing and difficult situation are mostly directed towards easier options like relief, compensation and social safety measures. Demand is also made from time to time to raise farm subsidies, offer higher prices for farm produce and ensure minimum income to the farmers. Providing relief to the sector or households who suffer erosion in their income due to events like crop failure, market failure, and tragedy like suicides, is important short term measures, but, it does not offer solution for the problem. It is also noted that despite increase in safety net and relief measures in recent years, agrarian distress has been spreading and becoming more severe. Therefore, there is a need to do a rethink on the responses to agrarian distress and follow a development strategy that can address the root causes and prevent agrarian distress in the country.

A thinking is developing in the country that agrarian distress can be addressed by providing compensation, relief, free or subsidised inputs, liberal financial support to farmers. These measures are important to provide succour and immediate help to those severely affected by distress, like farmers suicide, crop damage. Such help must be provided quickly but it cannot make agriculture sector distress free. Unfortunately, the quick fix and populist measures are being emphasised more than the development strategy. The reason is that competitive populism followed in the country has created strong 'sops psyche' and weakened 'development psyche'. This is evident from the resources we allocate to subsidies and investment in agriculture. The amount spent on subsidies for agriculture sector by the Centre government alone is much higher than the amount spent on development of infrastructure, that create base for long run growth, by Central government and all the states taken together. When state level subsidies are added to Central subsidy, their level becomes further higher than the resources allocated for infrastructure development in agriculture.

Raising farm income through increase in productivity require increase in use of modern inputs, irrigation and new knowledge and technology. There is a sop route and there is a development route to raise use of modern inputs and irrigation. The sop route is to give subsidy to farmers on seed, fertiliser, chemicals growth hormone and such inputs. Anything that is to sell at a below market price has a hazard of rent seeking and is prone to dilution in quality, as seen recently in case of subsidy on seed and chemicals in cotton in Punjab that caused widespread damage to cotton crop by white fly. Anecdotal and oral evidence indicate that a large chunk of subsidies on seed, equipment, chemicals is siphoned off by dealers and department officials and farmers get small share and inferior product. The development approach is to promote competitive market and to monitor and regulate quality. Similarly, for irrigation, the populist approach is free power leading to over-exploitation and uneconomic use of water, higher investment in submersible pump going beyond the reach of small farmers. In contrast, reliable and assured power supply and use of modern irrigation technologies lead to sustainable use of water.

On output side, demand is rising for effective and higher MSP for more crops in all states. The common perception is that MSP is higher than market price. This is true only in some cases. In a large number of cases, farmers get prices higher than MSP even under existing market imperfections. Enforcing MSP in such cases will not only distort market, it will also pull down prices. The alternative option of raising price realisation by farmers is to raise their share in price paid by consumers as is envisaged under e-NAM (national agriculture market). The electronic platform and unified NAM and some other market reforms can fetch much higher prices to the farmers, than MSP, by increased competition, better spatial integration of prices, reduced number of intermediaries and development of value chain. Detailed discussion on various sources for raising farmers income and doubling it by the year 2022 is provided in Chand (2017).

Recent Government Initiatives

During the last two years, the government has announced a number of initiatives for the development of agriculture which focus on production, efficiency, market, production risk, cost, price realisation by farmers, scale factor, and non-farm employment. These are listed below:

1. Pradhan Mantri Krishi Sinchayee Yojana (PMKSY)—It includes several components like *Har khet ko pani*, more crop per drop, renewal, renovation and repair of traditional water bodies, watershed development, convergence with MGNREGA, command area development.
2. Revamped and enlarged crop insurance scheme.

3. Soil health card.
4. Direct benefit transfer to replace input subsidies: pilot on reforms.
5. e-NAM for better prices and fair deal for farmers in market.
6. 100 per cent foreign investment in processed food retailing provided they are manufactured in India.
7. National Rurban Mission.
8. Reforms in agricultural markets.
9. Model Land Lease Law prepared by NITI Aayog.
10. Skill India Mission.
11. Startups in agriculture.

These are not sops but development initiatives to strengthen agriculture and to put it on sound growth path and make it attractive to farmers. The initiatives also include measures to shift workforce from farm sector to non-farm sector.

The big question is to make these initiatives deliver and this require strong collaboration and cooperation from States for these initiatives. The Central government can achieve some milestones in manufacturing and services on its own but any major success in agriculture require ideas, initiatives and resources from the Centre and their implementation by the States and with the contribution from the States.

Conclusion

Agrarian distress cannot be removed by doubling farm subsidies, raising MSP, and expanding MGNREGA, or food subsidies. The sustainable way to address this is to undertake development measures and policy reforms which can lead to fast growth in income per farmer.

Disclaimer: Views expressed in the paper are personal.

Note: A slightly different version of this paper was used for 23rd Dr B.P. Pal Memorial Lecture, Indian Agricultural Research Institute, 26 May 2016, New Delhi.

References

Chadha, G.K. (1986). "The Off-farm Economic Structure of Agriculturally Growing Regions: A Study of Indian Punjab", in R.T. Shand (ed.), *Off-farm Employment in the Development of Rural Asia.* Vol. 2 Canberra: Australian National University.

Chand, Ramesh (2017). "Doubling Farmers Income: Rationale, Strategy, Prospects and Action Plan", *NITI Policy Paper* No. 1/2017. New Delhi: National Institution for Transforming India, Government of India.

————. (2016). "Why Doubling Farm Income by 2022 is Possible", *Indian Express* (The ideas page), 15 April.

————. (2012). "Development Policies and Agricultural Markets", *Economic and Political Weekly, Review of Rural Affairs* 47(52): 53-63.

Chand, Ramesh, Raka Saxena and Simmi Rana (2015). "Estimates and Analysis of Farm Income in India, 1983-84 to 2011-12", *Economic and Political Weekly* L(22): 139-45, 30 May.

Guruswamy, Mohan (n.d.). "Look at the Issue Clearly, Farmer Suicides are Driven more by Psychology than Economics", Available at: *http://www.hindustantimes.com/analysis/look-at-the-issue-clearly-farmer-suicides-are-driven-more-by-psychology-than-economics/story- cESmrhVIYAOtCmSeDdneYJ.html*, accessed on 11.4.2017.

Gulati, Ashok and Shweta Saini (2016). "From Plate to Plough: Raising Farmers' Income by 2022", *The Indian Express*, 28 March.

Mellor, J.W., and U.J. Lele. (1973). "Growth Linkages of the New Food Grain Technologies", *Indian Journal of Agricultural Economics* 18(1): 35-55.

25

Emerging Water Crisis in India

Key Issues and Way Forward

ASHOK GULATI and PRITHA BANERJEE

Introduction

In the last two years, viz., 2014 and 2015, India faced back to back droughts. As a result, growth in agri-GDP (gross domestic product) collapsed to 0.5 per cent (average of FY15 and FY16), even below the rate of population growth of 1.4 per cent. Over that period, Maharashtra's Marathwada region, especially the Latur district, became somewhat synonymous with acute water crisis. The Marathwada region was facing severe drought and water in the reservoirs went down to less than 6 per cent of normal. The situation became precarious and Section 144 had to be imposed in Latur to keep law and order in place over water. Soon after, special trains carrying water ("*Jal doot*") were sent to the region. The pressure became so intense that the High Court had to intervene and asked for the upcoming IPL cricket matches to be held outside Maharashtra in order to save 60 lakh litres of water!

This back-to-back drought exposed the vulnerable water situation in 250 districts (out of 678, or almost 37%) in India. The situation was not totally new for India, but it did expose the strategic gaps in India's quest for development and food security. Wisdom lies in converting this type of a crisis situation into ushering major structural reforms in India's water sector, particularly where larger chunk of it is being used, that is, agriculture.

However, before one does that, it would be useful to understand the overall water situation in India, how it has been evolving over the recent past, and how it is likely to be in the coming decades.

India, like many other countries in South Asia, is going to be a water scarce country. In the last 50 years, per capita availability of water decreased by 70 per cent in South Asia, with India's per capita availability decreasing from about 5,200 cubic meters (m^3) in 1,951 to 1588 m^3 in 2010 (Varma 2011). Most of the water scarcity in India, unfortunately, is economic in nature and not physical.[1] This also indicates that our irrigation systems are not meeting the needs of farmers. This is clear from the fact that even after nearly 70 years of independence, only 46 per cent of India's NSA (net sown area) is irrigated. Much of the country's agriculture is still dependent on erratic rainfalls.

It has been observed during the times of green revolution (from late 1960s through 1970s) that with the application of HYV (high-yielding variety) seeds, fertiliser, and water, the productivity of wheat and rice can be increased substantially. Since these three inputs have to be applied together to get the desired results, it is difficult to separate the effects of these three on productivity, but the pivotal role played by irrigation in this cannot be denied (Gulati and Narayanan 2003). Thus, to ensure food security for the growing population in India, it is critical that enough water is available to farmers and it is used wisely so that agricultural productivity can be raised in a sustainable manner.

In this paper, we try to point out some of the key issues that are ailing this sector and based on our empirical analysis, we also suggest remedial measures that hopefully can make this sector deliver efficiently, equitably, and in a sustainable manner.

1. There is economic water scarcity when human, institutional, and financial capitals limit access to water even though water is available in nature locally to meet human demand. Less than 25 per cent of water is drawn from rivers for human purposes. There is physical scarcity of water when water resources development approaches or exceeds sustainable limits.

The paper is arranged as follows: section 2 discusses water resources and irrigation sector in India. Section 3 talks about key issues in the water (irrigation) sector. In section 4, we discuss and critically evaluate the approach of the Central government to solve the problems and whether they are enough. The last section suggests number of policy options to move forward with a view to ensure efficiency, equity, and sustainability in the use of water resources of India.

Water Resources and Irrigation Status in India

According to the estimates of the Central Water Commission (CWC 1993), the average annual water resources potential in the country is 1,869 BCM (billion cubic meter). Due to topographic, hydrological, and other constraints, the utilisable water is estimated at 1,123 BCM which comprises 690 BCM of surface water and 433 BCM of replenishable groundwater resources.

A country is termed water stressed if the annual per capita availability of water is less than 1,700 m^3 and water scarce if the same is less than 1,000 m^3. By that definition, India is already a water-stressed country and is going to face water scarcity as per its population projections. The average annual per capita availabilities of water in the country considering the population as per the 2001 Census, 2011 Census, and the population projections for the year 2025 and 2050 are 1816 m^3, 1545 m^3, 1340 m^3, and 1140 m^3, respectively.[2] Keeping in mind the need of the growing population, it is necessary that efficient use of water is ensured. As almost 78 per cent of the water is used in the irrigation sector, optimising water use in this sector is of prime importance.

Let us now focus our attention on the status of irrigation in the country to determine whether it is adequate to meet the needs of producing enough food, feed, and fibre for its people.

---

2. UNICEF 2013.

Ultimate Irrigation Potential

Given the current levels of technology, the UIP (ultimate irrigation potential) of India is estimated to be 139.89 million hectare (Mha).[3] Of this, 58.47 Mha (42%) is from MMI (major and medium irrigation) and the rest (81.43 Mha) is from minor irrigation. Of 81.43 Mha of minor UIP, 64.09 Mha is from groundwater and only 17.34 Mha is from surface irrigation (Figure 25.1).

Figure 25.1

Share of Major, Medium and Minor Irrigation in Ultimate Irrigation Potential

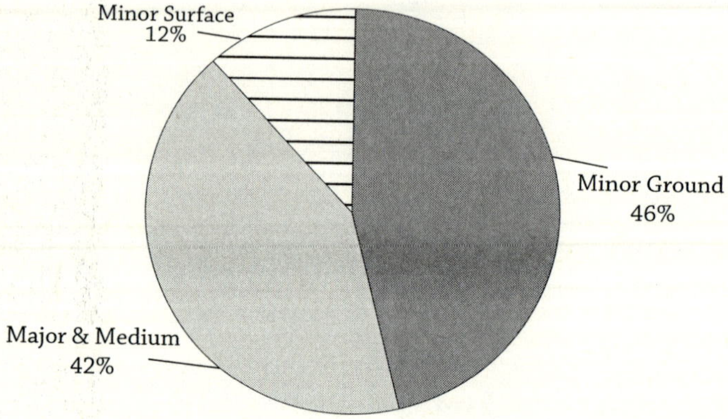

Source: Constructed using the data in *Water and Related Statistics 2015*, Central Water Commission.

Irrigation Potential Created and Utilised

Of the total 139.9 Mha UIP, 81 per cent or 113.5 Mha potential has already been created. Unfortunately, however, the potential utilised is still low. Till the end of the Eleventh Plan, only 87.9 Mha (provisional figure) of irrigated area has been utilised.[4] Appendix A-25.1 gives the plan-wise cumulative irrigation potential created and utilised in India. In the late 1960s, the gap between IPC (irrigation potential created) and IPU (irrigation potential utilised) started increasing, which became wider in the

3. If inter-linking of rivers is taken into account, the UIP is likely to go up to 170 Mha.

4. *Source*: *Water and Related Statistics 2015*, Working Group Report to 12th FYP—Minor Irrigation and Watershed Management.

late 1980s and early 1990s. However, recently, the gap has become significantly wide (Figure 25.2, Appendix A-25.1). This is a matter of concern. On the one hand, Indian farmers are heavily dependent on rainfall, while on the other, irrigation potential that has been created is not fully utilised. The reasons behind this might be lack of CAD (command area development) as also water guzzler crops occupying more area than initially planned in these projects, which reduces larger area planned for lightly irrigated crops.

Figure 25.2

Gap between Irrigation Potential Created and Utilised

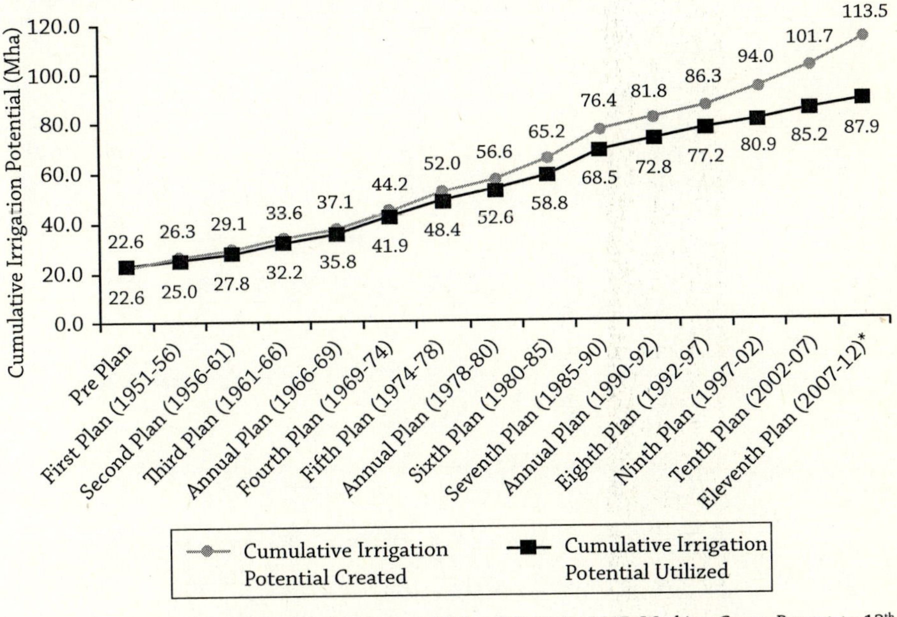

Source: Constructed from the data in *Water and Related Statistics 2015*, Working Group Report to 12th FYP-Minor Irrigation and Watershed Management.

Net Irrigated Area and Net Sown Area

Since 2000-01, the NIA (net irrigated area) has increased from 55.20 Mha to 65.26 Mha in 2011-12 but still it is only 46 per cent of the net sown area (Figure 25.3). GIA (gross irrigated area) increased from 76.19 Mha to 91.53 Mha over the same period. GIA is about 47 per cent of the gross cropped area. The intensity of irrigated cropping has increased marginally over the same period, from 138 per cent to 140 per cent.

Thus, there is still a lot of improvement to be done on that front. With climate change becoming a reality, which may lead to increasing frequency and intensity of droughts, there is an urgent need to focus on the fact that there is not enough irrigation in India and most of the farmers are dependent on erratic rainfall.

Figure 25.3

Change in Net Irrigated Area and Net Sown Area Over Last Decade

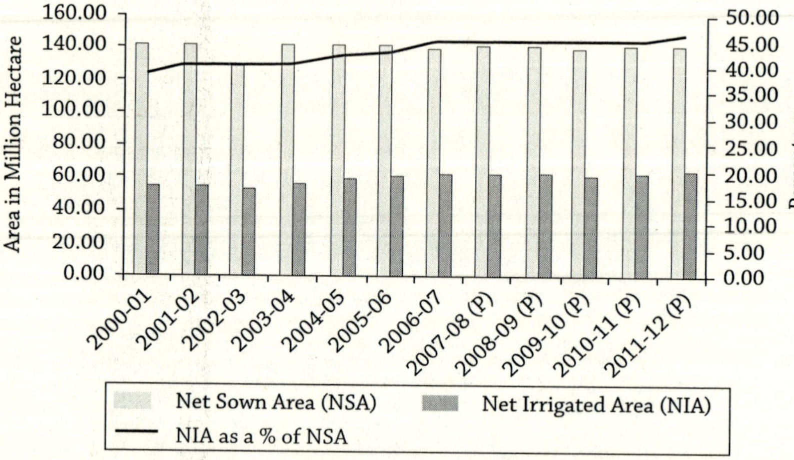

Source: Constructed using the data in *Agricultural Statistics at a Glance 2014*.

Key Issues in the Water (Irrigation) Sector

Water used in irrigation comes primarily from two sources: surface water (from canals, tanks etc) and groundwater (from wells and tube wells). Both the sectors are facing many problems arising primarily from policy decisions taken in the country. Key issues faced by the water (irrigation) sector in India are discussed below.

Low Pricing

In order to incentivise enough water in the fields, water charges have been kept at a low level. For some states, the water charge has not been changed since decades. For example, for flow irrigation, water rates have not been changed in Kerala since 1974, in West Bengal since 1977, in Tamil Nadu (TN) since 1987, and in undivided Uttar Pradesh (UP) since 1995. The most recent revision was done in Punjab in 2010. Since with passage of time, both the capital cost and working expenses of flow irrigation have increased significantly, the gross receipts in relation to the cost incurred are still at a very low level. Moreover, keeping water charges low for decades has not incentivised judicious use of water. Thus, inefficiency in water use has also become a pressing concern.

This again is only the surface water side. Low pricing is creating problems on groundwater side as well. SEBs (state electricity boards) supply power to the agricultural sector at a lower price than that supplied to other sectors. The price that is charged from the agricultural consumers is much less than the cost of power supply as well. For example, in 2013-14, the average cost of power supply in India was 593 paise per kWh (kilowatt-hour). However, SEBs charged only 183 paise per kWh (or, only 31% of the average cost of supply) from the agricultural consumers. They try to cross subsidise by charging a higher price to industrial and commercial consumers. However, most of the SEBs could not make up for the loss through this process. Almost all of them have incurred commercial losses without subsidy over past few years. The two exceptions are Delhi and West Bengal.[5]

There is a provision in the proposed amendments in Tariff Policy first announced by the Government of India in 2006 which states that:

> A higher level of subsidy could be considered to support poorer farmers of the region where adverse groundwater table condition requires larger quantity of electricity for irrigation purposes subject to suitable

5. Delhi is making commercial profit without subsidy since 2008-09 till 2011-2012 while West Bengal is making the profit even without subsidy at least from 2007-08 till projected estimates for 2013-14. With subsidy, Gujarat is making profit at least since 2007-08 till date and Karnataka is making profit since 2010-11. In 2013-14, Bihar is also expected to make marginal commercial profit with subsidy.

restrictions to ensure maintenance of groundwater levels and sustainable groundwater usage[6]

That is, in the poorer areas where groundwater levels are low, they would require using more electricity to extract groundwater from such lower levels. Therefore, the governments there are allowed to charge lesser tariffs for the agricultural sector. Punjab, TN, and Himachal Pradesh (HP) have taken this chance and have announced free power for the agricultural consumers. However, this step, even though taken with farmers' welfare in mind and not for political gain, has led to a problem in the groundwater situation which will be discussed later in this section.

Low Water Use Efficiency

Till date, the most commonly used method for irrigation in India is flood irrigation which has very low water use efficiency (65%). A country like India, which is moving fast towards water scarcity with increasing population, cannot afford to continue the use of inefficient ways to irrigate agricultural land. Irrigation efficiencies of various methods are presented in the Table 25.1.

Table 25.1

Different Irrigation Methods and their Efficiencies

Irrigation Methods	*Efficiency (%)*
Conveyance	
Through unlined canal for surface water	55-60
Through lined canal for surface water	70-75
Application for both surface and groundwater	
Flood irrigation	65
Furrow irrigation	80
Sprinkler	85
Drip	90
Overall efficiency for surface water system	30-65
Overall efficiency for groundwater system	65-75

Source: *Guidelines for Improving Water Use Efficiency in Irrigation, Domestic and Industrial Sectors*, CWC, 2014.

6. From Amendments Proposed in Tariff Policy, Ministry of Power, Government of India, accessed from *http://powermin.nic.in/upload/Amendments_proposed_in_the_Tariff_Policy.pdf* on 6 November 2015.

Using drips and sprinklers to apply groundwater is supposed to be more efficient. However, even our groundwater irrigation cannot reach the maximum potential efficiency. The main cause behind this is supplying power to the agricultural sector at highly subsidised prices which does not incentivise optimum use of groundwater.

High Cost of Surface Irrigation

Since independence, massive investments have been made to create canal irrigation. In the country's green revolution belt, irrigation has taken a driver's seat along with fertiliser and HYV seeds. Although econometrically it is difficult to separate the effect of those three on foodgrain production, the pivotal role of irrigation has been recognised by many studies. According to Svendsen and Gulati (1995),

> In case of canal irrigation, the nation spent more than ₹600 billion (at 1988-89 prices) between 1951 and 1990, taking the irrigation potential created from this source from 8.6 million hectares to about 32 million hectare.

While this increase is commendable, very few studies tried to find out the cost at which it was achieved. Most of the studies, be it Dhawan (1997) or CWC, find out the per hectare cost of major and medium irrigation by dividing the cost incurred in that year by the IPC. The Planning Commission also used to produce per hectare cost of MMI by this method. While that can give us an idea about the cost, there are two main problems in calculating the cost this way. First, as they are reported at current prices, they do not consider the inflation; and second, there is a gestation lag between the time at which the investment is made and the time at which the potential is created. Although, Dhawan (1997) considered costs at constant prices to deal with the inflation part, the gestation lag part is not captured in his writings.

Gulati et al. (1994) presented a methodological framework for addressing these problems. To arrive at the actual capital cost for MMI projects in India, they considered the inflation part and the gestation lag part as well as the SDR (social discount rate) to account for gestation lags. To find out the capital costs for MMI projects for the last decade or so, we follow this method to some extent. To adjust for the inflation part, we take the WPI (wholesale price index). We consider gestation lag as 12 years. According to Sharma et al. (1991) and Kula (2004), SDR for India can be considered 2.0 per cent and 5.2 per cent, respectively. We have calculated the capital cost for three SDRs, 2.0 per cent, 4.0 per cent, and 6 per cent for different states and regions of India. These are compared with the costs estimated without lags and SDR adjustments, but adjusted for inflation (Appendix A-25.2).

It is interesting to note that the all-India cost of creating one hectare of irrigation potential through major and medium schemes came to ₹3.51 lakh at 2014-15 prices, as against ₹1.72 lakh/ha in Gujarat, ₹1.62 lakh/ha in Bihar (including Jharkhand) and ₹1.58 lakh/ha in

Table 25.2

Gross Receipts and Components of Working Expenses

Year	Gross Receipts	Working Expenses (Crore ₹)			Direction and Administration as % of Total Working Expenses	Gross Receipts as % of Total Working Expenses
		Direction and Administration	Other	Total		
2000-01	754	993	7769	8762	11.34	8.60
2001-02	652	1397	6843	8239	16.95	7.92
2002-03	783	1445	7401	8846	16.33	8.86
2003-04	1048	1432	4862	6294	22.75	16.65
2004-05	1264	1557	5462	7018	22.18	18.01
2005-06	1195	2012	6204	8216	24.49	14.54
2006-07	1505	2442	7162	9604	25.43	15.67
2007-08	2045	3101	8798	11899	26.06	17.19
2008-09	1904	3565	8632	12197	29.23	15.61
2009-10	2351	4655	10266	14921	31.20	15.76
2010-11	2598	5505	11859	17364	31.70	14.96
2011-12	3893	6111	12610	18720	32.64	20.80

Source: CWC.

UP (including Uttarakhand). In Madhya Pradesh (MP) (including Chhattisgarh), which has one of the largest untapped potential of surface irrigation, the cost was ₹1.92 lakh/ha. In contrast, on the high end of the scale were states like TN with ₹12.9 lakh/ha and Maharashtra with ₹11.18 lakh/ha. These are costs per hectare of potential created. Since the gap between potential created and potential utilised has been increasing, the cost per hectare of potential utilised will obviously be much higher.

This is the capital cost side of surface irrigation. The working expenses side is also not free from problems. O&M (operation and maintenance) costs or working expenses are important to maintain efficiency of the created potential. However, almost one-third of working expenses is spent on direction and administration. The revenue receipts from pricing of water covers only about one-fifth (21%) of the total working expenses, and capital costs are deemed to be sunk costs for ever (Table 25.2).

Depleting Groundwater

With an intention to make groundwater more accessible to the resource-poor farmers, SEBs supply electricity to the agricultural consumers at a subsidised rate (in some cases, at zero prices). Since agricultural consumption is not metered in all the states and it is measured as a residual, it is generally assumed that 30 per cent of the power supplied to agriculture is diverted to other sectors such as household.[7] Assuming we calculate power subsidy to the agricultural sector,[8] we observe that at current prices, it increased from ₹16,852 crore in 2000-2001 to ₹46,892 crore in 2013-14 (Advance Prediction–AP). The increase is almost 2.8 times in current prices.

---

7. The 30 per cent overestimation assumption is made in 1988 domestic support notification to the World Trade Organization (WTO). It is also mentioned in the Annual Report on the Working of State Power Utilities and Electricity Departments 2011-12 that, "It is estimated that about 30 to 40 per cent of the consumption shown against the agricultural sector is an overestimate" (p.9).

8. Measured by multiplying the difference between cost of supply and agricultural tariff with the agricultural sales.

In 2014-15 prices, the increase is only 1.3 times: from ₹36,733 crore in 2000-01 to ₹47,842 crore in 2013-14 (AP) (Appendix A-25.4). Increased subsidy due to very low prices was not helpful in incentivising optimum use of groundwater. This, in fact, is the main cause behind depletion of groundwater resources in some parts of the country.

National Aeronautics and Space Administration (NASA) raised alarming signals on the rampant depletion of groundwater at the rate of one foot per year in the north-western India (in the period 2002-2008 when north-western India experienced almost normal rainfall and southern India experienced above average rainfall). Over the period, the north-western region saw a decrease of more than 109 cubic kilometer of groundwater. This rate of depletion is obviously not sustainable.

This situation matches with the situation of the stage of groundwater development as found by the Central Ground Water Board (CGWB) in various administrative blocks of India. The stage of groundwater development is defined as annual groundwater draft in an assessed administrative unit (blocks/*talukas*/*mandals*/districts) expressed as a percentage of annual groundwater availability in that unit. There are four stages of groundwater development depending on the percentage, namely, safe, semi-critical, critical, and overexploited. According to Dynamic Groundwater Resources 2011, out of 6,607 assessed units, 1,071 units were overexploited, 217 units were critical, 697 units were semi-critical, and the rest were safe. There were also 92 assessment units which were completely saline (Figure 25.4).

There is significant state-wise variation in the stages of groundwater development. In the north-western states like Punjab, Haryana, and Rajasthan; more than 80 per cent of administrative units are marked as overexploited, critical, or semi critical. The stages of groundwater development in Punjab, Haryana, and Rajasthan are 172 per cent, 133 per cent, and 137 per cent, respectively. In the states of TN, HP, and UP, and the UTs of Daman and Diu, Puducherry, and Lakshadweep, the stages of groundwater development were greater than 70 per cent. In the rest of the states and UTs, stages of groundwater development were less than 70 per cent. That is, on an average, those states could be categorised as 'safe'. Among these 'safe' states, however, Karnataka and Gujarat, with the stage of groundwater developments of 64 per cent and 67 per cent were very close to crossing the 70 per cent mark of being semi-critical (Appendix A-25.3).

Lack of Focus on Demand Side Management

It is no denying that there is a serious problem in the demand side management of groundwater. There are two prominent examples. One is that of rice in Punjab and the other is of sugarcane in Maharashtra. Rice is a water-intensive crop. A kilogram of rice needs almost 5,000 litres of irrigation water in the Punjab-Haryana belt. Rice is the main summer crop in Punjab and Haryana, where the groundwater level is already falling at an alarming rate.

The issue of sugarcane production in Maharashtra is another example of lack of demand-side management. Historically, Eastern UP and Bihar used to be the centre for sugarcane production since they are endowed with ample water. However, the licensing policy of prioritising cooperatives and to some extent necessary supply of electricity for sugar factories brought sugarcane cultivation to an area which does not have ample water resources. Now, sugarcane is produced in only 4 per cent of Maharashtra's area but takes up two-thirds of its irrigation water. Almost 100 per cent of Maharashtra's sugarcane area is irrigated whereas overall GIA as a percentage of GCA in Maharashtra was only 18 per cent in recent years. That means other crops do not get sufficient irrigation cover. Cotton, for example, in Maharashtra has only 3 per cent of its area irrigated. This is despite the fact that cotton needs just four to five rounds of irrigation while sugarcane is flooded with 25 to 30 rounds of irrigation. This tendency of using up larger portion of water resources for only one crop is neither very efficient, nor equitable, nor sustainable. In Gujarat, 57 per cent of

Figure 25.4

Categorisation of Groundwater Assessment Units

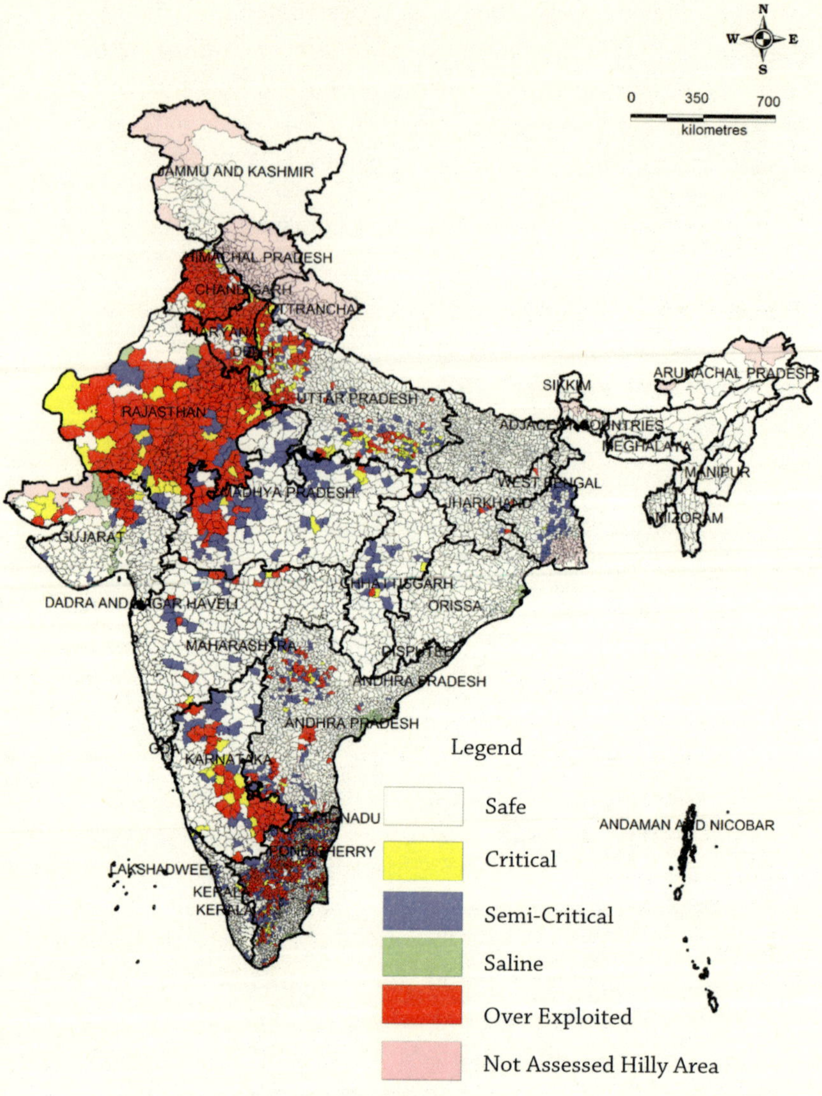

Source: Dynamic Groundwater Resources of India (As on 31st March 2011).

the cotton area gets irrigation and therefore the yield of cotton in Gujarat is almost double that in Maharashtra.

Approach of the Government and Harsh Reality

The current government, on many occasions has mentioned its priorities for the well-being of farmers.

Considering the fact that out of 140 Mha of NSA in India, only about 46 per cent or 65 Mha is irrigated, the government, with the objective of increasing irrigated cultivation, has announced Pradhan Mantri Krishi Sinchayee Yojana (PMKSY).

There are many existing schemes with the objective of enhancing irrigated area since proper irrigation is a main requirement to increase agricultural productivity. However, they have not been successful in increasing irrigated area at the desired pace thus leaving majority of farmers dependent on erratic rains. It is against this background that the scheme of PMKSY was initiated in 2014-15 keeping in consideration the importance of water and its efficient use in agriculture. This scheme is expected to provide an 'end to end' solution in irrigation supply chain (water resources, distribution network, and efficient on-farm use).

PMKSY has four programme components under three ministries namely, Ministry of Agriculture (Department of Agriculture and Cooperation), Ministry of Rural Development (Department of Land Resources) and Ministry of Water Resources, River Development and Ganga Rejuvenation. The components are:

- Accelerated Irrigation Benefit Programme (AIBP);
- PMKSY (*har khet ko pani*): this includes command area development; strengthening and creation of distribution network from source to the farm; and repair, restoration, and renovation of water bodies;
- PMKSY (per drop more crop): this includes programme management, preparation of State/District Irrigation Plans, approval of annual action plan, and monitoring; promoting precision water application devices like drips, sprinklers, pivots, and rain-guns in the farm (Jal Sinchan); construction of micro irrigation structures like tube wells and dug wells;
- PMKSY (watershed development; erstwhile Integrated Watershed Management Programme, or IWMP).

An outlay of ₹50,000 crore was announced for this project for the next five years, that is, from FY16 to FY20, the total allocation for FY17 being ₹5,767 crore.

However, two prominent questions arise. First is whether the Central government is allocating more for increase of irrigation than what they were before as claimed. To answer that, one has to see which old projects have been included in PMKSY. The old projects clubbed with PMKSY are as follows:

- Accelerated Irrigation Benefit and Flood Management Programme or, AIBFMP. This consists of four components.
  - AIBP and National Projects,
  - Command Area Development and Water Management (CAD&WM),
  - Flood Management Programme (FMP), and
  - Repair, Renovation, and Restoration of water bodies (RRR); and
- Integrated Watershed Management Programme.

Apart from that, PMKSY has allocations under the Ministry of Agriculture and Ministry of Water Resources, River Development and Ganga Rejuvenation also. The 12th Plan outlay (FY13-FY17) for AIBFMP alone was ₹86,435 crore (₹55,200 crore, ₹15,000 crore, ₹10,000 crore, and ₹6235 crore, respectively for AIBP, CAD&WM, FMP, and RRR, respectively) against five-year outlay of ₹50,000 crore for PMKSY as a whole in FY16. Also, if one compares budgeted and actual expenditures for the schemes for last three years with a budgeted figure of FY17, one can see that there has been, in fact, a sizeable decrease in terms of budgeted figures. In comparison with actual figures or revised estimates also, the announcement of ₹5,767 crore (budgeted) for the current financial year is less than what it was for the last three years (except for FY16, from which the budget estimate has undergone minor increase) (Figure 25.5). True, the current budget mentions that ₹12,517 crore is allocated through budgetary support and market borrowings; it is not clear whether this support is for the Ministry of Water Resources as a whole, or PMKSY or only for AIBP. Either ways, the allocation is less than what is mentioned as 'required' in the current budget speech.

The BE (budget estimate) for PMKSY in FY17 is 31 per cent, 43 per cent, and 109 per cent, respectively of BE for FY14 and FY15 and FY16. If we consider actual expenditure for FY14, FY15, and RE (revised estimate) for FY16, BE for PMKSY is 83 per cent, 103 per cent, and 76 per cent of them, respectively. One can see that the increase in actual or REs has happened only once in the last three years and the BE has increased marginally in the current year after decreasing for the last three years. And now, we have a lesser BE for a scheme (the allocation through market borrowing is not clear) which is supposed to be more extensive with the explicit goal of supplying water to every plot of land (*har khet ko pani*).

Figure 25.5

Budget Estimates, Revised Estimates and Actual Expenditure on Irrigation Schemes Included in PMKSY

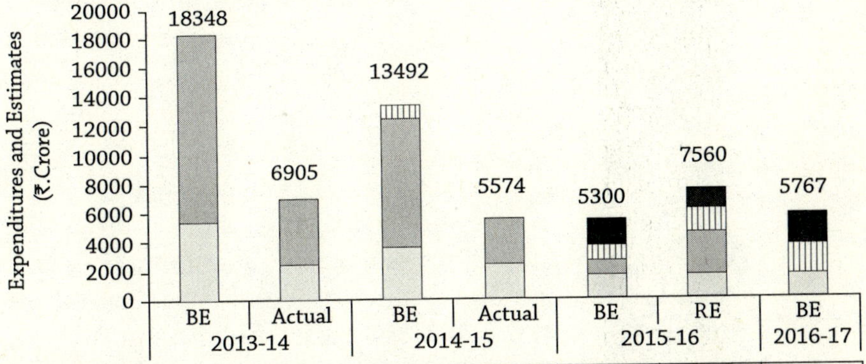

PMKSY (MoA)					1800	1550	2340
PMKSY (MoWR)			1000		1000	1500	1877
AIBFMP (MoWR)	12961	4630	8992	3261	1000	3010	
IWMP (DoLR)	5387	2275	3500	2313	1500	1500	1550

□ IWMP (DoLR) ▩ AIBFMP (MoWR) ▥ PMKSY (MoWR) ■ PMKSY (MoA)

Note: BE: Budget Estimate; RE: Revised Estimate.

Source: 1. *Expenditure Budget*, Volume II, 2015-16 and 2014-15, GoI.

2. For figures of Projects under AIBFMP:

a. For RRR: *Annual Report 2013-14*, Ministry of Water Resources, Government of India.

b. For AIBP, CAD&WM and FMP: Website of Ministry of Water Resources.

Second, it may be noted that the main expenditure on public irrigation comes from the states and not from the centre. During FY16, the irrigation expenditure budgeted by all states together was roughly at ₹104,605 crore during FY16 (Appendix A-25.5). This is roughly 18 times more than the allocation under PMKSY. However, even at this level of expenditure for public irrigation, it will take more than 3 decades to fully utilise the remaining potential of public irrigation. In view of this, one can easily see that PMKSY is no game changer. In fact, it is only very miniscule component of total expenditure that is needed to exploit the untapped potential of irrigation in the country.

The Way Forward

Due to back to back droughts in the last two years (2014 and 2015) and its repercussions, the problems of water sector are being highlighted. As mentioned earlier, the present government announced PMKSY in late 2014 to consolidate all existing irrigation schemes and also to provide 'end-to-end' solution in the irrigation supply chain. Although this is a welcome step, much remains to be done if we need to reduce the dependence of our farmers on the whims of nature.

Some steps to move forward are mentioned below:

Price Reform

Water charges for surface irrigation are very low in the country. The charges have remained same in many states even for decades. Since state irrigation departments are unable to recover even O&M costs, they have to turn to State government for even the O&M costs and since the state governments are generally on a budget strain, they have to cut down expenditure for further expenditure on irrigation. Water charges need to be raised in sync with better-quality service so as to recover at least the full O&M costs.

Electricity for agricultural use is mainly used to extract groundwater. As discussed earlier, it is also heavily subsidised in all the states. We have seen that this pricing has led to overexploitation of groundwater. The situation, therefore, needs to change. Like in the surface irrigation sector, the power sector also needs a price reform in sync with improved and better quality power.

Direct Benefits Transfer

We recommend a switch from price policy (subsidy) approach to income policy approach through DBT (direct benefit transfer) to the accounts of the farmers on per-hectare basis. This will be more efficient and equitable. If water charges are levied so as to recover the full O&M costs, cash can be transferred to the beneficiary account on a per-hectare basis so that they can afford the increased water charges. The amount of cash transferred can be revised after a certain interval of time. If increased water charges are levied, it must incentivise lower wastage of irrigation water. However, at present, the quality and quantity of irrigation supply is also poor. Before water charges are increased, government must ensure improving the situation so that farmers are willing to pay a higher price for an improved service.

In case of electricity sector also, direct cash transfer to the accounts of beneficiaries might help. Instead of charging abnormally low amounts for agricultural uses, agricultural sales could be metered properly by separating feeders for supply, use tamper proof meters to address the theft and pilferage problem, and then fix an upper limit of usage. A per hectare basis amount can be transferred into farmers' accounts directly as electricity subsidy and then supply can be charged at least to cover the cost of supply. Alternatively, in dealing with our problem of excess extraction of groundwater, the Chinese experience of rewarding farmers for using electricity less than a ceiling level could come handy.

Finishing Ongoing and Spillover Irrigation Projects in Mission Mode

According to the Report of the Working Group on Major and Medium Irrigation and Command Area Development for the Twelfth Five Year Plan (2012-

2017), there are 337 spillover projects, of which about 56 per cent are not approved by the erstwhile Planning Commission. Moreover, overall financial requirement for the major, medium and ERM (environmental resources management) projects likely to be spilled over to Twelfth Plan or to be taken up new is ₹184,000 crore. Thus, the government should be very careful announcing any new major or medium projects. Also, spillover projects should be completed in mission mode. This would create new irrigation potential as well as combat the problem of cost escalation for the projects ongoing for decades.

Proper Emphasis on Command Area Development

One of the major pressing problems of the sector is the increasing gap between IPC and IPU especially since the last two or three plan periods. To ensure *Har Khet ko Pani*, we need to address this problem as soon as possible and that can be done by putting proper emphasis on CAD. If the government is not being able to develop command areas to ensure supply of water to the field, private players could be encouraged to manage transmission and distribution of surface water from canals/tanks to fields.

Addressing Demand Side Management Problems

Producing water-intensive crops in water-scarce regions just for higher returns is creating problems for the sector. We have discussed the problems of producing rice in Punjab and sugarcane in Maharashtra earlier in this paper. However, the question is, how do we tackle demand side management problems? In the background of acute drought in Marathwada, the government has taken a welcome step of not allowing new sugar factories to be set up in that region, but that is clearly not enough. One way of addressing this problem could be levying water charges progressively with increased water use. Given current political situation, however, that is not a feasible solution, at least in the short run. An alternative could be to make the use of drip irrigation compulsory for at least 50 per cent to 75 per cent of the sugarcane area in the next 5 to 7 years and provide disincentives (like not allowing to produce at all) to those who do not comply. Drip irrigation can save 40 to 50 per cent of water and the saved water could be channelised to irrigate other crop areas. Crop diversification should be encouraged including those that yield fodder for cattle. Excess expenditure for drip irrigation can be borne partly by centre and partly by states with contributions from sugar factories and farmers as well.

Government should also think about a nation-wide land use policy. Only those cropping patterns in line with natural resource endowment in a state are to be encouraged in that state. The fact that the cost of surface irrigation is much higher in Maharashtra than in Uttar Pradesh should appear in the efficiency calculations. The government might consider whether Maharashtra (or for that matter, any given state) is more suitable for industry or agriculture and formulate a land-use policy on that basis.

Increasing Use of More Efficient Existing Technologies

In case of drip and sprinkler irrigation, the water use efficiencies are 90 per cent and 85 per cent, respectively whereas in case of flood irrigation, the same is only 65 per cent.[9] Also, if procedures like fertigation, that is, the process of injecting fertiliser in the field through drip irrigation can be encouraged, that will not only increase the efficiency of water use, but also the efficiency of fertiliser consumption.[10] Although there have been talks of making such facilities available to farmers since long, its spread has not gained any significant momentum. It is now essential that the usage of drips and sprinklers should also be encouraged since they increase the efficiency of water use considerably.

9. CWC (2014).

10. This process increases the nutrient use efficiency to a significant amount, as high as 95 per cent in case of nitrogenous fertilisers; from *http://agritech.tnau.ac.in/agriculture/agri_nutrientmgt_fertigation.html* accessed on 20 November 2015.

Following International Best Practices

To combat our own problems, we should also look for best international practices in this field and try to learn from their experiences.

Israel

A country like Israel, 60 per cent of which is desert, does not believe that there exists any correlation between drought and good harvest. Israel recycles sewage water, desalinates sea water, and harvests rainwater making the most of every drop of water. It makes use of 80 per cent of recycled waste water in agriculture. Like Israel, India should also try to conserve each drop of this precious resource.

China

A new irrigation technique has been developed in China. It is called 'trace irrigation system'. It is said to be even more efficient than drip irrigation. This system is based on capillary force principle. There is a water control tap buried near the root of the plants. It can sense the change in water level and supply water to the plant accordingly. When plants receive enough water, supply stops. The inventor of this system, Zhu Jun has patented it in New Zealand and Japan and in many countries, including the United States, the application is pending.[11] In India, we could also take the help of such systems to enhance the efficiency of water use.

Japan

Japan uses a technology called 'solar sharing'. PV (photovoltaic) cells are used in this method. The concept was developed by Akira Nagashima of Japan in 2004. The structures are made of pipes and rows of PV panels. These again are arranged with certain intervals to allow enough sunlight to hit the ground for photosynthesis. Also, these are used to produce electricity which is to be

---

11. *http://www.pri.org/stories/2013-06-17/low-water-lunch-chinese-breakthrough-irrigation* accessed on 4 April 2016

used for irrigation water extraction purposes. If there is excess electricity, farmers can also sell that to the grid to increase their income. Considering the necessity of raising farm incomes in India, this alternative can be used after proper cost–benefit analysis.

These are a few examples of best practices followed in many countries so as to optimise the use of water resources. India must follow their path before severe water crisis affects its population and economy.

Following State Best Practices

Not only international experience, India should also learn from the best practices followed in this area by different states. Learning from Gujarat's experience in feeder separation in rural area for domestic use and agricultural use, a scheme for feeder separation has been announced under Deen Dayal Upadhyay Gram Jyoti Yojana (DDUGJY). Some states have also done this following Gujarat and some others are in the process. This is also necessary to implement properly to have an idea about the actual agricultural usage of electricity. Gujarat also had success constructing check dams. Other states with water scarcity might follow in their path to confront this problem.

Artificial Water Recharge

As mentioned in the *Manual on Artificial Recharge of Groundwater* (2007),[12]

> Natural replenishment of groundwater reservoir is a slow process and is often unable to keep pace with the excessive and continued exploitation of groundwater resources in various parts of the country. This has resulted in declining groundwater levels and depletion of groundwater resources in such areas. Artificial recharge efforts are basically aimed at augmentation of the natural movement of surface water into groundwater reservoir through suitable civil construction techniques.

12. Central Groundwater Board, Ministry of Water Resources, Government of India.

There are many advantages of artificial water recharge including negligible evaporation losses, improvement in quality by infiltration through the permeable media, high biological purity, and no adverse social impacts such as displacement of population, and loss of scarce agricultural land.

Central Groundwater Board (CGWB) has done various impact assessment surveys of artificial groundwater recharge in all the states including 16 surveys in Rajasthan, 10 in AP, 8 in Kerala, and 7 in MP. In all the cases, positive changes were observed. For example, in AP using percolation tanks and check dams, more than 5,500 cubic meters of run-off water could be recharged in one year. In Kerala, using check dams, 5,100 to 30,000 cubic meters of runoff water was recharged in one year. In Rajasthan, check dams helped increase 88,000 cubic meter runoff water was recharged in one year. The water level was raised by 0.65 m. Through sub-surface barriers in Rajasthan, 2,000 to 11,500 cubic meter runoff water was recharged in one year. Water level rose from 0.25 m to 0.60 m.

Following these success stories and the manual provided by CGWB for artificial groundwater recharge, more states should be encouraged to follow the methods and save their water resources.

Ensuring Timely and Adequate Power Supply

Electricity supply in rural India including the agricultural sector is inadequate in most of the states. There is no or insufficient electricity supply for a considerable period during the day leading to farmers using diesel pumps for irrigation purposes. This practice is costly for farmers as well as the environment. Under DDUGJY, majority of the villages now have power supply grids. It is to be ensured that timely and adequate power is supplied to those grids for the proper use of electric pumps. Timely power supply will also help food processing industries in rural areas.

Investing in Extension Services

It is necessary to increase awareness among the farmers about the necessity of judicious water use. As mentioned earlier, India will soon become a water-scarce country and hence using water efficiently is of utmost importance. In our country, extension services are inadequate. In most cases farmers get information from local product dealers. However, educating them about the advantages of efficient water use is also important and encouraging them in using more efficient technologies to save water should be done by government.

J.F. Kennedy once said, "The Chinese use two brush strokes to write the word 'crisis.' One brush stroke stands for danger; the other for opportunity." India recognises the danger. The recent budget has paid heed to the importance of irrigation in the wake of drought conditions. However, the real game changer lies in the hands of our leaders in seeing this crisis situation as an opportunity of introducing some path-breaking reforms in the irrigation sector.

References

CWC (2014). *Guidelines for Improving Water Use Efficiency.* Accessed from *http://wrmin.nic.in/writereaddata/Guidelines_for_improving_water_use_efficiency.pdf* on 15 November 2015.

Dhawan, B.D. (1997). "Large-Scale Canal Irrigation-How Cost Effective", *Economic and Political Weekly* 32(26).

Government of India (2002). *Annual Report (2001-02) on the Working of State Electricity Boards and Electricity Departments.* New Delhi: Planning Commission, Power and Energy Division, Government of India.

———. (2007). *Report of the Expert Group on "Ground Water Management and Ownership"*. New Delhi: Planning Commission.

———. (2010). *Financial Aspects of Irrigation Projects in India.* New Delhi: Information Technology Directorate, Information System Organization, Water Planning and Project Wing, Central Water Commission.

———. (2011a). *Report of the Working Group on Major & Medium Irrigation and Command Area Development for the XII Five Year Plan (2012-2017).* New Delhi: Ministry of Water Resources, Government of India.

———. (2011b). *Final Report of Minor Irrigation and Watershed Management for the Twelfth Five year Plan (2012-2017).* New Delhi: Planning Commission, Government of India.

———. (2012). *Annual Report (2011-12) on the Working of State Power Utilities and Electricity Departments.* New DElhi: Planning Commission, Power and Energy Division, Government of India.

———. (2014a). *Agricultural Statistics at a Glance*. New Delhi: Agricultural Statistics Division, Directorate of Economics and Statistics, Department of Agriculture and Co-operation, Ministry of Agriculture.

———. (2014b). *Annual Report (2013-14) on the Working of State Power Utilities and Electricity Departments*. New Delhi: Planning Commission, Power and Energy Division, Government of India.

———. (2014c). *Ground Water Year Book 2013-14*. Faridabad: Central Ground Water Board, Ministry of Water Resources, Government of India.

———. (2014d). *National Accounts Statistics 2014*. New Delhi: Central Statistical Organisation, Ministry of Statistics and Programme Implementation.

———. (2015). *Water and Related Statistics*. New Delhi: Water Resources Information System Directorate, Information System Organization, Water Planning and Project Wing, Central Water Commission.

Gulati, A. and S. Narayanan (2003). *The Subsidy Syndrome in Indian Agriculture*. New Delhi: Oxford University Press.

Gulati, A., and P. Banerjee (2016). "Irrigation and Power Subsidy in India", *ICRIER Working Paper* (Forthcoming).

Gulati, A., M. Svendsen and N.R. Choudhury (1995a). "Capital Costs of Major and Medium Irrigation Schemes in India", in M. Svendsen and A. Gulati (ed), *Strategic Change in Indian Irrigation*. New Delhi: MacMillan India Limited.

———. (1995b). "Operation and Maintenance Costs of Canal Irrigation and their Recovery in India", in M. Svendsen and A. Gulati (ed.), *Strategic Change in Indian Irrigation*. New Delhi: MacMillan India Limited.

———. (1995c). "Towards Better Management of Major and Medium Irrigation Schemes in India", in M. Svendsen and A. Gulati (1995), *Strategic Change in Indian Irrigation*. New Delhi: MacMillan India Limited.

———. (1994). "Capital Costs of Major and Medium Irrigation Schemes in India", *Working Paper* No. 47. NCAER.

Kula, E. (2004), "Estimation of a Social Rate of Interest for India", *Journal of Agricultural Economics* 55: 91-99.

Sharma, R. A., M. J. McGregor and J. F. Blyth (1991). "The Social Discount Rate for Land Use Projects in India", *Journal of Agricultural Economics* 42(1): 86-92.

Svendsen, M. and A. Gulati (ed.) (1995). *Strategic Change in Indian Irrigation*. New Delhi; MacMillan India Limited.

UNICEF, FAO and SaciWATERs (2013). *Water in India*, Situation and Prospects.

Varma, H.K. (2011). "ADB's Water Sector Operations in India: Review and Way Forward", *ADB South Asia Working Paper Series*. Accessed from *http://www.adb.org/sites/default/files/publication/29246/adb-water-sector-operationsindia-review-forward.pdf* on October 15, 2015.

Online Resources:

Central Water Commission: *http://www.cwc.nic.in/*

Central Ground Water Board: *http://www.cgwb.gov.in/*

Department of Agriculture and Cooperation: *http://agricoop.nic.in/*

Ministry of Water Resources: *http://wrmin.nic.in/*

Press Information Bureau: *http://pib.nic.in/newsite/mainpage.aspx*

Reserve Bank of India: *https://www.rbi.org.in/*

Appendix A-25.1

Plan-wise Cumulative Irrigation Potential Created and Utilised in India

Area in Million Hectares

Plan	*Irrigation Potential Created (Cumulative)*				Total	*Irrigation Potential Utilised (Cumulative)*				Total
	Major & Medium	*Minor*				*Major & Medium*	*Minor*			
		Surface	*Ground*	*Sub-total*			*Surface*	*Ground*	*Sub-total*	
Pre plan	9.7	6.4	6.5	12.9	22.6	9.7	6.4	6.5	12.9	22.6
First Plan (1951-56)	12.2	6.43	7.63	14.06	26.26	10.98	6.43	7.63	14.06	25.04
Second Plan (1956-61)	14.33	6.45	8.3	14.75	29.08	13.05	6.45	8.3	14.75	27.8
Third Plan (1961-66)	16.57	6.48	10.52	17	33.57	15.17	6.48	10.52	17	32.17
Annual Plan (1966-69)	18.1	6.5	12.5	19	37.1	16.75	6.5	12.5	19	35.75
Fourth Plan (1969-74)	20.7	7	16.5	23.5	44.2	18.39	7	16.5	23.5	41.89
Fifth Plan (1974-78)	24.72	7.5	19.8	27.3	52.02	21.09	7.5	19.8	27.3	48.39
Annual Plan (1978-80)	26.61	8	22	30	56.61	22.57	8	22	30	52.57
Sixth Plan (1980-85)	27.7	9.7	27.82	37.52	65.22	23.5	9.01	26.24	35.25	58.75
Seventh Plan (1985-90)	29.92	10.9	35.62	46.52	76.44	25.4	9.97	33.15	43.12	68.52
Annual Plan (1990-92)	30.74	11.46	38.89	50.35	81.09	26.25	10.29	36.25	46.54	72.79
Eighth Plan (1992-97)	32.95	12.51	40.8	53.31	86.26	28.38	11.07	37.7	48.77	77.15
Ninth Plan (1997-02)	37.05	13.6	43.3	56.9	93.95	30.95	11.44	38.55	49.99	80.94
Tenth Plan (2002-07)	41.64	N.A	N.A	60.1	101.74	33.68	N.A	N.A	51.48	85.16
Eleventh Plan (2007-12)*	47.97	N.A	N.A	65.56	113.53	34.95	N.A	N.A	52.91	87.86

Note: *Provisional

Source: *Water and Related Statistics 2015*, Working Group Report to 12th FYP-Minor Irrigation and Watershed Management

Appendix A-25.2

Regional Variation in Costs per Hectare of Major and Medium Irrigation Potential Creation

(Potential Created in Million Ha, Cost in ₹ Per ha)

State/Region	Potential Created over Last 10 years	K (Lag and Inflation Adjustment)	K1 (Lag, Inflation and SDR Adjusted (2% SDR)	K2 (Lag, Inflation and SDR Adjusted (4% SDR)	K3 (Lag, Inflation and SDR Adjusted (6% SDR)	Per Ha Cost without Adjustment	
						Current Prices	2014/15 Prices
	MHa			₹/Ha			
Haryana	0.11	295104	374263	472471	593807	481393	715565
Himachal Pradesh	0.02	74736	94784	119655	150384	315895	445775
Punjab	0.14	516574	655140	827051	1039448	115002	187895
Uttar Pradesh+Uttarakhand	1.39	69378	87988	111077	139602	104685	158564
Jammu & Kashmir	0.15	24124	30595	38624	48543	36449	56451
Northern Region	1.80	114330	144997	183045	230053	210685	312850
Assam	0.21	43613	55311	69825	87757	18271	27579
Bihar+Jharkhand	0.55	119986	152172	192102	241436	104619	161920
Orissa	0.32	269680	342019	431766	542649	269174	399363
West Bengal	0.22	90573	114868	145010	182250	28043	43728
Eastern Region	1.30	139506	176927	223353	280713	118275	178746
Andhra Pradesh	1.50	102976	130598	164868	207208	427406	629604

contd...

.contd...

State/Region	Potential Created over Last 10 years	K (Lag and Inflation Adjustment)	K1 (Lag, Inflation and SDR Adjusted (2% SDR)	K2 (Lag, Inflation and SDR Adjusted (4% SDR)	K3 (Lag, Inflation and SDR Adjusted (6% SDR)	Per Ha Cost without Adjustment	
						Current Prices	2014/15 Prices
	MHa			*₹/Ha*			
Karnataka	0.84	230129	291860	368445	463066	364508	559073
Kerala	0.11	313597	397717	502080	631020	109899	179657
Tamil Nadu	0.03	667997	847182	1069485	1344141	830310	1290554
Southern Region	2.48	161904	205334	259214	325783	397105	594050
Gujarat	2.25	95425	121021	152778	192013	115986	171785
MP+Chhattisgarh	1.47	63498	80530	101662	127770	127198	192196
Maharashtra	0.89	299283	379563	479162	602216	729441	1118408
Rajasthan	1.17	127681	161931	204422	256920	83510	134033
Western Region	5.77	125262	158862	200548	252052	206812	315229
All-India	11.0	136357	172934	218312	274377	232931	351475

Source: Potential Created: Water and Related Statistics 2015; Cost: Financial Aspects of Irrigation Projects in India 2010, Central Water Commission.

Appendix A-25.3

Stages of Groundwater Development in the States and Union Territories

States/Union Territories	Stage of Groundwater Development (%)	No. of Assessed Administrative Units	Overexploited (No.)	Critical (No.)	Semi-Critical (No.)	Percentage of Overexploited, Critical and Semi Critical Units in Administrative Units
			States			
Andhra Pradesh	45	1110	83	15	97	17.57
Arunachal Pradesh	0.08	11	0	0	0	0.00
Assam	14	27	0	0	0	0.00
Bihar	44	533	0	0	11	2.06
Chhattisgarh	35	146	1	2	18	14.38
Delhi	137	27	18	2	5	92.59
Goa	28	20	0	0	0	0.00
Gujarat	67	223	24	5	13	18.83
Haryana	133	116	71	15	7	80.17
Himachal Pradesh	71	8	1	2	0	37.50
Jammu & Kashmir	21	14	0	0	0	0.00
Jharkhand	32	210	6	0	5	5.24
Karnataka	64	270	63	21	34	43.70
Kerala	47	152	1	2	23	17.11
Madhya Pradesh	57	313	24	4	67	30.35
Maharashtra	53	353	10	2	16	7.93

contd...

.contd...

Manipur	1.02	8	0	0	0	0.00
Meghalaya	0.08	7	0	0	0	0.00
Mizoram	3.52	22	0	0	0	0.00
Nagaland	6.13	8	0	0	0	0.00
Orissa	28	314	0	0	0	0.00
Punjab	172	138	110	4	2	84.06
Rajasthan	137	243	172	24	20	88.89
Sikkim	26	4	0	0	0	0.00
Tamil Nadu	77	1129	374	48	235	58.19
Tripura	7	39	0	0	0	0.00
Uttar Pradesh	74	820	111	68	82	31.83
Uttarakhand	57	18	0	2	5	38.89
West Bengal	40	271	0	1	53	19.93
Total States	62	6554	1069	217	693	30.20

contd...

.contd...

Union Territories						
Andaman & Nicobar	4.44	36	0	0	0	0.00
Chandigarh	0	1	0	0	0	0.00
Dadra & Nagar Haveli	22	1	0	0	0	0.00
Daman & Diu	97	2	1	0	1	100.00
Lakshadweep	67	9	0	0	3	33.33
Puducherry	90	4	1	0	0	25.00
Total Union Territories	36	53	2	0	4	11.32
All India	62	6607	1071	217	697	30.04

Note: Assessed administrative units:

Blocks: Bihar, Chattisgarh, Haryana, Jharkhand, Kerala, M.P., Manipur, Mizoram, Orissa, Punjab, Rajasthan, Tripura, UP, Uttarakhand, WB

Taluks (Command/Non-Command): Karnataka

Mandal : Andhra Pradesh

Taluks: Goa, Gujarat, Maharashtra

Districts (Valley): Arunachal Pradesh, Assam, Himachal Pradesh, Jammu & Kashmir, Meghalaya, Mizoram, Nagaland, Sikkim, Tripura

Islands: Lakshadweep, Andaman & Nicobar Islands

Firka: Tamil Nadu

Region: Puducherry

Tehsil: NCT Delhi

UT : Chandigarh, Dadar & Nagar Haveli, Daman & Diu

Source: Dynamic Groundwater Resources of India (As on 31 March 2011).

Appendix A-25.4

Electricity Subsidy in Current and Constant (2014-15=100) Prices

(Subsidy in ₹ Crore)

Year	*Apparent Subsidy*	*Electricity Subsidy-Current Prices (with Adjustment Factor 0.7)*	*WPI (2014-15 Base)*	*Electricity Subsidy (Constant Price)*
2000-01	24074	16852	45.9	36733
2001-02	24013	16809	47.5	35368
2002-03	21845	15292	49.1	31114
2003-04	23346	16342	51.8	31531
2004-05	25240	17668	55.2	32014
2005-06	23833	16683	57.7	28937
2006-07	26606	18624	61.5	30307
2007-08	33363	23354	64.4	36285
2008-09	39391	27574	69.5	39648
2009-10	45530	31871	72.2	44146
2010-11	44662	31263	79.1	39525
2011-12	57901	40531	86.2	47038
2012-13 RE	62053	43437	92.5	46957
2013-14 AP	66988	46892	98.0	47842

Source: Reserve Bank of India, Power Division of Planning Commission, GoI 2011, 2014b.

Appendix A-25.5

Expenditure on Public Irrigation by All States Taken Together

Year	*Capital Expenditure In ₹ crore*	*Revenue Expenditure In ₹ crore*	*Total Expenditure In ₹ crore*	*WPI (2014-15=100)*	*Total Expenditure in Constant Prices (2014/15=100) In ₹ crore*
2000-01	8760.30	11644.49	20404.79	45.88	44477.41
2001-02	9740.00	10998.65	20738.65	47.53	43635.71
2002-03	12230.11	11670.02	23900.13	49.15	48629.54
2003-04	16812.25	8905.82	25718.07	51.83	49621.34
2004-05	21123.12	9905.20	31028.32	55.19	56223.32
2005-06	26136.27	11394.60	37530.87	57.65	65098.21
2006-07	31552.99	13280.88	44833.87	61.45	72958.22
2007-08	37005.03	16367.94	53372.97	64.36	82925.46
2008-09	43692.46	17387.67	61080.13	69.55	87827.42
2009-10	41447.72	20645.75	62093.47	72.19	86008.43
2010-11	43249.06	24258.36	67507.42	79.10	85346.90
2011-12	46728.00	26060.33	72788.33	86.17	84474.25
2012-13	49701.75	29259.76	78961.51	92.50	85360.40
2013-14	50746.12	31076.78	81822.90	98.01	83481.47
2014-15 (RE)	64608.10	34940.53	99548.63	100.00	99548.63
2015-16 (BE)	71068.51	33536.93	104605.44		

Note: RE: Revised estimates; BE: Budget estimates.

Source: Reserve Bank of India.

26

Institutional Failures in Rural India

V.S. VYAS

I am happy that the Academic Foundation is publishing a book on Indian economy in memory of its founder late Shri Raj Kapila. I knew him as a highly enterprising publisher, who together with his very capable spouse, Uma Kapila, established a successful publishing house. I, as several of my friends, felt privileged to be published under its banner. It was only later that I came to know that he was a very well trained economist with deep insights in Indian economy, particularly its industrial sector. This, coupled with his warmth and human qualities endeared him to a large number of social scientists in the country. I dedicate this paper to the memory of an exemplary entrepreneur, a fine scholar and an excellent human being.

I

There are two incontrovertible facts about rural India. In the first place, the gap between the rural and the urban sector is widening, not only in the availability of social and economic overheads but also in household income. Secondly, the amount spent on various programmes of rural development by the Central and the State governments is progressively increasing. Naturally, the question arises, why investment in money and manpower on such a large scale has failed to bridge the gap between the rural and the urban sector. This puzzle can be solved if we look into the policies designed for the rural areas, and weakness in the principal rural institutions. This paper is addressed to the latter aspect i.e., the delivery systems to reach the rural population, particularly the rural poor. However, a word on the former may also be appropriate.

Most of the policies of rural development are geared towards making the goods or services cheaper by subsidising them under one plea or the other, be it credit, fertilisers or power. There is ample evidence to show that a large part of these subsidies, with few exceptions, are preempted by 'non-poor', and eventually filter back to urban manufacturers, traders or service providers.

Another major policy failure is the emphasis on supply aspect while ignoring the demand aspect. This can be best illustrated in case of credit, where supply of credit is increasing by leaps and bounds, but the beneficiaries, again, are 'non-poor'. The aspect of the demand for the credit does not figure in the credit policy (Vyas 2017). With such policy biases, only a trickle of funds is left for the people at the margin in the rural areas. These funds are handled by agencies that are not attuned to serve the bulk of the population. The main components of the delivery system in the rural areas are: bureaucracy, *panchayats* and cooperatives.

Most of the funds are channelled through bureaucracy at various levels, which has proved to be unequal to its tasks, especially at the lower level. *Panchayats* have emerged, in a number of states, as vehicles for implementation of a number of government schemes. They are highly politicised and partisan. Till recently, an important institution in the village India was the cooperative. These too are in a state of decay, both because of government interference, and politicisation. Let me briefly review the evidence of the decay in two major institutions, *panchayats* and cooperatives, at the village level; the role expected from them and the reasons for their failure.

Panchayats

Panchayat is the oldest institution in rural India. Historically five elders of the village acted as the representatives of the village population while dealing with the higher administrative authorities, and were also responsible for settling disputes among the villagers. Mahatma Gandhi idealised this institution and advocated that it should be the cornerstone of the state, a unit of self-government, a miniature state in itself.[1] It was thought to be a body of wise people respected and obeyed by all villagers. Its main economic function was to ensure 'self-sufficiency' in basic necessities i.e., food and clothing.

This idealised version of *panchayat*, influenced the policymakers after the advent of Independence. It found a place as article 40 in the Directive Principles of state policy. After several incarnations, it was consolidated in a three-tier *panchayati raj* system, as recommended by the Balwant Rai Mehta Study Team (1957). All political parties endorsed the concept of *panchayati raj* suggested by this team. In more recent years, it is touted as the basic unit of 'decentralised planning' with the hope that it will be able to articulate priorities of the village people, harness local resources, supplement resources devolved from higher units of governance and ensure that benefits of growth are availed by every villager irrespective of class or creed. It was also to be used as a delivery vehicle for various government schemes and programmes.

These hopes are largely belied. There was only a brief period, from 1959 to 1964, when the PRIs (panchayati raj institutions) showed some vigour (Ashok Mehta Committee 1978)[2] Since then a declining phase has started which continues till today. A serious attempt was made, with 73rd Amendment of the Constitution, to revive *panchayati raj*. However, it has hardly made any difference. There are only a few states, most notably, Kerala, where at least for a limited number of functions, especially as delivery system and to some extent as the basic unit of planning, *panchayats* have emerged as viable institutions. In most of the states, they never took off as vibrant units of planning or governance, or even delivery for a sustained period.

1. Gandhian view is discussed in detail by Narayan (1946).
2. Government of India (1978).

Functioning of the *panchayats* can be examined at three levels: as political entity, as local level planning agency and as delivery mechanisms for reaching the development initiatives of the states to the grass root level.

The idealised version of *panchayats* assumes that as the basic unit of governance it will give voice to every inhabitant of the village and will reflect their views on the development and governance of the village. The principal mechanism to ensure this role is the *gram sabha*, meeting regularly, having universal and well-informed participation. The executive body of a *panchayat* is supposed to implement the decisions arrived at by fair and full consultation in the *gram sabha*. The situation at the ground level does not evenly broadly meet these requirements. The *gram sabhas* do not meet; proceedings are fictitiously recorded and then forgotten. It is no exaggeration to say that the *panchayats* are controlled by a coterie of influential people for whom these serve as a forum to enhance their influence and rise to higher levels of the political ladder.

As a basic unit of planning, their second role, *panchayats* are found to be too weak and inadequate. They have proved incapable to assess resource endowment of the village, and allocation of these resources for inclusive development. At best they compile the wish list and transmit it to the higher tier of the PRIs. State level planning agencies hardly give importance to these 'wish lists', not withstanding the rhetoric about decentralised planning. The concept of decentralised planning and development to be carried out by the *panchayats* as the basic planning unit, has proved more fictitious than real.

Most of the *panchayats* today are limited to performing the agency function, i.e., to implement policies and programmes of the state at the grass root level. In this respect also, their efficacy is limited. It is only the schemes such as Mahatma Gandhi National Rural Employment Guarantee Act (MGNREGA), which are based on rights and entitlement, that the *panchayats* in some states have been able to perform their agency role more or less satisfactorily. In other types of schemes, particularly those involving subsidies, the benefits are pre-empted by the influential sections of the village society, either directly or through their proxies.

It bears repetition that the above description is not applicable to all five lakh odd *panchayats* in the country. However, the fact that this applies to the vast majority of these institutions can be substantiated by innumerable studies and reports, including those by the authors who are sympathetic to the concept of a village level institution as a pillar of democracy and a viable unit for decentralised planning.[3]

The necessity for a representative institution at the village level has justification both on the political grounds, to ensure democratic participation at the grass root level, and on the economic ground, to reach the benefits of development to every inhabitant of a village. Therefore, it is important to understand why we do not have such an institution.

The first mistake which was made at the very inception of *panchayati raj*, and is continued to be made, is the assumption of a homogeneous village society, where the interests of all inhabitants of the village are identical and that people who are elected as *panchas* can be relied upon to articulate and act upon a common agenda. In a caste ridden, economically unequal society this is, at best, a facile assumption. In such a society, a common agenda can be forged only if those who are disadvantaged assert themselves and those with wherewithal are persuaded that to a large measure their interests coincide with the common interests. It is possible only by a strong popular movement. This is what happened in Kerala where the civil society as well as the political parties took upon themselves the task of educating the people. It is no surprise that *panchayats* in Kerala are able to perform much better compared to any other state in the country, despite social

3. See, for example, Mani Shankar Aiyar Committee Report, Government of India ((2013). However, this report puts blame for the current state of *panchayats* on the bureaucracy and politicians at the centre and states level.

and economic inequalities.[4] In hardly any other state, there has been concerted effort from civil society, states or the Centre to strengthen the role of *panchayats*.

Secondly, neither the state level politicians nor higher-level bureaucracy are willing to shed their authority to the *panchayats* on the plea that they are highly politicised, and there is serious deficit of knowledge required for planning and implementation of the development programmes, in an effective way. When some functions are allocated to *panchayats*, necessary funds and functionaries are not provided. Only limited devolution of resources and personnel is made to manage the state level schemes. Even in such cases higher authorities retain the hold over the purse strings, and personnel continue to belong to their respective departments who control their posting and promotions.

The task of village level planning is much more difficult than what is generally assumed. Apart from mapping the village resources, which need considerable expertise, the main difficulty is in priority setting. In any case, the exercise becomes futile as the state level plans hardly take cognizance of even district plans; leave apart the block or *taluka* level plans.

All these handicaps ultimately are reflected in dysfunctional, faction-ridden *panchayats*.

Cooperatives

The cooperative as an institution is a product of British era. Some enlightened British officers who witnessed the highly exploitative terms on which credit was made available to Indian villagers, thought that the institutions on the model of German and British cooperatives would be an answer to the usurious moneylenders. By the time of our Independence, cooperatives were recognised as important institution of rural reconstruction. Although efforts were made to organise cooperatives in other areas, in agricultural marketing, in sugar, in dairying, and also

4. Issac and Harilal (1997).

in joint farming, apart from credit, however, none, the possible exception of dairy cooperatives have proved to be a success.

Right from the beginning, emphasis was on credit cooperatives, and that has continued since then. By the 1950s, it was becoming clear that even in the credit sector, the role of cooperatives was not promising. To look into the defects in the organisation and functioning and to suggest measures for reorganising them, the Reserve Bank of India (RBI) took the initiative and appointed A.D. Gorwala Committee.[5] The committee gave the famous slogan "cooperatives have failed, but cooperatives must succeed". Gorwala Committee's major recommendation was to provide substantial funds to cooperatives, and to induct government representatives on the boards of the managing committees to supervise their activities. They wanted better integration of long-term finance and the short-term finance provided by cooperatives. To make the operations viable, they recommended large cooperative societies covering several villages. In short, they gave major responsibility to state governments to supervise the activities of the cooperatives, under the garb of state partnership with the cooperative movement, and the RBI to liberally finance their operations.

Serious scholars of rural economy such as Prof M.L. Dantwala[6] were critical of this approach, which they thought would discourage member ownership of their cooperatives, provide bureaucratic stranglehold on their activities and facilitate the entry of free riders. One may also add that by opting for large cooperatives, the character of the cooperatives as a member owned village level institution was abandoned. With all the suggested 'reforms', the cooperative movement could not be revived. It was plagued with all the shortcomings, which Gorwala Committee was trying to remove.

---

5. *All India Rural Credit Survey* (Chairman: A.D. Gorwala,), Reserve Bank of India, Bombay.

6. Dantwala (1961).

Since then the Government of India, RBI and the National Bank for Agriculture and Rural Development (NABARD) constituted several committees under the chairmanship of distinguished academics and administrators.[7] Each successive committee reiterated the shortcomings in this sector and suggested measures, which were in essence 'more of the same.'

A significant departure was the report of the task force appointed by the Planning Commission (1991) under the chairmanship of Choudhari Bram Prakash. The report of the task force not only brought out the deficiencies in the structure of the cooperative movement, but also suggested a Model Cooperative Act to make cooperatives members-driven, autonomous institutions, more importantly, free from interference by non-producer politicians. The then chief minister of Andhra Pradesh, Rama Rao, made a beginning in implementing the new model cooperatives in the state. However, the move was soon aborted by vested interests.

In the beginning of this millennium, a task force was appointed by the Government of India under the chairmanship of A. Vaidyanathan. The task force suggested a revival package, which was discussed with the stakeholders, including state chief ministers, and consensus was achieved. The revival package for cooperative credit structure (short term) aimed at introducing legal and institutional reforms to enable cooperatives to function as autonomous member-centric and member-governed institutions. The reforms included wider access to financial resources as well as investment opportunities, removal of geographical restrictions on affiliation to federal structure and, administrative autonomy to cooperatives at all levels. The package also provided for technical enhancement

7. Since 1954, a number of Committees were appointed to improve the functioning of cooperatives. These include the Rural Credit Review Committee (RBI 1969), the Hazari Committee (RBI 1976), the Sivaraman Committee (RBI 1984), the Khusro Committee (NABARD 1989), the Jagdish Capoor Committee (NABARD 1999) Vyas Committee (NABARD 2001) and the Task Force headed by Vaidyanathan (Government of India 2005).

and computerisation of operations. Government of India accepted recommendations of the task force, persuaded states to follow the same, and made necessary budgetary provisions for the revival package. States were encouraged to sign a memorandum of understanding to incorporate the basic suggestions in their cooperative acts. NABARD was designated as implementing agency for the revival package.

After a lapse of seven years, the chairman of the task force (Vaidyanathan 2013) had to admit that "implementation is tardy and there are instances of reverting to old ways after receiving the financial assistance from the Centre. In short, interference of the state governments remains unabated." He finds all the defects underlined by previous committees, viz., undemocratic structure, hegemony of well-to-do sections, inefficient lending operations, weak capital base, near total dependence on government funding, inability to reach the asset-less and asset-poor people, continue to plague these institutions.

The defects, pointed out by the critics of the cooperative credit sector are present in the cooperatives in other sectors more or less to the same extent, with some exceptions like the dairy sector. In a vast country like India, there are bound to be some stray examples of genuine cooperative efforts right at the village level. But these are rare exceptions rather than the general rule.

Over the period of time with infiltration of the politicians in management, unimaginative bureaucratic controls, neglect of technical improvements and, growing proportion of free riders, effectiveness of the cooperatives is continuously declining. In credit, as in marketing areas, the public and the private sector firms have become the dominant players. Cooperatives have been able to retain their hold in the marketing of a few commodities, such as dairy products and sugarcane, and that too in few regions of the country.[8] In the credit sector, they are largely acting

8. See, various issues of the *Annual Reports* of the NABARD.

as the conduit to distribute loans obtained from financial institutions, principally from the NABARD.

With multi-agency approach to credit, they are losing their preeminence as the major credit disbursing institution in the rural area. Although the credit disbursed by cooperative credit societies is subsidised by the government, yet the share of cooperatives in disbursement of credit has stagnated at 17 to 18 per cent for the last five years, whereas the total amount of credit for agriculture and other rural activities is increasing year after year, at a fast pace.

The government has also recognised that the cooperatives as they exist today are not only inefficient vehicle for pursuing government policies, they are porous and unreliable. This was made obvious recently while demonetising higher denomination currency notes. Unlike commercial banks, District Cooperative Banks were not recognised to accept demonetised currency.

Concluding Remarks

Logic for a village level institution to give voice to common people provides justification for a tiered *panchayati raj* system with village *panchayat* as the base. It could be agreed that other tiers will be as strong as the base of the pyramid i.e., the village *panchayat*. Similarly, progressive growth of small farm sector in Indian agriculture, logic for organising collective action at the village level is unassailable. Producers find themselves in an unequal bargaining position vis-á-vis credit agencies, input suppliers and market functionaries. Nor can they make effective demands on the extension and research agencies. On the other hand the marketing firms, credit and extension agencies find dealing with the bulk of the small farms individually disadvantageous due to high transaction costs and higher risks. Similar unequal relationship exists as far as village artisans and craftsmen are concerned. *Panchayats* as the political face and cooperatives as economic arm have the possibility of empowering rural population, particularly its marginalised sections. Moot question is, why it is not happening?

Apart from tardy execution of legal provisions and indifference, if not hostility, of the bureaucracy and politicians, there are some unresolved questions at the conceptual level, as well as some strategic failures. Let me touch on both the aspects.

Let me take the case of *panchayats*. There is no clarity on the precise role of this institution as political entity, as a planning unit or an effective delivery system. Discussion on the political role of the *panchayats* should not lose sight of the fact that Indian Constitution by itself advocates, in essence, a top down approach. In this context, can *panchayats* emerge as an institution for self-governance at village level, or should it restrict itself as an effective conduit to carry forward the voice of the villagers to higher political bodies, at the district and state level?

On its planning role, is it realistic to assume that they will be able to asses the natural and human resources of the village and set out the priorities that are commonly accepted, or reflect villagers' views on components of the state plans, which directly affect them. As an agency, or a delivery mechanism, what are its responsibilities, how it is accountable, and to whom? Unless we find satisfactory answers to these questions, it will be futile to think of a vibrant, efficient and democratic institution at the village level.

Apart from the lack of clarity on the role and functioning of the village *panchayats*, two strategic interventions are largely missing. In a faction-ridden society with big divides in terms of class and castes, it requires a huge effort by civil society to emphasise the need for common action. This is amply borne out by the 'success' of *panchayats* in Kerala, where establishment of *panchayati raj* especially the decentralised planning component, was preceded by a massive and effective public movement spearheaded by some of the well known figures in the social and political spheres in the state. No other state seems to have taken this route. A peoples' movement is much more than PR (public relations) efforts made by the *panchayati raj* departments of the states or the Centre.

Second tactical mistake is the way 'training' is imparted to *panchayat* representatives. Apart from inadequacy of such training for functional purposes, the biggest deficiency is its partial approach. If the *panchayats* are entrusted with some important functions like education and health, the functionaries who have to assist the *panchayats* also need training to work in the public sphere. Experience in some states such as Rajasthan is illuminating in this respect. On the recommendation of the State Planning Board, the State government gave 'functions with funds and functionaries' to the *panchayats* to manage programmes in five important areas e.g., primary education, primary health, women and child upliftment, agriculture etc. With all this the results were not at all satisfactory. Partly, because the *panchayat* functionary had no understanding about the functioning of the concerned departments, and lower level government officials were equally ignorant about the intricacy of the functioning with an elected body at the village level. What is needed, therefore, is a 'system approach' in training, which should aim at improving capabilities of all the components of the system.

The main defects of the existing cooperative societies are well known: over dependence on government resources, infiltration of politicians at all levels, increasing number of free riders, lack of internal democracy etc. Many of these defects are due to lack of clarity on the structural issues. We are not clear whether we want 'one village one society', or large societies. Is it important to concentrate on one function and specialise, or go for a multipurpose society at the village level? Is it important to have separate organisations for short-term and long-term credit? Is it important to have three-tier structure or one of the tiers, i.e., district cooperative bank or the state cooperative bank can be eliminated. How close should be the relations between the three tiers? Can a village cooperative, say a credit cooperative, has to affiliate with the next tier in the area i.e., a District Central bank, or can it have freedom to affiliate with an organisation even outside the cooperative structure.

Outside the conventional cooperative framework, there are models of self-governing democratic institutions, such as SHGs (self-help groups) or farmers cooperative companies. Is it possible to incorporate some of the features, which have made these experiments reasonably successful in the traditional cooperatives?

The deficiencies in the village cooperatives are not exclusively due to structural or design related aspects. The basic defect is that like *panchayats*, cooperatives are also mandated from top. Examples of well-informed people coming together on their own and then asking for some assistance from the government are rare. It is also clear that civil society has not included strengthening village cooperatives as a part of their agenda, thus leaving it to the mercy of the politicians and bureaucrats. Preventing enforcement of a progressive legislation such as the 'model cooperative act' illustrates that there is no effective coalition to fight the entrenched vested interests and remove the well-known defects of the existing cooperative structure?

Sad plight of the village level institutions is mainly because it is assumed that the locus of the decision-making is with the top policymakers and senior civil servants. Unfortunately, they have frequently changed their views and embarked on the experimentation in the structure and functioning of the village institutions, with very little positive results. There is need to address the conceptual, structural and technical questions jointly with the villagers who would be the principal beneficiaries, or sufferers, of the changes in these institutions, and to create a consensus for reforms. If Kerala's experience in strengthening PRIs is any guide, it is important to have massive involvement of civil society along with the state in rejuvenating these moribund institutions.

References

Dantwala, M.L. (1961). "Agrarian Structure and Economic Development", *Indian Journal of Agricultural Economics* 16(1).

Government of India (1978). *Report of the Committee (Chairman: Asoka Mehta) on Panchayati Raj Institutions*. Ministry of Agriculture and Irrigation. August.

———. (2013). *Report of the Expert Committee (Chairman: Mani Shankar Aiyar) on Leveraging Panchayats for Efficient Delivery of Public Goods and Services*. Ministry of Panchayati Raj.

Issac, T.M. Thomas and K.N. Harilal (1997). "Planning for Empowerment: People's Campaign for Decentralized Planning in Kerala", *Economic and Political Weekly* 32(1/2), 4-11 January.

Narayan, Sriman (1946). *A Gandhian Constitution in Independent India*. Allahabad: Kitabistan.

Vaidyanathan, A. (2013). "Future of Cooperatives in India", *Economic and Political Weekly* XLVIII(18): 33, 4 May.

Vyas, V.S. (2017). "Capacity of the Rural People to Absorb Credit", in Preet Rastogi (ed.), *Rural Development: Contemporary Issues and Challenges in India—Essays in Honour of Professor Surjit Singh* (to be published).

27

Growth, Productivity and Job Creation in Indian Manufacturing

BISHWANATH GOLDAR

Introduction

At the present juncture of India's economic development, an accelerated, fast growth of the manufacturing sector and large scale creation of jobs in Indian manufacturing is quite essential for attaining and sustaining a rapid and inclusive economic growth in India, which would greatly help in alleviating poverty in the country. Large increases in employment in Indian manufacturing are critical for providing job opportunities to the youth (especially the uneducated or less educated youth) who will be entering the labour force in large numbers in the coming decades. The need for stepping up the rate of growth in manufacturing output and creating manufacturing jobs on a large scale in India is widely recognised, both in academia and in government policy circles.

The emphasis placed by the government on manufacturing sector growth and creation of manufacturing sector jobs is clearly reflected in the National Manufacturing Policy (NMP) of 2011 and the Make-in-India initiative launched in 2014. The NMP had, in 2011, set a target of raising the share of manufacturing in aggregate GDP (gross domestic product) from about 15 per cent (as prevailing at that time) to about 25 per cent in a period of about 10 years (by 2022 or so) and creating 100 million new jobs in that process. Attainment of this target of NMP requires a marked acceleration in the growth rate of manufacturing. Goldar (2015a) has observed that if the average growth rate of aggregate GDP is taken to be about 8 per cent per annum till 2022, then the manufacturing sector needs to grow at the rate of about 13 per cent per annum for reaching the target manufacturing share in GDP of 25 per cent by 2022. It may be added here that if a slightly longer period is considered for the attainment of the goals of the NMP, and it is assumed that the average growth rate in aggregate GDP would be about 8 per cent per annum during the period 2016-17 to 2025-2026, then for reaching the target share of 25 per cent by 2025-26, the required growth rate in manufacturing is around 12 per cent per annum. Indeed, as one of its key objectives, the NMP sought to enhance the growth rate of manufacturing to 12-14 per cent per annum in the medium term. By contrast, in the recent past, 2011-12 to 2015-16, the average annual growth rate in manufacturing real GVA (gross value added) was about 7 per cent per annum.[1] Evidently, a significant step up in the growth rate in manufacturing real GVA is required for attaining the targets of the NMP.

Several Indian economists have emphasised the need for stepping up the manufacturing sector growth and bringing about a shift from a services-led growth towards a manufacturing-led growth in the Indian economy. To give one example, the *India Employment Report of 2016* (Ghose 2016) underscores the need for a rapid growth in the manufacturing sector and associated increases in manufacturing sector jobs. The report draws attention to the growing imbalance between domestic absorption and domestic production caused by a services-led growth and it has been argued that this imbalance has led to growth deceleration. Accordingly, a case is made for a rapid growth in manufacturing and a transition from a services-led

1. This is based on data on real GVA of manufacturing provided in *National Accounts Statistics, 2016* (Central Statistics Office, Government of India) and official press note on national accounts dated 28 February 2017.

growth to a manufacturing-led growth. Similar views have been expressed in Ghose (2015a, 2015b).[2]

Against this backdrop, as outlined above, this paper is devoted to an analysis of growth, productivity and job creation in India manufacturing during the period 1980-1981 to 2014-15. The focus is mostly on the organised (or registered) manufacturing sector[3] which dominates Indian manufacturing in terms of invested capital, output and value added. Trends in RVA (real value added), employment and TFP (total factor productivity) in organised manufacturing are analysed for the period 1980-81 to 2014-15, and sub-periods within this period.

For studying trends in manufacturing employment, it is not enough to consider the number of persons engaged by organised manufacturing. This is so because the unorganised manufacturing sector dominates in terms of jobs provided by manufacturing, accounting for about 75-80 per cent of total manufacturing employment. Accordingly, for the sake of completeness, an analysis of trends in employment in unorganised manufacturing is undertaken, confining attention to the 2000s.

The rest of the paper is organised as follows. The next section deals with the basic data sources used for the study and measurement of variables. The subsequent three sections are devoted respectively to: (a) an analysis of trends in real value added and employment in India's organised manufacturing, (b) an analysis of TFP growth in India's organised manufacturing, undertaken at level of two-digit industries, according to National Industrial Classification (NIC) 2004, and at the aggregate level, and (c) estimates of employment function for organised

2. The importance of shifting to a manufacturing-led growth process in India has been noted by Mitra (2015), among others. See also Mitra (2016), for a detailed discussion on manufacturing-led growth in India.

3. Organised or registered segment of India manufacturing in the official data sources refer to those manufacturing establishments which are registered as 'Factories' under the Indian Factories Act, 1948 (which applies to factories employing 10 or more workers with the use of power or 20 or more workers without the use of power). The same definition is adopted here.

manufacturing based on two-digit industry level panel data, with a view to providing some explanation for the observed trends in employment growth. The sixth section presents an analysis of employment growth in unorganised manufacturing during the 2000s. The final section of the paper summarises the main findings and concludes.

Data Sources and Measurement of Variables

Sources of Data: Organised Manufacturing

As mentioned above, the analyses presented in the next three sections are for the organised sector of Indian manufacturing. The basic source of data for these analyses is the Annual Survey of Industries (ASI) published by the Central Statistics Office (CSO), Government of India. The Economic and Political Weekly Research Foundation (EPWRF) has prepared a time-series dataset of ASI, using the published ASI results for different years, from 1973-1974 to 2014-15. For the analysis of trends in RVA, TFP and employment in organised manufacturing presented in the next three sections, the RPWRF data series at two-digit industry level[4] for the years 1980-81 to 2014-15 are used.[5]

The two-digit level series on ASI data prepared by the EPWRF uses NIC-2004. This classification was used by ASI for the years 2004-05 to 2007-08. ASI data for the period after 2007-08 are available according to NIC-2008. Data for the period 1998-99 to 2003-04 are available according to NIC-1998. In the preceding period, NIC-1970 was used from 1970-71 to 1988-89 and NIC-1987 from 1989-90 to 1997-98. Thus, the EPWRF staff have taken detailed ASI data for different years and built a series on various key variables, after working out concordance among different industrial classifications. This time series prepared by the EPWRF is used for the present analysis.

---

4. The two-digit industries covered in the paper are listed later in Table 27.3 in Section 4. It should be pointed out here that, for the aggregate level analysis, manufacturing is defined as the total of two-digit industries 15 to 36 (according to NIC-2004).

5. The author is grateful to Dr J. Dennis Rajakumar of EPWRF for making available the latest two-digit level ASI data series for this study.

Measurement of Output and Inputs: Organised Manufacturing

For the analysis of TFP growth in organised manufacturing, the growth accounting methodology is applied, making use of a gross output function framework, with KLEMS (capital, labour, energy, materials, and services) being taken as five inputs. The Translog (or Tornqvist) index of TFP is computed. The basic study methodology and the measures of output, inputs and factor income shares used for the analysis are almost the same as used in Goldar (2015b) and do not require a detailed discussion here.[6] It would suffice to note that nominal value of gross output given in the EPWRF series based on ASI data has been deflated and the deflated value is taken as a measure of output. Similarly, the nominal value of materials consumed has been suitably deflated to obtain a measure of materials input and the nominal value of fuels consumed has been suitably deflated to obtain a measure of energy input. The nominal values of materials and fuels consumed have been subtracted from the nominal value of total input to derive a measure of the nominal value of services input (as done in some earlier studies based on ASI including Banga and Goldar 2007), which has then been suitably deflated to obtain the real value of services input.

Number of persons engaged has been taken as the measure of labour input. Net fixed capital stock at constant (2004-05) prices has been taken as the measure of capital input. This has been constructed by the perpetual inventory method.

Nominal values of materials consumed, fuels consumed and services used have been divided by the nominal value of gross output to derive the income share of materials, energy and services inputs, respectively. The income share of labour has been obtained by dividing total emoluments

6. In Goldar (2015b), a distinction has been made between domestically sourced materials input and imported materials inputs. No such distinction has been made in the analysis presented here, except for crude oil used in petroleum refining.

by the nominal value of gross output. The income shares of materials, energy, services and labour have been added and then subtracted from one. The balance is taken as income share of capital input, as the income shares of the five inputs must add up to the value of one under the assumption of constant returns to scale which underlies the Translog index of TFP.

Analysis of trends in RVA undertaken in the third section of the paper requires the construction of a value added series for aggregate organised manufacturing at constant prices. To build such a series, output price index (with base 2004-05) has been formed for each two-digit industry making use of the group-wise and item-wise official WPI (wholesale price index) series with base 2004-05 (Office of the Economic Adviser, Ministry of Commerce and Industry) and such series on wholesale prices indices for earlier years. Then, the value added series for each two-digit industry has been deflated by the output price index relevant to that industry. In the next step, the RVA series for different industries belonging to manufacturing have been added together to obtain the RVA series for aggregate organised manufacturing. This procedure is called single deflation. The series built in this manner is hereafter referred to as single-deflated GVA. As an alternative, the double-deflated GVA series has been constructed. This is explained later. Some additional information about the construction of output and intermediate input deflators is provided in the Annexure A-28.1.

Basic Source of Data: Unorganised Manufacturing

The analysis undertaken for unorganised manufacturing basically uses the National Sample Survey Office (NSSO), Government of India survey results for unorganised manufacturing undertaken for the year 2000-01 (NSS 56th round) and the NSSO survey results for unincorporated non-agricultural enterprises (excluding construction) for the year 2010-11 (NSS 67th round) which covered both manufacturing and non-manufacturing unorganised sector enterprises except those in construction. The component relating to manufacturing in the 67th round survey is used for the present analysis.

Unlike the analyses for the organised manufacturing sector in the next three sections of the paper which cover real GVA growth, employment growth and TFP growth, the analysis for unorganised manufacturing presented subsequently is narrowly focused on employment growth, and therefore data on the number of workers and its composition have been taken.

Growth in Real Value Added and Employment in Organised Manufacturing

Trends in real GVA growth and employment growth in India's organised manufacturing during the period 1980-81 to 2014-15 are analysed in this section. For this purpose, the period under study, 1980-81 to 2014-15, has been divided into three sub-periods: (i) 1980-81 to 1993-94, (ii) 1994-95 to 2002-03, and (iii) 2003-04 to 2014-15. The choice of sub-periods follows that adopted by Panagariya et al. (2014, Chapter 2). These three sub-periods correspond to three distinct periods of growth of the Indian economy since 1980. The third sub-period has been sub-divided into two parts: (i) 2003-04 to 2007-08 and (ii) 2008-09 to 2014-15. The rationale for this sub-division of the third sub-period is the global economic slowdown that has taken place since 2008. It is important to find out whether and how far the growth rates in real GVA and employment in Indian manufacturing have been impacted by the global economic slowdown.

In what follows, trends in employment are analysed first, and after that, the analysis of trends in RVA is undertaken because, for RVA, there are alternate series to be considered.

Table 27.1 shows the trend growth rates in employment and real GVA in India's organised manufacturing in the period 1980-81 to 2014-15 and the four sub-periods mentioned above. The trend growth rates in sub-periods have been estimated by using the kinked exponential model for growth rate estimation (Boyce 1986). Employment growth rates have been computed by using the series on the total number of persons employed. The time series on real GVA in organised manufacturing formed by the single deflation procedure (as explained above) has been used for computing the real GVA growth rates shown in Table 27.1.

It is seen from Table 27.1 that employment growth rate in organised manufacturing was rather slow during the periods 1980-81 to 1993-94 and 1994-95 to 2002-03. The trend growth rates for these two periods were 1.45 and 0.08 per cent per annum respectively. By contrast, the trend growth rate in employment in organised manufacturing in the periods 2003-04 to 2007-08 and 2008-09 to 2014-15 were significantly higher at 5.71 per cent and 4.07 per cent per annum respectively. The trend growth rate in employment during 2008-09 to 2014-15 was lower than that during 2003-04 to 2007-08, but it was well above the trend growth rates during the periods 1980-1981 to 1993-94 and 1994-95 to 2002-03. Clearly, despite the adverse effects of the post-2008 global economic slowdown on Indian manufacturing, the upward trend in employment in the organised manufacturing sector which prevailed during 2003-04 to 2007-08 has continued in subsequent years.

Table 27.1

Trend Growth Rate (% p.a.) in Employment and Real GVA in Organised Manufacturing

Period	*Employment*	*Real GVA (single deflation)*
1980-81 to 1993-94	1.45	8.22
1994-95 to 2002-03	0.08	5.05
2003-04 to 2007-08	5.71	12.93
2008-09 to 2014-15	4.07	6.20
1980-81 to 2014-15	1.98	7.60

Note: Trends growth rates for sub-periods have been computed by using the kinked exponential model.

Source: Author's computations based on ASI data.

Dividing the period under study into two parts, 1980-1981 to 2002-03 and 2003-04 to 2014-15, it is found that the trend growth rates in employment in these two periods were 0.93 per cent and 4.53 per cent per annum respectively. The difference in the growth rates between these two periods is statistically significant. It is evident that in the latter period, 2003-04 to 2014-15, there was a marked acceleration in the growth rate in employment in India's organised manufacturing. This is revealed also by Figure 27.1 which depicts the movements in organised manufacturing employment over time during 1980-81 to 2014-15.

Turning now to real GVA growth, it is seen from Table 27.1 that the trend growth rate in real GVA in organised manufacturing was 8.22 per cent per annum during the period 1980-81 to 1993-94, which fell to 5.05 per cent per annum during the period 1994-95 to 2002-03. It is interesting to note that despite the major economic reforms initiated in India from 1991, there was no significant step up in the trend growth rate in real GVA in organised manufacturing in the initial phase of post-reform era.

Figure 27.1

Employment in Organised Manufacturing: 1980-81 to 2014-15

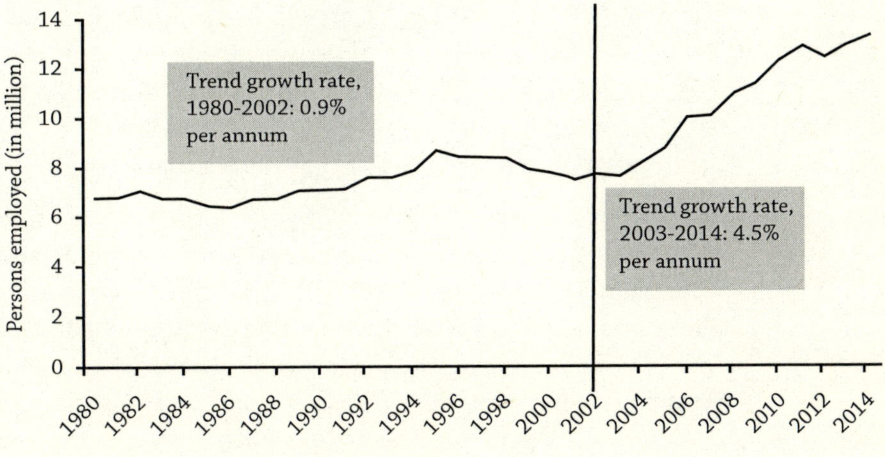

Source: Author's computations based on ASI data.

From 2003-04 began a period of rapid growth in organised manufacturing. The trend growth rate in real GVA in organised manufacturing was 12.93 per cent per annum during the period 2003-04 to 2007-08, which was well above the growth rates achieved during 1980-81 to 1993-94 and 1994-95 to 2002-03. The trend growth rate in real GVA in organised manufacturing came down after 2007-08. It was 6.20 per cent per annum during the period 2008-09 to 2014-15, which is significantly lower than the trend growth rate achieved during the period 2003-04 to 2007-08. Presumably, this fall in real GVA growth rate has been caused primarily by the global economic slowdown.

The hike in the growth rate of real GVA of organised manufacturing during the period 2003-04 to 2007-08 seems to be attributable in a large measure to the economic reforms undertaken in India since 1991. Drawing on the logic behind the J-curve hypothesis of growth and productivity of Virmani and Hashim (2011) postulated by them in the context of economic reforms in India, it may be argued that India's economic reforms needed some time for their intended beneficial effects on the economy to show up, and therefore it is the lagged effects of economic reforms which are manifested in the surge in the manufacturing sector growth that took place since 2003-2004. This, however, may not be the only factor underlying the hike in manufacturing sector growth rate since 2003. Perhaps, a favourable global economic situation during 2003 to 2007 (a faster growth in world GDP during 2003-2007 than during 1994-2002) had also contributed to the accelerated growth of India's organised manufacturing.

The trends in RVA in organised manufacturing are examined further in Table 27.2, making a comparison among alternate RVA series. The table presents average annual growth rates in real GVA of organised manufacturing during the period 1980-81 to 2014-15 and various sub-periods. For RVA series based on ASI data, a comparison is made between the single deflation and the double deflation procedures.[7] The table also shows, for the sake of comparison, the growth rates obtained by using data on real GVA in organised manufacturing (or registered manufacturing) from National Accounts Statistics (NAS) (CSO, Government of India).[8] It should be pointed out here that the data on real GVA in manufacturing in NAS are based on the single deflation procedure.

The need for using double deflation for deriving RVA in the Indian economy has been receiving attention lately in the context of the new series on national accounts (see, for example, Rajakumar and Shetty 2015). In a situation where the prices of products produced by a manufacturing industry grow on average at a rate much lower than (or much higher than) the average growth rate of prices of its intermediate inputs, the single deflation procedure will not correctly measure the growth rate in RVA and the double deflation procedure is more appropriate. The procedure of double deflation which involves separate deflation of output and intermediate inputs is data intensive. Another serious problem or difficulty is that double deflated GVA may turn out to be negative for a specific industry for a particular year, which would not be meaningful. For these

7. To compute double deflated GVA, for each two-digit industry, output and intermediate inputs have been deflated separately by suitable price indices, and then the latter series has been subtracted from the former series. Having obtained the real (double deflated) GVA series for different two-digit industries belonging to manufacturing, these have been added together to derive the real (double-deflated) GVA series for aggregate organised manufacturing.

8. The new series on NAS with base 2011-12 does not provide data on GVA in organised manufacturing. Instead, GVA data are provided for the corporate and households segments of manufacturing. For the years 2012-13, 2013-14 and 2014-15, the growth rate in real GVA for the corporate segment of manufacturing (which includes organised manufacturing mainly but also includes a part of unorganised manufacturing known as quasi-corporate) has been computed and this has been treated as the growth rate in real GVA in organised manufacturing. Another point that should be noted in this connection is that for the period 1980-81 to 2011-12, data on GVA in registered manufacturing have been taken from the earlier NAS series (with base 2004-05). The estimate of real GVA in registered manufacturing in 2011-12 given in earlier series on NAS was primarily based on ASI results for 2011-12. A correction was made to ASI data for 2011-12 by the CSO in January 2016. Accordingly, the figure on GVA of organised manufacturing in 2011-12 in the earlier NAS series has been corrected for this study by taking into account the correction in ASI.

reasons and possibly some other reasons, the double deflation procedure has not yet been brought into use in the Indian national accounts, though in many G-20 countries, manufacturing real GVA is being computed by the double deflation method (see Alexander et al. 2017).

It is seen from Table 27.2 that the growth rate in double-deflated GVA is higher than the growth rate in single deflated GVA for each of the sub-periods considered. For the entire period under study, 1980-81 to 2014-15, the growth rate in single-deflated GVA in India's organised manufacturing is found to be 7.5 per cent per annum, whereas the growth rate in double-deflated GVA is about 10.3 per cent per annum, i.e. about 3 percentage points higher. The growth rate in single-deflated value added obtained by using ASI data is close to that obtained by using NAS data (which is also based on single deflation). It appears that because of the use of single deflation procedure, the growth in RVA in India's organised manufacturing is getting underestimated in India's national accounts.

Table 27.2

Average Annual Growth Rate (% p.a.) in Real GVA of Organised Manufacturing

Period	*Based on NAS Single Deflated*	*Based on ASI Single Deflated*	*Double Deflated*
1980-81 to 1993-94	7.00	7.74	10.53
1994-95 to 2002-03	7.00	5.26	5.32
2003-04 to 2007-08	9.92	13.32	20.45
2008-09 to 2014-15	6.45	5.79	8.85
1980-81 to 2002-03	7.00	6.72	8.40
2003-04 to 2014-15	7.90	8.93	13.68
1980-81 to 2014-15	7.32	7.50	10.26

Notes: Average annual growth rates have been computed by taking a simple average of annual growth rates. The annual growth rates have been obtained by taking log-difference to maintain consistency with the growth rates shown in Table 27.1. For some details regarding growth rates based on NAS, see footnote 8.

Source: Author's computations based on NAS and ASI data.

For the period 1980-81 to 2002-03, the gap in the growth rates in RVA obtained by single deflation and double deflation is about 2.0 percentage points per year. But, for the period 2003-04 to 2014-15, the gap is much larger. It is about 5.0 percentage points per year. This is due to differences in the rates of increase in prices of products produced by the manufacturing sector and the prices of intermediate inputs used by manufacturing—the prices of intermediate inputs have grown much faster than the prices of products produced.[9] The single deflated GVA series indicates that the step-up in annual growth rate in the period 2003-04 to 2014-15 vis-à-vis the period 1980-81 to 2002-03 was about 2.0 percentage points. The double deflated GVA series indicates that the step-up in the growth rate of real GVA was much higher, at about 5.3 percentage points.

Considering Tables 27.1 and 27.2, the following inference may be drawn regarding real GVA growth in India's organised manufacturing: (a) The economic reforms initiated in 1991 did not result in any significant surge in the growth rate in real GVA of India's organised manufacturing in the initial phase of the post-reform period, (b) A marked acceleration in real GVA growth in India's organised manufacturing took place from 2003-2004 onwards which appears to be attributable mostly to the lagged effects of economic reforms, (c) The global economic slowdown that took place since 2008 had a significant adverse impact on the growth rate in real GVA in India's organised manufacturing, and (d) the use of single deflation procedure which is being followed in India's national accounts has caused an underestimation

9. To illustrate this point, it may be noted that the WPI for manufactured products has increased by 55 per cent between 2004-05 and 2014-15. During the same period, raw cotton prices have grown 106 per cent, raw jute prices have grown 188 per cent, groundnut prices have grown 110 per cent, sugarcane prices have grown 107 per cent, iron ore prices have grown 407 per cent, bauxite prices have grown 70 per cent, copper ore prices have grown 211 per cent, and coal prices have grown 90 per cent. With raw materials and energy prices growing faster than finished manufactured product prices, the use of single deflation procedure will lead to underestimation of growth in real GVA.

of growth rate of organised manufacturing, which is substantial for the period since 2003-04.

The above analysis has brought out that the growth rate in real GVA in India's organised manufacturing during 2003-04 to 2014-15 was higher than that during 1980-1981 to 2002-03, especially if one considers double deflated real GVA which is arguably a better indicator of the true value added growth achieved. How is this acceleration in value added growth to be explained? A question of particular interest is whether the acceleration in value added growth is traceable largely or substantially to acceleration in TFP growth. In the next section, therefore, trends in TFP growth in India's organised manufacturing are analysed and an attempt is made to provide a supply-side explanation for the post-2003 growth acceleration in organised manufacturing sector real GVA.

Productivity Growth

As mentioned earlier, TFP growth has been measured for individual two-digit industries (belonging to manufacturing) by applying the growth accounting methodology and using the gross output function framework. Table 27.3 shows the average annual growth rates in TFP in various two-digit manufacturing industries for the period 1980-81 to 2014-15, and two sub-periods, 1980-81 to 2002-03 and 2003-04 to 2014-15.

It is seen from Table 27.3 that in a majority of industries (14 out of 20), the growth rate in TFP during the period 2003-04 to 2014-15 was higher than that during the period 1980-81 to 2002-03. The increase in the growth rate of TFP in the latter period was relatively large in the cases of following industries: wearing apparel, printing and publishing, petroleum refining, and computers, office equipment and electronic products. For these industries, the difference in the annual growth rates in TFP between the two periods is two percentage points or higher. By contrast, the annual TFP growth rate in tobacco products industry came down in the latter period by about two percentage points.

Table 27.3

TFP Growth Rate, by Two-digit Industries

NIC code	Industry Description	TFP Growth Rate		
		1980-81 to 2002-03	2003-04 to 2014-15	1980-81 to 2014-15
15	Food Products and Beverages	1.42	0.95	1.25
16	Tobacco Products	-0.80	-2.79	-1.50
17	Textiles	1.45	0.64	1.17
18	Wearing Apparel, Dressing and Dyeing of Fur	-0.42	2.92	0.76
19	Tanning and Dressing of Leather, Manufacture of Luggage, Handbags, Saddlery, Harness and Footwear	0.35	1.38	0.71
20	Wood and Products of Wood and Cork, except Furniture, Articles of Straw and Plating Materials	-1.83	-0.85	-1.49
21	Paper and Paper Products	0.46	1.15	0.70
22	Publishing, Printing and Reproduction of Recorded Media	-2.88	0.08	-1.84
23	Coke, Refined Petroleum Products	-0.79	1.49	0.01
24	Chemicals and Products	0.45	1.80	0.92
25	Rubber and Plastic Products	0.45	1.06	0.67
26	Non-Metallic Mineral Products	0.75	0.95	0.82
27	Basic Metals	0.43	0.55	0.47
28	Fabricated Metal Products, Except Machinery and Equipment	0.73	2.28	1.28
29	Machinery and Equipment N.E.C	0.23	1.44	0.66
31	Electrical Machinery and Apparatus N.E.C.	1.83	1.71	1.79
30+32+33	Office, Accounting and Computing Machinery, Radio, Television and Communication Equipments and Apparatus, Medical, Precision and Optical Instruments, Watches and Clocks	3.22	6.26	4.29
34	Manufacture of Motor Vehicles, Trailers and Semi-Trailers	0.43	1.93	0.96
35	Manufacture of Other Transport Equipment	1.55	1.33	1.47
36	Manufacture of Furniture; Manufacturing N.E.C.	0.70	-0.56	0.26

Note: Industries 30, 32 and 33 have been combined to ensure better inter-temporal comparability of data.

Source: Author's computations based on ASI data, along with other supplementary data.

Considering the entire period under study, 1980-81 to 2014-15, the growth rate in TFP is found to be relatively high for computers, office equipment and electronic products, electrical machinery and manufacture of transport equipment other than motor vehicles. On the other hand, a decline in TFP at the average annual rate of over one per cent per annum during the same time period is found for tobacco products, wood and wood products, and printing and publishing (in spite of the improvement made between the two sub-periods).

The aggregate level TFP growth performance of the organised manufacturing sector may be taken up next. Since there is considerable amount of inter-industry transactions within manufacturing, it is not right to use the gross output function approach for measuring TFP at the aggregate manufacturing level, even though this is an appropriate framework to use for measuring TFP growth for individual two-digit industries (see Goldar 2015b: 110). Accordingly, two different approaches have been taken to measure aggregate level TFP growth rate of the organised manufacturing sector. The first approach is to apply Domar aggregation on the two-digit industry level TFP estimates (see Domar 1961, Jorgenson et al. 2005: Chapter 8 and Das and Kalita 2011). The second approach is to use the value added function framework with RVA being obtained by double deflation procedure (used in several earlier studies on TFP in Indian manufacturing, including Rao 1996, Trivedi et al. 2000, Goldar and Kumari 2003 and Goldar 2015b).

After applying Domar aggregation on industry level TFP estimates, the growth rate in TFP in aggregate organised manufacturing is found to be 3.2 per cent per annum during the period 1980-81 to 2002-03 and 7.3 per cent per annum during the period 2003-04 to 2014-15. When the value added function approach is taken with real GVA measured by the double deflation procedure, the growth rate in TFP in organised manufacturing is found to be 3.5 per cent per annum during 1980-81 to 2002-03 and 6.01 per cent per annum during 2003-04 to 2014-15. In terms of broad order of magnitude, the two sets of estimates are similar. Both indicate that there was a significant increase in the growth rate in TFP in organised manufacturing in the latter period.[10]

Figure 27.2 shows the contributions of labour input growth, capital input growth and TFP growth to GVA growth in India's organised manufacturing. The decomposition is shown separately for the periods 1980-81 to 2002-03 and 2003-04 to 2014-15. For this decomposition, the TFP growth estimates based on the value added function are used.

Figure 27.2

Source of Growth in GVA in Organised Manufacturing, 1980-81 to 2014-15

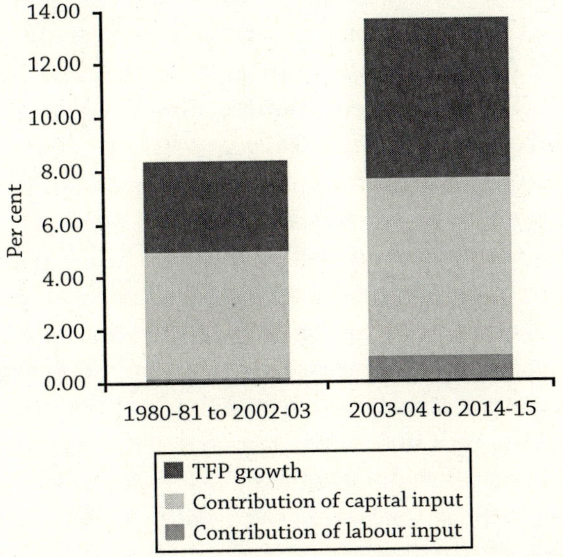

Source: Author's computations based on ASI data, along with other supplementary data.

It is evident from Figure 27.2 that the contributions of TFP growth and capital input growth to real GVA

10. The estimates of TFP growth in India's organised manufacturing during 1999-2000 to 2011-12 presented in Goldar (2015b) using value added function with double deflated value added is 6.7 per cent per annum. If the same period is considered, then the estimate obtained in this study based on value added function and double deflated value added is 6.5 per cent per annum. These two estimates are quite close.

growth went up substantially in the latter period (2003-2004 to 2014-15). The increase in the rate of TFP growth contributed nearly half of the 5.3 percentage points increase that took place in the growth rate of real (double deflated) GVA. The increased contribution of capital input growth accounted for about 37 per cent of the hike in the growth rate in GVA.

It has been noted earlier that the growth rate in employment increased from about 0.9 per cent per annum during 1980-81 to 2002-03 to about 4.5 per cent per annum during 2003-04 to 2014-15. This is obviously a major jump in the growth rate of employment. Yet, the contribution of employment growth (i.e. labour input growth) to GVA growth has not increased much between the two periods under consideration (see Figure 27.2). The acceleration in employment growth has caused a hike in the growth rate of real GVA of organised manufacturing by about 0.8 percentage points per annum; by contrast, a faster TFP growth has added about 2.5 percentage points to annual real GVA growth and increased contribution of capital input growth has added about 2.0 percentage points. The relatively low impact of accelerated employment growth on real GVA growth is explained by the fact that, in the growth accounting methodology, factors of production are given weights according to their income share, and in the case of labour in India's organised manufacturing, its income share has fallen over time, from about 44 per cent in 1980-81 to about 19 per cent in 2007-2008, which subsequently increased to about 27 per cent in 2014-15. Because of a low and falling weight of labour input, reflecting a low and falling elasticity of output (value added) with respect to labour, a large increase in the growth rate of labour input has had only a modest impact on value added growth.

Explaining Employment Growth Acceleration in Organised Manufacturing

Attention is now shifted to a different question. After two decades of slow employment growth in organised manufacturing (trend growth rate of about 0.9 per cent per annum during 1980-81 and 2002-03), what caused a steep hike in the growth rate in employment in organised manufacturing, bringing it to 5.7 per cent per annum during 2003-04 to 2007-08, followed by a trend growth rate of about 4.1 per cent per year during 2008-09 to 2014-15. A thorough investigation of this issue is outside the scope of this paper. However, an attempt is made below to provide some possible explanations.

For this purpose of studying the determinants of employment growth in organised manufacturing, an employment function has been estimated. The model is specified as:

$$lnE_{it} = \beta_0 + \beta_1 \ln V_{it} + \beta_2 \ln w_{it} + \theta \ln E_{i,t-1} + \lambda t + u_{it} \quad (1)$$

In this equation, t denotes time or year, E_{it} denotes employment (or labour input) in i'th industry in year t, V_{it} denotes real GVA in i'th industry in year t, and w_{it} denotes real product wage rate in i'th industry in year t, i.e. wage rate[11] deflated by the output price index of i'th industry. $L_{i,t-1}$ is employment in i'th industry in year $t-1$, i.e. lagged employment. The random disturbance term is denoted by u_{it}.

The model in equation (1) or its variant has been applied in several earlier studies (for example, Bhalotra 1998). This equation may be derived from a CES (constant elasticity of substitution) production function. The presence of the lagged employment term in the equation involves the assumption that the firms are not able to adjust their employment to the desired or optimum level immediately, and are able to do so with some lag. The process of adjustment of actual employment (E) to desired employment (E*) is assumed to take the following form (δ=1-λ):

$$\frac{E_t}{E_{t-1}} = \left[\frac{E_t^*}{E_{t-1}}\right]^{\delta} \qquad 0 < \delta \leq 1 \quad (2)$$

11. Wage rate is obtained by dividing total emoluments by total number of persons employed.

The coefficient of ln$V$, i.e. β_1, is the short-run elasticity of employment with respect of output (value added). The coefficient of ln$w$, i.e. β_2, is the short-run elasticity of employment with respect to real product wage. The numerical value of β_1 should be positive and the numerical value of β_2 should be negative. The parameter δ represents the ease of making adjustment in employment. The higher the value of δ (and the lower the value of λ), the easier it is for the firms to adjust their employment to the desired level. The long-run elasticities of employment with respect to output (value added) and wage rate are given by $\beta_1/(1-\lambda)$ and $\beta_2/(1-\lambda)$ respectively. These may be derived from the estimates of β_1, β_2 and λ.

Panel data for 20 two-digit industries (see Table 27.3) have been used for estimating the above model. For the variable V, the single deflated value added series is used. Since lagged employment is taken as an explanatory variable, the estimation of the model has been done by the Arellano-Bond GMM (Generalized Method of Moments) estimator. The model has been estimated separately for the periods 1980-81 to 2002-03 and 2003-04 to 2014-15 in order to find out if the parameters have changed between the two periods which are marked by a huge difference in employment growth rates. The estimates of the employment function are presented in Table 27.4.

The estimated coefficients of GVA and real product wage rate obtained for the two periods have the right sign and are of plausible numerical magnitude. The estimates for the two periods do not differ much. The estimated coefficient of the lagged employment variable is higher in the model estimate for the period 1980-81 to 2002-03 than in the model estimate for the period 2003-04 to 2014-15. This result indicates that industrials firms enjoyed relatively greater flexibility in adjusting the numbers of workers employed by them in the latter period, i.e. during 2003-04 to 2014-15 than during 1980-81 to 2002-03.

The long-run elasticity of employment with respect to GVA is found to be 0.84 for the period 1980-81 to 2002-03 and 0.64 for the period 2003-04 to 2014-15. Even though

Table 27.4

Estimates of Employment Function, Organised Manufacturing

Explanatory Variables	*Period: 1980-81 to 2002-03*	*Period: 2003-04 to 2014-15*
Logarithm of Real Gross Value Added	0.263 (6.79)	0.301 (25.78)
Logarithm of Real Product Wage Rate	-0.249 (-7.19)	-0.331 (-10.03)
Time (year)	-0.005 (-2.15)	0.012 (6.59)
Logarithm of Employment in Previous Year	0.686 (11.03)	0.531 (20.35)
Constant	12.92 (2.64)	-20.89 (-6.08)
No. of Observations	420	240
No. of Instruments	234	241
Sargan Test, Chi-square and Prob.>Chi-square in Bracket	19.13 [1.00]	17.25 [1.00]
AR(1) Test, Value of z and Probability in Bracket	-2.98 [0.003]	-2.16 [0.03]
AR(2) Test, Value of z and Probability in Bracket	2.13 [0.033]	1.62 [0.11]
Wald Chi-square and Prob.>Chi-square in Bracket	4388.0 [0.000]	5578.3 [0.000]

Note: Model estimation has been done by the Arellano-Bond GMM estimator. The figures in parentheses below the coefficients are t-statistics.

Source: Author's computations based on ASI data.

the elasticity is relatively lower in the latter period, the fact that the annual growth rate in real GVA measured by double deflation went up by 5.3 percentage points means that a faster real GVA growth in the latter period would itself explain a substantial part of the increase in the growth rate in employment.

It is interesting to note that the coefficient of time variable is negative and statistically significant in the estimates of the employment function for the period 1980-1981 to 2002-03, but it is positive and statistically significant in the estimate for the period 2003-04 to 2014-15. One possible interpretation of this result is that there was a labour-saving bias in the technological change that took place in India manufacturing during the period 1980-81 to 2002-03, but this bias disappeared or became weak during the period 2003-04 to 2014-15. If this interpretation is considered valid, then one may argue that the moderation in the labour saving bias of technological change in Indian manufacturing would provide an explanation of the observed trends in employment in organised manufacturing—slow growth during 1980-81 to 2002-03 and rapid growth during 2003-04 to 2014-15.

The first component of the assertion made above that during 1980-81 to 2002-03, technological change in Indian manufacturing had a labour saving bias is empirically supported by the findings of Bhandari and Heshmati (2005). Based on their analysis of labour demand in India's organised manufacturing industries during the period 1980-81 to 2001-02, Bhandari and Heshmati found that there was a labour saving bias in technical change in Indian manufacturing. This finding of Bhandari and Heshmati is consistent with the model results for the period 1980-81 to 2002-03 presented in Table 27.4.

However, for the second component of the assertion made above that labour saving bias of technical change in Indian manufacturing became weak or was absent during 2003-04 to 2014-15 remains speculative as no corroborative evidence can readily be furnished. This issue obviously needs careful econometric investigation to reach any definite conclusion.

An alternative interpretation of the positive coefficient of time variable in the employment function estimates for 2003-04 to 2014-15 is that the coefficient is capturing not only the impact of technological change, but also the influence of certain other development in Indian manufacturing in the 2000s and later. Perhaps, the developments had a strong influence on employment and have prevailed over the labour saving bias of technological change. One such development is the enormous increase that has taken place in the use of contract workers (i.e.

workers employed through contractors).[12] Kapoor (2014) notes that the number of directly employed workers have grown at the rate of about 3.7 per cent per annum during 2000-01 to 2010-11 and the number of contract workers have growth at a much faster rate of 13.7 per cent per annum. Das et al. (2015) report that the share of contract workers out of total workers employed in organized manufacturing has increased from about 21 per cent in 2000-01 to about 35 per cent in 2011-12.[13] Their analysis reveals that while the number of directly employed workers per factory has gone down slightly, the number of contract workers employed per factory has gone up substantially between 2000-01 and 2011-12.

Goldar and Ghosh (2015) have studied econometrically the growth in employment in about 10,000 manufacturing plants between 2002-03 and 2007-08 and have found that the change in the ratio between contract workers and directly employed workers is an important determinant of employment growth. According to their econometric results, an increase in the share of contract workers out of total workers employment tends to raise the growth rate in employment in factories. This empirical finding implies that certain developments[14] which have made it possible for industrial firms to use contract labour on a large scale have contributed to the steep increase in the growth rate of employment in organised manufacturing that has taken place from 2003-04.

---

12. There have been a large number of studies on contract labour use in India's organised manufacturing. These include Kapoor (2014), Hoda and Rai (2015), Das et al. (2015), Chaurey (2015), Sapkal (2015) and Goldar (2016).

13. Using ASI data for 2014-15, the share of contract workers in total workers engaged in organised manufacturing is found to be about 35 per cent, which is about the same as in 2011-12.

14. Drawing attention to a ruling by the Supreme Court in 2001 which interpreted the Contract Labour Act, 1970 in the case of Steel Authority of India versus National Union Water-Front Workers, Das et al. (2015) have argued that this judicial interpretation has led to increased flexibility in the Indian labour market enabling firms to employ 'contract' workers widely. In many cases, it has become possible to employ contract workers in jobs where they work alongside permanent workers.

Growth in Unorganised Manufacturing Employment

The analysis presented above has brought out that since 2003-04, employment in organised manufacturing has grown rapidly. The trend growth rate in employment during 2003-04 to 2014-15 was over 4.5 per cent per annum. It is important to draw a contrast here between organised and unorganised manufacturing because the latter dominates over the former in terms of employment generated and has recorded a rather poor growth performance in employment. This is discussed further below.

In 1999-2000, total employment in manufacturing was about 36.8 million (Ghose 2016: 126, Table S.1). Employment in organised manufacturing according to ASI data was about 7.9 million, accounting for about 21 per cent of aggregate manufacturing employment. Using unit-level data of Employment-Unemployment Survey (EUS) of NSSO, Ghose (2016) estimates that employment in organized manufacturing in 1999-2000 was about 9.5 million which comes to about 26 per cent of aggregate manufacturing employment. Thus, going by these two estimates, unorganised manufacturing accounted for about three-fourths to four-fifths of aggregate employment in manufacturing in 2011-12.

The growth rate in employment in unorganised manufacturing in the 2000s has been very low if not negative and this has pulled down the growth in overall manufacturing employment. If the results of NSSO survey of unorganised manufacturing for 2000-01 are compared with such results for 2010-11, the growth rate in employment in unorganised manufacturing is found to be negative, at about -0.6 per cent per year (Goldar and Sengupta 2016: 50, Table 3.3). An alternative possibility is to take the estimate of aggregate manufacturing employment from EUS of NSSO (for 1999-2000 and 2011-12), and then subtract the estimate of employment in the organised sector based in ASI and thus derive employment in unorganised manufacturing. Going by this method (with suitable interpolation of the estimate of aggregate manufacturing employment), the growth rate in employment in unorganised manufacturing between 2000-01 and 2010-11 was about 1.5 per cent per annum (Goldar and Sengupta 2016: 50, Table 3.3). A third possibility is to use the unit level data of EUS of NSSO to estimate employment in organized and unorganised employment, as done by Ghose (2016) and Goldar and Aggarwal (2017). According to the estimates of Ghose (2016), employment in unorganised manufacturing was about 27.3 million in 1999-2000 which increased to about 33.3 million by 2011-12. The growth rate comes to about 1.7 per cent per annum. Evidently, the available data indicate that there was sluggish growth in employment in unorganised manufacturing during the 2000s, lagging far behind the employment growth performance achieved by organised manufacturing.

What explains the sluggish growth in employment in unorganised manufacturing in the 2000s? A thorough investigation of this question is beyond the scope of this paper. Nonetheless, some hypotheses regarding the possible reasons for slow employment growth are advanced below and some sketchy evidence relating to these hypotheses is presented.

The first hypothesis is that employment growth in unorganised manufacturing has been slow mainly because the unorganised manufacturing sector has undergone a structural change in the 2000s. The own account manufacturing enterprises (units that do not use any hired workers) has been partly replaced by establishments (units that employ hired workers, up to nine such workers). Since employment to value added ratio is relatively higher in own account enterprises, the change in the structure in favour of establishments has adversely affected employment growth.

To provide some data in support of the above hypothesis, it may be pointed out that according to NSS data on unorganised manufacturing enterprises, employment in own account enterprises has fallen at the rate of 1.8 per cent per annum between 2000-01 and 2010-

2011 while employment in establishments has increased by about 1.6 per cent per annum in that period, i.e. the employment composition has changed. Also, employment in rural areas has fallen by 2.6 per cent per annum while employment in urban areas has increased by 2.3 per cent per annum during 2000-01 to 2010-11.

Goldar and Aggarwal (2017) observe that across states, there is a positive correlation between the change in the share of unorganised sector in manufacturing employment and the change in the share of own account enterprises in unorganised sector manufacturing employment. The correlation coefficient is 0.21. This supports the hypothesis that a restructuring within unorganised manufacturing from own account enterprises to establishments has been responsible for a fall (or sluggish growth) in unorganised sector in manufacturing employment.

The second hypothesis is that the significant decline in female labour force participation rate in rural India which took place between 2004-05 and 2011-12[15] has adversely affected employment of women in unorganised manufacturing in rural areas, leading to a downward pressure on employment growth in unorganised manufacturing. It may pointed out in this context that, according to NSS data, female employment in rural unorganised sector manufacturing fell by 2.4 per cent per year between 2000-01 and 2010-11.

Goldar and Aggarwal (2017) have presented some econometric evidence that indicate the employment in unorganised manufacturing is related with female labour force participation rate. They have estimated regression equations in which the rate of change in the share of unorganised sector in manufacturing employment (between 1999-2000 and 2011-12, taking industry by state data) has been taken as the dependent variable which has been regressed on a set of explanatory variables

15. Female labour force participation rate in 15+ population has fallen from 497 per thousand in 2004-05 to 358 per thousand in 2011-12 in rural areas and from 246 per thousand in 2004-05 to 205 per thousand in 2011-12 in urban areas (Sanghi et al. 2015).

which include the state level female labour participation rate. The econometric results indicate a significant positive relationship between female labour force participation rate and the share of unorganised sector in manufacturing employment. The interpretation of this result is that a fall in female labour force participation rate would lower the share of unorganised sector in manufacturing employment, presumably by lowering the growth rate in employment in unorganised manufacturing.

The third hypothesis concerns the use of contract labour in organised manufacturing. As mentioned earlier, during the 2000s, there was a marked increase in the employment of contract workers in organised manufacturing. Arguably, this has reduced the pressure on the organised sector manufacturing firms to opt for outsourcing. In the absence of a large scale increase in contract workers in organised manufacturing, there would have been a greater degree of outsourcing to unorganised manufacturing. In a sense, therefore, the use of contract workers in organised manufacturing has adversely impacted the growth of employment in unorganized manufacturing. This is an interesting hypothesis. It needs a detailed empirical analysis for its verification, which is beyond the scope of this paper. However, one piece of evidence may be presented in support of the hypothesis. Taking state-wise data on growth rate in unorganised manufacturing employment between 2000-01 and 2010-2011 and the share of contract workers in total workers in organised manufacturing in 2010-11, it is found that there is a positive correlation between the two variables. The correlation coefficient is 0.33.

Conclusion

An analysis of growth, productivity and employment generation in Indian manufacturing during 1980-81 to 2014-15 was undertaken in this paper, focusing mostly on the organised sector of manufacturing which dominates Indian manufacturing in terms of invested capital, output and value added. The analysis revealed that growth in

RVA (real value added) in India's organised manufacturing accelerated significantly since 2003-04. The growth rate in single deflated value added in organised manufacturing was found to be 6.72 per cent per annum during 1980-81 to 2002-03, which increased to 8.93 per cent per annum during 2003-04 to 2014-15. There was a much sharper increase in the growth rate of double deflated value added in organised manufacturing, which is a more satisfactory measure of RVA. The growth rate in double-deflated value added in organised manufacturing was found to be 8.40 per cent per annum during 1980-81 to 2002-03, which increased to 13.68 per cent per annum during 2003-04 to 2014-15, a hike of about 5.3 percentage points. The analysis of RVA growth in organised manufacturing clearly indicated that the use of single deflation procedure in India's national accounts is leading to an underestimation of manufacturing sector growth, especially for the period from 2003-04.

It was found from the analysis that there was a surge in the growth rates in employment and TFP in India's organised manufacturing during the period 2003-04 to 2014-15. While the trend growth rate in employment in organised manufacturing was less than one per cent per annum during 1980-81 to 2002-03, in the subsequent period, 2003-04 to 2014-15, it was more than 4.5 per cent per annum. As regards TFP, the growth rate went up from 3.2 per cent per annum during the period 1980-1981 to 2002-03 to 7.3 per cent per annum during the period 2003-04 to 2014-15 according to one set of TFP estimates, and the increase was from 3.5 per cent per annum during 1980-81 to 2002-03 to 6.01 per cent per annum during 2003-04 to 2014-15 according to an alternate set of TFP estimates. Nearly half of the hike in real (double deflated) value added growth achieved by India's organised manufacturing in the period 2003-04 to 2014-15 was found to be traceable to accelerated TFP growth.

To look into the reasons for the sharp increase that took place in the growth rate in employment in organised manufacturing in the period since 2003-04, an employment function was estimated econometrically using industry-wise panel data. Based on the estimated elasticity of employment with respect to RVA, it was inferred that the hike in employment growth in the period 2003-04 to 2014-15 is partly attributable to the hike in the RVA growth rate.

In the employment function estimates, the coefficient of the time trend variable was found to be negative and statistically significant for the period 1980-81 to 2002-2003 and positive and statistically significant for the period 2003-04 to 2014-15. One possible interpretation of this result is that there was a significant labour-saving bias of technical change in the period 1980-81 to 2002-2003, which became non-existent or weak in the period 2003-04 to 2014-15. If this interpretation is taken as right, then the hike in employment in the period since 2003-04 may be explained by a change in the nature of technological change. An alternative interpretation of the positive coefficient of time trend in the estimated employment function for the period 2003-04 to 2014-15 is that it reflects an important development in organised manufacturing, namely the growing use of contract labour. There is basis to believe that growing use of contract labour has had a favourable impact on employment generation. Thus, these two factors, one connected with nature of technological change and the other connected with growing use of contract labour may provide a part explanation of the observed significant hike in the rate of employment growth in organised manufacturing in the period since 2003-04.

While there was a marked acceleration in employment growth in organised manufacturing since 2003-04, the unorganised manufacturing sector which dominates in terms of the jobs provided by manufacturing, accounting for about 75-80 per cent of total manufacturing employment, experienced a sluggish or negative growth in employment in the 2000s. Three possible reasons for the sluggish or negative growth in employment in unorganised manufacturing in the 2000s were given and some empirical evidence was provided in support of the arguments. These three possible reasons are: (i) structural changes within unorganised manufacturing, away from own account enterprises to establishments, causing employment per unit of output (value added) to fall, (ii) fall in female labour force participation rate in rural areas in the latter half of the 2000s which probably adversely impacted use of female workers in own account enterprises and thus caused employment growth in unorganised manufacturing to come down, and (iii) growing use of contract labour in organised manufacturing firms, lowering their incentive for outsourcing, which in turn would have adversely impacted job creation in unorganised manufacturing.

References

Alexander, Thomas, Claudia Dziobek, Marco Marini, Eric Metreau and Michael Stanger (2017). "Measure Up: A Better Way to Calculate GDP", *IMF Staff Discussion Note* no SDN/17/02. January. International Monetary Fund. (available at: *file:///C:/Documents%20and%20Settings/uits/My%20 Documents/Downloads/sdn1702.pdf*, accessed on 10 May 2017).

Bhalotra, Sonia R. (1998). "The Puzzle of Jobless Growth in Indian Manufacturing", *Oxford Bulletin of Economics and Statistics* 60(1): 5-32.

Boyce, James K. (1986). "Kinked Exponential Models for Growth Rate Estimation", *Oxford Bulletin of Economics and Statistics* 48(4): 385-91.

Banga, Rashmi and Bishwanath Goldar (2007). "Contribution of Services to Output Growth and Productivity in Indian Manufacturing: Pre- and Post-Reform", *Economic and Political Weekly* 42(26): 2769-77, 30 June.

Bhandari, Amit K. and Almas Heshmati (2005). "Labour Use and its Adjustment in Indian Manufacturing Industries", *IZA Discussion Paper* no. 1596. Bonn: Institute for the Study of Labor (available at: *http://ftp.iza.org/dp1596.pdf*, accessed on 12 May 2017).

Chaurey, Ritam (2015). "Labor Regulations and Contract Labor Use: Evidence from Indian Firms", *Journal of Development Economics*, 114: 224-32.

Das, Deb Kusum and Gunajit Kalita (2011): "Aggregate Productivity Growth in Indian Manufacturing: An Application of Domar Aggregation", *Indian Economic Review* 46(2): 275-302.

Das, Deb Kusum, Homagni Choudhury and Jaivir Singh (2015). "Contract Labour (Regulation and Abolition) Act 1970 and Labour Market Flexibility: An Exploratory Assessment of Contract Labour use in India's Formal Manufacturing", *Working Paper* no. 300. New Delhi: Indian Council for Research on International Economic Relations.

Domar, E.D. (1961). "On the Measurement of Technological Change", *Economic Journal* 71(284): 709-29.

Ghose, Ajit K. (2015a). "India Needs Rapid Manufacturing-led Growth", *Working Paper* no. 01/2015. New Delhi: Institute for Human Development.

Ghose, Ajit K. (2015b). "Services-led Growth and Employment in India", in K.V. Ramaswamy (ed), *Labour, Employment and Economic Growth in India.* Delhi: Cambridge University Press. pp.57-90.

Ghose, Ajit K. (2016). *India Employment Report 2016.* Institute for Human Development. Published by Oxford University Press, New Delhi.

Goldar, Bishwanath (2000). "Employment Growth in Organised Manufacturing in India", *Economic and Political Weekly* 35(14): 1191-95

———. (2014). "Productivity in Indian Manufacturing in the Post-Reform Period: A Review of Studies", in V. Kathuria, S.N. Rajesh Raj and K. Sen (ed.), *Productivity in Indian Manufacturing.* New Delhi: Routledge. pp.75-105.

———. (2015a). "Sustaining a High Rate of Growth in India in the Next 10 Years", in Pradeep Agrawal (ed.), *Reviving Growth in India.* Delhi: Cambridge University Press. pp.47-81.

———. (2015b). "Productivity in Indian Manufacturing (1999-2011): Accounting for Imported Materials Input", *Economic and Political Weekly* 50(35): 104-11, 29 August.

———. (2016). "Use of Contract Labour in India's Organized Manufacturing: Role of Import Competition and Labour Regulations", Paper presented at the National Seminar on *Role of Public Policy in Development Process: Emerging Economic/Social Scenario in the Indian Economy* held at the Sardar Patel Institute of Economic and Social Research, Ahmedabad, 4-5 January.

Goldar, Bishwanath and Suresh Chand Aggarwal (2017). *Structural Changes in Manufacturing Employment in India, 1999-2011* (available at *SSRN:https://ssrn.com/abstract=2964373*).

Goldar, Bishwanath and Maitri Ghosh (2015). "Employment Growth in India's Organized Manufacturing: Trends and Determinants", *Review of Development and Change* 20(2): 277-302.

Goldar, Bishwanath and Anita Kumari (2003). "Import Liberalization and Productivity Growth in Indian Manufacturing Industries in the 1990s", *Developing Economies* 41(4): 436-60.

Goldar, Bishwanath and Sreerupa Sengupta (2016). "Post-Reforms Trends in Growth and Productivity in Indian Manufacturing", in C. Veeramani and R. Nagaraj (eds.), *International Trade and Industrial Development in India.* New Delhi: Orient BlackSwan. pp. 45-102

Goldar, Bishwanath and Suresh R. (2017). "Contract Labour in Organized Manufacturing in India", in K.P. Kannan, Rajendra P. Mamgain and Preet Rustagi (eds.), *Labour and Development: Essays in honour of Professor T. S. Papola.* New Delhi: Academic Foundation. pp.357-86.

Hoda Anwarul and Durgesh K. Rai (2015). "Labour Regulations and Growth of Manufacturing and Employment in India: Balancing Protection and Flexibility", *Working Paper* no. 298. New Delhi: Indian Council for Research on International Economic Relations.

Kapoor, Radhicka (2014). "Creating Jobs in India's Organized Manufacturing Sector", *Working Paper* no. 286. New Delhi: Indian Council for Research on International Economic Relations.

Jorgenson, D., M.S. Ho and K.J. Stiroh (2005). *Information Technology and the American Growth Resurgence.* Cambridge MA: The MIT Press.

Mitra, Arup (2015). "Manufacturing-Led Growth, Competition and Challenges", *Yojana* 59 (April): 13-16.

———. (2016). *Industry-led Growth, Issues and Facts.* Springer Brief in Economics. Singapore: Springer.

Panagariya, Arvind, Pinaki Chakraborty and M. Govinda Rao (2014). *State Level Reforms, Growth and Development in Indian States*. Oxford: Oxford University Press.

Rajakumar, J.D. and S.L. Shetty (2015). "Gross Value Added: Why Not the Double Deflation Method for Estimation?" *Economic and Political Weekly* 50(33): 78-81.

Rao, J. M. (1996). "Manufacturing Productivity Growth: Method and Measurement", *Economic and Political Weekly* 31(44): 2927-36.

Sanghi, Sunita, A. Srija and Shirke Shrinivas Vijay (2015). "Decline in Rural Female Labour Force Participation in India: A Relook into the Causes", *Vikalpa* 40(3): 255-68.

Sapkal, Rahul Suresh (2015). "Labour Law, Enforcement and the Rise of Temporary Contract Workers: Empirical Evidence from India's Organised Manufacturing Sector", *European Journal of Law and Economics* (Published on line: 14 September 2015, available at *http://papers.ssrn.com/sol3/papers.cfm?abstract_id=2661050SSRN*, accessed on 17 March 2016).

Trivedi, P., A. Prakash and D. Sinate (2000). "Productivity in Major Manufacturing Industries in India: 1973-74 to 1997-98", *Development Research Group Study* No 20. Mumbai: Department of Economic Analysis and Policy, Reserve Bank of India.

Virmani, Arvind and Danish A. Hashim (2011). "J-Curve of Productivity and Growth: Indian Manufacturing Post-Liberalization", *IMF Working Paper* no. WP/11/163. International Monetary Fund.

Annexure A-27.1

Output and Intermediate Input Deflators

Construction of deflators for this study has been done in a manner very similar to that in Goldar (2015b). Deflators for value of output and value added have been constructed from the official WPI (wholesale price index) series brought out by the office of the Economic Adviser, Ministry of Commerce and Industry, Government of India. For each two-digit industry, a suitable price index or deflator has been formed from the item-wise and group-wise wholesale price indices from the official series. In some cases, the price index for the two-digit industry could be found in the official WPI series directly. In other cases, these were derived from item-wise wholesale price indices by taking a weighted average (weights taken from the official WPI data).

The WPI with base 2004-05 have been used to construct deflators for two-digit industries for the years 2004-05 to 2014-2015. In the same way, the official WPI series for earlier years (for example, the series with base 1993-94 and the series with base 1981-82) have been used (with splicing) to build similar deflator series for the years 1980-81 to 2004-05. After building the price index for output of a two-digit industry for the years 1980-81 to 2004-05, the base of that series has been shifted to 2004-05. Then, the two series, one for the years 1980-81 to 2004-05 and the other for the years 2004-05 to 2014-15 have been joined together.

Turning now to intermediate inputs, deflators for materials input, energy input and services input have been formed for each two digit industry. One set of deflators have been formed for the years 1980-81 to 2004-05 and another set has been formed for the years 2004-05 to 2014-15. For the first set, the input-output table (absorption matrix) for 1998-99 has been used to compute weights. For the second set, the input-output table (absorption matrix) for 2007-08 has been used to compute weights.

For each input-output sector, price indices have been formed. In the cases of commodities, the best available price index from the WPI series has been taken. In the case of services, implicit deflators have been computed from the NAS and those have been applied. For each two-digit industry, the price index for energy input has been formed by taking a weighted average of price indices for coal, petroleum products, natural gas and electricity, the weights being derived from the corresponding column(s) in the input-output table. Similarly, data on the various services used by the industry is taken from the input-output table, these are used for computing weights and then the price indices of different services are combined using those weights so as to form the deflator for services input used by the industry.

The computation of material input deflator is similar to that of energy and services input. The weights are taken from the input-output table. Two additional points to be noted in this connection are: (a) in certain cases, petroleum products are not treated as energy but as feedstock and hence included in material (e.g. naphtha used for fertiliser industry), and (b) for crude oil used in petroleum refining industry, the domestic and imported crude oil have been separated and different price indices have been used.

28

Threshold Effects of Indian Labour Laws

A Critical Review of Some Recent Research

ADITYA BHATTACHARJEA

For over a decade, several articles in some of the world's leading academic journals have tried to show that India's supposedly archaic labour laws have been a major obstacle to industrial growth and employment creation. Following from the seminal contribution of Besley and Burgess (2004), most of the results in this literature seem to show that states that have reformed their labour laws so as to weaken the rights of workers have done better than those that have failed to reform. In three earlier papers (Bhattacharjea 2006, 2009, 2014), I have criticised the major contributions to this literature on a variety of grounds. In this short note, I assess the methodology employed by some recent papers which go a step further. They try to establish that 'pro-worker' labour regulation has more severe adverse effects on industrial establishments whose larger size brings them under more restrictive regulations.

The authors of these studies have econometrically estimated the impact of demand volatility and/or inter-state differences in labour regulation on various outcome variables, in the course of which they have examined differential effects on establishments of different sizes. The thresholds used to categorise establishments along the

---

Dedicated to the memory of my mother, Sunanda Bhattacharjea (née Surkund), who was a classmate of Shri Raj Kapila in the M.A. class of the Delhi School of Economics, 1953-1955.

size dimension are employment levels of 50 and 100, based principally on the authors' interpretation of different provisions of Chapters V-A and V-B of the Industrial Disputes Act (hereafter IDA). These chapters are regarded as EPL (employment protection legislation), because they impose restrictions on the ability of industrial establishments[1] to carry out layoffs, retrenchments, and plant closures (hereafter LRC),[2] with the severity of the restrictions increasing with establishment size, as measured by employment. All the studies find stronger adverse effects for larger plants. The inferences drawn from these findings is that size-dependent EPL either forces plants to remain sub-optimally small,[3] or inhibits their response to demand fluctuations (Adhvaryu et al. 2013), or to expand employment by disproportionately hiring contract workers (Chaurey 2015, Ramaswamy 2015).[4] In the context of Indian manufacturing, these

---

1. In the context of manufacturing, 'industrial establishments' in the IDA are factories as defined in the Factories Act: units employing at least 10 workers with the use of electric power, or at least 20 without power. This is conventionally regarded as the definition of the registered, formal, or organised manufacturing sector. I shall hereafter use establishments, plants and factories interchangeably.

2. It is important to understand these terms. A layoff is a temporary refusal of an employer to give employment to his workers; this is permitted only for certain reasons beyond the employer's control, which are laid down in the IDA itself. Retrenchment is a permanent cessation of the employment relationship, for reasons other than indiscipline. Closure of a factory necessarily involves retrenchment of its workers, although only those who can prove that they have worked for a certain minimum length of time are entitled to the protection of the IDA.

3. There are, however, other reasons for staying small. Using data from the 2005 Economic Census, Amirapu and Gechter (2017) show that the establishment size distribution reveals a significant discontinuity just below the level of 10 workers. This corresponds to the threshold of applicability of the Factories Act and several other pro-worker laws that impose other requirements on establishments, concerning occupational health and safety, payment of social security taxes, and maternity benefits. The authors demonstrate quite persuasively that the disincentive to expand beyond 10 workers is not so much the cost of complying with these requirements as the costs of harassment and extortion by inspectors once a factory is registered. Interestingly, the authors find no comparable discontinuity at the IDA Chapter V-B threshold of 100 workers, confirming the earlier finding of Hsieh and Olken (2014), which was based on ASI data for 2011.

4. The two studies that investigate this phenomenon in relation to threshold effects come to somewhat different conclusions. Ramaswamy (2015) finds that the ratio of contract workers to total (contract + 'regular') workers is

are workers hired through registered labour contractors. They are not borne on the rolls of the factories in which they work, and are therefore not protected by the IDA. They constitute a growing proportion of the workforce in organised manufacturing, exceeding one-third of all workers in recent years. As these workers typically have no job security, lower wages and fewer benefits, it is argued that pro-worker regulation actually harms the interests of workers.

Reliance on contract workers also has adverse effects on efficiency, because their productivity is lower: neither they nor the factories in which they work have any interest in developing their firm-specific human capital. The evidence on this is weak, however. Of the studies reviewed here, only Dougherty et al. (2014) examines threshold effects of labour market reforms on TFP (total factor productivity).[5] In a regression that attempts to identify the determinants of plant-level TFP, the estimated coefficients on a dummy variable representing states with 'flexible EPL,'[6] as well as on its interaction with dummy variables representing factories in the employment size categories of 50-100 and 100-250 workers, are insignificant. But the triple

---

contd...

actually highest for the size class of 50-99 regular workers. He interprets this result to mean that such establishments hire contract workers in order to stay below the employment threshold of 100 at which the most stringent provisions of Chapter V-B become applicable. On the other hand, Dougherty et al. (2014: 29) define contract worker intensity as the share of contract labour in total expenses of a manufacturing plant, and find that this ratio is strictly increasing in plant size. The two findings are consistent if larger plants pay relatively higher wages to contract workers.

5. Sofi and Sharma (2015a) show that industries located in states with 'rigid' EPL and exhibiting greater output volatility have higher contract labour intensity (the share of contract workers to total workers). Sofi and Sharma (2015b) show that rigid EPL has adverse effects on TFP, but these disappear after controlling for contract labour intensity. These papers, however, use industry-level data and therefore cannot examine plant-level threshold effects.

6. As their primary measure of labour law reforms, Dougherty et al. (2014) use a dummy variable for 'flexible EPL' states based on the OECD index, which tries to capture the variation across states in the extent of reform in a range of labour laws as well as actual implementation. To check for robustness, Dougherty et al. also use an alternative dummy variable based on an updated version of the Besley and Burgess classification of states, and interestingly they find the corresponding coefficient to be insignificant in relation to TFP.

interaction of the flexible EPL dummy with the dummy for plants employing over 250 workers and another dummy variable for labour-intensive industries is negative and significant. This means that pro-employer labour reforms have smaller effects on the TFP of large plants in labour-intensive industries. The authors relate this result to their independent finding that these plants have a higher propensity to hire contract workers, so they benefit less from such reforms. But no additional clause of the IDA takes effect once the Chapter V-B cutoff of 100 workers is crossed, and 250 does not correspond to the threshold of applicability of any other law, so it is not clear what is driving this result.

All these papers sub-divide Indian states into two categories, 'flexible' and 'inflexible', using some version of the 'regulatory measure' devised by Besley and Burgess (2004) to capture interstate differences in labour regulation. All of them acknowledge my earlier critique of this measure, and modify it by making some minor adjustments based on some errors that I had pointed out.[7] Although my critique of Besley and Burgess went far beyond just pointing out a few coding errors in their index, I do not intend to return to those broader issues here. Rather, I intend to assess only the specific issue of how size thresholds are used in the more recent literature. My criticism of this approach is two-pronged. First, I show that the increasing severity of EPL at employment thresholds of 50 and 100 is inaccurately matched to the text of the IDA. Second, I show that the way in which employment is supposed to be calculated for the purpose of determining whether or not an establishment meets the IDA thresholds does not correspond to the employment levels reported in the Annual Survey of Industries (ASI),

7. In order to demonstrate the robustness of their results, Adhvaryu et al. (2013) use a modified labour regulation measure which they call 'Bhattacharjea's Recoding of Besley and Burgess (2004)'. I would like to set the record straight on this: I never offered such a recoding. As Adhvaryu et al. mention elsewhere in their paper, the modified measure that they name after me was in fact constructed by Ahsan and Pages (2008), based on a few of the errors in the Besley and Burgess coding that I had pointed out.

which is the data source used by these authors. Therefore, factories covered by the ASI cannot be accurately divided into size-classes that match the coverage of different chapters of the IDA.

Employment Thresholds in the Industrial Disputes Act

All the papers surveyed here assert that Chapter V-A applies only to establishments with 50-99 workers, and smaller establishments are therefore outside the scope of the restrictions on LRC. For example, "the regulations in section V-A cover industrial establishments in which more than 'fifty workmen on an average per working day have been employed in the preceding calendar month' (section 25A, chapter V-A)" (Adhvaryu et al. 2013: 726). The same authors further claim that "factories with employment lower than 50 face no firing costs" (p.733), and that this class constitutes "factories that were exempt from the regulation" (p.737). Chaurey (2015: 225) claims that "Section V-A lays down regulations for establishments with 50 or more workers", and that "IDA regulations do not apply to small firms" (p.227) (i.e., those with less than 50 workers). Dougherty et al. (2014: 28) state that the 50 worker cutoff "corresponds to the presence of a few labour laws that are enforced starting at this establishment size". Finally, according to Ramaswamy (2015: 243), "Chapter V-A of the IDA requires notice and compensation for lay-off, retrenchment and closure if the firm employs not less than 50 workers." I shall now show that all these interpretations are inaccurate.[8]

Chapter V-A comprises sections 25A to 25J. Section 25A,which was incompletely quoted by Adhvaryu et al. (2013), actually excludes industrial establishments having fewer than 50 workers only from the application of sections 25C to 25E. These sections are very specific. Section 25C entitles workers to half their wages while they are laid off, provided they were on the muster roll of the establishment

8. I must admit that I made a similar mistake in Bhattacharjea (2006: 216) by referring to "establishments covered by Chapter V-A (those employing at least 50 workers)", although I was not analysing threshold effects.

and have completed a year of continuous service. Section 25D requires employers to maintain a muster roll. Section 25E disallows layoff compensation for workers who refuse alternative employment offered to them, or who do not present themselves for work at least once a day, or in case of a strike in another part of the establishment. Apart from these three sections, section 25FFA also does not apply to undertakings with less than 50 workers. This section requires employers to give 60 days' notice to the government before closing down 'any undertaking'. Thus, industrial units with less than 50 workers are exempted only from the requirements of paying layoff compensation, maintaining muster rolls, and giving 60 days' notice before closure.[9] In principle, all the other sections (25F to 25J) of Chapter V-A apply to all undertakings with less than 100 workers, not only to those with 50-99 workers. These sections require employers to give one month's notice and compensation (severance pay) at prescribed rates, in cases of retrenchment, or closure/transfer of ownership of an undertaking. Some other restrictions (such as 'last come, first go' in case of retrenchment) are also prescribed. Moreover, section 25A also specifies that exclusion from applicability of sections 25C to 25E applies only to 'industrial establishments', defined as in the Factories Act (see note 1 above). In contrast, 25F and its various sub-sections, which require notice and compensation, refer to workers in an 'industry' or 'undertaking', not in an industrial establishment. Thus, in principle, even units in the unregistered manufacturing sector are covered.[10] Thus, the IDA does impose restrictions ('firing costs') on employment flexibility even in units with less than 50

9. I would like to thank Prof K.V. Ramaswamy for correcting my understanding of some of these clauses.

10. In fact, the broad definition of 'industry' in section 2(j), and its even broader interpretation by courts, has allowed employees of small government agencies, *panchayats*, and societies to obtain retrenchment compensation, and sometimes even reinstatement with back wages since the date of illegal retrenchment.

workers.[11] Another way of putting this is that the increase in employment inflexibility mandated by the IDA at an employment level of 50 workers is not as sharp as what the authors assume.[12]

The restrictions on employment flexibility imposed by the infamous Chapter V-B of the IDA are far more stringent. They require industrial establishments with 100 or more workers to obtain government permission, and also prescribe longer notice periods before undertaking LRC. This threshold is much less subject to misinterpretation, although Dougherty et al. (2014: 28) inaccurately claim that the employment cutoff of 100 that they use "is consistent with IDA's national threshold set in 1982." In fact, as clearly stated in section 25K of the Act, the cutoff is applicable only to Chapter V-B of the IDA, and it was actually reduced from 300 to 100 with effect from 1984, not 1982. But these are minor issues that have no implications for their methodology. The more serious problems arise in trying to group factories into size-classes on the basis of employment data reported in the ASI. I now turn to this issue.

IDA Thresholds and ASI Employment Data

There are several problems here, the first two of which were pointed out in Bhattacharjea (2009) but not fully

11. However, while section 25D requires maintenance of muster rolls "for the purposes of this Chapter" (i.e. Chapter V-A, not just the sections governing layoffs), 25A exempts industrial establishments with less than 50 workers from this requirement. Under the various other sections of V-A, only workers with at least a year of continuous service are eligible for notice and compensation in case of retrenchment. In the absence of a muster roll, it would be difficult for them to prove their eligibility.

12. Ramaswamy (2015: 244) points out that in addition to the IDA, "others like the Industrial Employment (Standing Orders) Act that lays down terms and conditions of work come into force if the firm employs more than 100 workers or less depending on the state law in which the firm is located." However, this Act only requires employers to draft 'standing orders' that regulate the classification of workers, working conditions (shifts, working hours, wage rates, holidays, leave, transfers, etc.) and rules of discipline in their establishments; get the orders certified by a government official; and post them prominently near the gate of the establishment. This would certainly reduce arbitrariness on the part of employers, but it is not in the same league as the restrictions on LRC laid down in the IDA.

taken on board by later authors. First, section 2(ka) of the IDA, and some court judgements, require that distinct units (including non-industrial divisions) should be included as part of an industrial establishment or undertaking, if 'functional integrality' or lack of 'severability' between them can be established. Thus, ASI manufacturing units reporting less than the threshold specified by a particular section of the IDA may yet be covered by it, by including the employment of their affiliated marketing or accounting firms, even if they are nominally separate entities.

Second, but working in the opposite direction, is the fact that contract workers are not protected by the IDA if they are not borne on the rolls of the factories in which they work. However, their employment is supposed to be included in the figure for total workers reported to the ASI. Therefore, a researcher using the latter figure for establishing the threshold effect of a particular IDA section would unwittingly include units that are not covered by it. Chaurey (2015) and Ramaswamy (2015) do exclude contract workers while classifying factories by size class, but the others do not.[13]

A further problem is the mismatch in the technique of calculating employment as between the IDA sections and the ASI. The ASI calculates average daily employment as the total number of man-days worked over all shifts divided by the number of working days in the accounting year (usually April to March) to which the survey relates. Now compare this to the employment threshold for Chapter V-B, specified in section 25K: "The provisions of this Chapter shall apply to an industrial establishment ... in which not less than one hundred workmen were employed on an average per working day *for the preceding*

13. Chaurey (2015) however wrongly refers to non-contractual workers as 'permanent'. The employment returns in the ASI classify workers as those employed through contractors, and those employed directly. The latter need not be permanent: they may include apprentices, casual and daily-wage workers. On a related issue, none of the studies recognised that Rajasthan has to be treated differently because of an amendment to section 2(s) that it passed in 1958, extending the definition of 'workman' in the IDA to include contract labour.

twelve months" (emphasis added), i.e. the 12 months preceding the date of the LRC. Researchers will assign a plant to the above or below 100-worker category based on its average direct (non-contractual) employment as reported to the ASI for an accounting year. But whether or not Chapter V-B is applicable to a factory's LRC carried out in the early months of that year will be largely based on its employment levels during the preceding year. (This argument would not necessarily hold if the factory has significantly increased its direct employment in the current year. But such a factory would be unlikely to be proposing an LRC so soon.)

The employment threshold above which factories become liable for compensating laid-off workers, as laid down in section 25A of the IDA, gives rise to a different problem: "Sections 25C to 25E inclusive shall not apply to industrial establishments to which Chapter V-B applies, or (a) to industrial establishments in which less than fifty workmen on an average per working day have been employed in the *preceding calendar month*". Clearly, employment in the preceding month has no necessary relationship with the ASI figure for average employment in that year.

Conclusions

The papers reviewed above have tried to establish negative economic outcomes for firms exceeding employment levels of 50 and/or 100 workers, supposedly corresponding to the thresholds at which different sections of the IDA become applicable. In this paper, I have tried to show that these thresholds are inaccurately mapped from the IDA, and that the classification of factories into the corresponding size classes is also inaccurate because of different methods of calculating employment in the IDA and the ASI. The thresholds therefore represent boundaries that are fuzzy rather than sharp.

Does all this really matter for the results of these studies? After all, a vast amount of research on social and political behaviour, and the effectiveness of various policies, uses categories based on consumption, income, and age, even though we know that the interval boundaries are arbitrary, and the assignment of individuals or households to the resulting categories is prone to recall errors and wilful misreporting. My primary objection to the academic literature on EPL, as spelt out in my earlier papers, is directed at the use of an index based on a mechanical reading of a single labour law to represent labour market rigidity or flexibility. This paper has a different orientation, but I have tried to show once again the pitfalls involved in 'leximetrics', which in this context involves the mapping of dense legal texts into numbers or categories. As acknowledged above, I made a similar mistake in some earlier work on labour law. The purpose of this note is not to argue against quantification, without which economic analysis can make little progress. Rather, we all need to be more careful in our understanding of laws and data sources.

This caveat should be kept in mind while analysing the effects of a major policy change that is beginning to unfold. In 2014, the states of Rajasthan and Madhya Pradesh diluted the employment protection that the IDA provides, by raising the threshold of applicability of Chapter V-B from 100 to 300 workers, thereby restoring the pre-1984 situation. Some other states are reportedly considering similar amendments. In econometric terms, this will provide a suitable 'treatment' for examining threshold effects as compared to the 'control' states, after we have accumulated a few years of data. Meanwhile, in 2015, the Central government published a draft "Labour Code on Industrial Relations Bill,"[14] which would replicate the same change at the national level (see Section 85 of Chapter X of the Code, which corresponds to Chapter V-B of the IDA). To sweeten the pill, it also proposes to triple the prescribed rate of retrenchment compensation. However, section 74 of the Code exempts industrial establishments with less than 50 workers from all of

14. See *http://www.prsindia.org/uploads/media/draft/Labour%20Code%20on%20Industrial%20Relations%20Bill%202015.pdf*

Chapter IX (corresponding to IDA Chapter V-A), not just from the sections that correspond to the existing sections 25C to 25E. This would mean that workers in small units would no longer be entitled to notice and compensation for LRC. Tracing the effects of these changes would call for empirical investigation, with some attention being paid to the issues discussed in this paper.

References

Adhvaryu, Achyuta, A.V. Chari and Siddharth Sharma (2013). "Firing Costs and Flexibility: Evidence from Firms' Employment Responses to Shocks in India", *Review of Economics and Statistics* 95(3): 725-40.

Ahsan, Ahmad and Carmen Pagés (2008). "Are All Labor Regulations Equal? Evidence from Indian Manufacturing", *IZA Discussion Paper* 3394.

Amirapu, Amrit and Michael Gechter (2017). "Labor Regulations and the Cost of Corruption: Evidence from the Indian Firm Size Distribution", Revised *IED Working Paper* 166. Boston University. *https://sites.google.com/site/amritamirapu/research*

Besley, Timothy and Robin Burgess (2004). "Can Labour Regulation Hinder Economic Performance? Evidence from India", *Quarterly Journal of Economics* 119(1): 91-134.

Bhattacharjea, Aditya (2006). "Labour Market Regulation and Industrial Performance in India: A Critical Review of the Empirical Evidence", *Indian Journal of Labour Economics* 49: 211-32.

———. (2009). "The Effects of Employment Protection Legislation on Indian Manufacturing", *Economic and Political Weekly* 44(22): 55-62.

———. (2014). "Comments" [on Dougherty et al. 2014], in Shekhar Shah, Barry Bosworth and Arvind Panagariya (eds.), *India Policy Forum* 2013-14. New Delhi: Sage. pp.49-52.

Chaurey, Ritam (2015), "Labor Regulations and Contract Labor Use: Evidence from Indian Firms", *Journal of Development Economics* 114: 224-32.

Dougherty, Sean, Veronica Frisancho and Kala Krishna (2014). "State-level Labor Reforms and Firm-level Productivity in India", in Shekhar Shah, Barry Bosworth and Arvind Panagariya (eds.), *India Policy Forum* 2013-14. pp.1-44.

Hsieh, Chang-Tai and Benjamin Olken (2014). "The Missing 'Missing Middle'", *Journal of Economic Perspectives* 28(3): 89–108.

Ramaswamy, K.V. (2015). "Employment Protection Legislation and Threshold Effects", in K.V. Ramaswamy (ed.), *Labour, Employment and Economic Growth in India*. New Delhi: Cambridge University Press. pp.239-64.

Shah, Shekhar, Barry Bosworth and Arvind Panagariya (eds.) (2014). *India Policy Forum* 2013-14. New Delhi: Sage.

Sofi, Irfan Ahmad and Pritee Sharma (2015a). "Labour Laws and Informalisation of Employment: Panel Evidences from Indian Formal Manufacturing Sector", *Asian Journal of Law and Economics* 6(1): 65-84.

———. (2015b). "Does Employment Protection Legislation Matter in Dualistic Labor Market? Panel Evidence from Indian Manufacturing Sector", *Labor Studies Journal:* 1-20.

29

Bank Debt and Neoliberal Growth

C.P. CHANDRASEKHAR and JAYATI GHOSH

While India is being lauded for being the fastest growing economy in the world, the government is grappling with a bad debt problem that threatens the solvency of at least some of its banks. A feature of recent Indian development has been the persistence of high growth despite fiscal contraction and the absence of any export boom under neoliberalism in India. But that growth has been accompanied and driven by a credit boom. And a consequence of that credit boom has been the return of large NPAs (non-performing assets) in the banking system despite reform and recapitalisation and the reduction of NPAs. That is, the early success of banking reform in reducing NPAs was followed by the subsequent dismal failure of reform to keep NPAs from rising once again.

According to the various editions of the Reserve Bank of India's (RBI's) biannual *Financial Stability Report*, GNPAs (gross non-performing assets) of the SCBs (scheduled commercial banks) rose sharply from 5.1 per cent of gross advances at the end of March 2015 to 7.6 per cent at the end of March 2016, 9.2 per cent in September 2016 and 9.6 per cent in March 2017. Thus, the problem is not just the volume of bad assets, but the rapid growth in such assets. According to answers to two questions (Nos. 1759 and 2526 of August 2016) in Rajya Sabha (upper house of the Indian parliament), while the total GNPAs of PSBs (public sector banks) stood at ₹4,768 billion at the end of March 2016, the NPAs that were reported by them in the second half of financial year 2015-16 alone amounted to ₹2,770 billion.

This crisis created by NPAs on the balance sheets of commercial banks, especially PSBs, does not go away. It only intensifies. An environment that triggered large inflows of foreign capital and a surge in credit after 2003 encouraged banks to explore new areas and terms of lending, which are responsible for the large exposures that are now turning bad. Having encouraged that environment with its policies, the government had been pretending that the problem is not serious enough to warrant emergency action. The reason was that it wanted to do the impossible: resolve a big problem with little money. But now time seems to be running out.

Data for all banks (public and private) relating to December 2016, compiled by Care Ratings (and reported in *The Indian Express*, 20 February 2017) pointed to a 59.3 per cent increase over the previous 12 months to touch ₹6,97,409 crore. That amounts to 9.3 per cent of their advances, compared with an NPA to advances ratio of 3.5 per cent at the end of 2012. The annual increment in the NPA ratio, which stood at around one-half of a percentage point in the years ending December 2013 and December 2014, rose rather sharply to 1.6 percentage points and 3.3 percentage points respectively in the years ending December 2015 and December 2016.

Some observers argue that this rapid growth of bad debt is not as alarming as it seems. This is because a substantial part of the increase in NPAs was the result of an asset quality review mandated by the RBI in 2015, which forced banks to shift a substantial number of stressed assets that had been recorded as 'restructured standard assets' to the NPA head in their books. Restructured assets are those for which a default threat has been addressed with corrective measures such as lowered interest rates and easier terms of repayment. When NPAs and restructured assets are combined, the ratio of aggregate stressed assets to advances rose only marginally. But there is reason to believe that NPAs are still on the rise for reasons other than reclassification.

Even ignoring this trend, the rise in NPAs due to reclassification is not without implications for the health of India's predominantly public banking system. Once assets are recorded as non-performing, banks need to write off loss assets. They must also provide for the implicit decline in the value of doubtful and sub-standard assets. This adversely affects the profitability of banks. Even though much less than the RBI mandated 70 per cent of NPAs have on average been provided for by Indian SCBs, the RoA (return on assets) and the RoE (return on equity) of the group fell between end-March 2015 and end-March 2017, from 0.8 to 0.4 per cent in the case of the former and from 9.3 to 4.3 per cent in the case of the latter. Underlying this profit squeeze was large growth of risk provisions and increase in write-offs, which together contributed to a fall in profits after tax. Given the uneven distribution of this hit across banks, 21 SCBs accounting for 37 per cent of the total assets of all SCBs recorded negative RoA values over the financial year 2015-16.

This slump in profits or transition to loss-making status of Indian banks is only likely to accelerate, given the vulnerable position of many of the corporates that the banks are exposed to. A study on the "Performance of Private Corporate Business Sector during 2015-16", published in the *RBI Bulletin* for October 2016, reports that an analysis of the financial statements of 1,707 manufacturing companies shows that the number of 'vulnerable companies', or those whose debt-equity ratio is more than 200 per cent and interest coverage ratio (or ratio of earnings before interest, taxes, depreciation and amortisation to interest payment due) is less than one has been increasing continuously between 2012-13 and 2015-2016. The debt held by this set of companies (numbering 283 in 2015-16), or the 'debt at risk' because of their vulnerability, amounted to 30 per cent of the debt of all 1,707 companies. A similar study of a larger sample of 3,700 companies with an aggregate debt of around $500 billion, found that companies with an interest coverage ratio of less than one, accounted for as much as 39 per cent of the debt of the sample companies.

Neoliberal Growth and the NPAs

A question that arises therefore is whether there is a relation between the nature of recent high growth in India and the return to high NPAs in a 'reformed' financial structure. Kalecki[1] had argued that in a capitalist economy the, "rate of growth is ephemeral in the sense that any deviation from the path determined by it renders the system stationary—i.e., subject to cyclical fluctuations but no trend." In the event, "the system cannot break the impasse of fluctuations around a static position unless economic growth is generated by the impact of semi-exogenous factors." The formulation emerged from a system based on an investment function in which investment decisions today, that materialised in capital formation with a lag, were endogenously induced by the level of investment and the rate of change of investment.

This system tends to be subject to cyclical fluctuations around a static position, and a trend if any is observed is ephemeral and non-significant. Any trend growth requires exogenous or semi-exogenous stimuli. Exogenous stimuli are factors which raise aggregate demand but are not themselves dependent upon the fact that growth has been occurring in the system; that is, they operate irrespective of whether or not growth has been occurring in the system. The exogenous stimuli normally referred to in the literature are external markets, state expenditure, and innovation. Innovation, while relevant, is not really the driver of capitalist growth in post-WWII industrialisers, given the scope for catch up, in which already existing innovations are exploited. Exports are an obvious and important 'external' inducement to investment, but India's record here has been wanting relative to the export-

1. Kalecki, Michal (1943/1971). "Political Aspects of Full Employment,", Chapter 12 in *Selected Essays on the Dynamics of a Capitalist Economy 1933-1970*. Cambridge: Cambridge University Press. pp.138-45

led industrialisers. A third important source of stimulus to capitalist accumulation is State expenditure. State expenditure contributes directly to increases in demand as a result of purchases made. It also contributes indirectly since the expenditure increases public employment and incomes. Hence public expenditure is an obvious source of inducement to invest for the private sector.

Not itself being induced by current and/or past incomes or profits and capable of being financed with debt that is serviced through taxes imposed on the output increases, it results in such expenditure which is in large part autonomous. In the event, state expenditure by acting like an internal/external market, serves as an exogenous stimulus for capitalist growth. This has been a crucial driver of growth in India for a long period of time. However, for sometime now, the rhetoric of neoliberalism and its practice in India after the adoption of the Fiscal Responsibility and Budget Management (FRBM) Act in 2003, have implied fiscal reform that stifles the role of government spending as a stimulus for growth.

There is reason to argue, however, that financial expansion and deepening, that leads to a credit boom, can be considered as being akin to an exogenous stimulus, since it allows in certain circumstances the level of consumption and investment to be untethered from current income and its rate of change. There can be periods of easy money when individuals and firms can access credit in excess of what may be 'warranted' by their levels of current income at relatively low rates of interest. This matters because, to recall, the term exogenous is used here in the sense that the demand that provides the stimulus in question is independent of the actual level of present or past income.

Domestic demand comes from two sources: investment and consumption. If investment expands autonomously, as happens, for example, when governments decide to invest heavily in infrastructure, such investment directly and indirectly (through its multiplier effects) expands demand and induces further rounds of investment and growth. This is the 'internal', exogenous stimulus discussed earlier.

As compared to this, private investment is most often seen as induced and not autonomous, needing some external stimulus to occur. However, if governments adopt a strategy of implicitly or explicitly guaranteeing a minimal, acceptable return in particular sectors, and back this guarantee with easy access to adequate credit, debt financed private investment can also function as a source of autonomous demand. Infrastructure is a case in point.

Consumption Demand

The more difficult case to understand is the one where growth is not only based largely on domestic demand, but much of that demand takes the form of consumption expenditure. Increased consumption, since it is tethered to increases in income, is not normally seen as a stimulus to investment and growth, but an outcome of the latter. However, there is one way in which consumption can be 'autonomous' in the sense that it is not tethered to current income. That would be true if a significant share of incremental consumption is financed with credit.

In recent times, credit has played an important role in financing personal investment (in housing) and consumption in developed economies. This trend is also seen in developing countries after financial liberalisation. To the extent that this tendency operates, 'autonomous' consumption can spur demand and growth. This, however, is problematic, since households unlike governments cannot keep borrowing on the grounds that they can generate tax revenues partly because of and partly independent of the growth that their debt-financed expenditure stimulates.

Debt helps smoothen consumption and therefore partly dissociate levels of consumption from fluctuating incomes, but there are limits to household debt imposed from the side of lenders and/or borrowers, which should be determined by the magnitude and stability of expected household incomes. That makes it difficult for this kind of debt to serve as an exogenous driver of growth. But debt can be a persisting and even increasingly strong stimulus driving capitalist growth for a relatively prolonged period of time because of financial innovation, which helps transfer credit risk.

Securitisation, which allows different credit assets to be bundled, makes debt a tradable asset, and permits risk to be transferred away from those creating the credit assets in the first place. This allows mortgage companies and the banks that finance them to create far more credit assets than they would do if they had to carry all the credit risk To keep this process going, there needs to be adequate, reasonably cheap liquidity in the system, ensured in practice by a loose monetary policy on the part of central banks. Monetary policy rather than fiscal policy underlies this stimulus.

But there are other constraints to this process, since increasing the volume of credit assets requires expanding the universe of borrowers. This requires bringing into the credit net those who would earlier have been considered high risk or even unworthy of credit—the so-called sub-prime borrowers. This can go on only until at some point of time the share of sub-prime borrowers and assets in total debt exposure crosses some threshold (varying with historical circumstances). The process becomes unsustainable because the volume of simultaneous default crosses some level where the solvency of intermediary institutions is in question.

In the final analysis, this stimulus cannot be sustained and the crisis that ensues would be much more severe than the growth slowdown associated with the weakening of other kinds of exogenous stimuli, because the downturn is aggravated by a process of deleveraging, as levels of debt are sought to be brought down in ways that intensify the recession. But in the interim, for a reasonably long period, the demand infused into the system by debt financed private expenditure that is autonomous of income, induces investment and drives growth.

Revisiting the NPAs

This is exactly what has happened in India under financial liberalisation. The credit boom of the 2000s was the result of the easy liquidity situation that a surge in capital inflows created. Combined with banking policy liberalisation, this triggered a credit spiral that was based on an expansion of the universe of borrowers that brought in clients who were more prone to default.

There were two ways in which financial liberalisation facilitated a process of debt-financed, private expenditure-led growth. First, was increased lending in the form of retail loans, for housing investments, automobile and consumer durable purchases, or in the form of credit card receivables or personal loans to meet education and health expenses. The second was lending for infrastructural investments increasingly being undertaken by private investors directly or through PPP (public-private partnership) projects.

Expanding retail lending rapidly inevitably requires expanding the universe of borrowers, bringing in the process for those for whom the probability of default would be higher, given the level and stability of their incomes. As for infrastructural projects, these are the ones to which banks should not be lending without guarantees, since they are characterised by lumpy investments, long gestation lags and illquidity, whereas funds sourced by banks are substantially from saving households, looking for safety and liquidity, besides a small return over short-time intervals. The resulting maturity and liquidity mismatches, make lending to infrastructural projects too risky for banks, as opposed to investors in bonds and DFIs (development finance institutions). Since India does not have a developed corporate bond markets, and has shut down its DFIs as part of the neoliberal financial liberalisation programme, PSBs have been forced to take on the responsibility.

These factors were ignored because of the real economy boom that the credit spiral set off. But, a large number of projects to which money had been lent during the boom period that preceded 2011-12, when investment rates rose sharply, were not ones to which the banking system should have been exposed. As many of these projects found themselves unable to service their debt, loans are turning non-performing in quick succession. This trail of defaults is ensuring that the NPA ratio is continuously rising.

Fragility is also the result of the nature of the loans involved. A large part of this credit was from the PSBs to the corporate sector. In a written reply to a question posed in Rajya Sabha, submitted in July 2015, Minister of State for Finance, Jayant Sinha, reported that as of the end of March 2015 outstanding corporate loans with the PSBs stood at ₹23,522 billion. A few of these loans were individually in excess of ₹50 billion. State Bank of India had advanced 39 such loans totalling ₹4,422 billion, Canara Bank to two totalling ₹226 billion, and Bank of Baroda, Bank of India and Union Bank of India to one each amounting to ₹56.42 billion, ₹100.34 billion and ₹69.75 billion respectively. These 44 loans totalled ₹4,875 or a little more than a fifth of total lending by these banks.

The overall debt pile was also a cause for concern because it was concentrated with only a few, highly leveraged firms. Back in April 2015, the International Monetary Fund (IMF) had estimated that 37 per cent of corporate debt in India was at risk. About a third of corporate debt in India was with companies that had debt-to-equity ratios in excess of three, which was the highest in the Asia Pacific region. Moreover, a significant share of debt was with companies in whose case the profit-to-interest expenses ratio was less than one—that is, they were not generating sufficient revenues to pay the interest on their accumulated debt.

This situation is seen as having led to a large volume of corporate defaults that have showed up as either NPAs or restructured assets in the balance sheets of banks. The rapid rise was partly the result of an asset quality review mandated by the previous RBI Governor, Raghuram Rajan, which resulted in a recategorisation of a chunk of 'restructured standard assets' as NPAs in the books of the banks. Restructured assets are those in whose case, default had been postponed by adopting measures such as lowered interest rates and easier terms of repayment. But figures reported by Reuters indicate that stressed assets (or the sum of restructured and bad assets) on the books of the banks had risen from ₹8,060 billion at the end of December 2015 to ₹9,220 billion at the end of June 2016. So loans that were bad or near-bad are on the rise.

According to the RBI, GNPAs of the PSBs stood at ₹2,670 billion at the end of March 2015 as against ₹2,400 billion a year ago. The restructured advances of all banks were over ₹4,310 billion as of end-March 2015. The GNPAs of all SCBs as a percentage of gross advances stood at 4.5 per cent in March 2015 and stressed advances (which included restructured loans) at 11.1 per cent of total advances. The PSBs recorded the highest level of stressed assets at 13.5 per cent of total advances as of March 2015, as compared to 4.6 per cent in the case of private banks.

A lot of these stressed assets were on account of large borrowers, likely to be corporates. According to data reported to Parliament in early March 2015, the top 30 NPAs of PSBs totalled ₹951 billion in value as on December 2014. The total number of borrowers with loans of ₹100 million and above that had turned non-performing as at the end of September 2014 stood at 2,897 with total debt outstanding with them placed at ₹1,601.6 billion. More recently, as of March 2016, large borrowers (with liabilities of ₹5 crore and above) accounted for 58 per cent of SCB advances and 86.4 per cent of GNPAs. The top 100 borrowers accounted 16 per cent of total advances and 22.3 per cent of GNPAs. Indeed, the GNPA ratio of the top 100 borrowers rose from just 3.4 per cent in September 2015 to 22.3 per cent in March 2016, with the reclassification of restructured assets.

Unfortunately, the borrower's details in respect of defaulters against whom suits have not been filed are not disclosed as per Section 45E of the RBI Act, 1934 and other banking laws, which oblige a bank or financial institution to maintain secrecy regarding its clients. However, that corporate loans are involved here is clear from the fact that, five sub-sectors, namely, mining, iron & steel, textiles, infrastructure and aviation, which together constituted 24.8 per cent of the total advances of SCBs, had a much larger share of 51.1 per cent in the total stressed advances. Among these five sectors, infrastructure and iron & steel had a significant contribution to total stressed advances accounting for nearly 40 per cent of the total.

The fragility that this creates is worsened by the fact that in recent years, the exposure of corporates relying on borrowing to external debt has increased, because of the much lower interest rate on borrowing abroad for large firms. Many of them resorted to such borrowing without hedging against exchange rate risk, and would incur an enhanced rupee payment burden when the rupee depreciates. According to estimates from Fitch Ratings, the outstanding foreign currency debt of the 500 biggest corporate borrowers was around ₹4,000 billion as of end-March 2014. In the case of 234 of these, which accounted for 45 per cent of the total consolidated debt of the 500 and 37 per cent of their foreign currency debt, the fact that they were net foreign currency spenders in their operations made them even more vulnerable to rupee depreciation. A sharp depreciation can damage their bottom line severely.

Thus, excess debt accumulation is a major problem confronting the corporate sector that chose to expand operations to exploit the benefits of liberalisation during the high growth years between 2004 and 2010. But with India's growth slowing, even if not as much as elsewhere, the volume of that debt and its composition threatens profitability and even survival.

As the *Economic Survey 2016-17* recognised, under normal circumstances, this would have threatened the banks concerned with insolvency, perhaps triggered a bank run, forced bank closure and even precipitated a systemic crisis. India is fortunate that a large part of its banking system is owned by the government. According to the Care Ratings figures referred to earlier, 24 PSBs accounted for

88.2 per cent of the total NPAs with the public and private banks. Their NPA ratio stood at 11 per cent at the end of 2016, indicating that they have a disproportionate share of bad loans in total advances. According to the Survey, since there is belief that these banks have the backing of the government, which will keep them afloat, the bad loan problem has not, as yet, become a systemic crisis.

Seeking equity support from the market, through a controversial dilution of the government share in stockholding to below 50 per cent, though advocated, does not seem feasible. Low profits and large NPAs preclude sale of equity at reasonable prices. This has made the government's recapitalisation strategy the only available solution. Having been through many rounds of recapitalisation earlier, the government did announce a special ₹700 billion recapitalisation plan to deal with the current bloat in bank NPAs. Though significant sums have been released for the purpose, they have proved grossly inadequate to address the problem at hand. India's banks seem destined to live under the fear of insolvency at a time when they were expected to shore up their capital to meet the more stringent capital adequacy norms specified under Basel III.

Recovery is a possibility because the bad assets accumulated in the course of the lending boom after 2003 were concentrated in large loans to the corporate sector. Unfortunately, the focus of the government and the RBI, is on finding ways in which the banks can help large business groups revive, rather than how banks can recover their dues and beef up their balance sheets. According to RBI data, the rate of recovery of NPAs of SCBs through various channels (Lok Adalats, Debt Recovery Tribunals and the SARFAESI Act) has fallen from 22 per cent of amounts involved in cases referred to these channels and being considered by them at the end of March 2013 to 10.3 per cent by end-March 2016. The referred cases themselves exhaust only a small proportion of aggregate NPAs in the system. In fact, actual recoveries constitute a small proportion of the reduction in NPAs. In 2012, actual recoveries accounted for 34.4 per cent of NPA reduction, 'upgradation' (from NPA status) for 34.5 per cent and compromises/write-offs for the remaining 31.1 per cent. In 2015, these figures stood at 32.6 per cent, 26 per cent and 41.5 per cent respectively. Write-offs are rising from already high levels.

This failure to recover money lent to top corporates, has been accompanied by an effort to sell-off assets to private ARCs (asset reconstruction corporations), who could acquire NPAs at a negotiated discount. They make an upfront payment of as low as 5 per cent of the sums due, with the balance covered by security receipts accepted by the banks from the ARCs, which need to be redeemed only when the ARCs manage to sell the assets concerned. Thus, the ARCs were being contracted to recover a small percentage of the total NPA value, with their fee depending on the difference between the acquisition and sale price. The result has been that when the discount on NPAs sold by banks was sought to be reduced, the volume of NPAs sold have come down.

It is in this context that the Economic Survey's case for the creation of a Public Sector Asset Rehabilitation Agency (PARA) has to be assessed. In the Survey's view:

> Cash flows in the large stressed companies have been deteriorating over the past few years, to the point where debt reductions of more than 50 per cent will often be needed to restore viability. The only alternative would be to convert debt to equity, take over the companies, and *then sell them at a loss* (emphasis added).

So the point here is that instead of recapitalising the banks, the government should recapitalise the companies at taxpayers' expense. The Finance Ministry's claim is that this is necessary because the companies cannot share any blame for their current position. The Survey argues:

> Without doubt, there are cases where debt repayment problems have been caused by diversion of funds. But the vast bulk of the problem has been caused by unexpected changes in the economic

environment: timetables, exchange rates, and growth rate assumptions going wrong.

This unabashed call for subsidising private sector losses comes at a time when the government claims it does not have enough money to recapitalise the banks. Government and RBI spokespersons have been recommending that PSBs should sell new equity and dilute government stake to strengthen their capital base. But if banks are not recapitalised, there may not be many buyers for their equity. Meanwhile, the Finance Ministry is suggesting making transfers to the private sector through a roundabout scheme that helps write off their debt.

30

National Development Banks and Sustainable Infrastructure in India

NAGESH KUMAR

in collaboration with Pradeep K. Keshari and Rohan Ray

Introduction: National Development Banks in India

NDBs (national development banks) have played an important role in India's development over the years. In the early period after Independence, the focus of NDBs was generally of supporting industrial development. Infrastructure development was supported by the budgetary financing by the governments. However, over time with the widening gaps in infrastructure requirements and staggering resources required to close them prompted governments to turn to mobilise private investments. Hence, NDBs began to be established for facilitating infrastructure development including sustainable infrastructure through PPPs (public private partnerships). In addition to the sectoral coverage, the sources of funds and business models have undergone substantial transformation. This paper summarises this transformation and reviews the financing of infrastructure and sustainable infrastructure. It also presents case studies of two key NDBs engaged in infrastructure financing. It concludes with a few policy lessons from Indian experience. There has been revival of interest in the NDBs all across the world in the context of the potential role that they can play in closing the infrastructure gaps and building sustainable infrastructure by supporting the PPPs.

The rest of the paper is structured as follows. Section 2 provides an overview of infrastructure gaps, financing challenges and NDBs before summarising the evolution of NDBs in India over the post-Independence period. Section 3 overviews the infrastructure gaps and financing challenges facing India. Section 4 reviews the issues involved in sustainable infrastructure development. Section 5 summarises the policy framework for infrastructure NDBs including the sources of finance and their financing models. Section 6 concludes the paper with a few lessons from Indian experience.

Infrastructure Gaps, Financing Challenges and NDBs

Table 30.1 shows that India continues to suffer from significant infrastructure gaps not only compared to global averages but also with respect to its Asian neighbours. Figure 30.1 shows the infrastructure scores and rank among countries in terms of infrastructure development. India ranks below Sri Lanka and Indonesia, its Asian neighbours and way below China, Malaysia and Thailand not to mention developed countries of the region namely Japan and Republic of Korea.

Closing the infrastructure gaps has needed staggering and rising requirement of resources over the years. World Bank has estimated that South Asia needs around US $2.5 trillion investments by 2020. India is expected to require around US$3.5 trillion in infrastructure investments by 2030 according to the Boston Consulting Group.

Given that overstretched budgets of the governments in the region have limitations in meeting such staggering requirements of resources, the attention has been focused on harnessing the potential of private investment for closing the financing gaps including through PPPs. India has already been quite advanced in mobilising PPPs having achieved financial closure for 847 projects (76% of total projects) amounting to US$ 338 billion since 2002 (Aggarwal 2015). Private sector enterprises tend to leverage their equity with borrowings, typically in a 30:70 proportion as in India. To facilitate flow of private

Table 30.1

Infrastructure Availability in Subregions in Asia and the Pacific and South Asian Countries

	Telecom Access (Per 100 people), 2013	*Electricity Access (% of population), 2011*	*Access to Improved Water (% of population) 2012*	*Access to Improved Sanitation (% of population), 2012*	*Internet Users (Per 100 people), 2013*	*Rail Density (km of railway per 1000 km²), 2012*	*Road Density (km of road per 1000 km²), 2011*	*Paved Roads (% of roads), 2012*
East Asia	114	98	93	69	50	8	400	64
South-East Asia	125	77	89	71	26	4.7	276	55
South Asia	74	73	91	40	14	19.4	1123	52
Bangladesh	75	60	85	57	7	21.8	1838	10
India	73	75	93	36	15	21.7	1578	54
Nepal	80	76	88	37	13	..	139	54
Pakistan	74	69	91	48	11	10.1	341	73
Sri Lanka	108	85	94	92	22	23.3	1819	15
World	109	78	89	64	38	9.1	275	57

Source: UNESCAP based on UNESCAP online statistical database.

Figure 30.1

Global Competitiveness Index 2015/16: Infrastructure Scores and Ranking of Selected ESCAP Countries

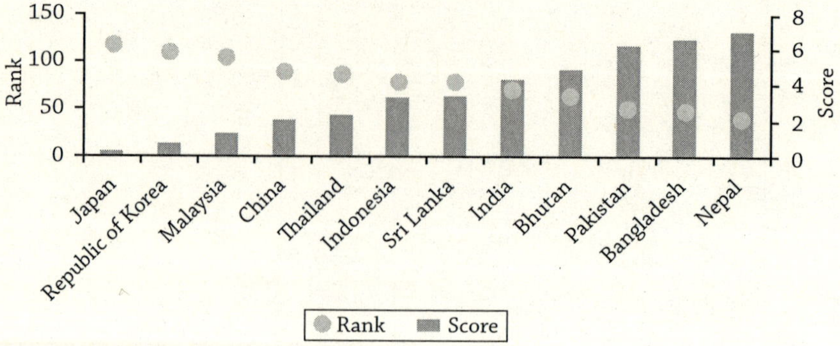

Source: Based on World Economic Forum (2015). *Global Competitiveness Report 2015-16*.

investments for infrastructure, therefore, it is important to create institutions that can arrange debt portion.

NDBs in India

India has pioneered NDBs from early post-Independence period. It would appear that most of the NDBs are government owned, some have started as government companies but were privatised or converted into public companies over time but a few of them are private sector initiatives. The other important observation from the list is that the early NDBs were established to promote industrialisation, the more recent ones are typically dedicated to infrastructure development. This transformation of NDBs from industry promotion to infrastructure financing is more clearly observed for India as summarised below.

Finally, South Asian countries have also established the SAARC Development Fund (SDF) within the SAARC framework headquartered in Thimphu, Bhutan in 2010. SDF has social, economic and infrastructure development windows for lending to projects in member countries that benefit more than one country. While the social window has been operating for the past four years, the other two windows are being operationalised in 2016. SDF will seek to catalyse the infrastructure investments in South Asia working with other multilateral and regional development partners.[1]

NDBs in India have evolved over the years in terms of number, scales of operation, range of activities, business models, with the changing policy focus as summarised below.

Changing Landscape of NDBs in India: Three Distinct Phases

NDBs in India have evolved over time through three distinct phases (see Table 30.2). In the early post-Independence period, the Indian government established three NDBs viz., the Industrial Finance Corporation of India (IFCI) in 1948, the Industrial Credit & Investment Corporation of India (ICICI) in 1955, and the Industrial Development Bank of India (IDBI) in 1964 to support the industrial enterprises as it was pursuing import substituting industrialisation strategy. The State governments also established the state financing corporations to complement the NDBs. The NDBs focused on providing term-loans to the manufacturing enterprises including heavy industries e.g. steel, cement, machinery, automotive, chemicals. To complement their main objective and ensure viability and security of their lending, these NDBs also offered technical services to industrial projects which included loan syndication, project appraisal (including managerial, market, industry, technology and financial appraisal), corporate advisory services, financial guarantees, public issue management, underwriting etc. There was a broad division of labour between the commercial banks which focused on short-term working capital requirements of the corporate sector while NDBs on longer terms loans. For their own resources, NDBs had access to soft window of long-term funds from the country's central bank, Reserve Bank of India (RBI) at concessional rate. They could also raise

1. *www.sdf.org*

funds through issue of bonds, investment into which by commercial banks qualified for SLR (statutory liquidity ratio) purposes imposed by Reserve Bank of India (RBI). They also had access to lines of credit from multilateral and bilateral agencies duly guaranteed by the Government of India.

During the 1970s and 1980s, a number of NDBs were established by the Indian government to serve specific purposes. These included refinancing institutions (National Bank for Agriculture and Rural Development [NABARD], Small Industries Development Bank of India [SIDBI], National Horticulture Board [NHB]) refinance for promoting specific activities. For instance, NABARD for promoting agriculture and rural development; SIDBI to promote SMEs (small and medium enterprises); NHB for housing. Other NDBs included Rural Electrification Council (REC) for supporting rural electrification; HUDCO for housing and urban development; EXIM Bank for providing trade finance; PFC for electricity generation, IREDA for non-renewable energy, among others.[2]

Following the initiation of economic reforms since 1991, the landscape of NDBs has changed dramatically. The first generation of NDBs namely the trinity of IFCI, ICICI, and IDBI lost their privileged access to low cost funds provided by the government by early 1990s, as a part of reforms. This put them at a disadvantage compared to commercial banks which had access to low cost funds from their retail and corporate customers through current accounts. This led them to raise capital through selling equity, by public deposits at higher interest, by issuing bonds, or external commercial borrowings devoid of government guarantees. Reforms and liberalisation unleashed in the domestic market also exposed their customers in the industrial sector to external competition. Those that could not compete had to close down leading to rising proportion of NPAs (non-performing assets). ICICI and IDBI converted themselves into full service

2. See RBI (2004), *Working Group on DFIs*, Section 1.4.3.

Table 30.2

Changing Landscape of NDBs in India, 1947-2015

Early post-Independence period, 1947-1969	Pre-reform years 1970s-1990	Post-reform 1991-
NDBs for supporting industrialisation	NDBs for specific sectors	Infrastructure financing institutions for supporting PPPs
IFCI (1948) ICICI (1955) IDBI (1964) + State Industrial Development Banks in different provinces	Rural electrification: REC (1970) Housing and urban development: HUDCO (1970) Agriculture & Rural Development: NABARD (1981) Trade: EXIM Bank (1981) Power: PFC (1986) Shipping: SCICI (1986) Renewable energy: IREDA (1987) Housing: NHB (1988) SMEs: SIDBI (1989)	IDFC (1997) IIFCL (2006) IL&FS, L&T Infra Finance, SREI Infra Finance (in the private sector) IDBI and ICICI turned into commercial banks IFCI enters infrastructure

Source: Author's compilation from various sources.

banks as a part of their strategy to obtain access to low cost funds. ICICI managed the transition to emerge as the largest private sector commercial bank. It became the first company from India to get listed itself in 1999 at New York Stock Exchange (NYSE). IDBI, on the other hand, has been struggling in this transition to become commercial bank since 2004. IFCI is the only one of the trinity of industrial NDBs that has stayed in its original form although it has diversified its portfolio towards infrastructure.

Given the need to mobilise staggering resources for infrastructure development from private sector, new NDBs were established—IDFC in 1997 and IIFCL in 2006. IDFC and IIFCL have both become important catalysts of infrastructure investments including sustainable infrastructure and have helped to mobilise funds from a wide spectrum of sources. There were other institutions established in the private sector namely IL&FS, L&T Infra Finance and SREI Infra Finance. In addition, the sectoral NDBs continue to support infrastructure development actively.

Infrastructure and Sustainable Infrastructure Financing Challenges in India

Since the onset of economic reforms in 1991, most of the infrastructure sectors have been thrown open for private sector including telecom, ports, roads, power generation and distribution. With the acceleration of economic growth following reforms, infrastructure scarcities started to become serious. Table 30.3 shows that the investment in infrastructure has doubled in every successive five year plan.[3] Over the years, it became increasingly difficult for the government to fund infrastructure investment through budgetary allocations as in the past. Hence, there has been an increasing reliance on private sector. Private sector investments in India tend to follow the debt to equity ratio of 70:30, as observed earlier. To facilitate flow of private investments for infrastructure, therefore, it is important to create institutions that can arrange debt portion. It is in this context that new age NDBs namely IDFC and IIFCL have been created in 1997 and 2006 respectively. IDFC and IIFCL have mobilised their resources from a variety of sources including sometimes unconventional innovative ones as discussed later. Given India's infrastructure financing requirements of around US$3.5 trillion by 2030, financial innovations to mobilise resources are going to be important for meeting the challenge of raising resources of that magnitude.

Table 30.3

Infrastructure Investments under the Five Year Plans, 2002-2017

	10th Five Year Plan 2002-2007	*11th Five Year Plan 2007-2012*	*12th Five Year Plan 2012-2017*
Infrastructure Investment (US$ billion)	240	500	1000
% of GDP	5	7	10
Budgetary Resources %	78	63	50
Private Sector/PPP %	22	37	48

Source: Author's compilation from various sources.

3. *Working Sub-Group on Infrastructure: Infrastructure Funding Requirements and its Sources over the implementation period of the Twelfth Five Year Plan (2012-2017)*, Planning Commission, Government of India.

In that context, establishment of the New Development Bank of BRICS and the Asian Infrastructure Investment Bank (AIIB) is an important development as it will help in expanding the availability of funds for infrastructure development in Asia.

Financing Needs in Key Infrastructure Sectors

Power: CRISIL Research expects investments of ₹8.2 trillion in the power sector over the next 5 years (2015-2016 to 2019-20). Generation segment investments (₹3.9 trillion) will continue to account for 48 per cent of total power sector investments but are expected to slow down due to drop in pace of capacity additions. On the other hand, investments in the transmission segment (₹2.4 trillion) are expected to witness strong growth over the next 5 years led by robust investments by Power Grid Corporation Limited coupled with steady investments from states including Maharashtra, Gujarat, Rajasthan, Chhattisgarh, Andhra Pradesh (AP) and Karnataka. Distribution segment investments (₹1.9 trillion) are expected to be driven by increased outlay from the Central government on various distribution related schemes.

Around 60 per cent of the total investment is expected to be funded through loans from SCBs (scheduled commercial banks) and central power financing institutions such as Power Finance Corporation (PFC) and Rural Electrification Corporation (REC). On the equity front while Central sector companies such as National Thermal Power Corporation (NTPC), National Hydroelectric Power Corporation (NHPC) and Power Grid Corporation of India Limited (PGCIL) have healthy cash position, few private sector companies such as Jaiprakash Power, GMR Infra and Lanco Infratech will opt for the 5:25 scheme as well as resort to asset sales to lower debt and fund under-construction projects.

Airports: The airport infrastructure sector received investments of ₹361 billion (at 2006-07 prices) in the Eleventh Five Year Plan (2007-08 to 2011-12). Of this, over 60 per cent was for development of metro airports under the PPP model; greenfield airports at Bengaluru and Hyderabad as well as brownfield airports at Delhi and Mumbai. These four PPP metro airports accounted for about 54 per cent of total passenger traffic in 2014-15. Other investments were directed towards modernisation of the airports at Chennai and Kolkata. Moreover an estimated ₹45 billion was allocated for modernising 35 non-metro airports. Till date the Airports Authority of India (AAI) has completed development works at 33 airports. Development work at Vadodara and Khajuraho airports is ongoing; modernisation at Vadodara airport is expected to be completed by first quarter of 2016-17.

The Twelfth Five Year Plan period (2012-13 to 2016-2017) forecasts investments of ₹675 billion for developing airport infrastructure. Of these, over 75 per cent would be via private participation/PPP with the rest through AAI. However, CRISIL Research expects just half of these investments to materialise over the plan period as most projects are greenfield ventures and hence take time to receive approvals and resolve land acquisition hurdles. Over 2015-16 to 2019-20, CRISIL Research expects investments in airports to the tune of ₹410-430 billion which is 1.4 times higher than the past five years.

Sea Ports: Majority of the investments in the last five years are estimated to have been pumped in by the private sector. Of the private sector investments, bulk of the investments have been driven towards non-major ports whereas public sector contribution in the investments has remained limited to maintenance of draft and building of allied infrastructure such as roads at major ports. Going forward, CRISIL Research estimates about ₹550-600 billion to be invested in the ports sector over the next 5 years. Odisha, Gujarat, AP and Maharashtra are the four states which will attract about 80 per cent of the investments. Around 60-65 per cent of the investment value is expected to come at non-major ports in contrast to major ports accounting for higher capacity additions (around 52% of total capacity addition). One of the key reasons for this is that the new LNG terminals that account for heavier capital expenses are expected to come at non-major ports like Dahej, Gangavaram, Kakinada etc. As part of assessing investment value, we have not included the non-core allied investments towards rail and road connectivity CFS (container freight stations) etc.

Sustainable Infrastructure Development in India

India recognised the relevance of renewable energy for its energy security way before the sustainability debates started especially in the wake of the two oil shocks of the 1970s. The Commission for Additional Sources of Energy (CASE) in the Department of Science & Technology was established in 1981 with the responsibility of formulating policies and programmes for development of new and renewable energy and coordinate R&D. In 1982, a new Department of Non-conventional Energy Sources (DNES) was created in the then Ministry of Energy. The Indian Renewable Energy Development Agency (IREDA) was established in 1987 to support renewable energy and energy efficiency projects under the DNES. In 1992, DNES evolved into the Ministry of Non-conventional Energy Sources which was renamed as the Ministry of New and Renewable Energy in 2006.

Table 30.4 summarises the status of renewable energy capacity and targets in India as in 2015 covering wind energy, small hydro power, solar energy, biomass and related sources. As on 31 March 2015, installed capacity in renewable energy sector stood at 38.7 GW of which wind energy had the highest share of 63 per cent followed by 11 per cent each in solar, small hydro power and biomass/cogeneration. However, in future a greater reliance has been put on harnessing the potential of solar energy with its cost going down and has set up a target of having 100 GW of solar capacity by 2022 besides 60 GW of wind energy. In its INDCs (intended nationally determined contribution) submitted to the United Nations Framework Convention on Climate Change (UNFCCC) on 1 October 2015, India has agreed to reduce its greenhouse gas emissions intensity of its GDP (gross domestic product) by

33-35 per cent by 2030 compared to 2005 levels. To meet this target, India will need to generate about 40 per cent of its electricity from non-fossil fuel sources as compared to 30 per cent presently. Thus, India has to increase its installed capacity of renewable power by 33 per cent to 300-350 GW by 2030, thus further doubling the renewable capacity from 175 GW in 2022. Achievement of INDCs target will require USD 2.5 trillion of investments as well as sourcing of an array of technologies from developed countries and collaborative R&D for their diffusion in the country. As a result, there is a currently a heavy focus on renewable energy especially solar energy.

Table 30.4

Renewable Energy Capacity in India, 2015

	Target FY- 2015-16	*Cumulative Capacity as on 30.09.2015*	*Target by 2022*
Wind Power	2400.00	24,376.26	60,000
Solar Power	1400.00	4,344.91	100,000
Small Hydro Power	250.00	4,146.90	5,000
Bio-power (biomass & gasification and bagasse cogeneration)	400.00	4,418.55	10,000
Total (including off-grid and waste to energy)	4590.00	38,683.70	175,000

Source: Ministry of New and Renewable Energy, Government of India.

Solar Energy: CRISIL Research expects 10-11 GW of solar PV capacity additions over 2016 to 2018 (refers to April-March). This will be driven by additions under National Solar Mission (NSM) Phase II—batch II, III and V coupled with capacities tendered by distribution companies in various states including Karnataka, Telangana, AP, Punjab, Madhya Pradesh (MP) and Tamil Nadu (TN). Capacities tendered by cash-rich PSUs (public sector undertakings) such as NTPC, Coal India Limited, ONGC and others will further support additions. Moreover government initiatives to facilitate land acquisition, improve transmission infrastructure and funding availability will support capacity additions.

Wind Energy: While wind power constituted only 8.6 per cent of the total power generation installed capacity (274 GW) in India as of June 2015, its share in renewable energy capacity (36 GW) was 65 per cent. Central government provides two incentives—AD (accelerated depreciation) benefit and GBI (generation-based incentive)—to encourage wind power capacity additions. AD benefit which was restored in August 2014 allows depreciation of 80 per cent on wind assets in the first year. In GBI, the generator receives ₹0.50 per unit of electricity generated subject to a cap of ₹10 million per MW. It is estimated that wind power accounted for about 3 per cent of the country's total power generated in 2014-2015. CRISIL research expects wind power capacity additions of 10-11 GW over the next three years (2016-2018) as compared to 7 GW over the last three years (2013-2015). Re-instatement of AD benefits in Union Budget 2014-15 led to a recovery with capacity additions of 2,300 MW in 2014-2015 (a 10% y-o-y increase). Capacity additions were led by states such as Karnataka, Rajasthan, MP, and AP which together contributed about 40 per cent of capacity additions (in 2014-15) driven by attractive preferential tariff and availability of sufficient evacuation infrastructure.

Some key lenders to wind projects include SBI, Axis Bank, L&T Infrastructure Finance Company Ltd., IREDA, and PFC Green Energy. While few players such as Ostro energy and Mytrah energy have received foreign funding from Actis LLP and Merrill Lynch respectively, the proportion of foreign funding is much higher in solar power projects since it is typically linked to import of solar modules. Till date most of the wind energy projects have been financed with recourse to the parent company's balance sheet and/or promoter's guarantees. Indian banks have financed most wind power projects on recourse basis at interest rates of 12-13 per cent. Bankers have been wary of extending project financing to these projects due to lack of region specific performance data risk related to variability of wind patterns and weak health of discoms.

Going forward, funding is expected to remain a critical factor to support capacity additions especially given the aggressive target of 60 GW by 2022 set by the government. However few large public sector banks (such as SBI), public sector financial institutions (such as PTC India Financial Services Ltd) and other large private sector banks (such as ICICI and YES Bank) have committed to fund renewable energy projects.

The PE (private equity) investors have evinced significant interest in the recent past in funding the wind power projects. Few companies such as Ostro energy (Funded by Actis LLP), Green Infra (Sembcorp), Renew Wind Power (Goldman Sachs Group Inc.) and Mytrah Energy (funded by Merrill Lynch and Apollo Global Management) are backed by the global private equity funds which typically funds projects at a lower interest cost. Actis LLP is funding $230 million of projects to be set up under Ostro energy in February 2015; Mytrah Energy raised about $70 million from Merrill Lynch and Apollo Global Management; Goldman Sachs bought $135 worth of equity in ReNew Wind Power in June 2013.

Biomass: As on 30 September 2015, the total installed capacity of biomass-based power has increased to 4.4 GW. Almost 413 MW of capacity has been added during the year of which nearly 295 MW was added by Maharashtra and Karnataka. Currently, Uttar Pradesh (UP) and Maharashtra lead the market with installed capacities of 776 MW and 940 MW respectively. The potential for power generation from biomass is nearly 17,500 MW (agro residue and plantations) while an additional 5,000 MW potential exists in bagasse-based co-generation.

Small Hydropower (SHP): The installed capacity of SHP plants has increased at a CAGR (compound annual growth rate) of 9.4 per cent to 4.1GW by September 2015 from 2,180 MW in 2007-08. Karnataka with an installed capacity of 1,031 MW has the largest SHP capacity in India. Ministry of New and Renewable Energy (MNRE) has set a target of achieving 5,000 MW of cumulative installed

SHP capacities by the end of the 12th Five Year Plan. Of this nearly 33 per cent of the potential SHP capacity lies in the northern region.

Sources of Finance for NDBs for Infrastructure Development and Business Models

As observed earlier, the early NDBs namely the trinity of IFCI, ICICI and IDBI depended largely on the government funds in the form of share capital and their access to low cost funds from commercial banks facilitated by the government policy. Government also helped them raise resources from MDBs (multilateral development banks) and external markets through guarantees. To support the financing of infrastructure investments, the Government through the central bank has created more flexible guidelines allowing the NDBs to raise external commercial borrowings and prudent lending norms by creating a new category of IFCs (infrastructure finance companies).

Policy Framework for Infrastructure Finance Companies

In 2010, the RBI created a new category of IFCs among the NBFCs (non-banking financial companies), a term that includes NDBs in India.[4] To qualify for an IFC, a NBFC should have a minimum of 75 per cent of its total assets in the form of infrastructure loans, it should not accept deposits from public, it should have owned funds of atleast ₹3 billion, and enjoy a minimum credit rating 'A' and have a CRAR (capital to risk assets ratio) of 15 per cent (with a minimum Tier I capital of 10%). As per these criteria, besides IDFC and IIFCL, a number of sectoral NDBs were recognised as IFCs including REC, HUDCO, IREDA, PFC, IRFC, IL&FS, SREI. Having been granted a bank license by RBI on 23 July 2015, IDFC has converted itself into a commercial bank, IDFC Bank, with effect from 1 October 2015.

4. RBI Circular No. RBI/2009-10/316 DNBS.PD. CC No. 168/03.02.089/2009-10 dated 12 February 2010.

IFCs are allowed to exceed the standard credit norms[5] and can lend to a single borrower up to 25 per cent of its owned funds as opposed to the earlier norm of 15 per cent, and to a single group of borrowers, up to 40 per cent from 25 per cent. IFCs are also permitted to avail of ECBs, including the outstanding ECBs (external commercial borrowings), up to 75 per cent of their owned funds, for on lending to the infrastructure sector as defined under the ECB policy.

Besides relying on the ECBs, the new generation NDBs namely IDFC, IIFCL as well as the sectoral IFCs have explored a variety of sources sometimes in an innovative manner as summarised below.

Foreign Exchange Reserves for Infrastructure Development: India has pioneered mobilisation of some of its foreign exchange reserves for infrastructure development through IIFC (UK) Ltd, a special purpose vehicle incorporated in London in April 2008 as a subsidiary of IIFCL. IIFC (UK) issues foreign currency denominated bonds for investment by the RBI. The funds, thus raised, are utilised by the company for on lending to the Indian companies, implementing infrastructure projects in India and/or to co-finance the ECBs of such projects for capital expenditure outside India in foreign exchange such as equipment purchase.[6]

Green Bonds and Infrastructure Bonds: NDBs active in renewable energy including PFC, REC, IREDA among others are raising low cost, long-term resources for investment in renewable energy generation through issue of tax free bonds, called Green Bonds.[7] Infrastructure NDBs including IIFCL, IDFC have also been raising resources from the market through issue of infrastructure

5. NBFCs (deposit accepting or holding) Prudential Norms (Reserve Bank) Directions, 2007.

6. *RBI Staff Studies* #SS(DEAP) 4:2010: 46-7.

7. REC, PFC, IREDA, others to raise ₹5,000 crores via tax-free bonds, *Live Mint*, 3 June 2015. Subsequently, the Securities and Investment Board of India issued guidelines for Green Bonds in December 2015.

bonds of 10 years duration that enjoy some tax benefits up to a limit of ₹20,000 per accounting year.

Infrastructure Debt Funds (IDFs): Infrastructure NDBs have been allowed to launch IDFs that serve as investment vehicles in which domestic/offshore institutional investors, specially insurance and pension funds can invest through units and bonds issued by the IDFs. IDFs would essentially act as vehicles for refinancing existing debt of infrastructure companies, thereby creating fresh headroom for banks to lend to fresh infrastructure projects or take over loans extended to PPP infrastructure projects. IIFCL, IDFC among other NDBs have launched their IDFs to mobilise resources through this route.

Intermediating Resources from MDBs (multilateral development banks) and Bilateral Donors: Some NDBs are intermediating the funds provided by MDBs for infrastructure development. IIFCL, for instance, has committed lines of long-term credit from ADB (USD$1.9 bn), World Bank ($195 mn), KfW (Euro 50 mn). It has also executed a financial agreement with European Investment Bank for Euro 200 mn. Multilateral funding agencies such as ADB and IFC and private equity funds are supporting a number of solar projects. In 2014-15, these agencies sanctioned approximately $610 million for various renewable energy projects.

National Investment and Infrastructure Fund (NIIF): NIIF is a fund being created by the Government of India, following the announcement in the Union Budget 2015-2016, for enhancing infrastructure financing in the country. Proposed to be set up as a trust, it would raise debt to invest in the equity of infrastructure NDBs. The initial authorised corpus of NIIF would be ₹40,000 crore, with Government's contribution of 49 per cent and rest open for contribution from others including sovereign wealth funds, public sector enterprises, domestic pension and provident funds and NSSF (national small savings fund). NIIF may utilise the proceeds of monetised land and other public assets for infrastructure development.

The establishment of NIIF was approved by the Securities and Exchange Board of India (SEBI) on 28 December 2015 (Sikarwar 2015).

National Clean Energy Fund (NCEF): Given the capital intensive nature of solar power, cost of capital plays an important role in determining viability. In order to provide funds for development of solar energy resources, the NCEF was established in 2010-11 and the total collection so far (till 2014-15) under the fund is ₹171 billion. As on September 2014, about ₹36 billion of budgetary allocations have been made from this fund to various renewable energy projects. In 2015-16, the budgetary allocation to renewable energy stood at ₹61 billion led by ₹20 billion allocation through NCEF. State Bank of India (SBI) has committed ₹750 billion in debt funding over the next five years to 15 GW of renewable energy projects.

Ujjawal Discom Assurance Yojana: Although not designed to be a source of funds for infrastructure, UDAY is a debt recast scheme for state-run power distribution companies which will receive funds from the government to repay debts owed to Power Finance Corporation (PFC) and Rural Electrification Council (REC). The PFC and REC in turn are planning to mobilise the funds received from the utilities to enhance their focus on renewable sector for supporting renewable energy investments including through refinancing and take-out finance. According to reports, the magnitude of such lending is likely to be around ₹1,000 billion (Singh 2016).

India Infrastructure Project Development Fund: One of the constraints for infrastructure development has been a lack of a pipeline of credible, bankable projects that can be offered to the private sector through competitive bidding process. To address this constraint, the Government of India established the IIPDF in July 2007 with an initial contribution of ₹1,000 million. IIPDF supports up to 75 per cent of costs for developing potential PPP projects through an advisory panel of pre-qualified experts as part of the overall PPP development framework. The IIPDF is open to access by all Central government and State government agencies that are willing to abide by specified criteria. The IIPDF may be replenished through recovery of costs from successful bidders.[8] One of the NDBs namely IL&FS has also established an India Project Development Fund (IPDF) towards funding project development expenses of large infrastructure projects, primarily in surface transport, ports, water and power infrastructure. IPDF meets all project development costs and takes on the development risk up to financial closure.[9] IDFC has also developed a project development arm, supporting projects through feasibility, structuring, and presentation to bidders.

Models of Infrastructure Financing

Besides direct lending to companies undertaking infrastructure projects, NDBs especially IIFCL, have evolved other modalities of promoting infrastructure financing including take-out finance and credit enhancement schemes as follows:

Senior and Subordinated Debt: As part of a consortium, IIFCL provides long-term funds to commercially viable infrastructure projects, taking an exposure of up to 20 per cent of total project cost (including subordinate debt and refinance, if any). Up to 31 December 2014, on a standalone basis, IIFCL has made cumulative gross sanctions of ₹602 billion under direct lending to 344 projects, and disbursements of ₹241 billion.

Takeout Finance: A large part of lending to infrastructure is still made by commercial banks. In order to address the asset-liability mismatch and exposure constraints faced by banks, IIFCL is taking over loans from the books of the banks and free up their funds for investing in newer infrastructure projects. IIFCL lends up to 30 per cent of total project cost (including direct lending). Up to 31 December 2014, IIFCL has made net sanctions of ₹97

8. *http://www.pppinindia.com/pdf/guideline_scheme_IIPDF.pdf*

9. *www.ilfsindia.com*

billion in 54 projects (after cancellation) and has disbursed ₹65 billion.

Credit Enhancement Scheme: Under this scheme, IIFCL provides its partial credit guarantee to enhance the credit rating of bonds (for refinancing of existing loans) of infrastructure companies. IIFCL can undertake credit enhancement to the extent which enhances the credit rating of the project bonds issued by the issuer up to maximum of AA subject to a maximum of 50 per cent of the total amount of project bonds issued. This enables channelisation of long-term funds from investors like insurance and pension funds in such bonds. ADB is providing backstop guarantee facility to IIFCL for up to 50 per cent of IIFCL's underlying risk pertaining to the credit enhancement scheme.

Refinance Scheme: IIFCL provides refinance to banks and other eligible financial institutions for their loans to infrastructure projects. Up to 31 December 2014, IIFCL had made cumulative disbursements of ₹62 billion as refinance. IREDA under its IREDA-NCEF refinance scheme refinances the 30 per cent of total loan disbursed by the SCBs/financial institutions to the clean energy project developers at concessional rate of interest.

Specialised Subsidiaries for Sustainable Infrastructure: Some NDBs are creating specialised organisations to focus on sustainable infrastructure. PFC India Limited, for instance, has set up a specialised subsidiary PFC Green Power to focus on renewable energy and had lent ₹174 billion to the renewable energy projects comprising 35 per cent of the outstanding loan book at the end of March 2014.[10]

To sum up therefore, NDBs are playing an important role in infrastructure and sustainable infrastructure development through catalysing larger investments. Catalyst role of NDBs through different modalities of financing infrastructure is clear from the fact that IIFCL,

10. See PFC *Annual Report 2013-14.*

for instance, has supported 342 projects up to March 2015 that would mobilise private investment of US$ 110 billion with an investment of $12 billion of which $7.6 billion has been disbursed. It has raised about $6.5 billion from domestic markets through a mix of infrastructure bonds and tax free bonds, long-term loans from insurance companies and small savings funds and has intermediated funds provided by MDBs and foreign exchange reserves through its UK based subsidiary. They are also providing technical expertise and funding for development of bankable projects.

Concluding Remarks

This paper has reviewed the role of NDBs in infrastructure financing in India in the context of need to close wide infrastructure gaps and staggering resource requirements to close them. It would appear that the NDBs have evolved in terms of their functions, sources of finance, business models and lending policies. Starting with the objective of supporting industrialisation, new age NDBs support infrastructure development and sustainable infrastructure investments through a variety of ways and through funds mobilised from diverse domestic and international sources. These NDBs are complemented by a number of NDBs catering to specific infrastructure sectors. The growing focus of the government on harnessing the potential of renewable energy is directing their activities to sustainable infrastructure.

NDBs are raising their funds from domestic and international markets backed by sovereign guarantees, through a mix of infrastructure bonds, green bonds, through new debt mutual funds that help to mobilise funds from insurance companies and pension funds. Besides ECB and intermediating the credit lines provided by MDBs, mobilisation of foreign exchange reserves for infrastructure investments has been pioneered in a very unconventional manner through a special purpose vehicle. Infrastructure financing is likely to be boosted further with the recent establishment of a major national infrastructure investment fund by the government to refinance NDBs resources.

NDBs are helping to address the issue of asset-liability mismatch inherent in bank-lending to infrastructure that continues to provide the bulk of debt to infrastructure investments. NDBs have begun to mobilise large scale longer term resources. They are also relieving the balance sheets of banks by through take-out finance and through credit enhancement strategies.

The experience shows that NDBs are able to catalyse very large scale of investments with relatively modest funds, working as a part of consortia which also help to diversify risks.

In terms of lessons from Indian experience, NDBs are highly sensitive to the enabling policy framework of the government that can make or mar their viability. Clear policy objectives, framework and support by the government are key to their success. Another constraint faced by NDBs has been a ready pipeline of bankable projects that has led NDBs to establish project development and technical advisory arms that support the project authorities in development of bankable projects. In recognition of this constraint, the government has also established a lending facility for project feasibility preparation. Therefore, NDBs' contribution to infrastructure development goes beyond providing financial resources.

Given the enormity of the infrastructure challenge faced by India requiring mobilisation of nearly $3.5 trillion by 2030, there is need for huge mobilisation of resources. In that context, establishment of new MDBs including NDB of BRICS and AIIB is an important development of interest for India. As a founder member of both the institutions, India has much to contribute to their evolution as robust financial institutions equipped to play an important development role complementing the existing MDBs. India has also much to benefit from arrival of the new players on horizon for lending for infrastructure development in developing countries. The new banks may draw upon the professional expertise available with Indian NDBs as they establish their own teams. They may also develop synergistic relationship with Indian NDBs like the existing MDBs have developed providing them lines of credit for infrastructure development for onward lending. In particular, there would be huge opportunities of cooperation between the Indian and South Asian NDBs and the new banks in the sustainable infrastructure development, given the huge requirements of funds in the region.

References

Aggarwal, Abhay (2015) *PPP Trends and Initiatives in South Asian Countries.* Presentation made at the Policy Dialogue on PPP for Infrastructure Development in South Asia Organized by UNESCAP 21-22 September, Kathmandu, Available at *http://www.unescap.org/sites/default/files/Day%201%20-%20Session%202.1%20-%20South%20Asia%20-%20EY.pdf*

Ahluwalia, M.S. (1997). "Financing Private Infrastructure: Lessons from India", in H. Kohli, A. Mody and M. Walton (eds.), *Choices for Efficient Private Provision of Infrastructure in East Asia.* pp.85-104.

Association of Development Financing Institutions in Asia and the Pacific (ADFIP), (2010). *Key Performance Indicators for Development Finance Institutions: A Complete User's Package.* Manila, Philippines: The ADFIAP Secretariat.

Cambridge Economic Policy Associates Ltd (2015). *Mobilising Finance or Infrastructure in Sub-Saharan Africa and South Asia: Literature Review.* Cambridge Economic Policy Associates Ltd.

Chaturvedi, R. (2011). "Funding Infrastructure", *Indian Infrastructure,* January. pp.88-89.

Das, S.B. and C.R. James (2013). *Addressing Infrastructure Financing in Asia.* Institute of Southeast Asian Studies.

Dasgupta, A. and H. Sahai (2013) "The Financing of Infrastructure Projects", *Live Mint.* Available from *www.livemint.com/*

Ministry of Finance (2015). *Project Information: Private Sector Infrastructure Projects (All India) Report ID: SD2.* Accessed on 24 October. Available at *www.InfrastructureIndia.gov.in*

Gutierrez, E., H. Rudolph, T. Homa and E.B. Beneit (2011). "Development Banks: Role and Mechanisms to Increase their Efficiency", *World Bank Policy Research Working Paper* No. 5729.

This paper is a shortened version of an earlier one presented at the Boston University-Brookings Institution Workshop on National Development Banks and Sustainable Infrastructure held in Boston, 15 November 2015 and issued in the BU Pardee Series. It has benefited from comments from Kevin Gallagher, Rogerio Studart, Amar Bhattacharya and other participants. The views expressed in this note are author's and should not be attributed to the United Nations ESCAP or its member states.

Heinz, R. (2009). 'State Financial Institutions: Mandates, Governance, and Beyond", *World Bank Policy Research Working Paper* No. 5141.

Infrastructure Development Finance Company Limited (IDFC) (2014a). *Scaling Up Renewable Energy Investments.* IDFC discussion note.

———. (2014b). *Sustainability Report 2012-14.* Chennai, India.

———. (2012). *Evolving Perspectives in the Development of Indian Infrastructure.* Volume 1&2. New Delhi: Orient Blackswan Private Limited.

India Infrastructure Financing Company Limited (IIFCL) (2013). *Environmental and Social Safeguards Frameworks.* New Delhi, India.

Kaur, G., L. Lakshmanan, R. Rajesh and N. Kumar (2010). "Infrastructure Financing: Global Pattern and the Indian Experience", *RBI Staff Studies* vol.4.

Kumar, N. (2014) "A Regional Financial Architecture for Sustaining Asia-Pacific's Dynamism in the Post-crisis World", in A. Hussain and M. Dubey (eds.), *Democracy, Sustainable Development, and Peace: New Perspectives on South Asia.* New Delhi: Oxford University Press.

Lall, R.B. and R. Anand (2009). "Financing Infrastructure", *IDFC Occasional Paper* series no.3.

Luna-Martinez, D. and Vicente, C.L. (2012). "Global Survey of Development Banks", *World Bank Policy Research Working Paper* no.5969.

Mahapatra, A. (2015). "Sharing India's PPP Experience", Presentation presented at the *UNESCAP Policy Dialogue on PPPs in Infrastructure,* Kathmandu, 22 September.

Nataraj, G. (2014). "Infrastructure Challenges in India: The Role of Public-Private Partnerships", *ORF Occasional Paper* no. 49, Observer Research Foundation.

Nayyar, D. (2015). "Birth, Life and Death of Development Finance Institutions in India", *Economic and Political Weekly* 50(33): 51-60.

NITI Aayog (2015). "Investment in Infrastructure: Strengthening PPP Policy Framework", *NITI BRIEF* # 5. New Delhi.

Observer Research Foundation (2015). "The New Development Bank: Identifying Strategic and Operational Priorities", *ORF Policy Brief* no. 17.

Ramakrishnan, T. (2014). "Financing Infrastructure Projects Through Public-Private Partnerships in India", *Transportation Research Record: Journal of the Transportation Research Board* no. 2450, pp.118-26.

Raychaudhuri, M. (2011). *Indian Infrastructure: A Trillion Dollar Opportunity.* PowerPoint presentation. BNP Paribas Securities India Pvt Ltd.

Reserve Bank of India (2010). *Infrastructure Financing: Global Pattern and the Indian Experience: RBI Staff Study*, Mumbai, India.

Sikarwar, Deepshikha (2015). "Modi Sarkar's Rs 40K cr Infra Fund Hits Road", *The Economic Times*, 30 December.

Singh, Sarita (2016). "PFC, REC to Lend Rs 1 Lakh Crore to Renewable Energy Sector", *The Economic Times*, 12 January.

Sinha, S. (2014). 'Long Term Financing of Infrastructure', *Indian Institute of Management W.P.* no.2014-03-23. Ahmedabad, India.

Spratt, S. and B. Barone (2015). "National Development Banks in the BRICS: Lessons for the Post-2015 Development Finance Framework", *IDS Policy Briefing* no.93.

Spratt, S. and L.R. Collins (2012). *Development Finance Institutions and Infrastructure: A Systematic Review of Evidence for Development Additionality.* Private Infrastructure Development Group Trust.

Tahilyani, N., T. Tamhane and J. Tan (2011). "Asia's $1 Trillion Infrastructure Opportunity", *McKinsey Quartely.*

Te Velde, D.W. and M. Warner (2007). *The Use of Subsidies by Development Finance Institutions in the Infrastructure Sector.* Overseas Development Institute.

UNDESA (2005). "Rethinking the Role of National Development Bank", Background Document for Ad Hoc Expert Group Meeting on *Rethinking the Role of National Development Banks.* New York, 1-2 December. New York; United Nations.

Williams, H.K. (2014). *Financing Sustainable Infrastructure.* Volumes I & II. International Development Finance Club Sustainable Infrastructure Working Group. October.

World Economic Forum (2015). *Global Competitiveness Report 2015-16.*

31

Living with Mega-Trade Blocs

India Needs a Strategy

RAJESH CHADHA and DEVENDER PRATAP

Backdrop

The multilateral trade discipline has been diluted by the emergence of bilateral and plurilateral preferential trade agreements. The web of preferential trading blocs has deflected the attention of most of the major players from consolidation of the multilateral trade discipline, which is the key goal of the World Trade Organization (WTO). The world trade discipline was on the path of multilateralism from the late-1950s until the United States (US) deviated in 1988 and signed a bilateral FTA (free trade agreement) with Canada (CUFTA) and expanded it in 1994 by bringing in Mexico (NAFTA). East Asia constituted the ASEAN[1] Free Trade Agreement (AFTA) in 1992. The European Union (EU) expanded its membership from 12 to 15 in 1995. All these developments occurred during and after the Eighth Round of trade negotiations (Uruguay Round 1986–1994).

Again, the United States (US) made an attempt to carve out a mega Free Trade Area of the Americas (FTAA) of 34 Western Hemisphere countries during 1994–2004, but hit a roadblock and failed to move forward. The EU expanded from 15 to 25 countries in 2004 and later to 27 in 2007.

The fizz of the Doha Development Round has been lost because of the long duration of its negotiations (2001–2015). The first four Rounds were completed in one year

1. ASEAN: Association of Southeast Asian Nations.

each, the following Dillon, Kennedy and Tokyo rounds took two, four and six years each, respectively, and the Uruguay Round was completed in eight years. In contrast, the Doha Development Round (Ninth Round) is yet to be signed.

Now that we have to live in a fractured world of trade discipline, India needs to give high priority to undertake policy research on its options for the future. The objective of this paper is to understand the need for entering larger trading blocs through tariff elimination in the mining and the manufacturing sectors, rather than to keep proliferating into bilateral trade agreements. While trade liberalisation is also important for agriculture, it continues to remain a sensitive sector under trade negotiations. The FTAs require the participating countries to lower/eliminate tariff barriers with each other. The member countries are expected to gain through efficient allocation of resources post-tariff liberalisation. This paper attempts to compute gains for India when it enters trading blocs with other countries in the Asia region along with Australia & New Zealand (ANZ). It is expected that the gains may arise from increased efficiency in the labour-intensive mining and manufacturing sectors. This may lead to an expansion of jobs. India may be able to leverage its wage rate advantage subject, of course, to building the requisite human skills, implementing factor market reforms, providing the requisite infrastructure, facilitating new investments and improving the ease of doing business.

In fact, India's unilateral trade liberalisation itself can lead to efficient allocation of resources and increase the output of labour-intensive sectors, viz., textiles, clothing, leather products and footwear (Chadha et al. 1998). Then, why should India be interested in regional trade FTAs? One important reason is that the multilateral trade discipline has become dormant. Bilateral, plurilateral and mega trade agreements have fast replaced the multilateral discipline in the world trade regime. Left alone, India may not reap the benefits it would have had if the multilateral trade discipline had been put in order under the WTO command.

The present paper contributes to understanding the impact of opening up of imports of mining and manufacturing sectors on resource allocation across sectors of production. India is expected to leverage its comparative advantage in labour-intensive sectors of production when its mining and manufacturing sectors are opened up to external competition, along with its trading partners also lowering their tariff barriers. Given the sensitivities, we have not simulated the impact of trade liberalisation in the agriculture sector and it is not feasible to model services given the scant data on their bilateral trade.

Literature Review: Mega Trading Blocs

The Asia-Pacific Economic Cooperation (APEC) forum was established in 1989 with a specific focus on trade and economic cooperation among 21 Pacific Rim countries: Australia, Brunei Darussalam, Canada, Chile, China, Hong Kong, Indonesia, Japan, South Korea, Malaysia, Mexico, New Zealand, Papua New Guinea, Peru, the Philippines, Russian Federation, Singapore, Taiwan, Thailand, United States of America and Vietnam. India is not a member of the APEC group of countries (Table 31.1).

The primary purpose of APEC was to create a seamless regional economy to facilitate economic growth and prosperity in the region. These objectives have been pursued through: (i) trade and investment liberalisation; (ii) business facilitation; and (iii) economic and technical co-operation. APEC's charter works through dialogue on non-binding commitments.

APEC endeavours to encourage trade at the borders, supply-chain integration across the borders and improved business environment behind the borders. While it supported multilateral trade discipline until the mid-2000s, it moved into discussions on regional trade agreements starting in 2005. The APEC leaders decided to promote high-quality PTAs (preferential trade agreements) with the long-term goal of creating a Free Trade Area of the Asia-Pacific, FTAAP (Tran and Heal 2014).

Table 31.1

Weaving Mega Trade Blocs from Enmeshed Thread Ball: Thread Shreds

		APEC	*ASEAN*	*RCEP*	*TPP*	*TTIP*
1	Australia	Yes		Yes	Yes	
2	Brunei	Yes	Yes	Yes	Yes	
3	Cambodia		Yes	Yes		
4	Canada	Yes			Yes	
5	Chile	Yes			Yes	
6	China	Yes		Yes		
7	European Union					Yes
8	Hong Kong	Yes				
9	India			Yes		
10	Indonesia	Yes	Yes	Yes		
11	Japan	Yes		Yes	Yes	
12	Laos		Yes	Yes		
13	Myanmar		Yes	Yes		
14	Malaysia	Yes	Yes	Yes	Yes	
15	Mexico	Yes			Yes	
16	New Zealand	Yes		Yes	Yes	
17	Papua New Guinea	Yes				
18	Peru	Yes			Yes	
19	Philippines	Yes	Yes	Yes		
20	Russian Federation	Yes				
21	Singapore	Yes	Yes	Yes	Yes	
22	South Korea	Yes		Yes		
23	Taiwan	Yes				
24	Thailand	Yes	Yes	Yes		
25	United States	Yes			Yes	Yes
26	Vietnam	Yes	Yes	Yes	Yes	

The post-2005 developments in the APEC region have enthused regional aspirations. Various trade agreements have been woven around APEC countries. While there are more than 100 small trade agreements in operation, two mega blocs have caused serious concerns for India, viz., the Trans-Pacific Partnership (TPP) and the Regional Comprehensive Economic Partnership (RCEP).

The TPP discussions commenced in 2005 through dialogue among four APEC member countries, viz., Brunei, Chile, New Zealand and Singapore. The US, Australia, Malaysia and Vietnam joined in 2010. Mexico and Canada joined in 2012 and Japan in 2013. The agreement was signed in the first week of October 2015.

RCEP is a more recent bloc, which commenced its negotiations in 2012. It includes 10 ASEAN member countries along with China, India, Japan, South Korea, Australia and New Zealand. Seven of the RCEP countries are also members of the TPP. These include four of the ASEAN member countries—Brunei, Malaysia, Singapore and Vietnam—and three non-ASEAN APEC member countries— Australia, Japan and New Zealand (Fukunaga 2014). The deal has reached mature status and is likely to be signed soon.

Conflicts may soon arise among the member countries of these mega trading blocs. The US is not a part of RCEP but of TPP, while China is a member of RCEP but is not in the TPP and Japan has taken membership in both clubs. Economic and trade tensions between China and the US are well documented, while political tensions between China and Japan have a long history. Japan would have to orchestrate its trade disciplines under two different mega trading blocs.

However, one of the major limitations of these mega trading blocs has been their lack of geographical coverage. South America (with the exception of Chile and Peru) and the whole of Africa, the Middle East and South Asia (with the exception of India) are out of any of the mega blocs. Can one still call these building blocks of multilateralism?

A report by the World Economic Forum (2014) states:

> There is no single view on the impact of mega-regionals on non-members and it is not the purpose of this report to present one. Rather, it showcases different angles of the discussion while

highlighting the relevance of consciously facilitating the relationship between mega-regionalism and the multilateral trading system, for the benefit of all countries.

India's Trade Agreements

India entered the race for preferential trade agreements starting in 2000. The India-Sri Lanka FTA became operational in 2000. Some other major Indian agreements that became operational in the 2000s include Thailand (2003), Singapore (2005), South Korea (2009), ASEAN (2009) and Japan (2011). Others under process include EU, Canada, Indonesia and Australia (Government of India 2015). More recent developments are provided in Annexure A-31.1.

One recent study has looked at the potential implication of India joining the TPP agreement (Narayanan and Sharma 2014). However, there have not been comprehensive ex ante and ex post studies on what could be or should be a preferred path of entering PTAs. The complications of the RCEP and TPP agreements are also causing serious worries. India is a member of RCEP but not of TPP, while seven Asian countries are members of both agreements, TPP and RCEP. The new developments in the Asia–Pacific and Transatlantic regions need to be watched and studied carefully.

India in the Asia FTA

In this paper, we undertake a hypothetical exercise to see the impact of India's mining and manufacturing sectors when India enters into a FTA with South Asia and then broaden this FTA to include China, ASEAN, NIEs (newly industrialising economies), Japan and Australia and New Zealand (ANZ), respectively, thus enlarging the bloc in a step-by-step manner. This paper builds on our paper on Titanic FTAs (Chadha and Pratap 2007). The two differences are that we use Global Trade Analysis Project (GTAP) model instead of the National Council of Applied Economic Research (NCAER)-Michigan model, and GTAP

2007 data instead of GTAP 2001 data. This exercise brings in its fold three major South Asian countries that are not included in any of the mega trading blocs, viz., Bangladesh, Pakistan and Sri Lanka. It is pertinent to have an economically well-integrated South Asian neighbourhood to reap economic and peace dividends through producing and trading 'more butter and less guns'.

General Equilibrium Modelling Analysis

The GTAP model is a multi-region, multi-sector CGE (computable general equilibrium) model (Hertel et al. 1997). The model is well grounded in economic theory. The GTAP database has 134 countries/regions and 57 sectors of production, which include 14 agriculture, 4 minerals, 24 manufacturing and 15 services. The model analyses trade flows across countries/regions of the world. Each country/region has 57 sectors of production. The inter-linkages across these sectors are captured through input-output databases specific to these countries/regions. Each country/region is assumed to have a single household that represents a consumer as well the provider of factor services. Goods produced by a specific industry across regions are imperfect substitutes between domestic and imported categories. The composite of domestic and imported goods is a CES (constant elasticity of substitution) function referred to as Armington elasticity (Saito 2004). The elasticity estimates differ across 57 sectors. Armington elasticity of substitution varies across sectors. Within manufacturing sectors, it varies from 1.1 for beverages to 2.1 for petroleum and coal products and 4.4 for metal products and electronic components. These composites are used by the households, government and firms for consumption, production and capital formation. The taxes are collected by the government and spent on public goods. The household preferences are based on the non-homothetic CDE (constant difference of elasticities) functional forms. The model assumes production technology under CRS (constant returns to scale). The inputs are used as a composite of intermediate inputs and primary factors of production. While the intermediate inputs are used in fixed proportions, the primary inputs are substitutable. The five primary factors of production are skilled and unskilled labour, capital, land and natural resources. Labour and capital are mobile across domestic sectors of production but immobile across regions. We use the comparative static version of the GTAP model, which provides post-simulation results of a new equilibrium.

The consumers are affected by resource allocation in the economy. More efficient allocation of resources adds to consumer welfare. The welfare gain from a policy simulation in the GTAP model refers to a money metric measure of the consumer's real consumption and saving due to changes in prices of commodities. We computed four components of such change: allocative efficiency, endowment effect, terms of trade effect, and investment-saving effect (Huff and Hertel 2007). We report the allocative efficiency gains in our results in macro and sectoral results.

In this study, we use the GTAP version 8.1 database for the reference year 2007 (Narayanan et al. 2012). We mapped GTAP 57 sectors into 27 sectors (Annexure Table A-31.1). The 14 sectors of agriculture were aggregated into one agriculture sector, the 4 sectors of mineral products were aggregated into 1 mineral sector, the 24 sectors of manufacturing were mapped one-to-one into 24 sectors, and the 15 sectors of services were compressed into 1 service sector.

The 134 countries/regions were compressed into 18 countries/regions (Annexure Table A-31.2). For the experiment, India, Bangladesh, Sri Lanka, Pakistan, China and Japan were taken as separate countries, and the other 14 countries were aggregated into three regions, namely, ASEAN, NIEs and ANZ.

The paper carries out a limited exercise. Ideally, simulations could be conducted for all sectors of production. We simulate the trade liberalisation experiments to the mining and the manufacturing sectors.

Computational Scenarios

The GTAP database (Release 8) used in this paper provides us with an approximation of the world trade configuration in 2007. The impact of the free trade arrangement within South Asia (India, Bangladesh, Sri Lanka, and Pakistan) and between South Asia and other Asian regions (China, ASEAN, NIEs, Japan, and ANZ) was analysed with the help of the GTAP model by simulating the possible elimination of import tariffs. We conducted a seventh simulation scenario for the formation of the Asian free trade area, namely South Asian Free Trade Area (SAFTA), through Simulation 7. This was a hypothetical experiment of open regionalism. The open regionalism scenario refers to member countries also liberalising trade with rest-of-the-world countries/regions even though the non-member countries do not lower their import tariff barriers.

Simulation 1: The four major South Asian countries (Bangladesh, India, Pakistan and Sri Lanka) mutually eliminate their import tariff barriers on mining and manufacturing sectors with one another while maintaining the existing barriers on imports from all other countries/regions (SAFTA).

Simulation 2: The experiment under Simulation 1 is run with China as the fifth country/region of the expanded SAFTA–China bloc.

Simulation 3: The experiment under Simulation 2 is run with ASEAN as the sixth country/region of the expanded SAFTA–China–ASEAN bloc.

Simulation 4: The experiment under Simulation 3 is run with NIEs as the seventh country/region of the expanded SAFTA–China–ASEAN–NIEs bloc.

Simulation 5: The experiment under Simulation 4 is run with Japan as the eighth country/region of the expanded SAFTA–China–ASEAN–NIEs–Japan bloc.

Simulation 6: The experiment under Simulation 5 is run with ANZ as the ninth country/region of the expanded SAFTA–China–ASEAN–NIEs–Japan–ANZ bloc (Asian-ANZ bloc)

Simulation 7: The experiment under Simulation 7 refers to open regionalism in which all six countries/regions of the Asian-ANZ bloc provide market access to other countries of the world as well while other countries do not remove their trade barriers on the Asian-ANZ bloc.

Computation Results

Macro Results

Annexure Table A-31.3 to A-31.11 report the results of our simulation experiments. Annexure 2.3 to 2.7 refer to the changes in macro variables across countries/regions of the world. These tables report changes in welfare, allocative efficiency, GDP (gross domestic product), output, imports and exports. Annexure Table A-31.8 to A-31.11 present sector-specific results in the Indian economy in terms of sectoral allocative efficiency, output, exports and imports.

Consumers are affected by resource allocation in the economy. More efficient allocation of resources adds to consumer welfare. While GDP gain is given in per cent terms, the welfare gain is presented in absolute terms. The GDP gain is higher in the case of South Asian countries than for others. In Simulation 7, India reaps a GDP gain of 2.8 per cent compared with 0.9 for China and 0.6 for Japan and ANZ.

Annexure Table A-31.3 shows that the absolute value of the welfare increases for all four South Asian countries under Simulation 1. India's gains are high, but Sri Lanka and Pakistan have lower welfare gains. China starts reaping significant welfare gains starting from Simulation 2 when it enters the expanding bloc. In the same vein, ASEAN starts gaining from Simulation 3, NIEs from Simulation 4, Japan from Simulation 5 and ANZ gains in Simulation 6. Almost all the non-member countries/regions lose welfare under Simulations 1–6. The results of Simulation 7 depict a win-win game for both member and non-member countries. The non-member countries/regions (except Brazil) also experience gains in welfare.

It may be observed that the South Asian countries face some reversal of welfare gain under Simulation 5. However, all the member countries gain in Simulation 6. Simulation 7 is a gaining proposition (compared with the results of Simulation 6) for all the countries/regions in the Asia–ANZ bloc (except NIEs). Japan, India and China are the major gainers.

The world welfare goes up from $1,565 million under Simulation 1 to $6.8 billion under Simulation 6 and then jumps to $14 billion in Simulation 7.

Annexure Table A-31.4 outlines the efficiency gain component of total welfare gain for all the countries/ regions. It clearly shows gains in Simulations 1 to 7 thus indicating efficient allocation of resources. It may be observed from Annexure Table A-31.5 that all the countries/regions of the Asia–ANZ bloc reap increasing gains in their real GDP. There are corresponding increasing gains in the trade of Asia–ANZ countries in Simulations 1–6 with some marginal dips in Simulation 7.

An important question is whether the model results indicate that India's participation in FTAs would lead to expansion of manufacturing relative to the other sectors, i.e, whether the manufacturing sector would grow relative to services or agriculture. This is not a pre-ordained result. In fact, under Simulation 7, the agriculture output grows by 0.3 per cent, services by 2.4 per cent and mining & manufacturing by only 0.4 per cent. The key to the gains lies in efficient allocation of resources. Some of the sectors gain while others lose.

Sectoral Results

Annexure Table 31.8 to 31.11 present the sector-specific results of Simulations 1 to 7 for India. The simulations were conducted by liberalising trade in the mining and the manufacturing sectors. Hence, we will focus on these sectors even though other sectors are also affected due to general equilibrium effects.

Trade liberalisation through removing import tariffs in the Asia–ANZ bloc leads to improved allocative efficiency in the mining and manufacturing sectors in all simulations (Annexure Table 31.8). Most of these sectors get continuously increasing allocative efficiency gains. The corresponding gains and losses in output do not correspond to similar directions. Increasing allocative efficiency may result in output gains for sectors in which India has a comparative advantage, but there are output losses in sectors where the partner countries have a comparative advantage over India.

It may be observed that the allocative efficiency in vegetable oils increases in Simulation 3 but then remains stagnant until Simulation 6. In the same simulation (Simulation 3), output declines by about 35 per cent, imports increase by about 55 per cent and exports increase by about 16 per cent. This indicates that India has high import tariffs on vegetable oils. As the tariffs are removed, imports increase and output declines. One interesting observation is that allocative efficiency registers a one-time jump in Simulation 3 and then remains stagnant until Simulation 6. In a similar vein, the output declines sharply in Simulation 3 but not more under Simulations 4 to 6. This happens because Indonesia and Malaysia account for more than 70 per cent of India's vegetable oil imports and these are included in ASEAN (Simulation 3). The values of vegetable oil output, export and import change once again in Simulation 7 because tariffs are removed for imports from two other sources, viz., Ukraine and Argentina, each accounting for about 12 per cent in India's vegetable oil imports.

India gains in producing labour-intensive goods including dairy products, sugar, textiles, wearing apparel, leather products, petroleum and coal products, transport equipment and other manufactures (not elsewhere classified). Outputs of wearing apparel and petroleum products register a major increase under open liberalisation (Simulation 7). Textiles and leather products also post significant gains under open liberalisation. The output losses are in sectors such as ferrous metals and metal products, and machinery and equipment (not elsewhere classified).

Limitations

The study works around a hypothetical scenario of India entering a mega trading bloc. It is subject to various limitations of the CGE modelling framework outlined in the methodology. Some of the major limitations are: i) the broad sectoral classification; ii) the use of the 2007 database; iii) issues of sensitivity analysis of various parameters; iv) assumptions of perfect substitution and product homogeneity; and v) assumption of comparative static framework.

The model allows for mobility of resources such as labour and capital across sectors within an economy. However, international flows of resources are not modelled. Gains from trade modelled here are mainly from resource reallocation and not expansion of capacity due to new investments.

The specification of the model and developing the parameters required for the model pose a challenge. The kind of data required for developing a global model is even more enormous. However, a lot of effort has gone into constructing the GTAP database, with contributions by country/region experts that were consolidated at the GTAP Center, Purdue University. The results of the model should be interpreted as indicative but not as forecasts.

Conclusions and Policy Implications

The present paper is a modest beginning towards the need to fill a major gap in India's strategy for moving forward in the era of mega trading blocs. This becomes even more important given the dormant multilateral discipline and dormant WTO. While most of the major economies in the world are busy signing up as members of one or more trading blocs, India has been signing bilateral trade agreements starting 2000s. It is only since 2013 that the discussions on India joining the RCEP have commenced. There has not been a comprehensive ex ante or ex post study to analyse India's preferential trade policy agreements.

Such studies are necessary for several reasons. One of the most important needs today is to generate productive jobs in labour-intensive manufacturing sectors that can absorb the surplus unskilled and semi-skilled labour force in the country. While these sectors can emerge successfully through a better domestic policy regime, external factors are also important. Open trade policies lead to efficient allocation of productive resources. Would India's joining one or more mega trading blocs help expand its labour-intensive manufacturing sectors? The model results indicate this can happen.

This study shows that trade liberalisation is expected to lead to positive outcomes by expanding sectors that produce manufactured goods in which the country has a comparative advantage due to its wage rate advantage. This does not mean that we are ignoring the importance of hi-tech, capital-intensive manufacturing sectors. The trade opportunities must be exploited through a well-chartered regional trade agreements route along with implementing the right domestic policy regime so as to leverage India's comparative advantage and economic growth along with rapid job creation.

References

Chadha R., S. Pohit, A. Deardorff and R. Stern (1998). *The Impact of Trade and Domestic Policy Reforms: A CGE Modelling Approach*. Ann Arbor: University of Michigan Press.

Chadha, R. and D. Pratap (2007). "Titanic FTAs: Is this Time to Establish PAN-Asia FTA?", *Margin: The Journal of Applied Economic Research* 1(1): 24-45.

Fukunaga,Y. (2014). *ASEAN's Leadership in Regional Comprehensive Economic Partnership*. Asia and the Pacific Policy Studies. Canberra: Australian National University.

Government of India, Ministry of Commerce and Industry (2015). *http://commerce.nic.in/ MOC/international_trade_agreements.asp* (last accessed on 12 November 2015).

Hertel, T.W., R. McDougall and T. Walmsley (2007). *GTAP Model version 6.2a*. GTAP Resource #2458. Available at: *https://www.gtap.agecon.purdue.edu/resources/res_display.asp?RecordID=2458*

Hertel, T.W. and M.E. Tsigas (1997). "Chapter 2: Structure of GTAP", in T.W. Hertel (ed.), *Global Trade Analysis: Modeling and Applications*. Cambridge University Press.

Huff, K. and T.W. Hertel (2007). "Decomposing Welfare Changes in GTAP Models", *GTAP Technical Paper* 5, Purdue University.

Narayanan, B., A. Aguiar and R. McDougall (eds.) (2012). *Global Trade, Assistance, and Production: The GTAP 8 Data Base*. Center for Global Trade Analysis, Purdue University. Available online at *http://www.gtap.agecon.purdue.edu/databases/v8/ v8_doco.asp*

Narayanan, B. and S. Sharma (2014). *An Analysis of Trans-Pacific Partnership (TPP): Implications for Indian Economy*. Centre for WTO Studies, Indian Institute of Foreign Trade.

Saito, M. (2004). "Armington Elasticities in Intermediate Inputs Trade: A Problem in Using Multilateral Trade Data", *Working Paper* WP/04/22. IMF.

Tran, D. and A. Heal (2014). "A Free Trade Area of the Asia-Pacific: Potential Pathways to Implementation", *Trade Insights* (Issue No. 2). ESCAP.

World Economic Forum (2014). *Mega Regional Trade Agreements: Game-Changers or Costly Distractions for the World Trading System*. Global Agenda Council on Trade & Foreign Direct Investment, WEF.

Review of Development & Change XX(2): 203-24, July-December 2015.

Annexure 31.1

India's Regional Trading Agreements: Recent Developments[2]

India-EU Bilateral Trade and Investment Agreement (BTIA): Negotiations commenced in June 2007 in the areas of goods, services, investment, sanitary and phyto-sanitary measures, technical barriers to trade, trade facilitation and customs cooperation, competition, IPRs (intellectual property rights), and GIs (geographical indications). Fifteen rounds of negotiations and a number of intersessional and Chief Negotiator-level meetings have been held till date. A Ministerial review meeting was held on 15 April 2013 at Brussels.

India-ASEAN Comprehensive Economic Cooperation Agreement (CECA)-Services and Investment Agreement: Conclusion of negotiations on Agreement on Services and Investment was announced at the ASEAN-India Commemorative Summit on 20 December 2012. Cabinet approved and ratified the Agreements on 19 December 2013. The ASEAN Secretariat has been asked to inform the dates for formal signing of the Agreements.

India-Thailand CECA: Early Harvest Scheme on 82 items implemented. The 29th round of the Trade Negotiating Committee (TNC) was scheduled on 16-18 December 2013, but was cancelled by Thailand on account of internal disturbances. Date for the next round is yet to be fixed.

India-EFTA BTIA: The 13th and final round of this BTIA with the European Free Trade Association (EFTA) was held on 25-29 November 2013. The areas covered include: trade in goods and services, investment, IPRs, sanitary and phyto-sanitary measures, rules of origin, trade facilitation, and customs cooperation.

India-New Zealand FTA/CECA: The ninth round of negotiations was held in Wellington, New Zealand, on 29-30 July 2013 followed by inter-sessional discussion on 9-10 December 2013 in New Delhi. The areas covered include: goods, services, investment and related issues.

India-Israel FTA: Eighth round of negotiations was held in Israel from 24-26 November 2013. The areas covered include: trade in goods, rules of origin, customs procedure, and movement of natural persons.

---

2. *Economic Survey (2013-14)*, Box 7.5 (p. 133).

India-Chile PTA: So far, five meetings of the Joint Administration Committee/rounds of negotiation have been held to discuss the expansion of the PTA. Official-level meeting was held between the two countries in February 2014 to discuss the issues of the India-Chile PTA. The areas covered include: trade in goods, rule of origin, SPS, and TBT.

India-Canada FTA: The eighth round was held in Ottawa, Canada, in June 2013. The next round will be held in New Delhi. The areas covered include: trade in goods, trade in services, rules of origin, SPS, and TBT.

India-Australia FTA/CECA: Five rounds of negotiations have so far been held. The fifth round was held in Canberra, Australia, in May 2013. The areas covered include: trade in goods and services, investment, and IPR-related issues.

Regional Comprehensive Economic Partnership (RCEP) Agreement: The RCEPAgreement is between ASEAN + six FTA Partners (Australia, China, India, Japan, South Korea, and New Zealand): Based on the Declaration of the leaders during the ASEAN Summit in November 2012, negotiations for a comprehensive economic partnership between the 10

ASEAN member states and its six FTA partners commenced in May 2013. The fourth round was held at Nanning, China, from 31 March-4 April 2014. The next round of negotiations is scheduled to be held in Singapore on 22-27th June 2014.

Annexure Table 31.1

Mapping of Model Sectors with GTAP Sectors

S. No.	*Sectors*	*Code*	*GTAP Model Sectors*
1	Agriculture and Allied Activities	agri	1. Paddy, 2. Wheat, 3. Cereal Grains Nec, 4. Vegetables, Fruit, Nuts, 5. Oil seeds, 6. Sugarcane, Sugar Beet, 7. Lant-based Fibers 8 Crops nec, 9. Cattle, Sheep, Goats, Horses 10. Animal Products nec, 11. Raw milk 12. Wool, silk-worm Cocoons, 13. Forestry 14. Fishing
2	Crude Oil and Minerals	min	15. Coal, 16. Oil, 17. Gas, 18. Minerals, n.e.c
3	Meat: Cattle, Sheep, Goats, Horse	cmt	19. Meat: Cattle, Sheep, Goats, Horse
4	Meat Products nec	omt	20.Meat Products Nec
4	Vegetable Oils and Fats	vol	21. Vegetable Oils and Fats
6	Dairy Products	mil	22. Dairy Products
7	Processed Rice	pcr	23. Processed Rice
8	Sugar	sgr	24. Sugar
9	Food Products Nec	ofd	25. Food Products Nec
10	Beverages and Tobacco Products	b_t	26. Beverages and Tobacco Products
11	Textiles	tex	27. Textiles
12	Wearing Apparel	wap	28.Wearing Apparel
13	Leather Products	lea	29.Leather Products
14	Wood Products	lum	30.Wood Products
15	Paper Products, Publishing	ppp	31.Paper Products, Publishing
16	Petroleum, Coal Products	p_c	32.Petroleum, Coal Products
17	Chemical, Rubber, Plastic Products	crp	33.Chemical, Rubber, Plastic Products
18	Mineral Products nec	nmm	34.Mineral Products Nec
19	Ferrous Metals	i_s	35.Ferrous Metals
20	Metals Nec	nfm	36.Metals Nec
21	Metal Products	fmp	37.Metal Products
22	Motor Vehicles and Parts	mvh	38.Motor Vehicles and Parts
23	Transport Equipment Nec	otn	39.Transport Equipment Nec
24	Electronic Equipment	ele	40.Electronic Equipment

25	Machinery and Equipment Nec	ome	41.Machinery and Equipment, nec
26	Manufactures Nec	omf	42. Manufactures, Nec
27	Services	svces	43. Electricity (ely), 44. Gas Manufacture, Distribution (gdt), 45. Water (wtr), 46. Construction (cns), 47.trade (trd), 48. Transport, n.e.c (otp); 49. Sea Transport (wtp); 50. Air Transport, 51. Communication (cmn), 52.Financial Services nec (ofi), 53. Insurance (isr), 54. Business services (obs), 55.recreation and Other Services (ros); 56. PubAdmin/Defence/Educate (osg); 57. Dwelling (dwe)

Source: GTAP Ver 8.1 Database.

Annexure Table A-31.2

Mapping of Model Region with GTAP Region

S. No	*Country/Region*	*Code*	
1.	India	India	India
2.	Bangladesh	Bangla-desh	Bangladesh
3.	Sri Lanka	Sri Lanka	Sri Lanka
4.	Pakistan	Pakistan	Pakistan
5.	China	China	China
6.	ASEAN	ASEAN	Indonesia (IDN), Malaysia (MYS), Philippines (PHL), Singapore (SGP), Hong Kong (HKG), Thailand (THA), Cambodia (KHM), Lao PDR (LAO), Vietnam (VTN)
7.	NIEs	NIEs	Hong Kong (HKG), South Korea (KOR) and Taiwan (TWN)
8.	Japan	Japan	Japan
9.	Australia and New Zealand	ANZ	Australia (AUS), New Zealand (NZL), Rest of Oceania (XOC)
10.	Other South & South-East Asia	OthS_SEAsia	Nepal (NPL), Rest of South Asia (XSA), Mongolia (MNG), Rest of East Asia (XEA)
11.	North America Free Trade Area (NAFTA)	NAFTA	Canada (CAN), United State of America (USA), and Mexico (MEX)
12.	Brazil	BRA	Brazil
13.	America Other than North America	A_N	Argentina (ARG), Bolivia (BOL),Brazil(BRA),Chile (CHL),Colombia (COL),Ecuador (ECU), Paraguay (PRY), Peru(PER),Uruguay (URY),Venezuela (VEN),Rest of South America (XSM), Costa Rica(CRI),Guatemala (GTM), Honduras (HND), Nicaragua (NIC), Panama (pan), El Salvador (SLV), Rest of Central America (XCA), Caribbean (XCB)

14.	European Union -27	EUN27	Austria (AUT), Belgium (BEL), Cyprus (CYP), Czech Republic (CZE), Denmark (DNK),, Estonia (EST), Finland (FIN), France (FRA), Germany (DEU), Greece (GRC), Hungary (HUN), Ireland (IRL), Italy (ITA), Latvia (LVA), Lithuania (LTU), Luxembourg (LUX), Malta (MLT), Netherlands (NLD), Poland (POL), Portugal (PRT), Slovakia (SVK), Slovenia (SVN), Spain (ESP), Sweden (SWE), United Kingdom (GBR), Bulgaria (BGR), Croatia (HRV), Romania (ROU)
15.	Rest of Europe	EUEFT	Switzerland (CHE), Norway (NOR), Rest of EFTA (XEF), Albania (ALB) , Belarus, (BLR),Ukraine (UKR),Rest of Eastern Europe (XEE), Rest of Europe (XER)
16.	Middle East and North Africa	MENA	Bahrain (BHR), Iran Islamic Republic of (IRN), Israel (ISR), Kuwait (KWT), Oman (OMN), Qatar (QAT), Saudi Arabia (SAU), Turkey (TUR), United Arab Emirates (ARE), Rest of Western Asia (XWS),Egypt (EGY), Morocco (MAR), Tunisia (TUN), Rest of North Africa (XNF)
17.	Rest of Africa	RofAFRICA	South Africa (ZAF), Rest of West Africa (XWF), Benin (BEN), Burkina Faso (BFA), Guinea (GIN), Togo (TOGO), Central Africa (XAC), Senegal (SEN), Ethiopia (ETH), Madagascar (MDG), Mozambique (MOZ), Tanzania (TZA), Uganda (UGD), Zambia (ZAM), Rwanda (RWA), Rest of Eastern Africa(X-EC), Malawi (MWI), (Cameroon (CMR), Cote d'Ivoire (CIV), Ghana (GHA),Nigeria (NGA), Kenya (KEN), Mauritius (MUS),Zimbabwe (ZWE), Botswana (BWA), Namibia (NAM),-South Africa (ZAF),Rest of South African Customs (XSC)
18.	Rest-of-World	ROW	Russian Federation (RUS), Rest of North America (XNA), Kazakhstan (KAZ), Kyrgyzstan (KGZ), Rest of Former Soviet Union (XSU), Armenia (ARM), Azerbaijan (AZE), Rest of the World (XTW

Source: GTAP Version 8.1.

Annexure Table 31.3

Absolute Change in Welfare (US$ million)

Country/Region	*SIM 1*	*SIM 2*	*SIM 3*	*SIM 4*	*SIM 5*	*SIM 6*	*SIM 7*
1 India	835	2136	11247	11417	11253	13683	24926
2 Bangladesh	636	627	773	814	812	799	1293
3 Sri Lanka	200	259	195	185	192	219	529
4 Pakistan	201	303	488	402	360	379	890
5 China	141	4852	10069	12873	14782	15598	21941
6 ASEAN	-86	-252	8002	10277	11291	11223	10350
7 NIEs	-61	-148	-1274	23320	20424	22124	23100
8 Japan	-49	-150	-1365	-3438	15616	16493	34154
9 ANZ	-7	-55	-182	-246	-819	4399	6646
10 OthS_SEAsia	-5	-15	-36	-38	-68	-63	290
11 NAFTA	4	-334	-756	-2076	-4755	-5535	3270
12 BRA	-8	5	-33	-137	-303	-350	-54
13 A_N	-10	-11	-206	-290	-718	-889	120
14 EUN27	-94	-503	-1228	-3846	-6275	-7088	4751
15 EUEFT	-7	-74	-121	-229	-407	-557	559
16 MENA	-92	-162	-119	279	-566	-1318	4459
17 RofAFRICA	-17	-38	-114	-141	-481	-800	1126
18 ROW	-15	-28	31	176	-234	-433	1357
Total	1565	6413	25370	49303	60104	67883	139708

Source: Authors' simulations based on GTAP model.

Annexure Table 31.4

Welfare Change due to Allocative Efficiency (US$ million)

Country/Region	*SIM 1*	*SIM 2*	*SIM 3*	*SIM 4*	*SIM 5*	*SIM 6*	*SIM 7*
1 India	342	1864	7308	7883	8373	9817	17630
2 Bangladesh	454	451	524	584	598	596	790
3 Sri Lanka	70	98	134	139	151	164	247
4 Pakistan	39	205	399	427	584	596	896
5 China	-47	859	2395	5285	7588	7831	14612
6 ASEAN	-16	-51	1661	3231	4474	4481	5212
7 NIEs	-13	-31	-284	6435	6579	7520	9857
8 Japan	-6	-23	-248	-547	3952	4755	13619
9 ANZ	-3	-25	-52	-78	-254	1824	3442
10 OthS_SEAsia	-1	-1	-9	-13	-20	-21	36
11 NAFTA	12	-80	-103	-169	-556	-687	671
12 BRA	-3	-8	-25	-70	-129	-148	-72
13 A_N	-3	-15	-64	-101	-193	-233	16
14 EUN27	-69	-248	-581	-1380	-2004	-2275	243
15 EUEFT	-3	-23	-41	-83	-135	-165	-9
16 MENA	-15	-90	-172	-292	-398	-455	425
17 RofAFRICA	-7	-29	-56	-93	-178	-240	168
18 ROW	-5	-29	-25	-22	-116	-159	283
Total	726	2823	10757	21136	28318	33201	68068

Source: Authors' simulations based on GTAP model.

Annexure Table A-31.5

Real GDP Growth (%)

Country/Region	*SIM 1*	*SIM 2*	*SIM 3*	*SIM 4*	*SIM 5*	*SIM 6*	*SIM 7*
1 India	0.04	0.22	1.07	1.12	1.15	1.36	2.79
2 Bangladesh	1.23	1.22	1.50	1.68	1.72	1.72	2.47
3 Sri Lanka	0.70	0.91	1.14	1.17	1.24	1.34	2.06
4 Pakistan	0.11	0.36	0.65	0.67	0.82	0.85	1.67
5 China	0.00	0.08	0.20	0.36	0.49	0.51	0.85
6 ASEAN	0.00	0.00	0.37	0.62	0.81	0.82	1.00
7 NIEs	0.00	0.00	-0.02	0.93	0.94	1.05	1.40
8 Japan	0.00	0.00	-0.01	-0.01	0.49	0.55	0.63
9 ANZ	0.00	0.00	-0.01	-0.01	-0.03	0.56	0.57
10 OthS_SEAsia	0.00	0.00	-0.01	-0.02	-0.02	-0.02	0.04
11 NAFTA	0.00	0.00	0.00	0.00	-0.00	-0.00	0.00
12 BRA	0.00	0.00	0.00	-0.01	-0.01	-0.01	-0.01
13 A_N	0.00	0.00	0.00	-0.01	-0.01	-0.02	0.00
14 EUN27	0.00	0.00	0.00	-0.01	-0.01	-0.01	0.00
15 EUEFT	0.00	0.00	0.00	-0.01	-0.01	-0.02	-0.00
16 MENA	0.00	0.00	-0.01	-0.01	-0.02	-0.02	0.02
17 RofAFRICA	0.00	0.00	-0.01	-0.01	-0.02	-0.03	0.02
18 ROW	0.00	0.00	0.00	0.00	-0.01	-0.01	0.02

Source: Authors' simulations based on GTAP model.

Annexure Table A-31.6

Change in Exports (%)

Country/Region	*SIM 1*	*SIM 2*	*SIM 3*	*SIM 4*	*SIM 5*	*SIM 6*	*SIM 7*
1 India	0.4	2.4	4.9	5.5	5.9	6.3	14.7
2 Bangladesh	9.6	9.5	11.2	12.8	12.7	12.7	13.7
3 Sri Lanka	0.5	0.8	2.7	2.7	2.5	3.0	2.7
4 Pakistan	0.9	4.3	7.1	7.7	7.8	8.1	11.3
5 China	0.0	0.6	1.5	3.0	4.1	4.2	5.8
6 ASEAN	0.0	0.0	1.6	2.2	2.4	2.5	2.1
7 NIEs	0.0	0.0	-0.2	3.5	3.7	3.8	4.0
8 Japan	0.0	0.0	-0.1	-0.3	2.1	2.4	2.3
9 ANZ	0.0	0.0	-0.1	-0.2	-0.4	2.8	2.2
10 OthS_SEAsia	0.0	-0.1	-0.4	-0.5	-0.9	-0.9	-0.2
11 NAFTA	0.0	0.0	-0.1	-0.2	-0.2	-0.2	0.5
12 BRA	0.0	0.0	-0.1	-0.1	-0.1	-0.1	0.3
13 A_N	0.0	0.0	-0.1	-0.2	-0.3	-0.4	-0.0
14 EUN27	0.0	0.0	-0.1	-0.2	-0.3	-0.3	0.3
15 EUEFT	0.0	-0.1	-0.1	-0.2	-0.4	-0.5	0.1
16 MENA	0.0	-0.1	-0.1	-0.1	-0.3	-0.4	0.3
17 RofAFRICA	0.0	0.0	-0.1	-0.1	-0.3	-0.4	0.1
18 ROW	0.0	0.0	-0.1	-0.1	-0.3	-0.3	0.2

Source: Authors' simulations based on GTAP model.

Annexure Table A-31.7

Change in Imports (%)

Country/Region	*SIM 1*	*SIM 2*	*SIM 3*	*SIM 4*	*SIM 5*	*SIM 6*	*SIM 7*
1 India	0.3	2.0	4.1	4.7	4.8	5.3	13.6
2 Bangladesh	8.6	8.5	10.2	11.6	11.5	11.5	13.1
3 Sri Lanka	1.7	2.4	3.3	3.3	3.3	3.6	4.4
4 Pakistan	0.7	2.9	4.4	4.7	4.9	5.1	8.1
5 China	0.0	0.7	1.8	3.9	5.4	5.6	7.9
6 ASEAN	0.0	-0.1	2.1	2.9	3.5	3.6	3.4
7 NIEs	0.0	0.0	-0.3	4.4	4.8	4.9	5.6
8 Japan	0.0	-0.1	-0.3	-0.7	4.4	4.8	4.1
9 ANZ	0.0	-0.1	-0.2	-0.3	-0.8	4.2	3.8
10 OthS_SEAsia	0.0	-0.2	-0.5	-0.7	-1.1	-1.2	-0.3
11 NAFTA	0.0	0.0	-0.1	-0.2	-0.5	-0.6	-0.1
12 BRA	0.0	0.0	-0.1	-0.2	-0.6	-0.7	-0.5
13 A_N	0.0	0.0	-0.1	-0.2	-0.6	-0.7	-0.4
14 EUN27	0.0	0.0	-0.1	-0.2	-0.4	-0.5	0.0
15 EUEFT	0.0	-0.1	-0.1	-0.3	-0.5	-0.7	-0.1
16 MENA	0.0	-0.1	-0.1	-0.2	-0.5	-0.6	0.1
17 RofAFRICA	0.0	-0.1	-0.1	-0.2	-0.5	-0.7	-0.1
18 ROW	0.0	0.0	-0.1	-0.1	-0.4	-0.5	0.0

Source: Authors' simulations based on GTAP model.

Annexure Table A-31.8

Sectoral Allocative Efficiency in India (US$ million)

Factor\Sector	*SIM 1*	*SIM 2*	*SIM 3*	*SIM 4*	*SIM 5*	*SIM 6*	*SIM 7*
1 Land	0	0	0	0	0	0	0
2 UnSkLab	6	28	183	185	181	218	525
3 SkLab	0	0	0	0	0	0	0
4 Capital	0	0	0	0	0	0	0
5 NatRes	0	0	0	0	0	0	0
6 agri	5	-6	-43	-48	-56	-55	-115
7 min	35	45	178	185	170	1055	1776
8 cmt	0	1	8	8	8	9	14
9 omt	0	1	1	2	2	2	6
10 vol	18	9	3736	3722	3695	3711	3880
11 mil	2	4	16	16	15	21	47
12 pcr	-4	-6	-28	-28	-27	-31	-54
13 sgr	6	7	19	19	19	19	58
14 ofd	3	16	61	63	63	68	144
15 b_t	3	5	32	32	30	41	210
16 tex	9	200	261	281	285	294	406
17 wap	-1	13	23	23	25	25	53
18 lea	0	26	42	40	42	43	76
19 lum	0	13	24	24	25	26	45
20 ppp	7	20	35	37	37	42	117
21 p_c	123	140	544	622	605	806	2364
22 crp	47	323	600	682	715	735	1419
23 nmm	3	35	53	56	59	62	135
24 i_s	7	99	190	226	268	284	684
25 nfm	-0	48	122	133	122	241	734
26 fmp	7	133	173	206	218	232	430
27 mvh	24	58	141	232	488	505	1072
28 otn	11	72	112	162	175	189	452
29 ele	2	15	29	38	40	45	90
30 ome	32	520	764	919	1094	1140	2649
31 omf	-2	45	84	91	98	108	511
32 Svces	-1	-0	-52	-48	-44	-47	-98
Total	342	1864	7308	7883	8350	9787	17630

Source: Authors' simulations based on GTAP model.

Annexure Table A-31.9

Sectoral Change in Output in India (%)

S. No.	Sector	Base Output US$ Mn	SIM 1	SIM 2	SIM 3	SIM 4	SIM 5	SIM 6	SIM 7
1	Agriculture and Allied Activities	267444	0.0	0.1	-0.1	-0.1	-0.1	0.0	0.3
2	Crude Oil and Minerals	41186	-0.1	0.1	0.2	0.3	0.4	0.0	-2.37
3	Meat: Cattle, Sheep, Goats, Horse	2469	0.0	0.5	8.0	8.2	8.5	8.5	10.9
4	Meat Products Nec	916	0.1	0.1	1.7	1.7	1.8	1.7	0.3
5	Vegetable Oils and Fats	16918	0.2	0.8	-34.7	-34.0	-33.6	-33.8	-40.4
6	Dairy Products	22449	0.2	0.3	1.1	1.2	1.2	1.2	1.8
7	Processed Rice	33218	0.2	0.3	1.0	1.0	1.0	1.1	1.9
8	Sugar	13772	0.7	0.8	2.1	2.1	2.1	2.1	2.0
9	Food Products Nec	45312	0.1	0.1	1.0	1.0	1.1	1.1	1.2
10	Beverages and Tobacco Products	14654	0.1	0.1	0.8	0.8	0.8	0.8	0.0
11	Textiles	59115	-0.1	-0.7	0.9	0.6	0.7	0.6	2.8
12	Wearing Apparel	15678	-0.5	1.6	3.6	3.6	4.1	3.9	8.3
13	Leather Prod-ucts	7434	-0.3	1.7	4.5	4.0	4.7	4.3	5.4
14	Wood Products	6841	-0.1	-1.1	-1.6	-1.6	-1.6	-1.6	-2.3
15	Paper Products, Publishing	16996	0.2	-0.2	0.1	-0.1	-0.1	-0.2	-2.8
16	Petroleum, Coal Products	108918	0.4	0.3	0.9	1.1	0.9	1.8	6.4
17	Chemical, Rubber, Plastic Products	116437	0.3	-0.1	0.4	0.1	-0.1	0.2	1.4
18	Mineral Products Nec	33742	0.0	-0.4	0.2	0.3	0.2	0.4	1.5
19	Ferrous Metals	58720	0.0	-1.1	-0.6	-1.2	-2.0	-1.6	-3.0
20	Metals Nec	21336	-0.3	0.6	2.7	2.4	2.4	-0.2	-5.0
21	Metal Products	45946	0.0	-1.1	-0.3	-0.4	-0.7	-0.2	1.0
22	Motor Vehicles and Parts	32487	0.4	0.8	1.5	0.9	-1.0	-0.8	-1.29

23	Transport Equipment Nec	19578	0.2	0.5	1.9	1.8	2.1	2.2	0.5
24	Electronic Equipment	23296	-0.1	-0.1	0.9	1.0	1.3	1.6	5.7
25	Machinery and Equipment Nec	101418	-0.1	-1.4	-1.0	-1.5	-2.2	-1.7	-3.6
26	Manufactures Nec	52075	-0.2	0.8	2.1	2.2	2.5	2.7	4.4
27	Services	1177403	0.0	0.2	0.8	0.9	0.9	1.0	2.4

Source: Authors' simulations based on GTAP model.

Annexure Table A-31.10

Sectoral Change in Exports in India (%)

S. No.	*Sector*	*Base Exports US$ Mn*	*SIM 1*	*SIM 2*	*SIM 3*	*SIM 4*	*SIM 5*	*SIM 6*	*SIM 7*
1	Agriculture and Allied Activities	6305	-0.5	-0.1	3.9	4.1	4.5	4.1	4.7
2	Crude Oil and Minerals	10443	0.1	1.4	3.5	3.6	3.3	7.5	38.1
3	Meat: Cattle, Sheep, Goats, Horse	964	-0.1	1.1	18.2	18.6	19.1	19.4	23.0
4	Meat Products Nec	25	1.2	2.4	34.8	35.7	39.7	37.5	13.7
4	Vegetable Oils and Fats	1897	3.3	6.5	16.4	20.4	21.4	20.5	17.5
6	Dairy Products	311	9.2	11.1	15.7	19.5	21.0	17.6	19.5
7	Processed Rice	2159	2.3	2.7	5.9	6.1	6.5	6.3	9.5
8	Sugar	1039	8.8	9.4	18.1	18.2	18.4	17.1	17.2
9	Food Products Nec	3263	0.5	1.2	6.1	7.3	7.7	7.1	6.7
10	Beverages and Tobacco Products	225	2.7	3.2	10.1	10.0	10.1	10.0	10.5
11	Textiles	13952	0.5	3.6	6.9	7.0	7.0	6.5	11.9
12	Wearing Apparel	8597	-0.9	2.6	5.3	4.9	5.5	5.2	11.6
13	Leather Products	3302	-0.3	5.3	9.8	8.8	9.8	9.3	13.6
14	Wood Products	686	-0.2	1.0	4.2	4.5	4.9	4.8	9.0
15	Paper Products, Publishing	792	5.2	7.0	9.1	8.2	8.3	8.0	13.3
16	Petroleum, Coal Products	22793	2.0	2.1	3.7	5.8	5.7	7.5	22.3
17	Chemical, Rubber, Plastic Products	20354	1.6	6.3	10.3	11.1	11.2	11.7	24.5
18	Mineral Products Nec	2324	0.5	1.8	3.4	3.6	3.6	3.8	10.6
19	Ferrous Metals	7987	0.3	2.2	5.4	5.5	5.4	6.1	15.1
20	Metals Nec	8325	-0.2	4.5	8.8	9.5	9.6	11.6	28.1
21	Metal Products	3959	0.7	3.1	6.2	8.4	8.9	11.0	25.1
22	Motor Vehicles and Parts	4171	2.9	5.1	9.6	11.0	10.0	9.9	16.9

23	Transport Equipment Nec	1878	3.4	5.7	11.6	13.6	15.2	15.1	26.7
24	Electronic Equipment	1911	0.1	5.7	8.9	10.7	12.5	12.7	24.0
25	Machinery and Equipment Nec	11174	0.3	5.1	9.1	10.3	11.7	13.1	27.7
26	Manufactures Nec	16929	-0.5	2.2	4.4	4.6	5.1	5.1	14.4
27	Services	66056	-0.3	0.2	1.0	1.5	1.9	1.7	4.3

Source: Authors' simulations based on GTAP model.

Annexure Table A-31.11

Sectoral Change in Imports in India (%)

S. No.	Sector	Base Imports US$ mn	SIM 1	SIM 2	SIM 3	SIM 4	SIM 5	SIM 6	SIM 7
1	Agriculture and Allied Activities	4944	0.5	0.3	-2.0	-2.2	-2.8	-2.4	-2.50
2	Crude Oil and Minerals	87458	0.4	0.3	1.5	1.6	1.2	1.7	11.2
3	Meat: Cattle, Sheep, Goats, Horse	18	0.7	2.4	2.0	1.6	1.7	20.6	42.9
4	Meat Products Nec	16	0.6	1.9	5.4	7.9	7.2	13.0	74.4
4	Vegetable Oils and Fats	4179	0.4	0.1	55.2	54.9	54.4	54.8	77.2
6	Dairy Products	63	0.6	1.7	3.6	3.3	2.5	13.9	78.4
7	Processed Rice	5	0.4	-0.1	30.6	30.2	29.8	30.0	58.9
8	Sugar	33	1.0	0.5	2.8	3.0	2.4	3.9	121.0
9	Food Products Nec	426	1.3	8.6	17.6	18.3	18.1	20.1	47.8
10	Beverages and Tobacco Products	216	0.9	1.4	3.7	4.5	4.1	7.0	50.5
11	Textiles	3192	2.0	27.1	30.1	33.9	33.8	35.4	43.2
12	Wearing Apparel	224	1.7	11.8	15.6	16.4	15.8	17.2	37.7
13	Leather Products	649	1.1	10.9	14.2	14.1	13.8	15.2	34.0
14	Wood Products	846	0.5	8.7	17.1	17.1	16.8	17.7	31.3
15	Paper Products, Publishing	3087	0.4	2.4	5.1	5.6	5.3	6.1	21.8
16	Petroleum, Coal Products	11116	0.3	1.4	3.9	5.4	5.9	4.9	10.7
17	Chemical, Rubber, Plastic Products	24765	0.4	4.7	7.7	9.1	9.5	9.5	19.1
18	Mineral Products Nec	1419	0.8	12.7	15.3	15.8	16.4	16.5	28.9
19	Ferrous Metals	8466	0.3	5.9	9.0	11.3	14.0	14.2	31.0
20	Metals Nec	19641	0.2	-0.2	0.6	0.6	-0.2	3.5	13.1
21	Metal Products	2915	0.4	16.0	18.1	21.0	22.1	21.6	32.3
22	Motor Vehicles and Parts	3130	0.3	2.0	5.3	11.8	20.4	20.9	40.5
23	Transport Equipment Nec	12234	0.2	0.2	0.5	0.7	0.3	0.4	6.7

24	Electronic Equipment	15983	0.2	1.3	1.9	2.0	1.5	1.7	1.2
25	Machinery and Equipment Nec	30072	0.3	5.5	7.8	9.4	11.3	11.2	25.9
26	Manufactures Nec	4447	0.3	2.5	3.0	3.3	3.0	3.3	34.5
27	Services	50417	0.3	-0.1	0.1	-0.2	-0.8	-0.5	-1.06

Source: Authors' Simulation based on GTAP model.